I0825312

This publication has been generously supported by
Major Patrons Jane Hains and Stephen Hains

Keith Haring

Jean-Michel Basquiat

Crossing Lines

Dieter Buchhart and contributors

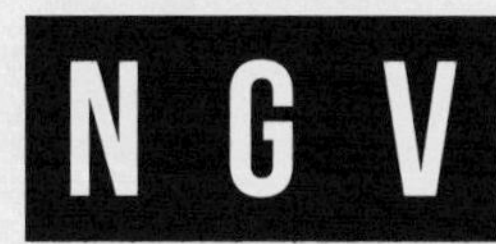

Contents

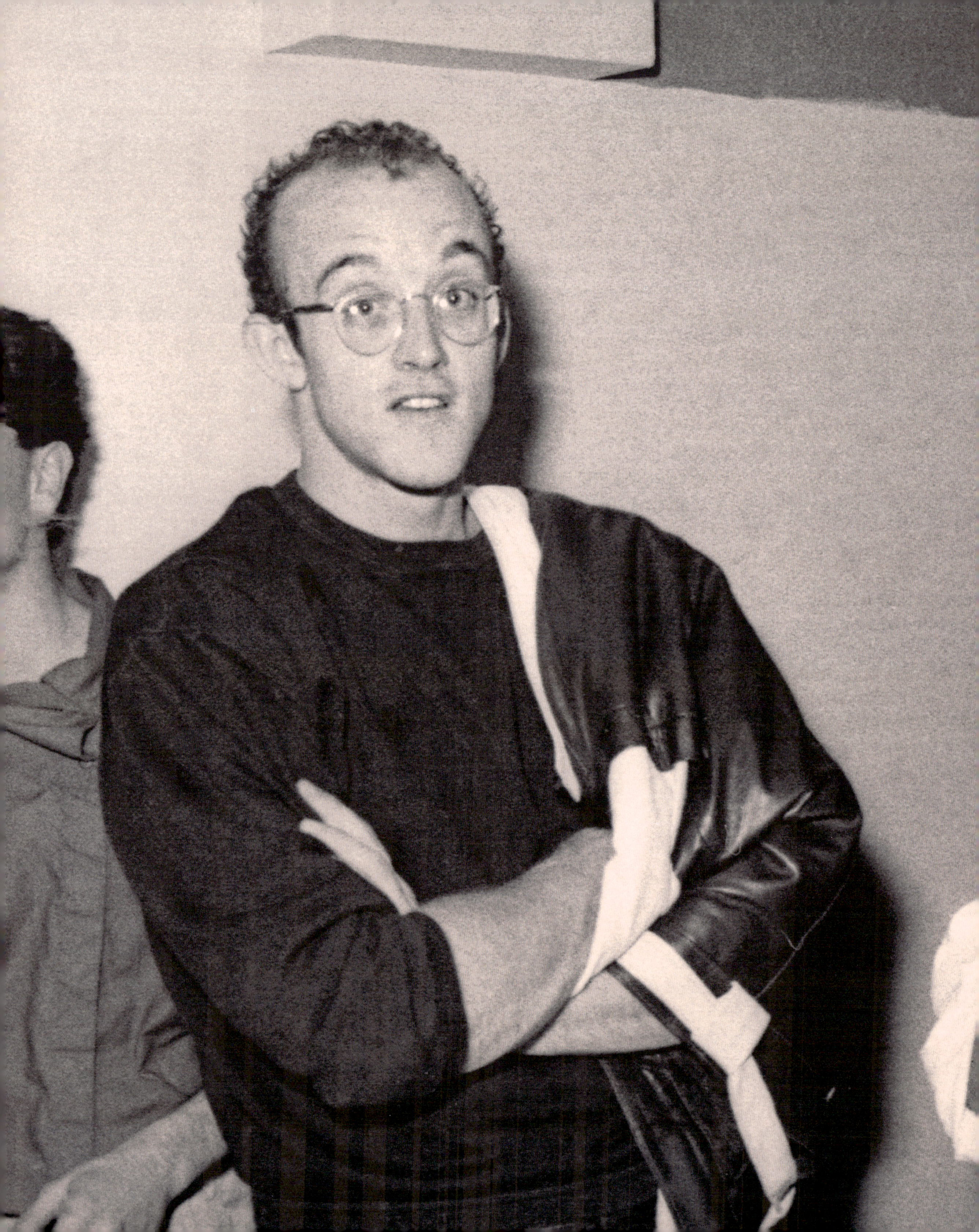

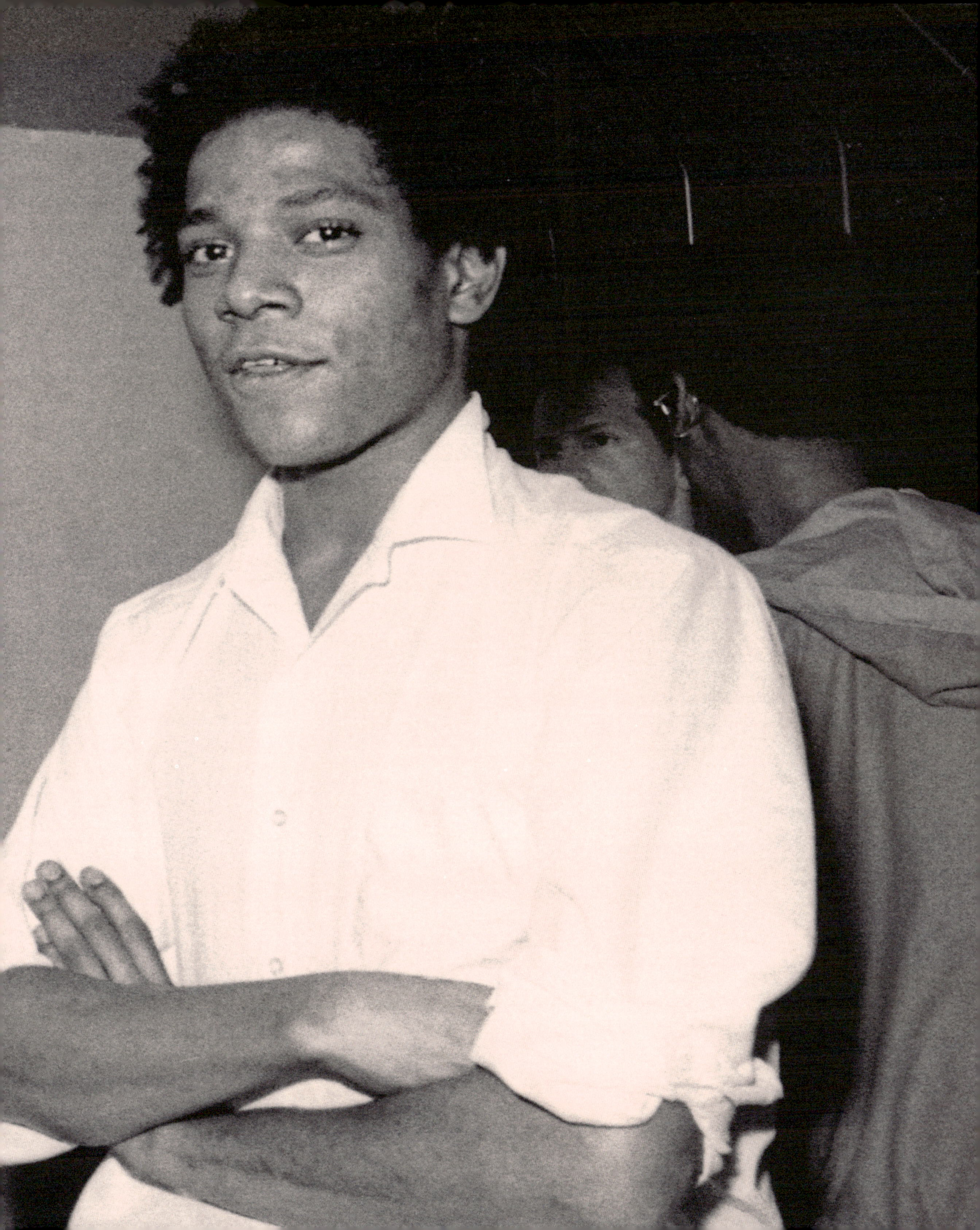

Foreword

The New York of the 1980s is rightly regarded as the epicentre of groundbreaking art of the time. The city pulsated with an atmosphere of enormous creativity and energy; all the while, barriers between society's elite and street culture were being broken down. Among many of the key figures to come out of that place and period were two who are now considered iconic: Jean-Michel Basquiat (1960–88) and Keith Haring (1958–90).

Both artists are known for their idiosyncratic imagery, radical viewpoints and complex sociopolitical commentary, with each employing signs, symbols and words to explore ideas around race, sexuality, spirituality and other aspects of contemporary life.

In 1984 the NGV was fortunate enough to host Keith Haring, who was given free rein to paint a mural across the entire Waterwall entrance. This work encapsulated his vast energy and thematic concerns. Although Basquiat never visited Australia, his influence here has been profound. A great many Australian artists have found relevance and inspiration in Basquiat's engagement with and artistic response to racial politics and issues of social justice.

The NGV is the first public art museum to present their work in dialogue. *Keith Haring | Jean-Michel Basquiat: Crossing Lines* draws out the many intersections between the two artists' lives, practices and ideas. This publication surveys each artist's career through more than 200 artworks, including works created in public spaces, paintings, sculptures, objects, works on paper and photographs. This wealth of imagery is augmented with interviews with some of Basquiat's and Haring's contemporaries, including gallerist Patti Astor, curator Diego Cortez, and artists Jenny Holzer and George Condo, as well as observations by experts on both artists' work. The exhibition's curator, Dr Dieter Buchhart, has contributed a detailed lead essay.

We are immensely grateful to the family of Jean-Michel Basquiat – Lisane Basquiat, Jeanine Basquiat and Nora Fitzpatrick – and the staff of the Keith Haring Foundation – Julia Gruen, Gil Vasquez, Annelise Ream and Anna Gurton-Wachter – for their generosity and openness in enabling this new perspective on these two artists to be developed and brought to fruition. David Stark, Sara Citarella and Alex de Ronde of Artestar have facilitated many aspects of the project and we are thankful for their efforts. We also thank Charles Buchan, Wiley Agency (UK), for his assistance with the publication.

I would also like to extend my thanks to the public institutions that have loaned works. Our appreciation also extends to the many private lenders who have so generously made their works available.

My sincere thanks go to Dieter Buchhart, Exhibition Curator, and Dr Anna Karina Hofbauer, Co-Curator, for their unstinting work on both the exhibition and publication. Jean-Michel Basquiat and Keith Haring have been of enduring professional interest to Dieter, who has previously curated acclaimed monographic exhibitions on both artists. In presenting the artists in tandem and in dialogue, Dieter has revealed new insights into both artists' work, further illuminating the significance of each artist's contribution to late twentieth-century art. Larry Warsh has served as Special Advisor on *Keith Haring | Jean-Michel Basquiat: Crossing Lines* and, through his valued contribution to this catalogue and the exhibition, has been a passionate advocate for the project over many years. We are sincerely grateful for his support.

We acknowledge the commitment and ongoing support the NGV receives from the Victorian Government, through the Honourable Daniel Andrews MP, Premier of Victoria; the Honourable Martin Foley MP, Minister for Creative Industries; and the Honourable Martin Pakula MP, Minister for Tourism, Sport and Major Events. We thank Presenting Partner Creative Victoria and Simon Phemister, Secretary, Department of Jobs, Precincts and Regions, and Andrew Abbott, Deputy Secretary, Creative, Sport and Visitor Economy and Chief Executive, Creative Victoria. We also thank Visit Victoria and CEO Peter Bingeman for their support.

(previous) Jean-Michel Basquiat and Keith Haring at Area (detail), New York, 1985

We recognise the Honourable Paul Fletcher MP, Minister for Communications, Cyber Safety and the Arts, and the Australian Government and its Australian Government International Exhibitions Insurance (AGIEI) Program. AGIEI was established by the Australian Government to provide funding for the purchase of insurance for significant cultural exhibitions, and without it the high cost of commercial insurance would prohibit the organisation of many touring exhibitions.

This exhibition has been made possible through the generous support of the corporate and philanthropic community. We extend our sincere thanks to Principal Partner Mercedes-Benz Australia/Pacific, and Managing Director, Mercedes-Benz Cars & CEO, Horst von Sanden, for their exceptional and longstanding support. We also thank Major Partners American Express and Managing Director – Australia & New Zealand Corrina Davison; Lavazza and Global Vice-Chairman Giuseppe Lavazza, Director Francesca Lavazza, and APAC Business Unit Director & Lavazza Australia Managing Director Silvio Zaccareo; and Telstra and CEO Andrew Penn. We thank our Learning Partner La Trobe University and Vice-Chancellor Professor John Dewar. We are very grateful to our Major Patrons Jane Hains and Stephen Hains for their support of this publication.

We acknowledge the support of our Media Partners: *Vogue Australia* and Editor-in-Chief Edwina McCann; *The New York Times* and General Manager, Australia, Adam Kershaw; Broadsheet and Director and Publisher Nick Shelton; smoothfm and CEO of Nova Entertainment Cathy O'Connor; Val Morgan Cinema Network and Managing Director, Guy Burbidge; and The Herald & Weekly Times and Victorian Managing Director, Editorial – NewsCorp Victoria Peter Blunden. Our thanks extend to our Tourism Partners Sofitel Melbourne On Collins and General Manager Clive Scott; and Melbourne Airport and CEO/ Managing Director Lyell Strambi.

We thank our supporters: Asahi Super Dry and Chief Operating Officer Robert Iervasi and Chief Strategy Officer Kazutomo Tamesada; MIMCO and Managing Director Sarah Rovis; and Dulux Australia and CEO Patrick Houlihan. Our sincere thanks go to Krystyna Campbell-Pretty AM and family for their ongoing support of the Schools Access Program. We are also grateful to our Event Partners Yering Station and winery owner Doug Rathbone AM; and Bombay Sapphire through Bacardi-Martini Australia and Managing Director Mauricio Vergara Herrera.

Finally, I would like to thank the NGV staff who have worked tirelessly on this project: Andrew Clark, Deputy Director; Don Heron, Assistant Director, Exhibitions Management and Design; Donna McColm, Acting Assistant Director, Curatorial and Collection Management; Miranda Wallace, Senior Curator, International Exhibition Projects; Meg Slater, Curatorial Project Officer, International Exhibition Projects; Pip Wallis, Curator, Contemporary Art; Georgia Jones, Senior Exhibitions Coordinator; Michael Varcoe-Cocks, Head of Conservation; Paula Nason, Head of Registration; Kathryn Kiely, Registrar; Ingrid Rhule, Manager, Exhibition Design; and Elizabeth White, Senior Designer, Exhibition Design.

Keith Haring | Jean-Michel Basquiat: Crossing Lines is both an exploration of and a tribute to the work of two of the most significant and influential artists of the late twentieth century.

Tony Ellwood AM
Director, National Gallery of Victoria

Keith Haring and Jean-Michel Basquiat at the opening reception for Julian Schnabel's exhibition at the Whitney Museum of American Art (detail), New York, 1987

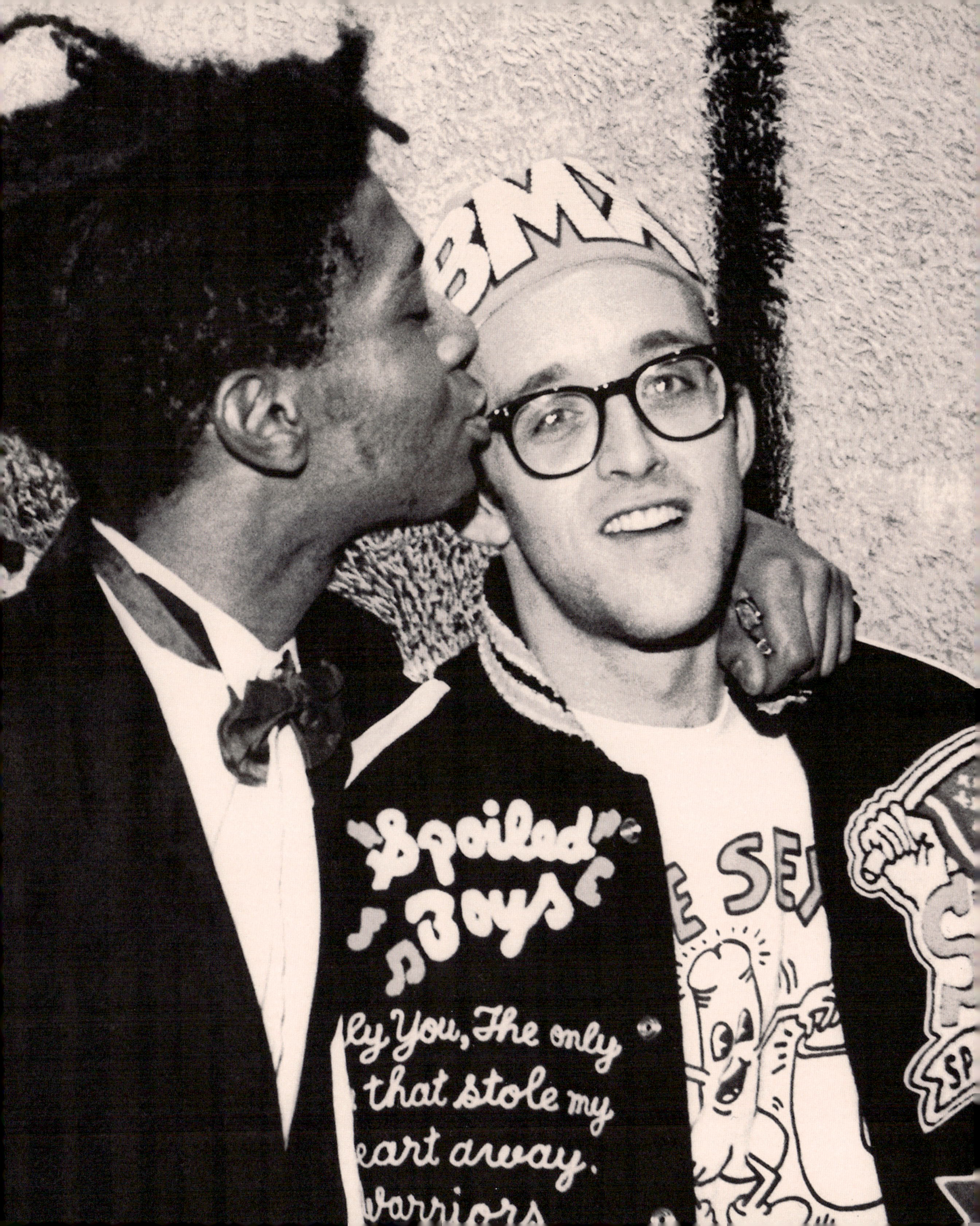
"Spoiled"
Boys
ly You, The only
that stole my
eart away.

Government Messages

Victorian Government

Our Government is proud to support the NGV's presentation of *Keith Haring | Jean-Michel Basquiat: Crossing Lines*.

The NGV's summer exhibitions have become a highlight in Victoria's events calendar, bringing some of the world's greatest masterpieces to our state. This year is no exception.

Transforming the art landscape of the 1980s, Haring and Basquiat tackled some of the most important issues of their day.

Decades on – and as this exhibition demonstrates – the artists' powerful work continues to resonate even now.

As a city and a state, we're proud to host this world-first exhibition – and we're prouder still to be Australia's cultural capital.

The Honourable Daniel Andrews MP
Premier of Victoria

Australian Government

I would like to congratulate the National Gallery of Victoria (NGV) on its new exhibition *Keith Haring | Jean-Michel Basquiat: Crossing Lines*.

The NGV has become well known for its presentation of work of some of the most significant artists of the twentieth and twenty-first centuries. Keith Haring and Jean-Michel Basquiat fall squarely into this category: both came out of a vital period of artistic activity in New York in the 1980s and went on to achieve great critical acclaim and fame. The themes of both artists' work have strong resonances in today's world, which makes this exhibition a timely one.

The exhibition and this publication are the result of the generosity of the Estate of Jean-Michel Basquiat and the Keith Haring Foundation, as well as the tireless work of a number of teams at the NGV. I sincerely thank all who have worked to bring this book and the exhibition to fruition.

I am delighted that the Australian Government has been able to assist this project through the support of the Australian Government International Exhibitions Insurance Program. It's wonderful to see the powerful and thought-provoking work of these two artists in our nation.

The Honourable Paul Fletcher MP
Minister for Communications, Cyber Safety and the Arts

Partners & Supporters

Principal Partner's Message

Mercedes-Benz is proud to be the Principal Partner of the world premiere exhibition *Keith Haring | Jean-Michel Basquiat: Crossing Lines* at the National Gallery of Victoria.

This exhibition pairs two of the most significant and talented artists of the late twentieth century in a dynamic and energetic exchange. Their iconic and innovative works reach a level of excellence that Mercedes-Benz greatly values. Their lasting influence continues to inspire successive generations, including our designers at Mercedes-Benz.

It is a privilege to enable the NGV to stage the first major exhibition of Basquiat's work, and the largest exhibition of Haring's work, ever displayed in Australia. We trust that audiences will be captivated by the exhibition and enjoy this publication.

Horst von Sanden
Managing Director, Mercedes-Benz Cars & CEO, Mercedes-Benz Australia/Pacific Pty Ltd

THE NGV THANKS ITS PARTNERS AND SUPPORTERS FOR MAKING THIS EXHIBITION POSSIBLE

PRESENTING PARTNER

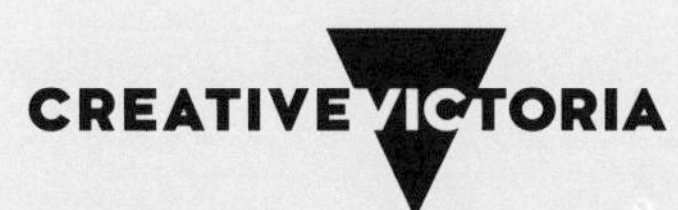

PRINCIPAL PARTNER

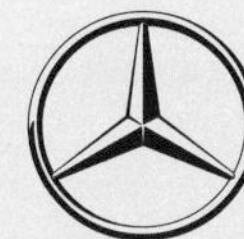

MAJOR PARTNERS

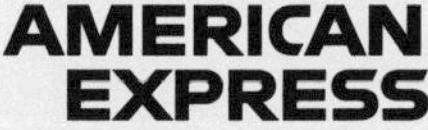

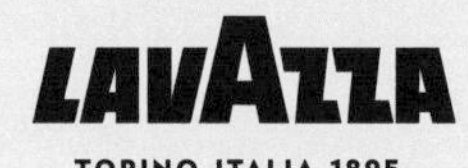

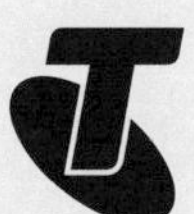

LEARNING PARTNER

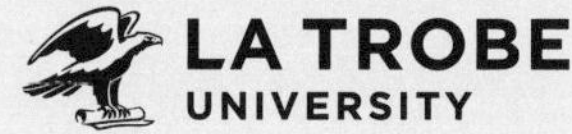

MAJOR PATRONS

JANE HAINS &
STEPHEN HAINS

MEDIA PARTNERS

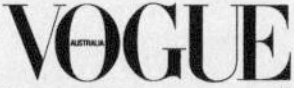

The New York Times

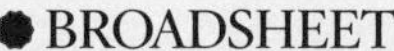

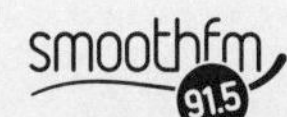

valmorgan

Herald Sun

TOURISM PARTNERS

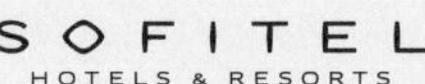

MELBOURNE AIRPORT

SUPPORTERS

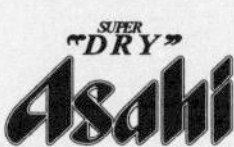

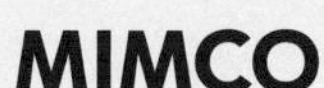

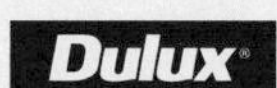

SCHOOLS ACCESS SUPPORTER

KRYSTYNA CAMPBELL-PRETTY AM
& FAMILY

EVENT PARTNERS

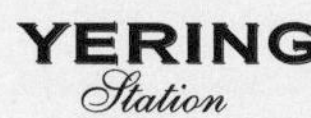

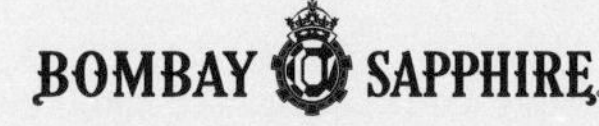

WITH THE ASSISTANCE OF

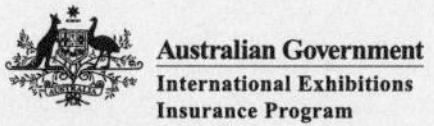

(opposite) Keith Haring and Jean-Michel Basquiat with group including David Hockney, Andy Warhol, Julian Schnabel, Kenny Scharf, Tony Shafrazi, Francesco Clemente and Robert Mapplethorpe at Mr Chow (detail), New York, 1985

(pp. 2–3) Jean-Michel Basquiat *Hollywood Africans in Front of the Chinese Theater with Footprints of Movie Stars* 1983 (detail), synthetic polymer paint and oilstick on canvas on wood panel, 90.0 x 207.0 cm, The Estate of Jean-Michel Basquiat, New York

(pp. 4–5) Keith Haring *Malcolm X* 1988 (detail), synthetic polymer paint, enamel, and collage on canvas, 152.4 x 152.4 cm, Private collection, New York

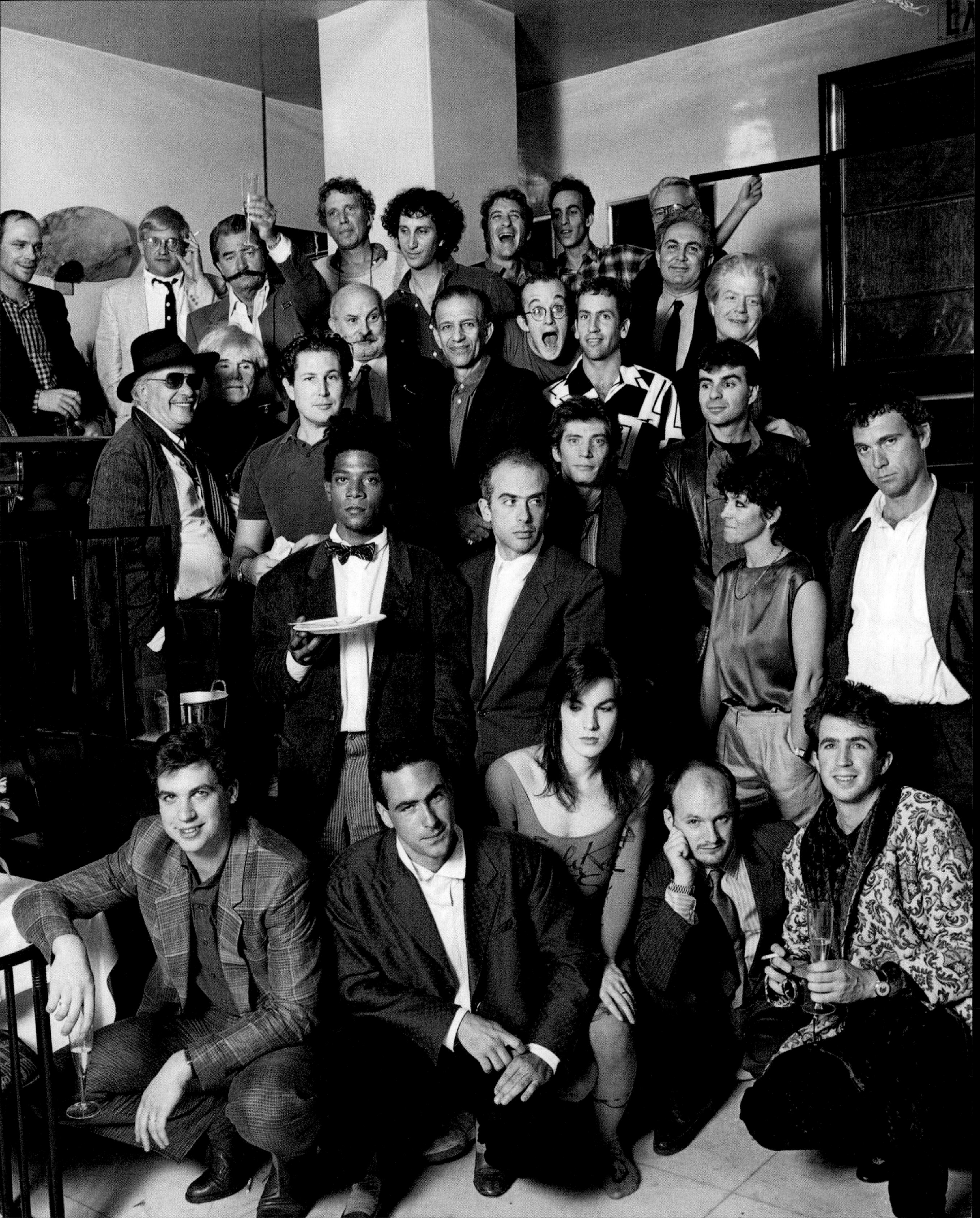

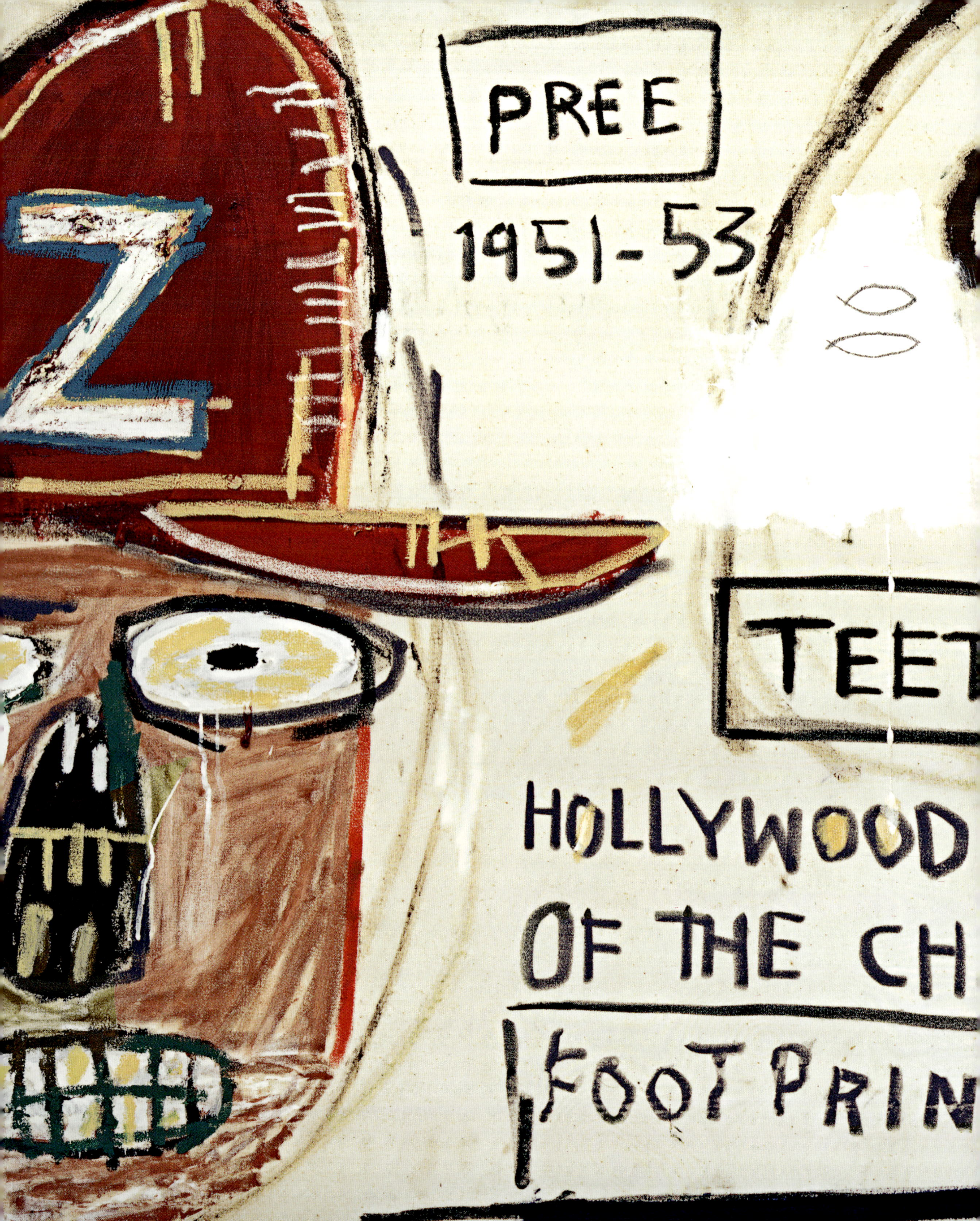
PREE
1951-53
TEET
HOLLYWOOD
OF THE CH
FOOTPRIN

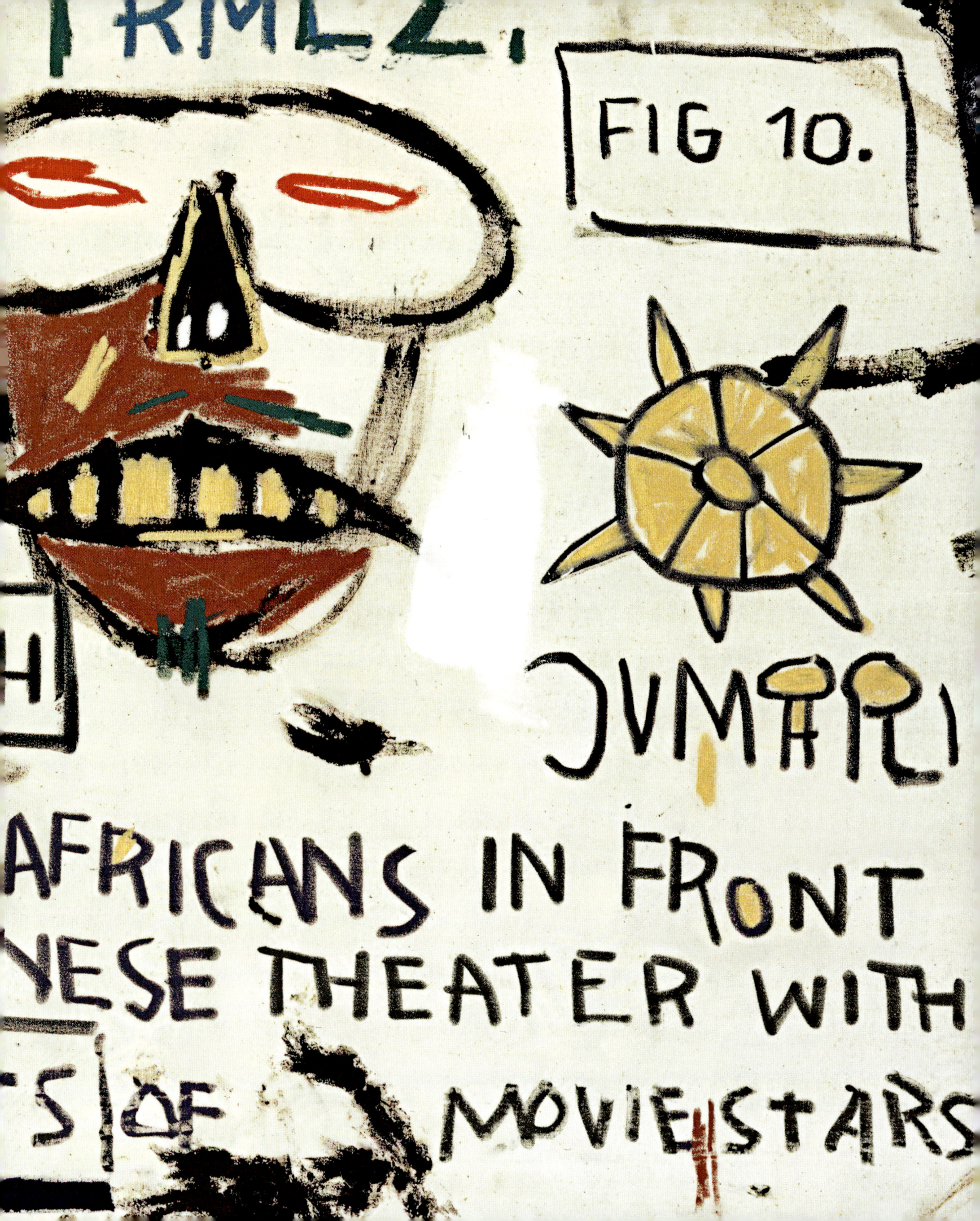

RMEZ.

FIG 10.

AFRICANS IN FRONT
NESE THEATER WITH
S OF MOVIE STARS

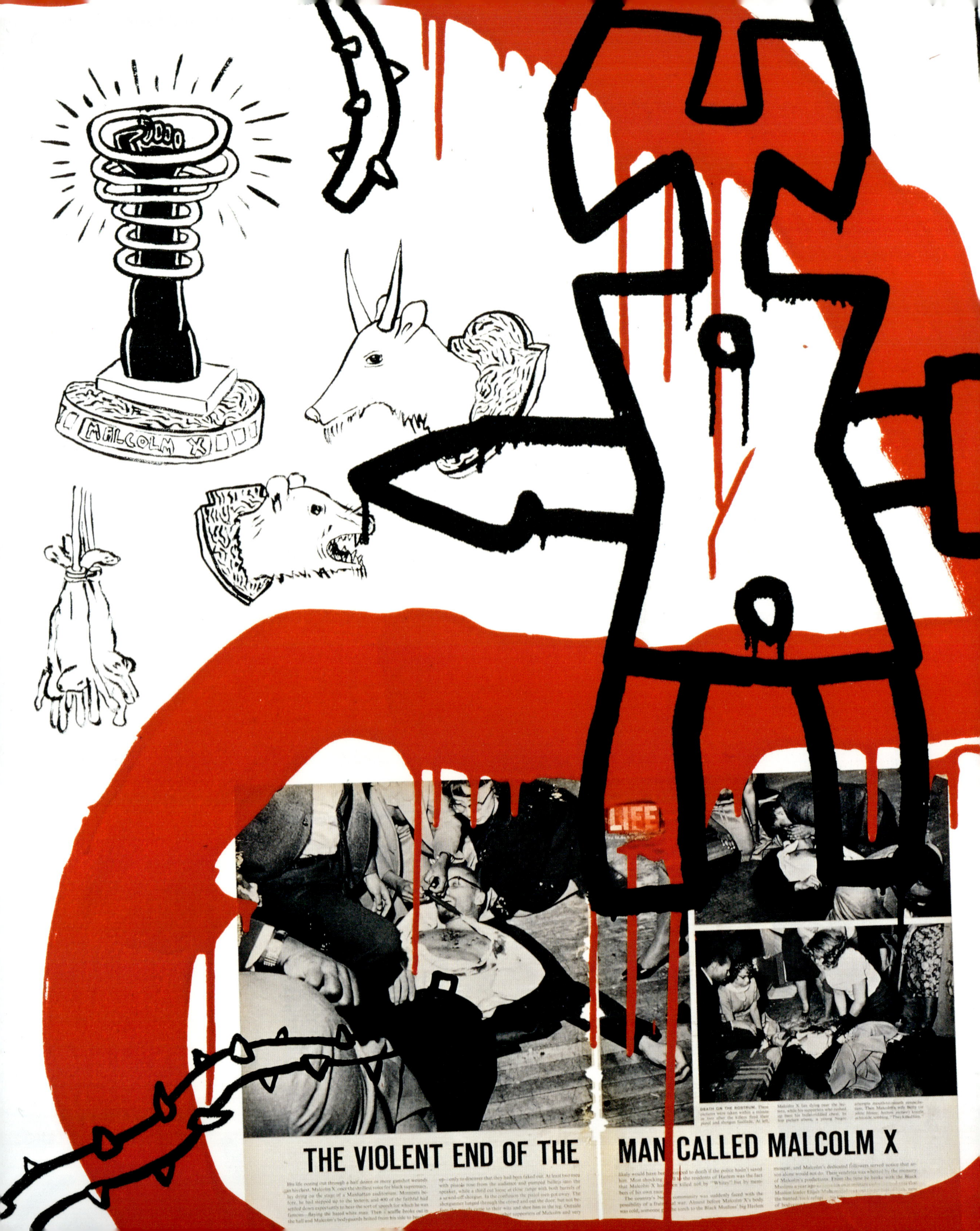
MALCOLM X
LIFE
THE VIOLENT END OF THE MAN CALLED MALCOLM X

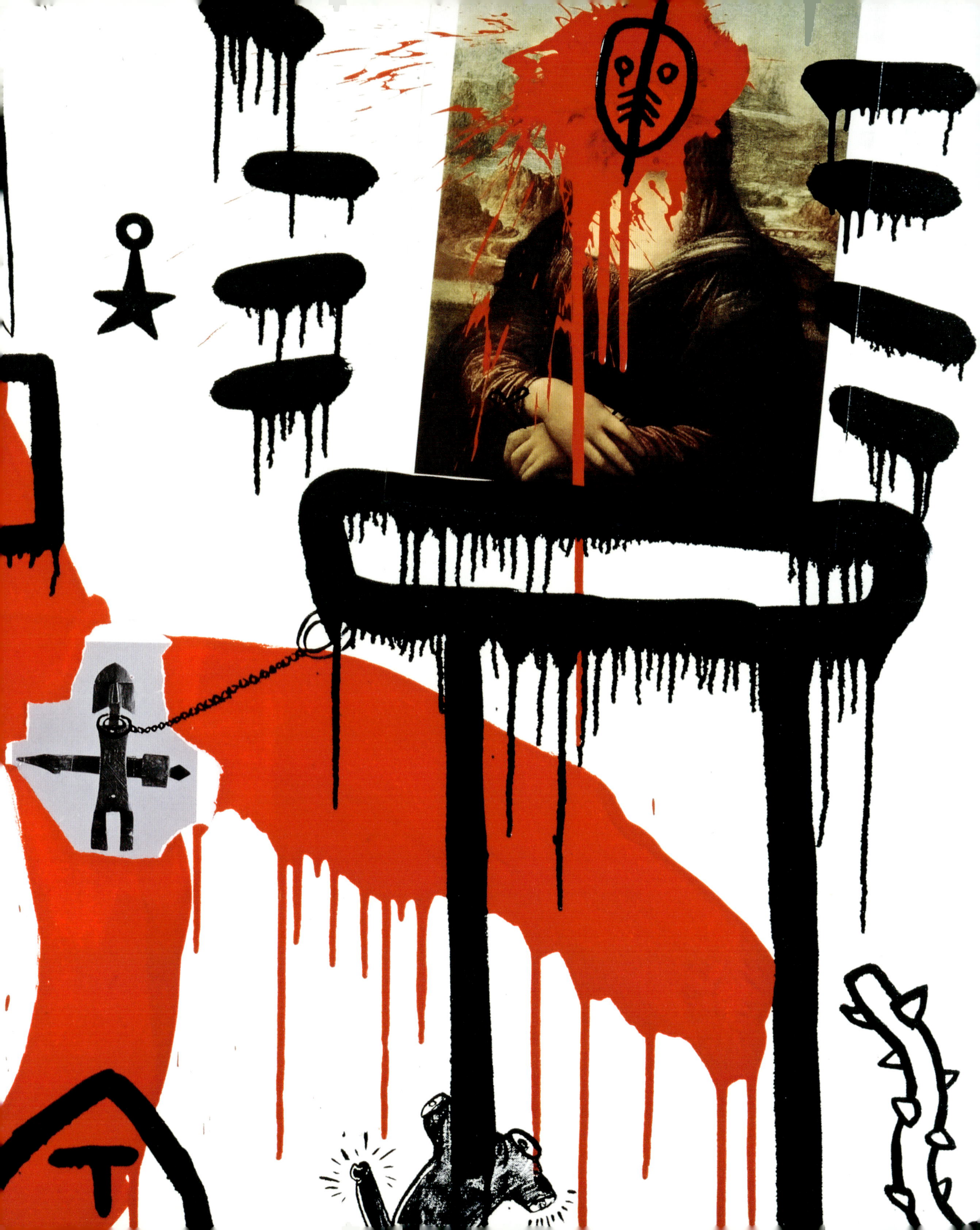

Keith Haring & Jean-Michel Basquiat: Crossing Lines

Dieter Buchhart

When you first see a new picture you are very careful because you may be staring at Van Gogh's ear.
Rene Ricard[1]

I've come to the realization that I can draw anything that I want to – never believing in mistakes.
Keith Haring[2]

Believe it or not, I can really draw.
Jean-Michel Basquiat[3]

Keith Haring and Jean-Michel Basquiat took the art scene of the 1980s by storm: first New York, then Europe, ultimately Japan and the rest of the world. In their works, saturated with signs, figures and words, the age found its symbols. But even thirty years after their all-too-early deaths, their postmodern, political line is stronger than ever. As predecessors of the copy-and-paste internet and post-internet society, they resonate with today's youth culture. Their art inspires the very youngest as well as millennials and the generations before that. With their collaged spaces of knowledge, Basquiat's works today command higher prices than the work of any other American artist, while Haring, with his image-words, could be seen to have contributed to the founding of our 'emoji culture', in which symbols have become a universal language.

After numerous comprehensive retrospectives over the past decade honouring both artists and changing our perspectives on them,[4] it seems important to take a look at these two pioneers together. Not only did they work at the same time in downtown Manhattan, but their personal and professional paths often crossed. Against the backdrop of this shared world, how can we describe the relationship between them? What are the similarities and differences between their work? And why has the significance of their art so drastically increased over the past decade? Now is the time to reveal the points of intersection in the two artists' lives, work and political perspectives.

Crossing lines: life and work

Haring, born on 4 May 1958, was two-and-a-half years older than Basquiat, who was born on 22 December 1960. When he began attending the School of Visual Arts (SVA) in downtown Manhattan, Haring had already encountered Basquiat's poetic, conceptual graffiti. As of 1977, Basquiat and street artist Al Diaz had already made a name for themselves under the pseudonym SAMO©, with concrete poetry like 'SAMO© SAVES IDIOTS AND GONZOIDS ...' or 'SAMO© AS

AN ALTERNATIV= 2 "PLAYING ART" WITH "RADICAL? CHIC" SECT ON DADDY'$ FUNDS ...' (p. 56). Impressed by their concrete poetry, Haring paid homage to SAMO© in an early work from 1979. Years later, in 1985, Haring looked back over his artistic beginnings:

—— A few years back, there were a lot of things in New York that influenced me: graffiti writers, and street artists. People like Jenny Holzer, who took propaganda-like texts onto the streets, which aroused the public curiosity. Samo, who used the whole of downtown Manhattan as his field of operation, was the first to write a sort of literary graffiti. He added a kind of message to his name which conveyed an impression of poetry: statements criticizing culture, society and people themselves. Since they were much more than ordinary graffiti, they opened up new vistas to me.[5]

Haring encountered Basquiat during his time at SVA, as he remembered in the spring of 1981:

—— The School of Visual Arts was ... actually where I met Samo (Jean-Michel Basquiat) for the first time. I let him into school without knowing who he was – because he was having troubles getting past a security guard at the front. I walked him in, and then later on I saw all this graffiti and found out he was the one who had done it ... some of his best stuff was in the School of Visual Arts – because he was at his peak ... He had things like 'Samo as an attitude towards playing art' or 'Samo as Vincent van Gogh' or 'They made you a second-class citizen' ... I had looked up to him for a while before I saw him, because I had been going to the Mudd Club. The whole route from the East Village to the Mudd was covered with [tags].[6]

After the two artists became acquainted with one another, they became fast friends, despite the fact that they circulated in two different artistic circles: Basquiat was separating himself from the graffiti scene, while Haring was embracing it; Haring had formal training, while Basquiat had none. Artist and mutual friend Kenny Scharf described their close association:

—— I met Jean-Michel when I was 19 and he was probably 17, and Keith was a year older. And even though we were still young we definitely knew that there was something really exciting going on, and we were immersed in art; even though our styles were so different we definitely connected, and I got a lot from them ... which is a kind of a competitiveness with people you think are really great, and you look up to, but you are still on the same level. So it created a tension that I thought was very healthy and exciting ... I never felt particularly part of a New York 'group' or a New York 'thing', I always felt a little individual ... The only thing I felt I belonged to was maybe the threesome: Keith, Jean-Michel, and me, but that was not stylistic. The three of us definitely rejected the elitist art of the time, and that's where we really had a bond.[7]

After *The Village Voice* unveiled the secret of the identity of SAMO© on 11 December 1978,[8] Diaz and Basquiat soon announced the end of their collaboration by spraying 'SAMO© IS D=AD' on building walls. Haring then exhibited Basquiat's works – the first time he did this – on 29 May 1980 at Club 57 in the group show he organised, the *Club 57 Invitational*, the next year presenting *Flats Fix*, 1981 (private collection, p. 10) in the *Lower Manhattan Drawing Show*, which he curated, at the Mudd Club from 22 February until 15 March.[9] During these years, Haring and Basquiat had their first more comprehensive exhibitions, both in alternative spaces as well as more established venues. The two attracted great attention in the art world with their participation in the *Times*

Square Show in June 1980 and then the *New York/New Wave* exhibition at the then P.S. 1 Contemporary Art Center in February 1981, in particular. On 30 October 1981, Annina Nosei opened the exhibition *Public Address*, in which the influential gallerist showed works by both artists along with works by artists like Jenny Holzer and Barbara Kruger. Nosei dedicated the entire rear space to Basquiat's standing black male power figures created on wooden doors, including *Irony of a Negro Policeman*, 1981 (p. 307). In December 1981, the legendary essay 'The radiant child' by Rene Ricard followed, which explored Basquiat and Haring in detail, the author noting that 'Jean-Michel's [works] don't look like the others'.[10] Basquiat 'evolved a vocabulary, and so in his way has Keith Haring ... His [Haring's] work is faux graphic and looks ready-made, like international road signs. This immediacy is his trump card'.[11]

Point of convergence: William S. Burroughs
As different as the origin and education of the two artists from middle-class families might have been – Haring was from Kutztown, Pennsylvania, while Basquiat was from Brooklyn – both developed their artistic repertoire out of the humus of the lively New York art scene that had been cultivated by Andy Warhol. Along with Warhol, concrete poetry and William S. Burroughs's cut-up technique left deep traces in the work of the young artists. In the early 1980s, during the emergence of hip-hop, with its cut-up, sample-heavy aesthetic, and the burgeoning 'copy-and-paste' society more broadly, Burroughs's practice of cutting up texts and arranging the parts to form a new text struck a nerve, and he met with late popularity. As the writer said, 'Life is a cut-up. As soon as you can walk down the street your consciousness is being cut by random factors.

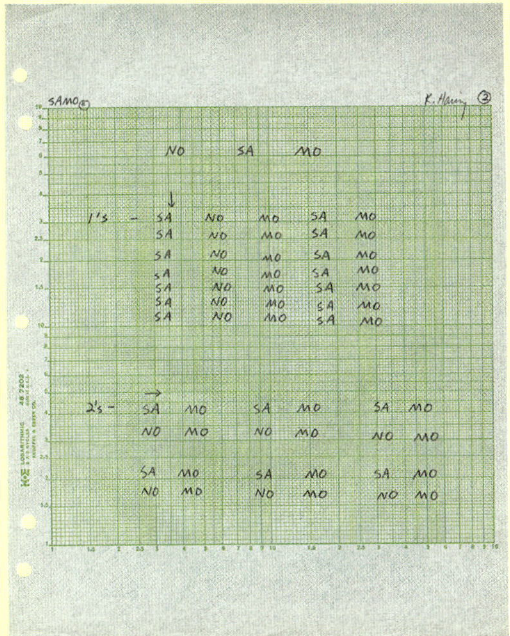

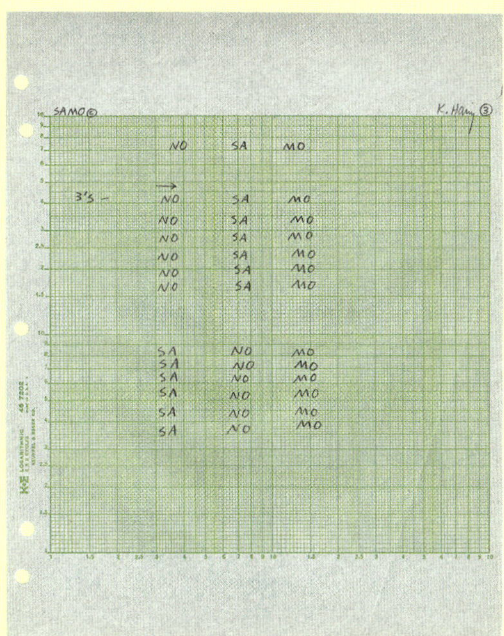

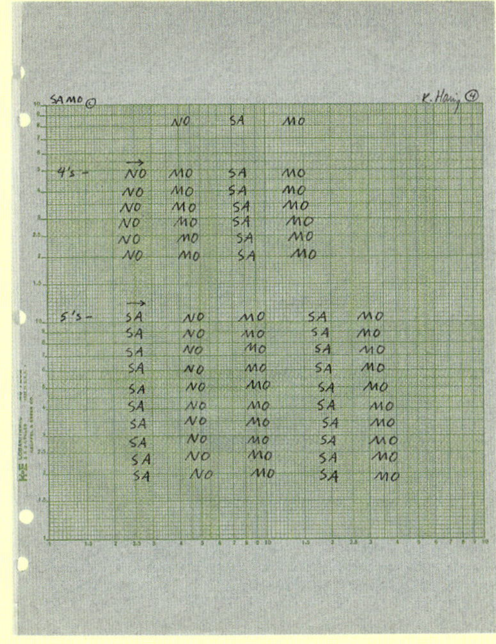

Keith Haring *The End of SAMO Dedicated to SAMO* 18 May 1979, (1-4) 27.94 x 21.59 cm (each), The Keith Haring Foundation, New York

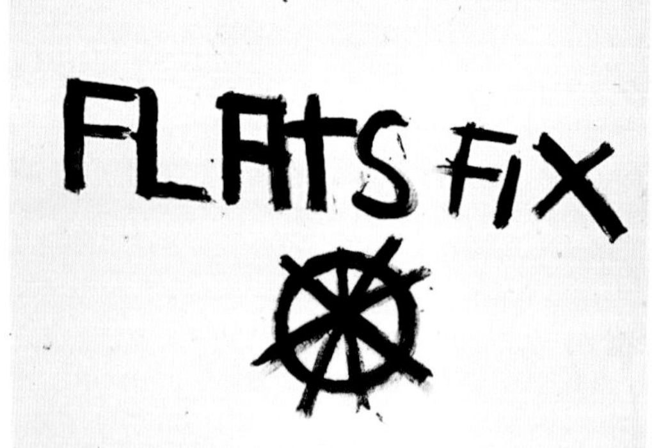

The cut-up is closer to the facts of human perception than linear narrative'.[12] Basquiat, aware of how fashionable Burroughs had become, noted,

— I was going to say Burroughs, but I thought I'd sound too young. 'Cause everybody [says] Burroughs all the time. But he's my favourite living author, definitely. I think it's really close to what Mark Twain writes, as far as the point of view. It's pretty similar, I think.[13]

Basquiat sampled from everything around him with all his five senses; he used the 'source material'[14] that always surrounded him to create his spaces of knowledge. Like Burroughs, he created new links between various contexts and ideas, opening new spaces of thought for the audience, such as Burroughs's basic idea that life itself is a cut-up. The influence of Burroughs on Haring's early text and collage works seems, in comparison, quite direct, in that the artist, also influenced by Jenny Holzer's 1978-87 series *Truisms*,[15] used the technique of cut-up to rearrange headlines from newspapers like the *New York Post*, which he affixed to paper using adhesive tape.[16] He applied hundreds of xeroxes of these 'headline' works, which made proclamations such as 'Reagan Slain By Hero Cop' or 'Reagan's Death Cops Hunt Pope' to lampposts and newsstands[17] in the summer and autumn of 1980, and in playing with the rearranged headlines took a clear position against authority, racism and discrimination (pp. 46–7).[18]

Burroughs himself paid his respects to the young artists. He met Haring personally in 1983,[19] expressing his deep admiration for his work and comprehensive subway drawing project:

— I think Keith is a prophet in his life, his person, and his work. In that way, he's like Paul Klee, who was probably the most influential artist of the twentieth century - certainly through his art, his writings, his teaching. Keith will influence other painters - probably profoundly. By association, Keith is part of the whole New York subway system. Just as no one can look at a sunflower without thinking of Van Gogh, so no one can be in the New York subway system without thinking of Keith Haring. And that's the truth.[20]

The two artists collaborated in 1988 on the print portfolio *Apocalypse*, 1988, and again in 1989 on *The Valley*. 'Our work was of equal weight and purpose ... My texts were perfectly understood and perfectly rendered',[21] Burroughs recalled later.

Photographic documentation shows that Burroughs also met Basquiat, who paid dubious homage to him in 1983 in his triptych *Five Fish Species*. Here he referred, with the words 'BURROUGH'S BULLET©' and '1951', to 6 September 1951, when Burroughs shot his wife, Joan Vollmer, dead in Mexico City, trying to replay the scene with the apple from Friedrich Schiller's drama *William Tell* while under the influence of drugs.[22] This radical and brutal dedication to Burroughs focuses, just like Burroughs's own merciless depiction of life's abysses, on the moment of his wife's death. Basquiat thus ruthlessly evokes Burroughs's eventful life, his rejection of social norms and his radical artistic innovations,

Jean-Michel Basquiat *Flats Fix* 1981, ink on paper, 91.5 x 122.0 cm, Private collection

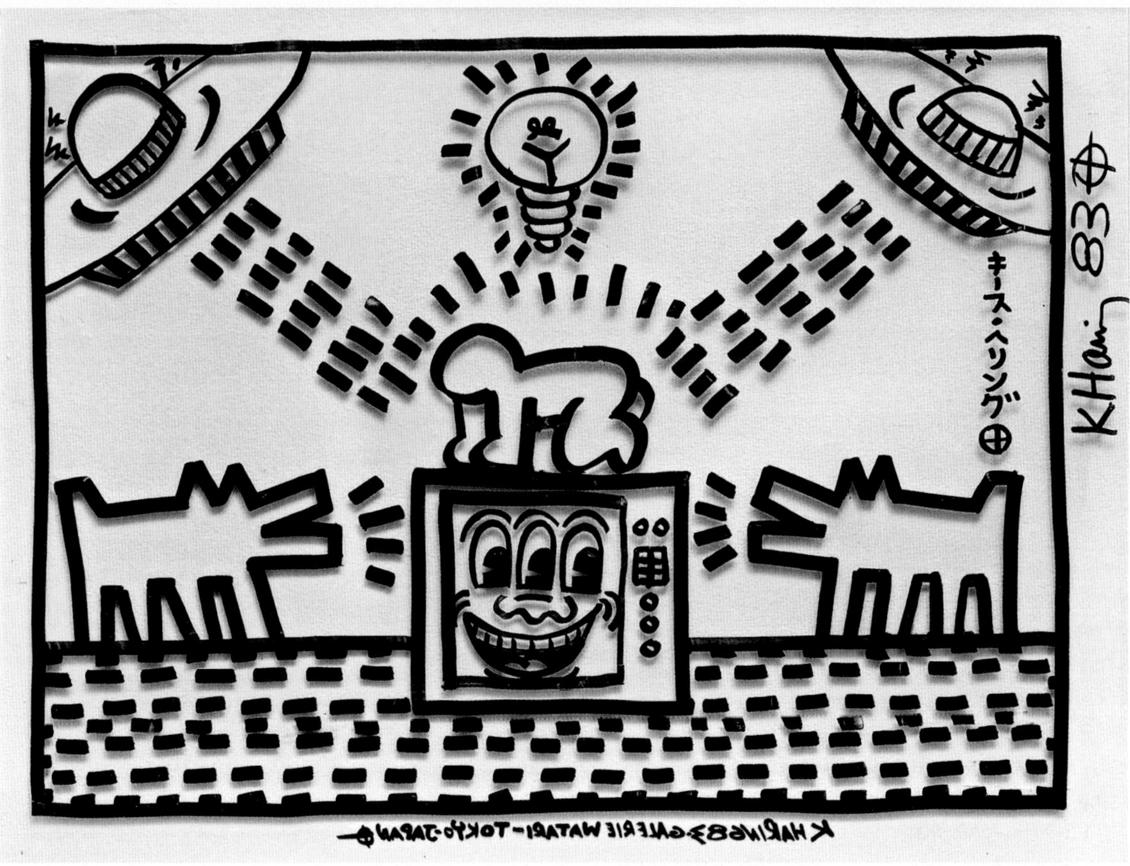

such as the idea of life as a permanent cut-up, in an artistic fulmination against racism, police violence, oppression and social injustice.

Crossing performance lines

Basquiat's early works are marked by the same immediacy and speed with which he wrote his concrete poetry on the walls of buildings, as is documented in the film *Downtown 81*,[23] shot during 1980 and 1981. Basquiat's right hand glides quickly along the wall, applying the spray-paint, while his body rhythmically follows. He developed his own style using the oilstick; he was freed from classical techniques of drawing, with awkward, sometimes dancing movements, as described by hip-hop pioneer and contemporary Fab 5 Freddy [Fred Brathwaite]:

— He would stick [the pencil] through the fourth finger ... so that when he drew, the pencil would just kind of slip out of his hand. He'd let it go that way, then grab it and bring it down, then let it drift. It was amazing, this whole dance he did with the pencil.[24]

With the movement of his hands, Basquiat made drawing a performance: the stick gliding across the picture support, the rhythm of the simple forms and the repetition of letters such as A, O or I. In contrast to the sometimes abrupt drawing rhythm of Basquiat, Haring let the stick or brush glide quickly across the paper or the picture support (here, there is a similarity with Basquiat's poetic graffiti). The speed with which Haring drew his lines was honed during his subway drawing project. Between 1980 and 1985, in a near-manic fashion, and always at risk of being arrested, he executed around 5000 to 10,000 drawings in the New York subway.[25] These works fit almost naturally into his daily

Keith Haring *Untitled* 1983, fibre-tipped pen on plexiglass, 76.2 × 96.5 cm, Private collection, New York, courtesy Martos Gallery, New York

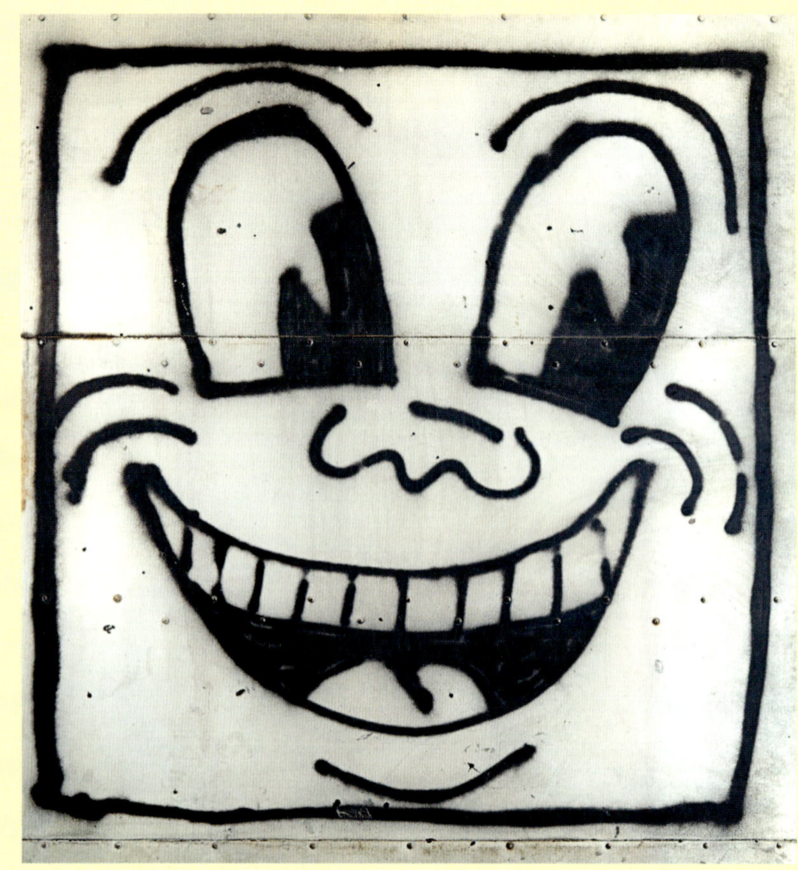

rhythm, when he would take the subway around New York. He used the ephemeral medium of white chalk on the black paper that was applied to advertising billboards temporarily not in use at subway stations.

—Drawing with chalk on this soft black paper was like nothing else I had ever drawn on. It was a continuous line, you didn't have to stop and dip it in anything. It was a constant line, it was a really graphically strong line and you had a time limit. You had to do these things as fast as you could. And you couldn't erase. So it was like there were no mistakes. You had to be careful to not get caught.[26]

Haring walked along the corridors of the subway, took a moment, covered the black paper with his drawings without interruption and at rapid speed, and continued his line on the next surface. Here, 'the man behind the subway drawings'[27] developed his own artistic vocabulary. Haring had studied the theory of semiotics at the SVA and developed his entire visual language from his understanding that images could operate like words.[28] The subway drawings became an essential foundation for his art: 'It sort of became the perfect environment or laboratory to work out all those ideas I was discovering'.[29]

Both Basquiat and Haring were manic draughtsmen who drew constantly, whether in the studio, on trips or at the homes of friends and acquaintances. The critic Robert Storr noted about Basquiat: 'Drawing, for him, was something you did rather than something done, an activity rather than a medium'.[30] The artistic result was of great importance to him, and the very act of drawing in itself was akin to an experience and confirmation of one's own being. The same was true for Haring, who as a twenty-year-old had pointed out that every individual line is already a complete drawing. In his sketchbook from 1978, Haring noted above a small drawing: 'Why didn't you "finish" it?' He answered himself underneath:

—The drawing is 'finished' from the time you start with the first line. There are places you can 'stop' the drawing and call it 'finished' until time and space itself are 'finished'. There are always infinitely more things you can do to the composition, trouble is knowing when to stop. The beauty is knowing when to stop. I choose when to stop. I choose when to stop, but my work is never 'finished' and always 'finished'.[31]

Haring's line is only interrupted to be taken up again at the very next moment, meaning that it continues endlessly. Beginning with an apparently random line, he was able to achieve a balanced composition in just one step, without any hesitation or interruption and without corrections. He created drawing installations as well as 'performance drawings'.[32]

Keith Haring *Untitled* 1982, spray-paint on metal, 213.4 x 190.5 x 5.0 cm, Collection of Larry Warsh

—The drawings which I do have very little in common with drawings in the classical sense as they developed during the Renaissance, and the drawings that imitate life or make a lifelike impression. My drawings do not try to imitate life, they try to create life, to invent life.[33]

So it is not just the resulting drawing, but also the performative act that creates and invents life. In 1980–81 Basquiat had already linked some of his paintings to his poetic graffiti, while Haring had also used spray-paint in his large-format ink drawings from 1980 to evoke the graffitied walls of downtown Manhattan. Created on rolls of paper, one after another like a comic strip or a storyboard, his symbols and acts – such as the activation of a nuclear reactor, the New York skyline, a dolphin, or a couple having sex – link up. While his depictions in the subway were linked to one another by viewers and passers-by, the artist could link individual scenes to visual stories on a single piece of paper.

The street and mutual respect

Parallel to his subway project, Haring applied his image-words to police barriers, construction trucks, containers and scrapped cars. He transferred found and everyday objects from their ordinary locations to the space of his art, and in so doing transformed all these locations into his art space, which he covered with his unique endless line. He thus transformed a US mail truck and dented taxi bonnets into artworks. Alongside found objects, his image-words also took over terracotta vases and fibreglass sculptures, working like a foil or projection over the three-dimensional volumes. Basquiat also painted and drew not only on everything that surrounded him in his friends' apartments – walls, refrigerators, televisions, radiators, pieces of clothing[34] – but also onto anything he found on the street: discarded windows and doors, a mirror, a cigar box, foam rubber, wood planks, old boards. He left his mark on the objects of everyday life among which he lived, and things that he found by chance. In this way, the objects from public space always remained metonymically tied to their place of origin, the street; the street as a concept and space of association remained an artistic subject.

Both artists had been transforming everyday objects and items from public space into artworks from the very beginning of their careers. Their mutual admiration came from their early perception of one another's work. Basquiat admired Haring as an artist, and also made portraits of him (p. 39), as Mary-Ann Monforton has stated: 'Keith Haring, whom Basquiat called his favourite artist, started out with wheat-paste postering and then devised a new semi-calligraphic drawing style with his abstract figures drawn in chalk on the black paper that replaced subway ads when their lease was up'.[35] Basquiat said about these drawings: 'I think I have to give [the street art] crown to Keith

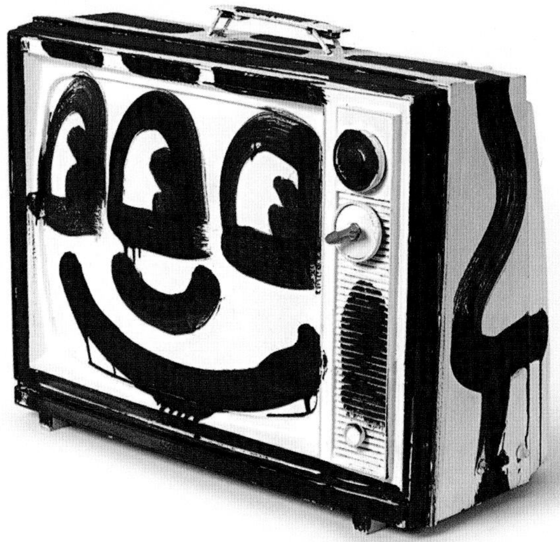

Keith Haring *Untitled* 1986 (detail), mixed media and paint on television and shopping cart, 101.6 x 71.1 x 35.6 cm, Collection of Larry Warsh

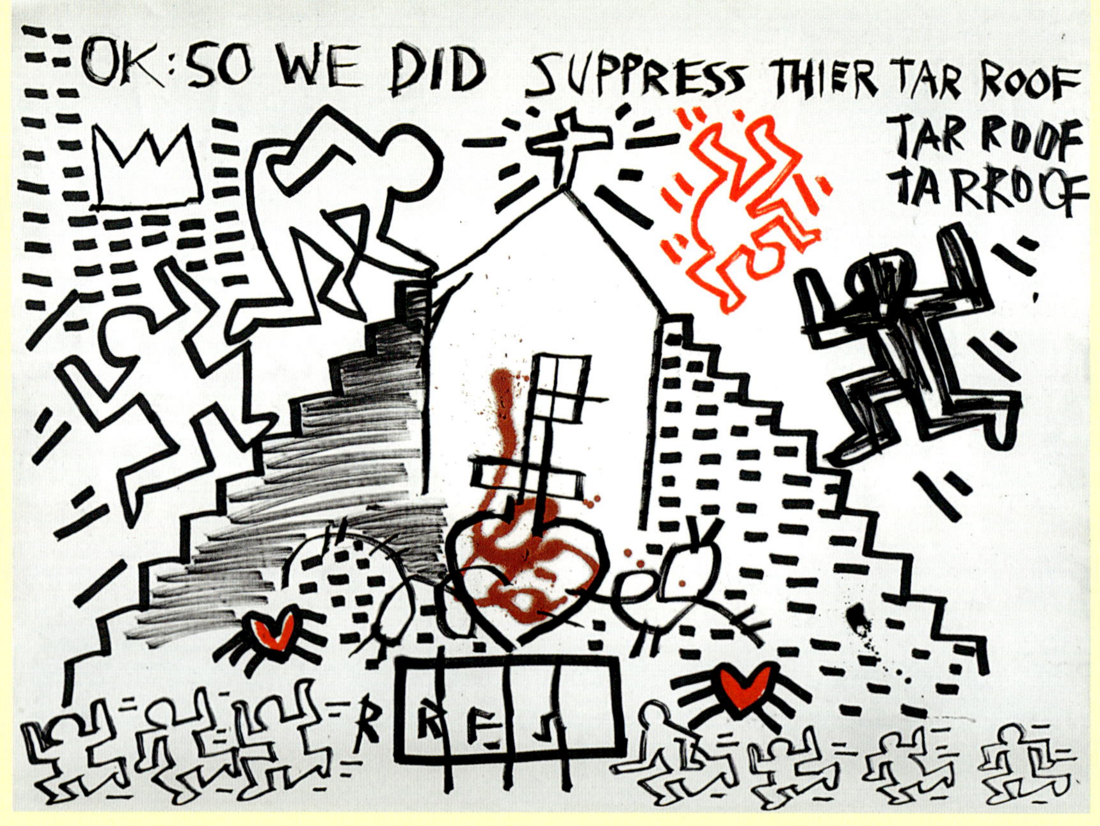

Haring. I haven't worked in the streets for so long'.[36] Haring, for his part, expressed the high esteem he felt for Basquiat in interviews and in his journal. In 1989, he noted once again: 'And there was this art out on the streets. Before I knew who he was, I became obsessed with Jean-Michel Basquiat's work ... From the beginning he was my favorite artist'.[37]

Collaborative lines

The two artists also expressed their mutual admiration in a series of collaborative works. Collaboration was popular among young artists at the time, particularly in the art scene in downtown Manhattan in the late 1970s and early 1980s, where practitioners worked in a range of artistic disciplines like painting, performance, music or film. An important model was surely Andy Warhol who, since the 1960s, had been working across artistic media and was constantly expanding his practice, which moved from painting, prints, drawings, photography and sculpture to film, fashion, television, performance, theatre, music, literature and digital art. Warhol thus broke through the traditional lines separating the individual disciplines and art scenes. Subsequently, artists followed his example. Basquiat was active as a draughtsman, painter, performer, actor, poet, musician, fashion model and DJ, while Haring performed art in public spaces, and produced paintings, drawings, sculptures and prints, and worked with language, video and photography, and also as a DJ. Haring created joint works with the graffiti artist Angel Ortiz, better known as LA II (LA standing for Little Angel),[38] as well as with artists and performers like Madonna, Grace Jones, Bill T. Jones, Timothy Leary, Jenny Holzer, Yoko Ono, Warhol and Burroughs. The artistic oscillation between different disciplines was virtually a natural undertaking, and anticipated the

Keith Haring, Jean-Michel Basquiat *Untitled* 1980, fibre-tipped pen on paper, 96.5 x 127.0 cm, Private collection

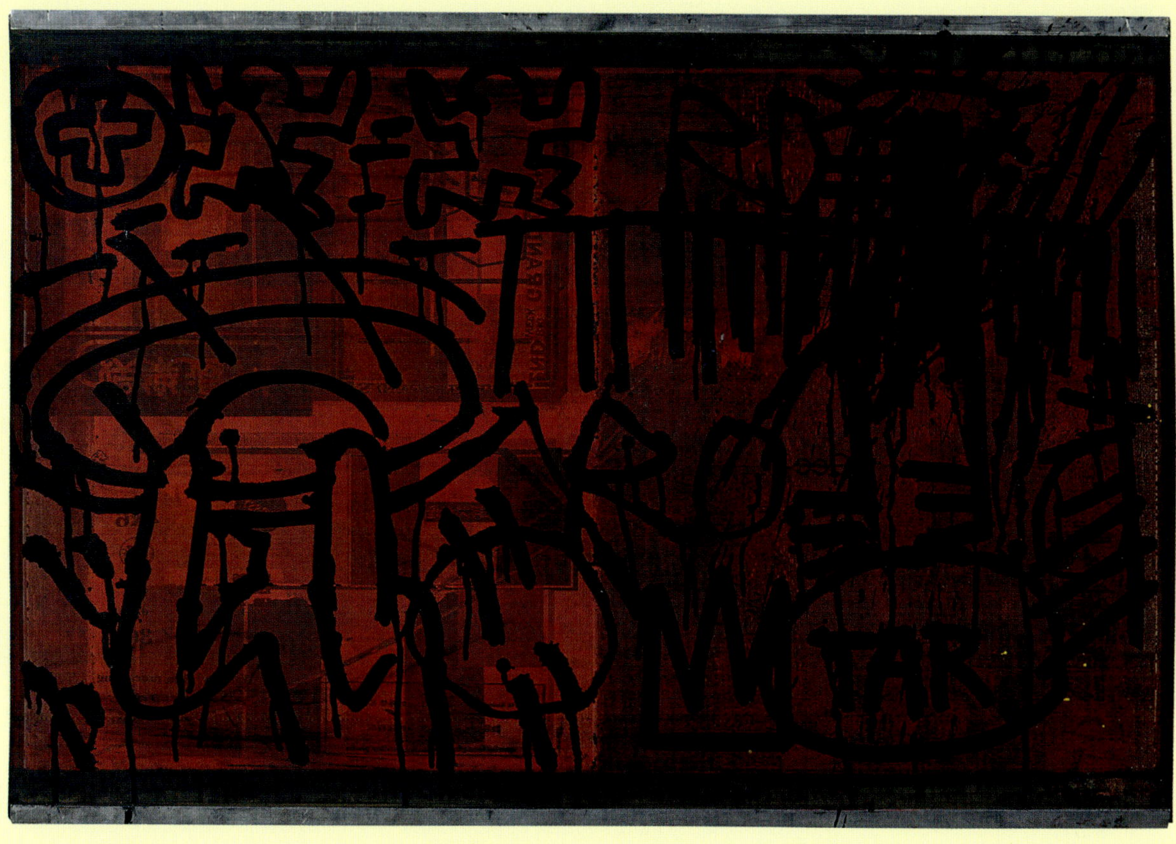

interdisciplinary practices of many artists in the 1990s.

In a collaborative work from 1982, Haring and Basquiat worked with the same ink, resulting in a largely unified appearance, but the artistic signatures of the two remain clearly distinguishable from one another: there are Haring's two-dimensional silhouettes of walking figures, and Basquiat's black angel balancing on the word TAR, an evocation of slavery, racism and lynching that he then obscures with several gestural ink strokes (above). This is in line with Basquiat's own understanding of his painting technique: 'I scratch out and erase but never so much that they don't know what was there. My version of pentimento'.[39] The overpainted or erased always remains decodable. In another collaboration, from 1980 (p. 14), three stick figures, one of which Basquiat filled with coarse black strokes, walk towards one another up opposite stairs that are linked at the top by a roof, topped off with a cross. The work features the words 'OK: SO WE DID SUPPRESS THIER TAR ROOF / TAR ROOF / TARROOF'. Haring added a white protagonist outlined in red that tumbles towards the black figure. The sacred heart, a combination of a heart with a cross, was a symbol of royalist-Catholic resistance among the rural population in France around 1793 against the compulsory military service ordered by the revolutionary government.[40] Here, it is countered to the cross on the ridge of the roof; Haring has added two flying hearts to the symbol of resistance. The confrontation on the roof, the grille, the barbed wire, the symbol of resistance combined with the Christian symbol of the cross and the words of oppression create a highly political work, in which the two humanists encounter one another via symbolic antagonists in the struggle against repression, police violence and the church.

Keith Haring, Jean-Michel Basquiat *Untitled* 1982, ink on rubber printing blanket, 62.9 x 88.9 cm, The Keith Haring Foundation, New York

At the time, Haring created joint works with LA II: 'We pursued our collaborations on vases, pillars, paintings and found objects. "Street tags" were finally placed in context where people were forced to see them as art'.[41] Gallerist Bruno Bischofberger in turn initiated fifteen joint works by Warhol, Basquiat and Francesco Clemente; Warhol and Basquiat continued the collaboration during 1984–85, producing more than 150 works. Basquiat's collaborations with Warhol can be read as a melange of each artist's visual language. Haring, who frequently visited Warhol's Factory 'while they were painting together',[42] described Basquiat and Warhol's collaboration in an essay entitled 'Painting the third mind'.

> —— Andy was amazed by the ease with which Jean composed and constructed his paintings, and was constantly surprised by the never-ending flow of new ideas. Each one inspired the other to outdo the next. The collaborations were seemingly effortless. It was a physical conversation happening in paint instead of words.[43]

As he did in his own art practice, Basquiat accentuated and obscured Warhol's visual creations by employing his own visual elements:

> —— Andy was intrigued and intimidated at the same time. Painting with Jean-Michel was not easy. You had to forget any preconceived ideas of ownership and be prepared to have anything you'd done completely painted over within seconds ... Andy loved the energy with which Jean would totally eradicate one image and enhance another ... They worked on many [canvases] at the same time, each idea inspiring the next. Layers and layers of images and ideas would build towards a concise climax.[44]

Haring summed up this highly intense collaboration, which thrilled and fascinated him, by referencing a term coined in a book by William S. Burroughs and Brion Gysin, *The Third Mind*, published in 1978:[45] 'They are truly an invention of what William S. Burroughs called the "Third Mind" (two amazing minds fusing together to create a third totally separate and unique mind)'.[46]

Like Basquiat, Haring was tied to Warhol both personally and professionally. Even at the start of their careers, Warhol served as a role model. Artist Jennifer Stein, who had produced postcards with Basquiat in 1979, noted: 'Of course, Warhol was his great hero'.[47] And art historian Robert Farris Thompson, who was also linked to both artists during their lifetimes, recalled:

> —— Nevertheless Haring, like Basquiat, loyally presents Warhol as his master: 'Andy's life and work made my work possible. Andy set the precedent for the possibility for my art to exist. He was the first *real* public artist in a holistic sense'.[48]

When Haring created 'Andy Mouse' in the mid 1980s, a synthesis of Mickey Mouse and Andy Warhol based on his earlier drawings of Mickey Mouse, he embodied his friend and great artistic model: 'I am seriously convinced that he is the greatest artist since Picasso'.[49] At the same time, Warhol almost

Keith Haring *Andy Mouse* 1985, fibre-tipped pen on plexiglass, 81.2 x 105.4 cm, Courtesy Laurent Strouk

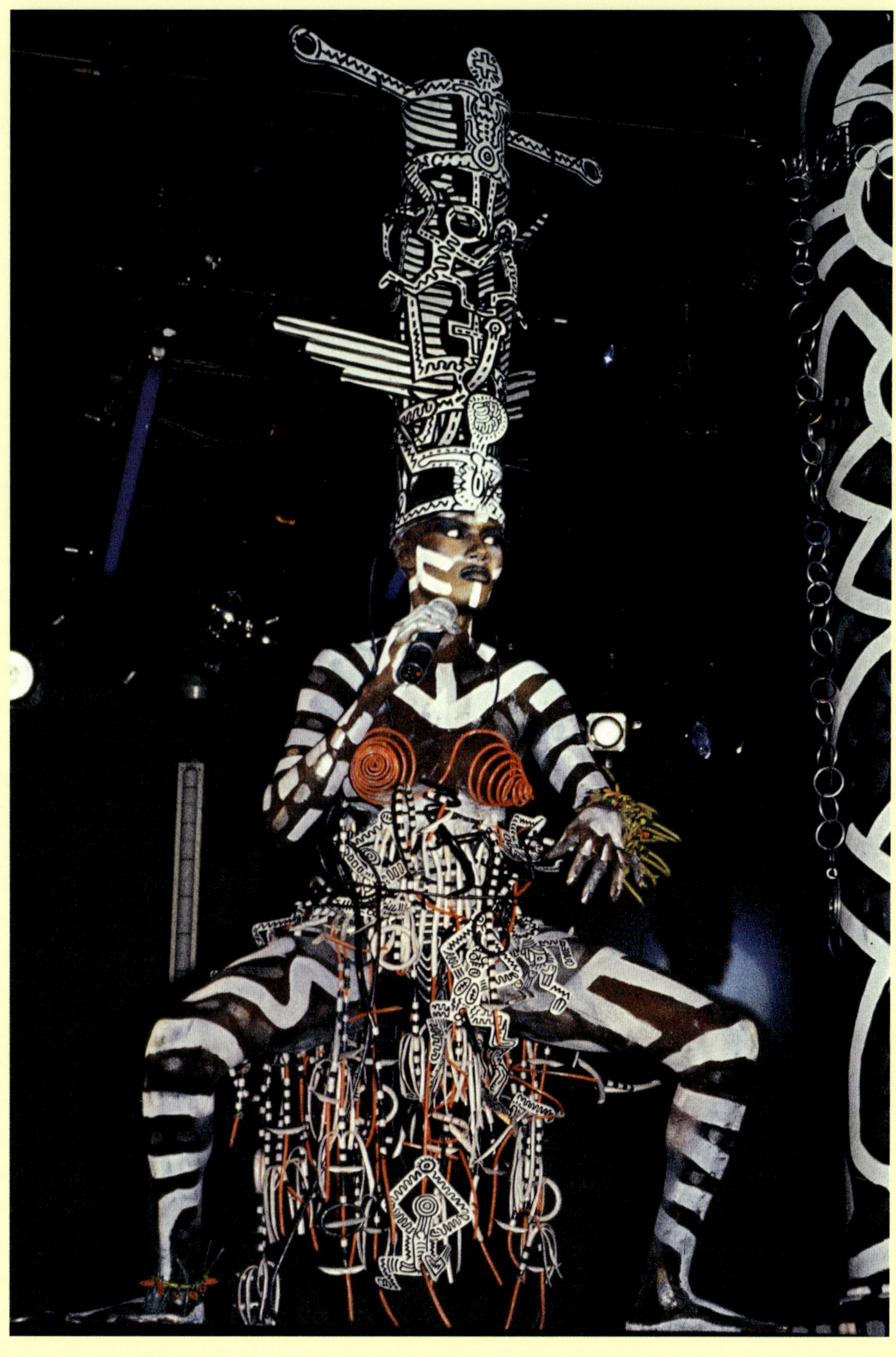

Grace Jones performing at Paradise Garage, New York, 1984

perfectly embodied the image of the artist as businessman and offered the ideal backdrop for Haring's critique of capitalism. Warhol's ambivalence about capitalism, which saw him veer between critique and supposed affirmation of capitalist methods of the exploitation of humanity by large corporations, was something that Haring was quite well aware of: 'He challenged the consumer orientation of the art world, beating it with its own weapons'.[50] When Haring finally created a series of prints of Andy Mouse in 1986, he signed them together with Warhol.[51] Warhol's unexpected death in 1987, due to complications resulting from an allergic reaction to penicillin during a gall-bladder operation, hit both artists very hard. While Basquiat created *Gravestone*, 1987 (private collection), a three-part assemblage dedicated to Warhol depicting a cross, a skull-like head, a black tulip and the word 'PERISHABLE', Haring created two drawings: the first was a portrait of Warhol as a woman with a large yellow banana, the second was a letter he received from a young fan, marking Warhol's death: 'KEITH / I AM UNHAPPY / TODAY WARHOL / IS DEAD I HAVE A / SAD DAY'.

Along with Haring's collaborations with Basquiat, Warhol and LA II, there was his work with performers like Madonna and Grace Jones, as well as the choreographer and dancer Bill T. Jones. In these projects, he transferred the visual language of his objects and two-dimensional drawings to three-dimensional installations, or imposed object-like space onto moving people. Painting human bodies became part of Haring's art practice and in 1984 resulted in him having the opportunity to paint Grace Jones's body (the meeting was arranged by Warhol): 'I was really interested in painting Grace Jones because to me hers seemed like the ultimate body to paint'.[52] The painted human being, in this case Jones, did not rigidify into a painted object, but became a body moving through space. The duration of the movement and the interaction between body and space became part of the artwork. In two performances at the New York club Paradise Garage, in 1984 and 1985, Jones appeared between two round columns covered in Haring's drawings (p. 17). She wore a totem-like headpiece and wire costume adorned with painted metal figures created by Haring and jewellery designer David Spada, and her body was partly surrounded by wires bearing several figures drawn by Haring (pp. 110–11). Here, music, movement, drawing and performance became a *Gesamtkunstwerk* (total work of art).

The next year, photographer Annie Leibovitz convinced Haring to participate in a photo shoot:

> — We decided that he would paint his torso for me. We shot it in the studio, on a set constructed to look like someone's living room, then painted it white. When Keith arrived he painted the room with black lines in less than forty-five minutes. Then he painted his upper body in about five minutes. When he came out of the dressing room he was wearing white painters' pants, but it just seemed obvious to both of us at that point that he should paint the rest of him. It's hard to paint yourself. Keith did only the front. I loved the way he painted his penis. It was so witty, with an elongated line. The pictures took only a few minutes, and when we finished, Keith didn't want to stop.[53]

Haring transformed the entire space into a total work of art, painting the sofa, the lamp, the coffee table, the television and himself, so that his body almost seems to disappear in the white space covered with his lines (see opposite). In this way, Haring transformed a stage into his art space.

Crossing political lines: symbols and words

Haring and Basquiat both developed their 'inimitable line' early on,[54] so unique that

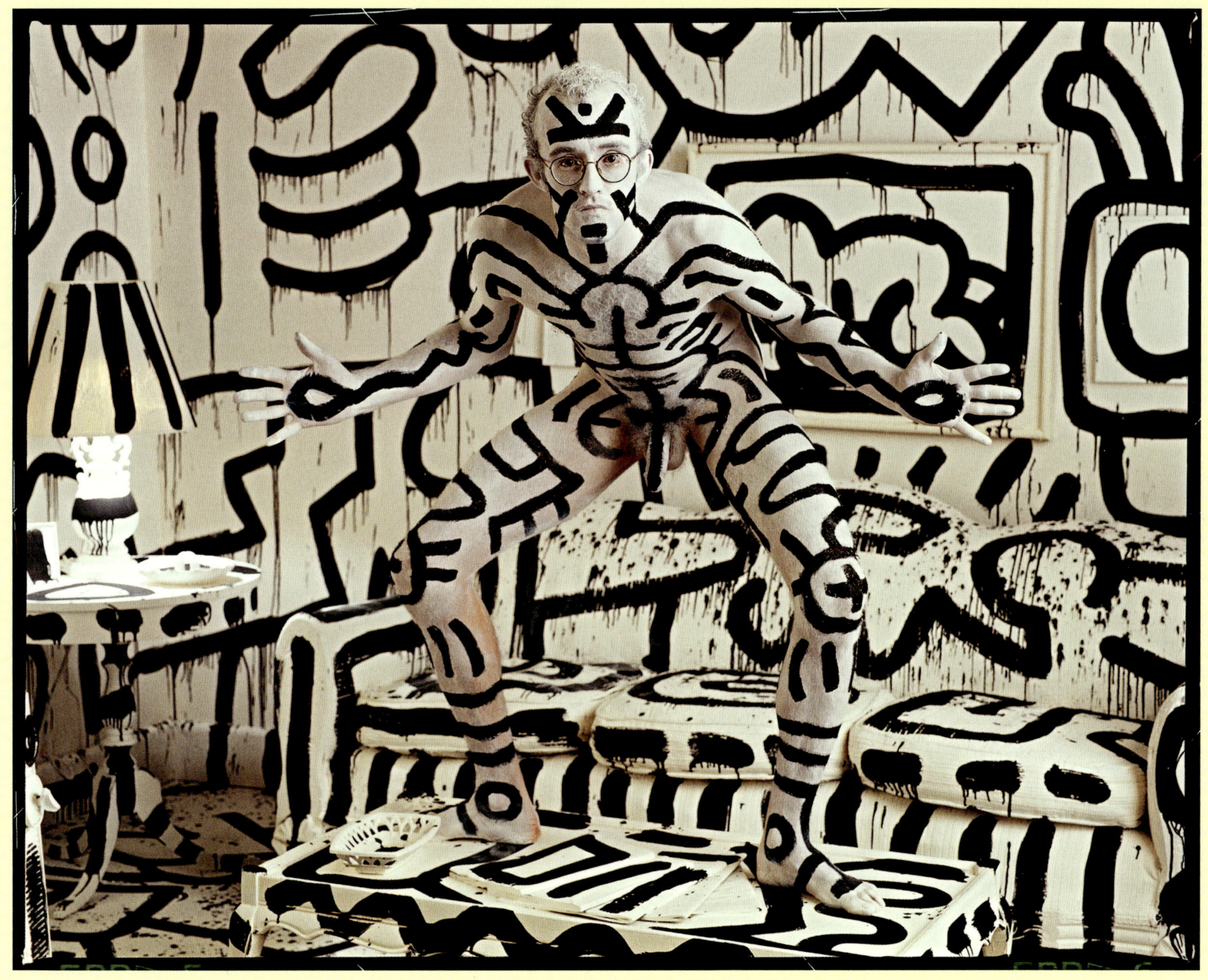

Keith Haring, 1986

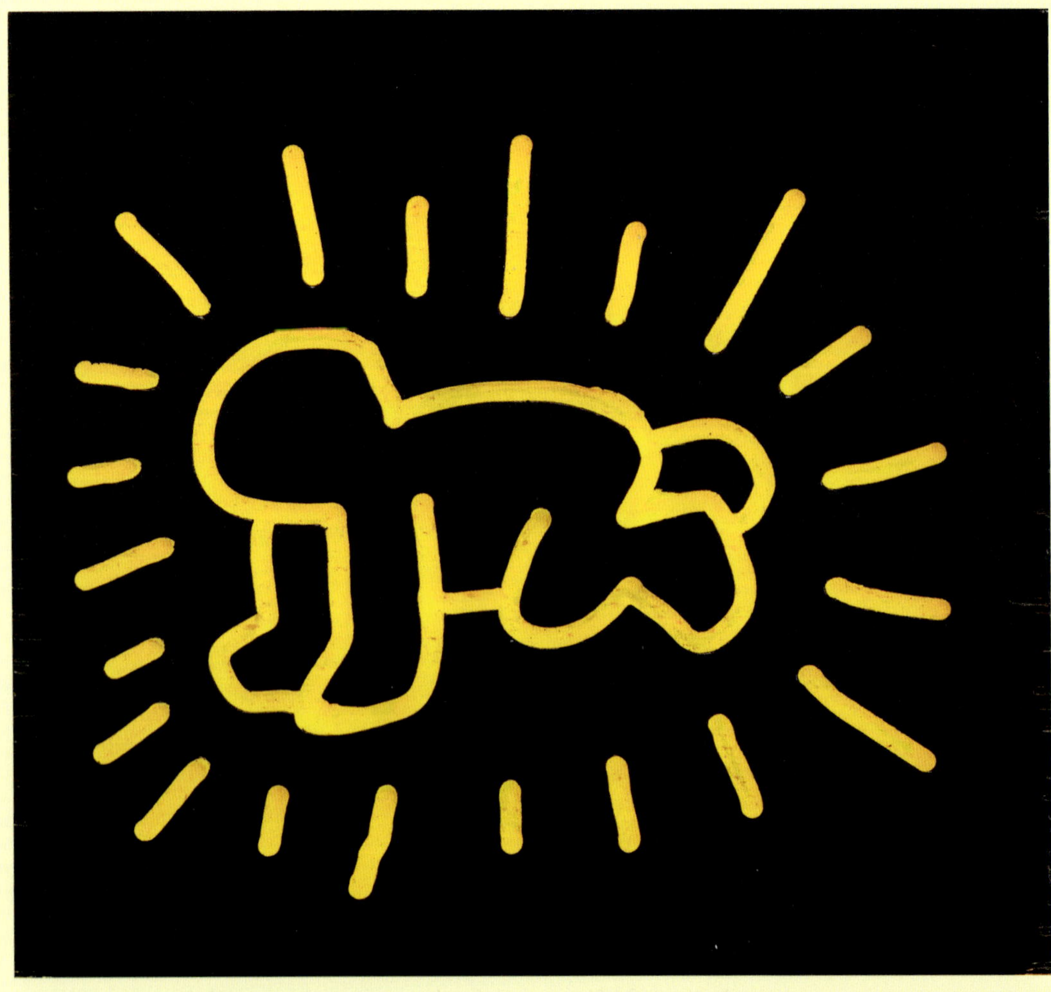

Ricard had already noted in 1981: 'This is no graffito, this is no train, this is a Jean-Michel Basquiat. This is a Haring'.[55] He recognised 'the Radiant Child on the button' as Haring's trademark, while Basquiat had appropriated both the copyright sign and that of the crown: 'he copyrighted the crown'.[56] Continuing his remarks on the copyright sign, Ricard wrote, 'It's the patent, the transition from the public sector into the private, the monopolizing personal usurpation of a public utility, of prior art; no matter who owned it before, you own it now'.[57]

A drawing of a human being crawling on all fours led Haring to the idea of the baby:

—— Babies represent the possibility of the future, the understanding of perfection, how perfect we could be. There is nothing negative about a baby, ever. The reason that the baby has become my logo or signature is that it is the purest and most positive experience of human existence.[58]

The baby thus became a symbol of Haring's uncompromising humanism.[59] The baby – the still malleable, neutral, primal form of the human being – marked the start of his development of an entire alphabet of image-words, including human silhouettes, dogs and dolphins, which were used to comment on the major subjects of the time: gayness;[60] the fear of machines and computers in the age of the mass media; religion, the church, television preachers, extremism, racism and apartheid in South Africa (all of which Haring examined with a critical eye); the AIDS epidemic; ecocide; the Cold War; and the end of humanity.

Keith Haring *Untitled* 1983, enamel on routed wood panel, 28.0 x 29.0 cm, Collection of Misha and Anna Moeremans d'Emaus

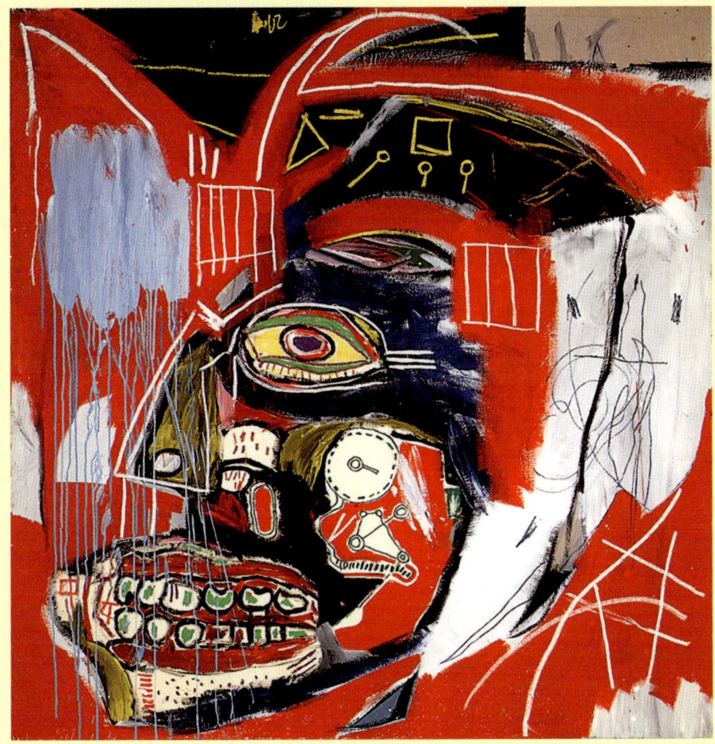

In turn, Basquiat, with his symbol-laden, often furious images, dedicated himself with great intensity to the struggle against capitalism, inequality and racism. Meanings and symbols can be found hidden behind emblems, concepts and words like 'SOAP' (for whitewashing), 'FOOL©' (for the tragic aspect of the black entertainer) and 'COTTON©' (for slavery). The highly political artist, with his inimitable line, established a link between new figurative, in part expressive, elements, and signs with the line, the word, collage and assemblage. The drawing is always the foundation of Basquiat's artistic practice,[61] while letters, words, lists and phrases are often an integral component of his art. Curator Klaus Kertess put it fittingly:

> —In the beginning of his creation, there was the word. He loved words for their sense, for their sound, and for their look; he gave eyes, ears, mouth – and soul – to words. He liked to say he used words like brushstrokes.[62]

Basquiat's line is the painful stake in the texture of his depictions of the black heroes, athletes and musicians he so admired. The standing black man is always presented full of emotion and eager to fight. He is both verbally and physically combat-ready: with arms stretched up in a victor's pose, his body sketched with rough strokes of the oilstick and delimited by an existential line, he is the hero. The nimbus, resembling a crown of thorns, also stands for Christ as martyr and a raging hero. Basquiat's personally and politically charged depictions of protagonists inspired by African-American boxers and heroes oscillate between victim and rebel.

Both men were deeply shocked by the death of African-American graffiti artist Michael Stewart in 1983 following his arrest by police in the New York subway: 'He [Basquiat] was completely freaked out', said Haring. 'It was like it could have been him. It showed him how vulnerable he was'.[63] In the painting *In This Case*, 1983 (private collection, above), Basquiat presents the brutally crushed skull of Stewart surrounded by blood. He highlights the police violence that marked the exclusion, oppression and exploitation of African Americans in the 1980s and which continues today. He saw his own vulnerability and endangerment. This work reflects a statement made by Basquiat about his own practice: 'It's about 80 percent anger'.[64]

Haring was also stunned and reacted with a demand for justice:

> —Today I read in the *New York Times* that all of the officers who killed Michael Stewart were *again* dismissed of charges. Continually dismissed, but in their minds they will never forget. They know they killed him. They will never forget his screams, his face, his blood. They must live with that forever. I hope in their next life they are tortured like they tortured him.[65]

Two years later, he proceeded to process the events with the greatest urgency in *Michael*

Jean-Michel Basquiat *In This Case* 1983, synthetic polymer paint and oilstick on canvas, 197.5 x 188.6 cm, Private collection

Stewart – USA for Africa, 1985 (private collection, p. 302). The monumental canvas tarp shows Stewart being strangled with a rope held by white hands and his foot being stomped upon by a white foot, while a hand extending out from a dollar sign and crosses also threatens him. In the upper right corner, our bursting globe can be recognised; a huge gush of blood emerges from it, drowning people all over the world. The apocalypse is presaged.

In *Untitled*, 1984 (Stedelijk Museum, Amsterdam), Haring took a defiant position against racism and apartheid in South Africa. An oversized black figure, being mistreated by a small white figure using a collar and a leash, kicks his oppressor in a gesture of liberation. Haring used this motif for a poster that he distributed in public spaces. In other representations, the leash – the instrument of oppression – becomes a snake and devours the white man. In *Prophets of Rage*, 1988 (p. 278–9), finally, the dice have been thrown. The oppressed black figure has tossed off his chains, reached for the crown and hung the white man from his feet, decapitating him. Haring's deep sense of outrage in the face of racism and violence finds its expression in a violent end for the oppressor.

Haring's image-words and apocalyptic pictures are explicitly political. Basquiat's line, in contrast, was ready for battle, razor sharp, injured and injurious at the same time, but what his father Gérard once said about him always held true: 'Jean-Michel was very bright, very social and very politically oriented. He didn't have to politicize through a microphone. The works possess messages and speak for themselves'.[66] Thus his existential line is located between powerlessness and self-empowerment, and between human existence and the pressing forces of everyday and institutional racism, oppression, violence and death.

Late works and a pile of crowns

The lifelines and performative, political, artistic and professional lines of Basquiat and Haring crossed from the time of their first personal encounters, whether at the Mudd Club or Club 57, on the street, at openings or in joint exhibitions. Their works were shown alongside those by artists including Joseph Beuys, Anselm Kiefer, Gerhard Richter, Cy Twombly and Warhol at *documenta 7* in Germany in 1982.[67] At the time the youngest participant in this international exhibition, Basquiat presented *Arroz con Pollo*, 1981, and *Acque Pericolose (Poison Oasis)*, 1981 (private collections), while Haring presented *Untitled*, 1984, another tarp work and one of his fibreglass vases.[68]

At the Fun Gallery, run by Patti Astor and Bill Stelling,[69] both artists held groundbreaking exhibitions. The legendary Basquiat exhibition took place between 4 November and 7 December 1982. The artist presented a new series in which he engaged clearly with the support of the artwork and its physicality, eschewing the norm of canvases stretched

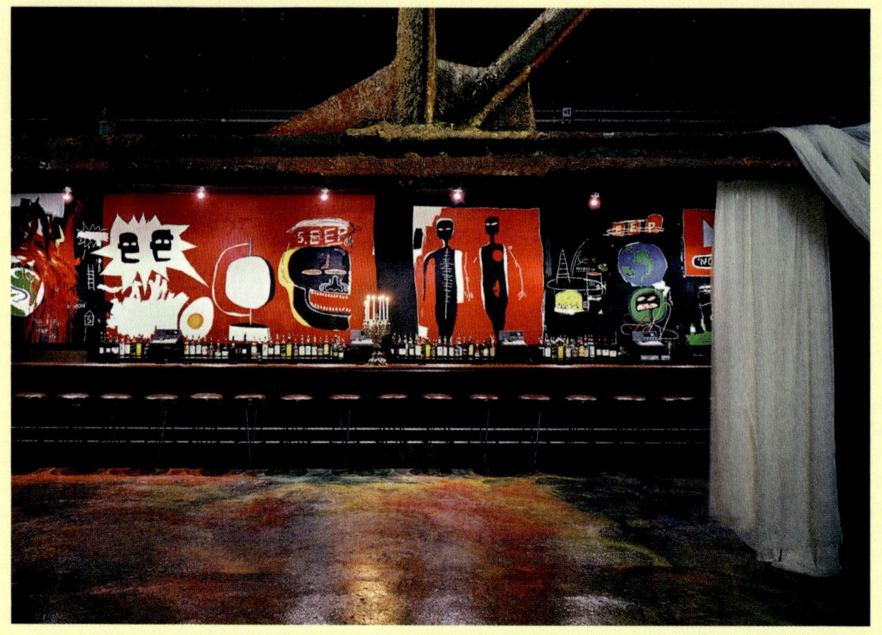

Interior of the Palladium nightclub, New York, with a mural by Jean-Michel Basquiat, 1985

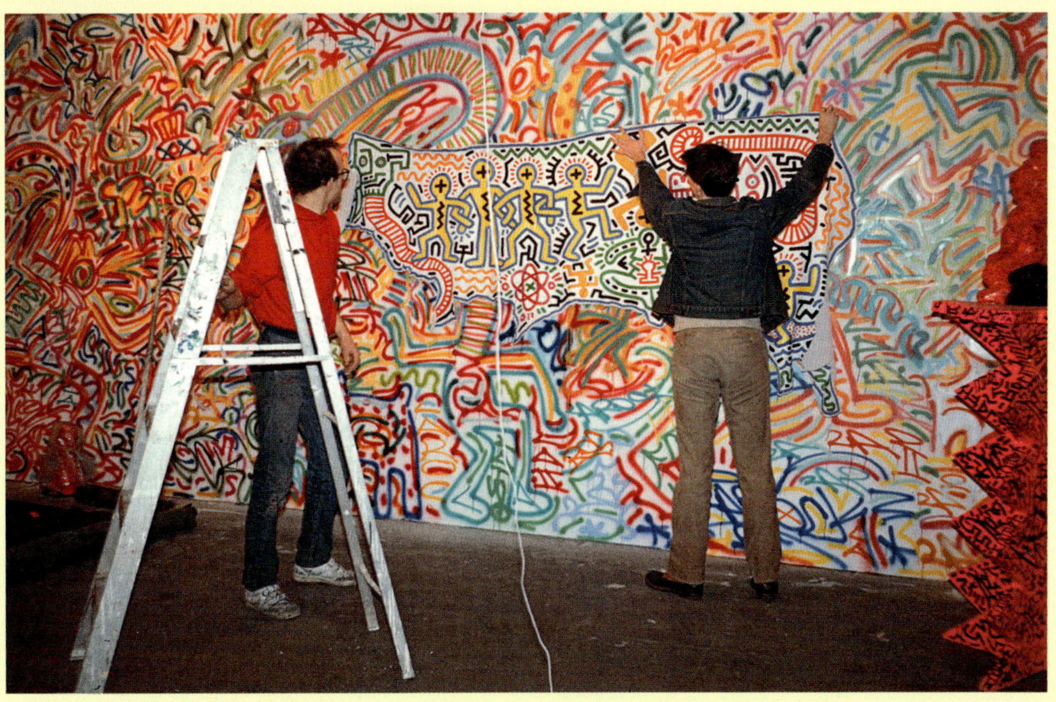

on standard frames. The canvases were instead affixed to pallets or wooden beams or slats that were bound with twine or nailed together. Elsewhere, an assemblage of doors was used and wooden elements or a sculpture of canvas and wood. Critic Cathleen McGuigan described the exhibition as 'bold and colourful, the canvases were crudely, irregularly stretched, and the works had more of the gritty immediacy of the paintings he had done before he joined the [Annina] Nosei Gallery, in part because he returned to a more intense drawing of words and symbols'.[70] And Bruno Bischofberger commented: 'I liked that show the best. The work was very rough, not easy, but likable. It was subtle and not too chic'.[71]

Haring's Fun Gallery exhibition was held between 3 and 27 February 1983. Together with LA II, Haring covered the entire gallery space, floor and walls, with colourful spray-paint pictures and tags. By then mounting works executed on synthetic and leather skins across this room covered in paint, he emphasised the installation-like character of his artistic practice. Haring and Basquiat were featured at the *Whitney Biennial* in New York that same year and two years later at the exhibition *5/5: Figuration Libre, France/USA* curated by Hervé Perdriolle for the Musée d'Art Moderne de la Ville de Paris. In 1985 they also exhibited at the New York nightclub Area,[72] created monumental works for a glamorous new nightclub, Palladium (opposite and p. 103),[73] and executed performance drawings on MTV.[74] In 1987, the two artists took part, along with Sonia Delaunay, Joseph Beuys, Kenny Scharf, Rebecca Horn, Georg Baselitz, David Hockney, Salvador Dalí, Jean Tinguely and Roy Lichtenstein, in André Heller's monumental project *Luna Luna*, which had been almost ten years in the making. *Luna Luna* (p. 117) was intended to create 'a huge terrain of modern art based on the centuries-old idea of the town fair that draws people of all age groups and educational backgrounds into playful processes'.[75] Basquiat was assigned the design of the Ferris wheel and Haring was assigned the carousel. This artistic laboratory remains unique today.

Neither the monumental outdoor sculptures in steel that Haring began creating in 1985 and showed in part at Leo Castelli Gallery, nor his legendary Pop Shops at 292 Lafayette Street and in Tokyo, which Castelli

Keith Haring, Fun Gallery Mural (collaboration with LA II), New York, 1983
(overleaf) Keith Haring, Pop Shop, Tokyo, Japan, 1988

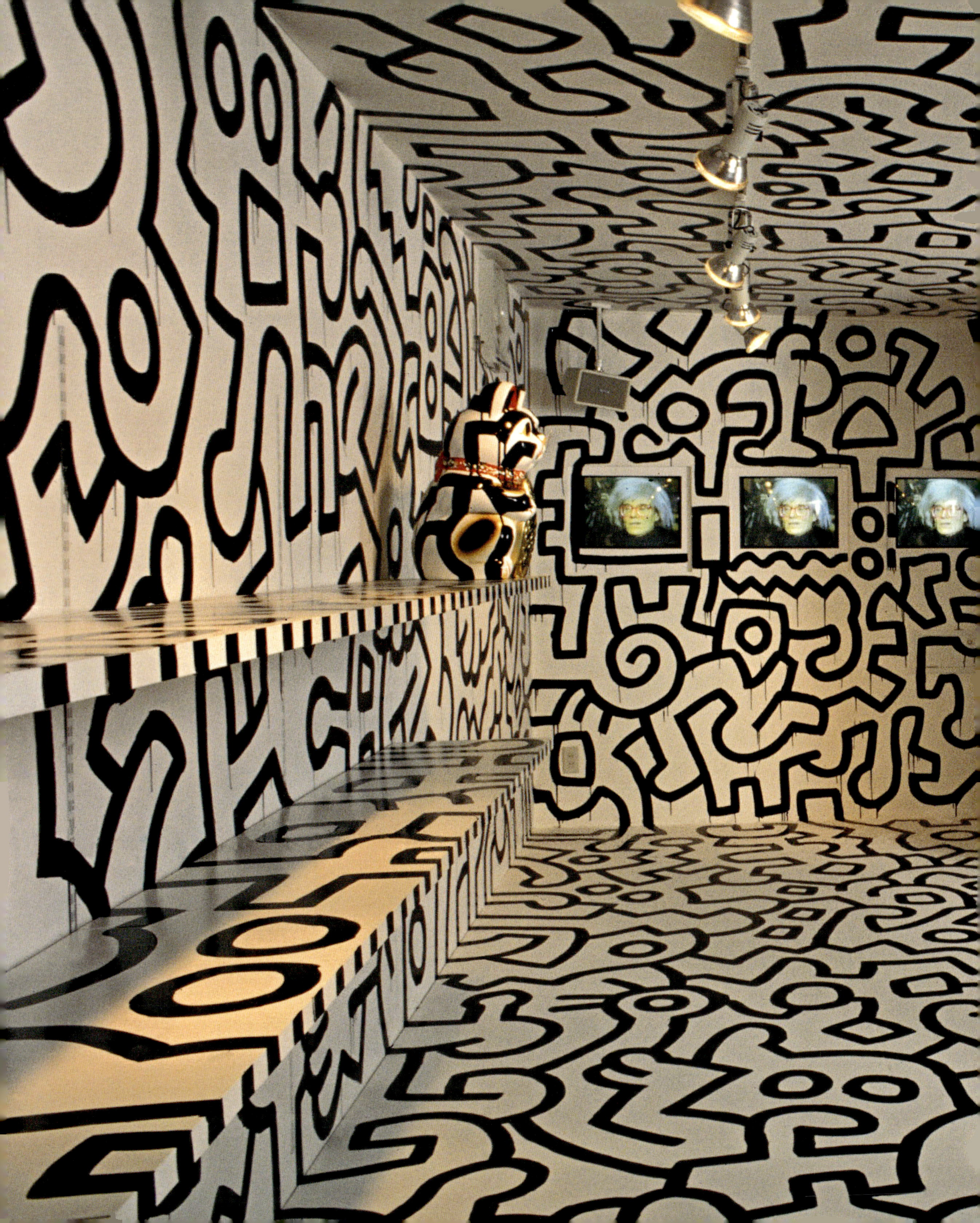

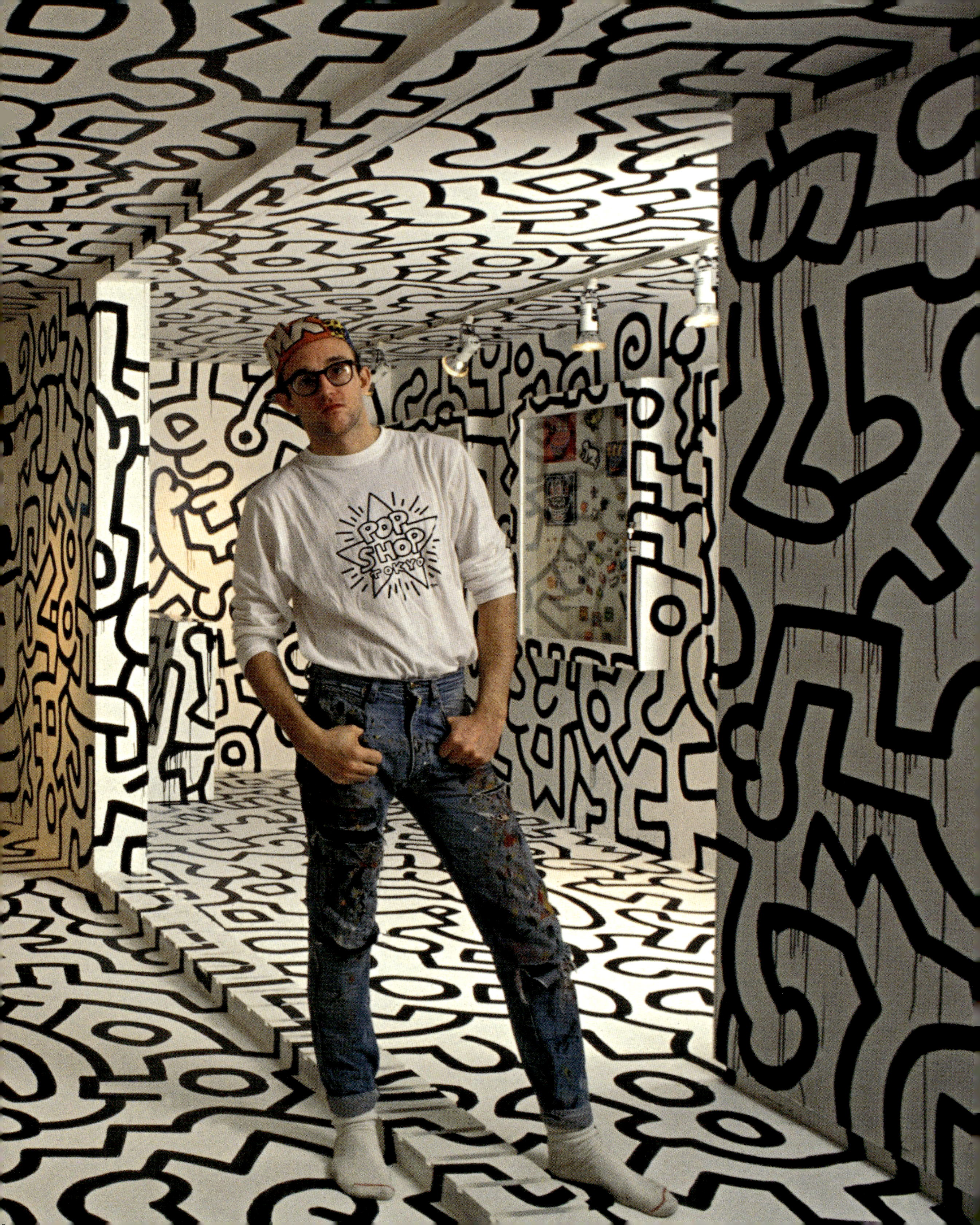
POP
SHOP
TOKYO

called artworks in their own right,[76] find reverberation in Basquiat's work. Basquiat's late works, from the years 1987 to 1988, which alternated between emptiness and a density grown out of a *horror vacui*, find parallels in Haring's last years of creation. Basquiat also created a new kind of representation of the figure and worked on an expanded repertoire of sources, symbols and content, while Haring in his last years expanded his alphabet of image-words between density and voids.

After Jean-Michel Basquiat died on 12 August 1988, Haring wrote a personal obituary for his friend for the November 1988 issue of *Vogue*, titled 'Remembering Basquiat: Keith Haring on a fellow artist – and a friend'.[77] Haring reworked the manuscript several times, as shown by the various versions in the archive of the Keith Haring Foundation. He finally sketched out Basquiat with the words:

> —The intensity and directness of his vision was intimidating. He was uncompromising, disobedient ... He revealed things. He removed the Emperor's clothes ... His expertise at the assembling and disassembling of language has revealed new meanings to old words. He used words like paint. He cut them, combined them, erased them, and rebuilt them. Every invention a new revelation.[78]

Haring was aware of his friend's significance: Basquiat always took an uncompromising position as an artist, innovator and humanist. His themes have lost none of their explosiveness today. His mode of working anticipated the current copy-and-paste society and his drawing presaged the madness of our contemporary culture of constant communication. Despite life's adversities, he was 'UNBREAKABLE', as he recorded in huge red letters on a densely painted monumental canvas (p. 28). 'Wielding his brush

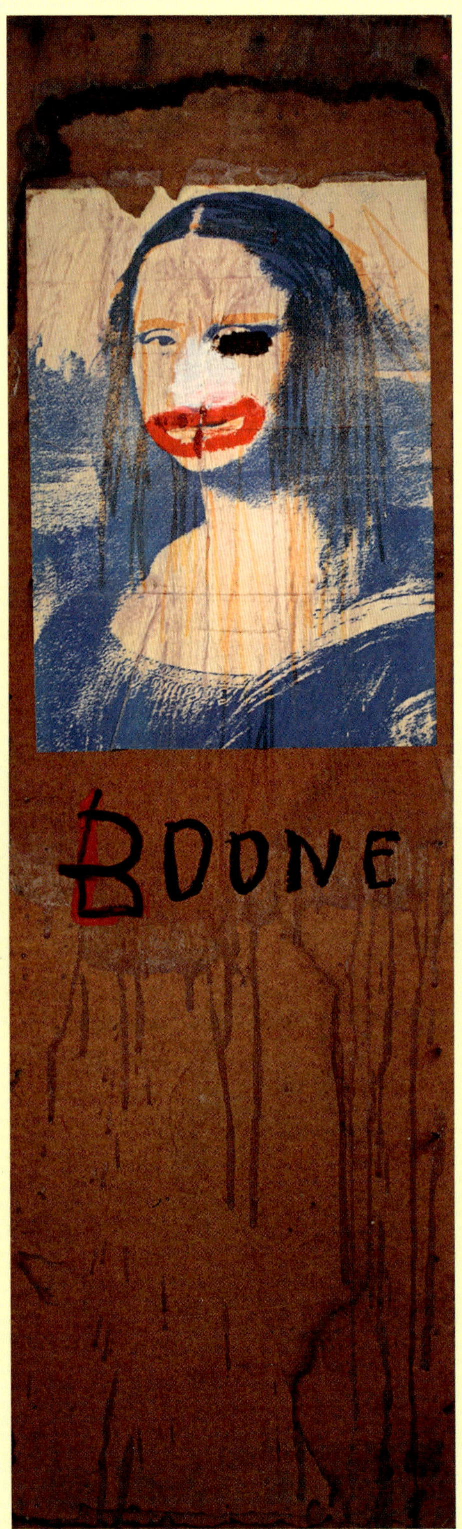

Jean-Michel Basquiat *Boone* 1983, paper collage, fibre-tipped pen and oil wax crayon on composition board, 104.0 x 30.5 cm, Private collection

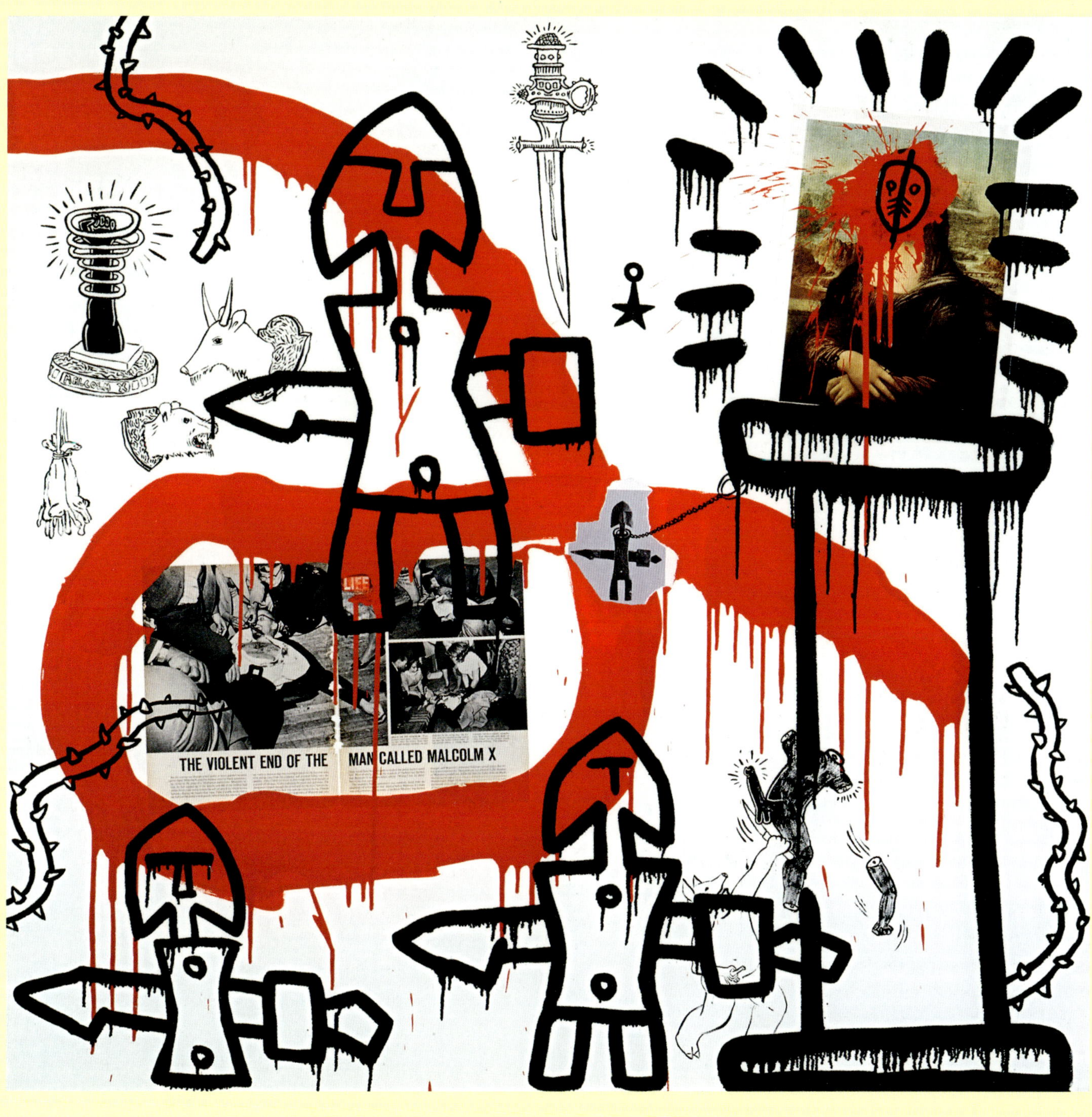

Keith Haring *Malcolm X* 1988, synthetic polymer paint, enamel and collage on canvas, 152.4 x 152.4 cm,
Private collection, New York

as a weapon',[79] along with his oilstick, he fought against exploitation, consumerism, oppression and racism. The ambiguity of his symbols and words open to the beholder a wide field of association and provide new space to think.

As an artistic homage, Haring painted *A Pile of Crowns for Jean-Michel Basquiat*, 1988 (pp. 298–9), where the pile of crowns is given a copyright sign and is stretched on a three metre-wide and ten centimetre-deep triangular frame. The crowns are piled up on an uneven ground and activated with beams emerging from them. According to Robert Farris Thompson:

> —— Basquiat saw himself in graffitero terms, as the king of the young painters. The word King, with its concomitant of sovereign composure, Cool or Kool, appeared with great frequency in New York City graffiti of the '70s. Haring saturates *A Pile of Crowns for Jean-Michel Basquiat*, 1988, with these understandings. He takes the signs of coronation seriously and transmutes them into an epitaph. The crowns are built up, like a mound of stones upon a sepulcher, as if honouring every painting Basquiat ever signed with this seal of assertion. Some of the crowns have fallen, however. The artist is gone, unable to tend his reputation. Haring causes the mound to shine with inner spirit, intuiting a lasting contribution to American painting.[80]

For Haring, Jean-Michel Basquiat was 'still the ♕ of art'.[81]

A few weeks before Basquiat's death, the two art stars accidentally met on the street. Haring asked to take a picture of Basquiat for a 'street fashion' report; the image shows Basquiat lying down, relaxed, on a grille. Basquiat asked Haring how he was feeling, since he had heard about Haring's HIV diagnosis. Haring's iconography had already changed markedly in 1985 after the loss of some of his acquaintances to AIDS. He composed images of the apocalypse: fantastic depictions with demons, mythical beings, flying skulls and corpses, which hardly allowed for any hope of saving humanity. In his last painting, from 1989, Haring shows, 'against all odds',[82] a celebrating mass of humanity, ready to take up the struggle against oppression, suffering, death and downfall. Keith Haring's own struggle ended on 16 February 1990. He continued his line almost until his last breath. Each of his lines is complete and incomplete at the same time.

After Haring's death, Francesco Clemente, a friend of the two artists, created a work that he dedicated to both of them (opposite). He translated Haring's homage to Basquiat, *A Pile of Crowns for Jean-Michel Basquiat*, into his own delicate watercolour painting, thereby honouring both Haring and Basquiat. While Haring had noticed on 16 June 1987 that Clemente's works looked wonderful 'between James Brown and Jean-Michel'[83]

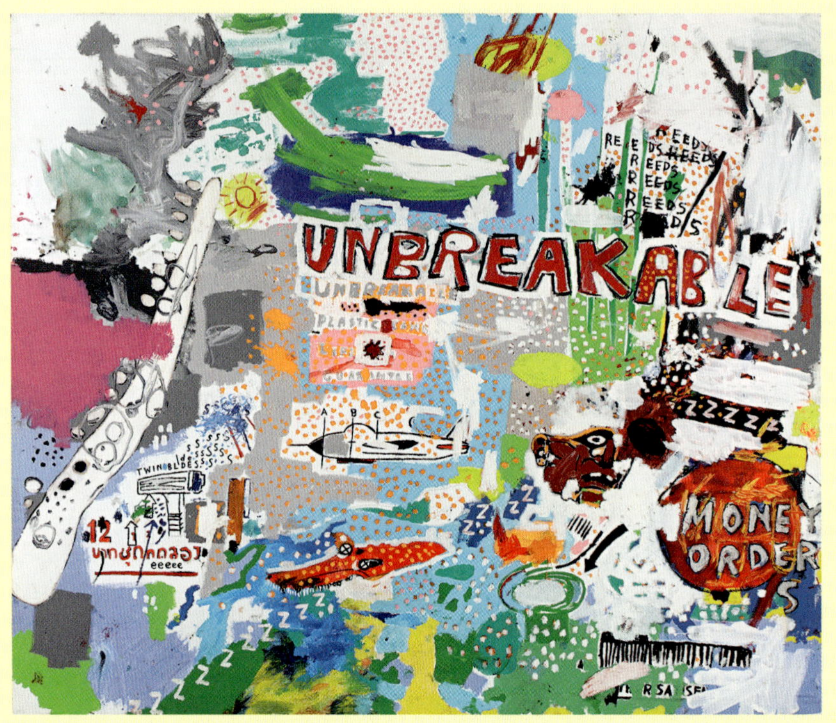

Jean-Michel Basquiat *Unbreakable* 1987, synthetic polymer paint, 249.0 x 284.0 cm, Private collection

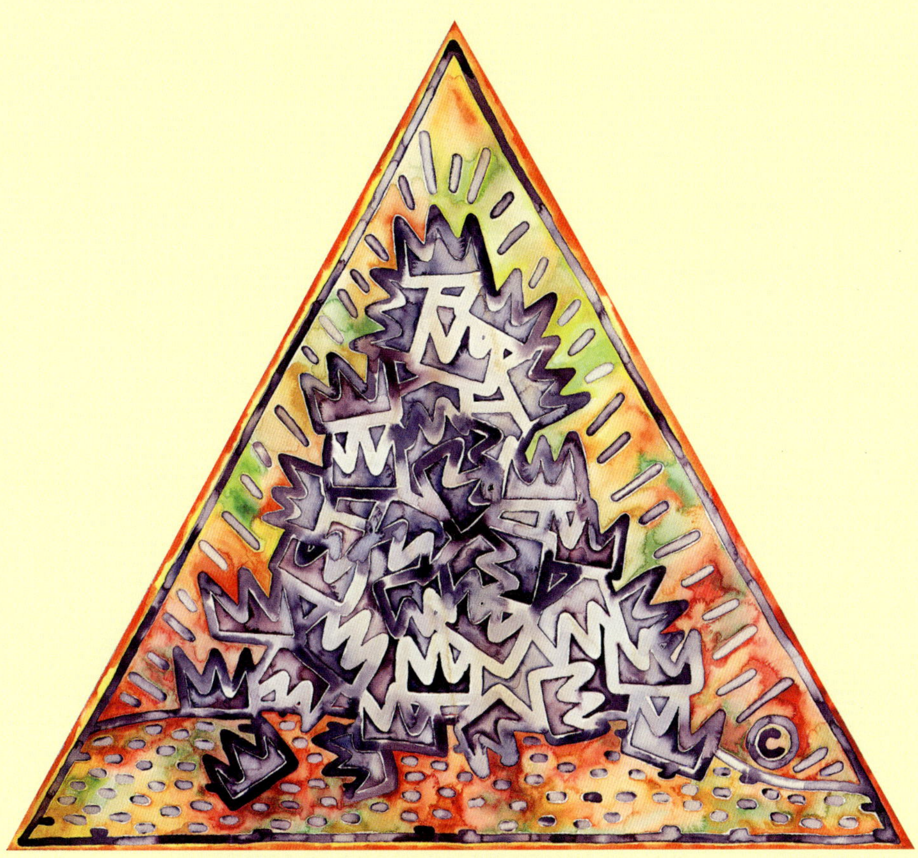

at Art Basel, now it was Clemente who was able to create a work reflecting both artists and the world around them.

Three decades after their deaths, it remains important to stress that Haring and Basquiat were always friends and rivals. As Haring recalled, 'I was always jealous of the attention that he would get in some circles, and he had similar feelings about me for other reasons, so it balanced itself out'.[84] Today, both are considered among the most influential artists of not only the 1980s but more broadly of our time. Both are still relevant to global youth culture today; in fact, they have never been more relevant. While Basquiat anticipated today's 'always-on' culture of communication and contemporary knowledge spaces, Haring foreshadowed emojis with his image-word alphabet. This universal system of communication remains, like his 'urban guerrilla art',[85] a positive, humanistic meme in the collective struggle against ignorance, fear and silence. As Richard D. Marshall has written:

> —These ... wise men, through their visual expression, sought to make art relevant to modern existence and offer enlightenment towards an improved society. Basquiat's determination to ennoble the rich history of black musicians and athletes while acknowledging the underlying persistence of discrimination; Haring's quest to promote individual rights and personal freedoms ... have all been achieved with great artistic style and strength ... Unfortunately, by the end of the decade of the 1980s, two of the wise men had died (and also their spiritual leader, Andy Warhol), but their statement is clear and strong, and their distinctive artworks survive in substance and prominence.[86]

The codes of humanism seem inherent in the practices of both of these influential artists. And their existential lines continue to burn in our brave new world of all-over surveillance. Their steadfastness gives hope that Martin Luther King Jr's call will finally be heard: 'Injustice anywhere is a threat to justice everywhere'.[87]

Francesco Clemente *Keith and Jean* c. 1990, gouache on paper, 108.0 x 119.0 x 4.0 cm, Collection of Larry Warsh

Notes

1 Rene Ricard, 'The radiant child', *Artforum*, vol. 20, no. 4, Dec. 1981, p. 40.
2 Barry Blinderman, interview with Keith Haring, 1981, quoted in Blinderman (ed.), *Keith Haring: Future Primeval*, University Galleries, Illinois State University, Normal, 1990, p. 104.
3 *Jean-Michel Basquiat: An Interview*, interview with Marc H. Miller, produced by Paul Tschinkel, United States, 34 mins, 1989 (no. 30a in the video series *ART/New York*). Distributed by Inner-Tube Films, New York. The interview was filmed in October 1982, but the complete unedited version was released in 1989 after Basquiat's death.
4 I have curated or co-curated exhibitions on Haring, including at Musée d'Art Moderne de la Ville de Paris (2013) and the de Young Museum, San Francisco (2014); the travelling exhibition *Keith Haring: The Political Line* (Kunsthal Rotterdam; Kunsthalle der Hypo-Kulturstiftung, Munich, 2016); and an exhibition at the Albertina, Vienna (2018). For Basquiat, these include pioneering exhibitions at Fondation Beyeler, Basel (2010), Musée d'Art Moderne de la Ville de Paris (2010–11), Guggenheim Bilbao (2015), Barbican Centre, London (2017) and Fondation Louis Vuitton, Paris (2018).
5 Haring quoted in Paul Donker Duyvis, 'Every station is my gallery: interview with Keith Haring', in Wim Beeren (ed.), *Keith Haring*, Stedelijk Museum, Amsterdam, 1986, p. 45.
6 Haring quoted in Vince Aletti, 'An interview with Keith Haring, spring 1981', in Blinderman, pp. 95–6.
7 Kenny Scharf quoted in 'Interview with Kenny Scharf', in William Jeffett, *Kenny Scharf: Pop Surrealist*, Salvador Dalí Museum, St. Petersburg, Florida, 1997, pp. 49–51.
8 Philip Faflick, 'SAMO graffiti: BOOSH-WAH or CIA?', *The Village Voice*, 11 Dec. 1978.
9 See John Gruen, *Keith Haring: The Authorized Biography*, Simon and Schuster, New York, 1991, p. 62, and 'Keith Haring: cut-up street works 1980', in Jeffrey Deitch, Suzanne Geiss & Julia Gruen (eds), *Keith Haring*, Rizzoli, New York, 2008, p. 48. Club 57 was located in the basement of a Polish church at 57 St Marks Place, while the Mudd Club was located further south, at 77 White Street.
10 Ricard, p. 41.
11 ibid. p. 42.
12 William S. Burroughs quoted in Tim Head, 'Interlude I: a chance encounter with William S. Burroughs', in Colin Fallows & Synne Genzmer (eds), *Cut-Ups, Cut-Ins, Cut-Outs: The Art of William S. Burroughs*, Verlag für Moderne Kunst, Nuremberg, 2012, p. 32.
13 'Jean-Michel-Basquiat interviewed by Becky Johnston and Tamra Davis, Beverly Hills, California, 1985: I have to have some source material around me', in Dieter Buchhart et al. (eds), *Basquiat*, Hatje Cantz Verlag, Ostfildern, 2010, p. xxx.
14 ibid. p. xxvi.
15 See 'Songs of innocence at the nuclear pyre', in Elisabeth Sussman (ed.), *Keith Haring*, Whitney Museum of American Art, New York, 1997, p. 12.
16 According to Haring; see Deitch, Geiss & Gruen, p. 52.
17 ibid. p. 53.
18 For more on projects in public spaces in 1980, see ibid. p. 53 and Sussman, pp. 12–14.
19 Gruen, p. 183.
20 ibid. pp. 183–4.
21 ibid. p. 183.
22 See 'William S. Burroughs chronology', in Fallows & Genzmer, p. 53.
23 *Downtown 81*, Edo Bertoglio, New York Beat Films LLC, United States, 72 mins, 2000. The film was produced by Maripol, and features Jean-Michel Basquiat and Debbie Harry, among others. It was shot in 1980–81, but due to a lack of funding was only completed twenty years later. Since the entire soundtrack was lost, the material (including Basquiat's voice) had to be dubbed: this information came from Suzanne Mallouk and Glenn O'Brien in conversation with the author, 18 Sep. 2009.
24 Quoted in Ingrid Sischy, 'Jean-Michel Basquiat as told by Fred Brathwaite a.k.a. Fab 5 Freddy', *Interview*, Oct. 1992, p. 122.
25 It is not known how many subway drawings Haring actually did, but an estimate of between 5000 and 10,000 seems realistic based on the 15,000 photographs that Tseng Kwong Chi took of them, in which several drawings are depicted in two or three photographs. Haring was arrested several times, but we do not know exactly how often. My thanks to Julia Gruen at the Keith Haring Foundation for this information.
26 Quoted in Jason Rubell, 'Keith Haring: the last interview', *Arts Magazine*, Sep. 1990, p. 59.

27 Gina Belafonte did the voice over in Aubert's documentary. See *Drawing the Line: A Portrait of Keith Haring*, Elisabeth Aubert, Kultur International Films, United States, 30 mins, 1989.
28 See Haring's statements, ibid.
29 ibid.
30 Robert Storr, 'Two hundred beats per min', in John Cheim (ed.), *Jean-Michel Basquiat: Drawings*, Robert Miller Gallery, New York, 1990.
31 This drawing comes from a sketchbook with drawings from Pittsburgh and New York. My thanks to Julia Gruen for the information.
32 Sussman, p. 12.
33 Keith Haring quoted in Germano Celant (ed.), *Keith Haring*, Prestel, Munich, 1992, p. 116.
34 Glenn O'Brien, 'SAMO©'s New York', quoted in Dieter Buchhart, 'Boom, boom, boom for real', in Dieter Buchhart & Eleanor Nairne (eds), *Basquiat: Boom for Real*, Prestel Verlag, Munich, 2017, p. 103.
35 Franklin Sirmans in conversation with Mary-Ann Monforton, 31 Jan. 1992, quoted in M. Franklin Sirmans, 'Chronology', in Richard Marshall (ed.), *Jean-Michel Basquiat*, Whitney Museum of American Art, New York, 1992, p. 235.
36 Henry Geldzahler, 'Art: from subways to SoHo: Jean-Michel Basquiat', in Dieter Buchhart et al., *Basquiat*, 2010, p. lviii.
37 David Sheff, 'Keith Haring: an intimate conversation', *Rolling Stone*, Aug. 1989.
38 See Keith Haring, 'About LA2', in *Keith Haring*, Tony Shafrazi Gallery, New York, 1982, p. 20.
39 Jean-Michel Basquiat to Suzanne Mallouk, quoted in Jennifer Clement, *Widow Basquiat*, Payback Press, Edinburgh, 2000, p. 62.
40 See Claudia Schlager, *Kult und Krieg. Herz Jesu – Sacré Cœur – Christus Rex im deutschfranzösischen Vergleich 1914–1925*, Tübinger Vereinigung für Volkskunde e.V., Tübingen, 2011, pp. 103–4 and Raymond Jonas, *France and the Cult of the Sacred Heart*, University of California Press, Berkeley, 2000, pp. 102–3.
41 Haring, 'About LA2', in *Keith Haring*, p. 20.
42 Keith Haring, 'Painting the Third Mind', in Joseph D. Ketner II (ed.), *Andy Warhol: The Last Decade*, Prestel, Munich, 2009, p. 208.
43 ibid.
44 ibid.
45 William S. Burroughs & Brion Gysin, *The Third Mind*, Viking Books, New York, 1978.
46 Haring, 'Painting the Third Mind', in Ketner, p. 208.
47 Jennifer Stein, in conversation with the author, 18 Jan. 2019.
48 Robert Farris Thompson, 'Introduction', in Keith Haring, *Keith Haring: Journals*, Penguin Classics, New York, 2010, p. xxviii.
49 Haring, *Keith Haring: Journals*, pp. 154–5.
50 ibid.
51 George Mulder in Gruen, p. 182.
52 'Grace Jones 1985', in Deitch, Geiss & Gruen, p. 266.
53 Annie Leibovitz, *At Work*, Phaidon, London, 2018.
54 'Cy Twombly: works on paper', in Roland Barthes, *The Responsibility of Forms: Critical Essays on Music, Art, and Representation*, trans. Richard Howard, Farrar, Straus and Giroux, New York, 1985, p. 170.
55 Ricard, p. 36.
56 ibid. p. 37.
57 ibid.
58 Thompson, 'Introduction', in Haring, *Keith Haring: Journals*, p. xxv.
59 See on this Anna Karina Hofbauer & Dieter Buchhart, 'Glossary', in Dieter Buchhart, Elsy Lahner & Klaus Albrecht Schröder (eds), *Keith Haring: The Alphabet*, Albertina, Vienna, 2018, p. 200.
60 For more on the preference for the term 'gay' over 'homosexual' among the LGBTIQ+ community, see Jeremy W. Peters, 'The decline and fall of the "H" word', 21 March 2014, *The New York Times*, <https://www.nytimes.com/2014/03/23/fashion/gays-lesbians-the-term-homosexual.html>, accessed 24 July 2019.
61 See Dieter Buchhart, 'Egon Schiele, Cy Twombly, Jean-Michel Basquiat: it's all drawing and the emancipation of dissonance', trans. Brian Currid, in Dieter Buchhart (ed.), *Poetics of the Gesture: Schiele, Twombly, Basquiat*, Nahmad Contemporary, New York, 2014, pp. 14–27.
62 See also Klaus Kertess, 'The word', in Larry Warsh (ed.), *Jean-Michel Basquiat: The Notebooks*, Art + Knowledge, New York, 1993, p. 17.
63 Anthony Haden-Guest, 'Burning out', *Vanity Fair*, Nov. 1988, p. 190.
64 Henry Geldzahler, 'Art: from subways to SoHo: Jean-Michel Basquiat', *Interview*, no. 13, Jan. 1983, p. 46.
65 Haring, *Keith Haring: Journals*, pp. 165–6.
66 Gerard Basquiat, 'Gerard Basquiat in his own words', in Jeffrey Deitch, Franklin Sirmans & Nicola Vassell (eds), *Jean-Michel Basquiat 1981: The Studio of the Street*, Charta, New York, 2007, p. 94.

67 *documenta 7* was held from 19 June to 28 September 1982.
68 Keith Haring, *Untitled*, 1982, vinyl ink on vinyl tarpaulin, c. 380 x 366 cm; Keith Haring, *Untitled*, 1982, marker and enamel on fibreglass, height: 99 cm, diameter: 71 cm.
69 Bill Stelling left the gallery in spring of 1985. My thanks to Patti Astor for this information.
70 Cathleen McGuigan, 'New art, new money: the marketing of an American artist', *The New York Times Magazine*, 10 Feb. 1985, p. 33.
71 Bruno Bischofberger quoted in McGuigan, p. 33.
72 Area, 157 Hudson Street, was famous for its theme parties and extravagant decoration. On the meaning of the club for the downtown art world, see Eleanor Nairne, 'The scene', in Buchhart & Nairne, p. 97.
73 Palladium, on East 14th Street, had an interior designed by Japanese star architect Arata Isozaki. Henry Geldzahler recommended Haring and Basquiat, as well as Francesco Clemente and Kenny Scharf, to the club owners Ian Schrager and Steve Rubell.
74 Basquiat participated in the pioneering series *Art Breaks* and Haring painted the studio set during an appearance of Duran Duran's Nick Rhodes and Simon Le Bon.
75 André Heller, *Luna Luna*, Wilhelm Heyne Verlag, Munich, 1987, p. 9.
76 Leo Castelli quoted in Aubert.
77 Keith Haring, 'Remembering Basquiat', *Vogue*, Nov. 1988, pp. 230, 234.
78 ibid.
79 ibid. p. 230.
80 Robert Farris Thompson, 'Requiem for the Degas of the B-boys', *Artforum*, May 1990, <http://www.haring.com/!/selected_writing/requiem-degas-of-the-b-boys>, accessed 29 May 2019.
81 Haring, *Keith Haring: Journals*, p. 161.
82 Keith Haring, *Against All Odds, 20 Drawings – Oct 3, 1989*, Publishing House Bébert, Rotterdam, 1990.
83 Haring, *Keith Haring: Journals*, p. 203.
84 Deitch, Geiss & Gruen, p. 455.
85 Sussman, p. 14.
86 Marshall refers to Haring, Basquiat and Kenny Scharf. See Richard D. Marshall, 'Three wise men: Basquiat, Haring, and Scharf', in *In Your Face*, Malca Fine Art, New York, 1997, p. 13.
87 'Letter from Birmingham Jail, April 16, 1963', in Martin Luther King Jr, *Why We Can't Wait*, Signet Classics, New York, 2000.

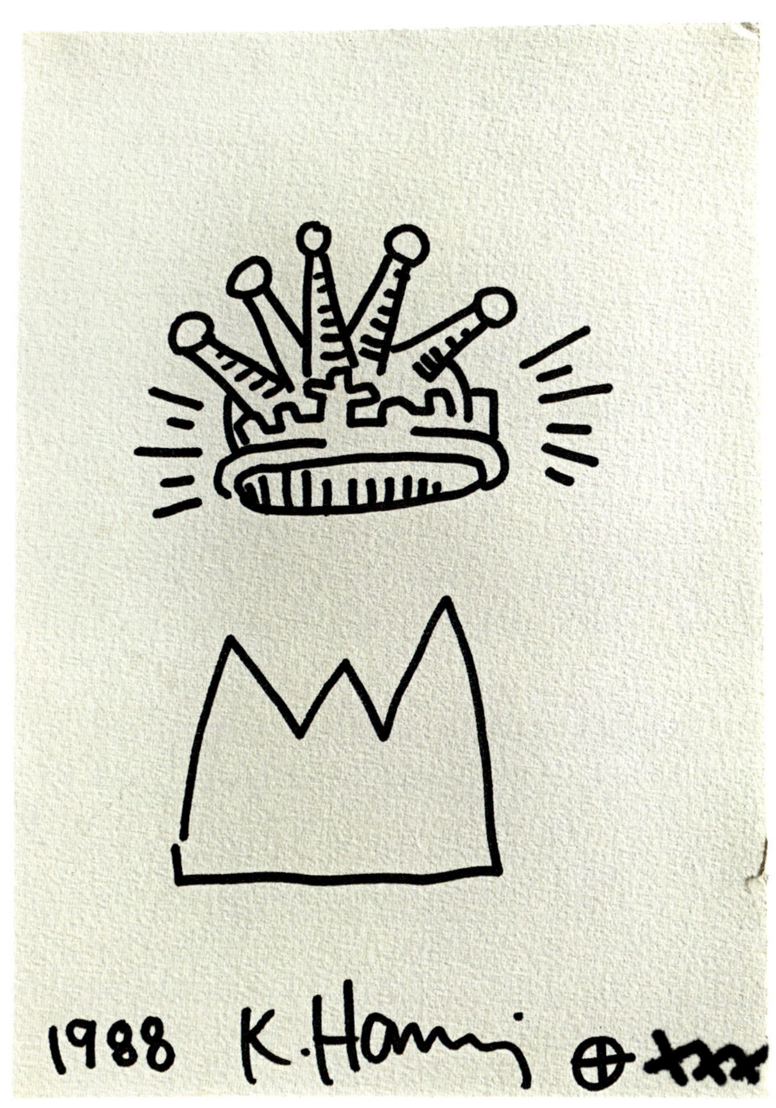

Keith Haring *Untitled* 1988, ink on paper, 26.0 x 17.8 cm, Collection of Kermit and Lisa Oswald

JEAN MICHEL BASQUIAT BORN DEC. 22/1960/BROOKLYN/N.Y.)

MOTHER: PUERTO RICAN (FIRST GENERATION)
FATHER: ~~HA~~ PORT-AU PRINCE, HAITI.
(DIVORCED)

[NAME OF THE TOWN]

ST. ANNS
?
P.S. 6
P.S. 101
P.S. 45
I.S. 293 ← (SOME CATHOLIC SCHOOL DURING YEAR + 1/2 IN PUERTO RICO)
CITY AS SCHOOL

11 TH GRADE DROPOUT
(1) PUT A BOX OF SHAVING CREAM IN PRINCIPAL'S FACE AT GRADUATION
NO POINT ~~IN GOOT~~ IN GOING BACK

FIRST AMBITION: FIREMAN
FIRST ARTISTIC AMBITION: CARTOONIST.

EARLY THEMES WERE ~~THE~~:

1. THE SEAVIEW FROM "VOYAGE TO THE BOTTOM OF THE SEA"
2. ALFRED. E. NEUMAN
3. ALFRED HICTHCOCK (HIS FACE OVER + OVER)
4. NIXON
5. CARS (MOSTLY DRAGSTER)S.
6. WARS
7. WEAPONS.

(8) MADE DRAWINGS OF OOPICK + FRITZ + HAIR + YABOO WITH MARC PROZZO.

(A.) SENT A DRAWING OF A GUN TO J. EDGAR HOOVER IN ~~3rd~~ Grd. THIRD GRADE
(NO REPLY)

TAUGHT SECOND GRADERS WHEN I WAS IN THE FOURTH GRADE. (CARS MADE OF PAPER CLIPS (MASKING TAPE + FASTENERS.

SCHOOLING: SOME ^ACADEMIC^ LIFE DRAWING IN NINTH GRADE.
(WAS THE ONLY CHILD THAT FAILED)

EARLY MUSIC INFLUENCES: WEST SIDE STORY
THE "WATUSI"
ROUND 'BOUT MIDNIGHT
WALKING HAPPY
BLACK ORPHEUS.

Jean-Michel Basquiat *Untitled (Biography)* 1983, oilstick on paper, dimensions and collection unknown

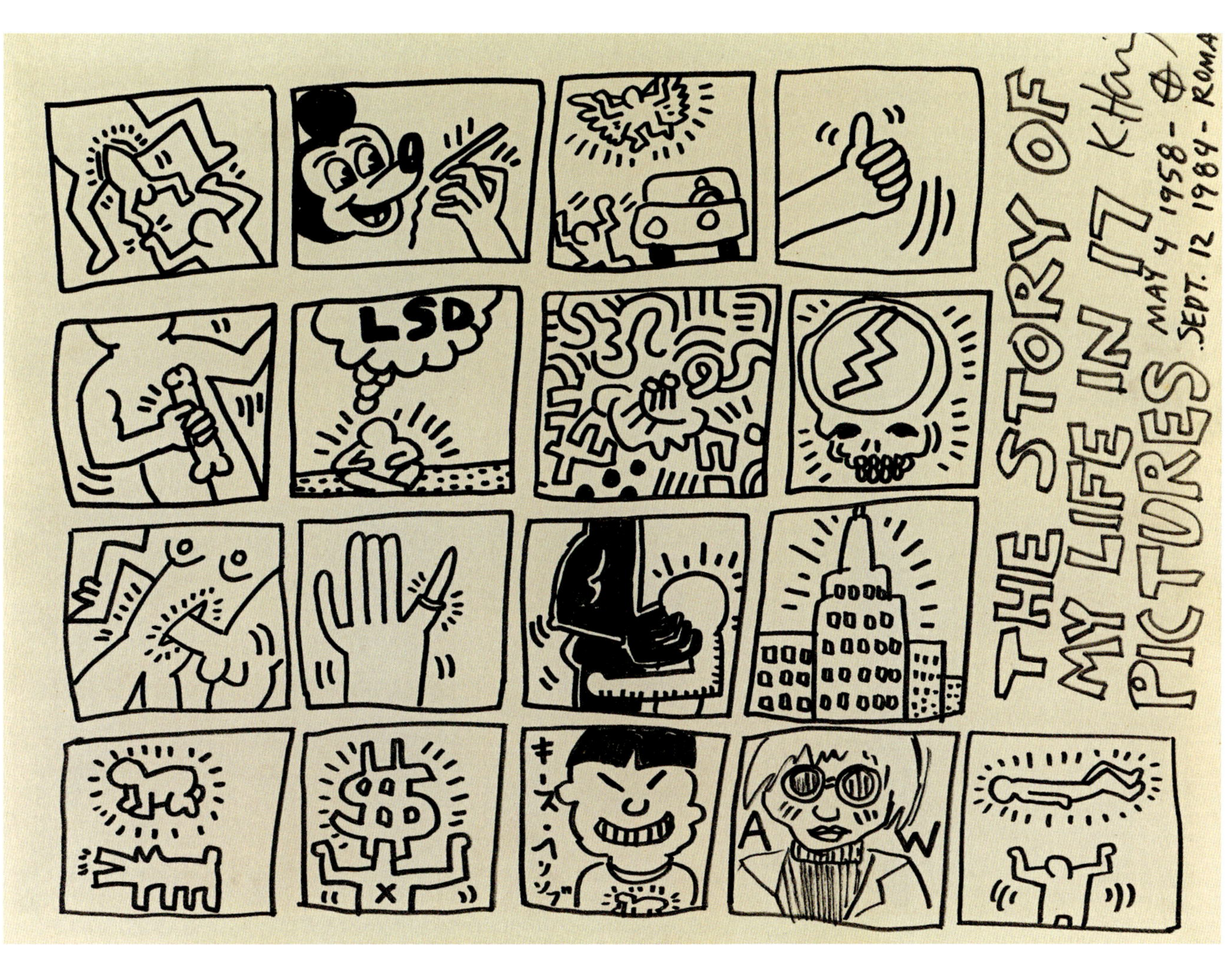

Keith Haring *The Story of My Life in 17 Pictures* 1984, ink on paper, 39.0 cm x 49.0 cm (framed), BvB collection, Geneva

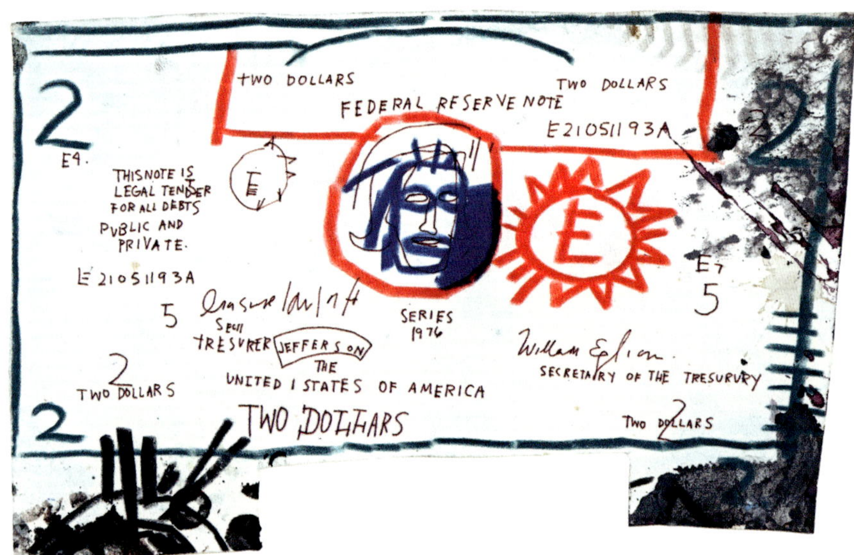

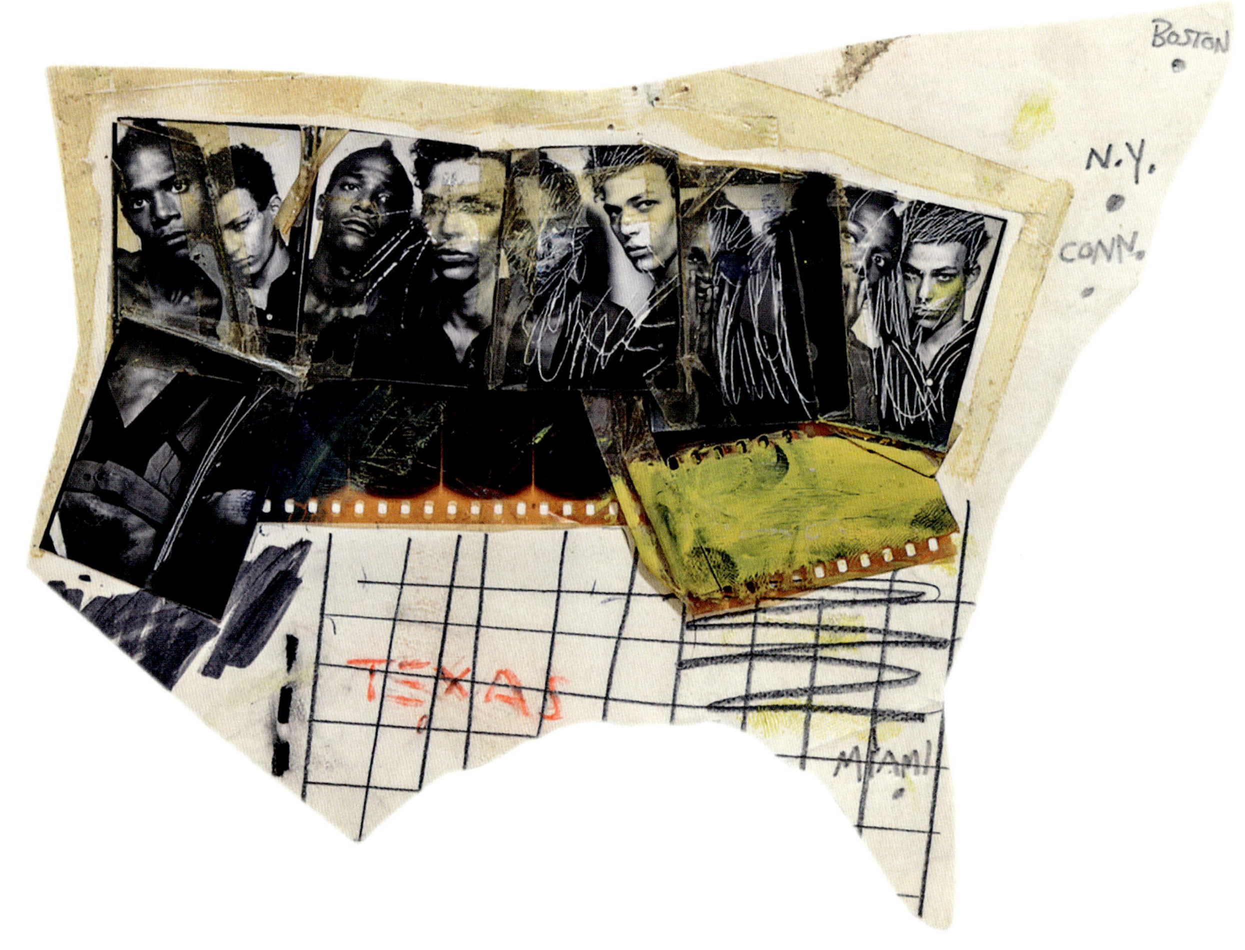

(top) Jean-Michel Basquiat *Untitled (E)* 1985, ink, oilstick and watercolour on paper, 15.6 x 23.5 cm, The Estate of Jean-Michel Basquiat, New York
(bottom) Jean-Michel Basquiat *Untitled (Map)* 1980, mixed media collage, 26.7 x 34.0 cm, Collection of Larry Warsh

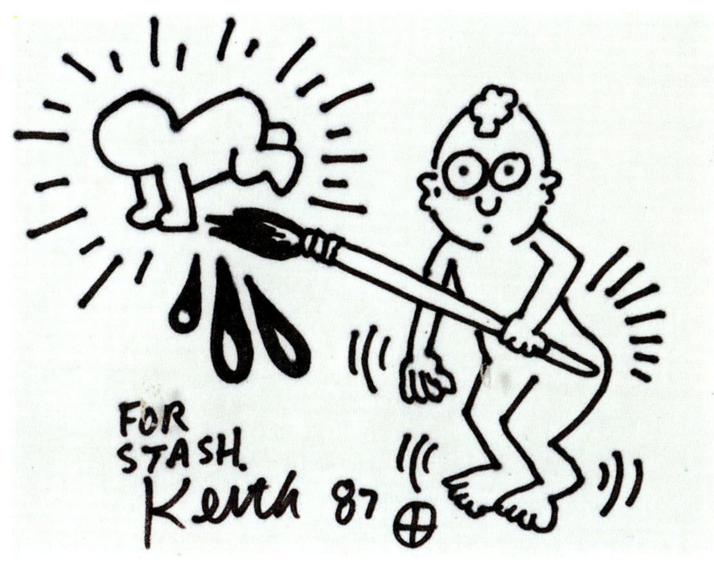

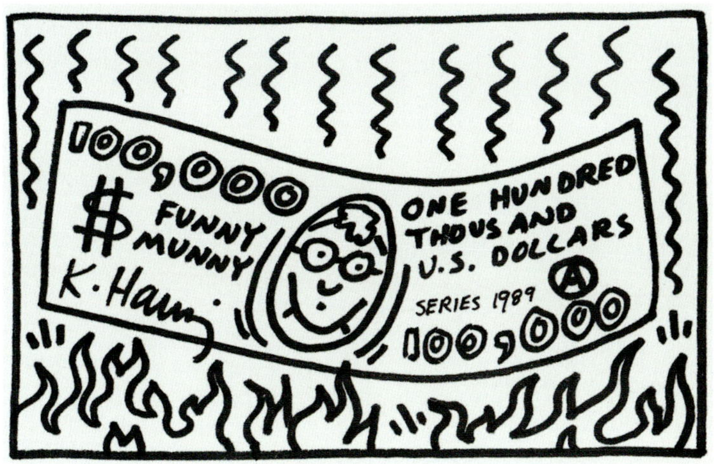

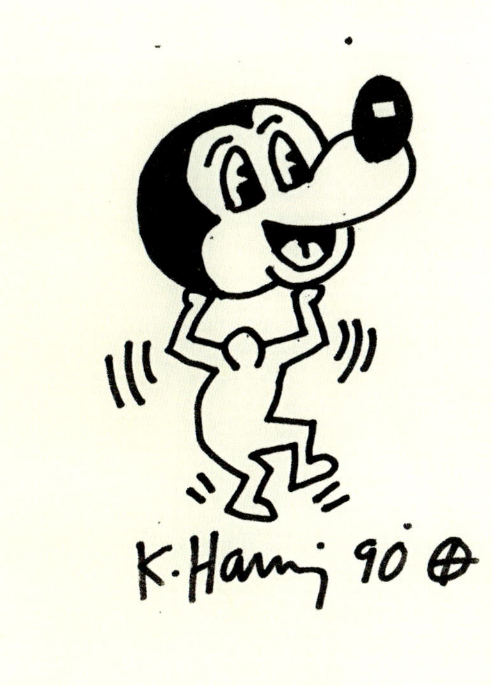

(clockwise from top left) Keith Haring *Untitled* 1987, ink on paper, 12.7 x 15.2 cm, Collection of Larry Warsh; *Untitled* 1990, ink on paper, 40.6 x 30.5 cm, Private collection; *Untitled* 1989, ink on paper, 11.4 x 15.2 cm, Collection of Larry Warsh

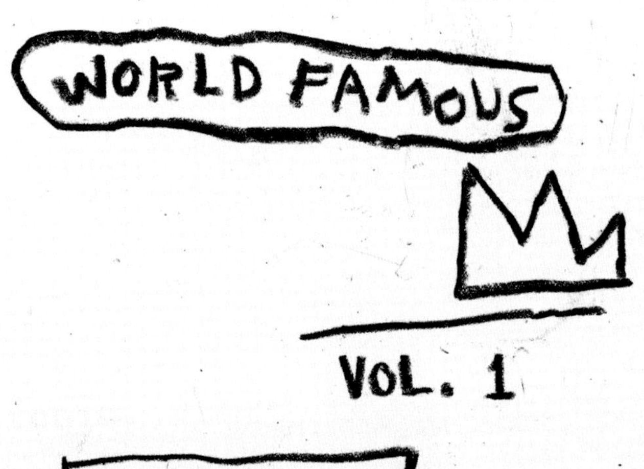

Jean-Michel Basquiat *Untitled (World Famous)* 1983 (detail), crayon on paper, 57.1 x 76.2 cm,
The Estate of Jean-Michel Basquiat, New York

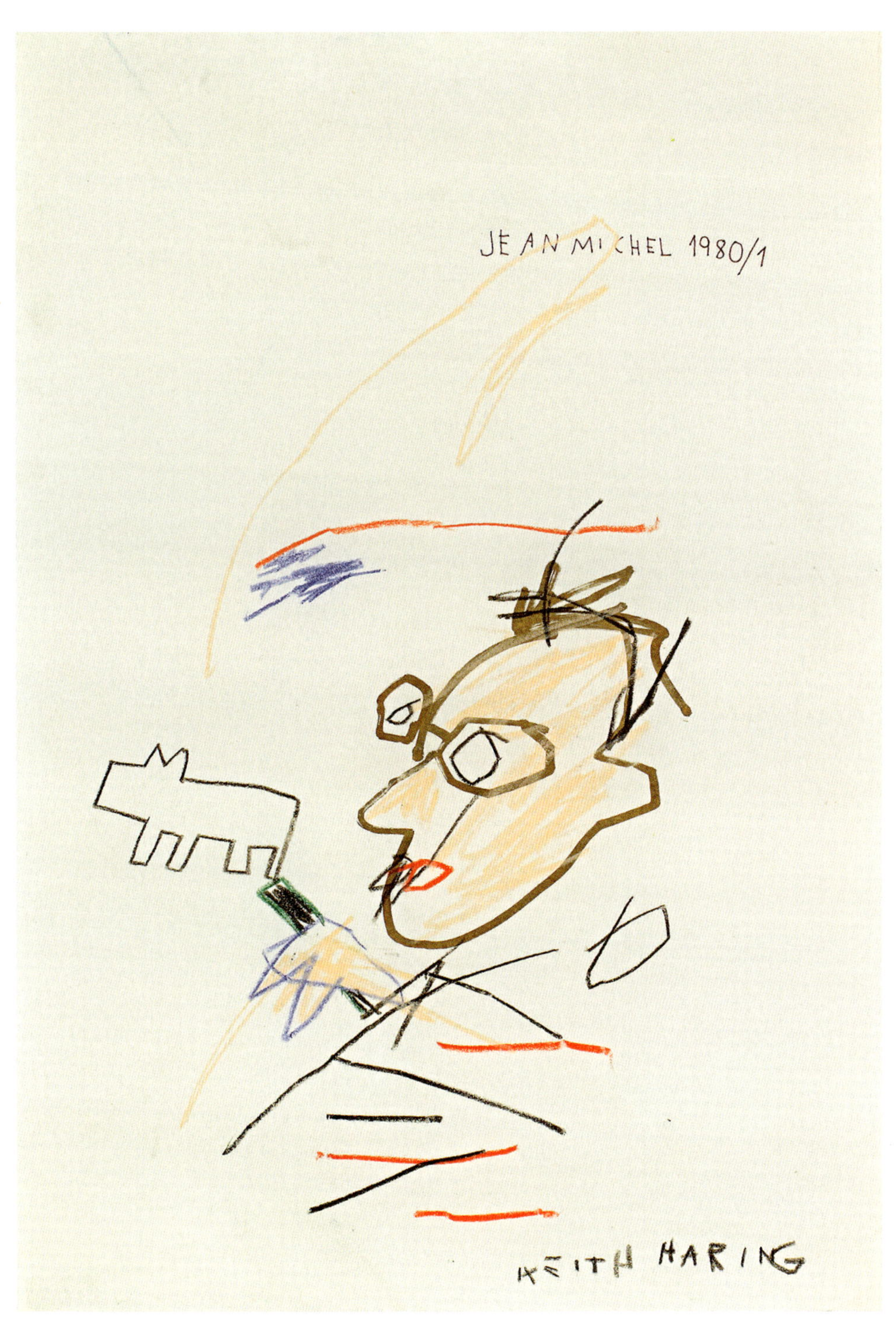

Jean-Michel Basquiat *Untitled (Keith Haring)* 1980–81, oilstick and fibre-tipped pen on paper, 45.7 x 30.5 cm,
Private collection, courtesy Tony Shafrazi Gallery, New York

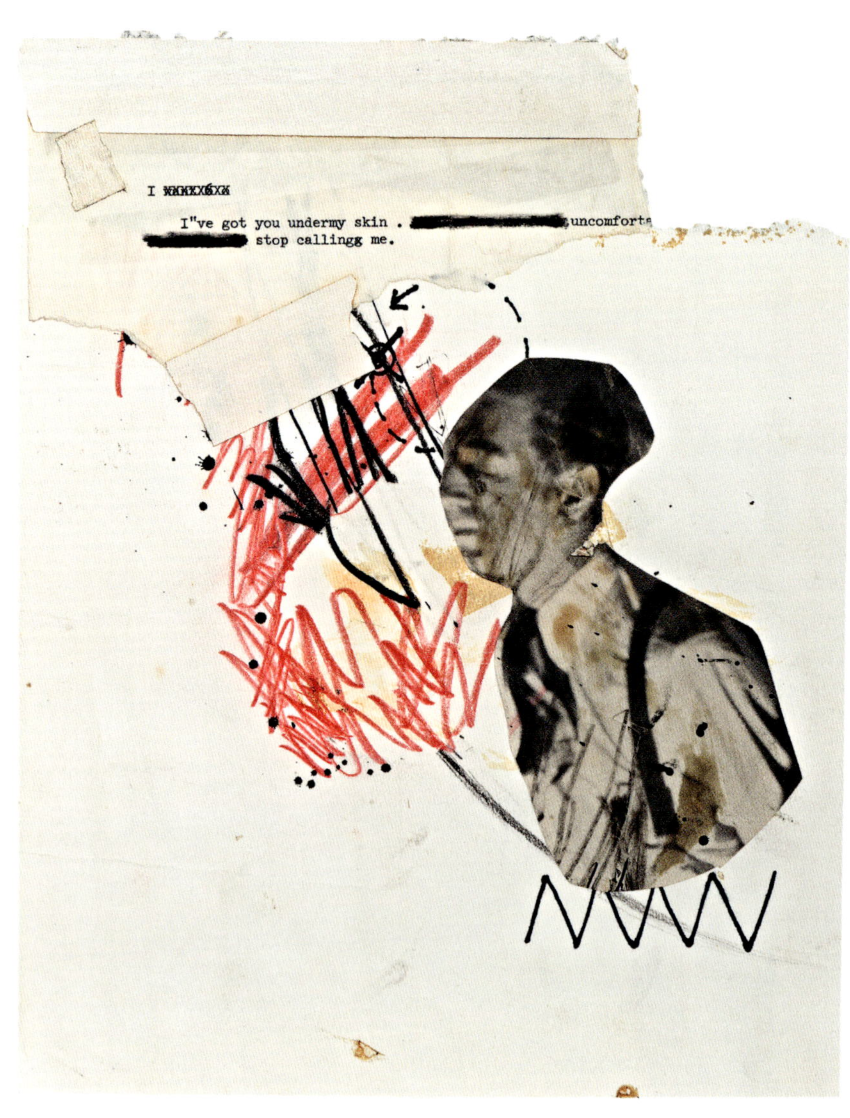

Jean-Michel Basquiat *Untitled (Duchamp)* 1980, collage on paper, 26.7 x 21.0 cm, Collection of Larry Warsh

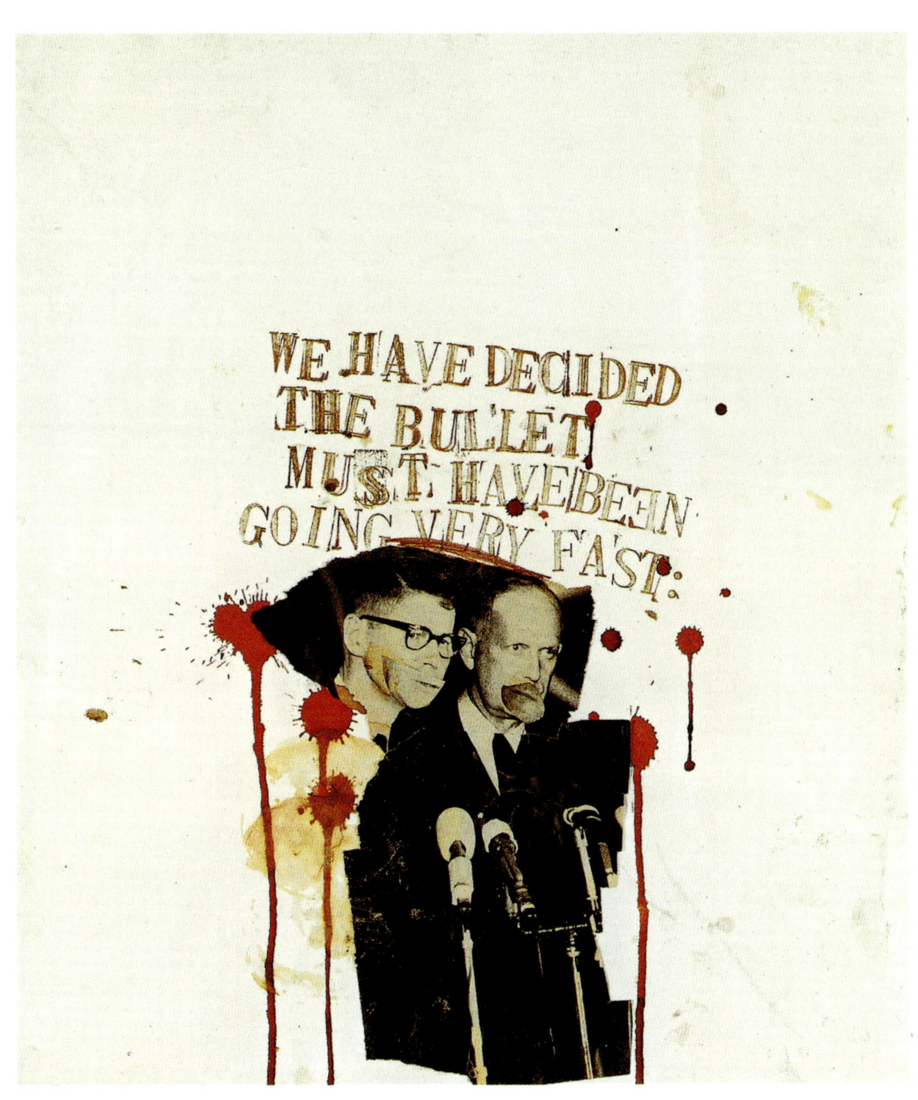

Jean-Michel Basquiat *We Have Decided the Bullet Must Have Been Going Very Fast* 1979–80, synthetic polymer paint, blood, ink and collage on paper, 42.5 x 35.5 cm, Private collection

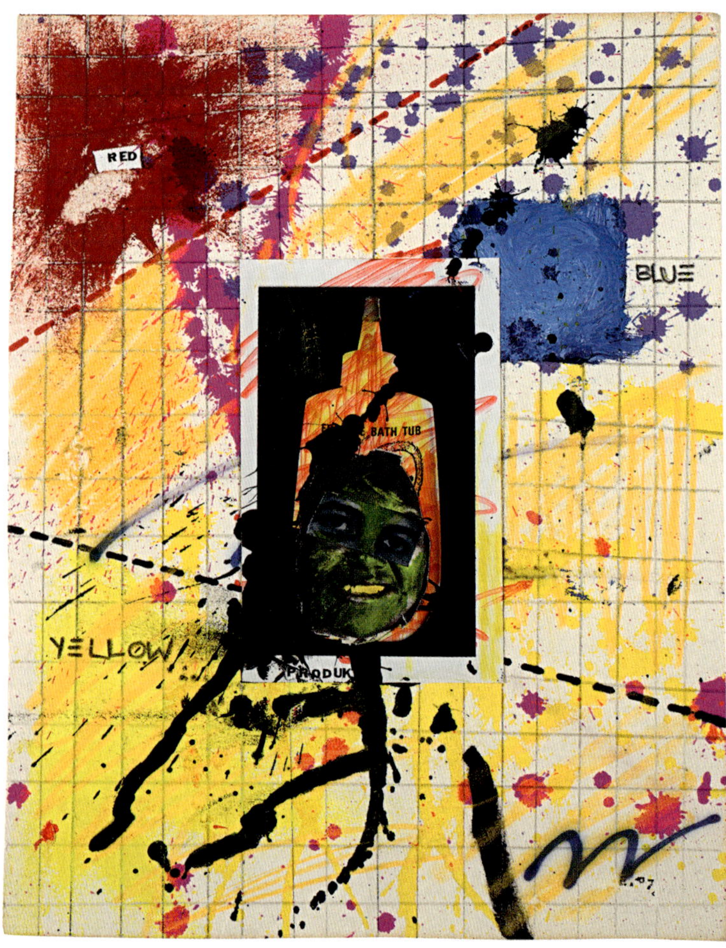

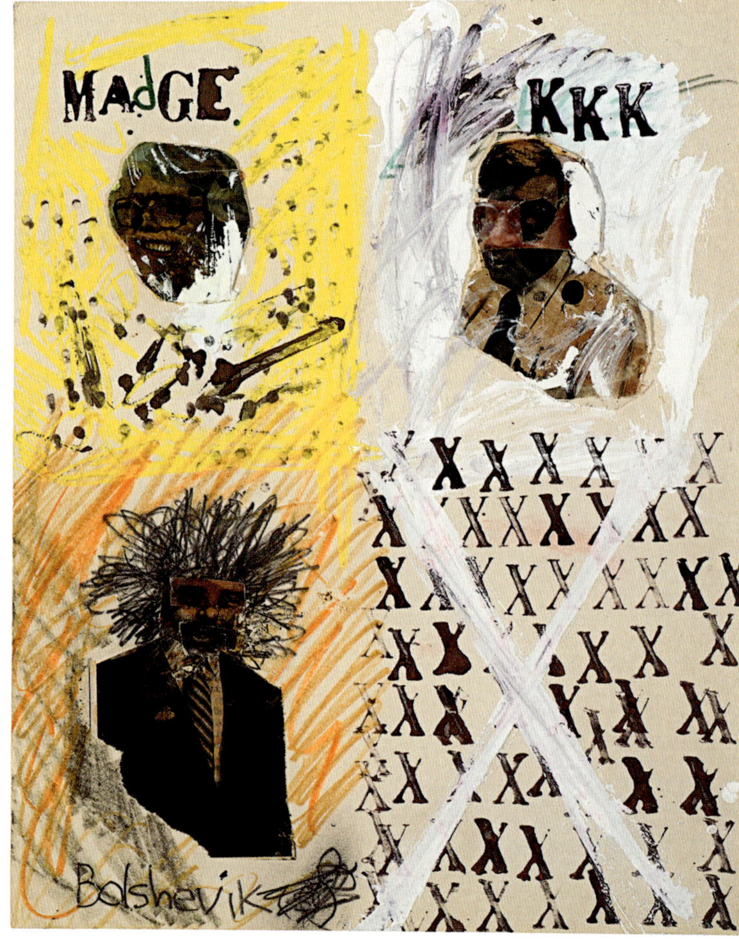

Jennifer Stein, Jean-Michel Basquiat from *Postcards* 1979, mixed media on cardboard, dimensions variable,
Collection of Jennifer von Holstein

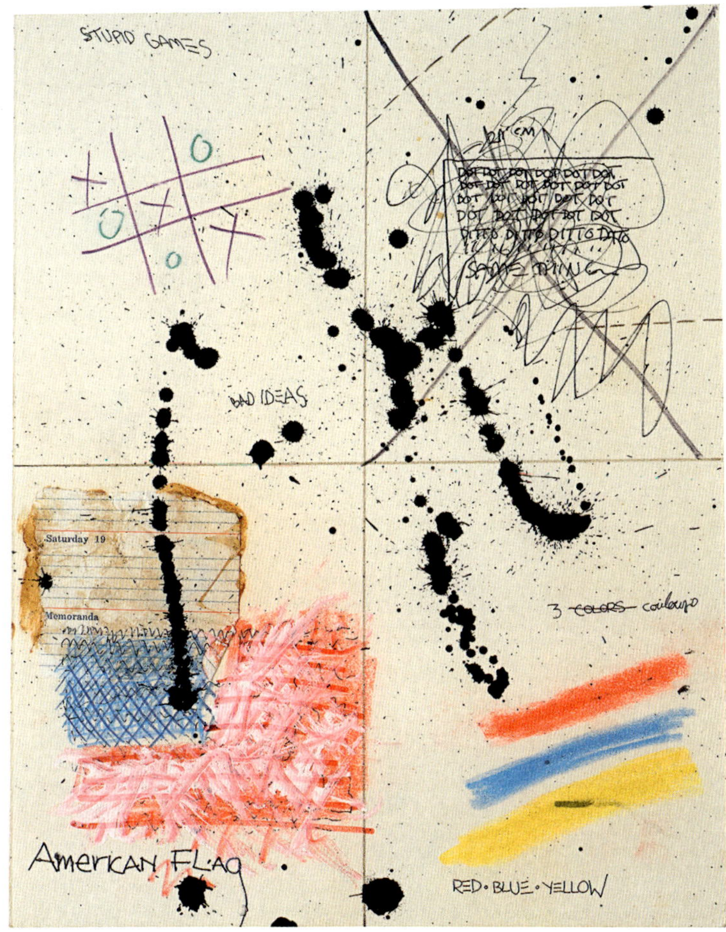

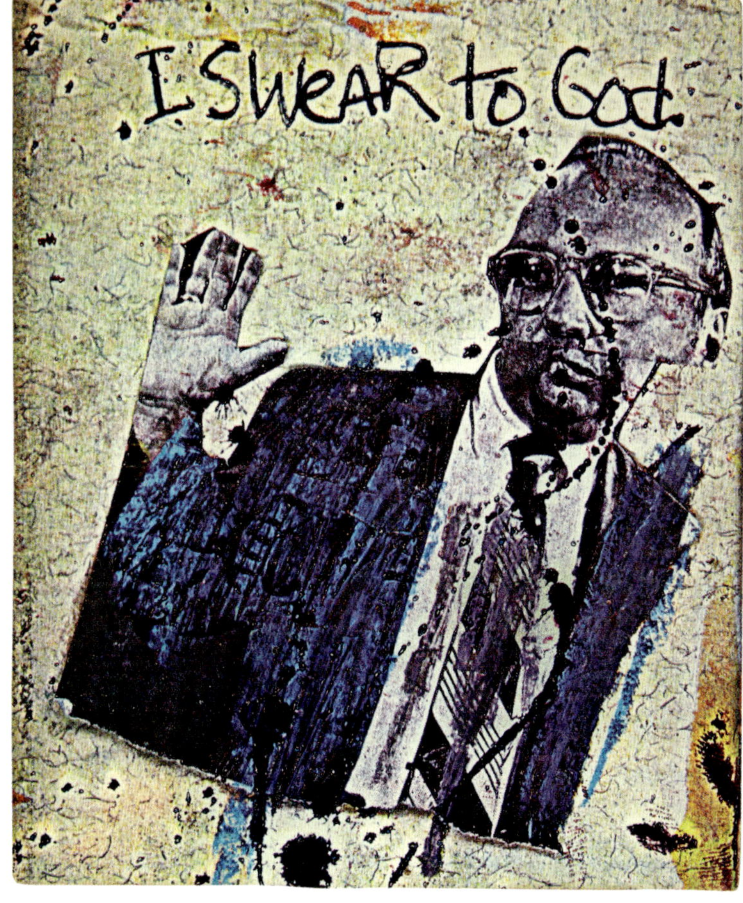

(top) Jennifer Stein, Jean-Michel Basquiat from *Postcards* 1979, mixed media on cardboard, dimensions variable, Collection of Jennifer von Holstein
(bottom) Jean-Michel Basquiat *Untitled (I Swear to God)* c. 1985, ink on postcard, 14.0 x 11.4 cm, Collection of Larry Warsh

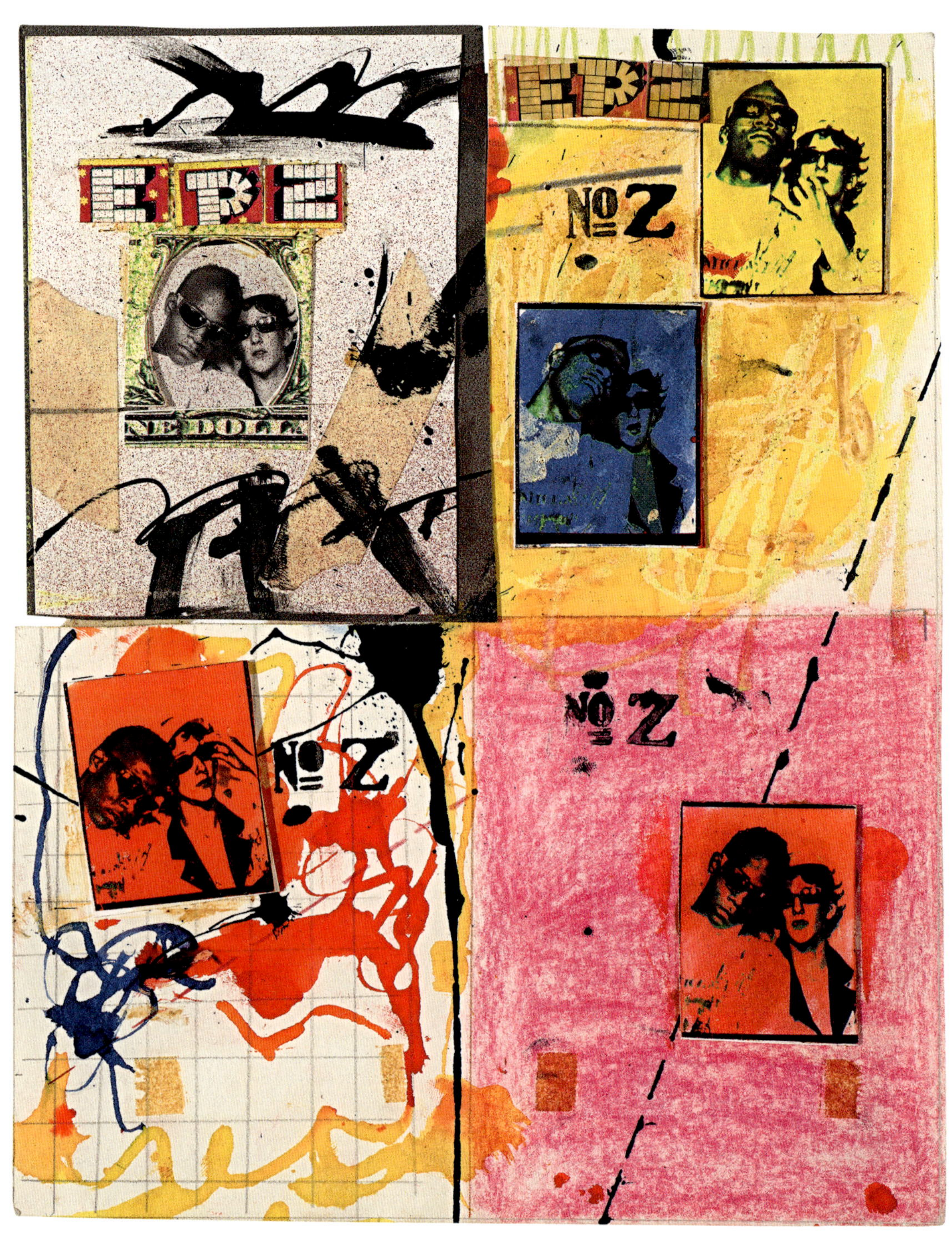

Jennifer Stein, Jean-Michel Basquiat from *Postcards* 1979, mixed media on cardboard, dimensions variable, Collection of Jennifer von Holstein

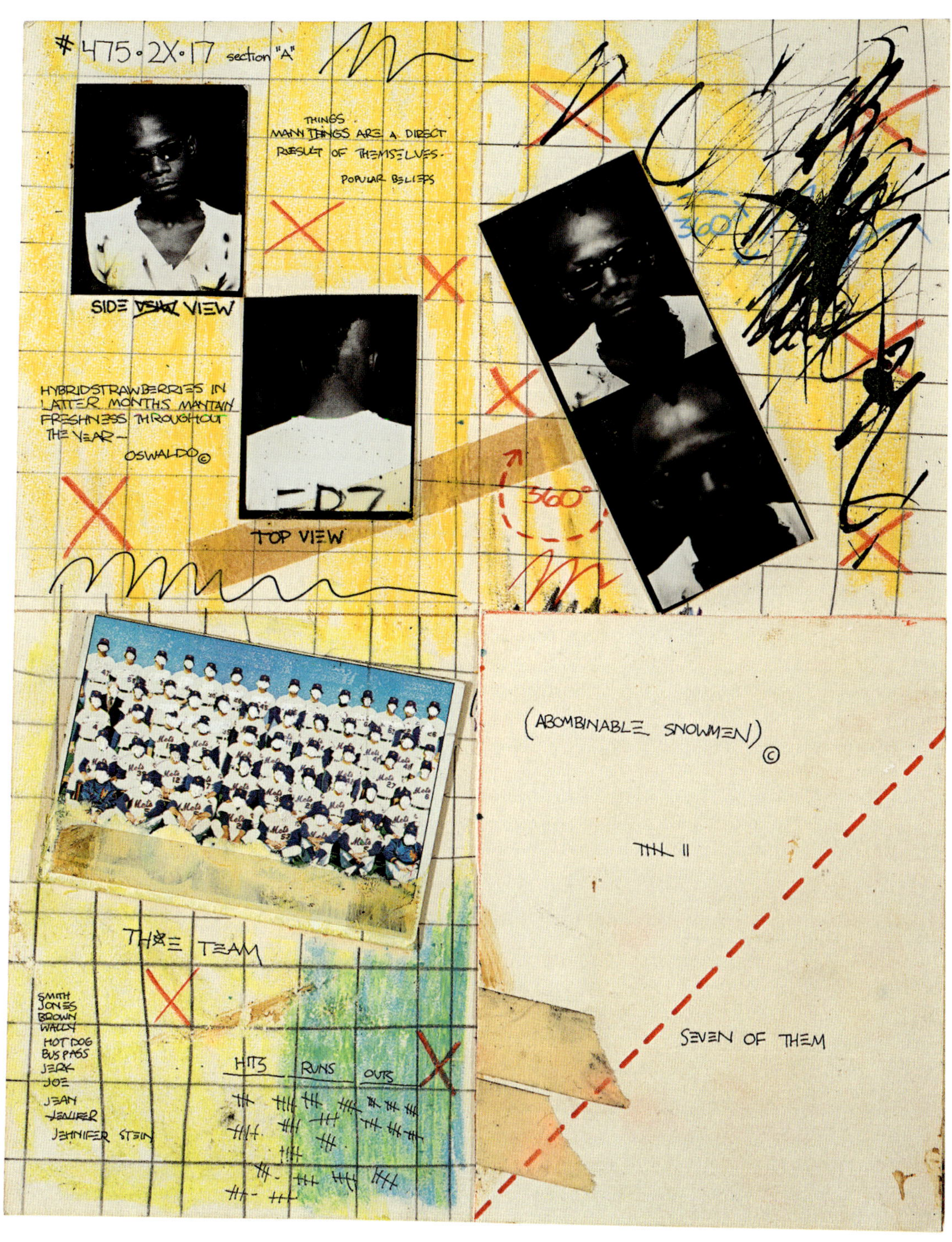

Jennifer Stein, Jean-Michel Basquiat from *Postcards* 1979, mixed media on cardboard, dimensions variable, Collection of Jennifer von Holstein

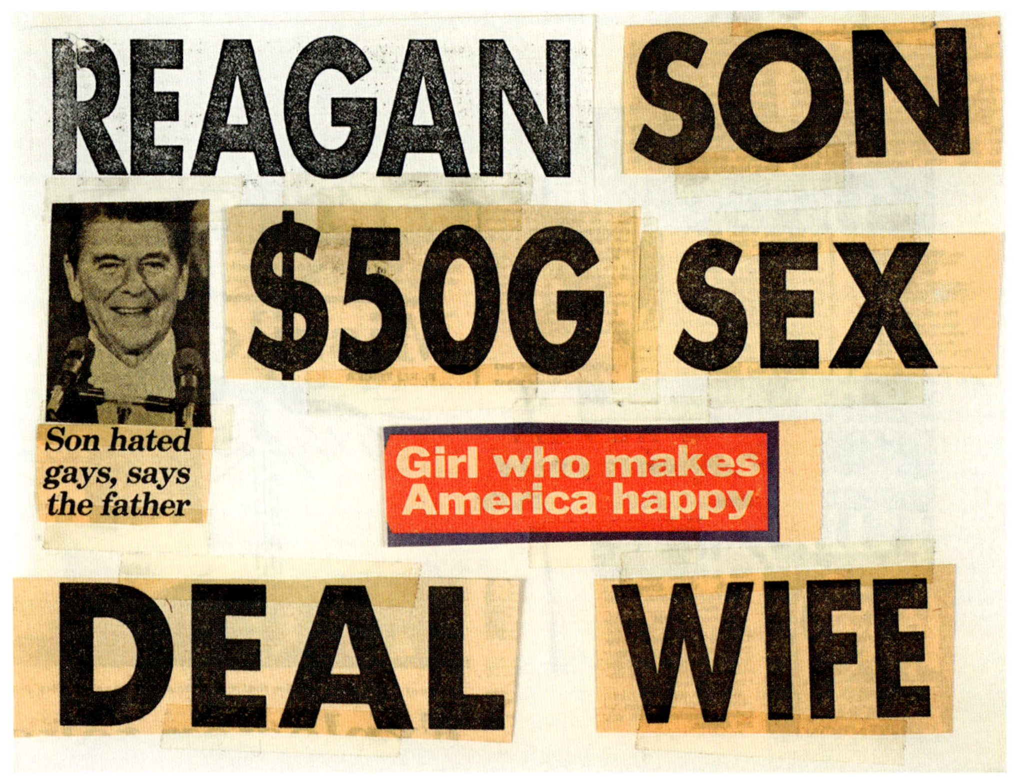

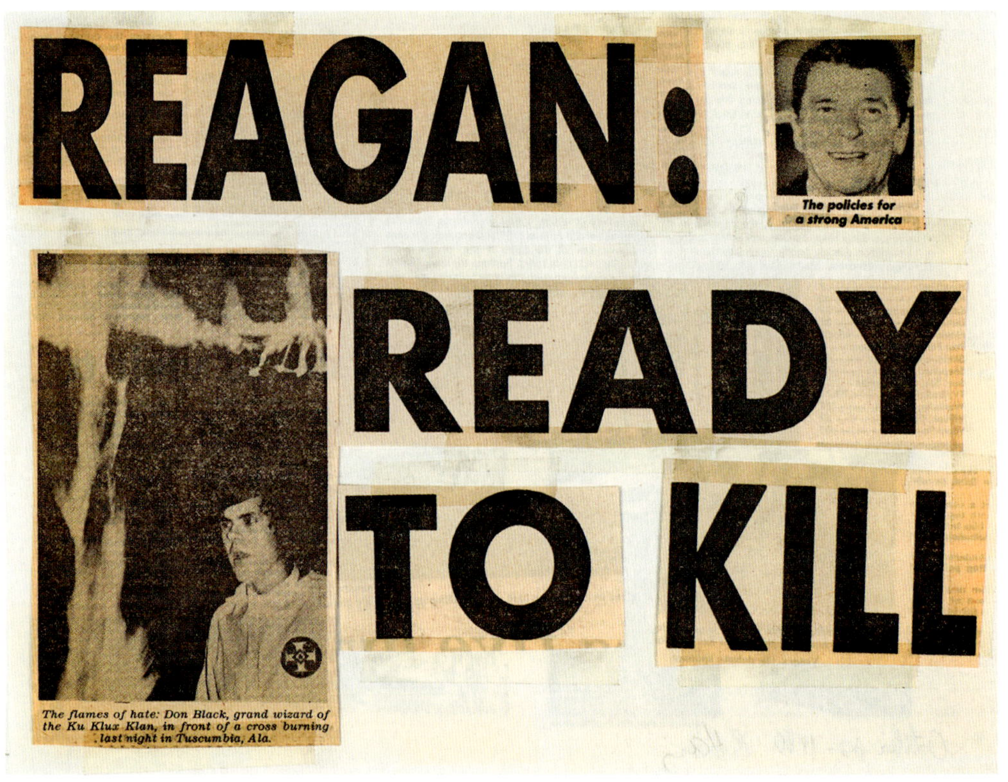

(top) Keith Haring *Reagan Son $50G Sex* 1980, newspaper collage, 21.6 x 27.9 cm, The Keith Haring Foundation, New York
(bottom) Keith Haring *Ready to Kill* 1980, newspaper collage, 21.6 x 27.9 cm, The Keith Haring Foundation, New York

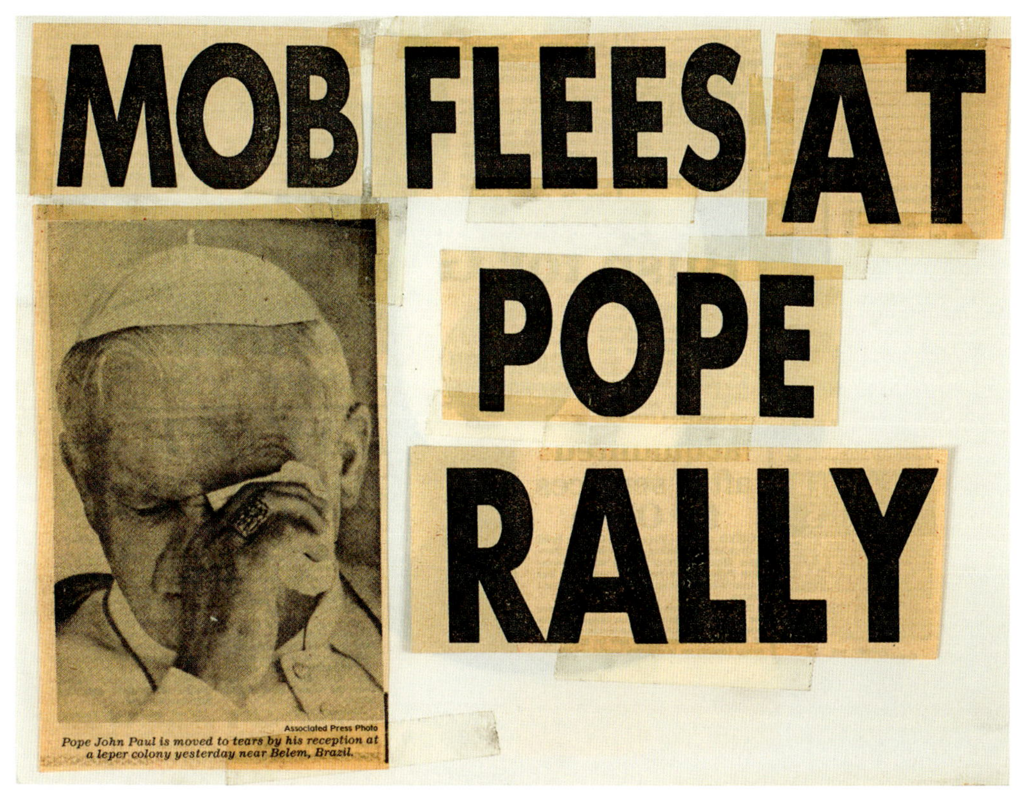

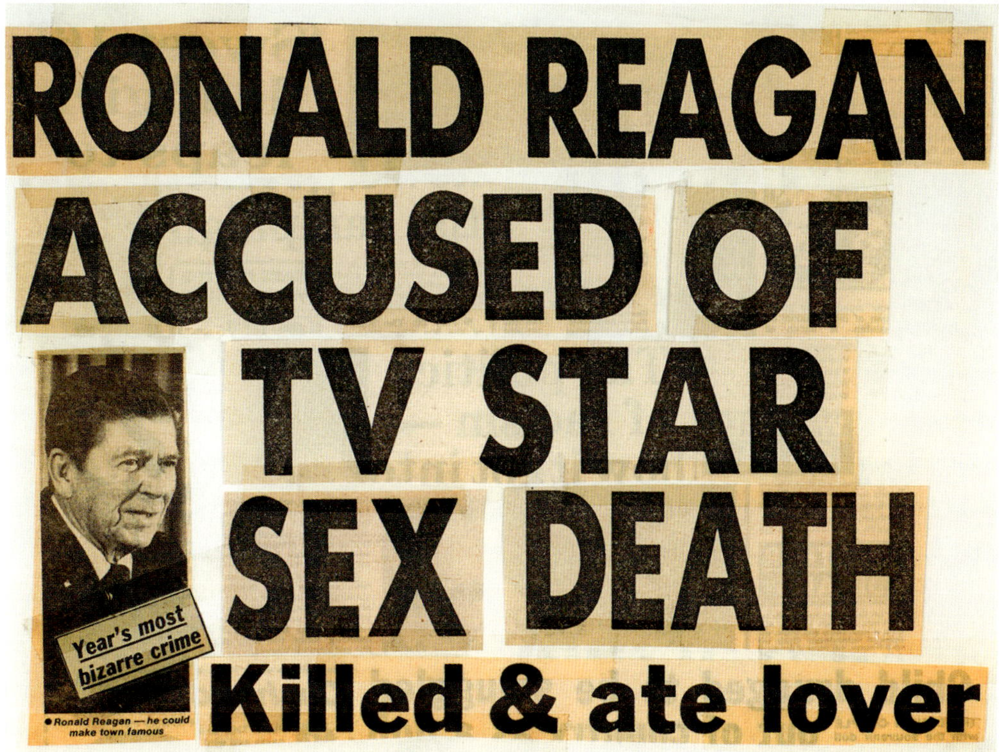

(top) Keith Haring *Mob Flees at Pope Rally* 1980, newspaper collage, 21.6 x 27.9 cm,
The Keith Haring Foundation, New York
(bottom) Keith Haring *Ronald Reagan Accused of TV Star Sex Death* 1980, newspaper collage, 21.6 x 27.9 cm,
The Keith Haring Foundation, New York

Interview: Jenny Holzer

Dieter Buchhart

Dieter Buchhart (DB): In October 1981 you exhibited with Jean-Michel Basquiat and Keith Haring in the group show *Public Address* at the Annina Nosei Gallery.[1] Can you share your impressions from the show?

—Jenny Holzer (JH): I don't remember much about that gallery show. What is still vivid is seeing Jean-Michel in the street routinely, because we both would go around in the middle of the night doing our work. We had a friendly, nodding acquaintance as we passed one another doing what we did [laughs]. That's more alive to me than what took place at Annina's.

DB: What were you working on at the time of these 'noddings in the night'?

—JH: I was sneaking around putting up posters. That was my intense postering period: first the *Truisms* and then the *Inflammatory Essays*. I would be relatively encumbered and a little slow, because I would have a bucket of wheat paste and a brush and my roll of posters. Jean-Michel would be fleet of foot with only his marker, doing SAMO©, so I was jealous that he was so fast!

DB: So, this must have been very early.

—JH: Yes, I started with the *Truisms* in the late 1970s, and I think I was on to the *Inflammatory Essays* by the time I met Jean-Michel. So probably it was the early 1980s. That's my guess.

DB: In 1980, before the election of Ronald Reagan, Keith Haring was also posting his collages of newspaper headlines in the streets. My impression was always that he was inspired by your *Truisms*, as well as by William S. Burroughs's cut-up technique. Do you recall ever speaking with Haring about the *Truisms*?

—JH: I would see Keith in the street as well, and we also had a wink and a nod and a wave acquaintance. I wish I'd talked with him about Burroughs. The first time I ever spoke to Keith at length was funny, because it was in Joseph Kosuth's class [at the School of Visual Arts]. Keith had invited me to be a visiting artist, and it was a nice loop because Kosuth's work had interested me when I was in school. To be with Joseph and Keith in the same place was not dull.

DB: That's interesting, because I heard that Basquiat also visited Joseph Kosuth's class.

—JH: I didn't know that. I was only there with Keith.

DB: Then Haring must have invited Basquiat to the class the same way he did with you.

—JH: It would be interesting to talk with Kosuth and learn what he remembers.

DB: Indeed. Especially in light of the crucial role that words play in Basquiat's work. The role of language seems much less relevant in Haring's work. But let's circle back to SAMO©, Basquiat and Al Diaz's conceptual poetic graffiti that you mentioned earlier. What were your thoughts about the project when you first saw it?

—JH: I am more engaged when there is more language. I appreciated the tagging, the simple SAMO©, but I like seeing riotous content. I'll often spend quality time with one of Jean-Michel's paintings where there are many words and images, sometimes words and images that resolutely don't match, but each a gift and each a language. There's a very good Basquiat painting in the Guggenheim Bilbao [*Man from Naples*, 1982]. When in Bilbao, I make a pilgrimage to stand and marvel again at the combination of Jean-Michel's hand and mind, the range of subjects, the choices for colour, the live lines. There is plenty to sustain interest for repeat visits. Good art has that magic, that irresistible unknowable quality. I, to this day, and after much study, don't know why this painting works so beautifully. But it does!

DB: I agree! The breadth of sources and references in his works is incredible.

—JH: His work is encyclopaedic but in a mysterious way.

DB: Absolutely! While Haring and Basquiat were always on friendly terms, it certainly seems like they were closest at the beginning of their careers. What was your impression of their friendship?

—JH: I don't have much firsthand knowledge, because I'm a little bit older, so I was at that stage of going home at night and feeding my dog as opposed to being on the circuit [laughs]. But yes, my sense is that they were tighter earlier and together a fair amount then. They were wild, busy, determined men out late at night in many of the same circles, and with Andy Warhol as a destination.

DB: The art scene of New York in the 1980s seems at once small and large; there were different groups, but Warhol seemed to be the god.

—JH: A god.

DB: *A* god! I like that! Can you describe your view of this scene a bit?

—JH: I was more involved with people who stayed in the street. I was outside high society and the glam scene, as were many friends and collaborators. We worked outdoors on purpose. We often had different trajectories, different goals, different subjects, different audiences. It wasn't 'holier than thou' but ours became distinct practices, inclined to public placement and tough content.

A number of people associated with Collaborative Projects [artists' group] weren't even self-defined as artists; they wanted to produce something interesting and potentially useful for any passer-by to the end of sharing concerns and offering possible courses of action.

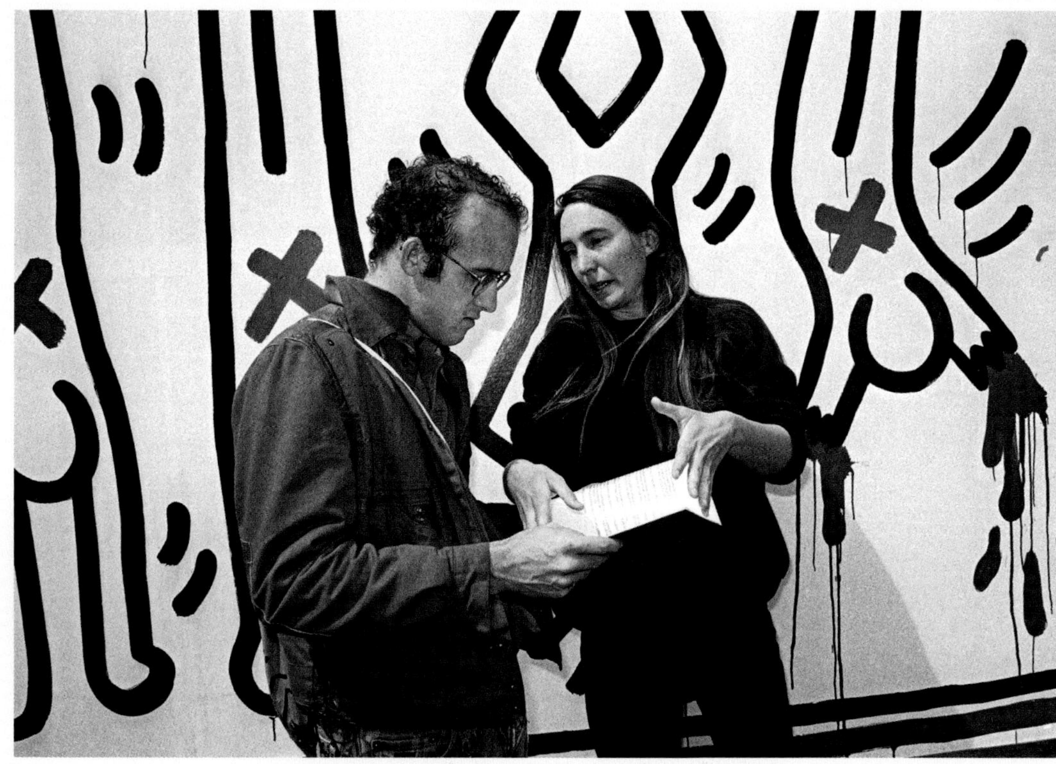

DB: Your collaboration with Haring, then, makes perfect sense. Basquiat, after he finished the SAMO© graffiti and stopped selling his postcards, quickly focused on gallery and museum shows and went in this direction.

—JH: Which I would say was his inalienable right. But others wanted to stay outside or work inside and out – whatever felt appropriate.

DB: And Haring did just that; he worked both in institutional places as well as outside. He explicitly stated that his *Subway Drawings*, for example, were aimed at everybody. So, I think a lot of the things you just mentioned resonate in his practice. Can you tell me a little bit about your collaboration with him in Vienna in 1986?

—JH: That collaboration was for the Wiener Festwochen.[2] I can report that Keith and I went to the opera and that he bought me something from the snack bar. What a gentleman! [Laughs.] It was not a safe period; there was of course the tragedy of Chernobyl and AIDS. So, we had opera and Chernobyl as a backdrop and then our respective bleak and sometimes lively concerns.

DB: Do you recall how people reacted to your work?

—JH: The goal of any street artist is to have people give what you've offered a little time, and people did stop and look. Keith by then was a celebrity, so there was celebrity attention as well as just, 'Oh, what is that?' The reactions were ones of surprise, with people laughing at the more comic bits and being backed up by the difficult drawings.

DB: Like your drawing *Protect Me From What I Want*.

—JH: That was good all-purpose advice.

DB: Did you make other works besides the official large-scale works?

Keith Haring and Jenny Holzer at the Wiener Festwochen, Vienna, 1986

—JH: We did little things here and there, on bus stops and so on, and there was the poster that we developed together.

DB: Do I interpret the poster correctly in stating that it was about religious or ideological traps?

—JH: You would have needed to ask Keith about religion – that cross was his contribution – but it's reasonable to imagine that neither Keith nor I were in favour of ideological traps. The 'Protect me from what I want' slogan is somewhere between a deadly serious and a slightly funny comment. The predictable part of it is anti-consumerist, but that is 5 per cent of the message at most. It has more to do with a subject of mine – sexual assault. That is the main deal. And 'Protect me from what I want' is generally applicable. Humans are curious and worse, and go to way too many places where they shouldn't. My offering was 'take a beat'. Consider for a moment whether you should have, think or do what you want.

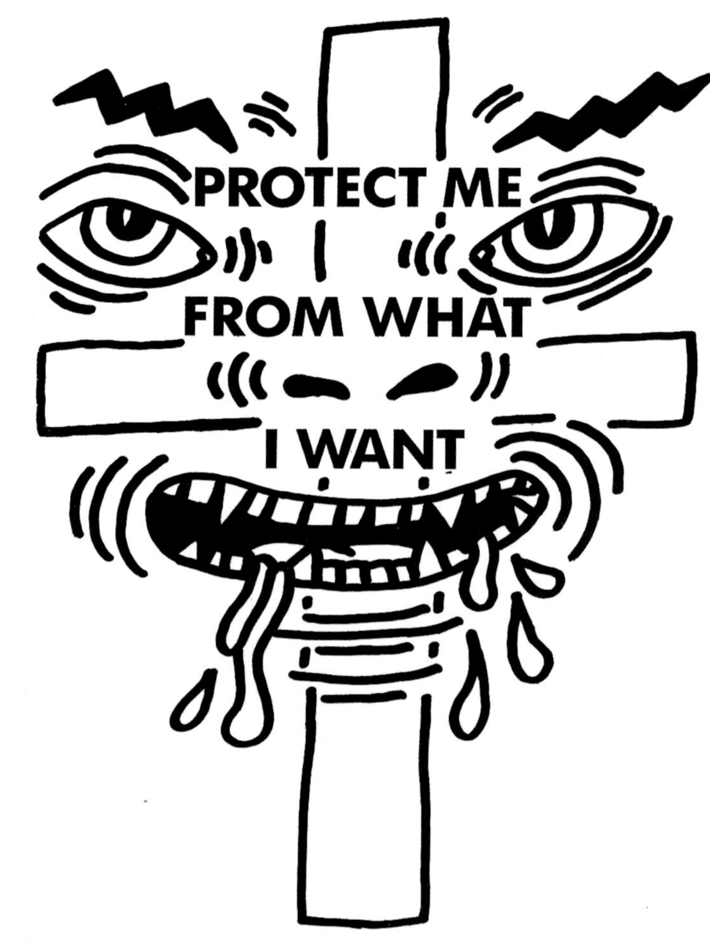

'SCHÜTZ MICH VOR DEM WAS ICH WILL', KEITH HARING – JENNY HOLZER, WIENER FESTWOCHEN 1986, AM HOF

DB: Did you collaborate with Haring on any other projects?

—JH: The happiest collaboration was *Sign on a Truck*, a project Keith and I, along with many other artists and passers-by, realised in the build-up to the 1984 presidential election. Keith was kind enough to make drawings and help with the soundtrack we played from the truck. The project was to have people thinking, talking and voting. It was the first time that a woman, Geraldine Ferraro, was running on a major party's ticket. There was debate, passion and optimism, but we got Ronald Reagan and George H. W. Bush as president and vice president.

I secured a very large and, for that time, 'techno-deluxe' truck with a big LED sign on it, which we parked in front of the Plaza Hotel and later on Wall Street. We screened pre-recorded contributions, like Keith drawing and showing people how to vote, and wonderful stuff by Vito Acconci, Barbara Kruger and Claes Oldenburg.[3] We had MCs who would roam the crowd live, and ask people not just for whom they would vote, but also, 'What frightens you? / What do you love dearly? / What do you want to see grow? / What is ghastly?' In Wall Street there was a guy who held up his wallet and said, 'I care what's in my wallet'; another guy said, 'I don't want a woman in the White House, she's a dummy!' An African-American woman declared the opposite: 'The white lady, she's okay because she's a woman'. Here was a representative sample of US politics at that

Keith Haring, Jenny Holzer *Protect Me From What I Want* 1986, poster, 83.8 cm x 57.2 cm, The Keith Haring Foundation, New York

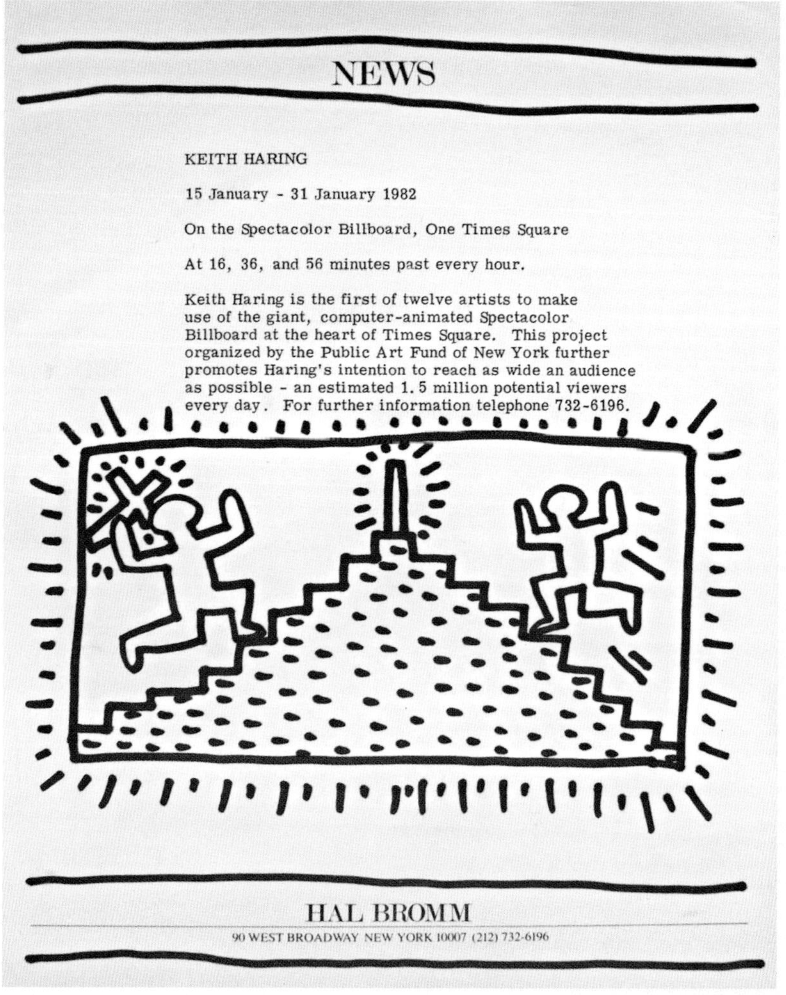

NEWS

KEITH HARING

15 January - 31 January 1982

On the Spectacolor Billboard, One Times Square

At 16, 36, and 56 minutes past every hour.

Keith Haring is the first of twelve artists to make use of the giant, computer-animated Spectacolor Billboard at the heart of Times Square. This project organized by the Public Art Fund of New York further promotes Haring's intention to reach as wide an audience as possible - an estimated 1.5 million potential viewers every day. For further information telephone 732-6196.

HAL BROMM

90 WEST BROADWAY NEW YORK 10007 (212) 732-6196

Keith Haring *Untitled* 1982, fibre-tipped pen on paper, 27.9 x 21.6 cm, Hal Bromm Gallery

time and what seems, in retrospect, to be a hint of the schism, the polarisation that's so obvious and painful now.

DB: When was the first time you collaborated with Keith Haring?

—JH: I believe our chat in Kosuth's class was the first offering – that's a collaboration of sorts [laughs]. I don't think we officially collaborated again after the 1986 Wiener Festwochen project.

DB: I believe you mentioned that Annina Nosei represented your husband, Mike Glier, at the same time as Basquiat?

—JH: Mike was working on a show for Annina and Jean-Michel was up next. Jean-Michel was working in Annina's basement – that famous story! Mike said Jean-Michel was almost always there with an entourage, that his posse formed early and that he had constant companionship, for better and for worse. And that he was enormously prolific, but doing work of the highest quality, which is a remarkable thing. Both Keith and Jean-Michel were fast, prolific and able.

DB: Did you go to openings, like Keith Haring's show at Tony Shafrazi in 1982, or Basquiat's at Mary Boone Gallery in 1984? Were they part of the scene at the time?

—JH: I would go to shows at Shafrazi sometimes, but not so much to Mary Boone's space. I liked a number of the women who showed at Metro Pictures, so I would enjoy their openings. I still am friendly with some of these Metro women. Although Haring, Basquiat and I were in different crowds, there was much overlapping for most of us downtown.

DB: When you say different crowds, can you describe your crowd?

—JH: I was most involved with people in Collaborative Projects. I also worked on paintings with two graffiti artists, Lady Pink and A-One. A friend of mine from Collaborative Projects, Ilona Granet, a radical artist who would contribute her own street signs to New York City, had a fantastic hand and she would paint the text on Lady Pink and A-One paintings. These people were more my group than the Warhol acolytes, [Julian] Schnabel and [David] Salle or the European painters – the Italians and the Germans. There was that painting revival at the time.

DB: Yes. People always tried to place Basquiat in that group, which was a problem for him.

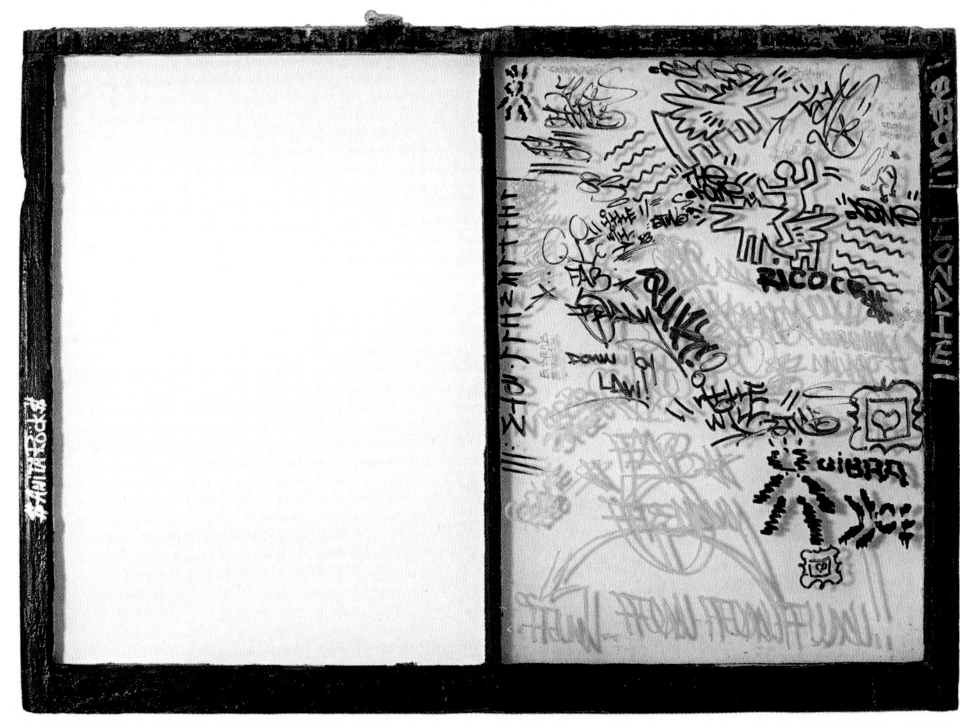

—JH: No, he was utterly himself. Bless him!

DB: Yes! And that's what makes him and his work so interesting and sustainable today.

—JH: We're looking at Basquiat because he wasn't a faint echo or a retro repetition as some of the European painters were. It was kind of silly how some painters, perfectly okay but with modest derivative skills, were heralded as the next great masters ... It was clear they weren't.

DB: People just love having easy paintings on the wall. That's it. Can you describe the reception of Haring and Basquiat in the 1980s?

—JH: In some quarters there was serious and proper recognition of their great abilities and their very real contributions. That was right. But a part of the response came to be Warholian society silliness without Warhol's brains and bite, and with a dose of sycophantic danger. Haring and Basquiat deserved the attention for all the good reasons, but there was a kind of cool-kid goofiness, too. Even that was eventually legit; they both deserved the love.

DB: And would you say that their strong political ideas were recognised in the 1980s?

—JH: At times it seemed the fluff took over. Which was unfortunate, because the important political and cultural content, the societal references that were in both men's work, were neglected in the party and money frenzy. You'd have to be dim to miss the gay pride and liberation message in Keith's work, and that Jean-Michel was a race man, but people didn't always talk about that.

DB: Thank you so much for sharing your memories and insight. Is there anything else you want to share?

—JH: I miss them.

(23 February 2019)

Notes

1 *Public Address*, 31 October – 19 November 1981, Annina Nosei Gallery, New York. The exhibition also included works by Bill Beckley, Mike Glier, Barbara Kruger and Peter Nadin.
2 The Wiener Festwochen is an annual, multidisciplinary art festival held in Vienna, Austria. It was founded in the 1950s.
3 Also among the contributors were artists Ida Applebroog and Leon Golub.

(above) Keith Haring, other artists *Untitled* c. 1985, fibre-tipped pen on window, 111.7 x 137.1 x 7.6 cm, Collection of Larry Warsh
(opposite) Keith Haring *Untitled* 1981, paint on wood panels, 215.9 x 152.4 cm, Collection of Larry Warsh

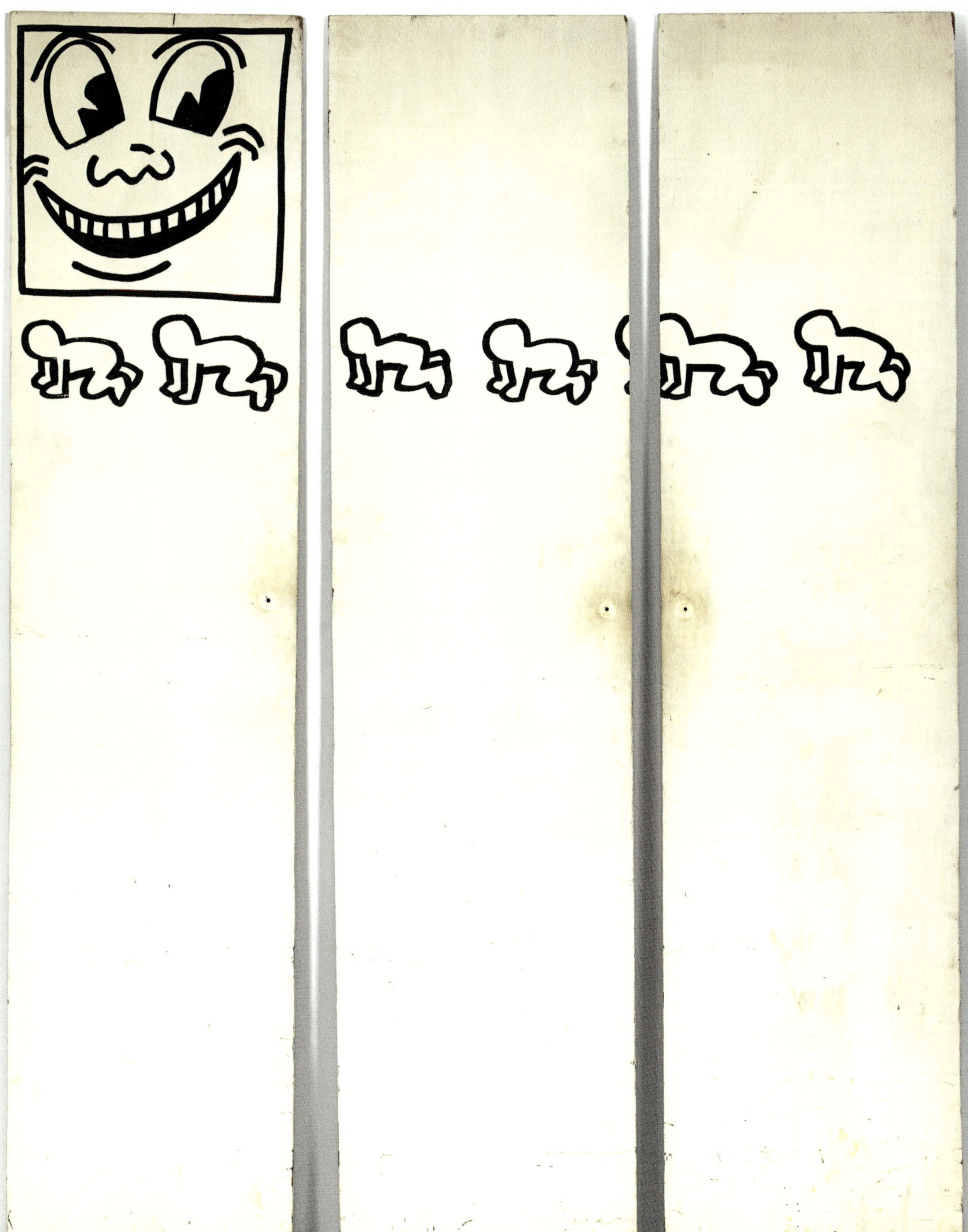

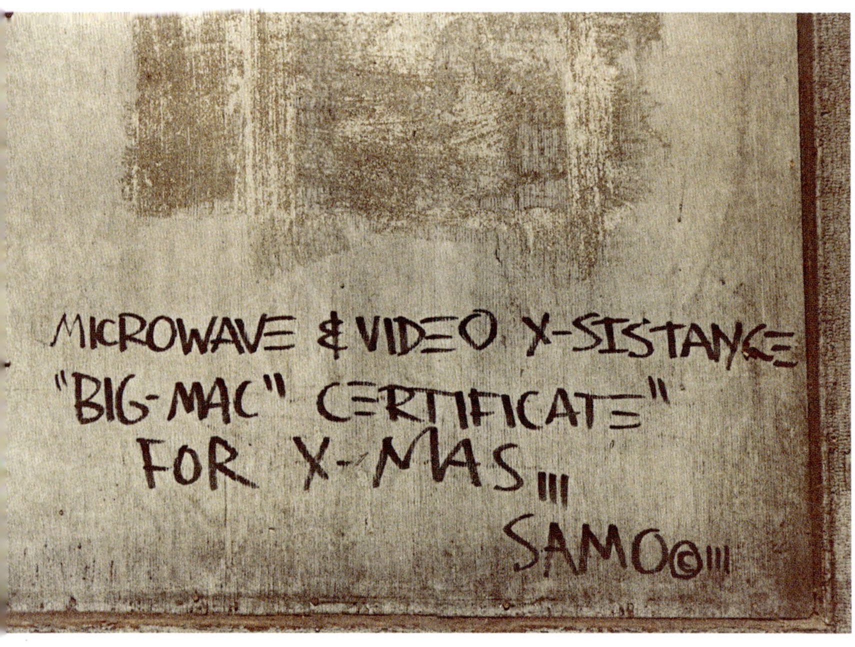

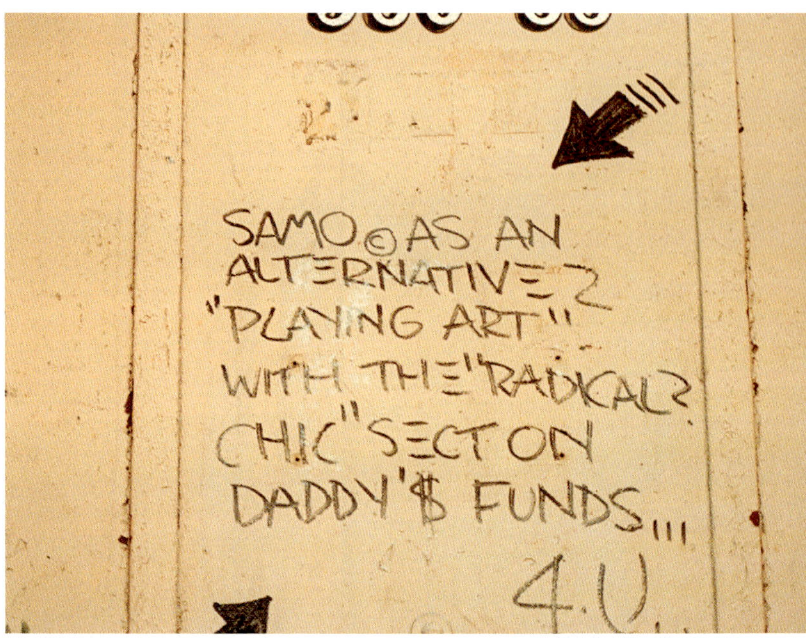

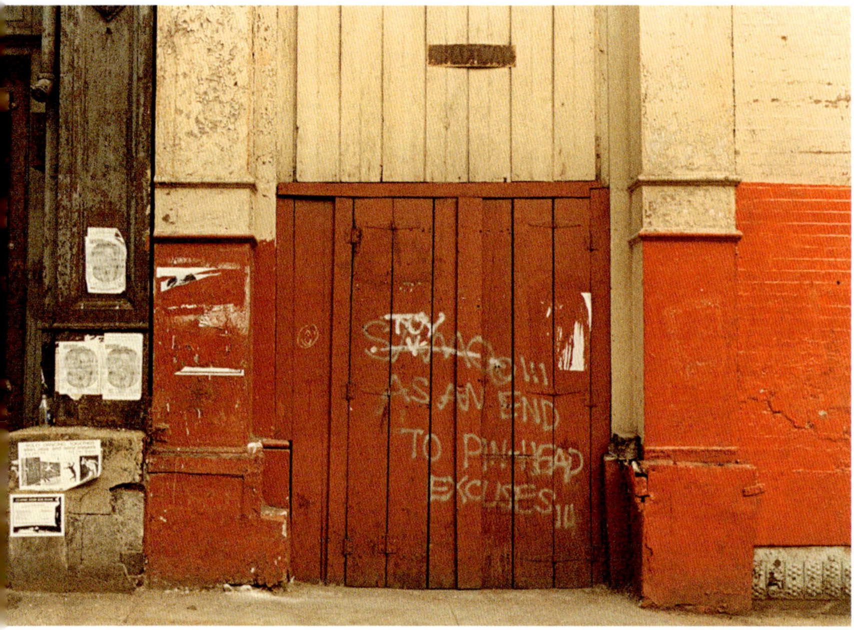

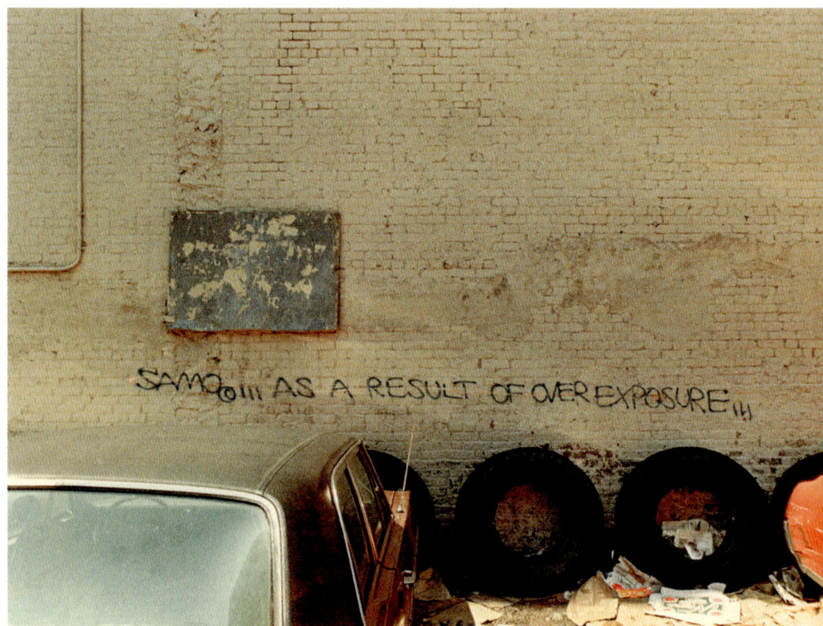

(clockwise from top left) Vijya Kern *SAMO© Microwave & Video*; *SAMO© as an alternative*; *SAMO© as a result of overexposure*; *SAMO© as an end to pin-head excuses*, all taken in New York, 1980, courtesy of Artstübli Gallery, Basel

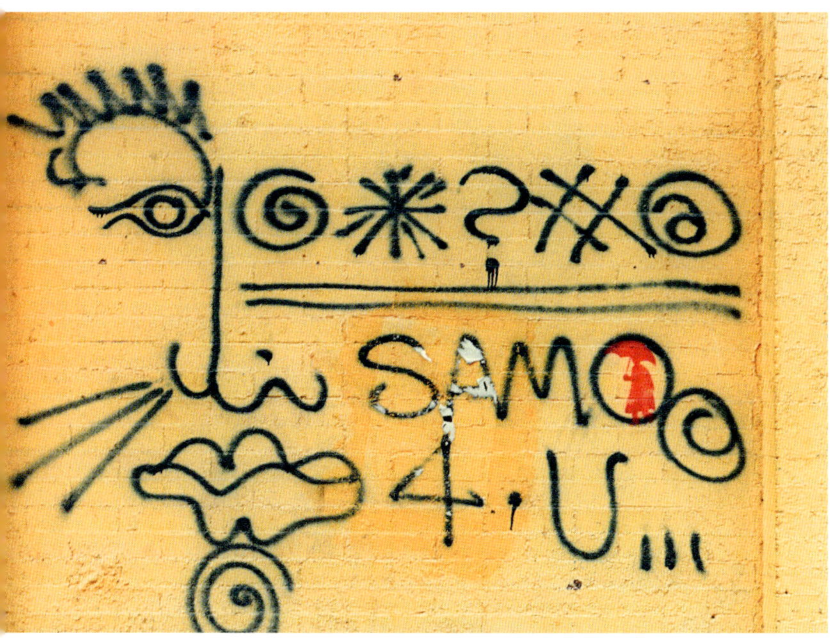

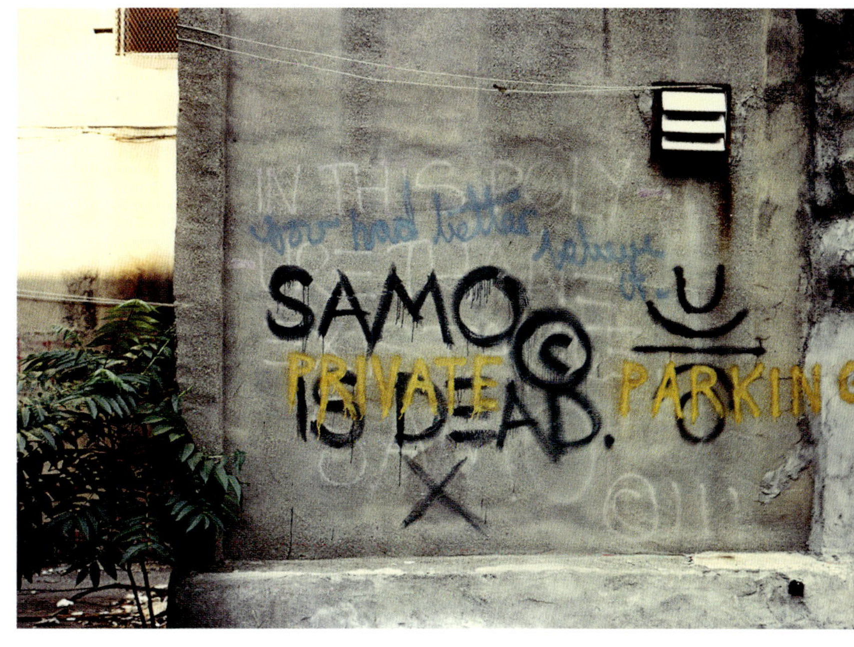

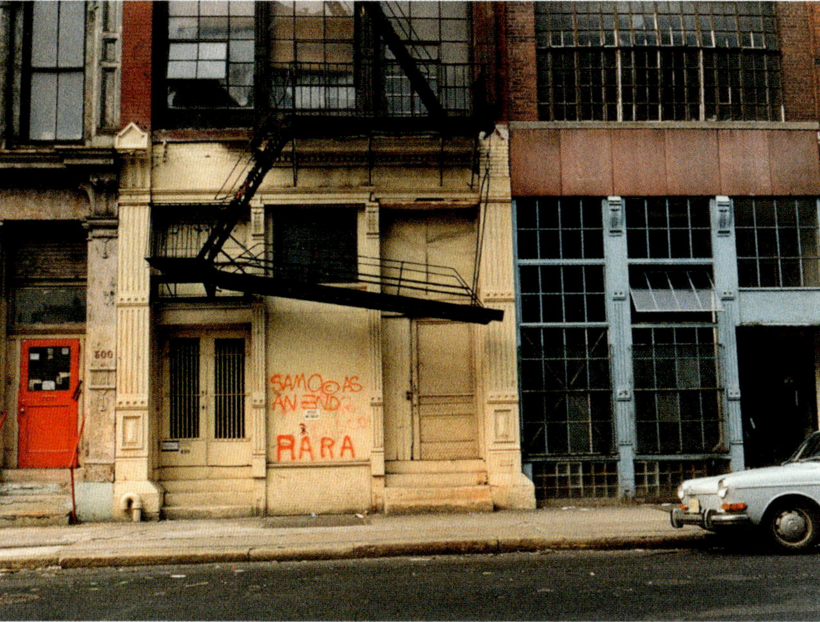

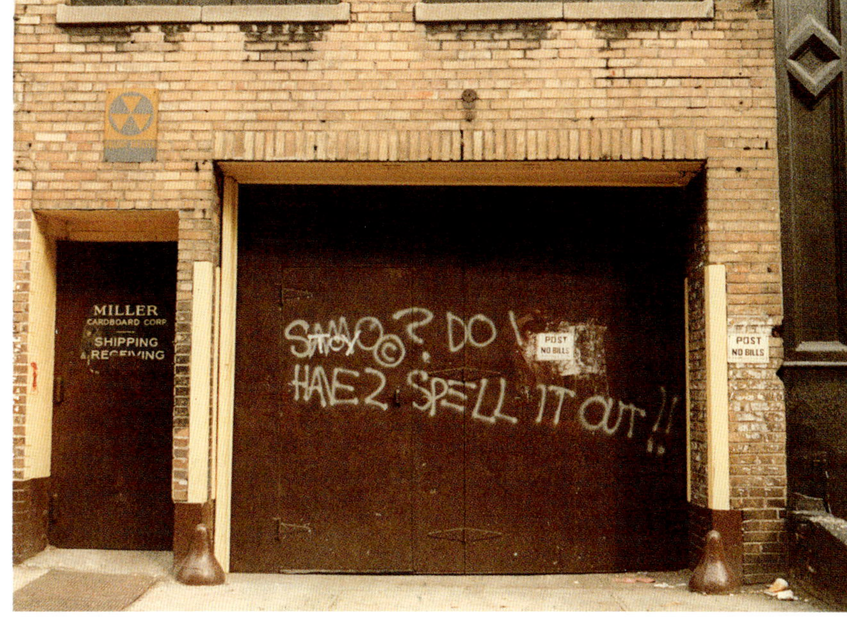

(clockwise from top left) Vijya Kern *SAMO© 4.U; SAMO© is Dead – private parking*; *SAMO© do I have 2 spell it out*; *SAMO© as an end – Rara*, all taken in New York, 1980, courtesy of Artstübli Gallery, Basel
(overleaf) Jean-Michel Basquiat on the set of *Downtown 81* 1980–81, directed by Edo Bertoglio

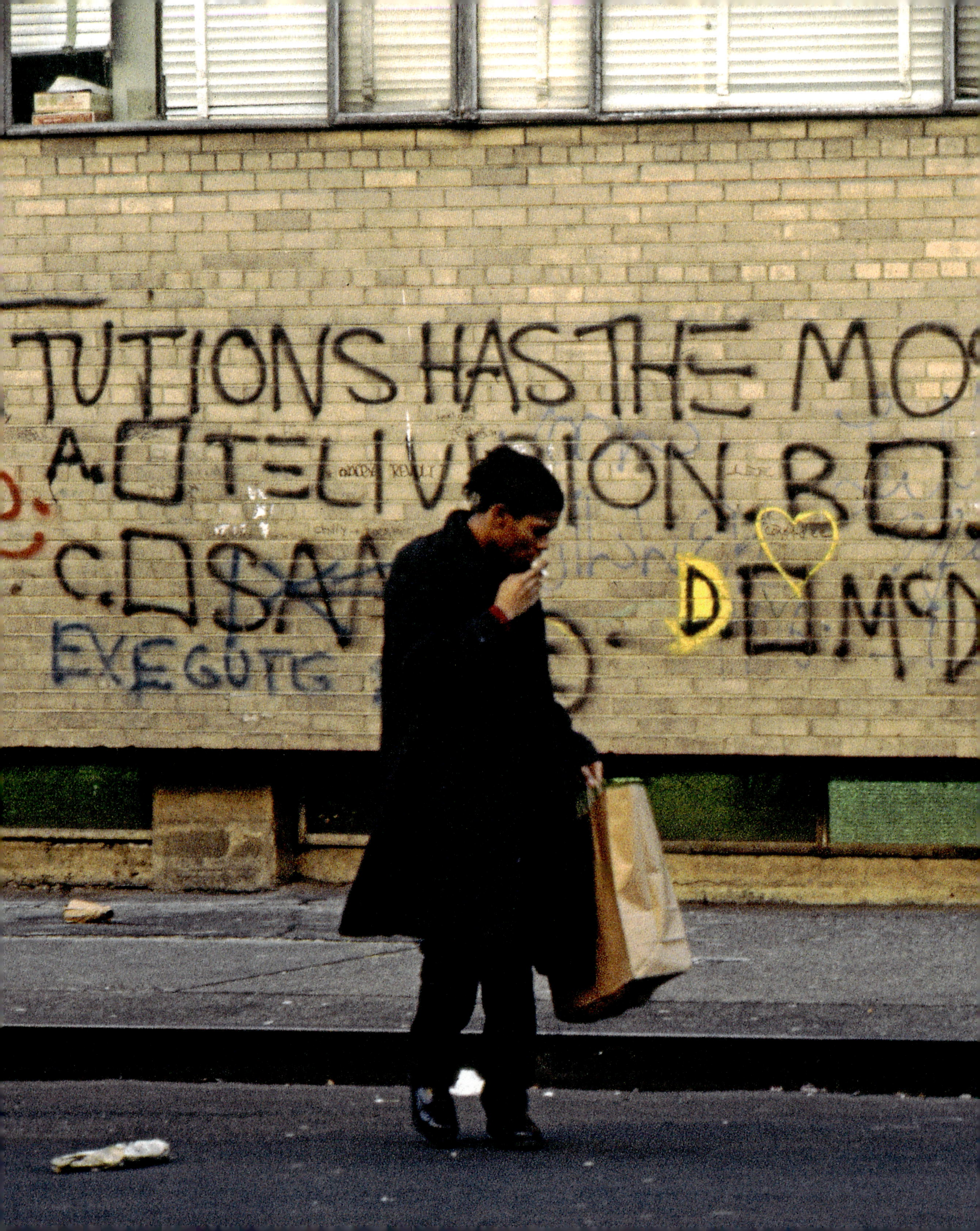
TUTIONS HAS THE MO

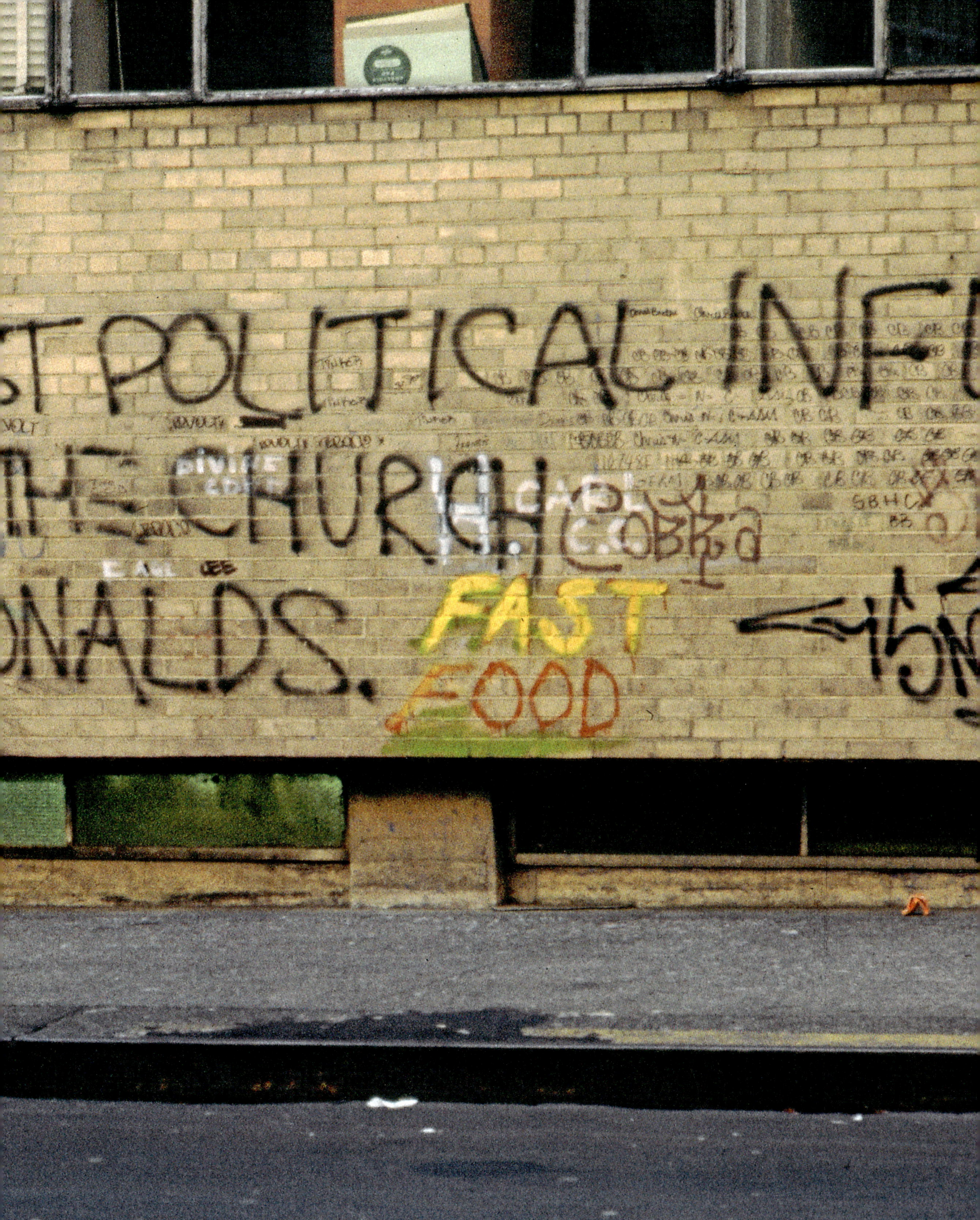
ST POLITICAL INF
HE CHURCH
ONALDS.
FAST
FOOD

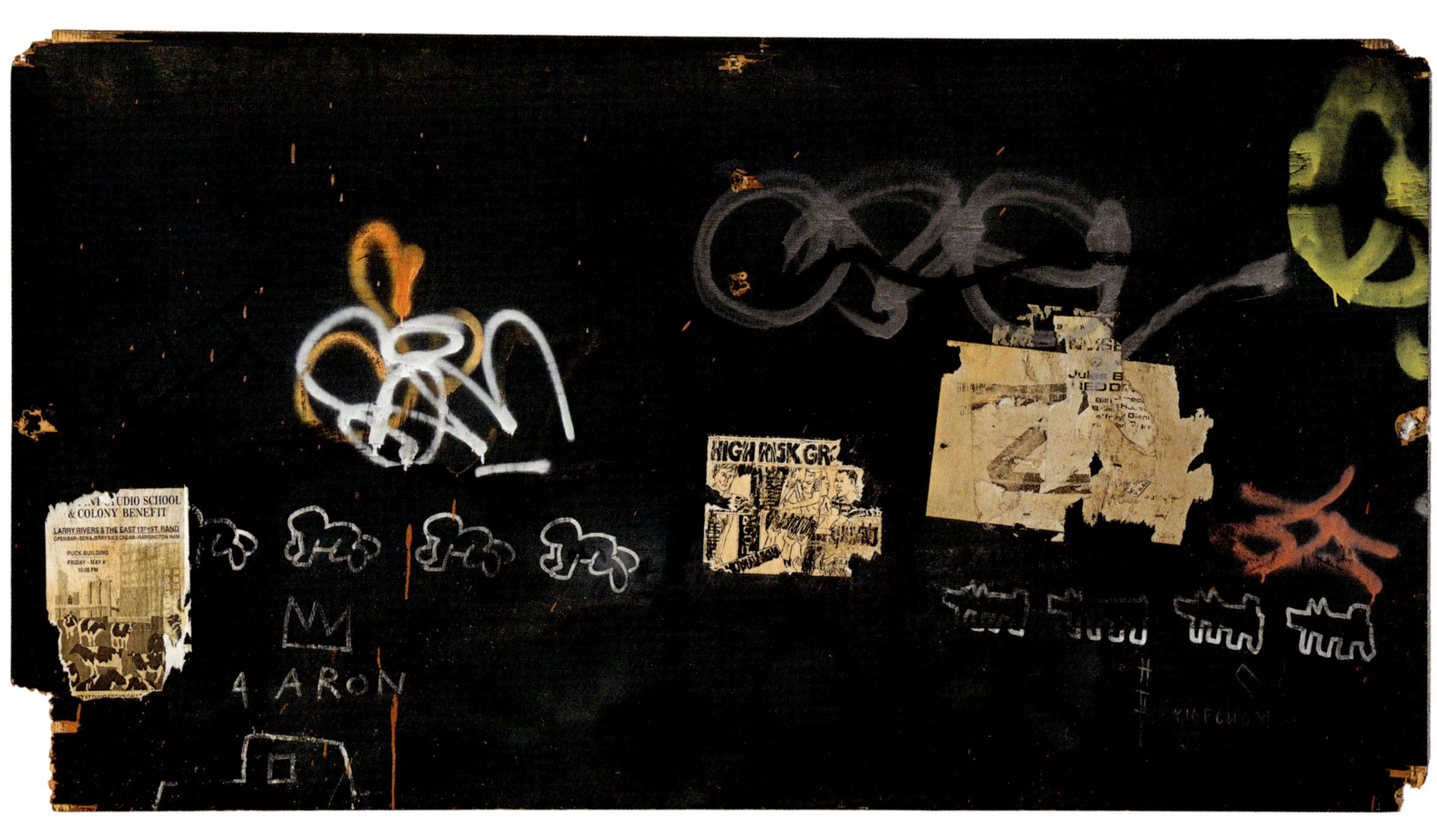

Keith Haring, Jean-Michel Basquiat, other artists *Untitled (Symphony No. 1)* c. 1980–83, mixed media, spray-paint and paper on plywood, 122.6 x 219.7 cm, Collection of Larry Warsh

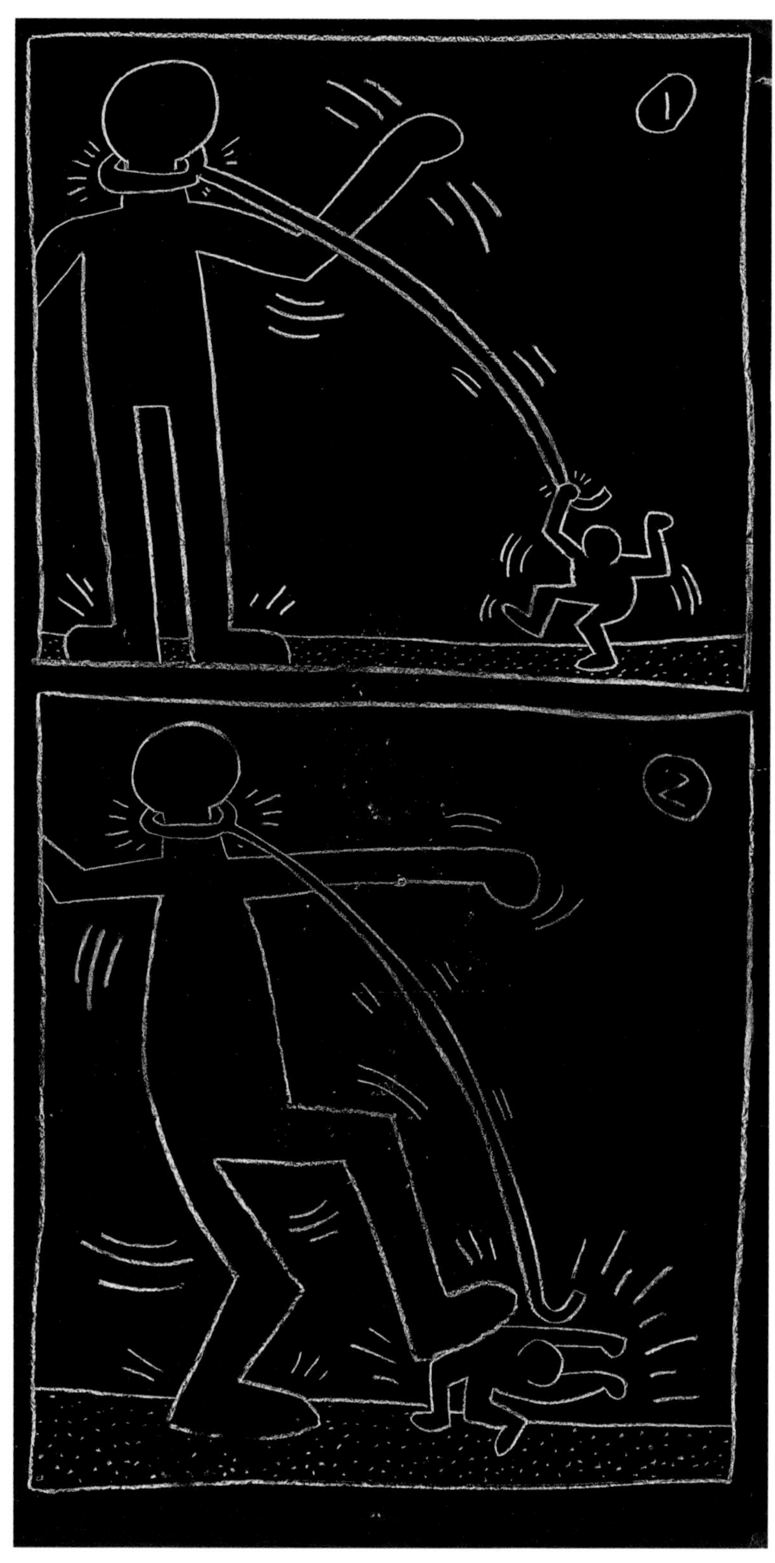

Keith Haring *Untitled* 1982, chalk on paper, 220.0 x 114.0 cm, Collection of Larry Warsh

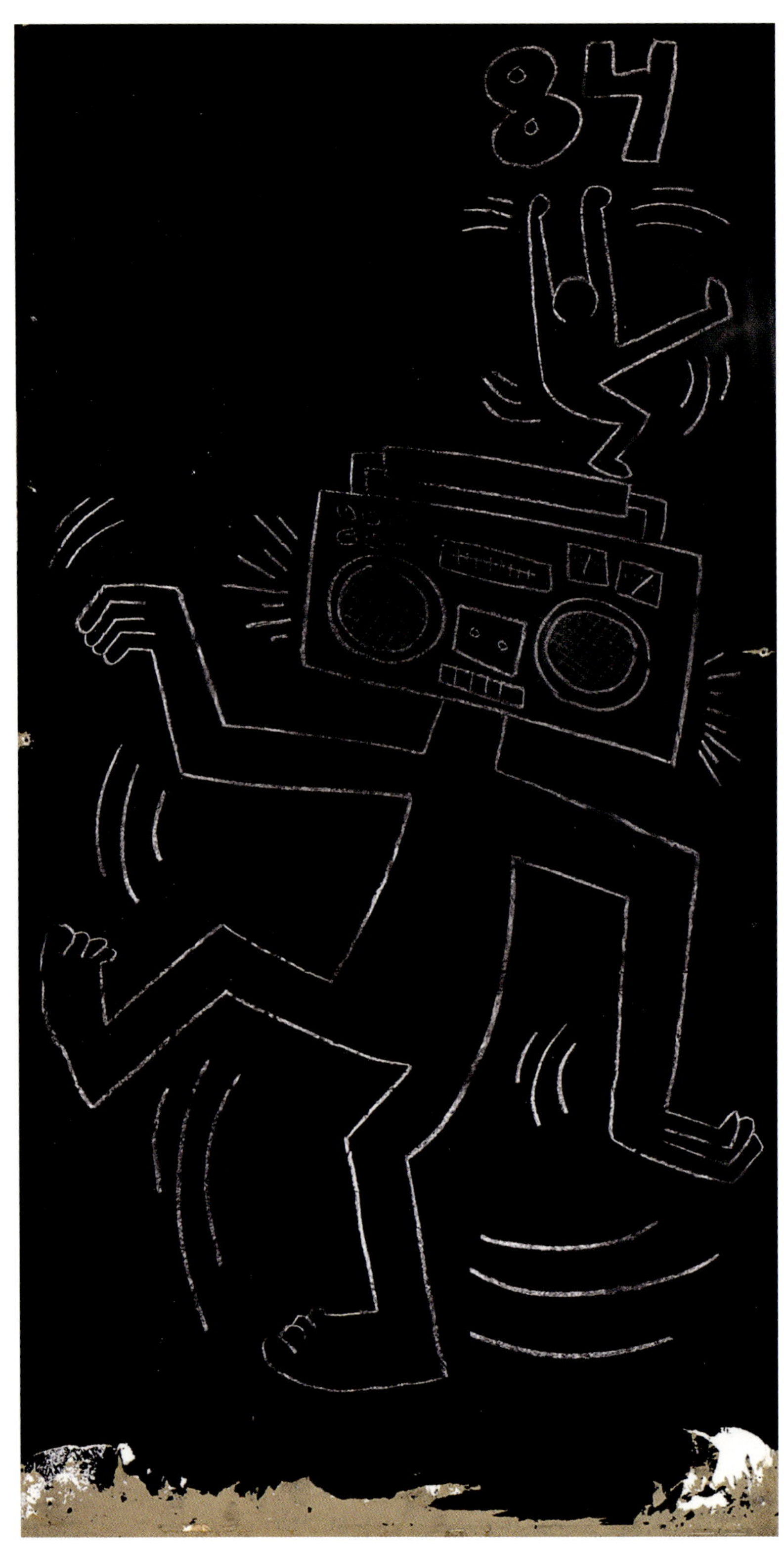

Keith Haring *Untitled* 1984, chalk on paper, 220.0 x 114.0 cm, Collection of Larry Warsh

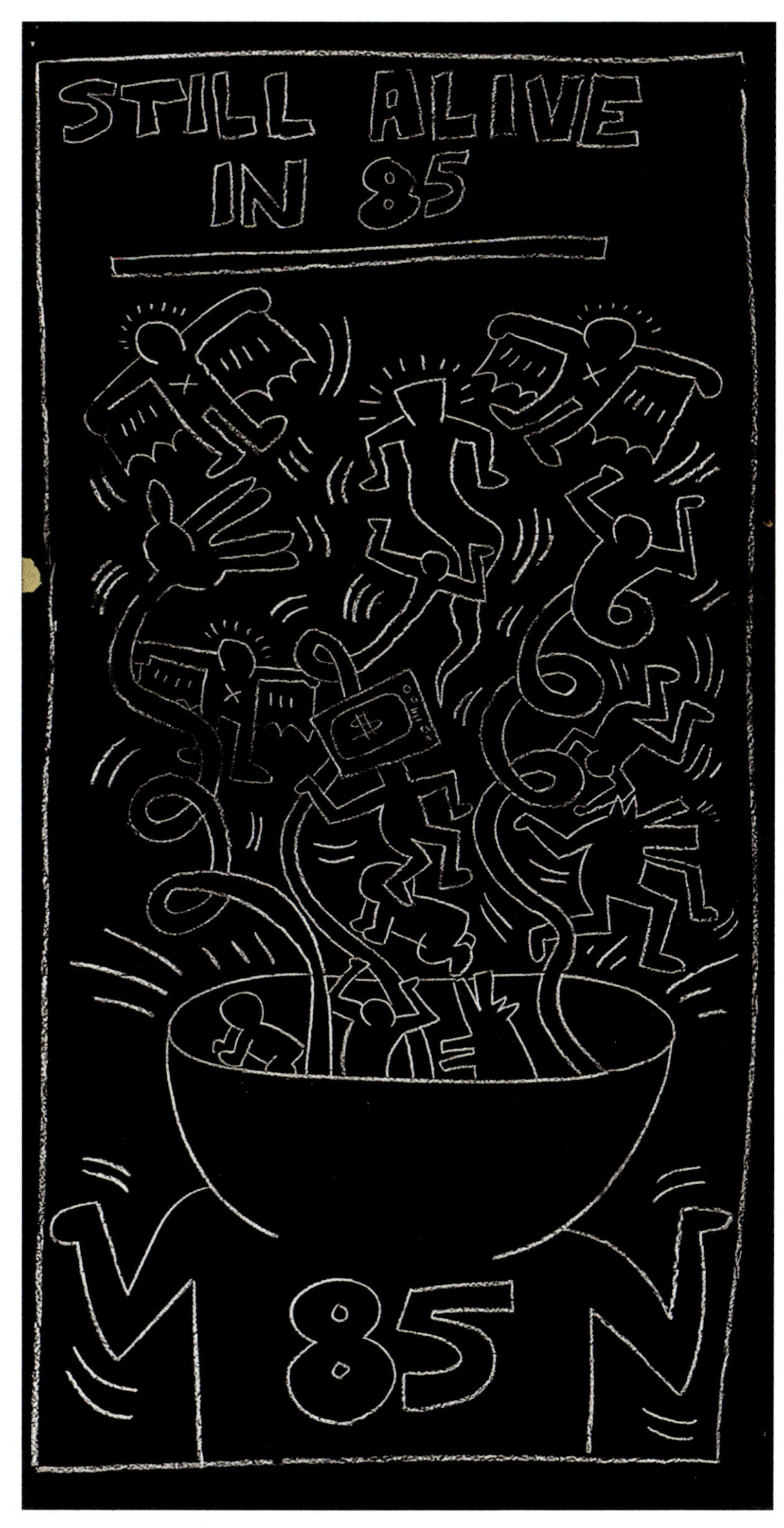

Keith Haring *Untitled* 1985, chalk on paper, 220.0 x 114.0 cm, Collection of Larry Warsh

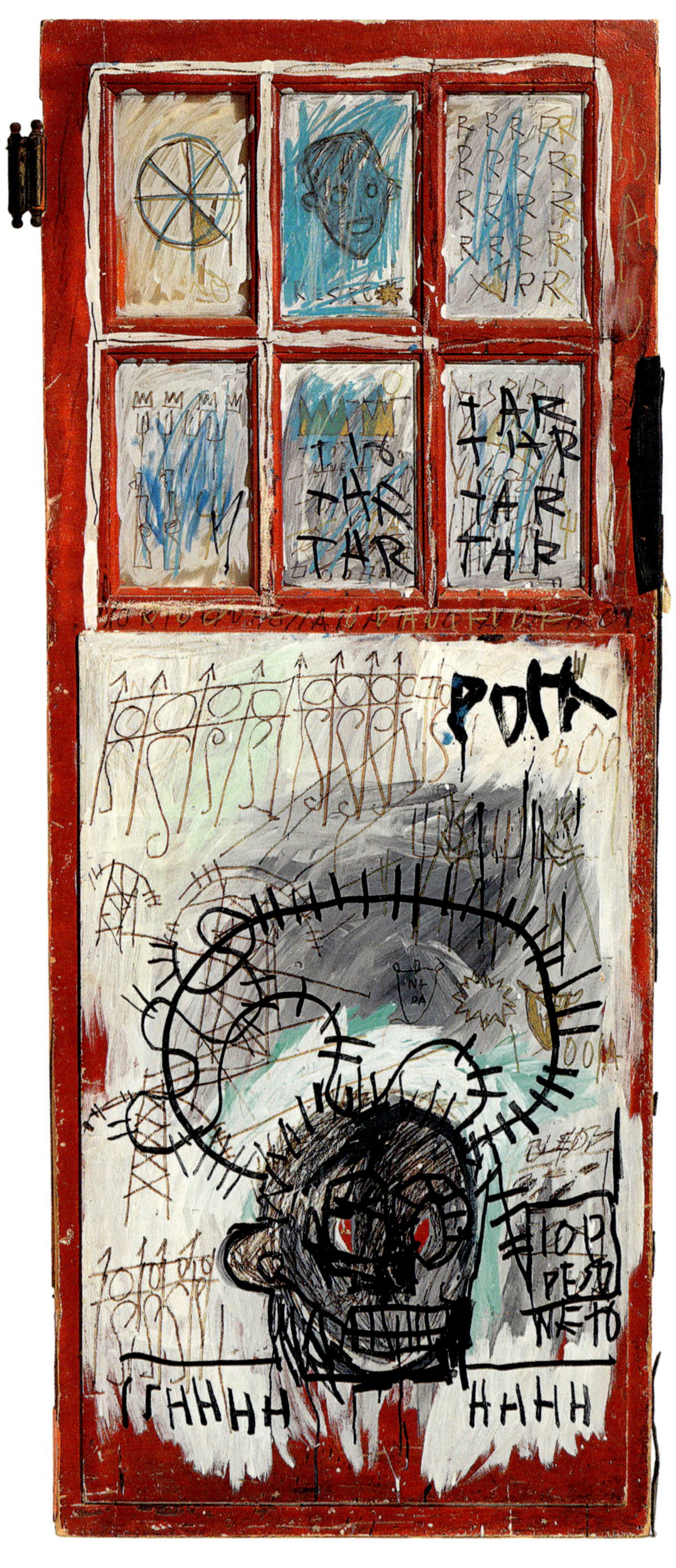

Jean-Michel Basquiat *Pork* 1981, synthetic polymer paint, oil and oilstick on wood and glass door, 210.8 x 85.4 cm, Private collection

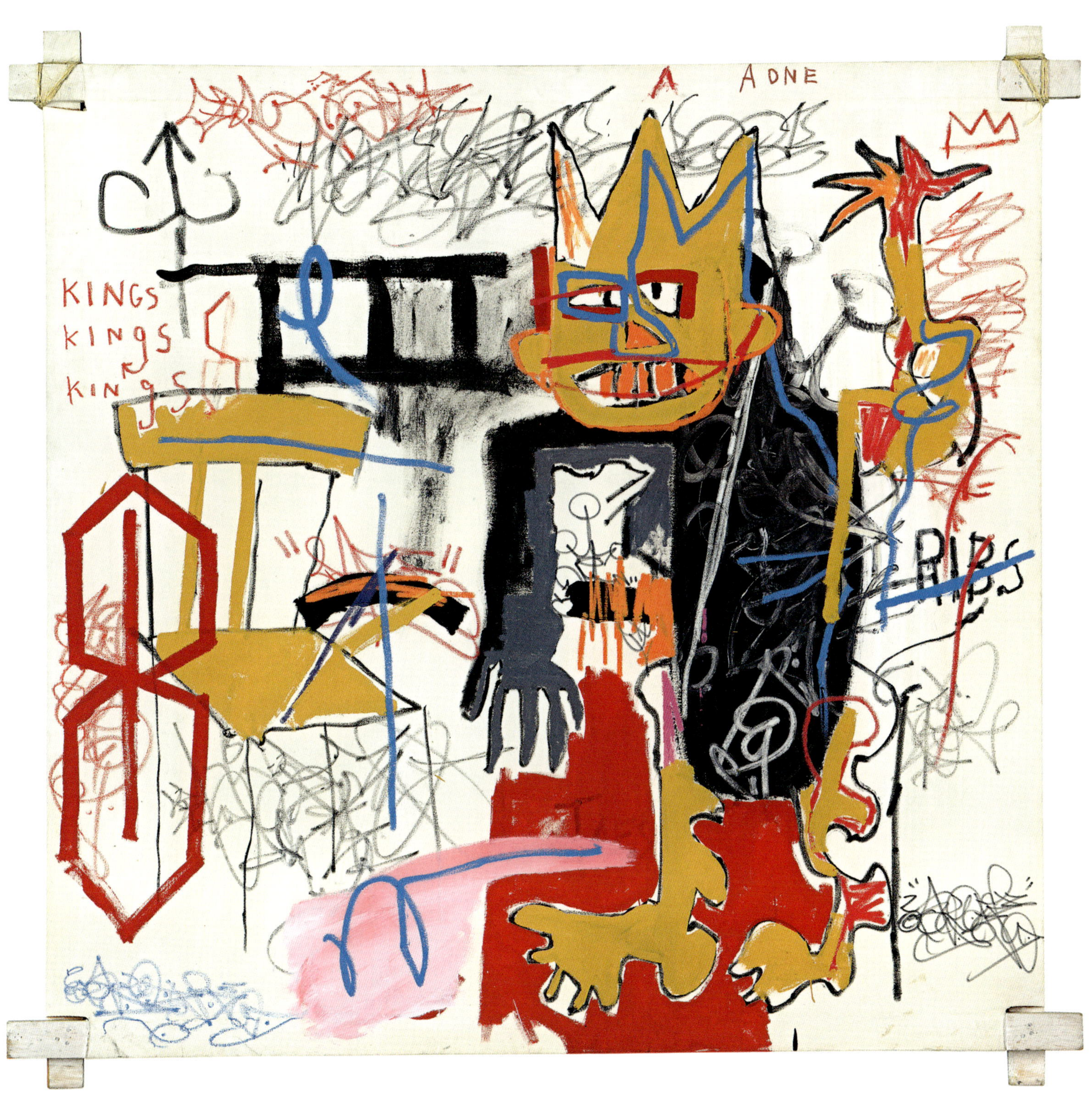

Jean-Michel Basquiat *Portrait of A-One A.K.A. King* 1982, synthetic polymer paint on canvas and wood, 182.8 x 184.0 cm, Private collection

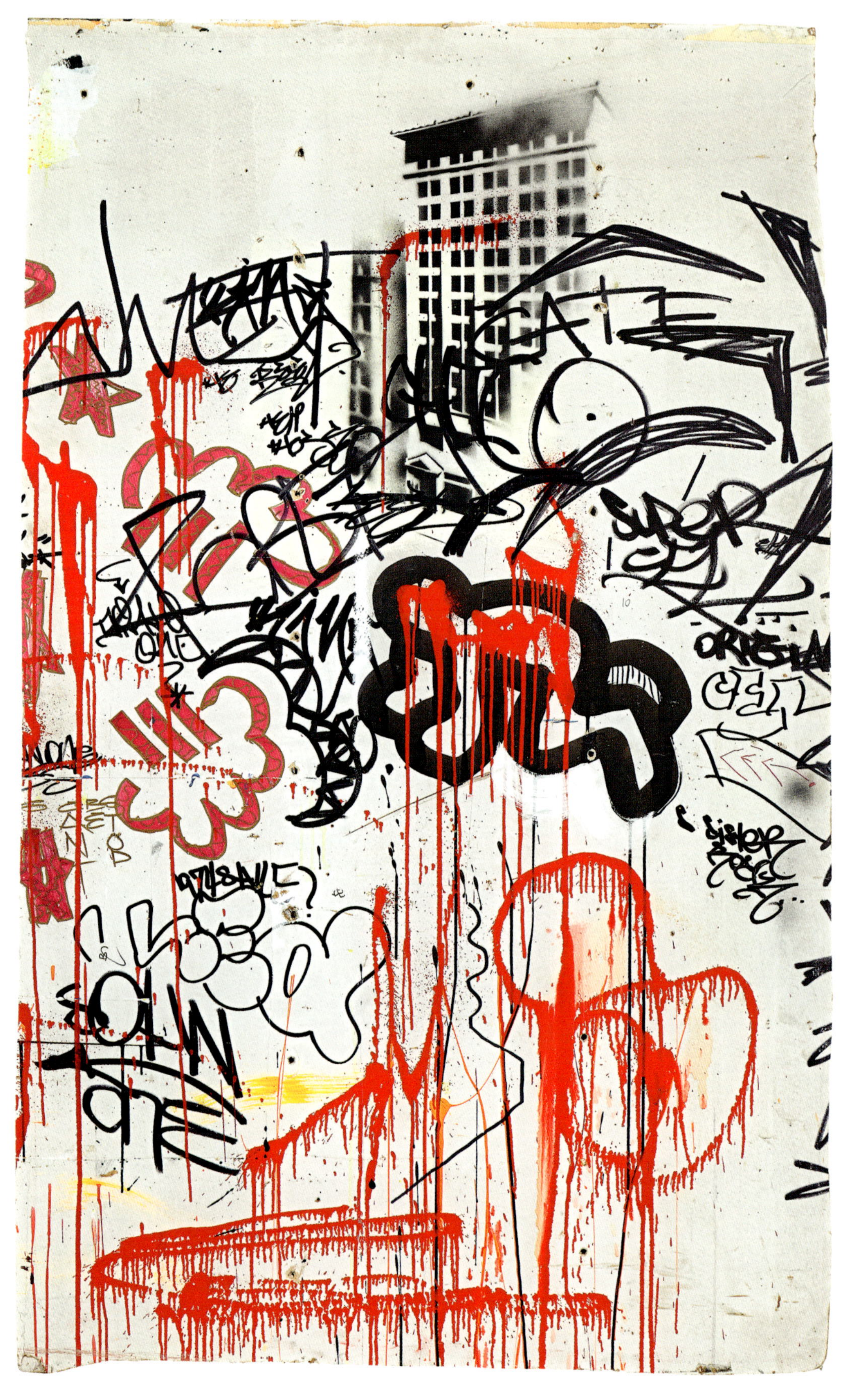

Keith Haring, other artists *Untitled* c. 1982, mixed media on composition board, 243.8 x 121.9 cm, Collection of Larry Warsh

Kenny Scharf, Fred Brathwaite, Jean-Michel Basquiat, LA II, other artists *Art is the Word* 1981, spray-paint and fibre-tipped pen on composition board, 186.7 x 121.9 cm, Noirmontartproduction collection

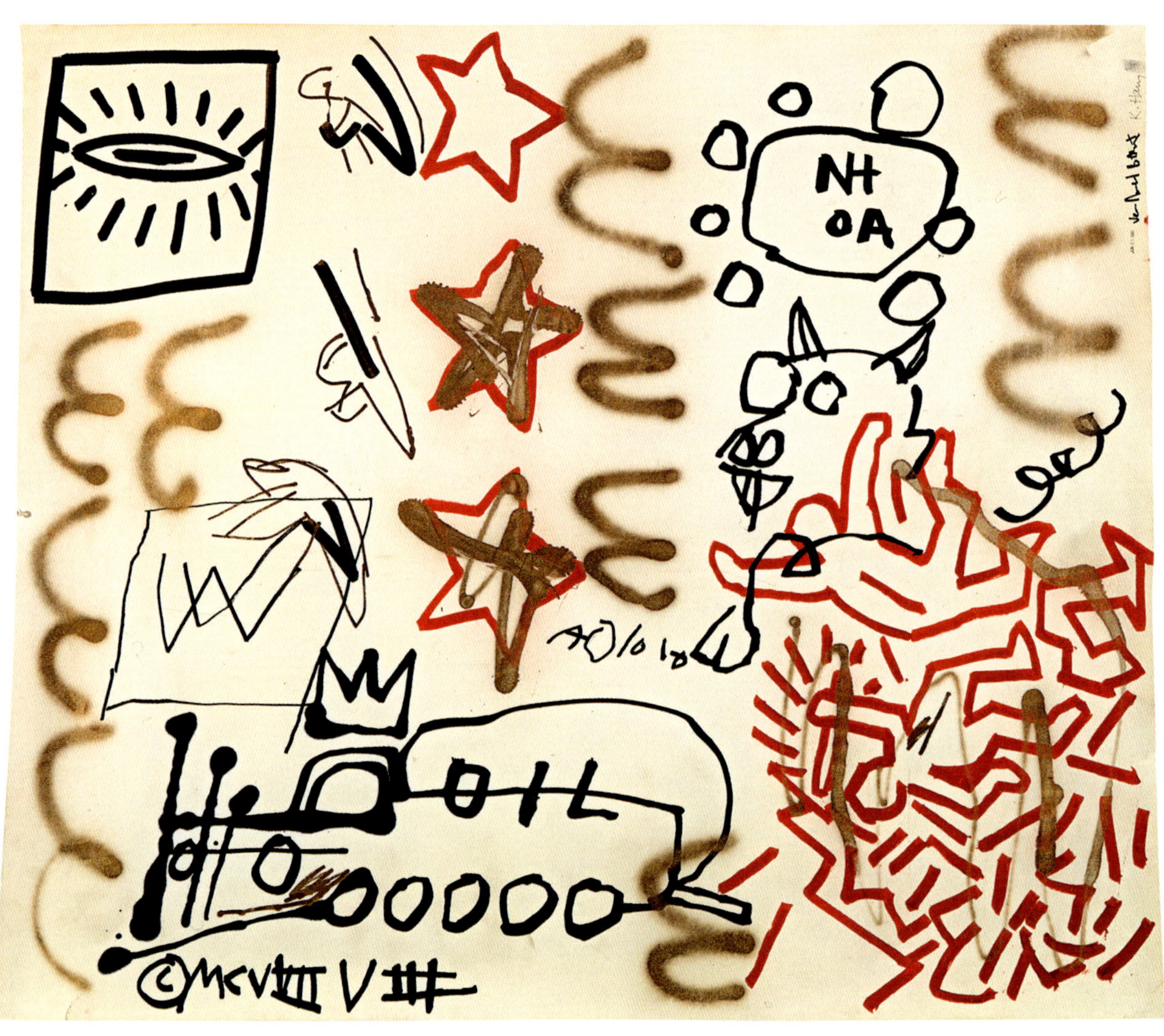

Keith Haring, Jean-Michel Basquiat *Untitled* 1981, fibre-tipped pen, spray-paint on paper, 106.7 x 121.0 cm, The Keith Haring Foundation, New York

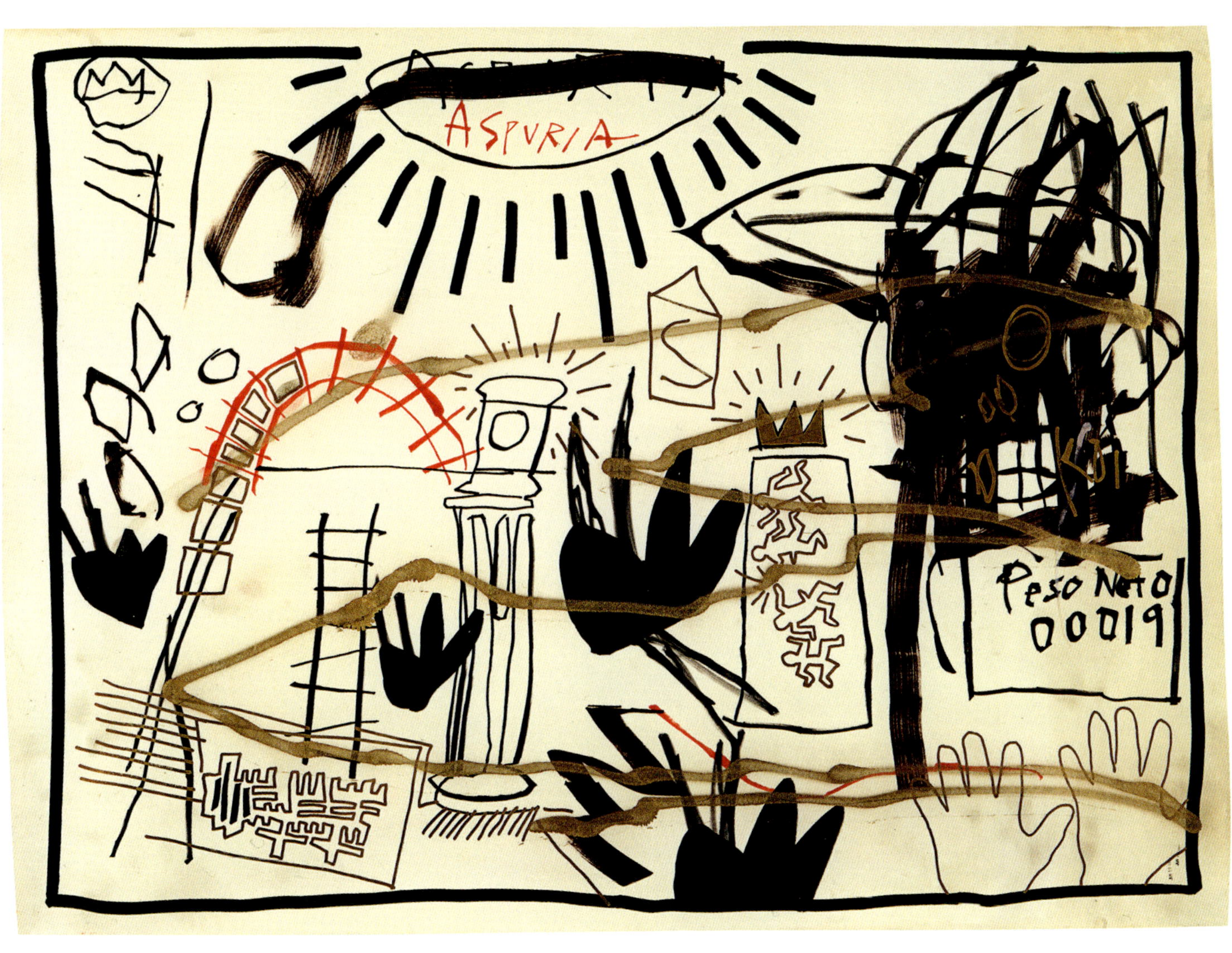

Keith Haring, Jean-Michel Basquiat *Untitled* 1981, fibre-tipped pen and spray-paint on paper, 106.7 x 142.3 cm, The Keith Haring Foundation, New York

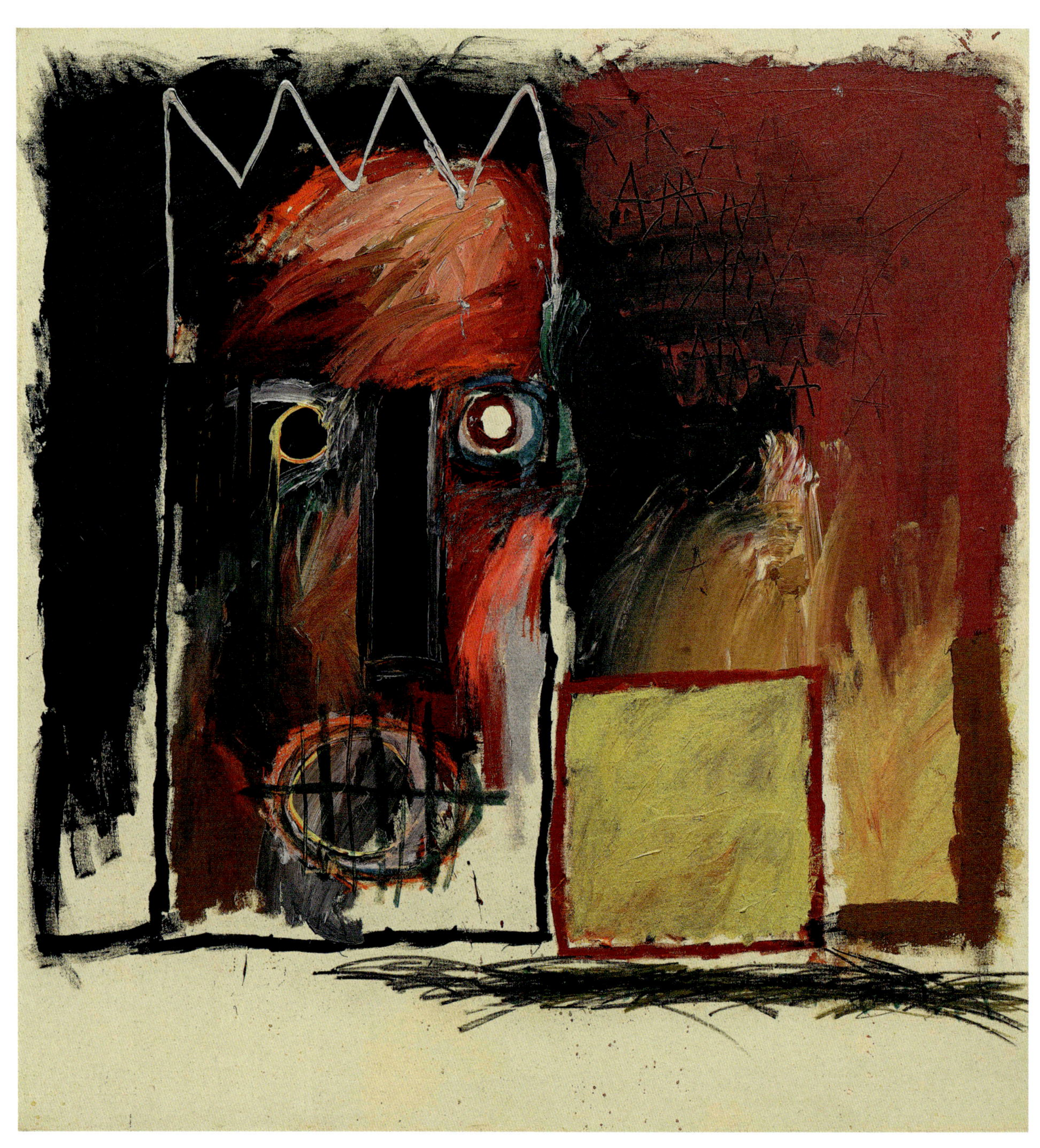

Jean-Michel Basquiat *Masque* 1981, synthetic polymer paint and oilstick on canvas, 142.0 x 125.0 cm,
Collection of Ben and Debra Ashkenazy, New York

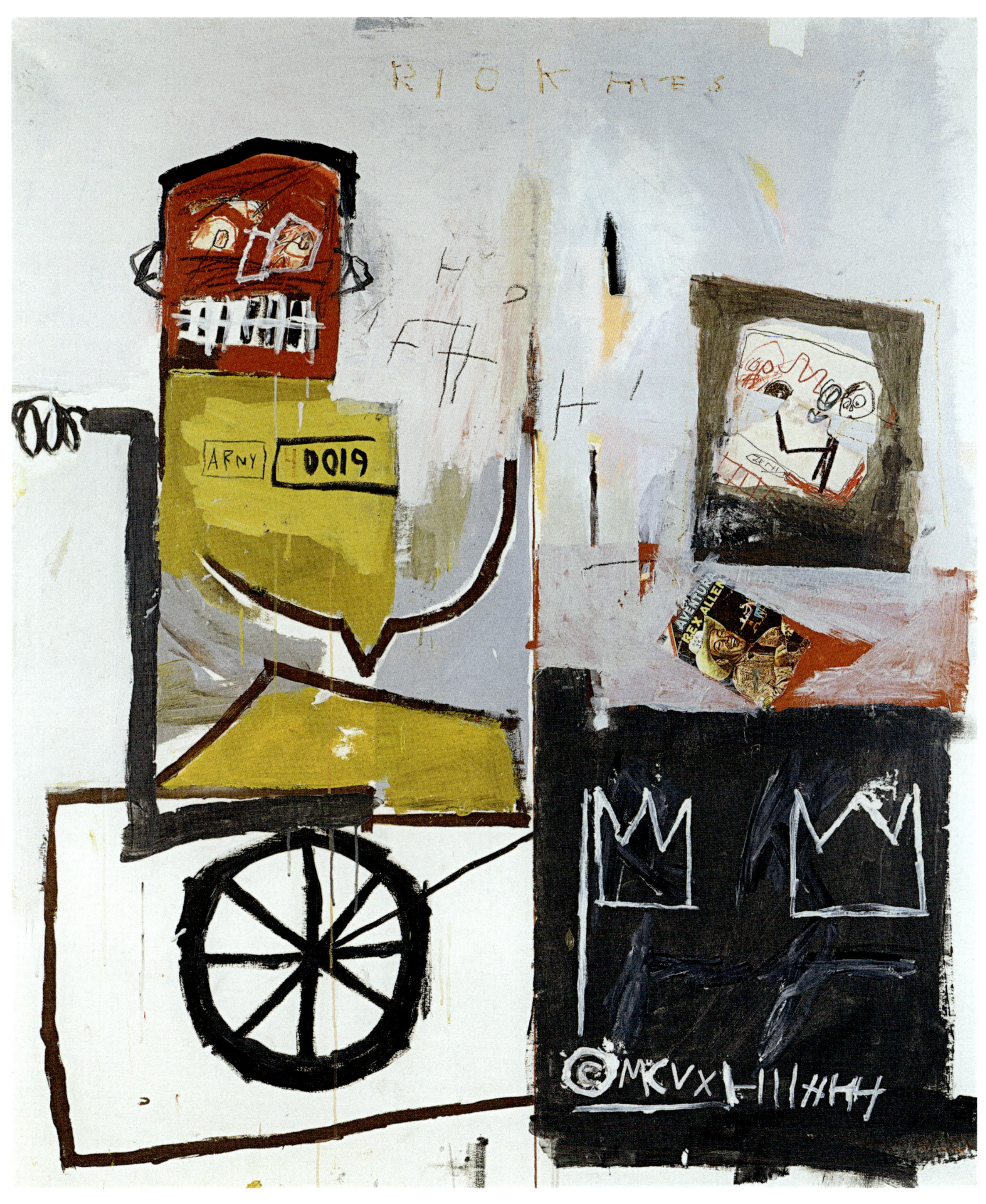

Jean-Michel Basquiat *Number 4* 1981, synthetic polymer paint, oilstick and paper collage on canvas, 167.0 x 137.0 cm, Collection of Andre Sakhai

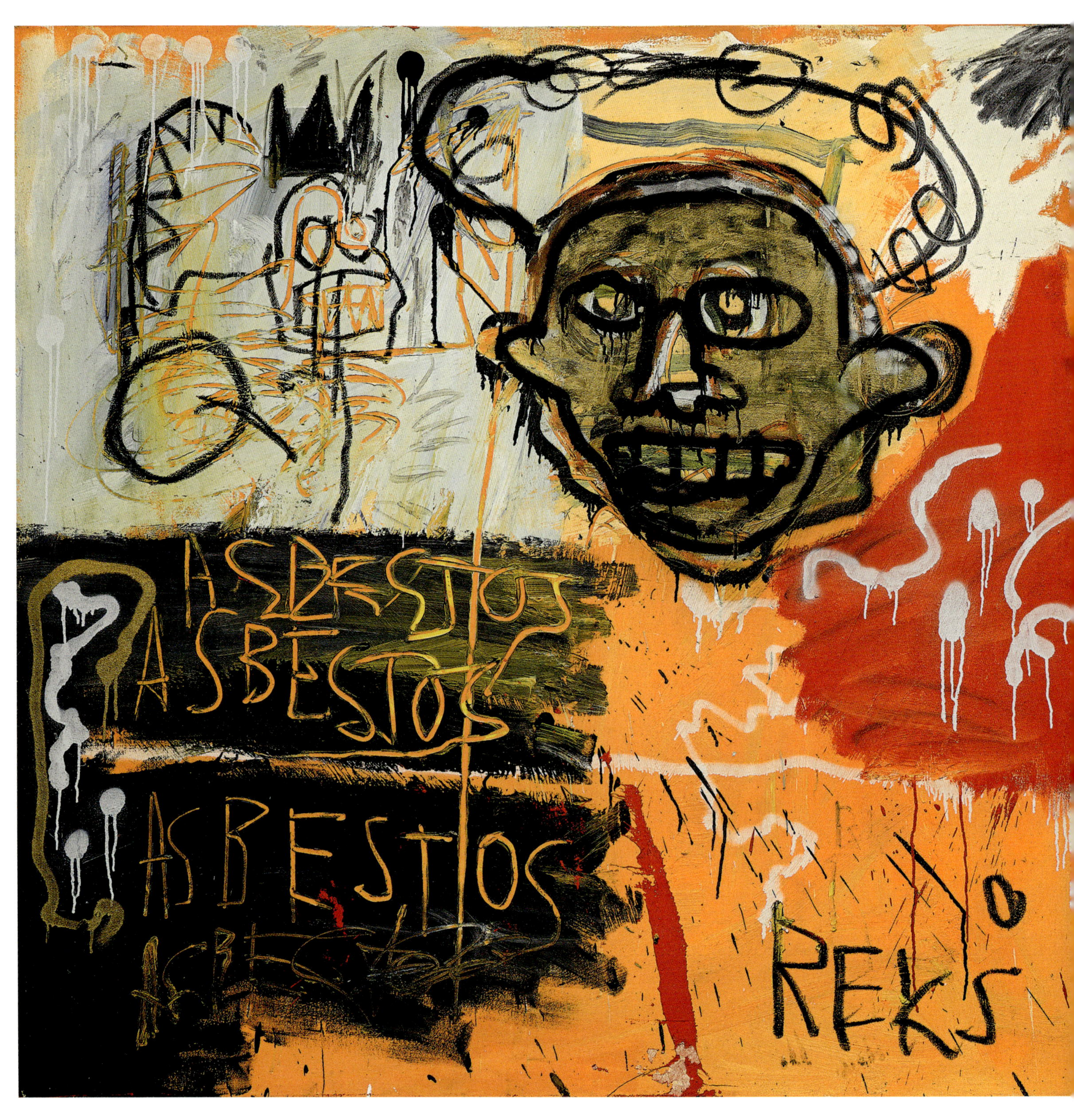

Jean-Michel Basquiat *Untitled (Pollo Frito)* 1982, synthetic polymer paint, oil and enamel on canvas, (a-b) 152.4 x 306.1 cm (overall), Private European collection, courtesy of John Sayegh-Belchatowski

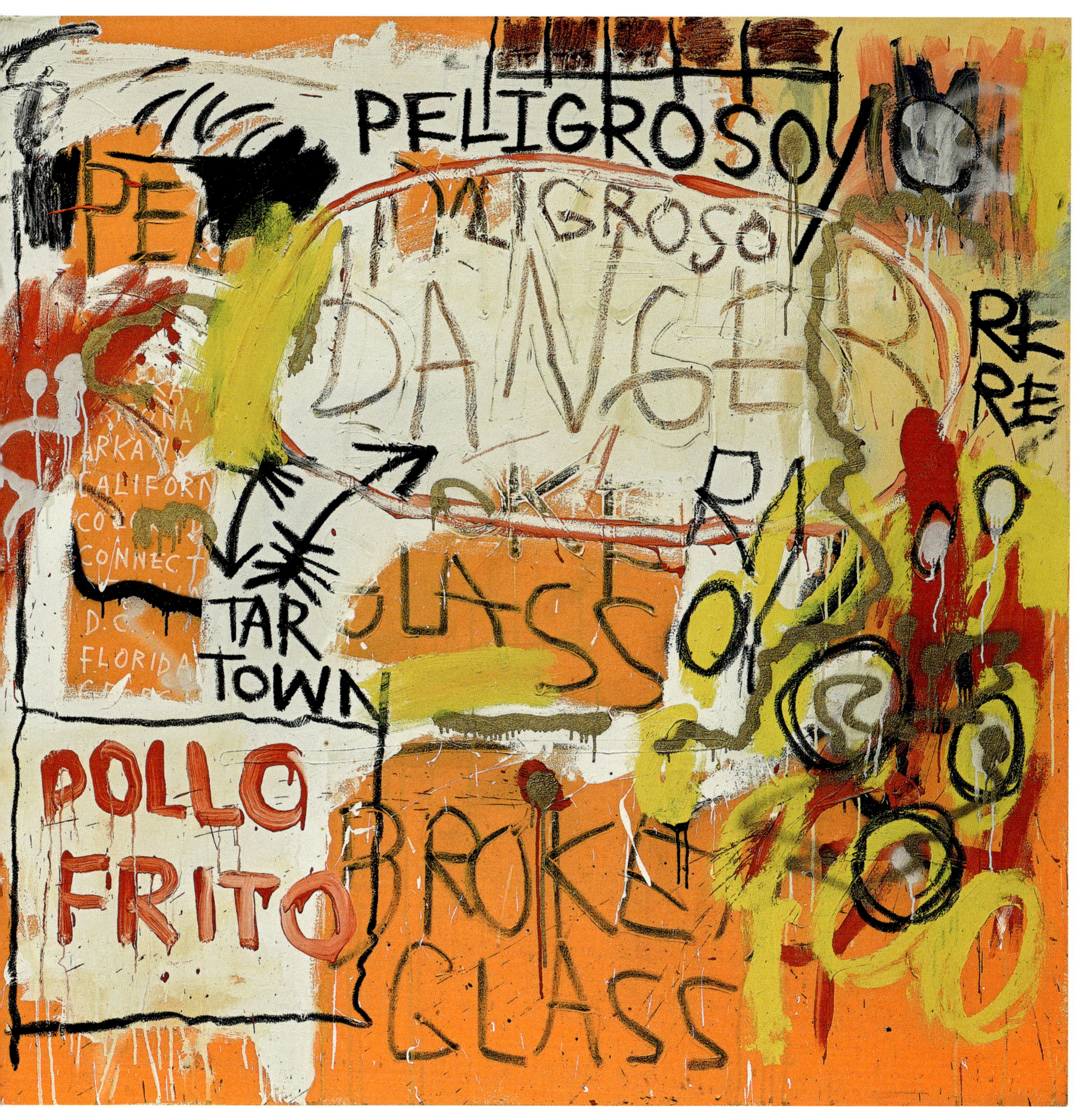
PELIGROSO
DANGER
RE
RE
ARKAN
CALIFORN
CONNECT
D.C.
FLORIDA
TAR
TOWN
GLASS
POLLO
FRITO
BROKE
GLASS

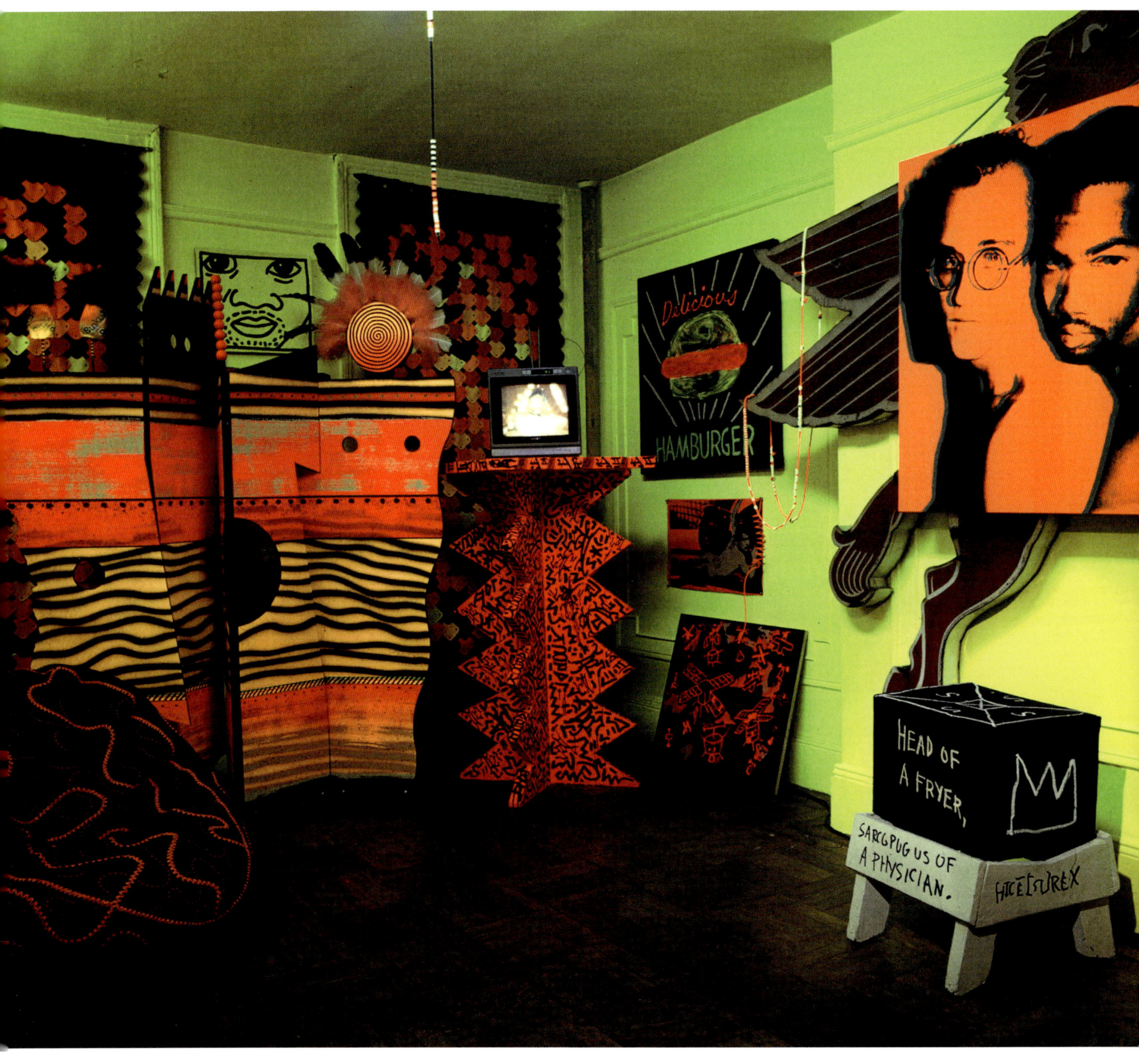

Keith Haring's Broome Street Apartment (detail), New York, c. 1983–84

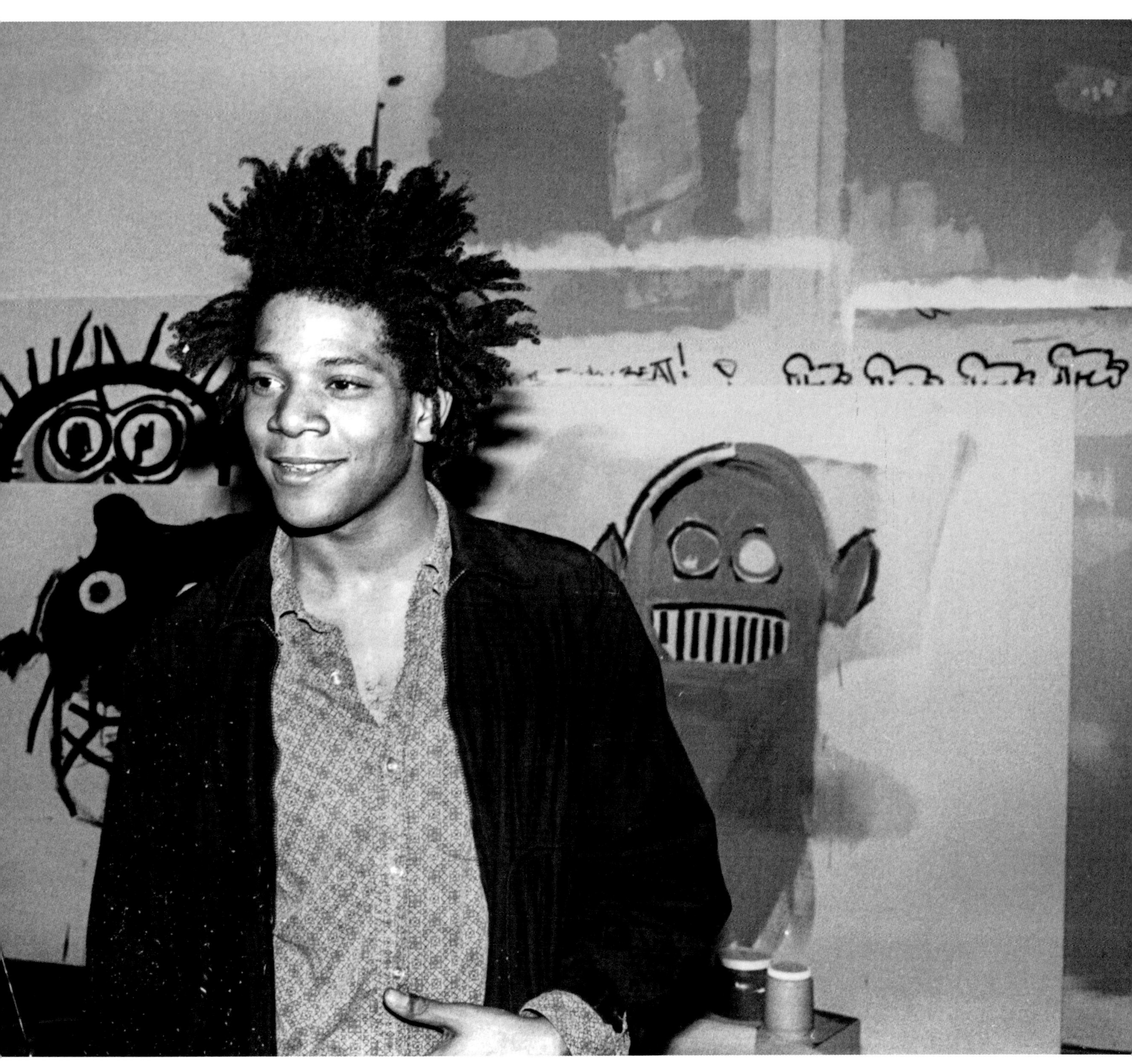

Jean-Michel Basquiat in his studio at the Annina Nosei Gallery (detail), May 1982

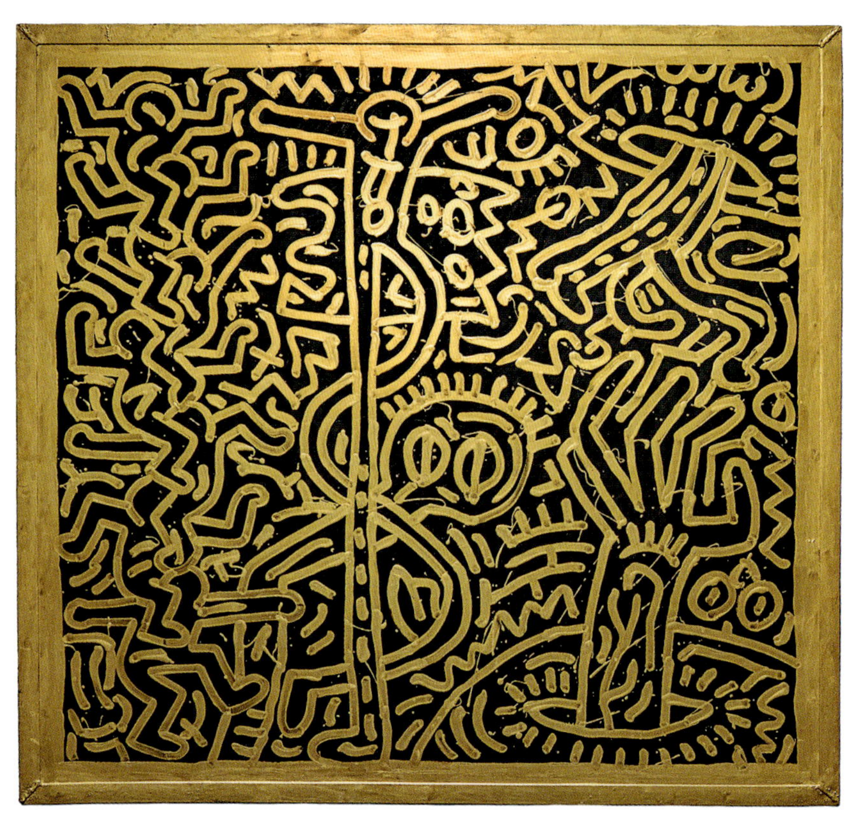

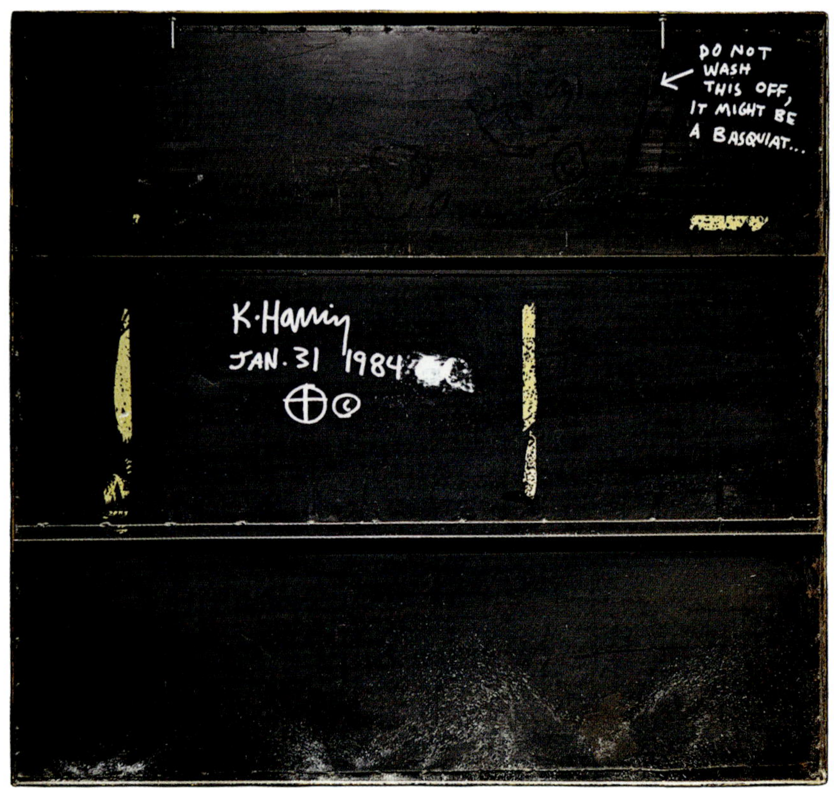

Keith Haring *Untitled* 1984 (front and back), enamel on sheet metal, 145.4 x 152.1 cm, Private collection

Keith Haring *Untitled* 1981, synthetic polymer paint on canvas, 127.0 x 127.0 cm, Private collection, New York

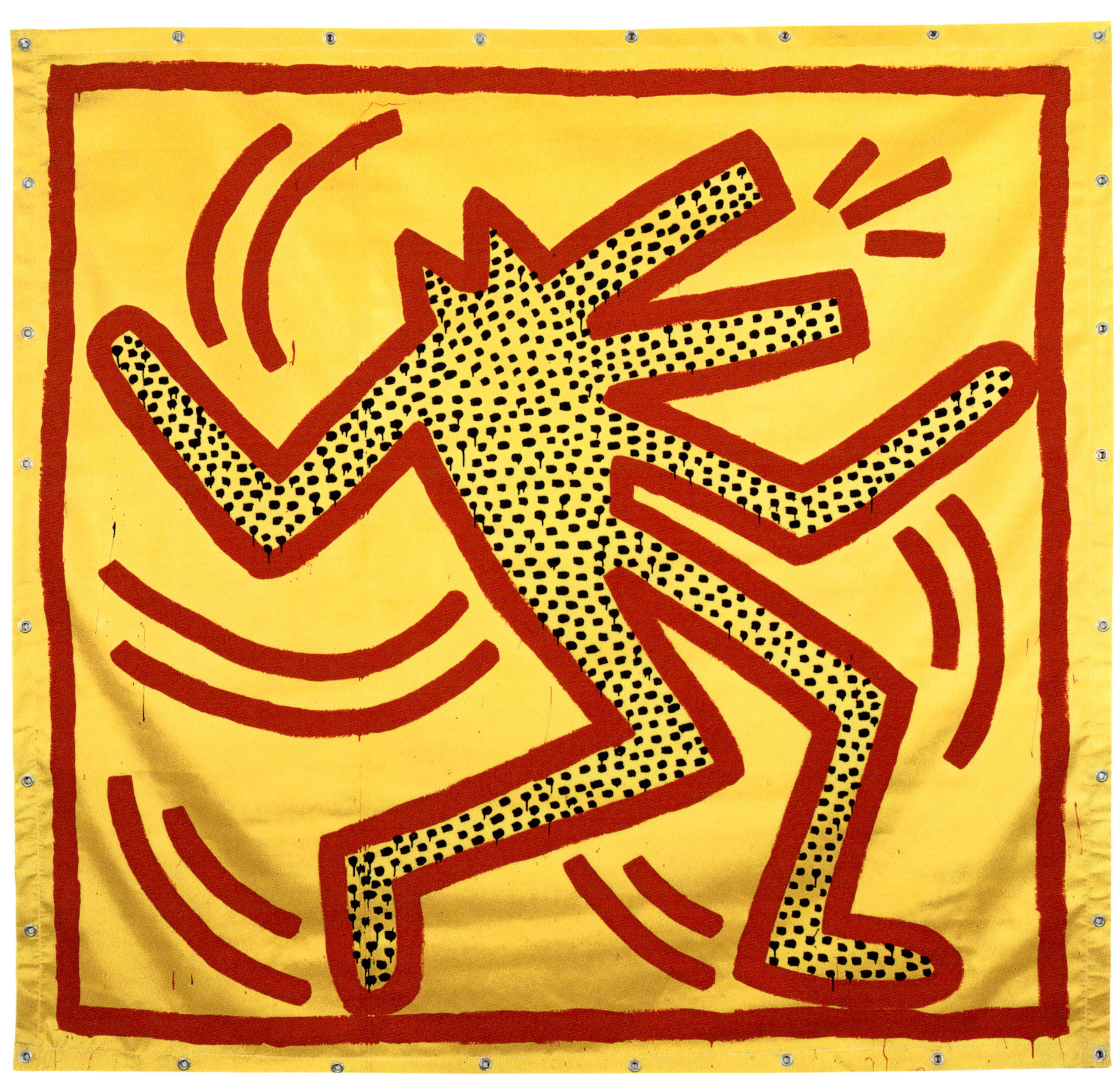

Keith Haring *Untitled* 1982, synthetic polymer paint on vinyl tarpaulin, 213.5 x 220.0 cm, J W Power Collection, The University of Sydney, managed by Museum of Contemporary Art, purchased with funds from the J W Power Bequest, 1982

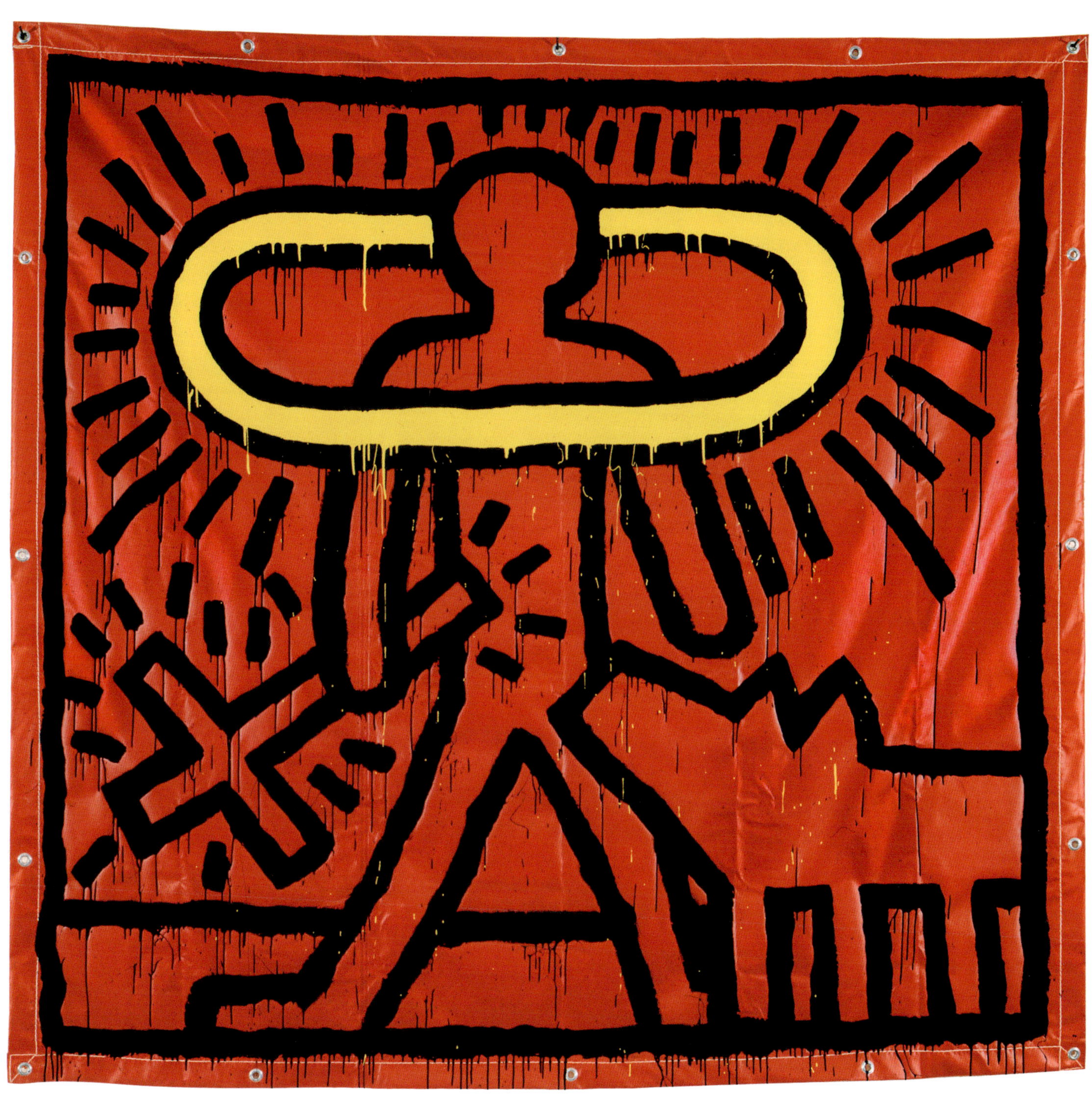

Keith Haring *Untitled* 1982, vinyl paint and vinyl ink on vinyl tarpaulin, 213.4 x 213.4 cm, Private collection

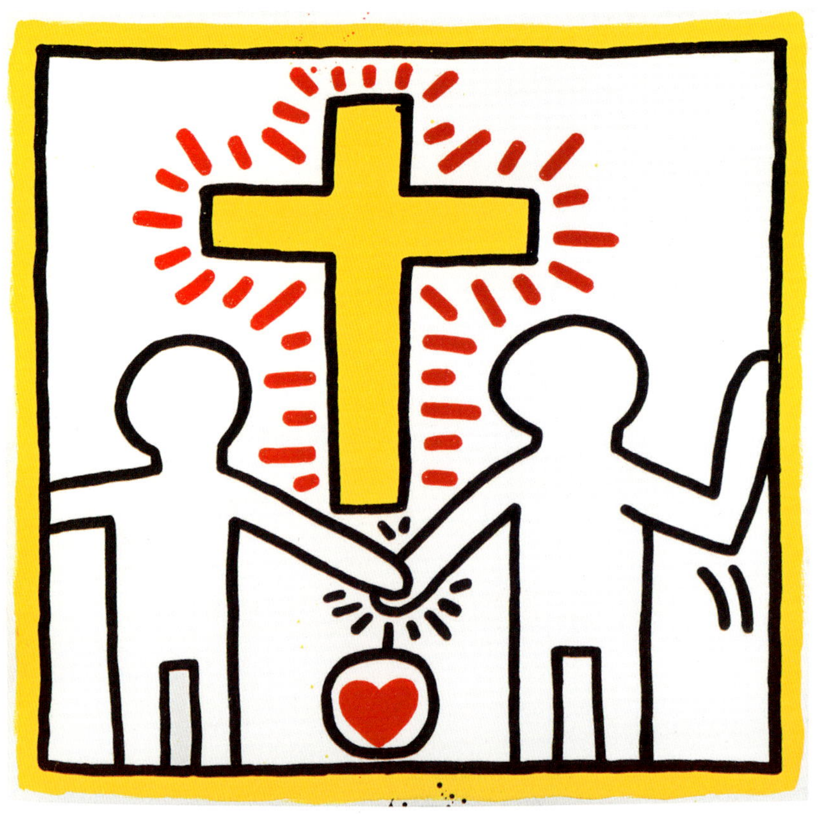

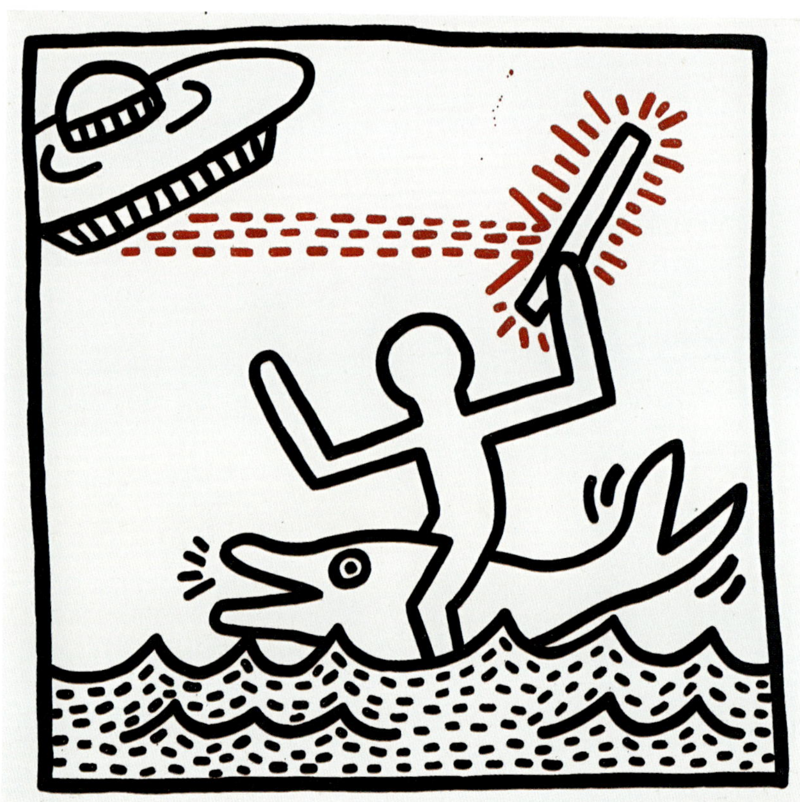

(top) Keith Haring *Untitled* 1982, baked enamel on metal, 109.2 x 109.2 cm, Museum MACAN, Jakarta, Indonesia
(bottom) Keith Haring *Untitled* 1982, baked enamel on metal, 109.2 x 109.2 cm, Collection of Larry Warsh

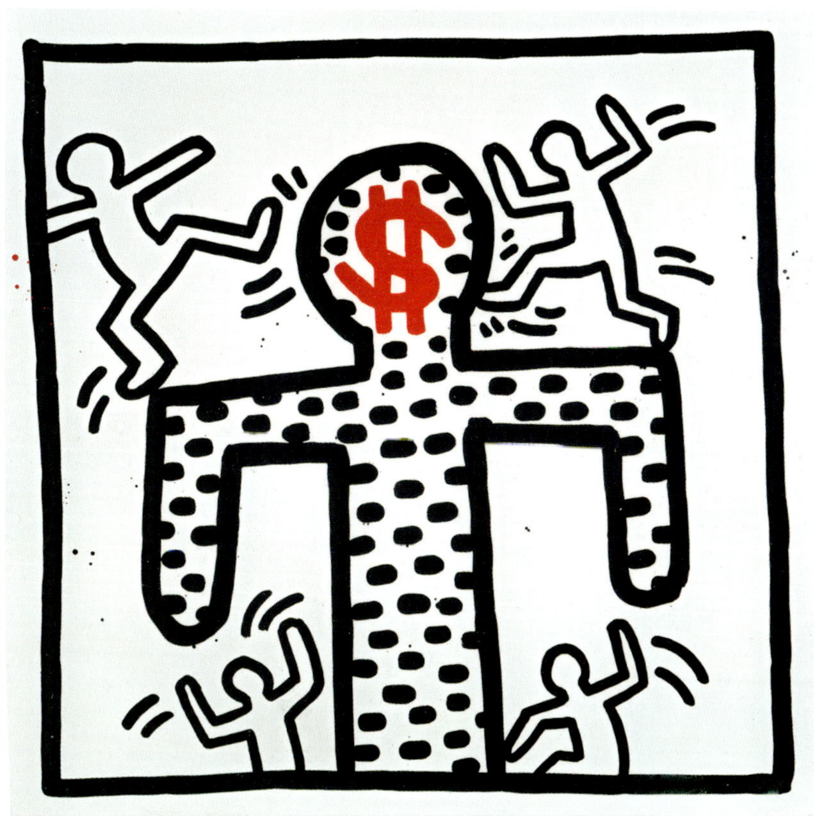

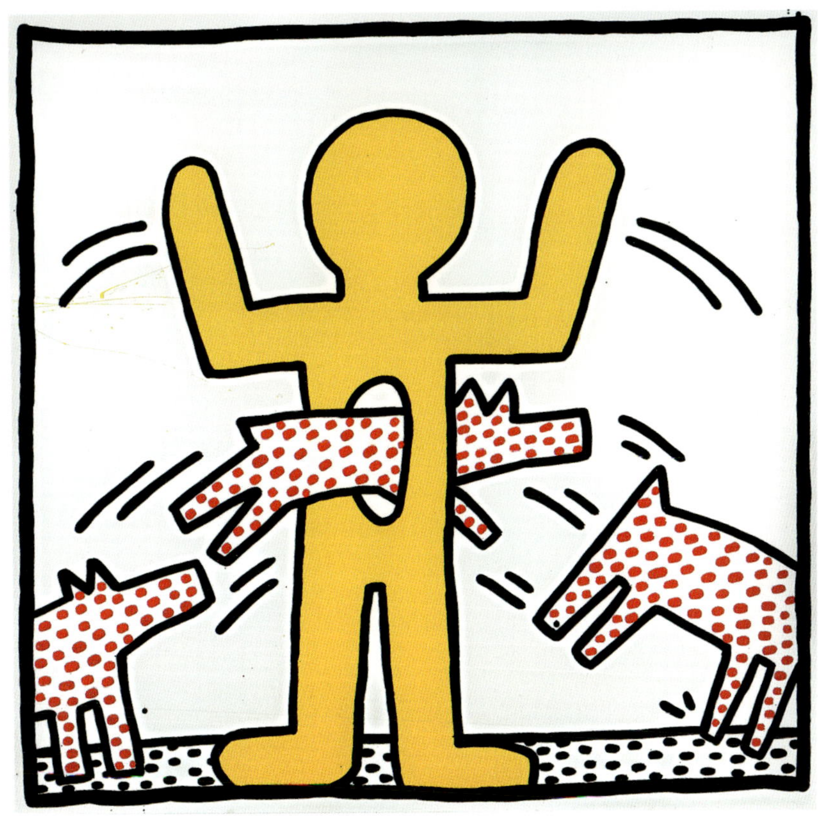

(top) Keith Haring *Untitled* 1982, baked enamel on metal, 109.2 x 109.2 cm, Private collection
(bottom) Keith Haring *Untitled* 1982, baked enamel on metal, 109.2 x 109.2 cm, Collection of Larry Warsh

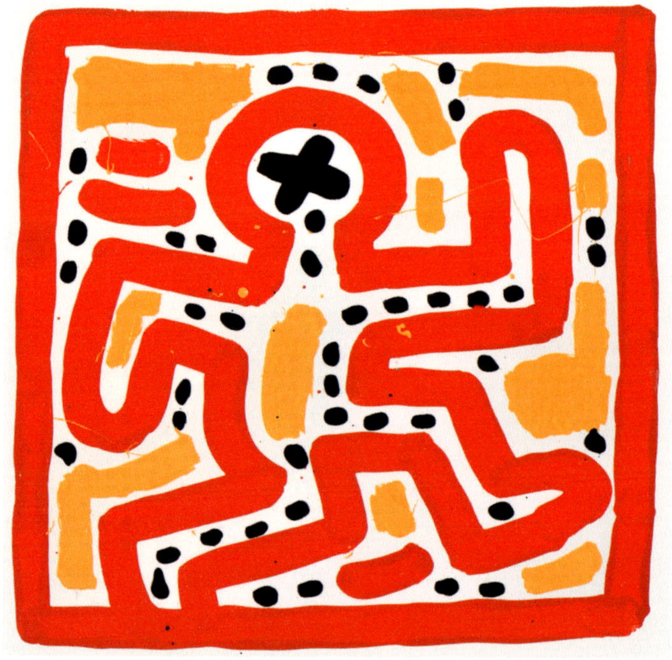

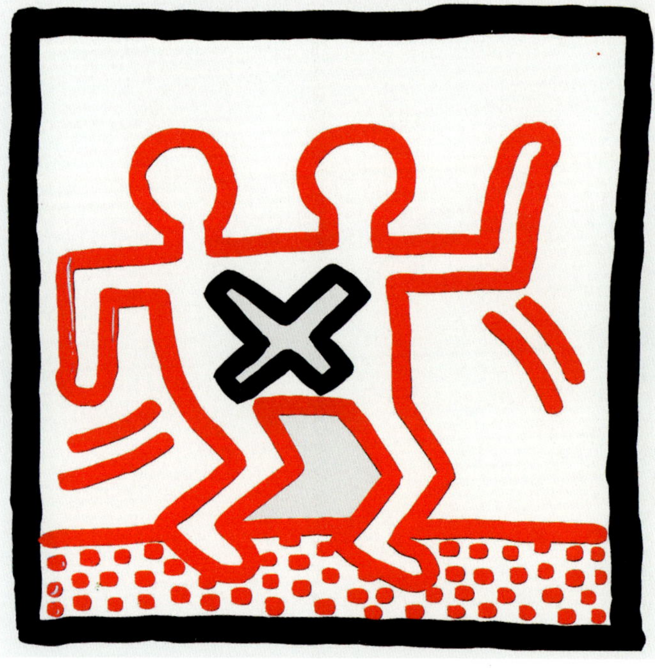

(clockwise from top left) Keith Haring *Untitled* 1982, baked enamel on metal, 30.5 x 30.5 cm, Collection of Larry Warsh; *Untitled* 1985 baked enamel on metal, 30.5 x 30.5 cm, Courtesy Laurent Strouk; *Untitled* 1982, baked enamel on metal, 30.5 x 30.5 cm, Collection of Larry Warsh

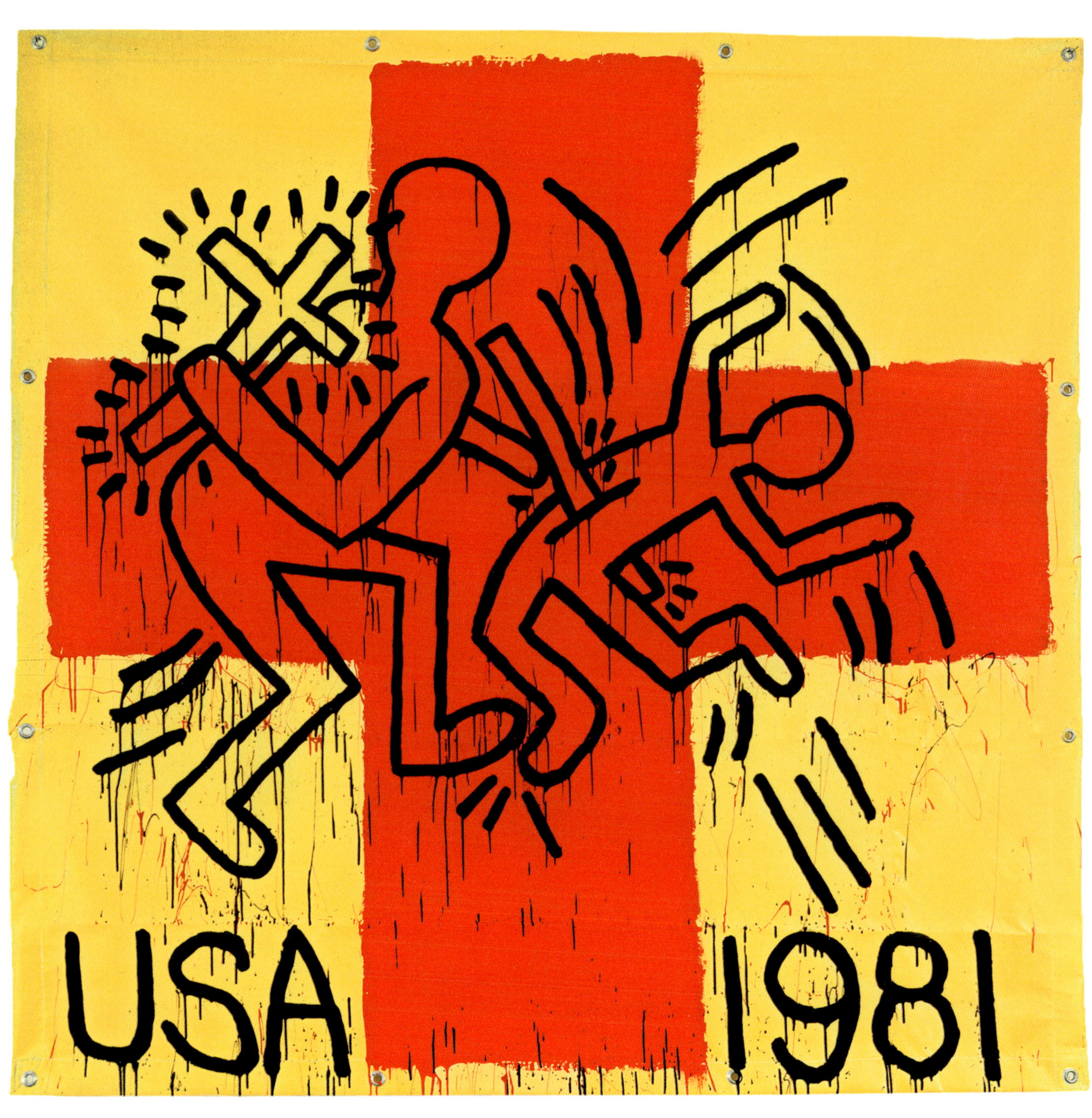

Keith Haring *Untitled* 1981, vinyl ink on tarpaulin, 182.8 x 182.8 cm, Private collection, Europe, courtesy Martos Gallery, New York

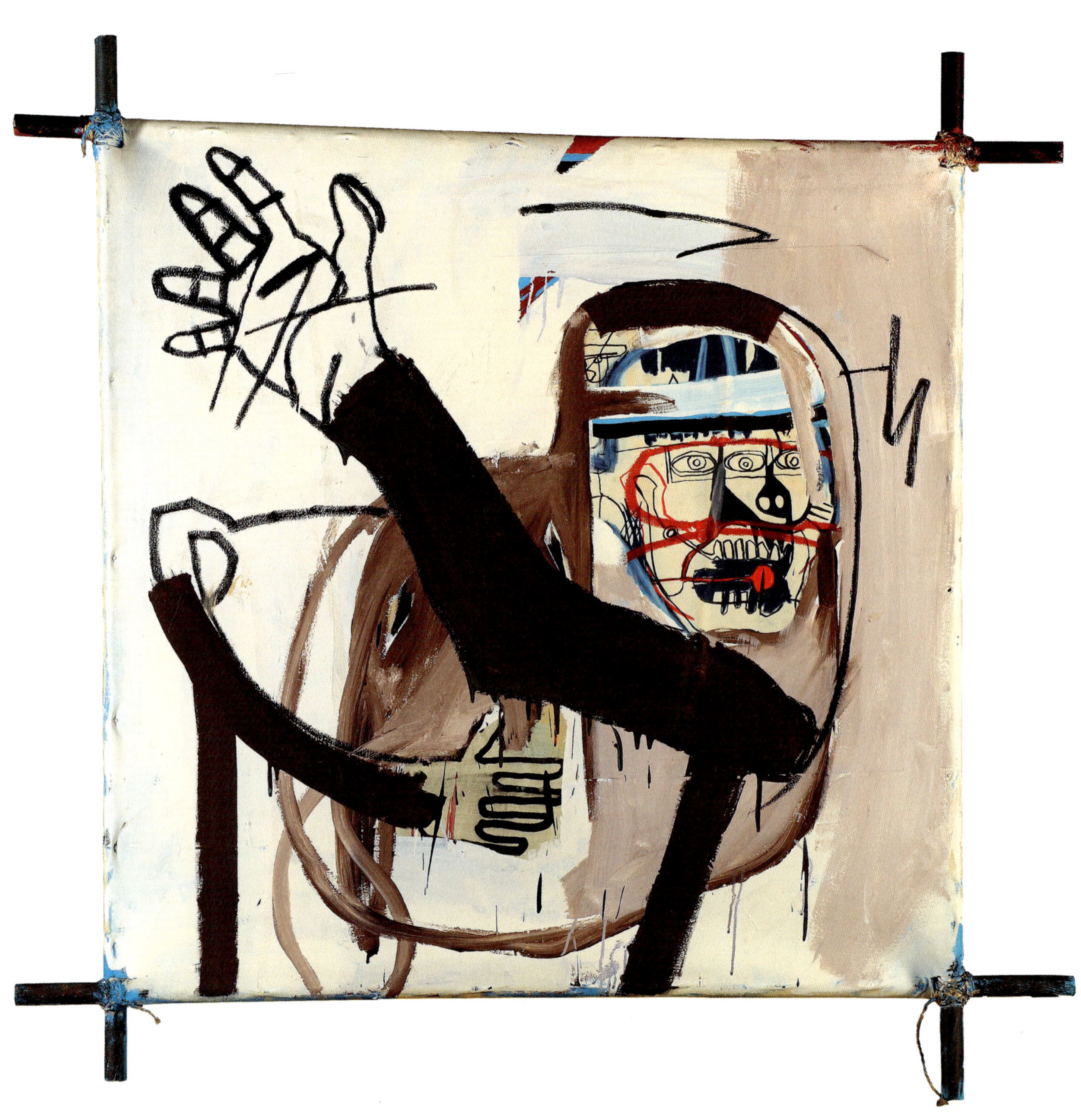

Jean-Michel Basquiat *Cantasso* 1982, synthetic polymer paint on canvas and wood, 156.0 x 156.0 cm, Collection of Georges Saier

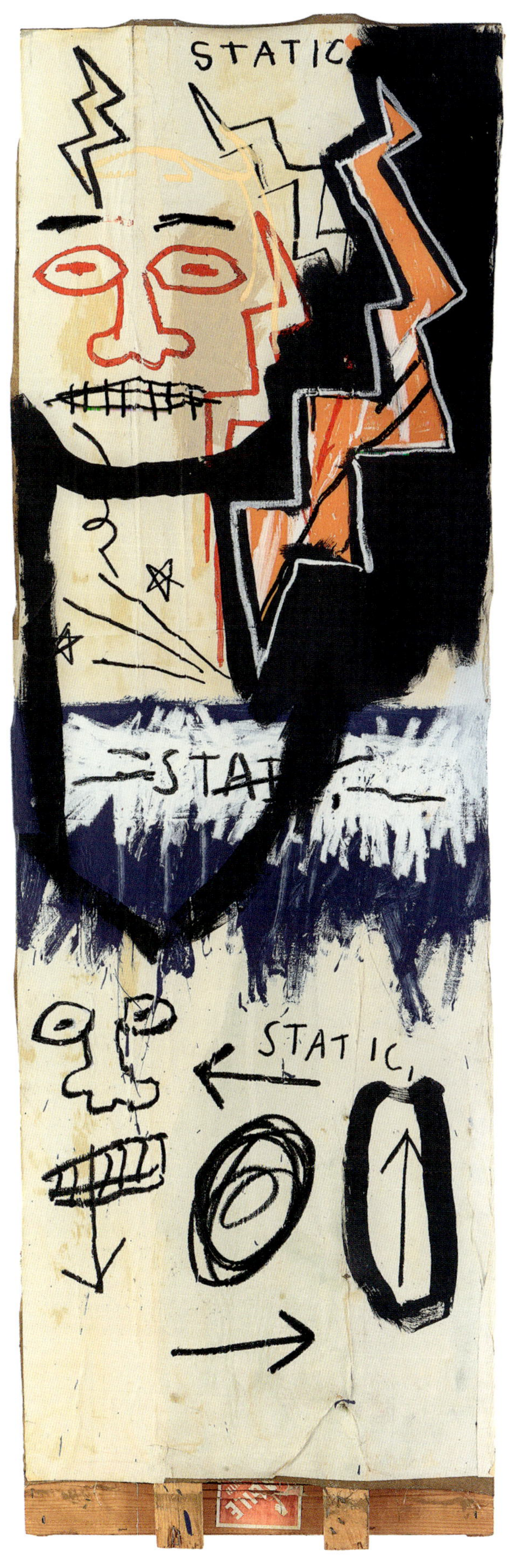

Jean-Michel Basquiat *Totem* 1982, synthetic polymer paint, oilstick and paper collage on canvas on wood panel, 203.0 x 63.5 x 10.0 cm, Collection of Yoav Harlap, Israel

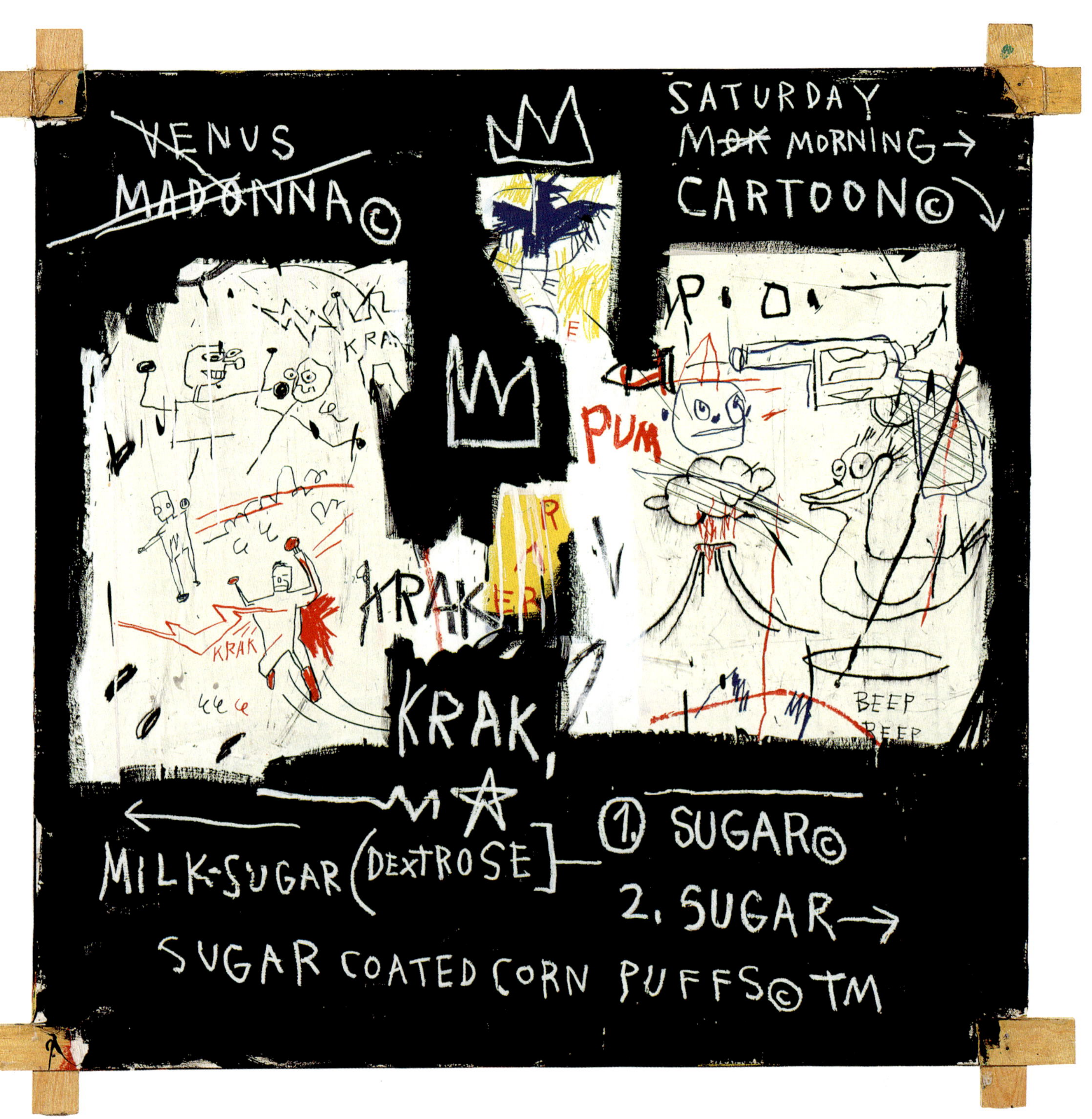

Jean-Michel Basquiat *A Panel of Experts* 1982, synthetic polymer paint and oil pastel on paper on canvas and wood, 152.5 x 152.0 cm, Montreal Museum of Fine Arts

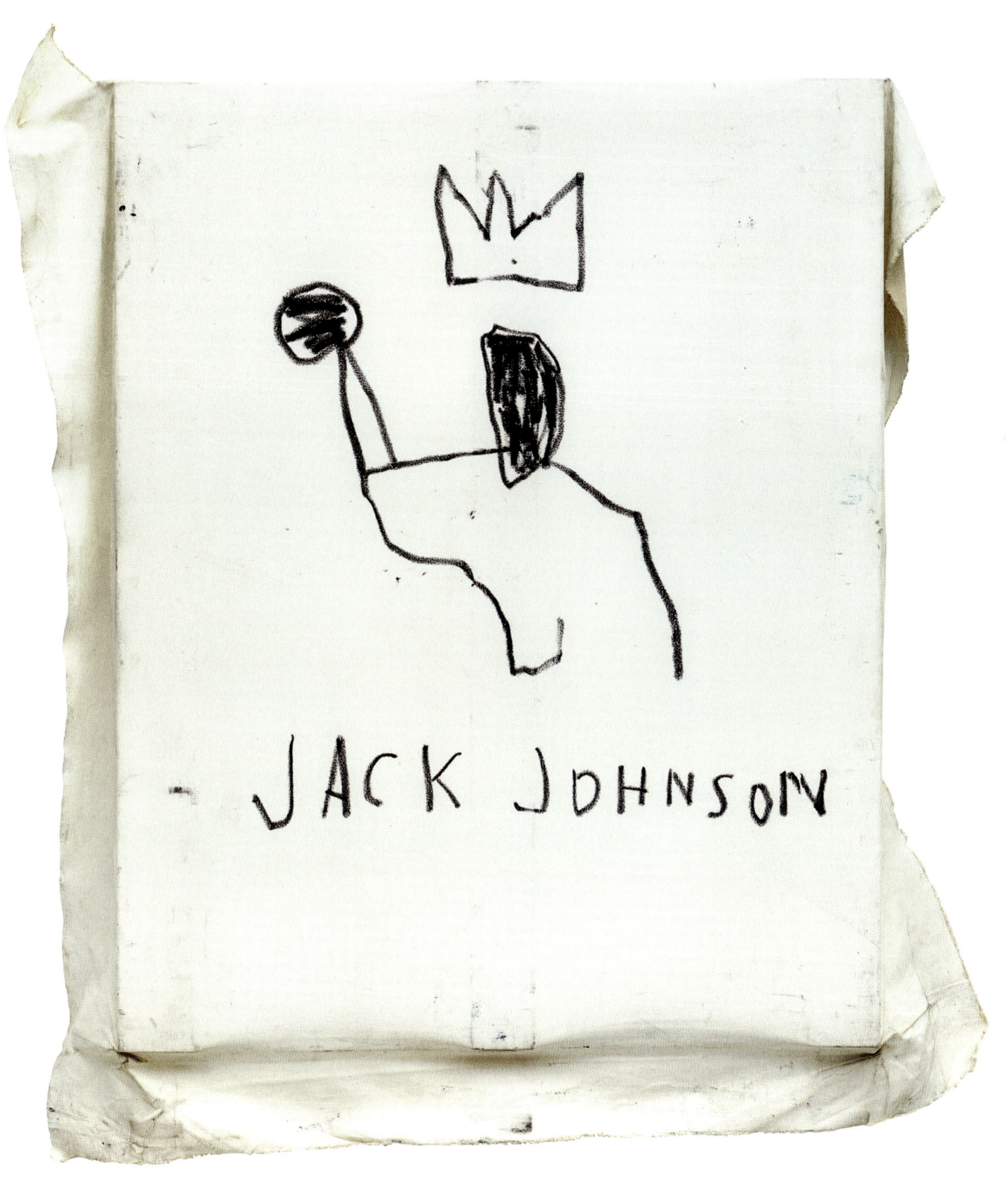

Jean-Michel Basquiat *Jack Johnson* 1982, synthetic polymer paint and oilstick on canvas, 120.5 x 96.5 cm, Private collection

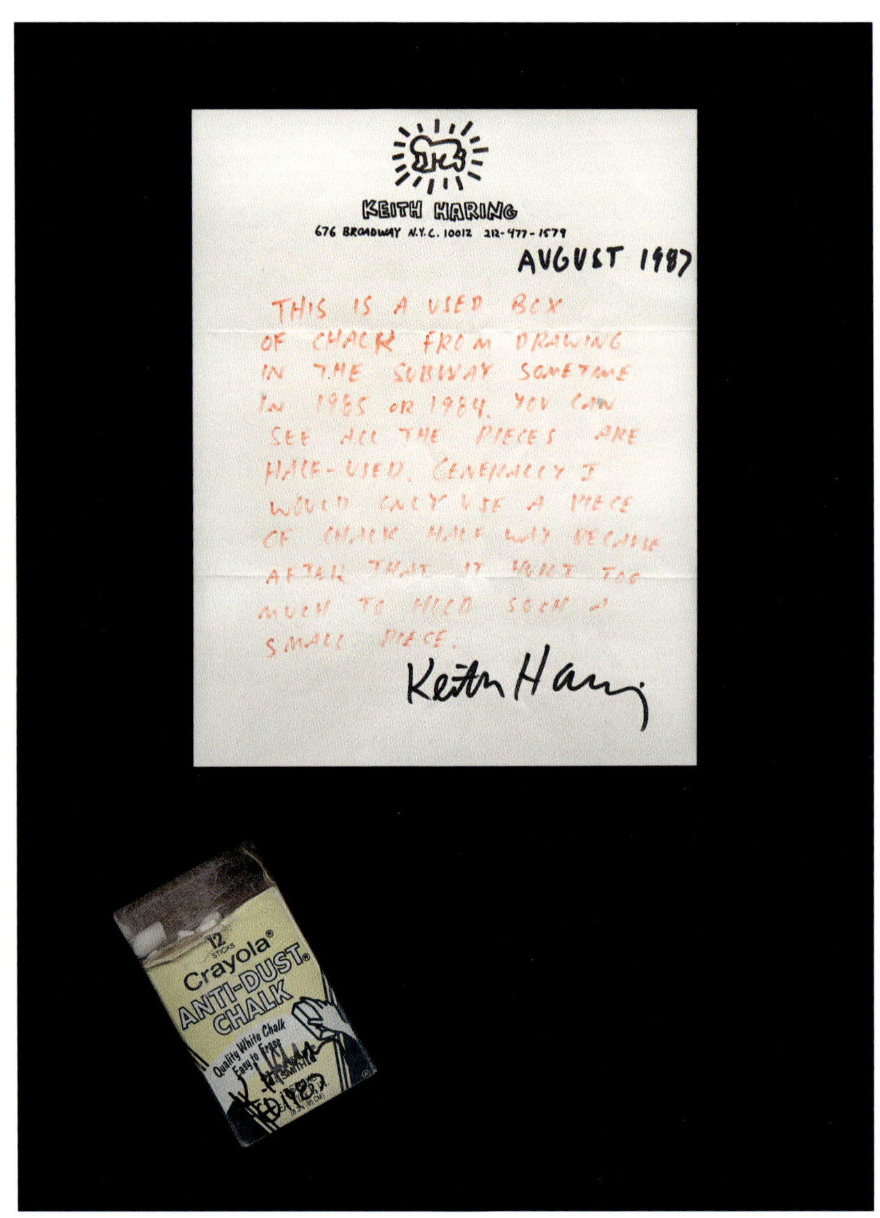

KEITH HARING
676 BROADWAY N.Y.C. 10012 212-477-1579

AUGUST 1987

THIS IS A USED BOX OF CHALK FROM DRAWING IN THE SUBWAY SOMETIME IN 1983 OR 1984. YOU CAN SEE ALL THE PIECES ARE HALF-USED. GENERALLY I WOULD ONLY USE A PIECE OF CHALK HALF WAY BECAUSE AFTER THAT IT HURT TOO MUCH TO HOLD SUCH A SMALL PIECE.

Keith Haring

Keith Haring *Untitled* 1987, ink on paper and box of chalk, 54.6 x 38.1 cm (overall), Collection of Larry Warsh
(opposite) Keith Haring in the New York City Subway, New York, 1984

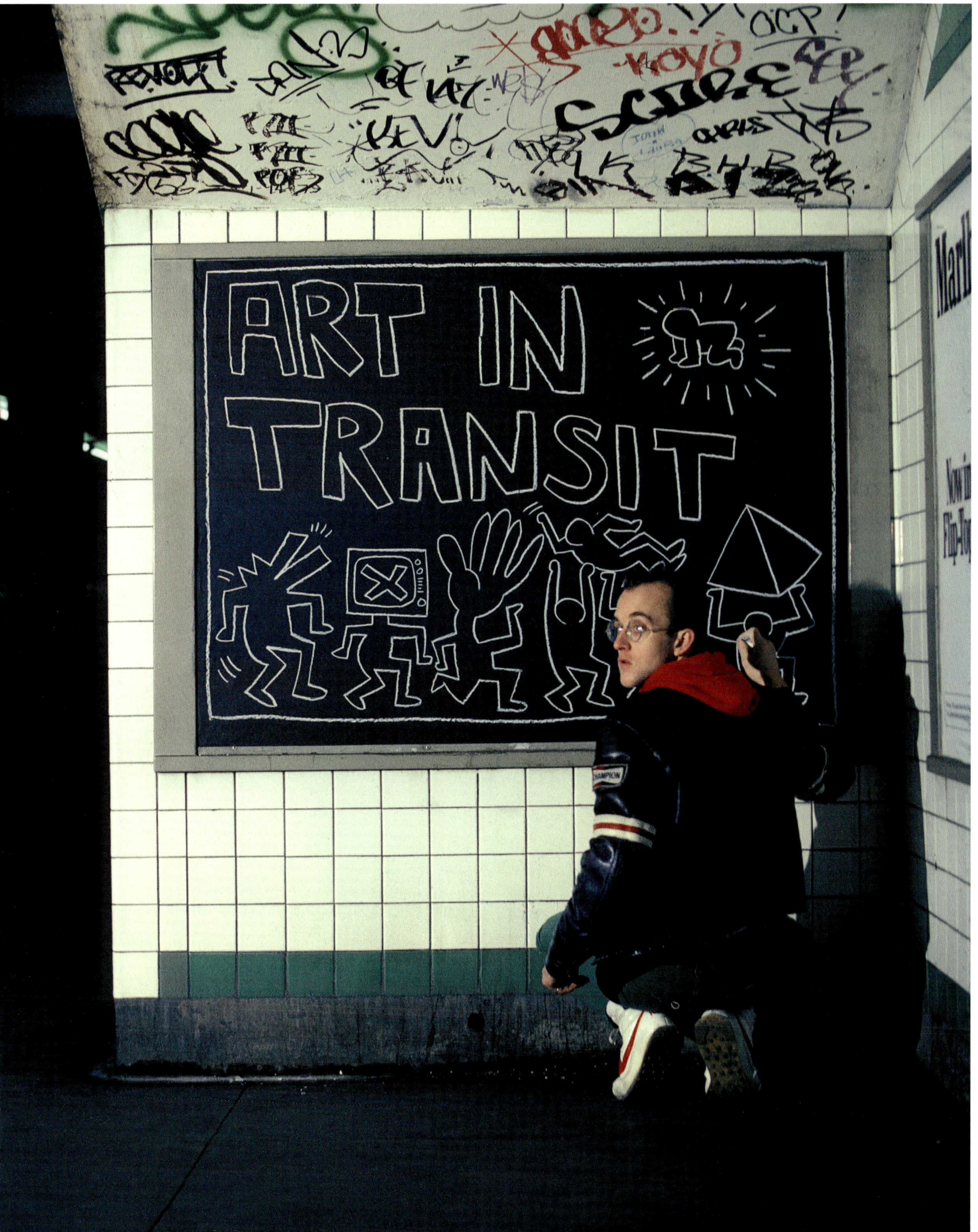
ART IN
TRANSIT

Interview: George Condo

Dieter Buchhart and Anna Karina Hofbauer

Dieter Buchhart (DB): With your recent participation at the Venice Biennale you have formed an impressive bridge between your early works from the beginning of the 1980s to what painting means today and is able to contribute to our contemporary art discourse. Your painterly style has evolved over your already long career but you remain true to painting as your main medium. Where do you see the importance and relevance of painting in contemporary art today?

—George Condo (GC): Painting is a direct contact with the canvas and the audience. It's like a sound, a visual sound that can instantly be read in pictorial space. I want the physicality of the paint to combine forces with the images in my mind and erupt onto the surface of the canvas like a volcano.

Anna Karina Hofbauer (AKH): You started painting at a key moment in twentieth-century art history and were part of the incredibly dynamic and vivid art scene of downtown New York. Can you briefly describe this scene?

—GC: The scene was dark and shady. Lots of homeless people, junkies and derelicts. Then there was the artistic side which had an urgency; we all felt a fast-track, impulsive need to be exhibited and seen. All of us were young, in our early twenties, literally just out of our teenage years, and we found the whole city to be alive and kicking. Some of it, like Times Square, felt like an old Edward Hopper painting, other parts felt like an underground world of wild punk music, art and revolt.

DB: You were friends with both Keith Haring and Jean-Michel Basquiat. How did you meet them for the first time?

—GC: I met JMB the first night I arrived in New York in 1979 when the experimental band I was in from Boston came down to play Tier 3. His band, Gray, opened for us. He was fidgeting with some gadgets on stage so we started up a conversation about electronic music. Later, he took me to the Mudd Club and told me I should move to New York ... so I did! Keith and I met in '83, some years later. I'd heard that he and Warhol went to a show I was in at the Anderson Theater Gallery and each of them bought four or five pictures. It was very exciting news. So later Keith and I connected and became the best of friends up until his death.

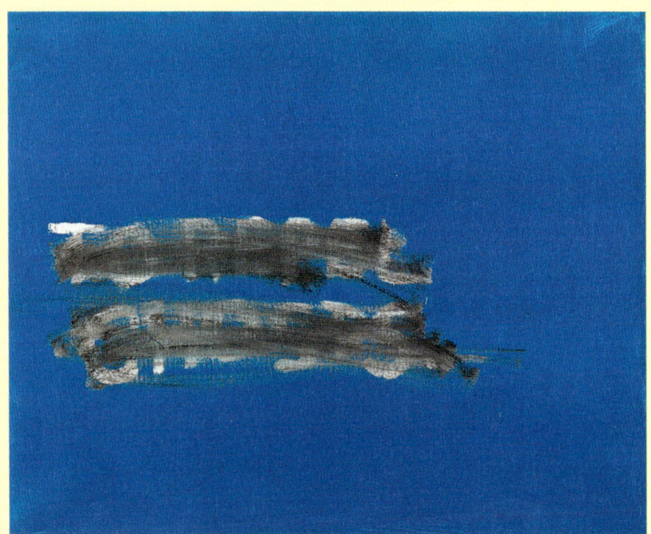

AKH: Perhaps one could speak of a triad: Haring, Basquiat and yourself. Do you feel that you influenced one another artistically?

—GC: I had a very different kind of approach, which did not impinge upon either of their styles. But the graffiti movement was in full swing, so I did in fact use the concept of the 'tag' and did some name paintings in 1984. Kind of Old Masters graffiti. Keith had symbols, as did Jean. Jean had the crown and Keith had the baby. I used symbols as well but painted them in a style that was fully realised in the traditional way of painting by Old Masters. I painted crowns, gold, jewels ... it was the thing that bonded our friendship, to be in a non-competitive stylistic approach. JMB and I were very into jazz. Keith was more into pop and all of us loved the new hip-hop movement that was evolving with Afrika Bambaataa and Run DMC. I remember seeing Herbie Hancock playing 'Rockit' with Jean at the Roxy. In the later paintings of JMB, such as *Eroica* (in reference to Beethoven's symphony; 1988, private collection) and *Riding with Death* (1988, private collection), there was the cross-influence of both classical music and Old Masters painting somehow involved. Keith, after seeing my Picasso-esque works from the early '80s, went through a phase of his own Picasso-esque works. So I would say yes, we did influence each other. In fact, in an ironic twist to JMB and Andy Warhol's collaborations, Keith and I did two paintings together in Paris and four box-top collaborations using the all-over imagery I was working on with my expanding canvases at that time in 1985.

AKH: The visual languages of Haring's and Basquiat's art differ greatly – what common ground did the two men share? What united them?

—GC: They were in fact very different in many ways. Jean was an expressionistic artist who used words, paint, collage, xerox

(above left) Jean-Michel Basquiat *To Repel Ghosts* 1986, oil on canvas, 40.6 x 35.6 cm, Collection of George Condo
(above right) Jean-Michel Basquiat *To Repel Ghosts* 1986, oil on canvas, 30.5 x 50.2 cm, Collection of George Condo

and very kind of jazz-related Afrocentric imagery, like in the Charlie Parker paintings. He did not want to be associated with a white upper-class environment, even if those were his patrons. His work was revolutionary and personal. His approach was like a cross between a scientist of random wordplay and a bebop saxophonist. Keith wanted to reach out to the general population and express his political ideas in reaction to the societal opposition to being gay and being free to be however he wanted. So much of his work had that element to it and it worked. It brought awareness and enlightened those out there who were stuck in some judgemental abyss that needed to be changed. Keith opened doors for that through his art. They were both fighters but for different causes.

AKH: Can you describe the relationship that Haring and Basquiat had with one another?

—GC: I never saw them together in all the years I knew them both. I was either with one or the other so I couldn't tell you. But I assume from the comments each made about the other that they were good friends.

DB: I remember from one of our previous conversations that Haring stayed with you for a longer period of time in Paris. Can you give us some insight into his practice at the time?

—GC: He worked in my studio on the Île Saint-Louis. He worked on the big mural for the Hôpital Necker-Enfants Malades and he was just on automatic pilot. I remember we made huge brushes together in my Paris apartment. We literally taped them onto a broomstick. We had so much fun in those days! He was incredibly systematic and inventive at the same time.

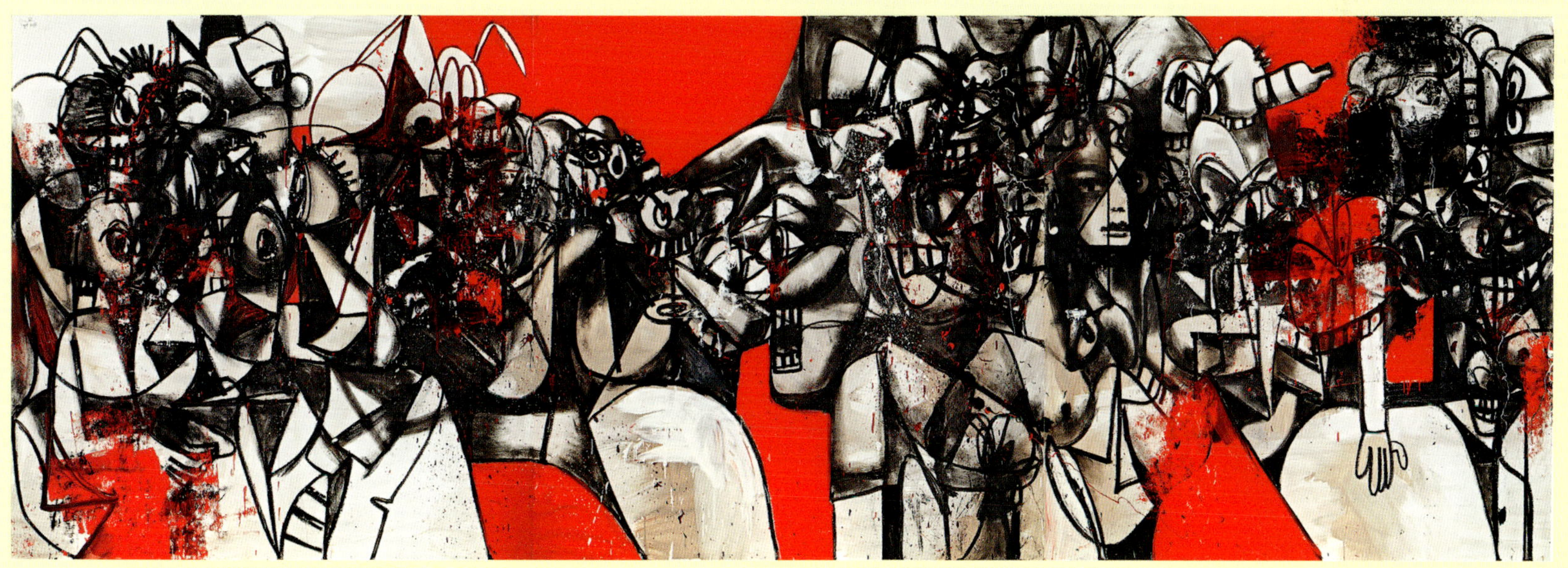

George Condo *Facebook* 2017–18, synthetic polymer paint, oil and pigment stick on linen, 203.2 x 571.5 cm (overall), Collection of George Condo

DB: I recall that Basquiat gifted you two small canvases, which both had the title *To Repel Ghosts*. Do you recall Basquiat's working process?

—GC: He did via Bruno Bischofberger. Bruno said, 'Here are a few pieces Jean left sitting around, take them if you want them'. So, in effect, really, Bruno gave them to me but Jean was glad I had them. I was at Basquiat's studio at the fire station on Great Jones Street [in Lower Manhattan]. He had a pyramid of books on the floor, everything from medical text books to classic novels, about five feet high. He would randomly pick one up and just write out something that was written there. He worked on numerous pieces simultaneously.

DB: You and I have recently had very animated discussions about our current times, which are so strongly shaped by social media and the possibility of instant communication, as well as by the phenomenon of 'fake news' and the power of the internet. These themes have led you to create a whole new body of works referencing the challenges of our time. Where do you see the importance of Haring and Basquiat today, and why are they such an integral part of today's youth culture? They seem to be even more relevant now than they were during their lifetimes.

—GC: They are always going to be relevant because each of them was a great artist. The trends in the media, which came more out of my concept of Artificial Realism, hadn't occurred to them. They were fighting for human rights. That will always be their strength. I fought a battle of awareness of a kind of philosophical nature. It was like the atomic bomb, an equation of thought processes that unfortunately exploded into politics and social media and has taken on a different role than its original meaning. I use languages of art to express images and memory to unlock subconscious behaviour and free the observer from his or her worst nightmare.

(June 2019)

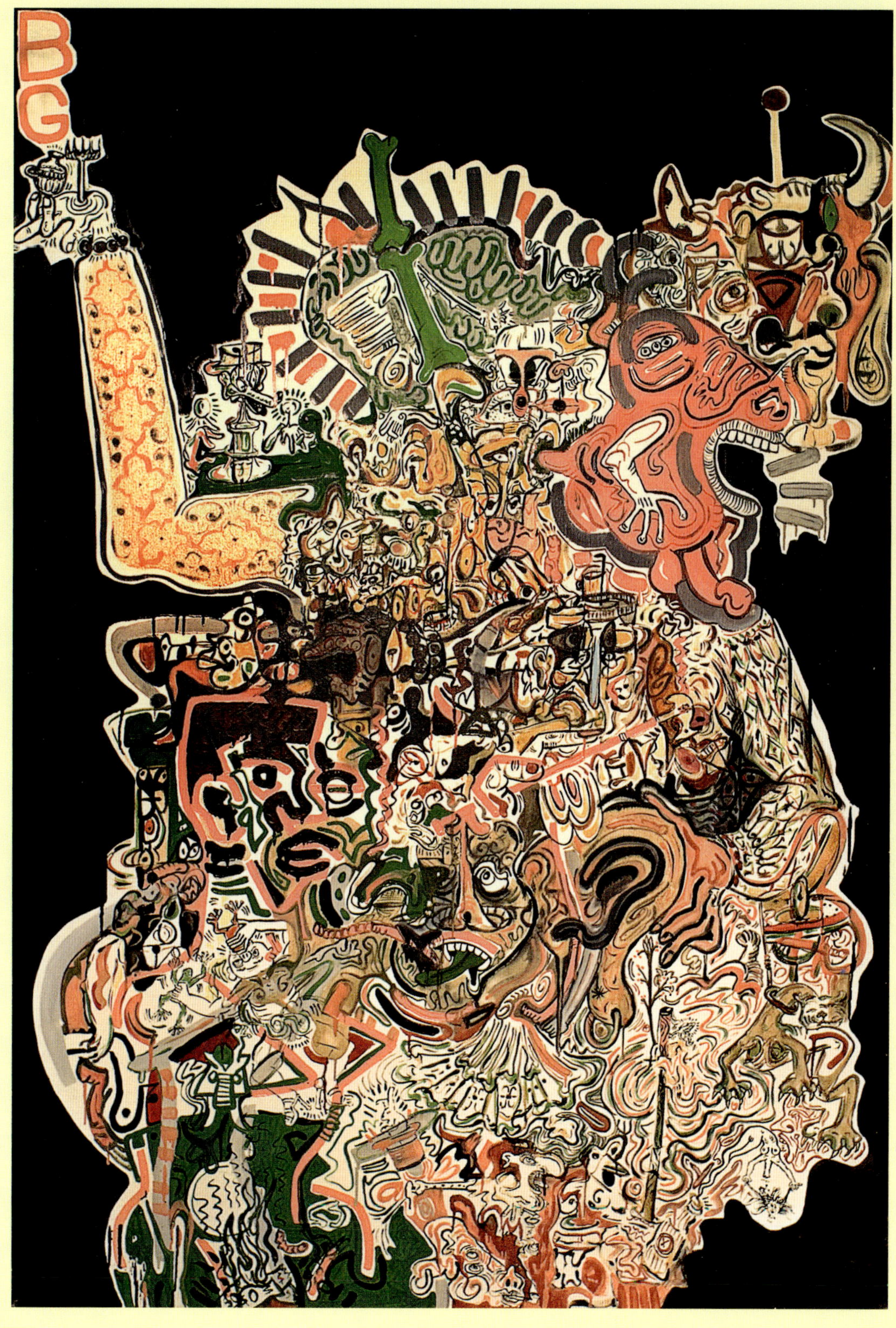

George Condo, Keith Haring *For Brion Gysin* 1985, oil on canvas, 194.3 x 129.5 cm, Private collection
(overleaf) Keith Haring outside the Palladium nightclub, 1985

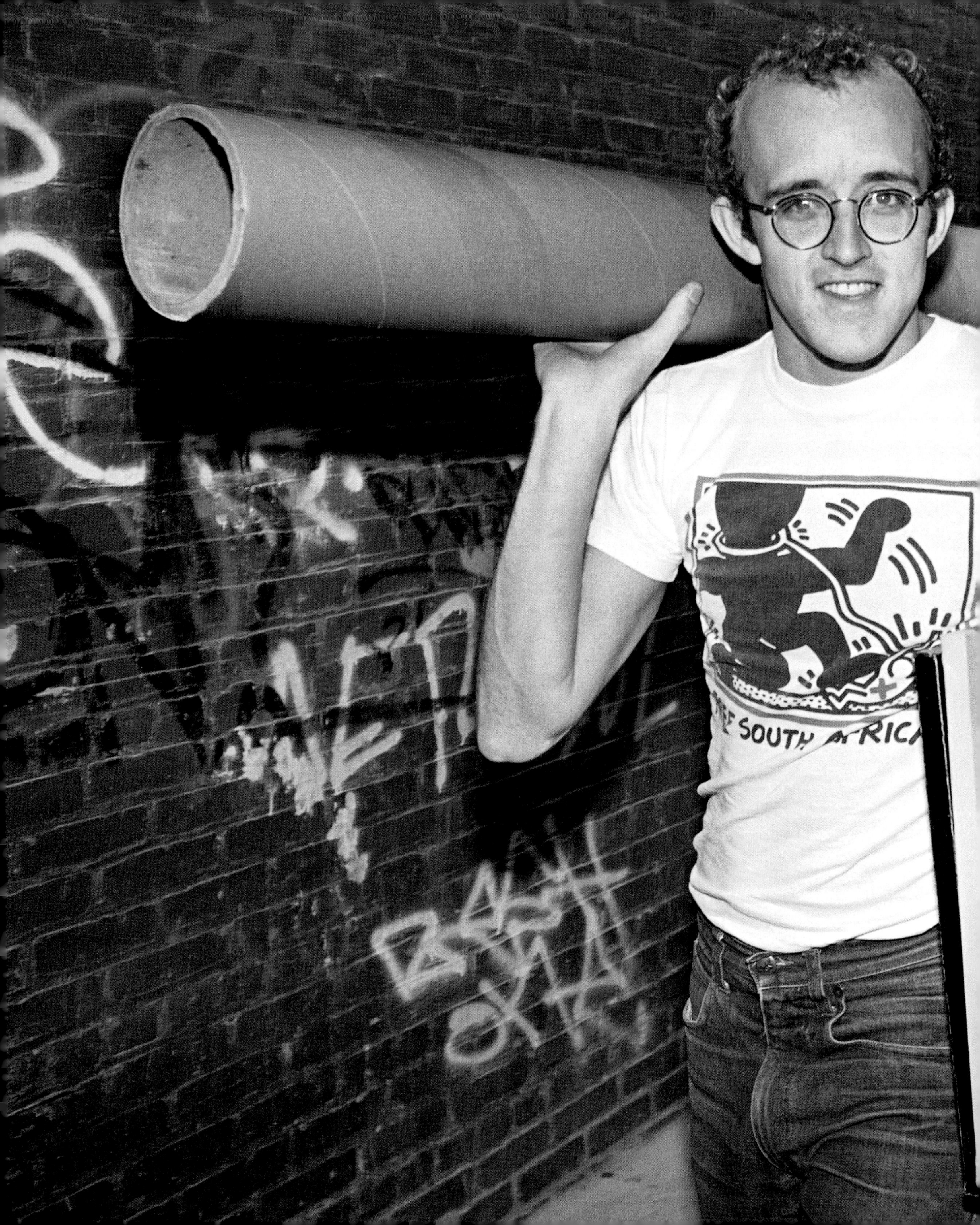

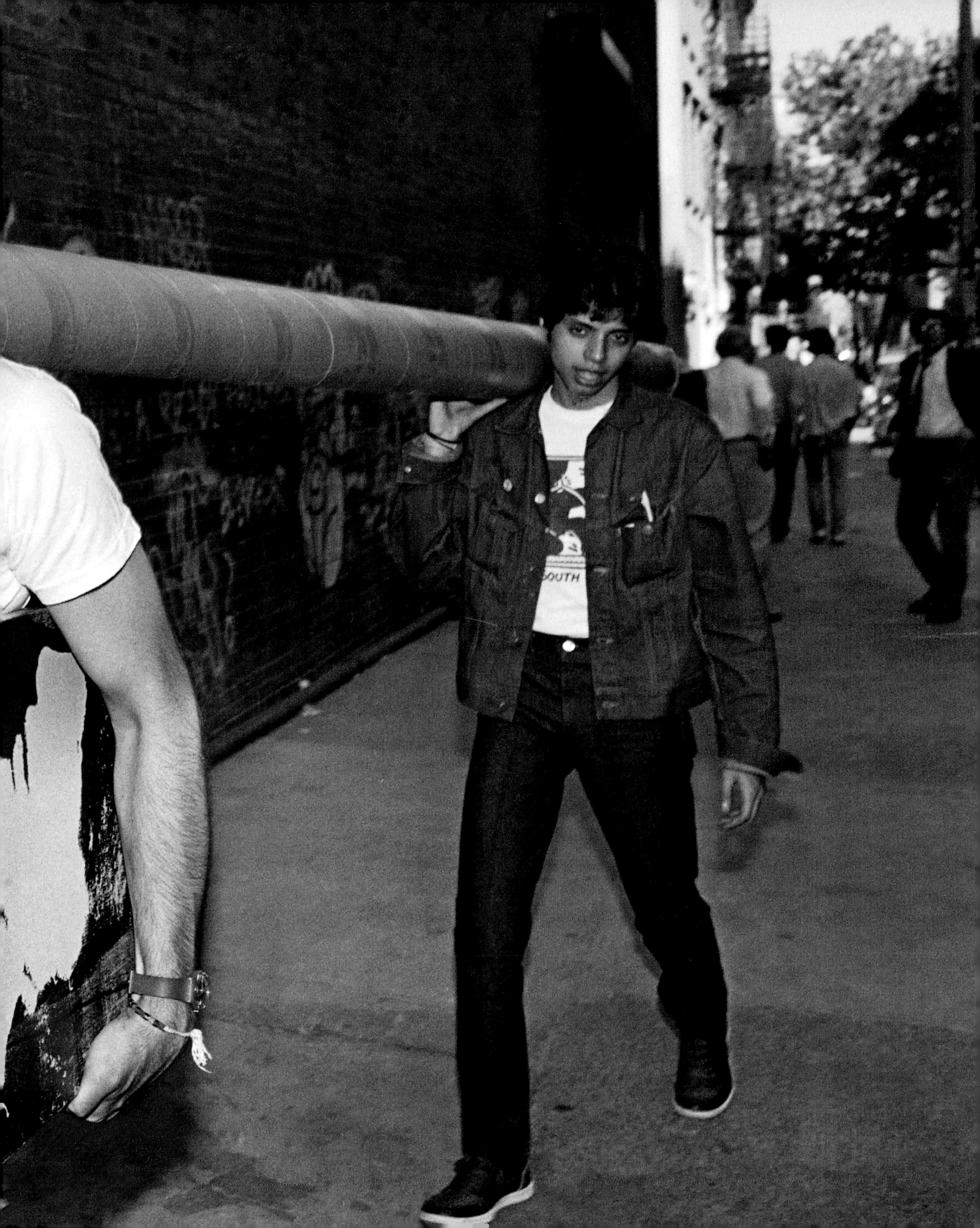
SOUTH

Interview: Diego Cortez

Dieter Buchhart

Dieter Buchhart (DB): Diego, you were not only friends with both Keith Haring and Jean-Michel Basquiat but also exhibited their work in your seminal show *New York/New Wave*. Can you tell me how that exhibition came about?

—Diego Cortez (DC): I curated *New York/ New Wave* in 1981, but the research started in 1979 when Renato Barilli and Francesca Alinovi invited me to curate a show at the Galleria d'Arte Moderna in Bologna. I gathered all the research, images, texts – everything. And then the local government changed and funding fell through. The show never happened in Italy. It would have been a much different show than what ended up at P.S. 1. I had all that material from the end of 1979. Then, eight months later, I bumped into [curator and Director of P.S. 1] Alanna Heiss and she said, 'Well, let's do it at P.S. 1'. That's how it happened.

DB: When did you first meet Haring and Basquiat?

—DC: I met Jean-Michel on the dance floor in 1979 at the Mudd Club. I founded the club with my roommate, Anya Phillips, and the owner, Steve Mass. I became friends with Jean-Michel. A few months later, I invited Keith and Kenny [Scharf] and some other friends from the SVA program [School of Visual Arts] to be in the show.

In the summer of 1980, after seeing the SAMO© tags on Prince Street, off the Bowery, I started working with Jean as an agent. I began to sell some paintings and drawings to people like Jeffrey Deitch, Henry Geldzahler, and Eugene and Barbara Schwartz. I separately brought Jeffrey and Henry to Jean's apartment, which he shared with Suzanne Mallouk. In 1981, Jean gave me many works to sell on consignment. Other collectors came to my place, a loft on 36th Street, which I shared with Columbia University French Studies professor Sylvère Lotringer. Later that spring, [gallerist] Emilio Mazzoli and [curator] Achille Bonito Oliva visited to look at works intended for Jean's first solo gallery show in Modena.

DB: Were you involved in Basquiat's work being included in the *Times Square Show*?

—DC: No. In fact, I disliked that show.

I was starting to sell Jean's works, not for a lot of money. Keith asked if I would also represent him. I agreed, as I loved his work. That was also the summer of 1980.

Jean-Michel was very trusting, very warm. He was like my brother, also Fab 5 Freddy [aka Fred Brathwaite], like family members. Both were wonderful people to know. Though I believed Keith to be a great artist and person, he was slightly micro-managing in the artist–agent relationship. He would call every couple of days to ask if I sold something. Finally, I said, 'No, I didn't sell anything and could you come pick up your works?' [Chuckles.] Then, I'd see him at different events and it was slightly cool. Finally, near the end of his life, at a party at [artist] Philip Taaffe's in Naples, Italy, he apologised for his attitude towards me all those years ago. He had never maltreated me but conversations were always awkward. Keith said, 'You helped me a lot and you did wonderful things with Jean'.

DB: Do you remember how and where Haring's and Basquiat's works were presented in *New York/New Wave*?

—DC: Keith had a lot of works, drawings and objects. Kenny [Scharf] was installed in the same room, a kind of party room alluding to the Club 57 scene. This room preceded the last room of the exhibition, which featured Jean-Michel. I can't remember who else was installed in the room with Jean-Michel but it was a little more like a straightforward gallery environment. The room on the other side of the Haring room included black-and-white photos by Robert Mapplethorpe and colour prints by the still photographer from *Saturday Night Live*, Edie Baskin. Just the two of them. Beautiful photographs, very elegant. Some rooms in *New York/New Wave* were very chaotic, some rooms very elegant.

DB: You also exhibited *Jimmy Best*, 1981 (private collection). If I remember correctly, Basquiat gave it to you as a gift?

—DC: Yes, and when he gave it to me, he said something like: 'You keep this because you're Jimmy Best'. He knew my birth name was Jimmy. He usually called me Jim. I don't remember him calling me Diego to my face.

DB: How did you decide that Basquiat would create the metal panel at the entrance?

—DC: I said, 'Let's do a title plate'. And he quickly did it in less than five minutes: *New York/New Wave*.

DB: You gave him a lot of space in the show. What was the reason for this?

—DC: Collusion [laughs]. No, it was because I always thought that he was the most important artist at that time. Like several of my closest friends – Maripol, Edo [Bertoglio], Glenn [O'Brien], Fred [Brathwaite], Keith and so forth – we all knew Jean would be huge. With due respect to artists of colour from the earlier part of the twentieth century, like [Jacob] Lawrence and [Romare] Bearden, I thought he could be the first major black artist in Europe or the States, which was major. I felt that this was a great opportunity and moment for him. His postcards were great, his sketchbooks, I mean, come on.

DB: Absolutely!

—DC: A true genius.

DB: Do you remember the relationship between Haring and Basquiat?

—DC: They were very close, from the beginning. But I wasn't with them all the time [laughs]. I always thought that Keith was likewise a genius. Once I lost twenty of his major parchment drawings, getting off the D train. The doors were closing when I remembered I left a tube of drawings on the train.

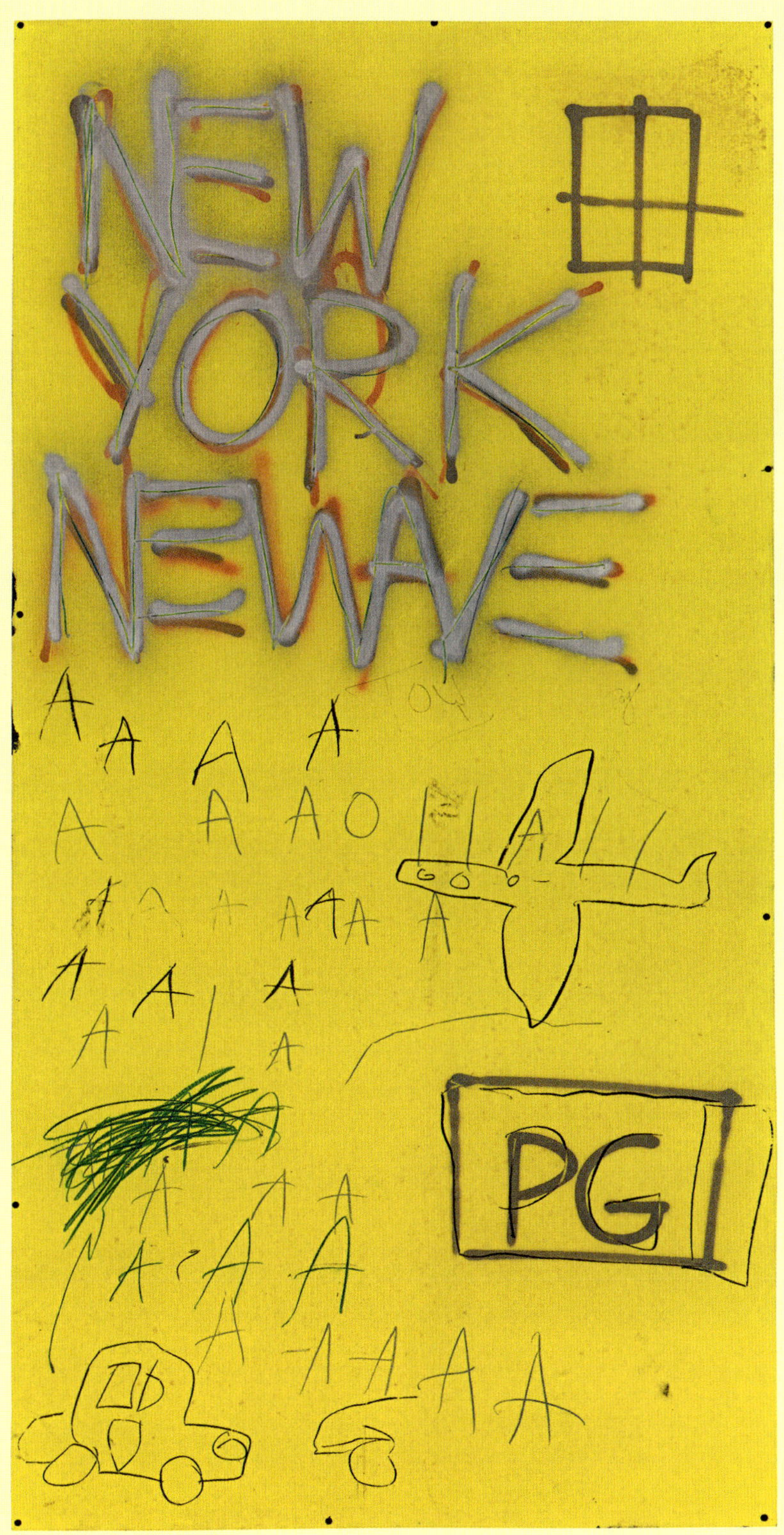

Most subway operators will open up the doors for people who are caught in the closing doors. I kept shouting to the other end of the train but the driver wouldn't open the doors. I never saw the drawings again. When I told Keith, he said, 'Oh, don't worry about it. I'll make more'. Bang, he didn't care.

DB: Did you see Basquiat perform with his band Gray?

—DC: Oh yeah. A few times. The performance I remember the most was at One University Place. That was great. It was a wild, kind of punky crowd, you know? I think that's when Rene Ricard slashed [author] Victor Bockris's face.

DB: Can you describe the differences between the crowds at the Mudd Club and Club 57?

—DC: After my CBGB days, I was in the Mudd Club scene where later I heard about Club 57. Perhaps Keith and Kenny [Scharf] invited me. I went to about thirty evenings at Club 57 with different themes – skits and things – and Jean-Michel went to some of those as well. They were incredible. The Mudd Club was not so much about that. Today, there would never be an exhibition at MoMA about the Mudd Club because it was just dancing and sound and hanging out. There were some exhibitions but it was more of a meeting place. Club 57 was also a much younger crowd, so it was much more playful and funny, artsy and very connected with kitsch and gay culture. The Mudd Club was not so much about gay culture or kitsch. It was connected to punk rock and new wave music: real music, live groups and rock dance music on the other side of the musical spectrum to Studio 54's thump-thump disco beat. We all hated Studio 54.

Jean-Michel Basquiat *Untitled* 1980, enamel, spray-paint and oilstick on enamelled metal, 243.8 × 122.1 cm, Whitney Museum of American Art, New York

DB: When you think back, what were the defining moments for you with regard to Haring's and Basquiat's work?

— DC: The first thing I saw from Jean was the SAMO© graffiti. It shocked me. It was totally intellectual. In the early days of Jean-Michel's career, I critically opposed people who labelled him a graffiti artist: 'No, no, no, he's a studio artist just like any studio artist, like Robert Rauschenberg or Cy Twombly'. They all worked in studios to make paintings. Yes, Jean-Michel's work does relate somewhat to the street art scene. Years later, when Jean's work had become fully established, I finally could admit that his relationship to graffiti was profound. But in the early days, I had to defend him as being a contemporary artist, a museum artist, for people to take him more seriously.

Keith's work – those early parchment drawings and then the *Subway Drawings* were absolutely brilliant. I never saw him as a graffiti artist; rather, a public artist. There were people like Joseph Kosuth doing billboards, or Jenny Holzer's work – that to me was public art. So, I saw Keith as part of that context.

DB: Why do you think both artists are still so relevant today?

— DC: You have to realise that they emerged just after Neo-Expressionism. Neither of them is a pure Neo-Expressionist artist; they're not like Anselm Kiefer, Francesco Clemente, Sandro Chia or Julian Schnabel. Looking at those artists in the history of art – they are very European.

Haring and Basquiat represent a younger generation and their work is a breakthrough on many levels. You know, I've always thought that art is not about meaning, it's about style. I think Basquiat's style is completely unique and it's all on the surface. I mean, I can stare at one painting and I have a hundred ideas. Great artists are those who conjure hundreds, if not thousands, of important ideas.

DB: True! And Haring also developed a very unique style.

— DC: Yes! There are some precedents for his kind of work, for example Pierre Alechinsky, but it is still new and unique. Haring's style was connected with a particular moment in New York: the nexus of graffiti, hip-hop and an emerging awareness of black and Latino culture. Keith's work is very related to black culture, even if he was white.

(4 April 2019)

Interior of the Palladium nightclub, New York, with installation by Keith Haring, 1985

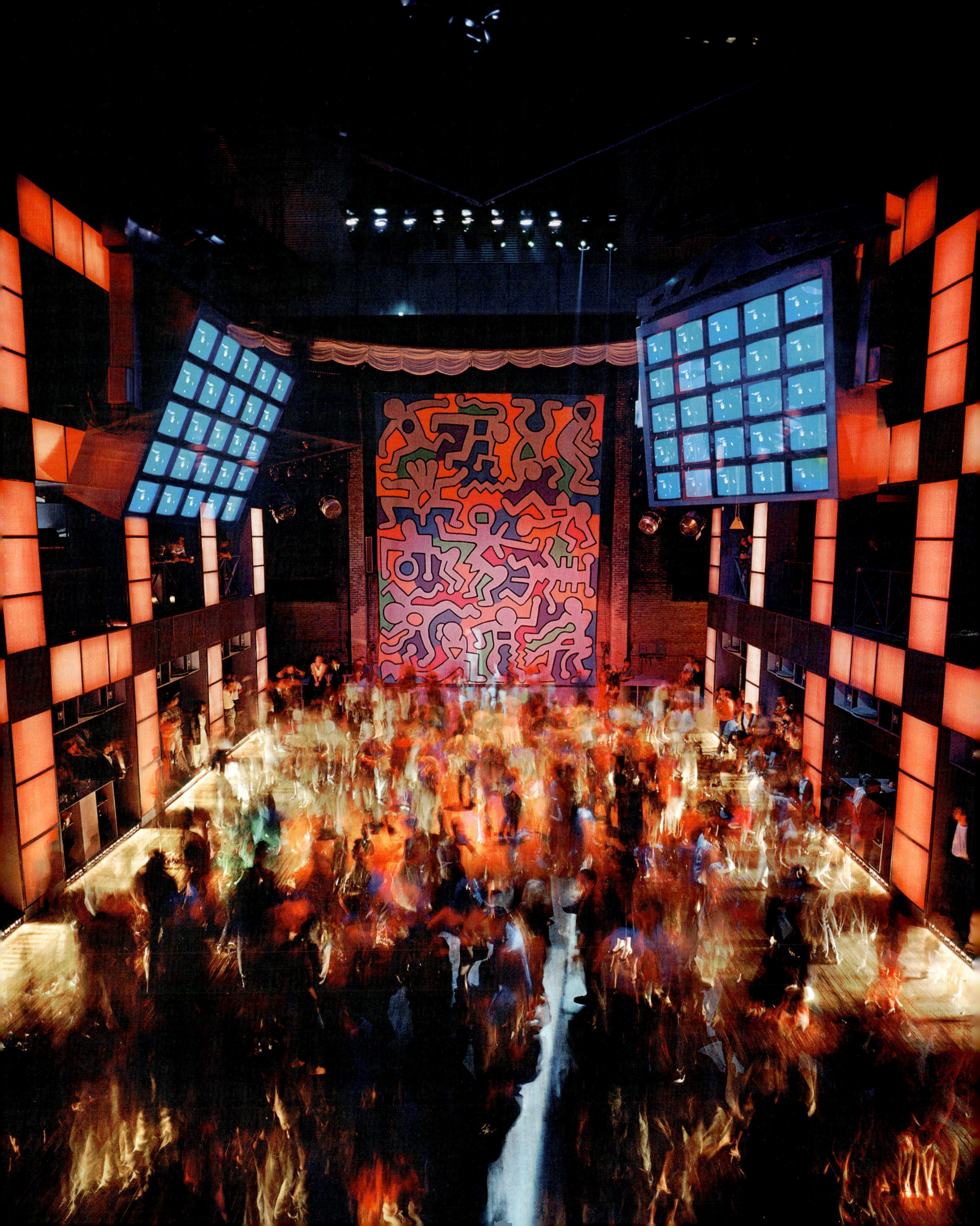

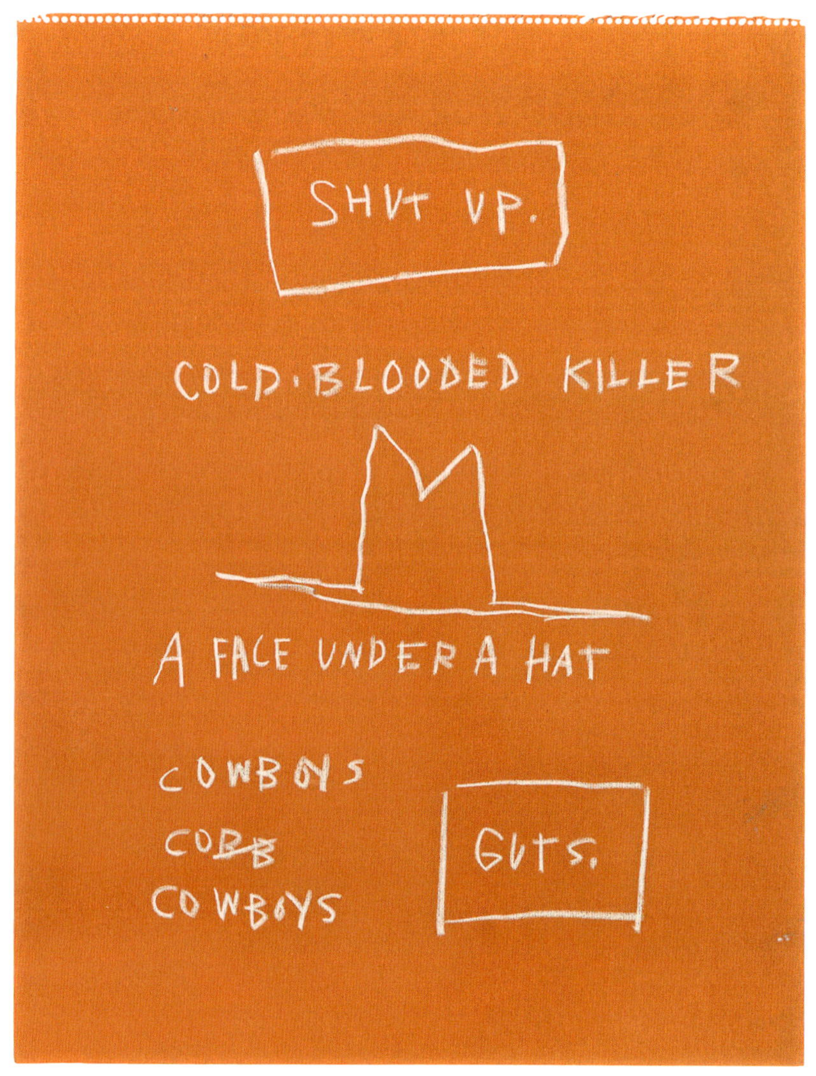

Jean-Michel Basquiat *Untitled (Cold Blooded Killer)* 1983, wax crayon on paper, 59.7 x 45.7 cm, Private collection

Jean-Michel Basquiat *Untitled #27 (Lee Harvey Oswald)* c. 1982, oilstick on paper, 55.9 x 76.2 cm, Private collection

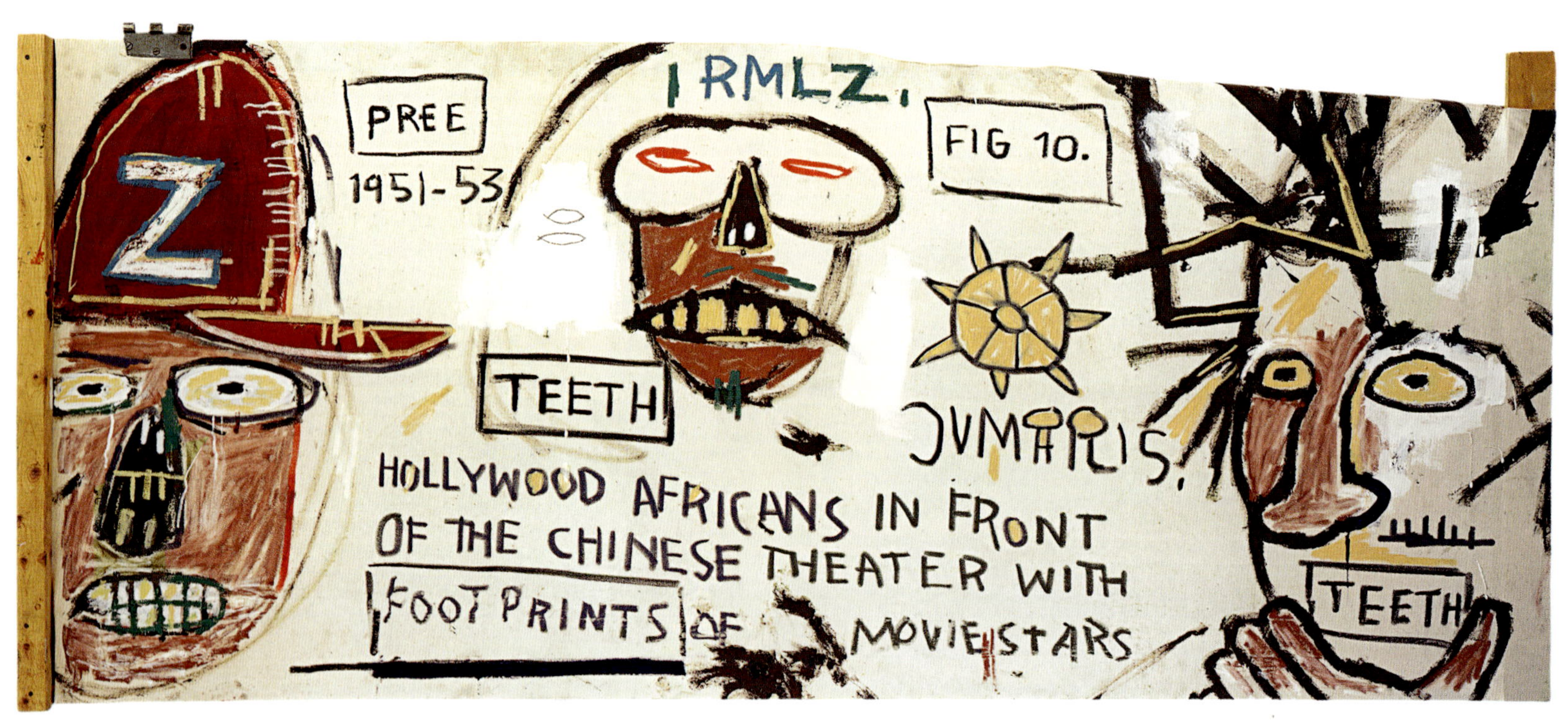

Jean-Michel Basquiat *Hollywood Africans in Front of the Chinese Theater with Footprints of Movie Stars* 1983,
synthetic polymer paint and oilstick on canvas on wood panel, 90.0 x 207.0 cm,
The Estate of Jean-Michel Basquiat, New York

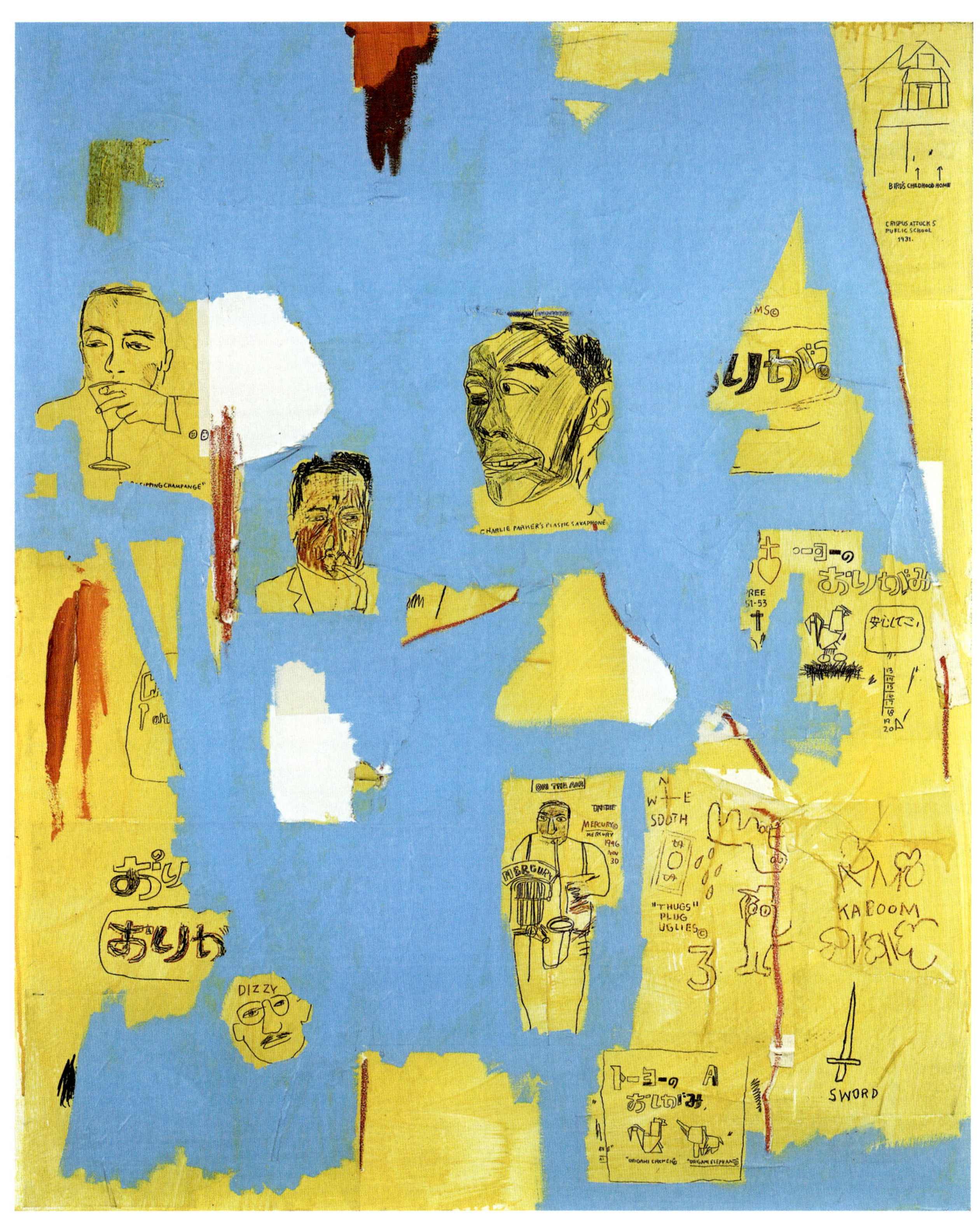

Jean-Michel Basquiat *Plastic Sax* 1984, synthetic polymer paint, colour oilstick, xerox paper and collage on canvas, 152.4 x 123.2 cm, agnès b. collection

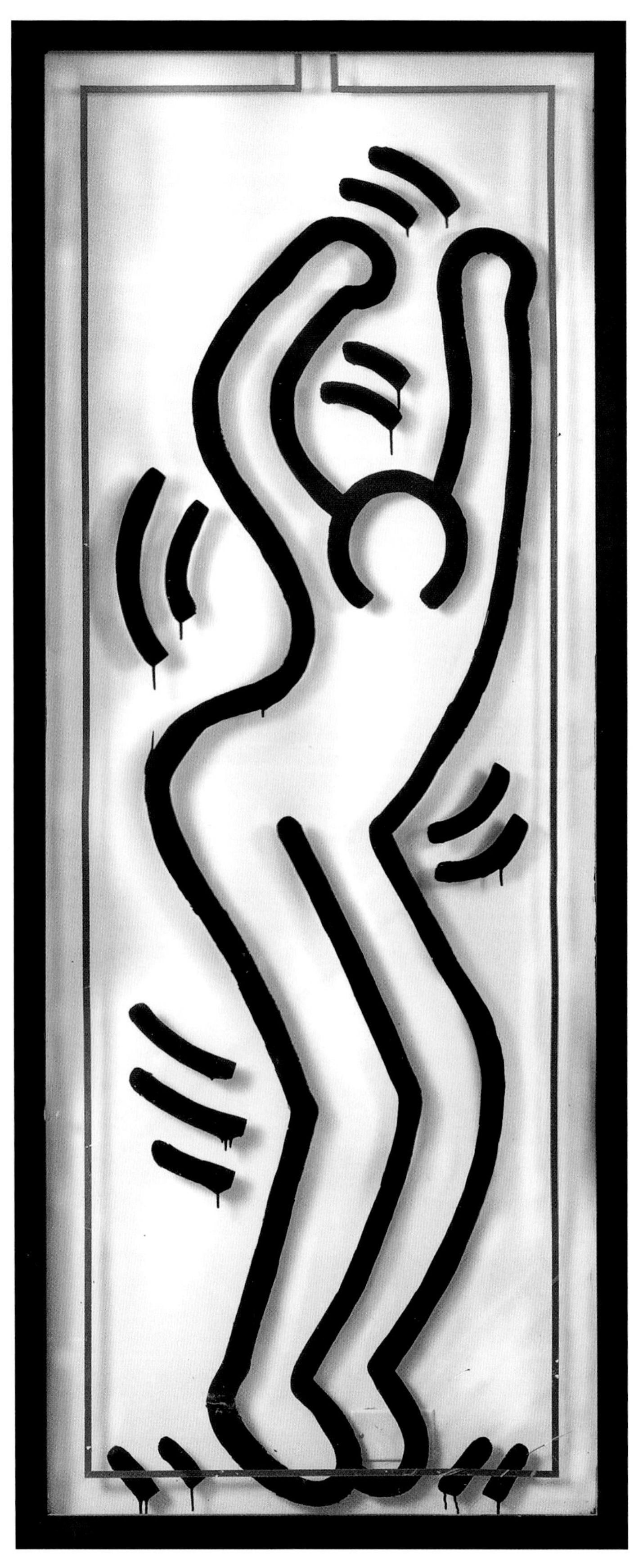

Keith Haring *Untitled* c. 1985, paint on glass, 208.0 x 76.2 x 5.0 cm, Private collection

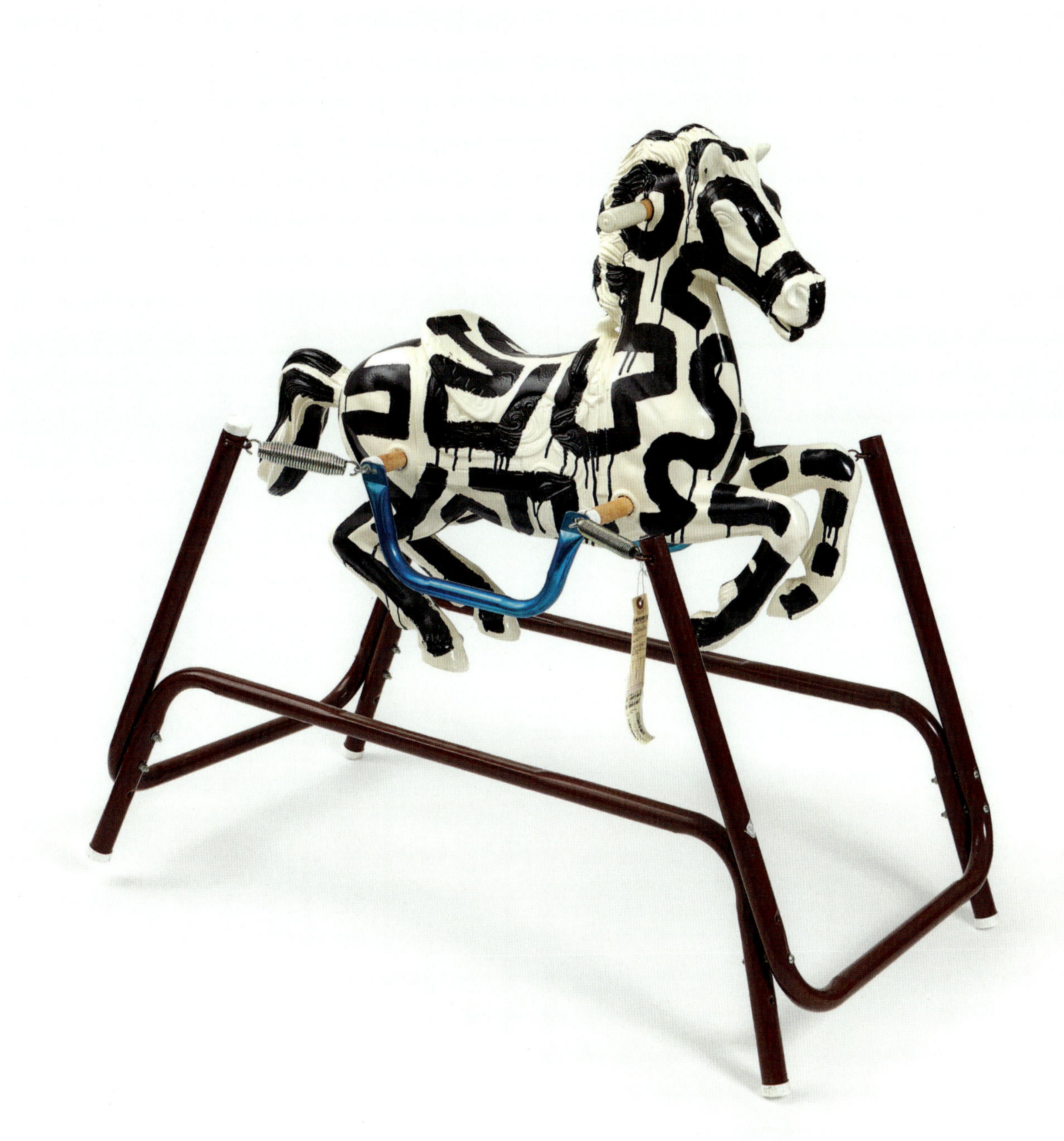

Keith Haring *Untitled* c. 1985, mixed media and paint on plastic and metal, 114.3 x 114.3 x 59.7 cm, Collection of Larry Warsh

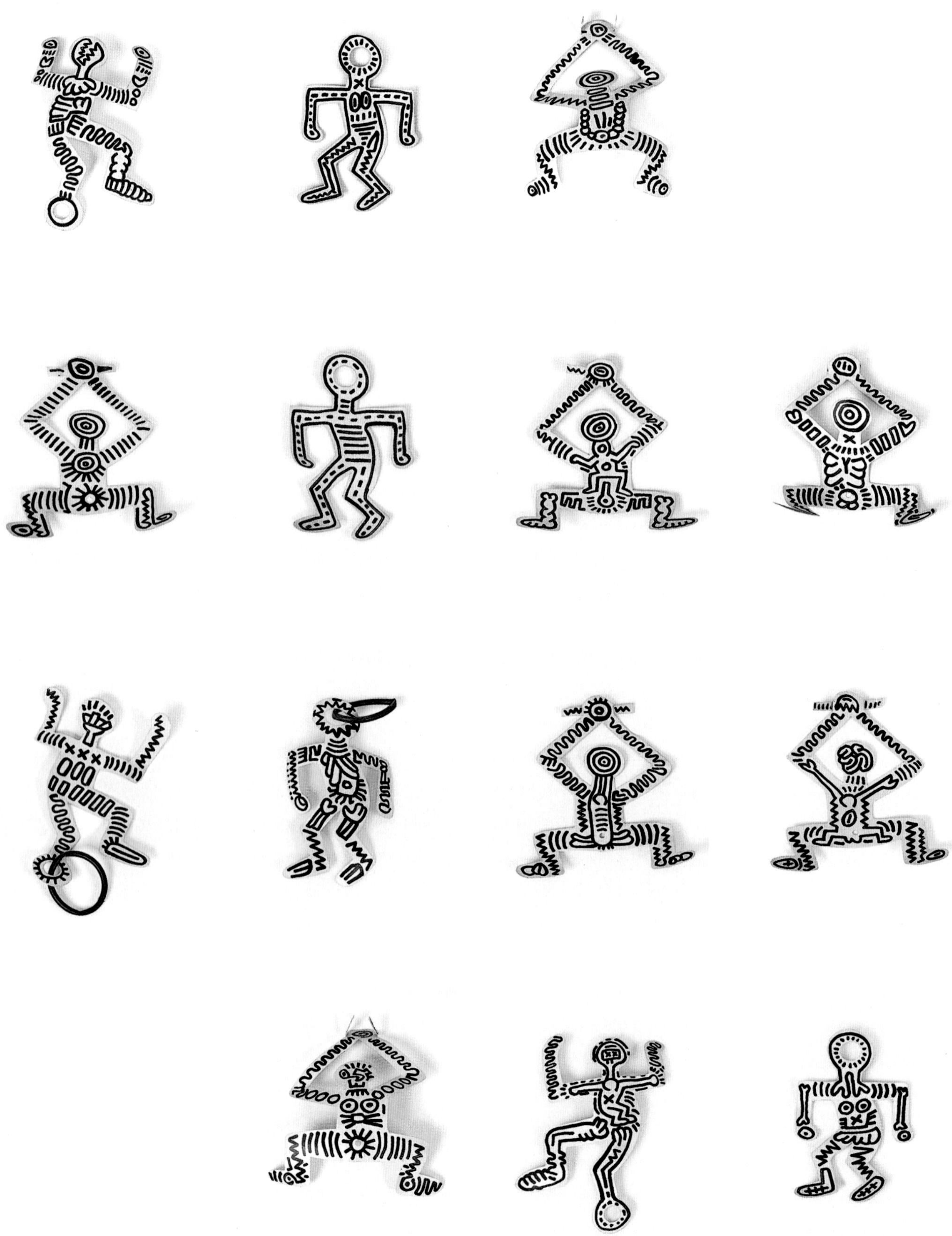

Keith Haring, David Spada *Ornaments for Grace Jones's costume* 1984, ink on metal, (a-n) 25.4 x 15.3 cm (variable) (each), Collection of Larry Warsh

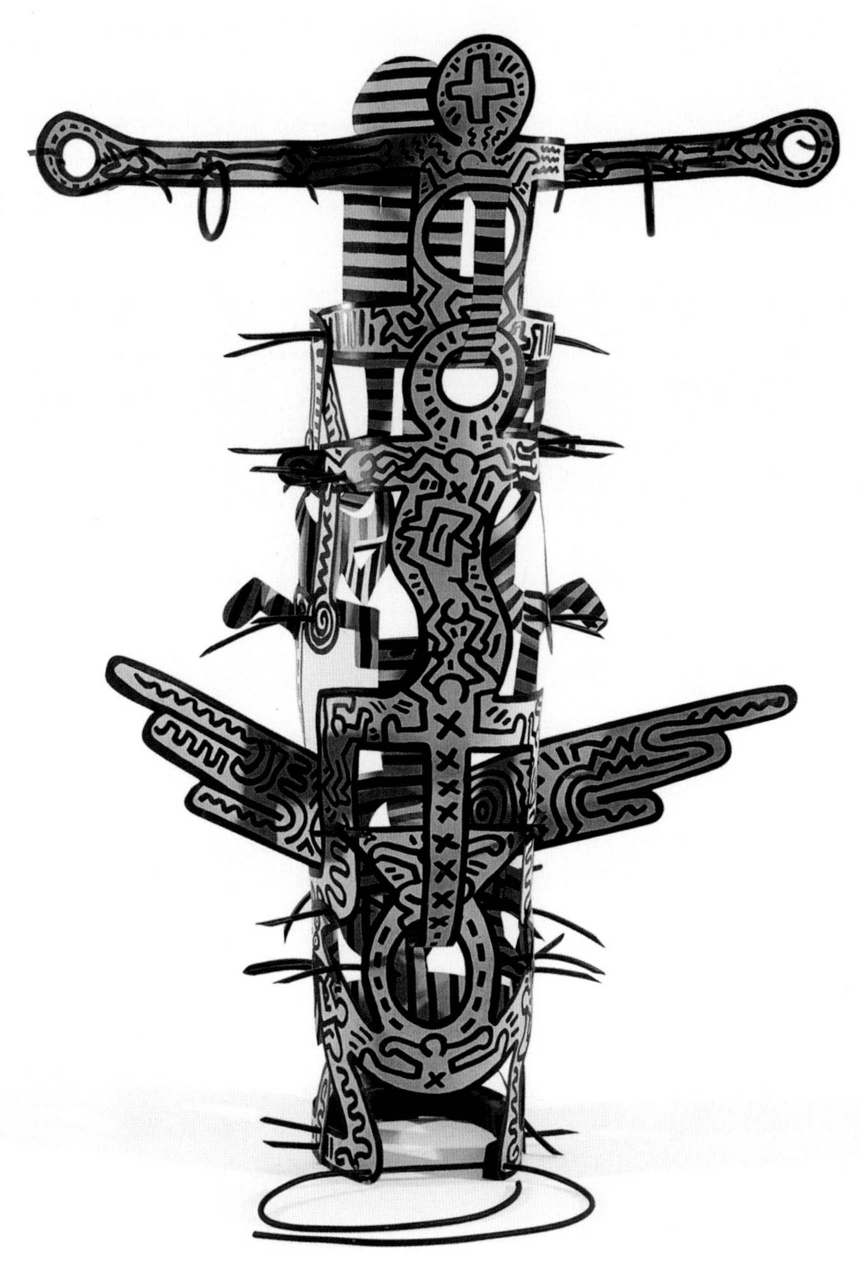

Keith Haring, David Spada *Grace Jones's Hat* 1984, ink on metal, 89.0 x 61.0 cm, The Keith Haring Foundation, New York

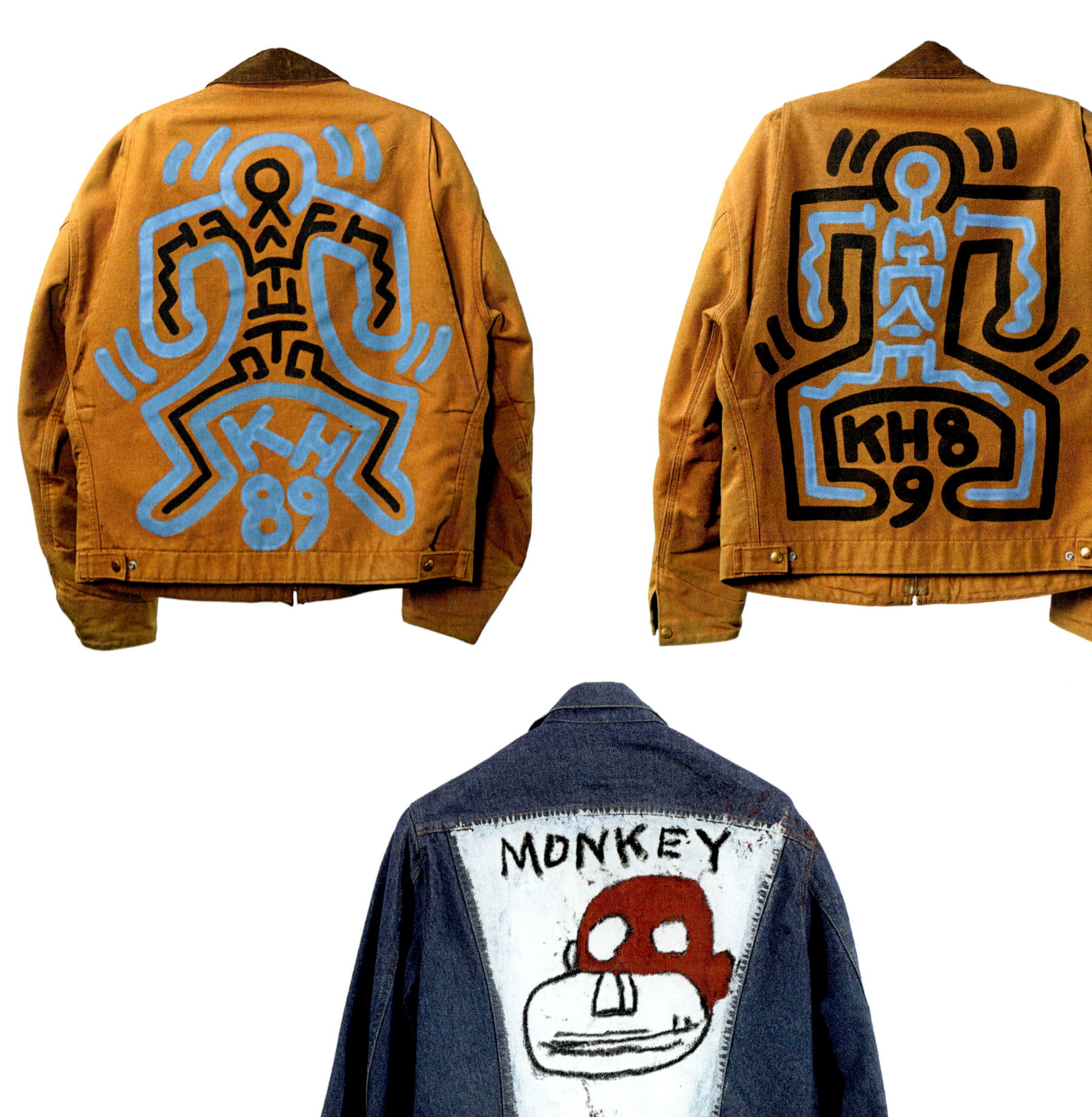

(top) Keith Haring *Untitled* 1989, paint on cotton jacket, (a-b) 63.5 x 55.9 cm (variable) (each), Collection of Larry Warsh
(bottom) Jean-Michel Basquiat *Untitled (Monkey)* 1986, oil on denim jacket, 81.3 x 62.2 cm, Private collection

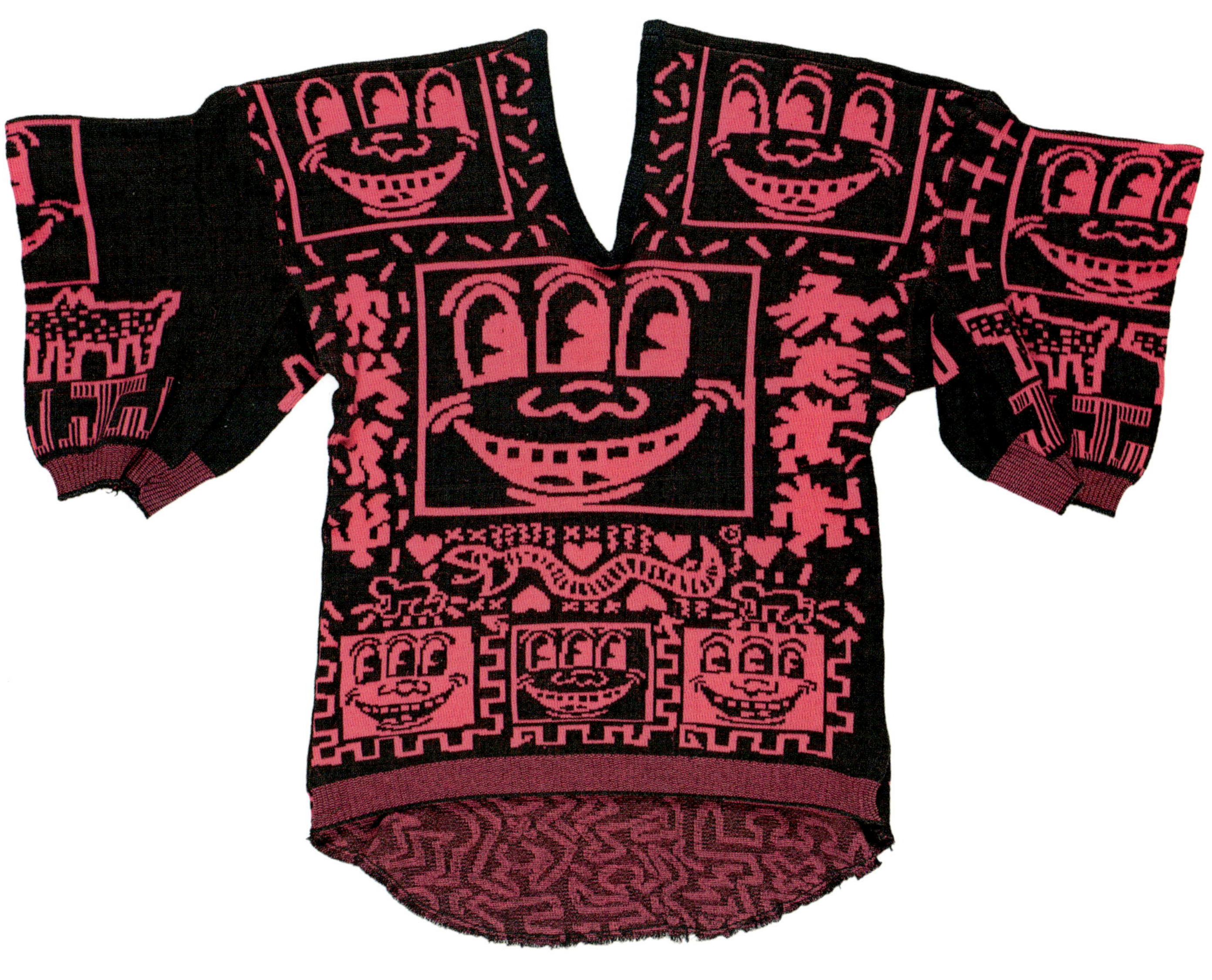

World's End, London (manufacturer), Vivienne Westwood (designer), Malcolm McLaren (designer), Keith Haring (designer) *T-shirt* 1983–84, autumn–winter *Witches* collection, cotton, 53.0 cm (centre back), National Gallery of Victoria, Melbourne

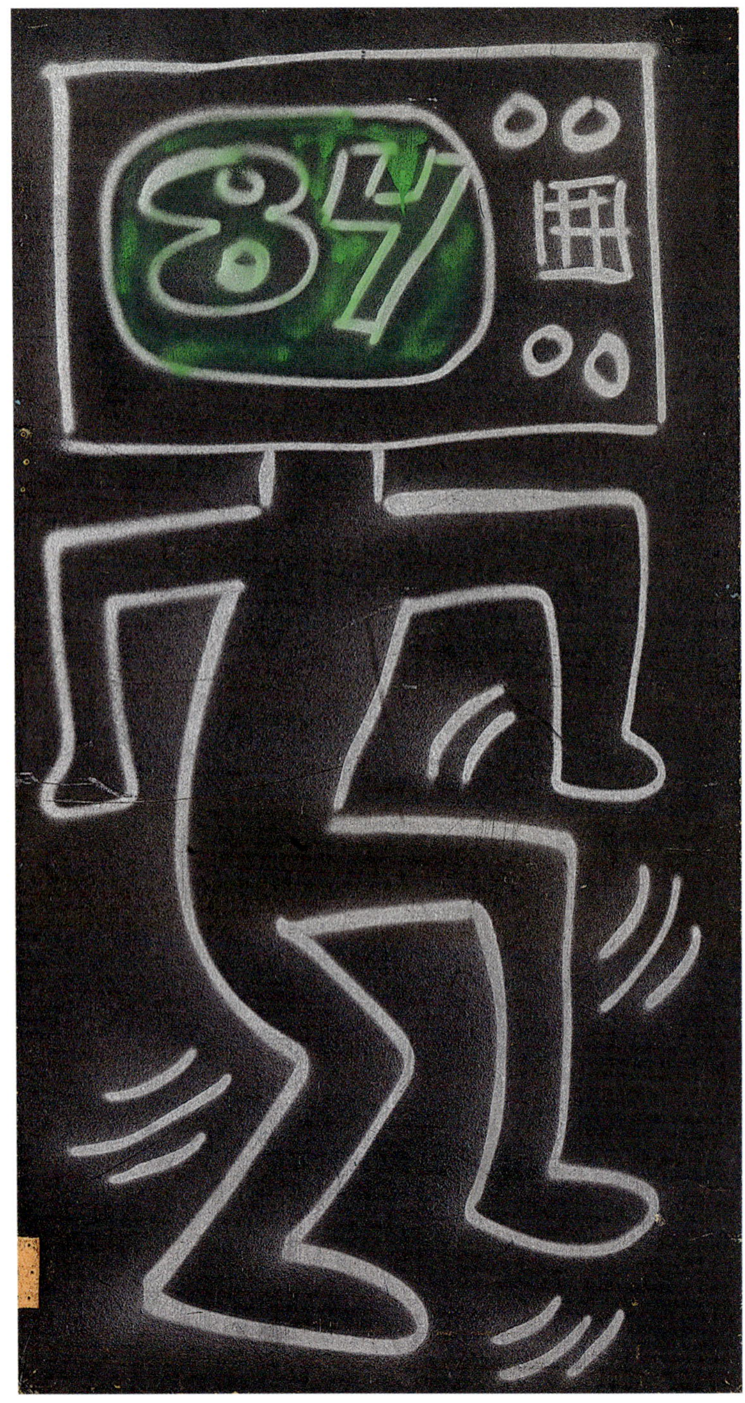

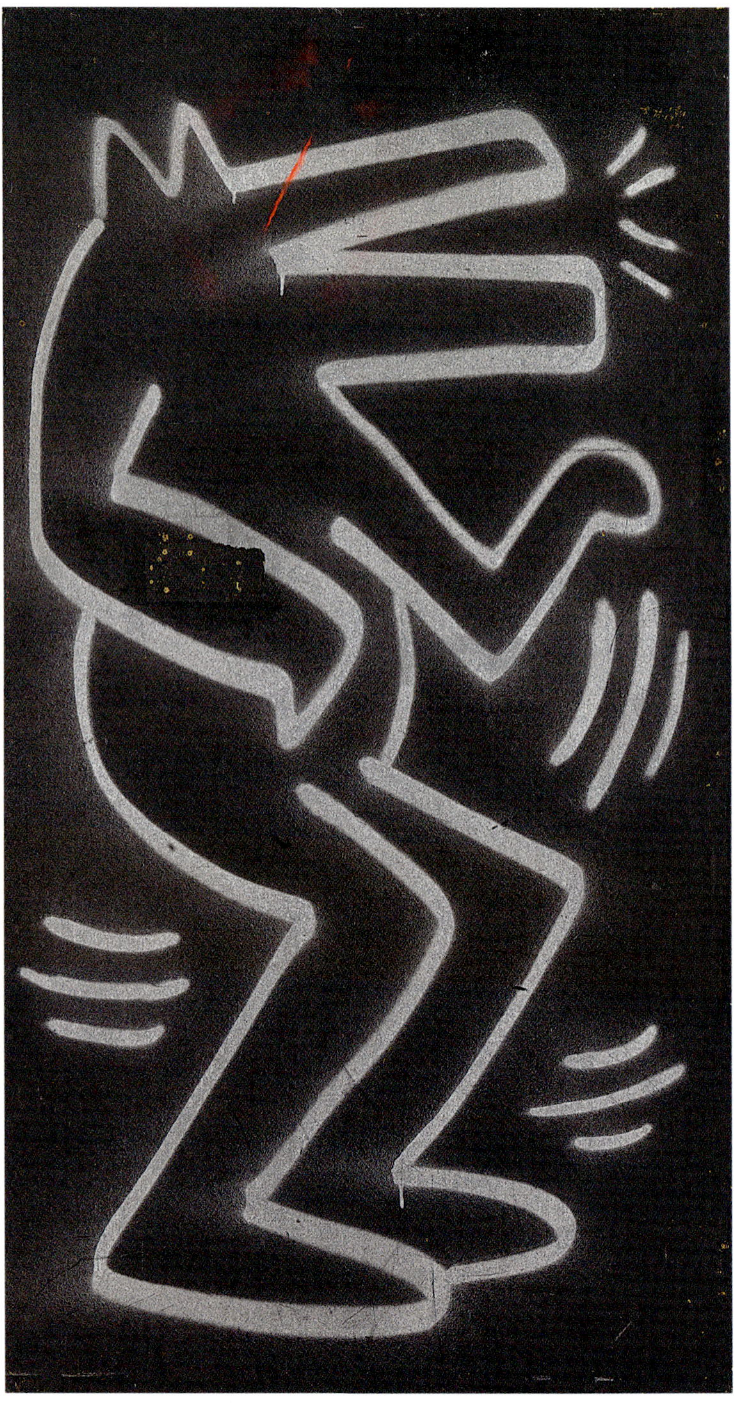

(left) Keith Haring *Untitled* 1984, metallic and enamel paint on composition board, 166.0 × 86.5 cm, National Gallery of Victoria, Melbourne
(right) Keith Haring *Untitled* 1984, metallic and enamel paint on composition board, 166.0 × 86.5 cm, National Gallery of Victoria, Melbourne

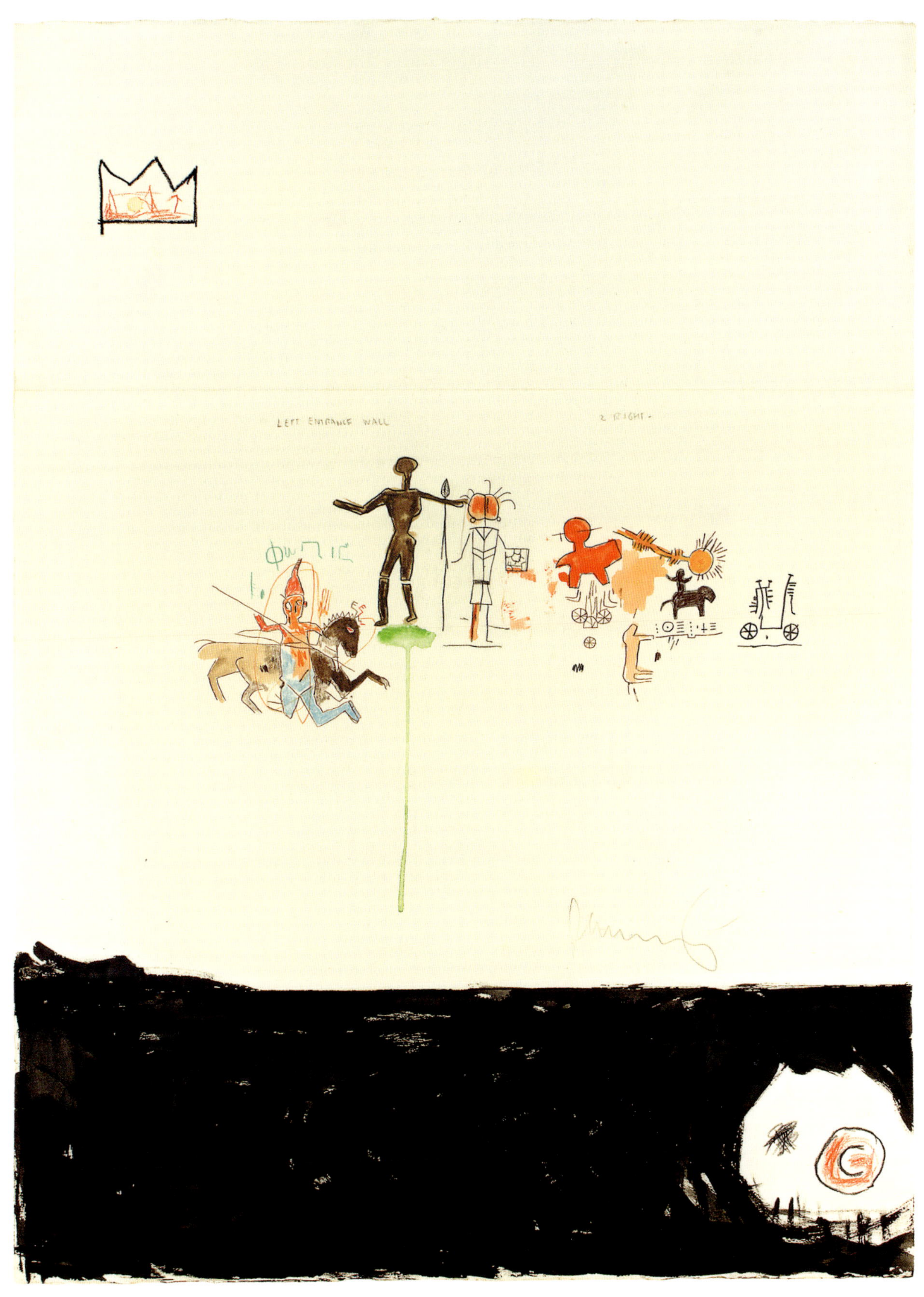

Jean-Michel Basquiat *Untitled (Left Entrance Hall)* 1986, pencil, oilstick and gouache on paper, 106.0 x 75.0 cm, Private collection

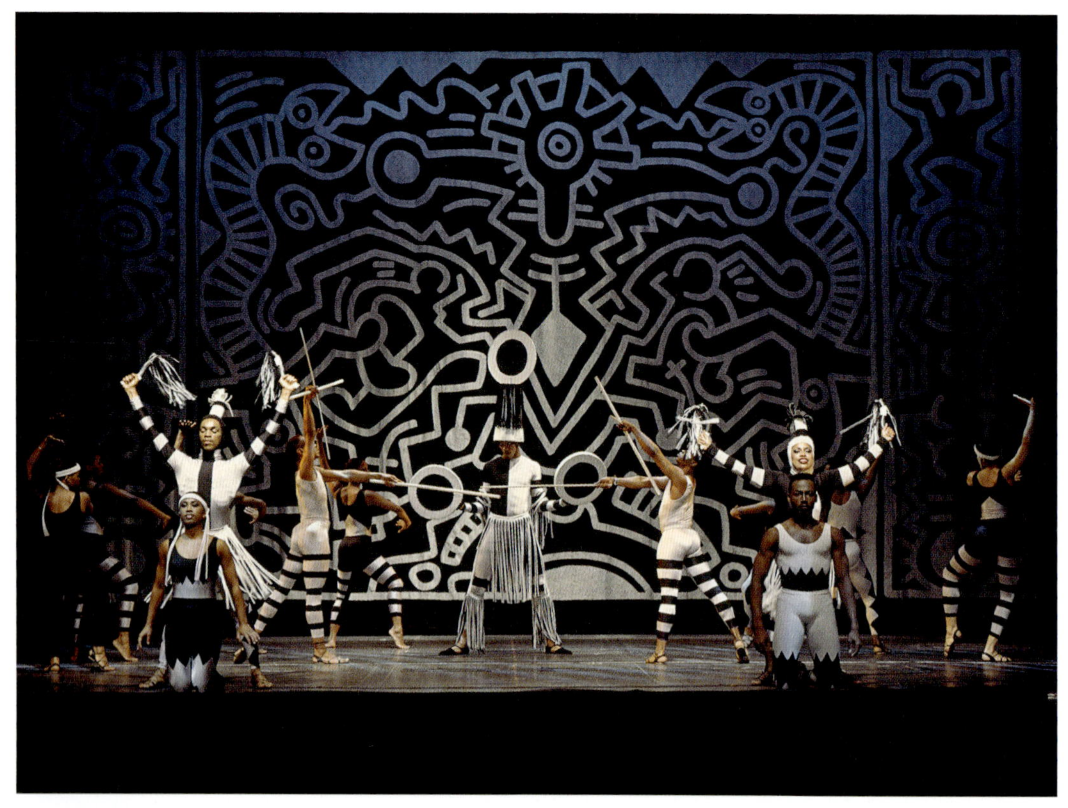

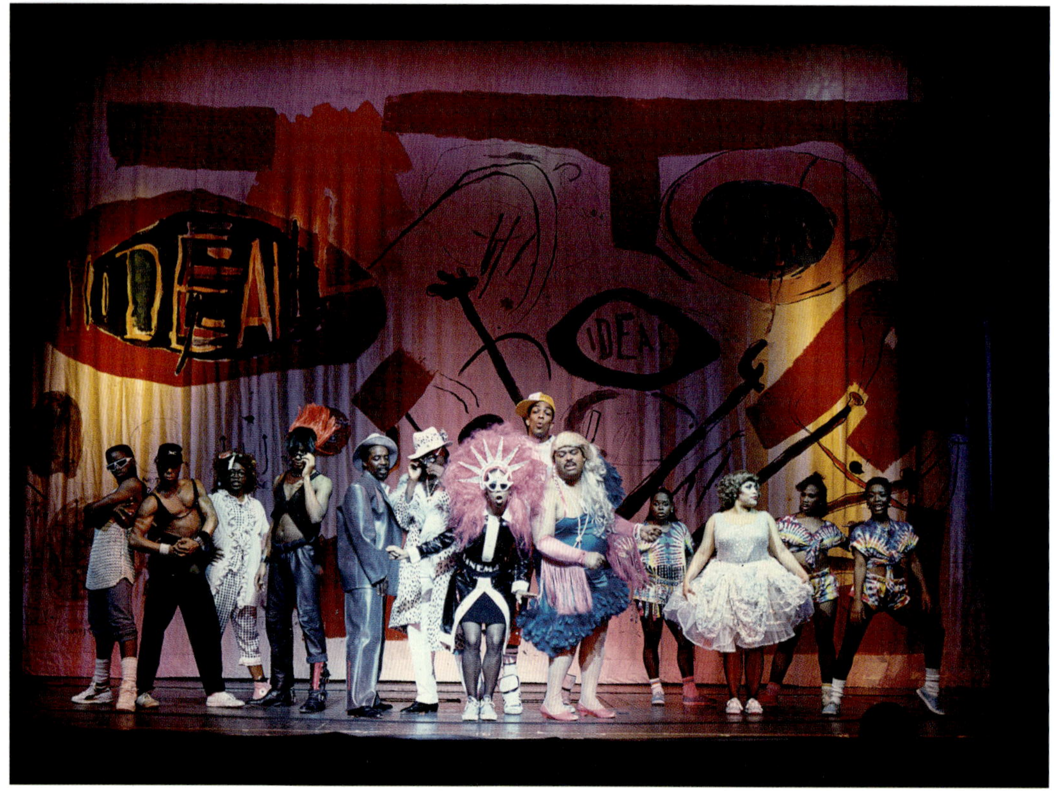

Body and Soul dance festival at the Deutsches Theater featuring painted backdrops by Keith Haring (top) and Jean-Michel Basquiat (bottom), Munich, Germany, 1988

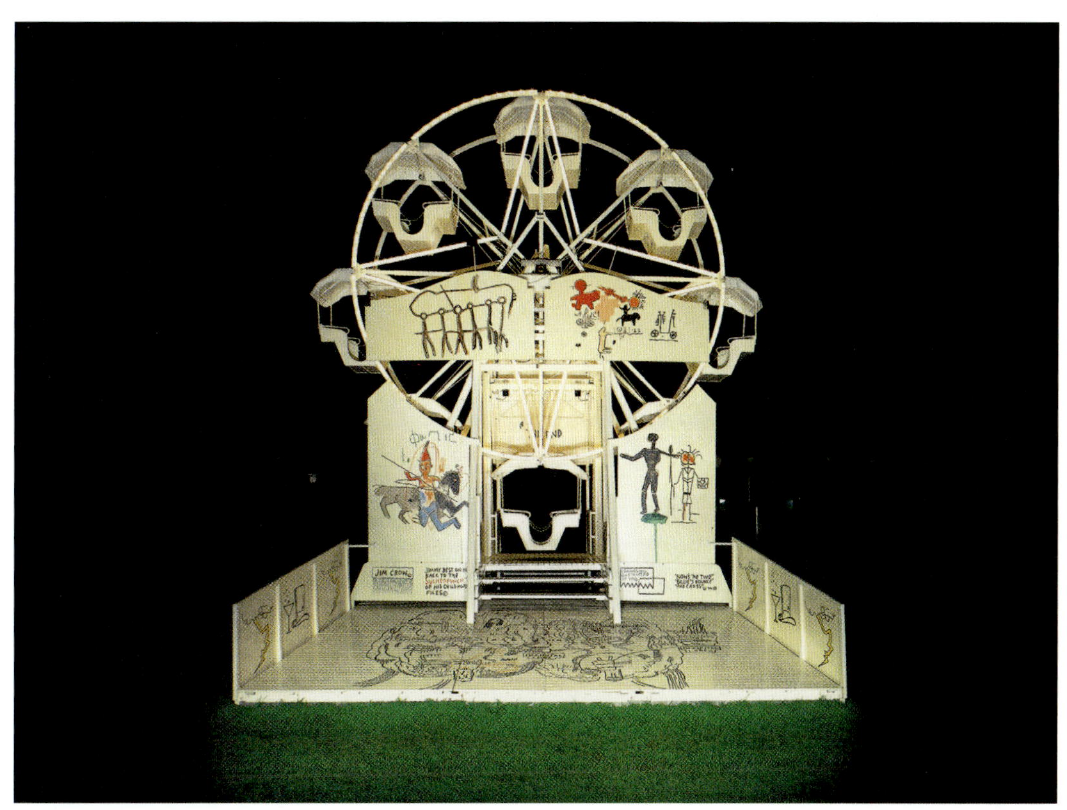

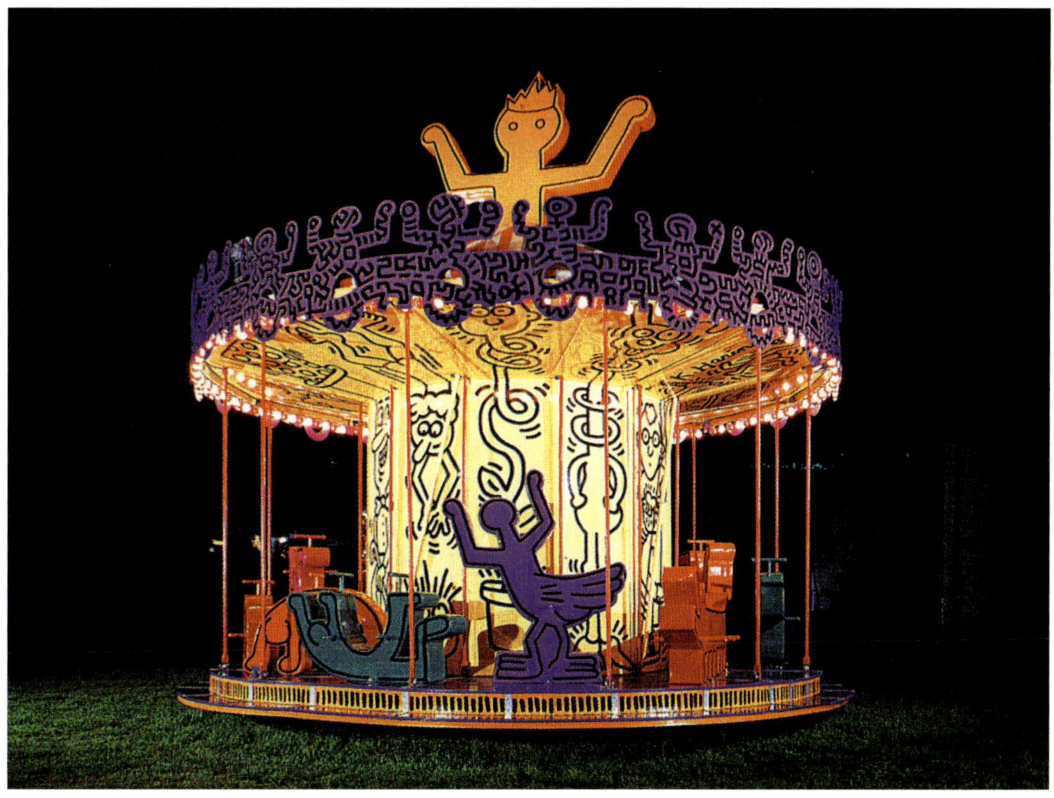

(top) Jean-Michel Basquiat's Ferris wheel (front view), *Luna Luna*, 1986
(bottom) Keith Haring's carousel, *Luna Luna*, 1986

Interview: Patti Astor

Dieter Buchhart

Dieter Buchhart (DB): Can you tell me a little bit about the downtown scene and how you started out in New York?

—Patti Astor (PA): I was never an art business person. I was a film actress, I wanted to be in movies. The first real official art opening I went to in New York was around 1974. My friend Don Rodan had a show with Leo Castelli, back when he had a gallery on the Upper East Side in his apartment.

I came to New York as a dancer in 1968 and lived there until about 1972, when I went on tour to Europe with my dance act *A Diamond as Big as the Ritz*. Then, in 1975, I came back to New York and ended up downtown because it was really cheap. The whole East Village scene was probably from 1975 to 1985. It really started in 1975. It was *the* spot, so we moved over there and everybody said, 'I'll never see you again because it's so dangerous over there! I'm not coming to visit you and you're gonna get killed anyway!' And I said, 'Okay! That sounds really good!' [Laughs.]

What people don't realise is that the scene was very small at the beginning, so we all just met. [Punk club] CBGB was the only place to go other than the Russian bars with the old men. Which were great! You would have a fifty-cent beer and play pool with the old Russian and Ukrainian guys in suits that were living in the East Village. And then you would go to CBGB. In 1976, I got cast by the director Amos Poe, whom I knew from CBGB, in the movie *Unmade Beds*. [Blondie singer] Debbie Harry was the star of the movie and I thought, 'I've made it!' [Laughs.]

This was the time of the transition from the Warhol era to our era. We started going to the big art openings because you could get free drinks. We would look for Andy and the Warhol [super]stars and that's how we met Rene Ricard. Those were our idols.

So anyway. Back to CBGB – that era went from 1975 to 1977. We were all running around and that's where I met [curator, agent] Diego Cortez, at CBGB. In New York, particularly back then, you would just be in the clubs every night. You're either on the street or you're in a club because you don't want to be in your apartment. Then, in 1978, my best friend, Anya Phillips – who was also in some movies with me – she and Diego [Cortez] decided to start the Mudd Club. So, everybody moved to the Mudd Club. And that was when the underground film scene really took off; between 1978 and 1980, I made twelve beyond-low-budget films.

Okay, so then we cut to 1980. Fab 5 [Freddy; aka Fred Brathwaite] decides that he is going to bring hip-hop to the world and comes to the East Village. And I have to give [writer] Glenn O'Brien, Debbie Harry and [Blondie guitarist] Chris Stein from the [public-access cable] show *TV Party* very much credit here. Because really the story here is the coming together of punk rock and hip-hop. And I think the things that are interesting about Keith and Jean are that they didn't come out of 'street art' – I can't stand the term – they came out of the club scene. They didn't come out of the ghetto and they didn't come out of hip-hop. But they definitely *learned* from those guys. Because the thing about punk rock and hip-hop is that nobody had any money: we were living in horrible ghettos, terrible tenement apartments, and it was pretty dangerous. So, everybody was just making their own story up.

But anyway, so Fred [Fab 5 Freddy; Fred Brathwaite] decides okay, now I gotta get in this whole downtown scene because it's really blowing up. I met him for the first time at a party that [writer] Duncan Smith, who was also a very good friend, was hosting. And Fred's there because he had come with Diego. They walked up to me – Fred had just seen the movie *Underground USA* – and he says, 'Patti Astor, you're my favourite movie star, can I have your autograph?' And I said, 'Yes, of course. You must be my new best friend'. And so that's how we met.

And then things jumped off. In 1980, nobody had heard of hip-hop, rap music, graffiti art, breakdancing, nothing. All of a sudden, 1981 was the year. And so that's kind of the timeline. So, it went from punk rock bands (1975–77), underground films (1978–80) and then the whole art scene took off (1981–85). So that's the three eras.

DB: When and where did you meet Keith Haring?

— PA: Keith was part of the second wave of people that came in around 1978 and 1979. They were younger, they went to art school, they were more organised about things. I mean, me and my people were just a bunch of dropouts and nutjobs. We were just crazy. Yeah, we were artists but we weren't the kind that went to school.

I don't know if I even met Keith until 1980. I was walking across Astor Place and Keith – he was wearing these handpainted day-glo glasses – and he just came up to me and said, 'Patti Astor, I'm Keith Haring. Can I take your picture?' The story of our meeting is one of my fondest memories because, after he took my picture, he gave me a button, the original 'Baby' one, and that was the first time I had seen it! So, that's how I met Keith.

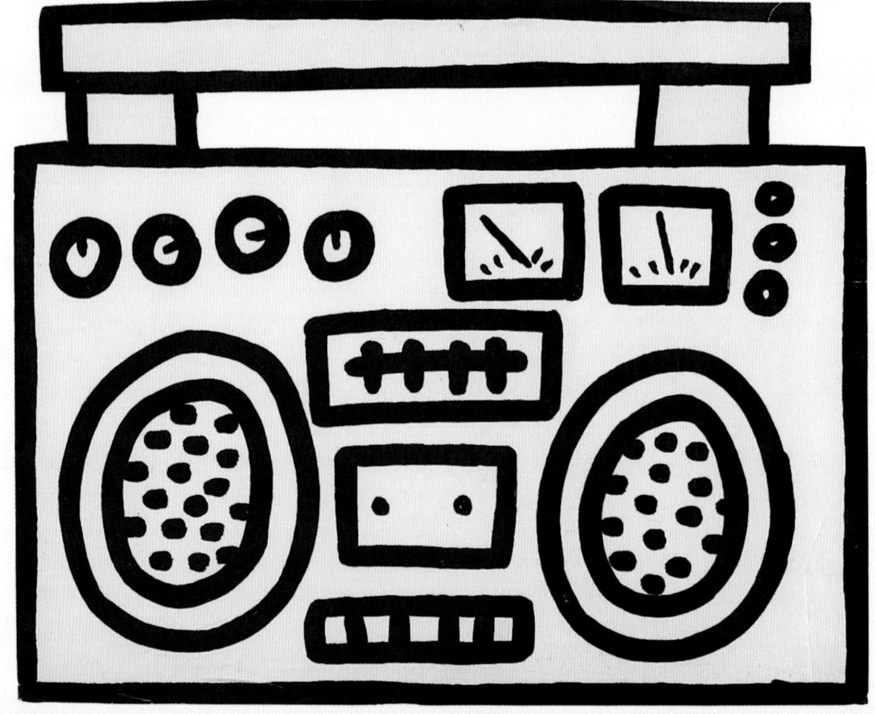

Keith Haring *Untitled* c. 1982, ink on board, 101.6 x 127.0 cm, Collection of Larry Warsh

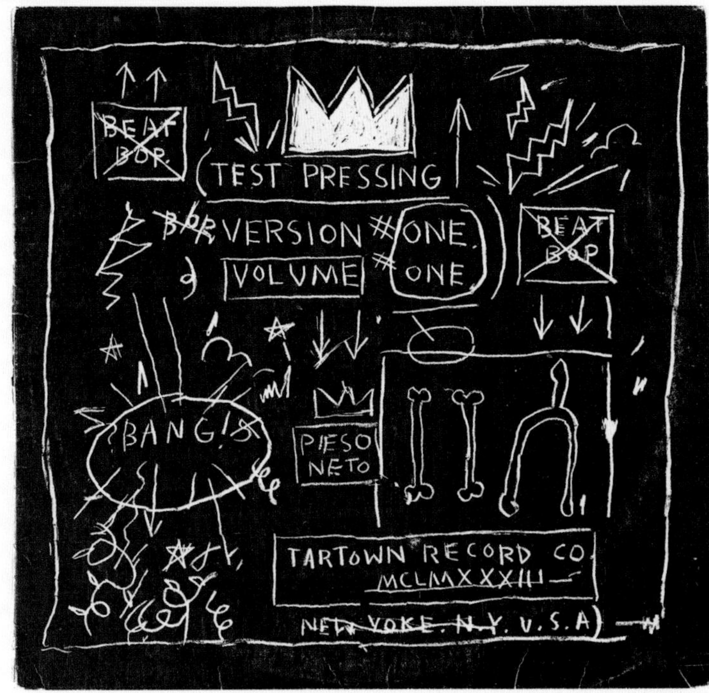

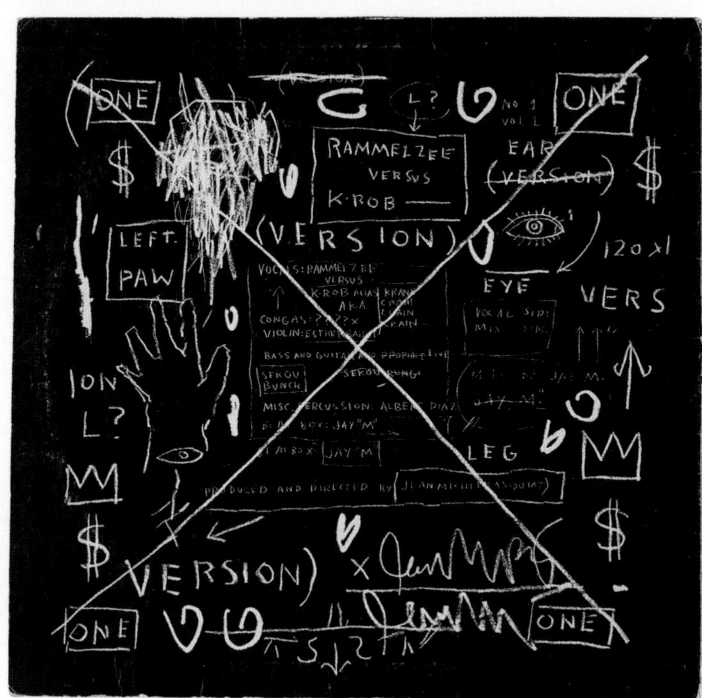

DH: And what about Jean-Michel Basquiat, how did you meet him?

—PA: I met Jean-Michel at the Mudd Club. He had just started hanging out there with his band, Gray. So, at first, I knew him as just this kid who had this band, Gray. The first time I saw him face to face was when we ran into each other on the stairs up to the VIP room of the club. And I started flirting and teasing him about his weird hairdo, and we just hit it off. That's how we met and then we became really good friends. I had a different relationship with him because I wasn't in the art business. Either I was at all of the events of his career or he told me about them. You know? Like, when he came back from Bruno's [Bischofberger, gallerist], when he came back from Larry's [Gagosian, gallerist]. We talked about his experiences.

At first, I didn't even know he was an artist. But then came the P.S. 1 show [*New York/New Wave*] and the *Beyond Words* exhibition. *Beyond Words* is what I considered the landmark show and it was held at the Mudd Club. The club had four floors and [co-founder] Steve Mass said, 'Keith, why don't you do a gallery here?' So, Keith did and he invited Futura [2000] and Fab 5 to come curate the show. Afrika Bambaataa was the DJ and that was the first time I saw these little kids running around with backpacks full of spray cans getting ready to go bomb [paint] trains in the yards. Jean had one drawing in the show called *Flats Fix* [1981, p. 10]. When I saw that drawing, I was like, oh, that's Jean? That guy's a genius. He's a genius.

DB: Can you tell me a little bit about how the Fun Gallery started out?

Jean-Michel Basquiat *Album cover for Ramm:ell:zee vs. K.Rob, Beat Bop* 1983 (front and back), 30.0 x 30.0 cm, Collection of Jennifer von Holstein

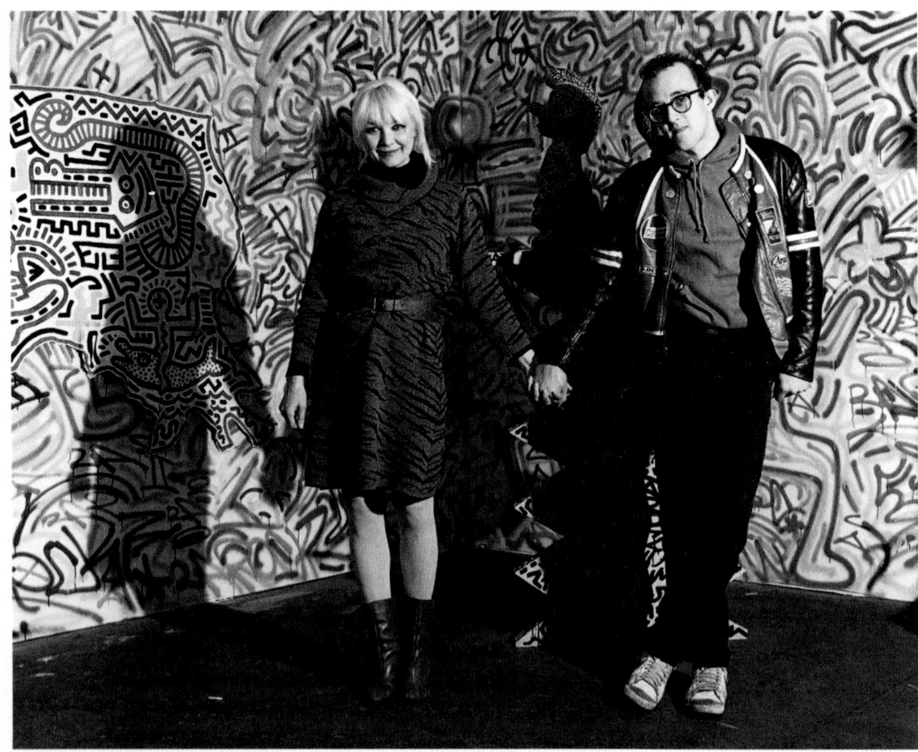

—PA: Our first space [at 225 East 11th Street] was tiny, 8 feet by 25 feet. Our first official show was Kenny Scharf in 1981 and he's the one that named it Fun Gallery. And then, the next show was Fred [Brathwaite]. We were only open on Sunday afternoon from 3 to 6 pm and I'm sitting there and all of a sudden this huge limousine pulls up and this guy that looks like Goldfinger gets out. He's got two babes with him, one on each arm. He comes in and he announces, 'I'm Bruno Bischofberger' [laughs]. Fred had hustled him somewhere and I had no idea who he was, I didn't know anything about the art world. He pulls out all these index cards and starts going through, 'Well, what do you think about graffiti in New York? Who do you think is good? And what do you think about this guy? And what do you think of Jean-Michel Basquiat?' And then, thank god, Fred showed up. After Bruno saw the show, they went over to the coffee shop right across the street where [actress] Jackie Curtis and all the fabulous drag queens hung out. I would have loved to have seen that scene!

DB: When did you decide to ask Basquiat to do an exhibition at the Fun Gallery?

—PA: That was later, when we had already moved to the second, bigger space [254 East 10th Street]. By this time, the Fun Gallery had taken off. People hung out there every day. I mean, you had the Beastie Boys – they were fourteen and so they weren't the Beastie Boys yet – in the backyard. You had the Rock Steady Crew breakdancing in the front, Fab [5 Freddy; Fred Brathwaite] would be on the boom box. It was just a scene. Rene Ricard loved it and became fascinated with the whole B-boy culture and everything, so by this time he basically lived at the Fun Gallery. And he just loved the whole thing. He had already written 'The radiant child' article on Jean and he worshipped him. At the time, Jean needed a place, Jean needed something, you know? And so, Rene just said to him, 'Jean, chill with Patti. Come home. Come on. She'll be straight with you'. That's how that show came about.

Patti Astor and Keith Haring at Keith's exhibition at Fun Gallery, New York, 1983

DB: How much time went into preparing the show?

— PA: It wasn't really that spur of the moment because we were already advertising. It probably was over the summer. Because it was a huge thing. I mean, he had a reputation and we did a huge installation.

DB: Did Basquiat specifically start with the exposed stretcher paintings for your show?

— PA: His whole idea was, we're going to make it really raw. So, [Fun Gallery co-founder] Bill [Stelling] and I started going down to Jean's loft. There were drawings all over the floor and Jean said, 'Bill, you guys should just take some drawings'. And Bill said, 'No, Jean, we're not here for that. We should really plan your show'. And that's how Jean and I came up with the idea of the sheetrock [drywall] installation for the walls. He came up with the deconstructed stretchers – we were really shocked but I loved them.

DB: So, it was all you doing the exhibition architecture and such?

— PA: Yes, it was me and Jean.

DB: Did he come with the paintings he wanted to show?

— PA: Yes. There were some thirty paintings in that show. The point of the Fun Gallery was that this was an artists' gallery. That's how we came up with the name Fun Gallery, because this was going to be different from Soho. The artists could do whatever they wanted to, including naming the gallery. That was the whole thing – that you would really be able to collaborate. That's why with Keith's show he did whatever he wanted to do. The shows, they usually took about a week to put together.

I remember building the sheetrock walls myself with a power nail gun. Bang, bang, bang! So, Basquiat brings up all his stuff and just moved in for at least three days before the opening. He was there twenty-four hours a day, wandering around barefoot in his Armani suit with a paintbrush and a can of black paint touching up the paintings. One night, it's two in the morning, and Jean declares, 'I have to have this painting from my studio'. Bill and I say, 'Okay. No problem'. We take a cab down to Crosby Street and this painting's eight feet long! So, Bill and I walked it all the way back. That was a fourteen-block walk. It was freezing, the wind was blowing something awful, it carried us along First Avenue like a giant sail! So, that was, basically, how it went.

DB: And how was the opening?

— PA: By this time, the openings were really insane. There would be a thousand people at these openings. The whole street outside would be packed, stacks of limos.

Paul Simon was there and said he wanted to buy [Basquiat's work] *St Joe Louis Surrounded by Snakes* [1982]. Rene Ricard was right there and he went into a huge screaming temper tantrum in the middle of the opening in front of Paul Simon and said, 'But that's my painting! Jean promised me that painting! If you sell that painting, I'm going to run onto the street and get run over by a car!' And then he runs out to the street and we hear this huge screech. Thankfully, he didn't get run over. But Paul Simon left.

Madonna was there as well. Jean and Madonna were dating, then. They had a huge fight.

DB: Do you remember if Keith Haring was there?

— PA: I'm sure he was. There's a photo of Keith, standing in front of [Basquiat's work] *Leonardo da Vinci's Greatest Hits* [1982, Schorr Family Collection].

DB: And then you arranged a Keith Haring show a couple of months later, in February 1983.

— PA: Keith and I were also very good friends. And Keith was so instrumental in developing that radical new scene. He did the black light art show at Club 57 that was so influential. Jean was the DJ for that show! Keith loved the Fun Gallery. He was there all the time. He was part of the regular hangout group. When we moved to the second space, he actually gave me this really beautiful drawing to sell and raise money to make the move.

After Jean's show he said, 'I want to do a show', and I said 'Of course'. That was, again, another whole week of installation with him and LA II [Angel Ortiz] spray-painting the walls. That wasn't even airbrush, it was all cans.

DB: Was that Haring's idea?

— PA: Yeah, that was Keith's idea. I mean, Keith was determined, we have to really cover everything. And he's the one that did the poster. Keith printed those and he said, 'We're just going to give them away'. Later, someone came running in: 'The neighbourhood kids are selling Keith Haring posters up on the corner for five dollars!' So, I had to go outside and tell them to cool it [laughs].

DB: How did the press react to Haring's and Basquiat's shows at your gallery? Bruno Bischofberger, for example, says that the best show he has ever seen of Basquiat was the one at the Fun Gallery. So, I was wondering, how were the reactions at the time?

— PA: You know, I can't specifically tell you, I don't have the press clippings. But Jean's show, even then, was recognised as a great show. But there was not the huge press that you get now. The most important was Rene Ricard's third *Artforum* article about me and the Fun, 'The pledge of allegiance' in November '82, where Whitney curator Richard Marshall described it as 'the most beautiful art exhibit I have ever seen'.

DB: Do you think that both artists, as well as Freddy and Kenny [Scharf], were creating more freely because the Fun Gallery was a different kind of gallery? It seems like your gallery model encouraged them to really develop a different kind of creativity with regard to the forms of display and the works that were shown.

— PA: Oh yeah, absolutely. Artist Peter Herley, who was a friend of Jean's, told me this really nice story that Jean said he was so happy to just feel free and easy about doing his artwork at the Fun Gallery. Because it was like there were no grown-ups [laughs]. For example, we had a big backyard at our second gallery, it was great. So, when Leo Castelli came down to see Jean's show, there were some breakdancing guys there and they put on an impromptu performance for him!

In the backyard is where we had the DJ for Keith's show – it was just a sea of people – and his boyfriend Juan Dubose was the DJ.

DB: Did you have a DJ for the Basquiat show as well?

— PA: We probably had something on boom boxes. That was the thing, the DJ for Keith, it was specific. You know, every show was a completely new adventure.

DB: Everything was designed specifically for the show?

—PA: Yes, for each individual artist I asked them, 'What do you want to do? I'll do anything you want to as long as you bring me your best'.

DB: Your two friends have been dead for nearly three decades now. When you think back, is there a beautiful memory you would like to share?

—PA: Oh, so many! One of my favourite ones with Jean is when he came back from doing the show with Emilio Mazzoli [in 1981] in Italy. We were sitting out in the bushes in front of Club 57 and he leans in conspiratorially and says, 'Patti, I have to tell you something. I just made $30,000'. And I exclaimed, 'Damn that's great', because that was the first time that anyone, particularly Jean, had made any real money. It's the middle of the night and there's music blasting. We talk it over, 'Oh wow, that's really big and I wonder what's gonna happen to your career now'. And since we were tripping on magic mushrooms at the time, I said, 'I think this means that you're going to become the Prince of Ethiopia', and he replied, 'Yes, I think you're right!'

I also remember going to his first one-man show at Annina Nosei. It was pouring rain and all these collectors were packed in there and I look around – 'Where's Jean?' So, I fight through the crowd and finally find him holed up in a little room in the back of Annina's and he's got his boom box on, listening to John Coltrane. I said, 'Jean, the show looks great! What's going on?' And he remarked bitterly, 'I can't stand those people and I'm not coming out until they're all gone'. So, I said okay and we just sat there and listened to John Coltrane until everyone left.

DB: And what about Keith Haring?

—PA: There's so many of Keith! When he did the installation at the Fun Gallery with LA II, I was wearing a white hoodie. They were so into painting that they took my sweatshirt and painted it too! This show was in February, it was cold! And they just kept spray-painting and finally they went outside and spray-painted all the snow piled up outside the Fun Gallery, too.

DB: Is there anything else about the two of them that you would like to add?

—PA: They were very good friends and I think that back then they were the first real superstars. They were the hot shots and there's a lot of pressure that comes with that. And I think that the two of them could share that. I mean, they had very different styles but they were in this incredible adventure together and they were just taking off. They were really shooting stars. And they had that in common.

What Keith and Jean – and I – shared was that we wanted to make our own art, we wanted to make our own world. Which in modern terms is what art is all about. That was our dream we all had in common: we're going to make the world a better place.

(2019)

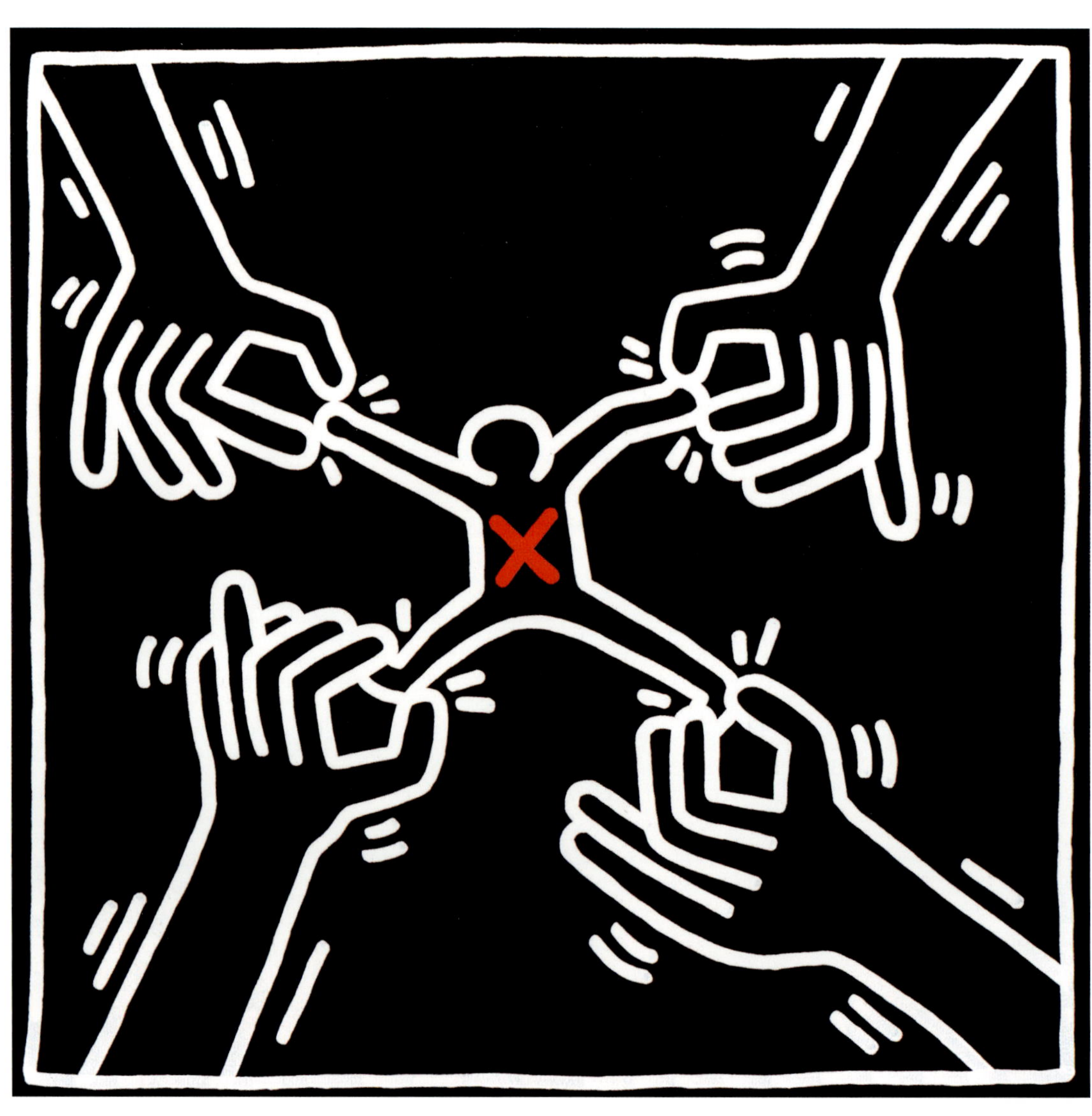

Keith Haring *Untitled* 1985, synthetic polymer paint on canvas, 150.0 x 150.0 cm, Collection of Ms Alona Kagan, USA

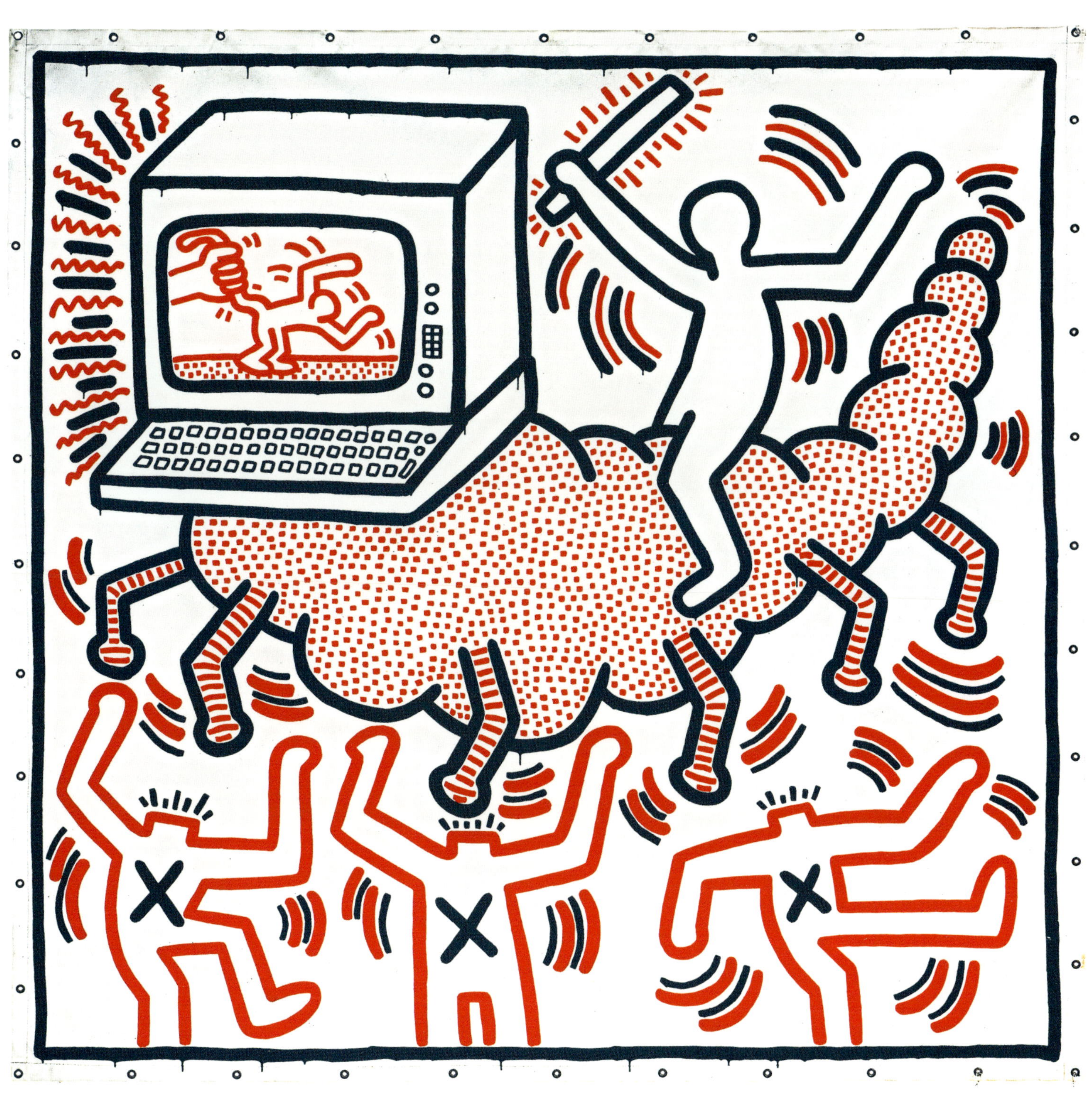

Keith Haring *Untitled* 1983, vinyl paint on vinyl tarpaulin, 307.0 x 302.0 cm, Collection of KAWS

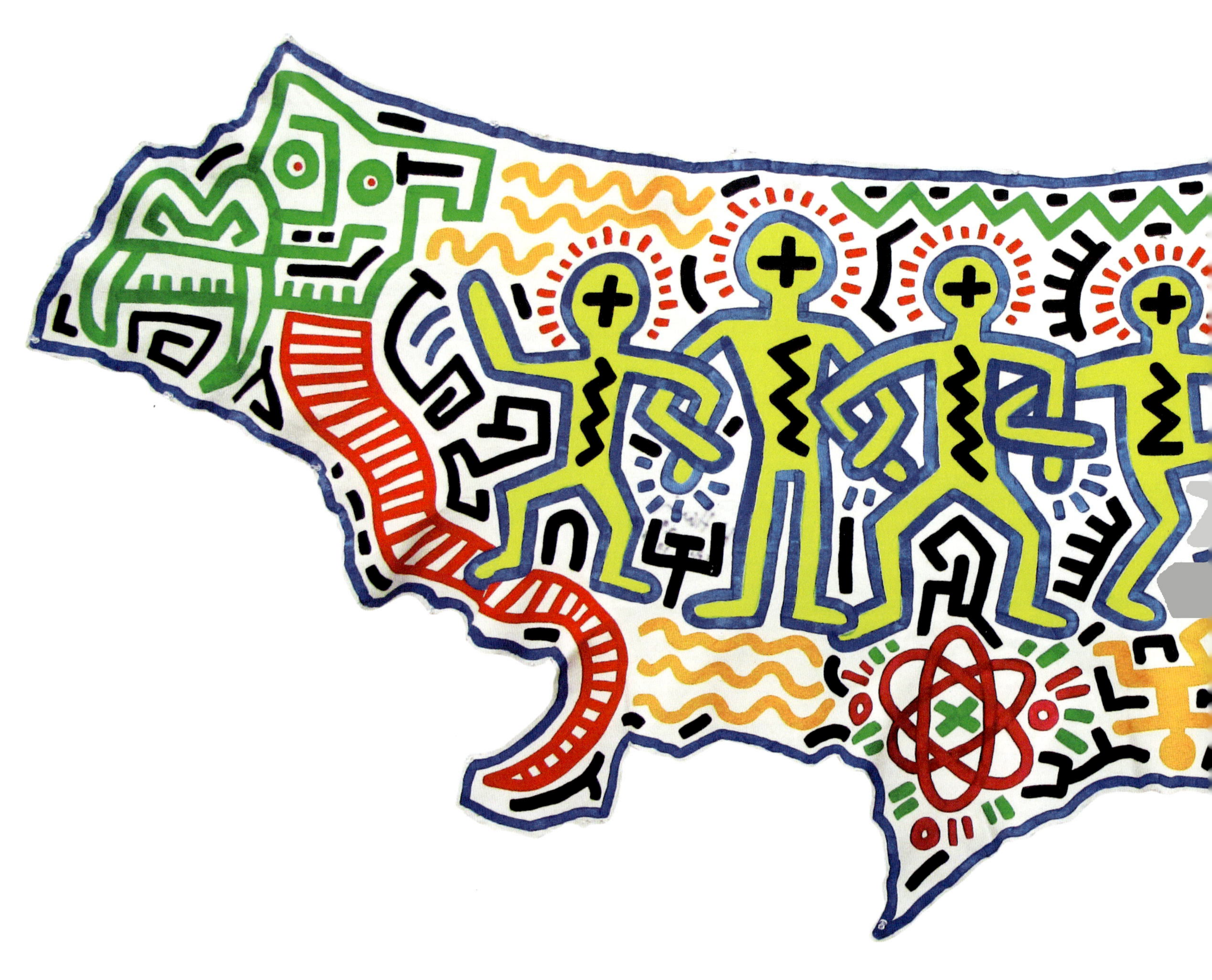

Keith Haring *Untitled* 1983, synthetic polymer paint on leather, 134.6 x 294.6 cm, Private collection

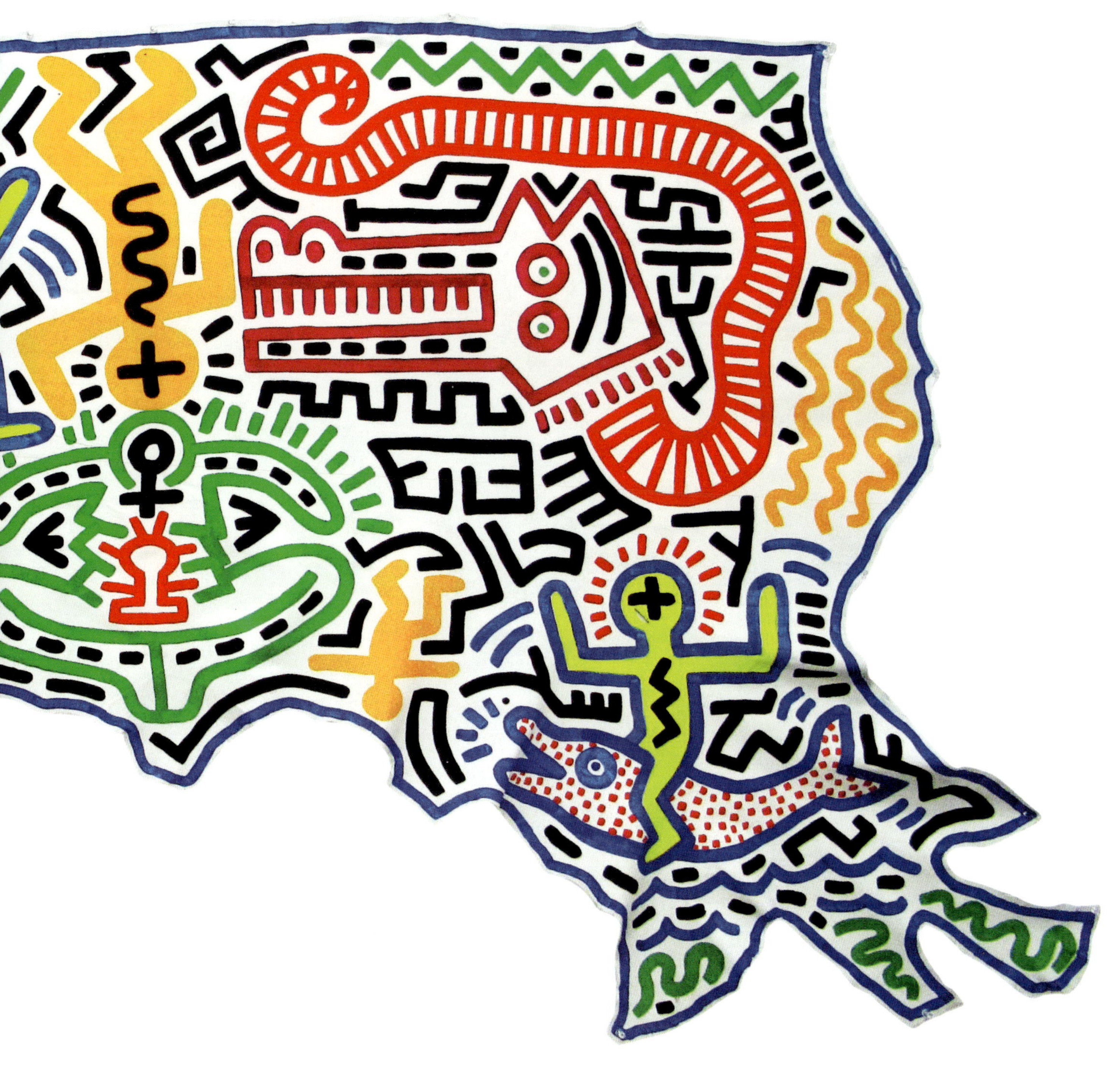

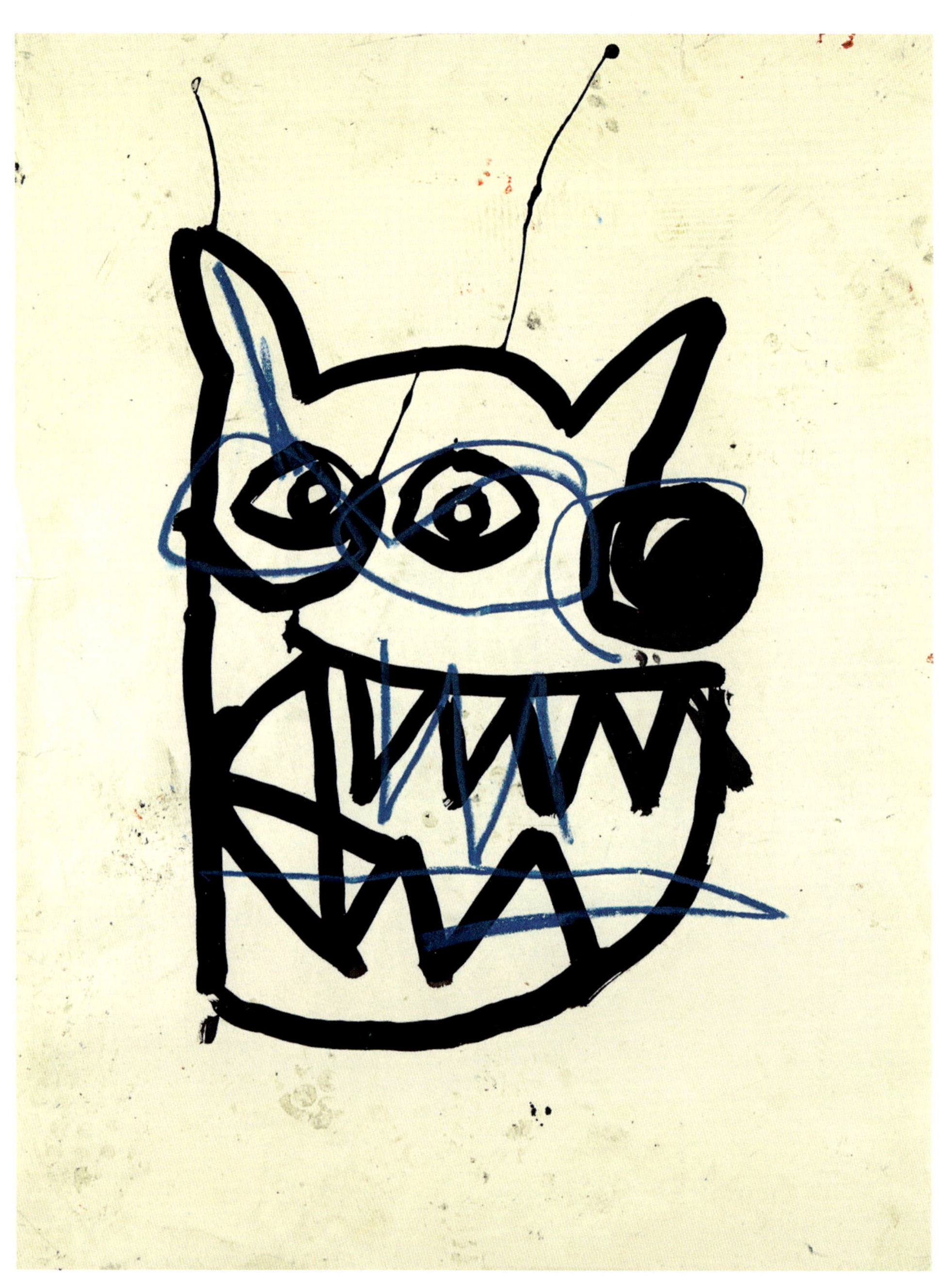

Jean-Michel Basquiat *Untitled* 1983, oilstick and ink on paper, 75.6 x 55.9 cm, Private collection

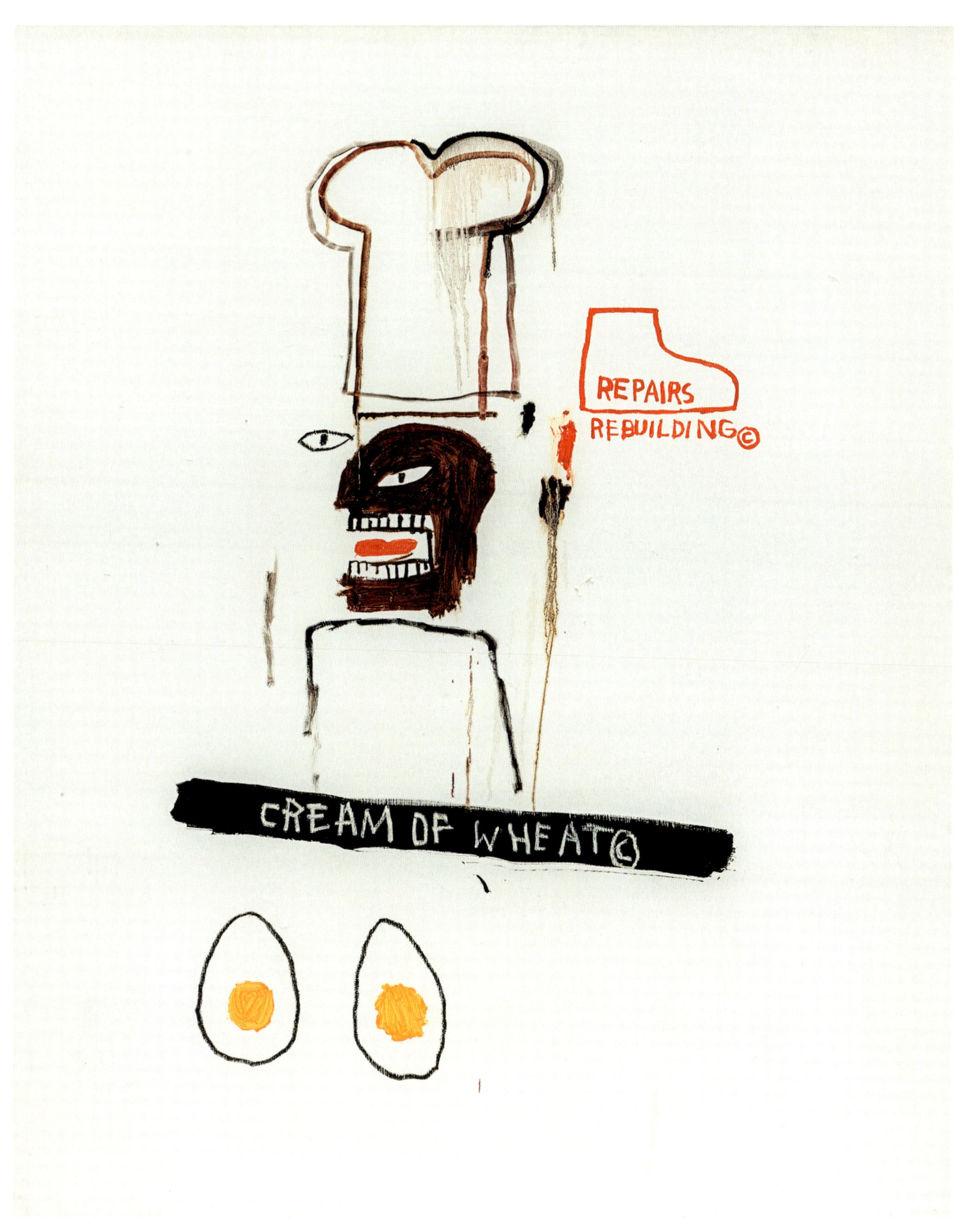

Jean-Michel Basquiat *Farina* 1984, synthetic polymer paint and oilstick on canvas, 218.4 x 172.7 cm, Collection of Sabina and Robert Franklin

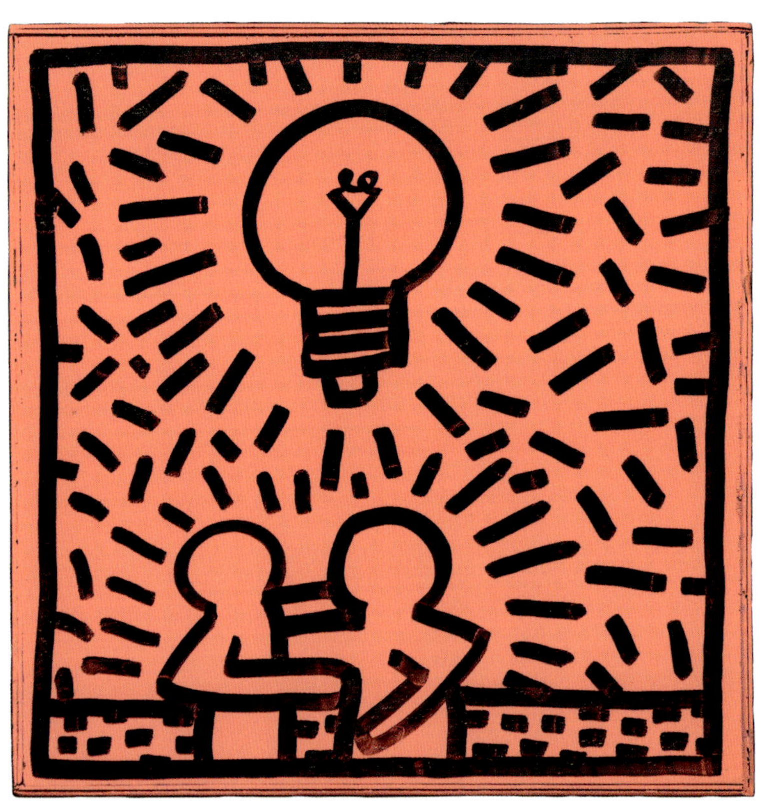

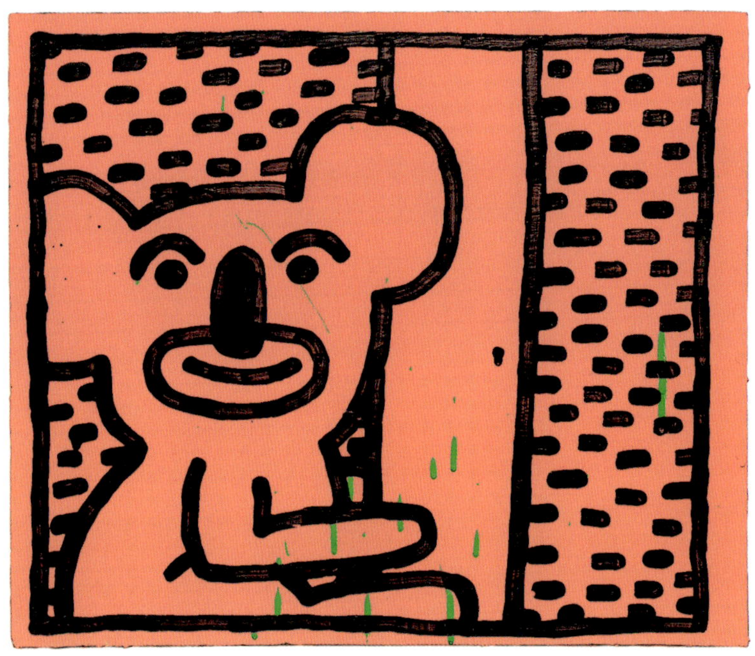

(top) Keith Haring *Untitled* 1981, enamel and ink on wood panel, 52.1 x 53.3 cm, Private collection
(bottom) Keith Haring *Untitled* 1982, oil on wood panel, 43.1 x 48.3 cm, Private collection

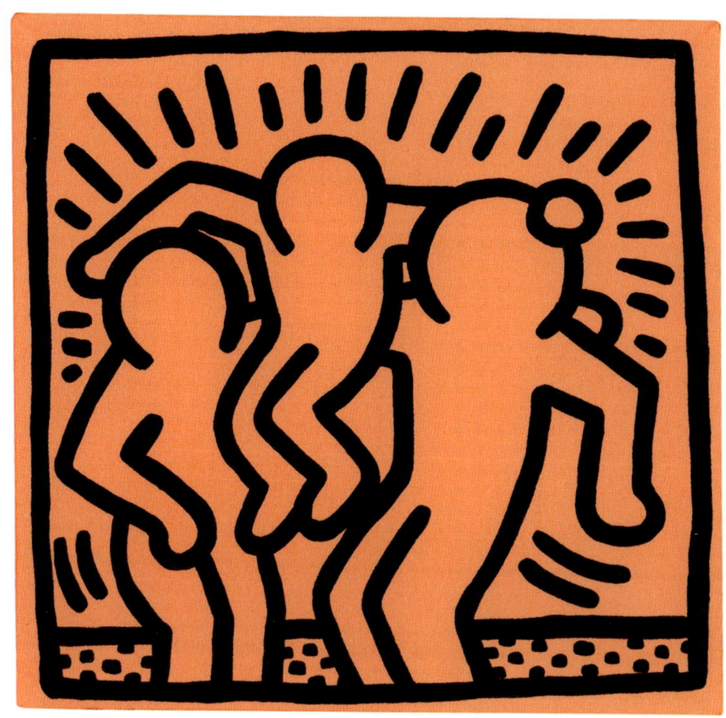

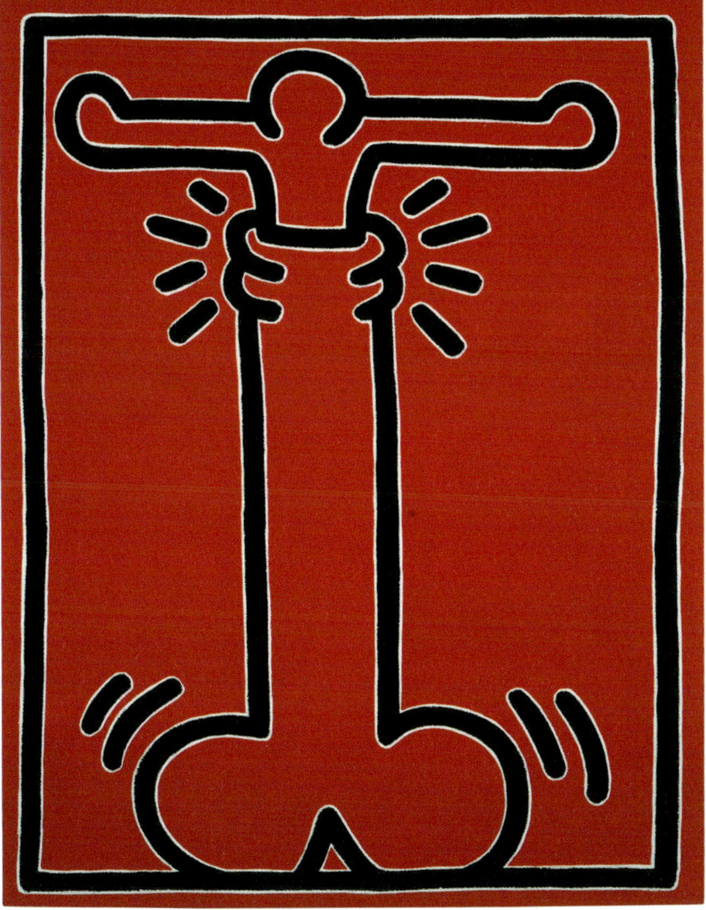

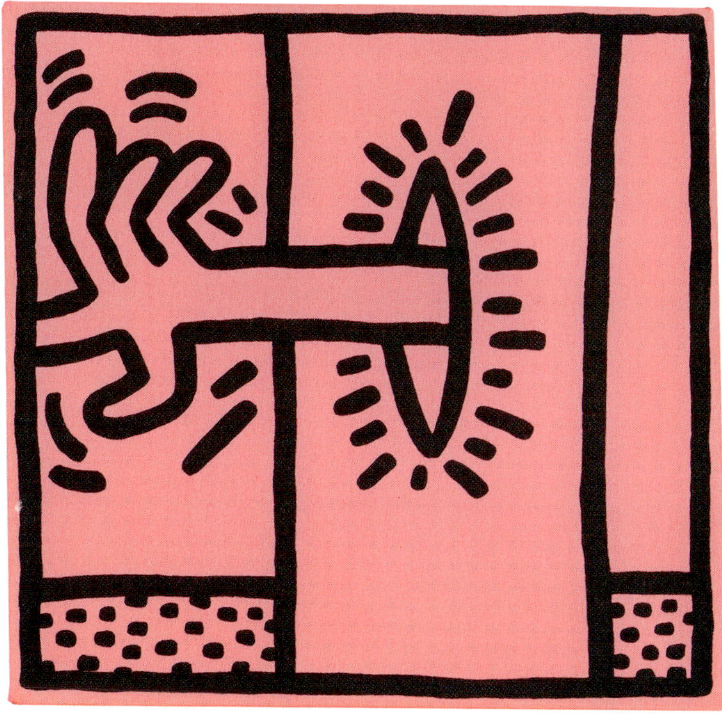

(clockwise from top left) Keith Haring *Untitled* 1984, synthetic polymer paint on canvas, 38.0 x 38.0 cm, Courtesy Laurent Strouk; *Untitled* 1988, synthetic polymer paint on canvas, 126.0 x 97.0 cm, Courtesy Laurent Strouk; *Untitled* 1984, synthetic polymer paint on canvas, 33.5 x 33.5 cm, Private collection

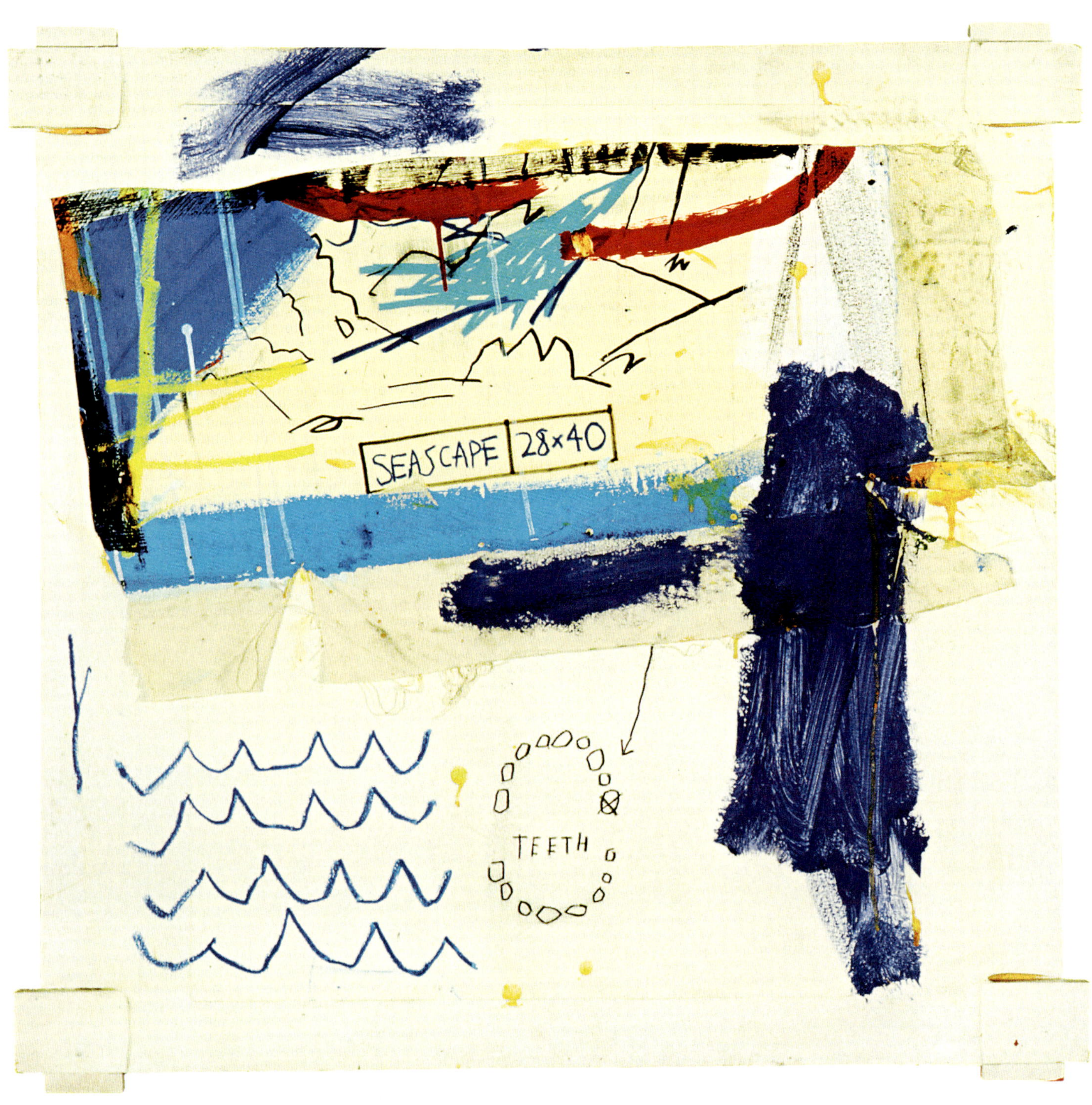

Jean-Michel Basquiat *Seascape* 1983, synthetic polymer paint and oil pastel on paper on canvas and wood, 92.4 x 91.2 cm, Montreal Museum of Fine Arts

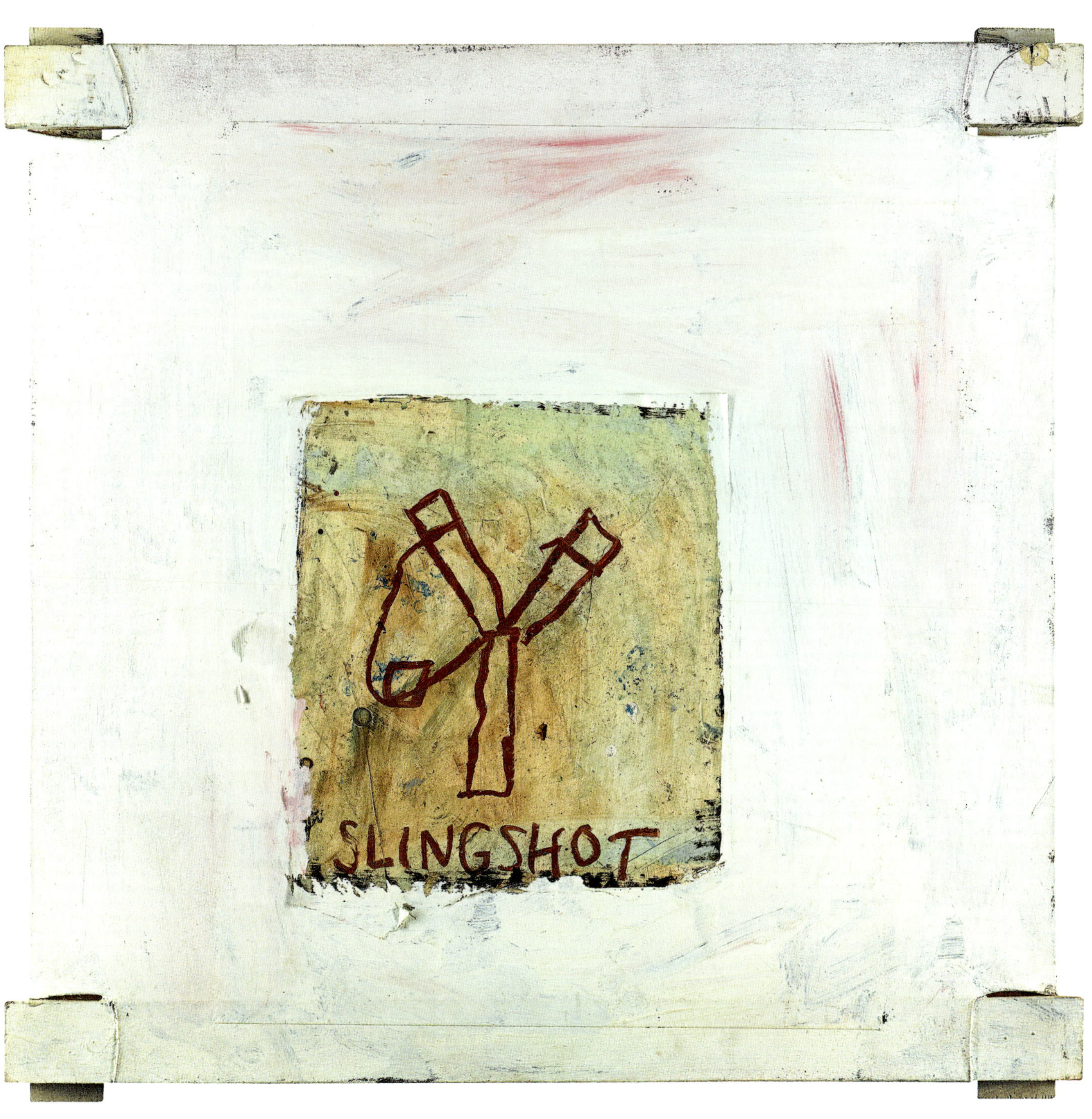

Jean-Michel Basquiat *Untitled* 1983, synthetic polymer paint and oilstick on paper on canvas and wood, 91.5 x 91.5 cm, The George Economou Collection

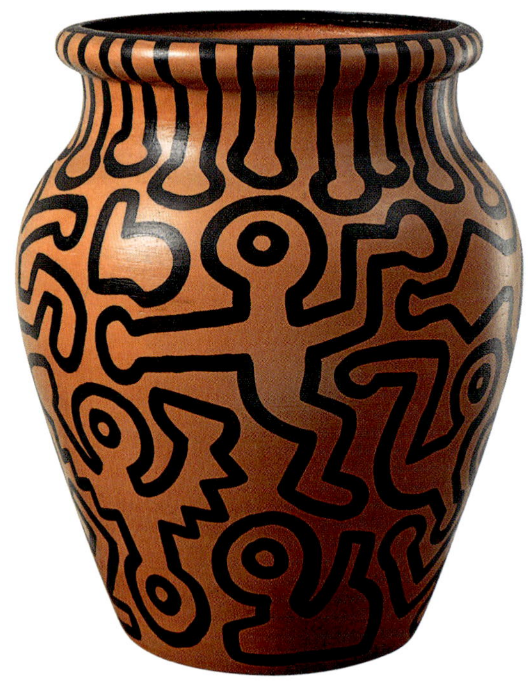

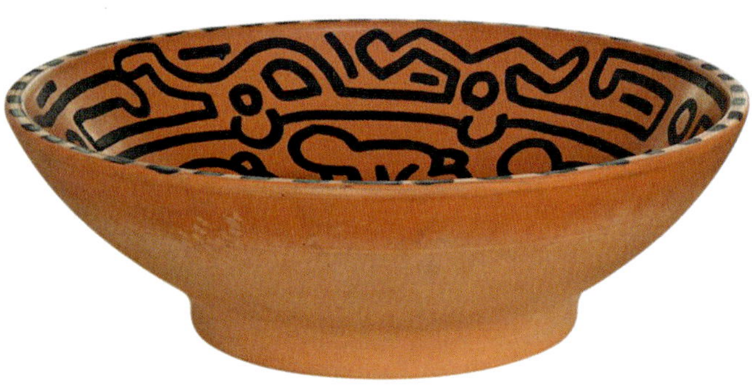

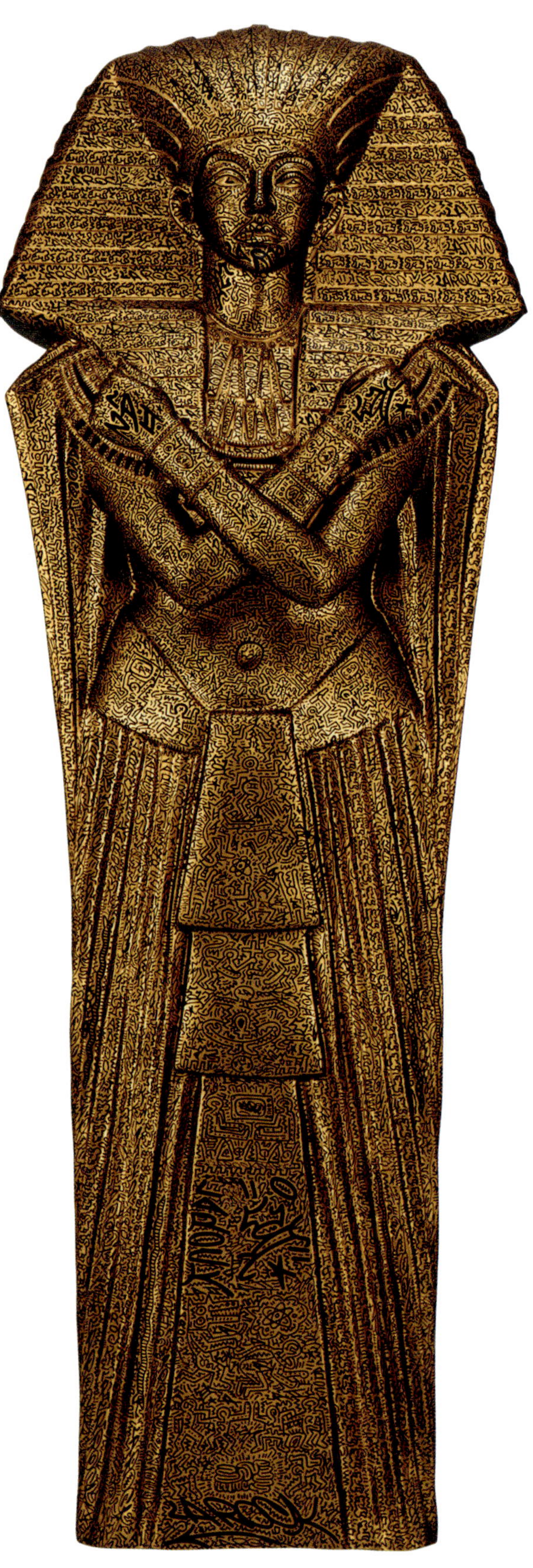

(clockwise from top left) Keith Haring *Untitled* 1989, ink on terracotta vase, 57.1 x 25.4 cm diameter, Private collection; Keith Haring, LA II *Sarcophagus* 1983, synthetic polymer paint and fibre-tipped pen on fibreglass, 249.0 x 86.0 x 56.0 cm, Private collection; Keith Haring *Untitled* 1988, ink on terracotta bowl, 50.8 cm diameter, Private collection

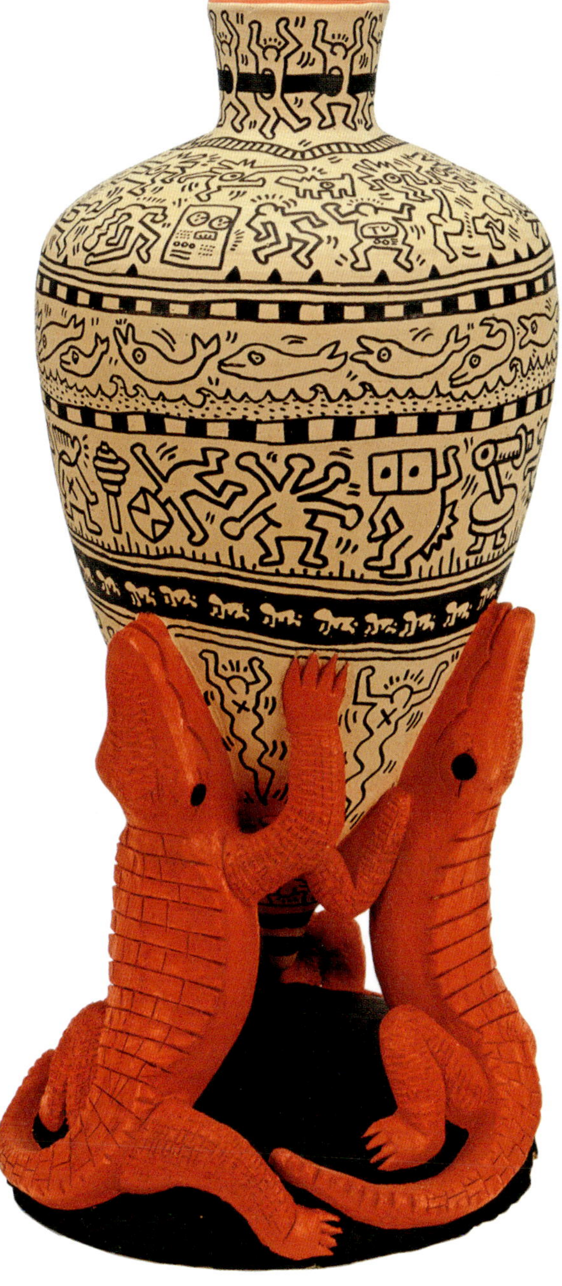

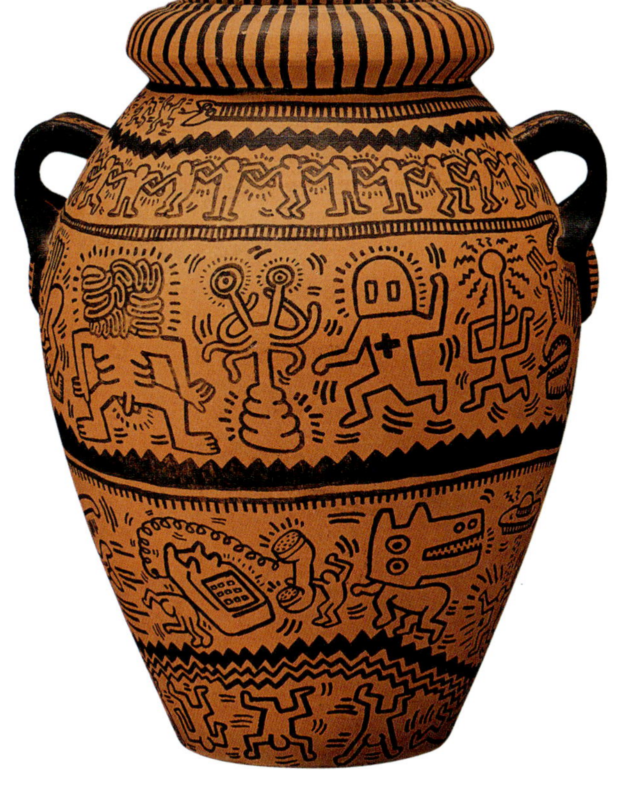

(above left) Keith Haring *Untitled* 1990, synthetic polymer paint and fibre-tipped pen on terracotta vase, 60.3 x 27.9 x 27.9 cm, Collection of KAWS
(above right) Keith Haring *Untitled* 1984, ink on terracotta vase, 54.6 x 44.5 x 44.5 cm, Collection of Larry Warsh

Jean-Michel Basquiat *Untitled (Pecho/Oreja)* 1982–83, synthetic polymer paint, oilstick and paper collage on canvas, 183.0 x 183.0 cm, Onyx Art Collection

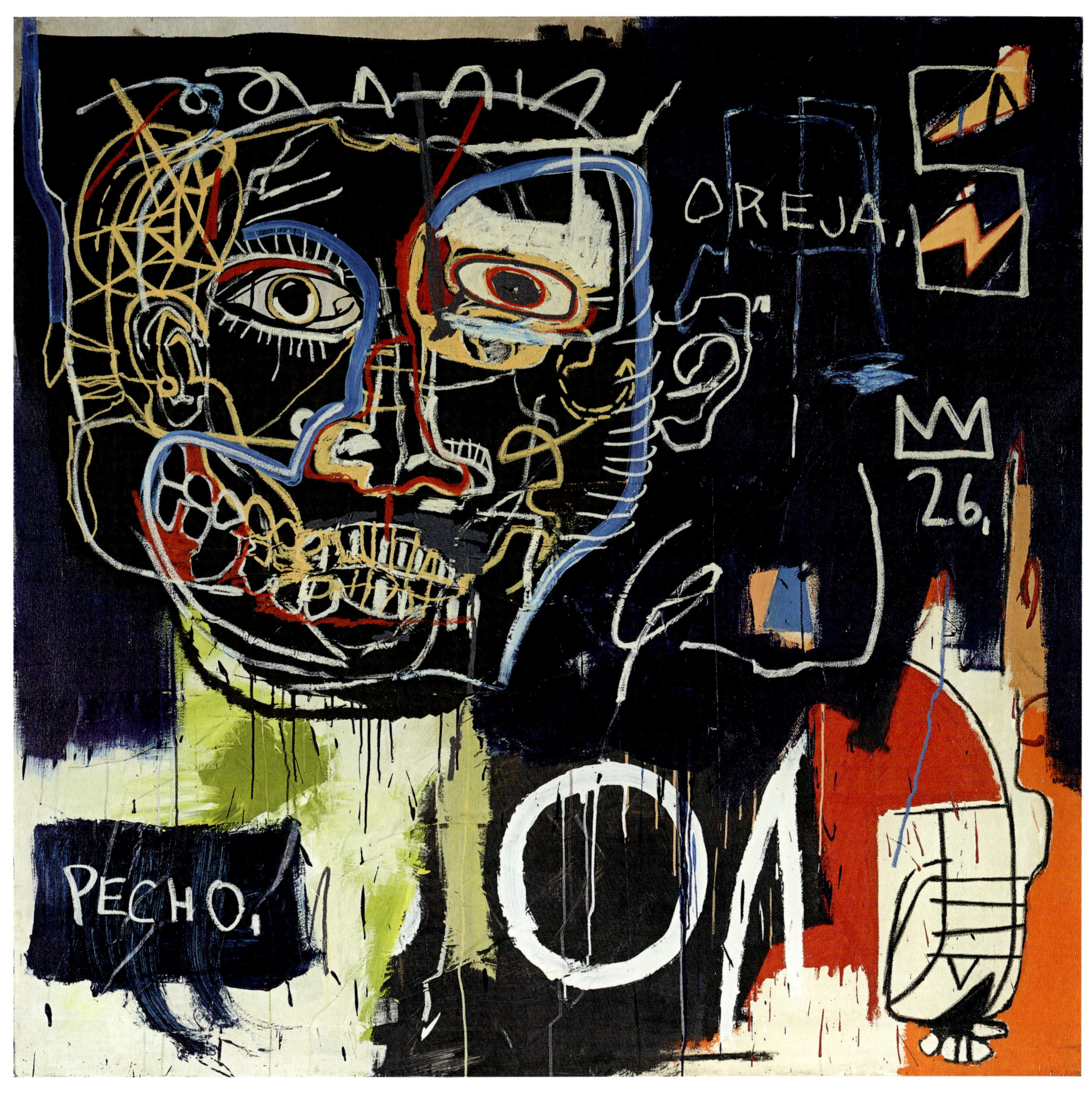
OREJA,
26,
PECHO,

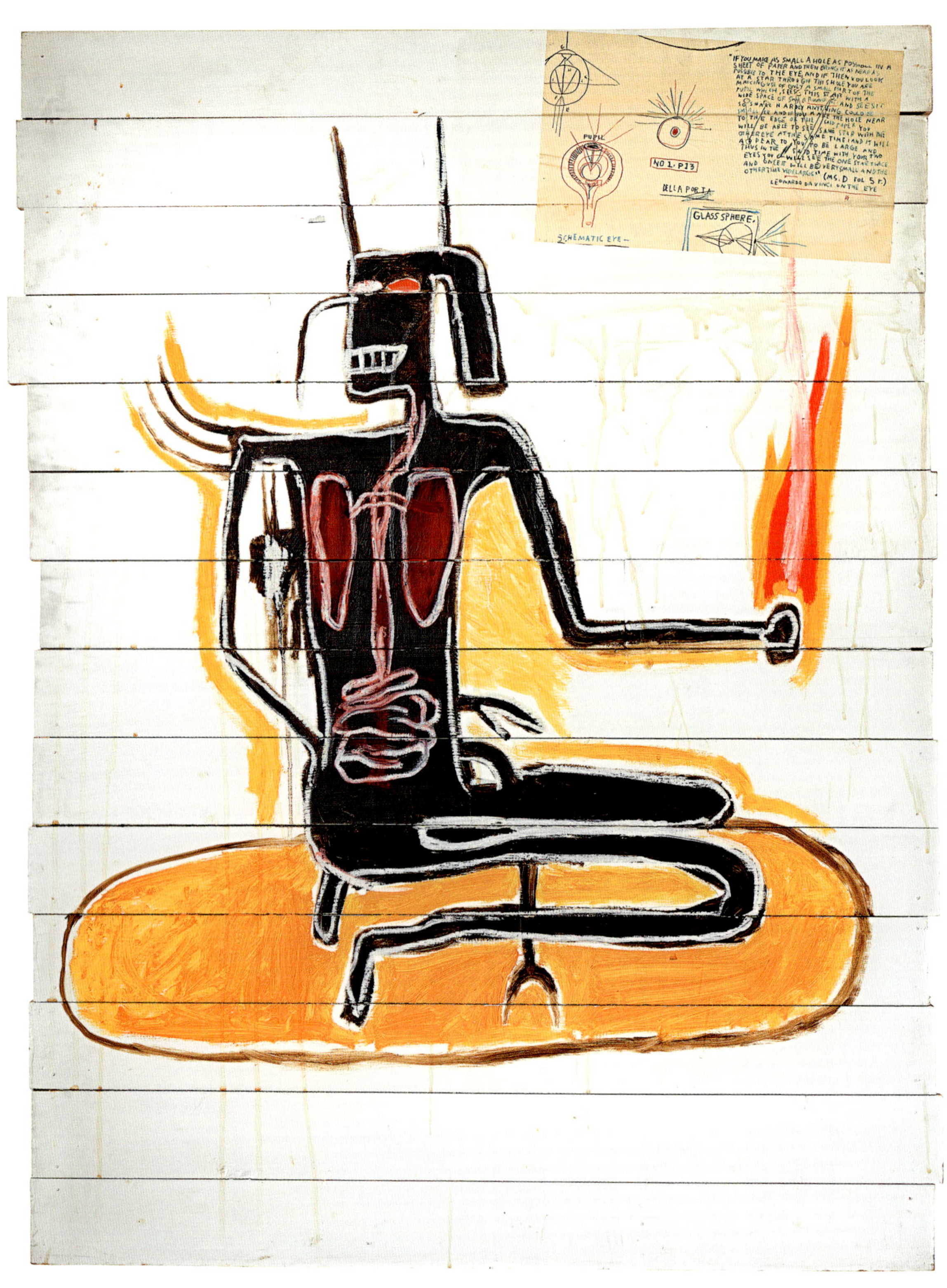

Jean-Michel Basquiat *Untitled* 1984, synthetic polymer paint, oilstick, and xerox collage on wood, 125.5 x 94.0 cm, Private collection

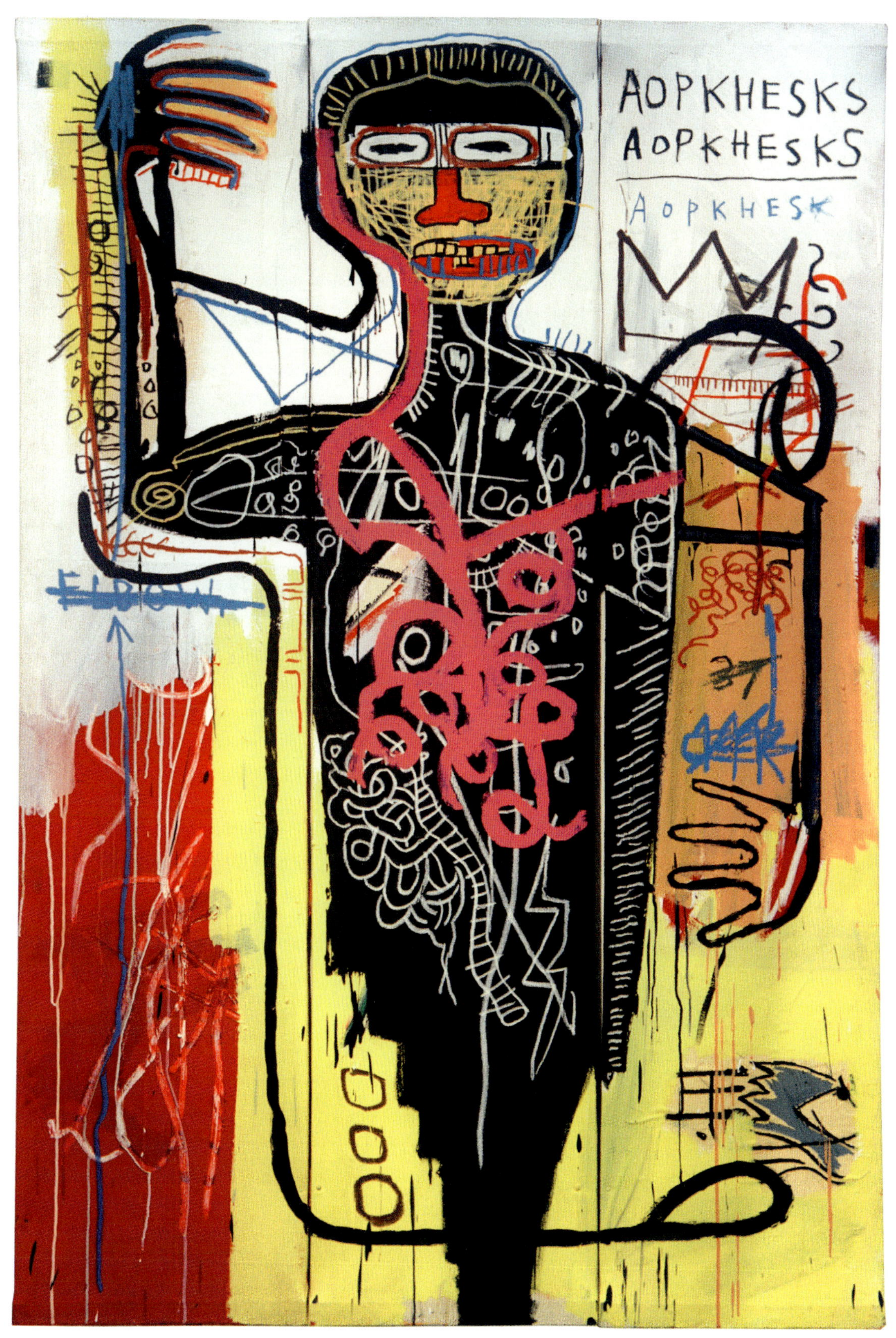

Jean-Michel Basquiat *Versus Medici* 1982, synthetic polymer paint and oil wax crayon on canvas, 213.0 x 136.0 cm, Private collection

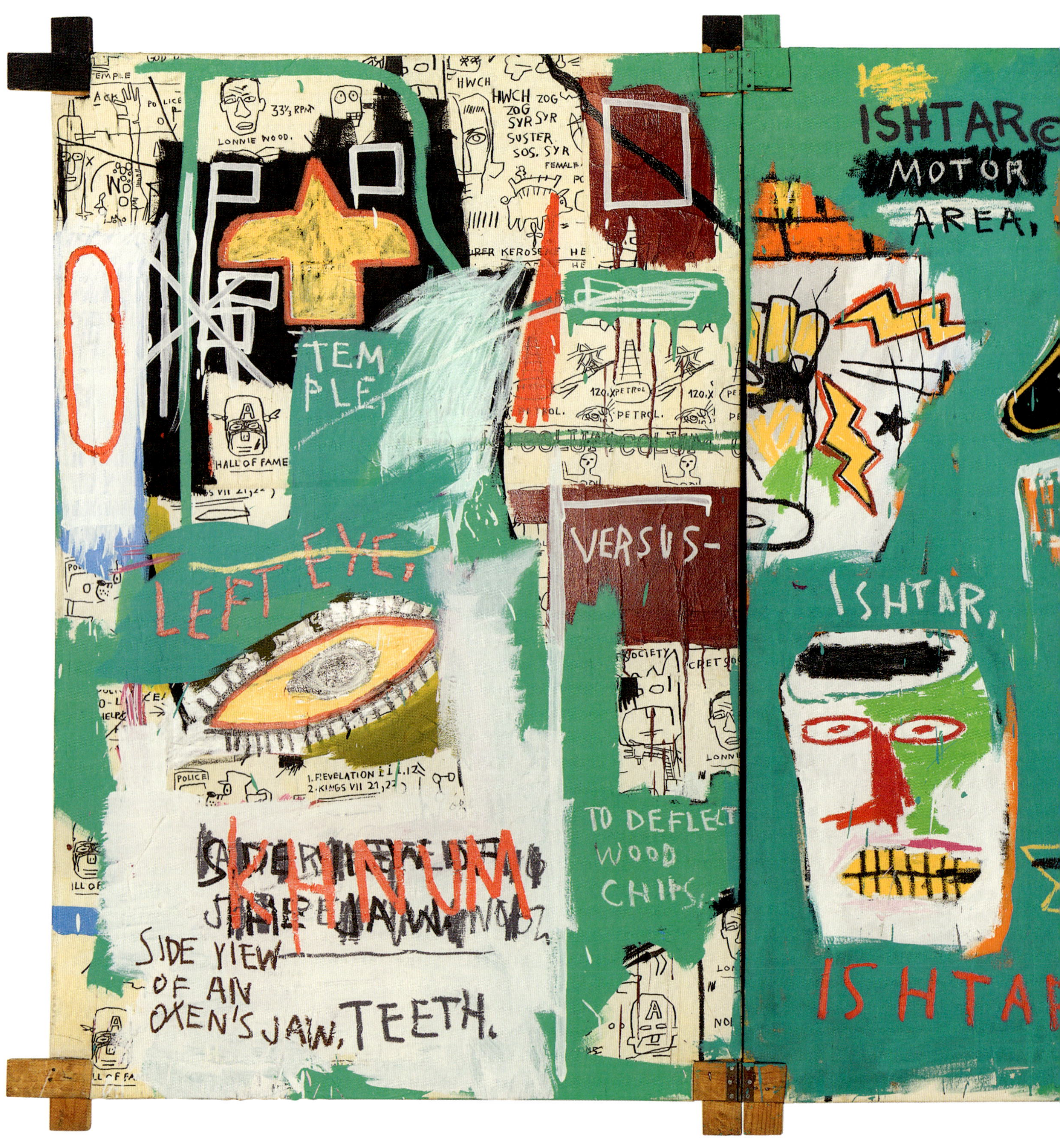

Jean-Michel Basquiat *Ishtar* 1983, synthetic polymer paint, wax crayon and photocopy collage on canvas and wood, 182.9 x 352.0 cm (overall), Collection Ludwig, Ludwig Forum für Internationale Kunst, Aachen

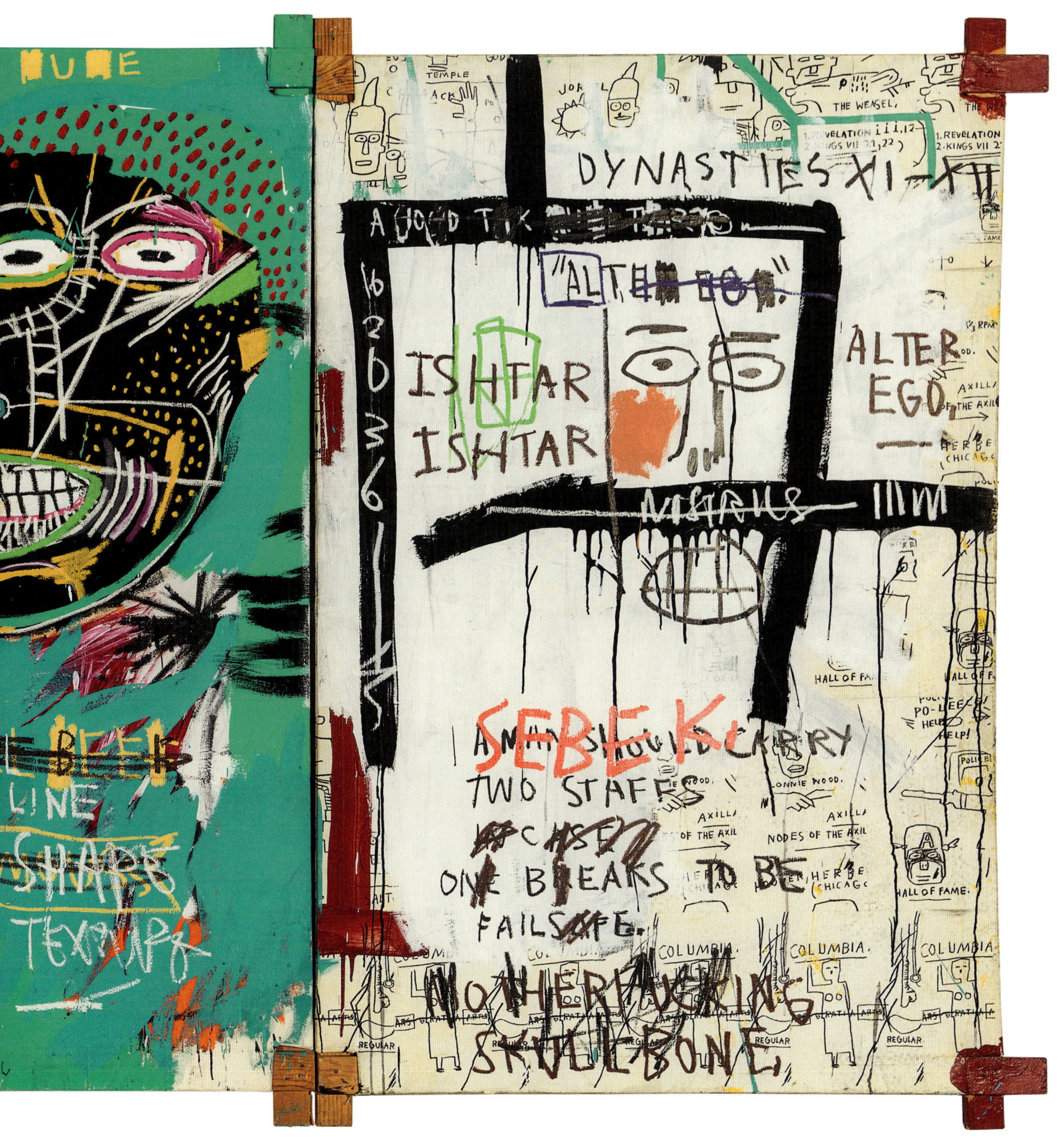
TEMPLE
THE WEASEL
1. REVELATION iii.12
2. KINGS VII 21,22
DYNASTIES XI-XII
ISHTAR
ISHTAR
ALTER
EGO.
AXILLA
HALL OF FAME
SEBEK
CARRY
TWO STAFFS
ONE BREAKS TO BE
FAILSAFE.
RONNIE WOOD.
NODES OF THE AXIL
POLICE
HELP!
COLUMBIA.
REGULAR
SKULLBONE.
LINE

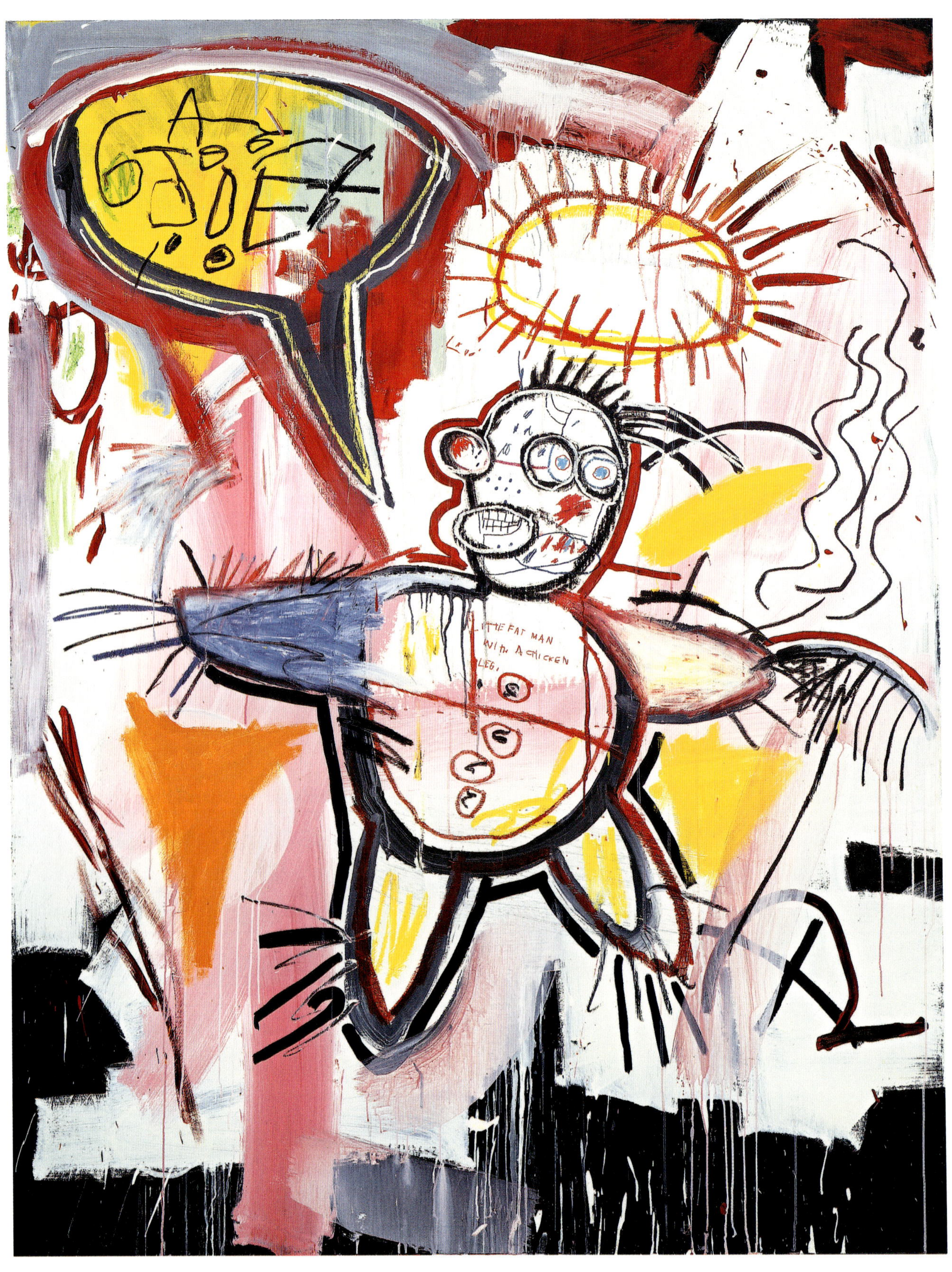

Jean-Michel Basquiat *Donut Revenge* 1982, synthetic polymer paint, oilstick and paper collage on canvas, 243.2 x 182.9 cm, Private collection

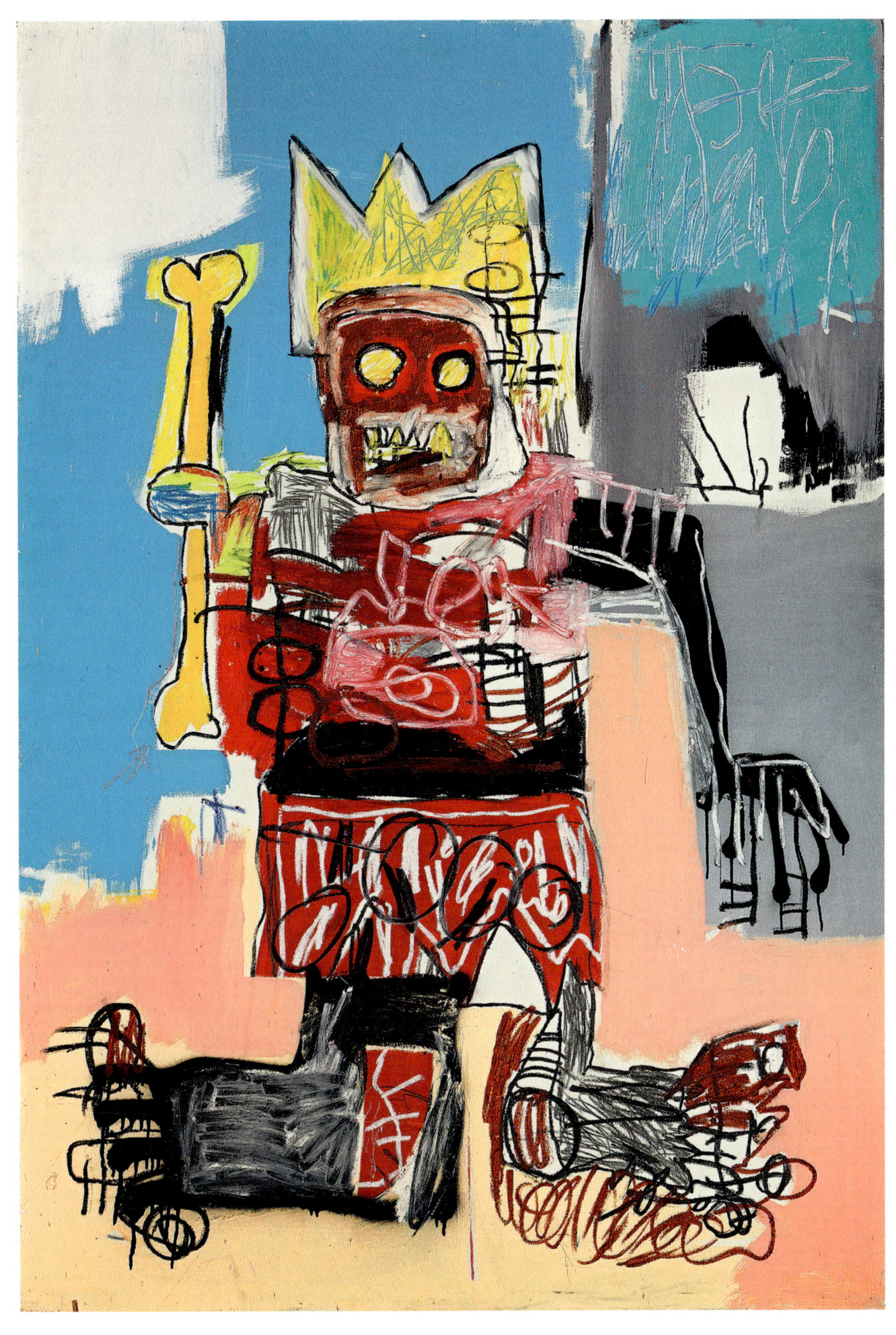

Jean-Michel Basquiat *Untitled* 1982, synthetic polymer paint and oilstick on wood panel, 183.0 x 122.5 cm, Private collection

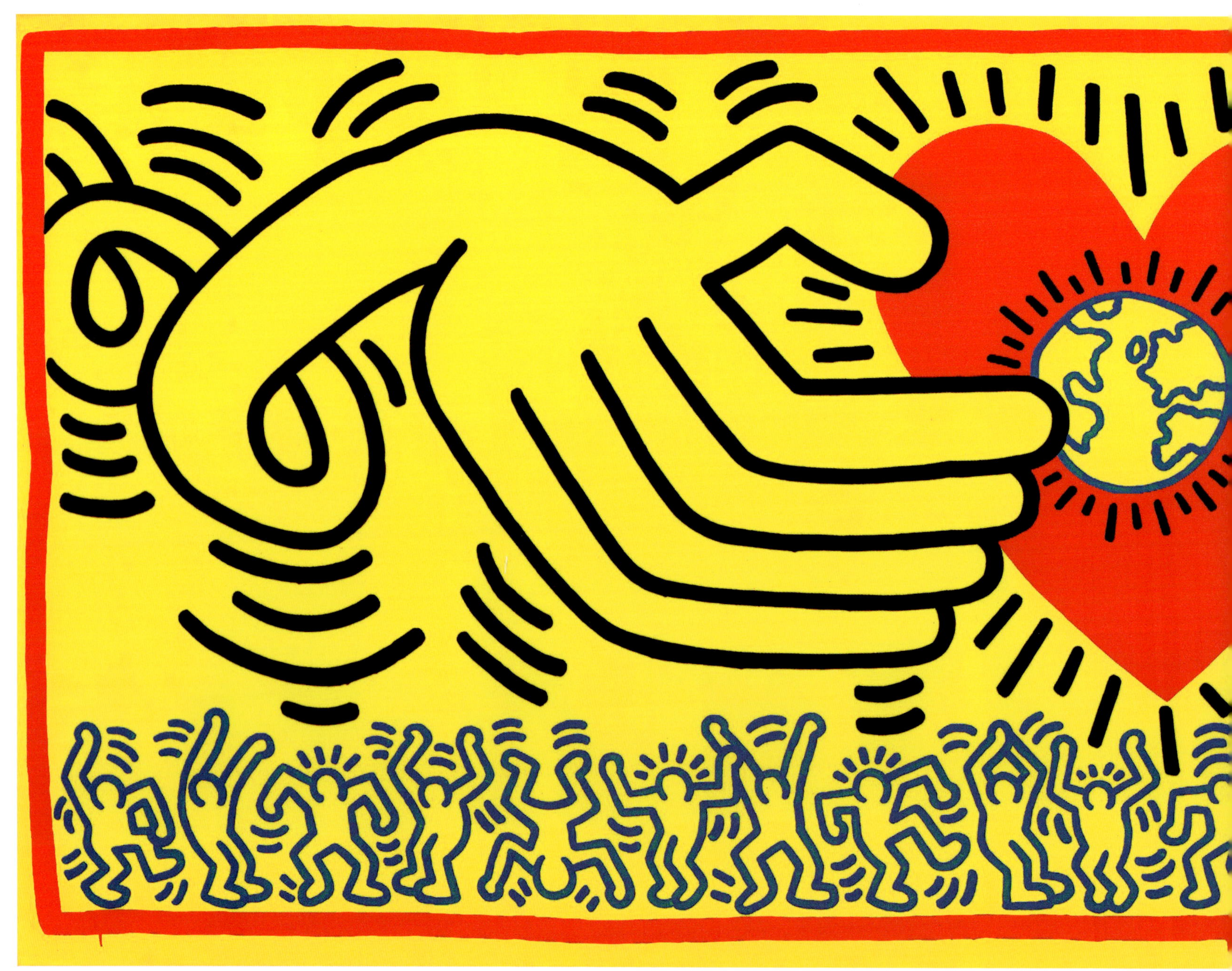

Keith Haring *Untitled* 1985, synthetic polymer paint on canvas, 228.6 x 599.4 cm,
Private collection, Europe, courtesy Martos Gallery, New York

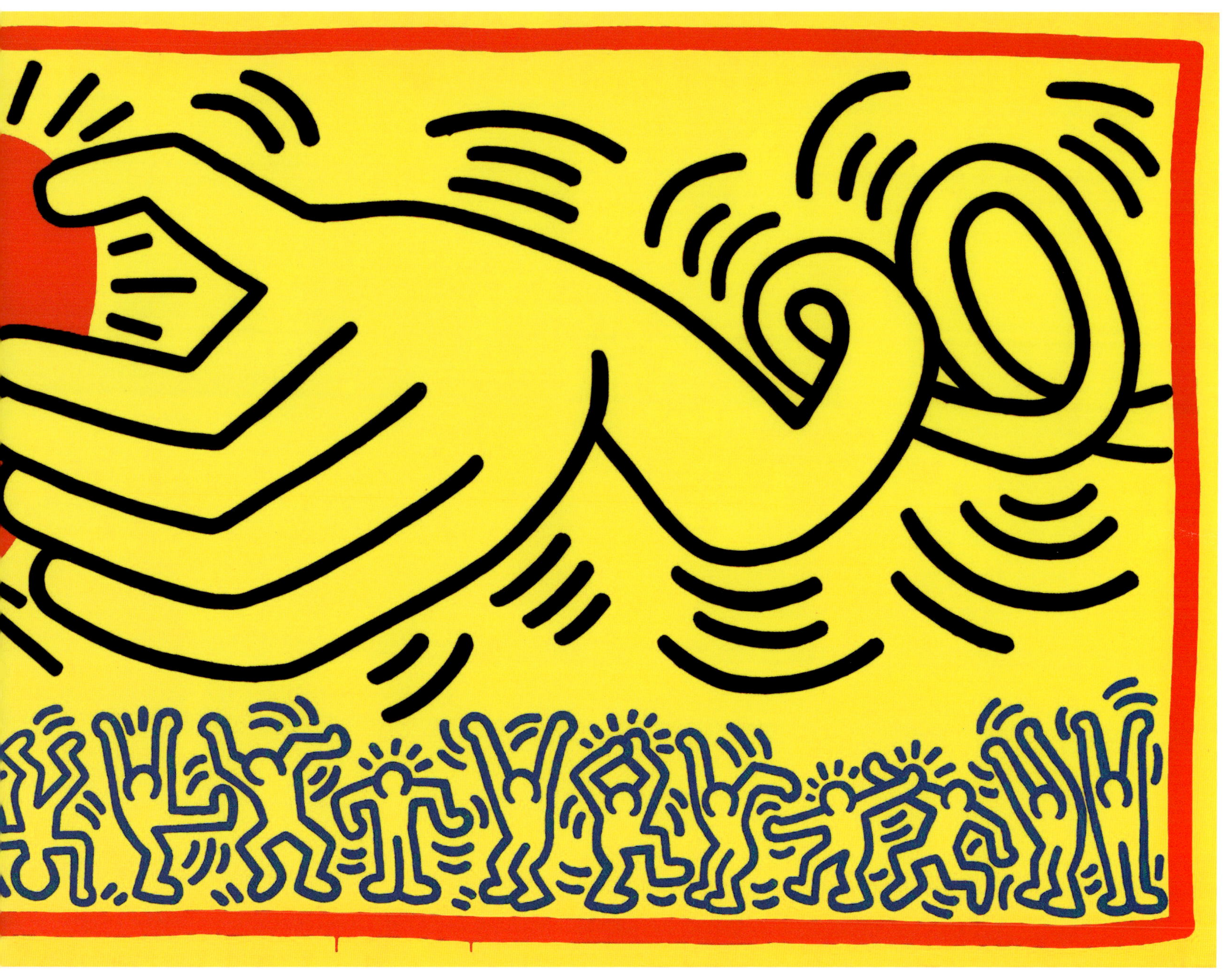

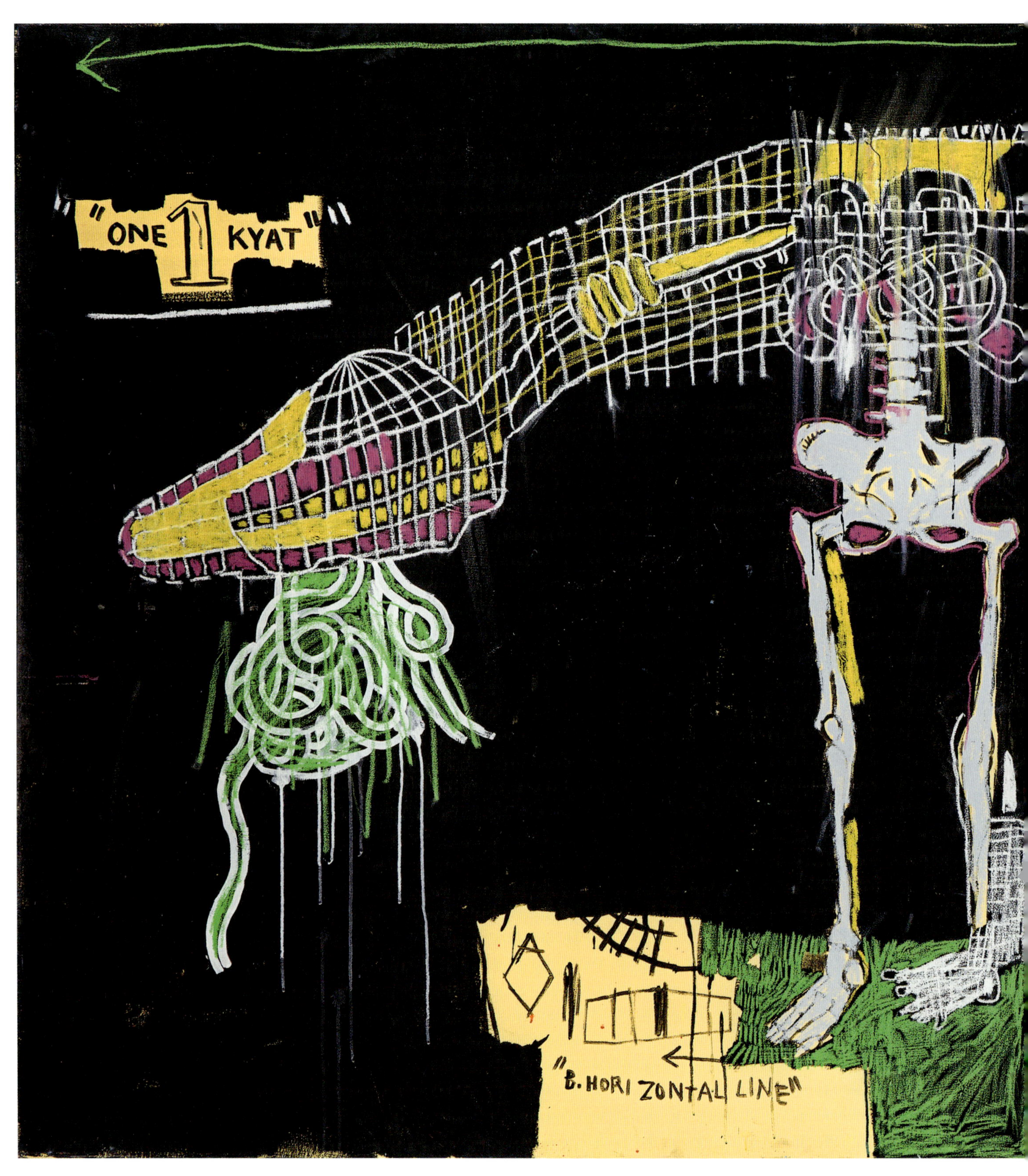

Jean-Michel Basquiat *Grazing - Soup to Nuts - MGM - 1930* 1983, synthetic polymer paint and oilstick on canvas, (a-b) 168.5 x 153.5 cm (each), Collection Ludwig, Ludwig Forum für Internationale Kunst, Aachen

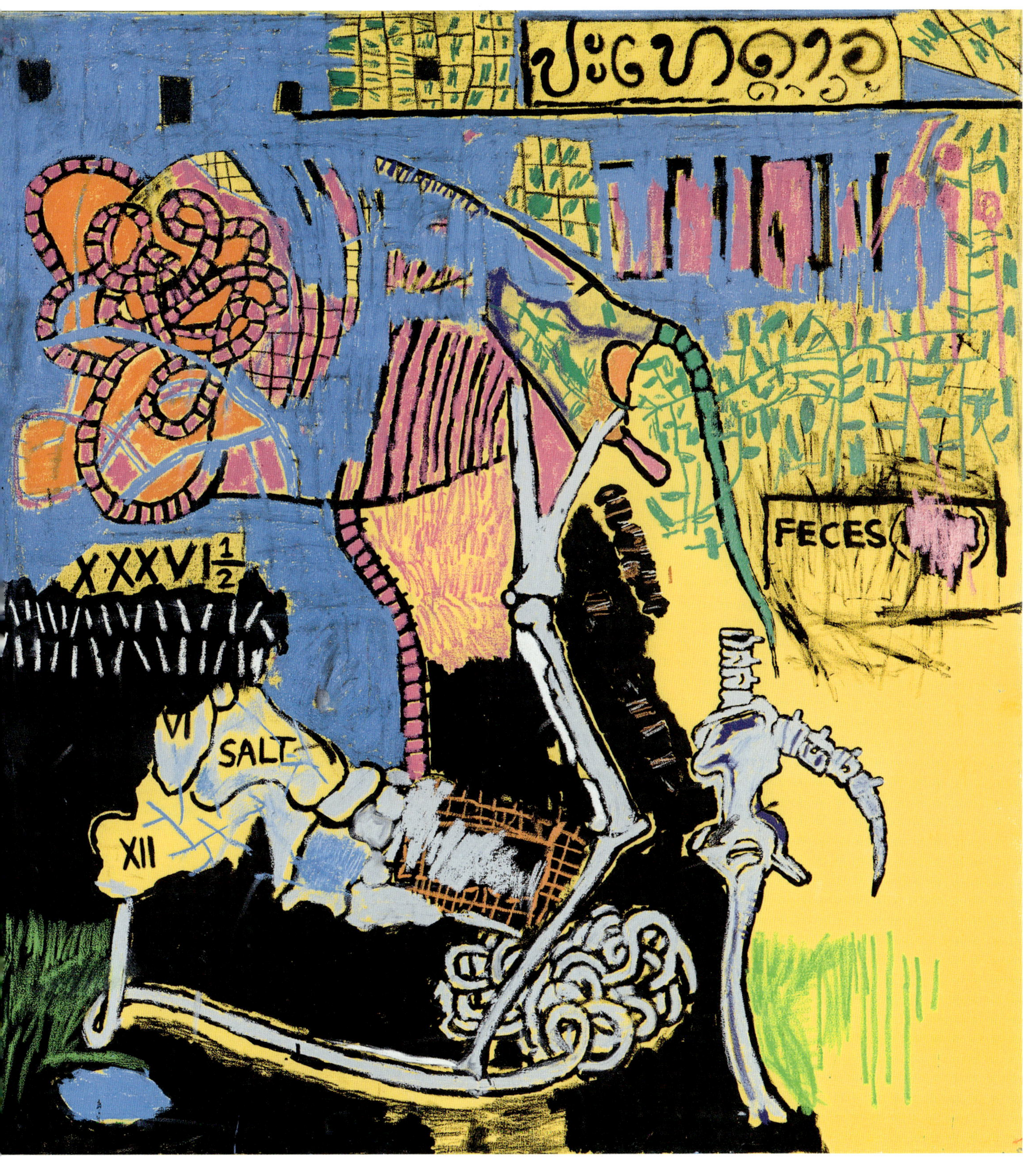
ປະເທດລາວ
XXXVI 1/2
FECES
VI
SALT
XII

In Others' Words: An Oral History of Keith Haring & Jean-Michel Basquiat

Linda Yablonsky

Keith Haring and Jean-Michel Basquiat both moved to Manhattan in 1978, Haring to attend the School of Visual Arts (SVA) and Basquiat to explore the university of the streets. For the rest of their brief, brilliant lives, they moved in parallel, sometimes overlapping, circles. Here, a few of their closest friends and associates vividly recall key moments in the development of their separate but ultimately twinned careers, and offer insight into the personalities of each artist.

Samantha ('Sam') McEwen (artist)
The first morning of my first day at SVA was a drawing class. The teacher had a stack of paper and boards on her desk and she said, 'Okay, everybody! I want you to get a board and a piece of paper, get a chair and go draw someone else in the room'. So, this guy got a board and came right across the classroom, dragging a chair behind him. He sat opposite me and he went, 'Hi, I'm Keith. Can I draw you?'

Very slowly, because I was so shy, we became friends. When I started going out with [artist] Kenny Scharf, Keith was sharing a loft that Kenny was subletting. When the sublet ended, Keith came to my apartment on Broome Street. That's how I really got to know him. We lived together for two or three years. And Jean-Michel came over quite a lot.

Kenny Scharf (artist)
I met Jean-Michel in the cafeteria at SVA. For him, it was a hangout. He wanted to see the portfolio I was holding. I showed him and he said, 'You're gonna be famous'. That was on his mind. We started drawing in the streets together and hanging out. He took me to a place in Chelsea, where he was staying with a guy who had a nice apartment. Jean had some collages and drawings on a wall in the kitchen. I almost fell on the floor. They were so powerful it was like they came off the paper. I'll never forget the feeling.

Tony Shafrazi (artist and art dealer)
I'd done galleries before, in London and Iran, but in 1979, having no other choice, I decided

to transform my apartment into a gallery. The artist Bill Beckley, a friend who was teaching at the School of Visual Arts, sent over two students to paint the walls. One was Keith Haring. While he worked, I noticed that he was remarkably agile. The way he painted was so organised and systematic, efficient and fast, washing all the tools and brushes afterward, laying them on the floor in an orderly fashion. That impressed me no end.

I asked about his art and he gave me a small white card with a drawing, as I remember, of a baby, and some text. It was the invitation to two exhibitions that he'd arranged for himself. One was at PS122, an old school on First Avenue and 9th Street, and the other at Westbeth, the artists' residence on the West Side Highway [both exhibitions took place in 1980].

At PS122, I saw sumi ink drawings on different-sized papers going all the way up to the ceiling in a cartoon-like, fragmented narrative of animated imagery – references to a science-fiction world, renderings of a baby crawling, or some erotica, [images] of gaining or losing power – drawn very quickly and left like that, all over the place. I remember doing a double take. If something is making me react that way, it has something that I have to recognise and respect. Within a year, everyone wanted to represent him.

Sam McEwen
The first time Keith drew figures was in the show at PS122. At art school, everything had been abstract. The drawings didn't have the confidence that he got later. They were sensitive – quite fragile – in a way. The exhibition was completely different from anything he'd done before and anything that anyone else was doing. That was the point where it all took off.

Kai Eric (artist)
In 1979, New York was covered with graffiti. There was one bit – bleak poetry, if you will – that was appearing side by side with the graffiti. That was Jean-Michel and his high school friend Al Diaz's statements as SAMO©. It was this new form of street art that wasn't the classic graffiti but was on the same walls.

One day, I was walking around Tribeca and there was Jean-Michel. He had a can of spray-paint in his hand and was mid statement. He had a mohawk haircut. It came to a point at the front of his head and he was wearing a second-hand overcoat that was the length of a duster.

Sam McEwen
The way Jean-Michel dressed was very strange. He didn't dress like an American. He had this beautiful, sort of Moroccan, hat and a big old wool overcoat. I don't know another guy who could look as good in that kind of coat. At the time, he was a very mysterious figure. Keith was always very open. Jean-Michel was about secrets. He would really lay on the mystery and it was very seductive. He was into being interesting.

Lee Quiñones (artist)
In the spring of 1979, Fred [Brathwaite; Fab 5 Freddy] and I were preparing paintings for our first show, in Rome, in a corner of the studio of Stan Peskett, a British artist who set up in a ginormous loft and put together posh, wild parties. Jean was sleeping on a sofa there, and Fred was in and out of his parents' home in Brooklyn and mine on the Lower East Side, kind of establishing a base camp, of sorts, to set off our ideas. For one of Stan's parties, we all ended up painting huge drop cloths together, 12 feet high by 15 feet long. They showcased Jean's work, probably for the first time.

I painted a background loosely referencing subway cars that I'd done several years before. It was a caricature of a train trucking to music. Then Jean would come up and

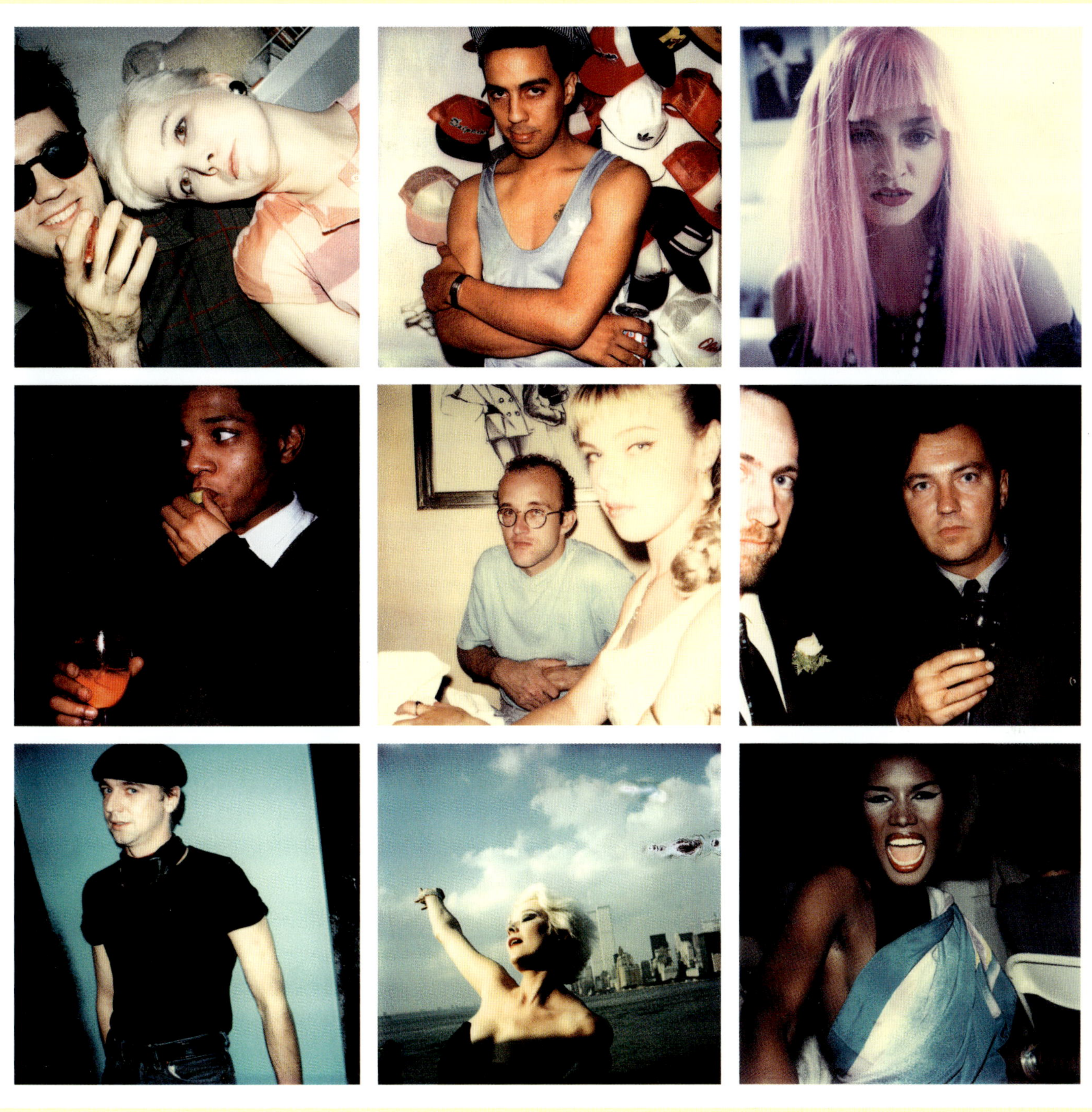

Polaroids taken by Maripol between 1976 and 1992, in New York, Los Angeles, and Tokyo
(top, left to right) Diego Cortez and Patti Astor, Futura 2000, Madonna
(middle, left to right) Jean-Michel Basquiat, Keith Haring and Debi Mazar, Kenny Scharf and Diego Cortez
(bottom, left to right) Rene Ricard, Patti Astor, Grace Jones

paint on top of that. I wasn't too happy about it, because in graffiti subculture it's sacrilegious to paint over someone else's work.

Jean was trying to discover what he was, what his work meant to him. It was a very difficult transitional stage for all three of us. We were like a tripod, leaning on each other for advice and recognition, and some sort of support. That's when Jean started doing his postcard pieces. It was almost at the end of the SAMO© campaign, when Al Diaz disappeared from the scene and Jean was writing 'SAMO© is dead'.

Diego Cortez (curator, agent)
Jean was at the Mudd Club when it opened, in the fall of 1979, when I was starting to research *New York/New Wave* for P.S. 1. I didn't see his SAMO© graffiti until the summer of 1980, when I started working with him as an agent, selling his works to collectors, and in February of 1981, I put him in *New York/New Wave*. I met Keith a year before the show's opening, but not through Jean. Jonny Rudo [Jon Rudowitz], an SVA student, took me to Keith's East Village apartment. Jon also told me about Kenny. I included both of them in my show. And I started hanging out at Club 57, which I thought was really ingenious.

Kenny Scharf
[Performance artist] John Sex, Keith and I had wandered into Club 57, in the basement of a church on St Marks Place. It was during the daytime. No one was in there, so we put a nickel in the jukebox and started dancing. All of a sudden [actor and comedian] Ann Magnuson comes out of nowhere and starts dancing with us. She had been to a show I did at Fiorucci with [vocalist] Klaus Nomi. And she said, 'Hey, you want to do some stuff here?' I did *Celebration of the Space Age*, where we were serving Tang and Space Food Sticks, and I had these paintings that I made in school out of Hostess snowballs. Keith was in the club every night. Jean-Michel came, but he wasn't a regular.

Diego Cortez
There was a kind of division between Club 57 and the Mudd Club, but then Fred [Brathwaite; Fab 5 Freddy] curated a graffiti show at the Mudd, *Beyond Words*, and Keith curated a drawing show. But they all had their own social circles.

Suzanne Mallouk
(former artist now psychotherapist)
I think Jean felt both superior and jealous of all those SVA artists, like Kenny and Keith, and the Club 57 people, because he had no money to go to art school and he was estranged from his family. He often told me art school 'ruined my eyes' and the eyes of all these Club 57 people. He believed that, but he also wished he could've gone. He had a fragile ego.

Sam McEwen
Club 57 was like a little family. Everyone was sleeping with each other, or in love with each other. Keith did a couple of amazing performances there. One was in Morse code. He was trying to work out if there was another way to communicate with people, apart from going up and talking to them. He was blocking out letters on subway ads, like one for Chardon jeans – a crotch shot of some guy in a pair of jeans. Keith blocked out the 'C' with a marker, so it said 'hardon'. It was really funny.

Kenny Scharf
At SVA, Keith was doing his kind of [artist Jean] Dubuffet rooms, painting himself into corners, with music, and studying semiotics. But in the summer of 1980, when Keith was doing his chalk drawings in the subway, we left school and were living together in a loft on Sixth Avenue, near Bryant Park, close

to Times Square. John Ahearn [artist and co-organiser of seminal 1980 exhibition the *Times Square Show*] had seen *Celebration of the Space Age* and invited me to the *Times Square Show*, and I just brought Keith and Jean with me. That's how they got into the show and that's where Keith met all the graffiti guys.

Fred Brathwaite (aka Fab 5 Freddy, artist)
At the opening party of the *Times Square Show*, I pitched the idea that became [hip-hop film] *Wild Style* to [director] Charlie Ahearn. He was like, 'Come back. Bring Lee Quiñones. I want to put you in the show'. So, I came back with Lee. We went up and installed these two paintings I had. This guy comes in and he goes, 'You guys should know Fred and Lee from the Fab 5. These guys are some of the most important graffiti people'. We're thinking, 'Is this a joke?' Then John Ahearn walks in, and he goes, 'Fred, Lee, are you happy with the installation?' And Keith flushes deep red, super embarrassed. He laughs. Me and Lee crack up. And that's how we meet and become really good friends.

Lee Quiñones
Shortly after that I introduced Keith to the concept of painting the walls of handball courts. The first one I did was a completely rendered caricature of Howard the Duck, 25 feet high by 30 feet long. Keith came and said, 'How did you do that?' I said, 'You get a ladder'. And he said, 'Oh!' Then he asked me about the double handball court at the corner of Bowery and Houston Street. He said, 'Do I have your permission to paint that wall?' 'Keith, it's not my wall. Get a ladder, and get some balls, and go up there!'

Fred Brathwaite
Keith hadn't figured out the crawling baby yet. His work at that time was inspired by [Belgian artist] Pierre Alechinsky's, whom he talked about a lot. He was fascinated by the graffiti scene, just enthralled. He wanted to be part of it, but he didn't want to be a white guy exercising what we now know as white privilege.

Sam McEwen
I don't know what Jean-Michel thought about being a black guy in a white world, but I do know that Keith found it enormously intimidating to be a white guy in the black or Hispanic graffiti world. He so wanted to participate, but he needed a tag, something he was prepared to repeat, so that everybody would read him. And SAMO© gave him the idea that he could, because that one tag was entirely different from the graffiti culture. He talked about whether the baby would be accepted, or if somebody would draw on top of it. That was how you could tell whether you were being allowed to participate. I mean, who was he to come and start drawing in this world, some white boy from Pennsylvania at art school?

Kai Eric
One night, Jean came into Club 57 with Suzanne Mallouk, a very pale, red-lipped beauty, on his arm. He asked if I'd be interested in buying one of his drawings. He had ten or fifteen there, and unfurled them. One was *Famous Negro Athletes* [1981]. I said, 'How much?' And he said, 'Ten dollars apiece'. I said, 'Jean, there's no way I'm going to pay you ten dollars for one of these drawings'. He looked crestfallen. 'I'm going to give you twenty-five dollars.' He was smiling. What he did was give me four. And we became very good friends.

Suzanne Mallouk
I met Jean early in 1981. He was living in the storefront that was the production office for the filming of *Downtown 81*, and he would come into Nightbirds, the bar on Second Avenue, where I was working days, and he would lean against the jukebox and just stare

(overleaf) Andy Warhol *Jean-Michel Basquiat, Little Angel (LA II), Keith Haring and Kenny Scharf* 1984, gelatin silver print, 20.3 x 25.4 cm, The Andy Warhol Foundation for the Visual Arts, New York

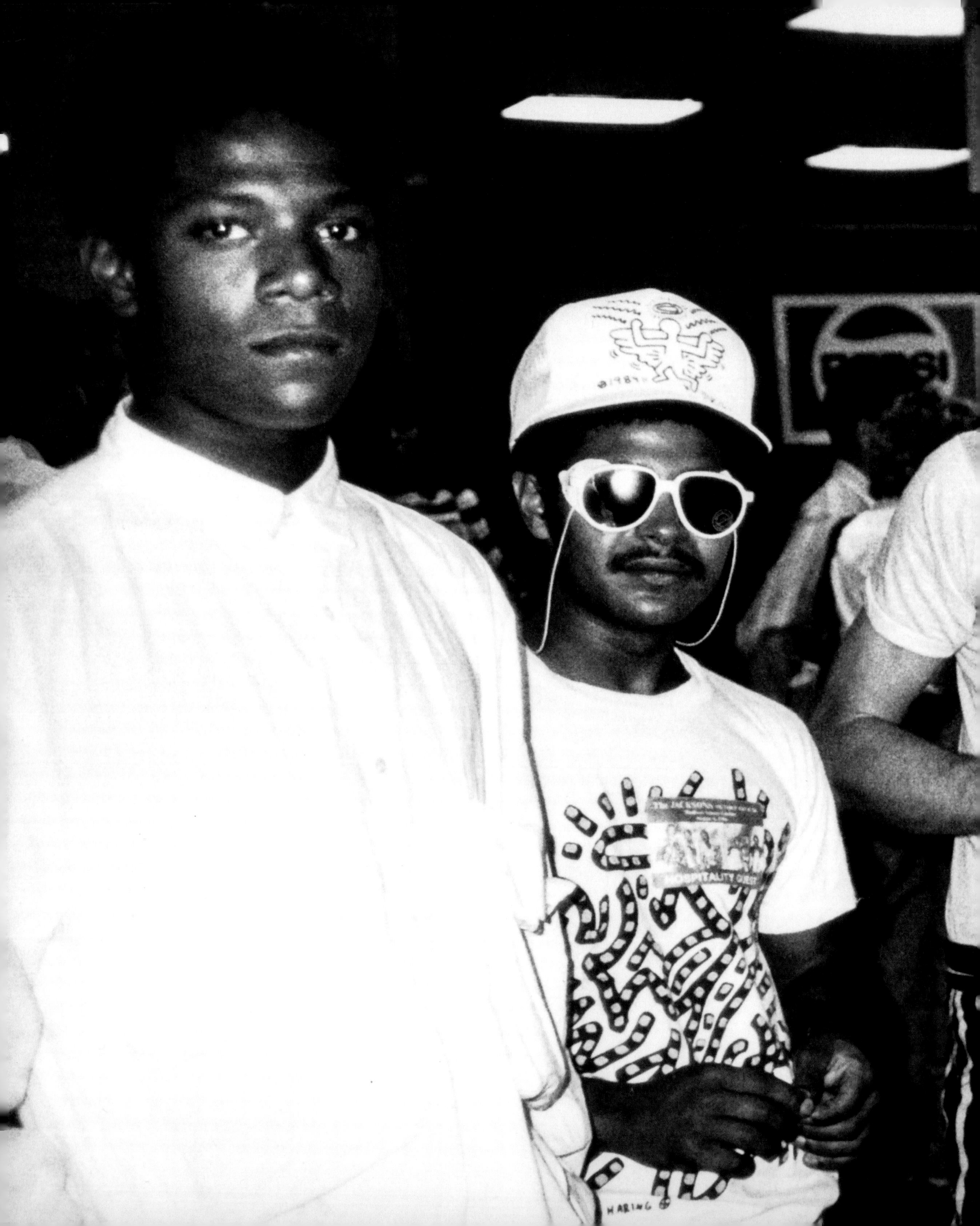
HARING

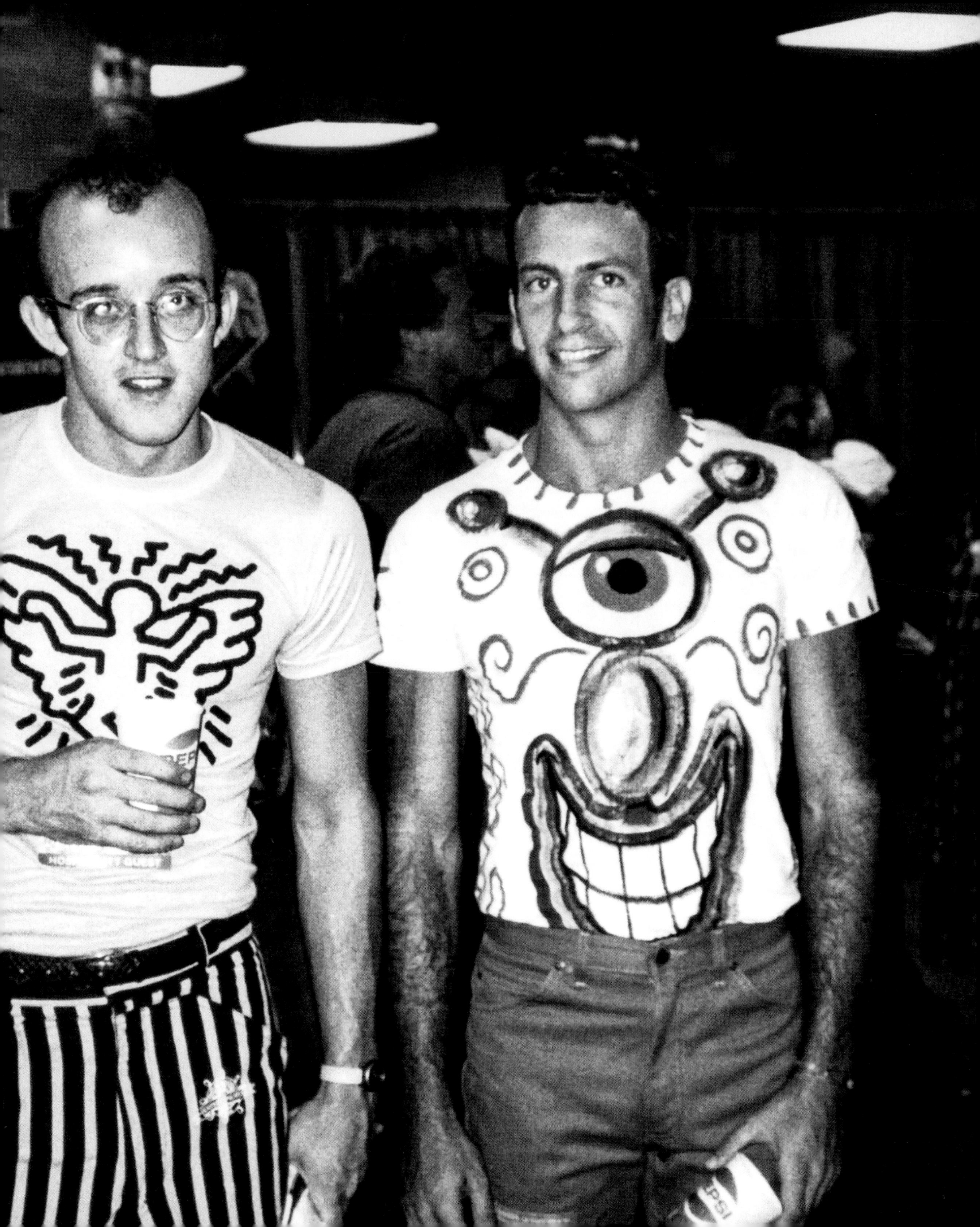

at me, and not talk. He did that for about a month. Finally, when he had a bit of money, he would come up to the bar and pay with coins. The first time, he was writing poetry in black-and-white notebooks and when he read the poetry to me, I realised, 'Oh my God, you're SAMO©!' And he said, 'Yes, but SAMO© is dead'.

At that point, he was starting to paint and not do street art. He felt it would be better for him to break away from the graffiti artists. He really struggled to let them know his SAMO© was like high-end poetry and sociopolitical commentary, not graffiti art. Plus, he didn't think graffiti art was fine art. He was very conflicted about that, but he needed to be seen as a legitimate artist.

One day, he came into the bar, excited. He had sold his first painting, probably for $200. He told me that Glenn O'Brien had sold it to [Blondie's] Debbie Harry and he took me out for dinner at a Chinese restaurant, which was such a treat for us. Two weeks later, he moved into my apartment, because he was homeless, living from place to place. It's not like I invited him. He just moved in.

Jeffrey Deitch (curator, art dealer)
I believe that I was the first person ever to buy work by Jean-Michel. I bought five drawings off the floor of Suzanne Mallouk's apartment. I paid fifty dollars a drawing. This was when Diego [Cortez] was handling things. And very early on, I bought wonderful works from Keith, marker on red plastic – classic Keith images of barking dogs and dancing dogs. I still have them all.

Suzanne Mallouk
We lived together off and on, in apartments all over 1st Street, in the Algonquin Hotel, in friends' apartments and then I moved to 101 Crosby Street with Jean. Brett De Palma was over at 101 Crosby a lot.

Brett De Palma (artist)
Diego introduced me to Jean-Michel at the opening of *New York/New Wave*, which I was in. I already knew Keith from the club scene and had seen his things over in Westbeth, early scroll pieces where he would paint on the floor. And everybody went to Keith's parties, where everything was red – the floor, the furniture, a Coke machine. Sometimes Jean would come to my loft and sleep on the couch or do drawings like he did everywhere, with everybody. He'd just leave things there. Both Keith and Jean gifted so many of us with their work. Keith painted a crib for our son when he was born and Jean left me a portrait of me as a negro that he did in [gallerist] Annina Nosei's basement. I was working at a gallery in Soho when Jean first got his studio there and I would go over and hang out with him, and later at Crosby Street, but everybody came to that basement. He was really cranking, producing really rapidly, and Annina was selling work right off the rack.

Tony Shafrazi
In 1981, I rented a space in Soho. Because the place was not ready, I got Keith a show in Holland [for 1982]. When he came back, in response to my suggestion to try making paintings, he discovered the tarpaulins that are used to cover trucks, which he could stitch with grommets to any size he wanted. These were twelve and ten feet tall. He also found an industrial paint he felt was perfect for the tarp. I had rolls of photographer's seamless paper, about seven or eight feet wide, and when Keith saw this paper he started using it to make large sumi ink drawings up to thirty feet long.

He didn't have room in his studio, so he worked in the basement of the gallery, maybe even before Jean-Michel was in the basement at Annina Nosei's. It had water on the floor and no heat. But nothing would stop this guy! We got ready to do his first big, one-man show, with a big beautiful pink catalogue, itself a work of art.

The show opened in the summer of 1982. The basement was a black light room, with artworks in fluorescent, day-glo colours. Upstairs were the tarpaulin paintings and lots of works on paper that were mounted all the way to the ceiling. A huge production. Nobody had done anything like that before. It was a blockbuster show, a real revolution in art. Everybody talked about it. Everyone came to the opening. Most people were out in the street, because there was no room to go inside, where there was a cool DJ, break-dancers and the smell of sweet ganja. The party went on till 7 am.

Fred Brathwaite

It was coincidental that Keith and Jean both were working in basements. When you hear basement, you think dark, dank cellar. Annina's basement was not that. It had windows, a lot of sunlight. The way people would talk about this young, wild black man that Annina Nosei has chained in the basement of her gallery was ignorant racism. I was one of the people that emphatically told Jean, 'You have to get out of here'.

Suzanne Mallouk

I remember one night when Jean went on a rant about the way white people in the art world regarded him as their black mascot. It caused him anguish. He did not want to be tokenised for his blackness. He couldn't get out of bed because of this issue.

Fred Brathwaite

A young black man making art? It took a while for people to get it. Very few in the art world had any sense of what was really going on. Keith never claimed to be a graffiti artist, nor did Jean, nor did I. But the press made that what we were – wild savages spray-painting everything. That was the general tone. There was no understanding of us in the context of art history, outside of our inner circle. Keith would often speak up to defend us, because he had an inherent understanding of the ways racism works.

Brett De Palma

When Larry Gagosian gave Jean his first show in LA, it pulled Jean a little bit away from Annina and he got pissed at Annina. He claimed she was selling things before they were done. That's when [art dealer and gallerist] Bruno Bischofberger moved on Jean-Michel and said, 'I can get you into Mary Boone [Gallery]. You want to go to Mary Boone?' Jean was like, 'Yeah. Yeah, let's go'.

Jean always could burn bridges and somehow have another platform to land on that was a step up.

Diego Cortez

Initially, after seeing the P.S. 1 show, Bruno Bischofberger wasn't interested in Jean. Neither was Annina Nosei. But then I organised Jean's first solo gallery show with Emilio Mazzoli [gallery] in Modena, Italy. Mazzoli scheduled it for May 1981 under the name SAMO© and it sold out.

Kai Eric

A team of people set up canvases in a hangar at the local airport in Modena and Jean got to work. He churned out at least eight major canvases in a month. Emilio Mazzoli paid him in cash. I think he had close to $200,000. Jean said, 'I think we should divide it up'. When we got to the airport, I raced off to return the car, and when I walked into the terminal, Jean was standing there in his paint-splattered overcoat and paint-splattered fishing cap, with his dread-locks coming from underneath, and Suzanne, the punk-chic ingenue, by his side. On either side of them were two Italian police holding submachine guns.

We were taken to the bowels of the airport, where the baggage comes in. Jean's luggage consisted of cardboard boxes that he wrapped with rope and tied with a bow. This is the way he packed. He threw in a couple of shirts. He threw in a bunch of cassettes. He threw in a beatbox and what looked like dirty laundry. It was a mess.

Suzanne Mallouk
We had money hidden all over us. I had it in the toes of my cowboy boots. I put it in my hair and teased my hair into a beehive hairdo. Jean had dreadlocks and looked crazy, and they searched us, and found the money. They thought we were drug dealers and they questioned us for hours. Emilio Mazzoli had to open a Swiss bank account for Jean, because we could not take all of that money out of the country.

Diego Cortez
Keith also had asked me to be his agent, but the interpersonal relationship between us fizzled. I never sold one piece by him. Then Jean joined Annina Nosei and when he left Annina in late spring of 1982, he asked me to be his agent again. And I said, 'No, Bruno Bischofberger wants to represent you'. Three days later Jean was with Bruno, who wanted to cancel Jean's Fun Gallery show, but it was already in the works and it ended up being the best work he ever did.

Bill Stelling (co-founder of Fun Gallery)
I think the reason Jean-Michel wanted to show at Fun was to establish his street cred, whereas Keith always had street cred. Jean-Michel had his show before Keith, in 1982. Keith's show was in February of 1983. [Keith and LA II] spray-painted the entire gallery – literally bombed the entire inside of the gallery with graffiti – the works 'on top' were on animal hides – and [Keith] placed his artwork on top of that, but instead of doing the lines in black and white, he did them in colour. Every day there would be forty young graffiti artists from the ages of ten to eighteen hanging out in the gallery, smoking pot and chewing grape-flavoured bubblegum. That's what I remember: the gallery smelling like bubblegum and marijuana.

Kenny Scharf
Patti Astor [co-founder of Fun Gallery] had seen one of my shows at Club 57 and told me that she had a space and did I want a show there. Of course, I did. I did a whole display in the window and named the gallery Fun. It was supposed to change with each artist, but it stayed. The gallery was great, because these graffiti kids didn't really have anywhere to go and all of a sudden there's this major cultural thing and people were coming from all over.

Jeffrey Deitch
This super success happened after the Fun Gallery shows, with Jean-Michel going with Bruno Bischofberger in St Moritz and Yvon Lambert [Gallery] in Paris. I went to a lot of Keith's shows in Europe, too. One, in Bordeaux, was a giant event. All the cool people from Paris came; Helmut Newton took a group photograph. Jacques Chaban-Delmas, the mayor of Bordeaux and former prime minister, was there and [banking family] the Rothschilds gave an incredible lunch at their chateau. I'd never experienced anything like this.

Sam McEwen
I don't think success affected Keith at all. I think he made some quite good friends in Europe and I think probably the biggest change was that he stepped out of the East Village and became somebody in the world.

Brett De Palma
I remember when Jean had Bruno Bischofberger and Mary Boone over to Crosby Street for lunch. He put two eels that weren't dressed on a platter with two carved tomatoes between them. In walked Bruno with Mary and Jean goes, 'Snakes for snakes'. I thought, 'Oh, my God'. But they got the message: put your money where your mouth is.

Suzanne Mallouk
When [African-American graffiti artist] Michael Stewart died [at the hands of the police] in 1983, I asked Jean to donate money for the legal defence fund that I had set up and he wouldn't do it. He was very careful to distance himself from these causes, particularly racially motivated police violence. Keith, being white, could do radical social work, particularly with [activist group organised by artists and writers] ACT UP and it wouldn't hurt his career. It would help.

Diego Cortez
I really loved Keith's aesthetic, which was different from Jean-Michel's, in terms of his engaging the community. Jean-Michel applied a graffiti mentality to the art world. But he was a studio artist, and private. Even though his subject matter supplied racial themes, he never talked about race or sociological matters in our conversations. Keith had more social consciousness built into his work. He was a brilliant public artist. Keith's isn't even all public art, but his work ended up serving a very public function with regard to gay culture, AIDS and black culture.

Kenny Scharf
We were super close, but there was a period where Jean-Michel did some crazy, sabotage-y stuff to me, like rip paintings off walls. Before he died, he apologised. He said, 'I'm sorry'. And I said, 'Why have you been this way?' It tormented me. And this is what really broke my heart. He said, 'It's because you're happy'. It was very emotional, our relationship.

Brett De Palma
Keith was much more an activist and wanted to organise. Jean-Michel had no interest in organising. He was more a social genius.

Both Keith and Jean changed my life, and so much for the better. They were artists who believed in their own independent vision. Both were intuitive. The genius just flows from someplace, the subconscious, or from the atmosphere of information that's in the universe. They both picked up on it and were able to translate it so that a massive audience could look at their work and go, 'Yeah, I recognise that. I don't know why'. It has the ring of the familiar, but it's very different and singular. They did something that was really very difficult to do and they made it look easy.

Kenny Scharf
I was with Keith on his deathbed. He couldn't talk, and he was really agitated. He was shaking. I held his hand and I said, 'Look, I know that you can hear me. You have to just let go and surrender'. I told him, 'Your legacy is so strong and it's just going to keep going and you've done a major thing'. All of a sudden his whole body relaxed. Then I left the room and he was gone an hour later.

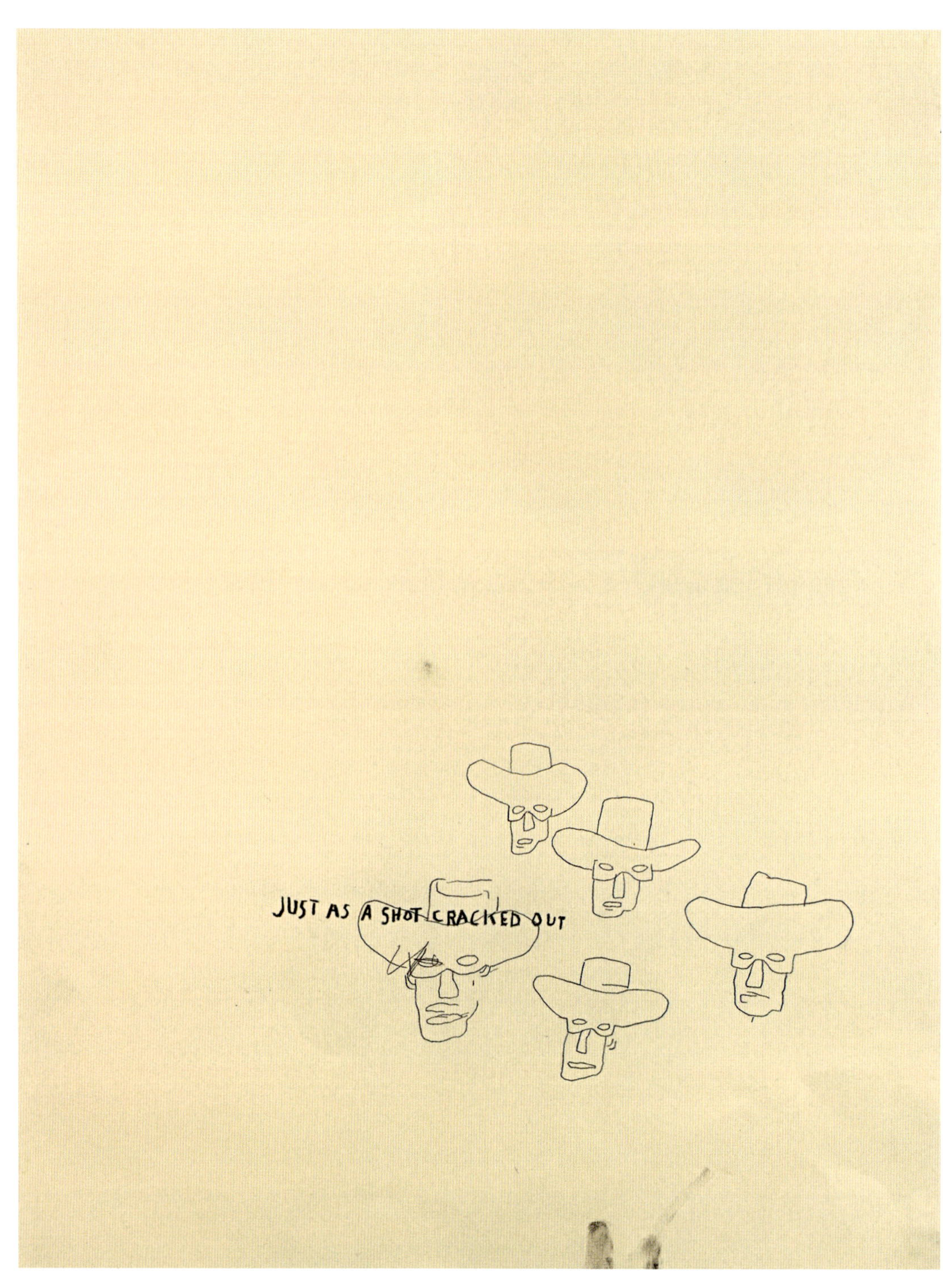

Jean-Michel Basquiat *Just as a Shot Cracked Out* 1981, pencil and oilstick on paper, 76.0 x 56.0 cm,
Collection of Diego de Noirmont

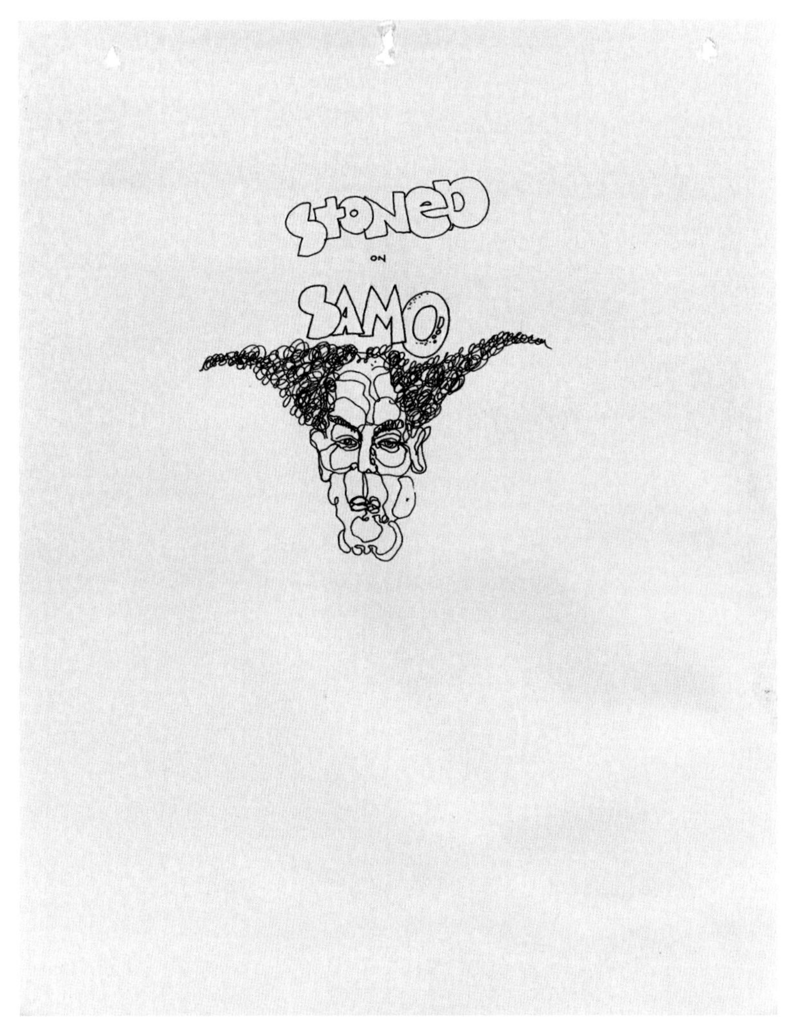

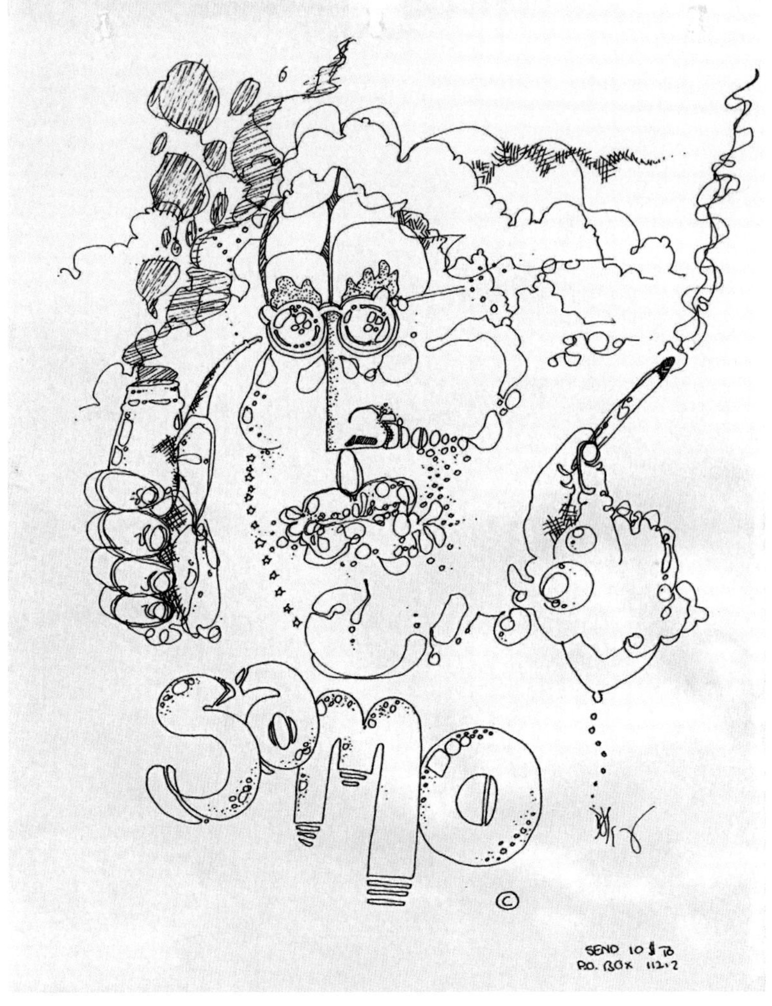

(above left) Jean-Michel Basquiat *Stoned on Samo* 1978, ink on paper, 30.5 x 22.9 cm,
Collection of Emmanuelle and Jérôme de Noirmont
(above right) Jean-Michel Basquiat *Samo* 1978, ink on paper, 30.5 x 22.9 cm,
Collection of Emmanuelle and Jérôme de Noirmont

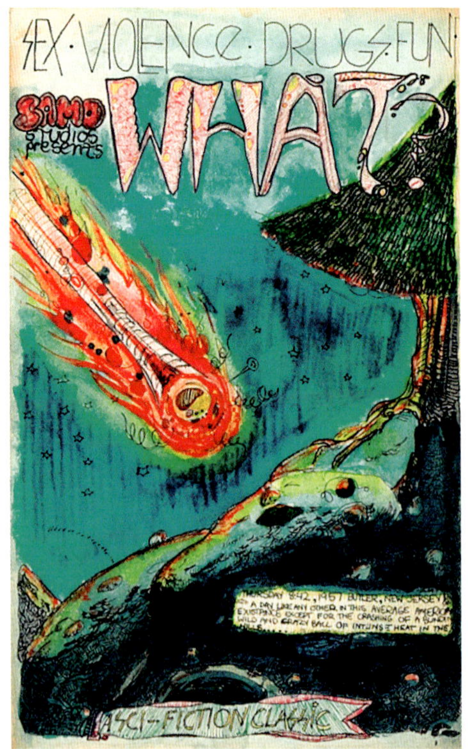

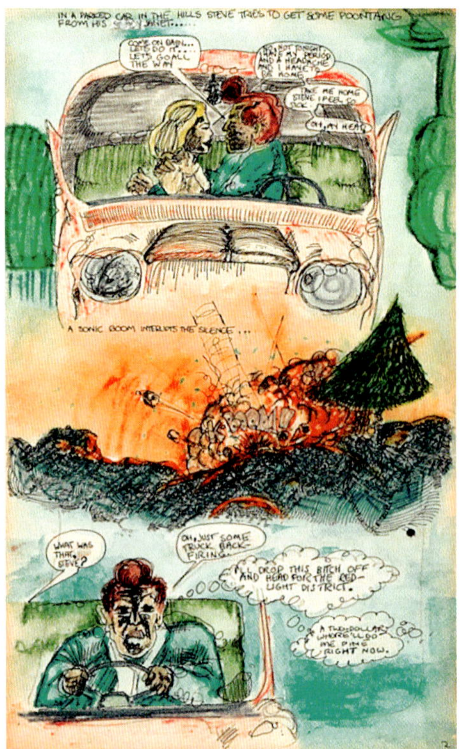

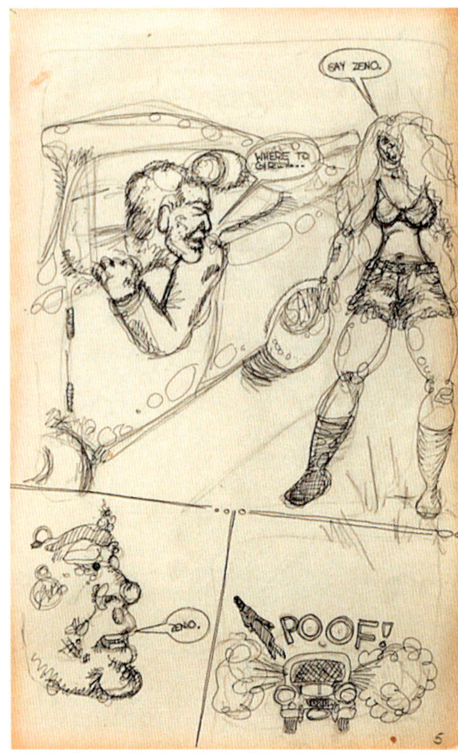

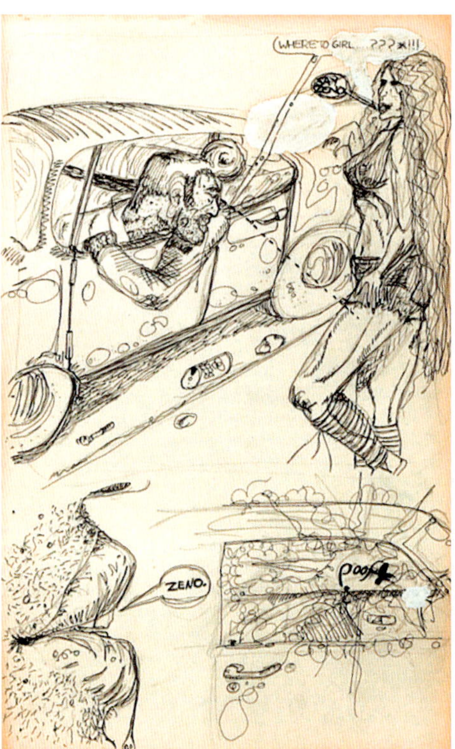

Jean-Michel Basquiat *The Comic Book* 1978, watercolour, ink and pencil on paper, (a–h) 35.6 x 21.6 cm (each), Private collection

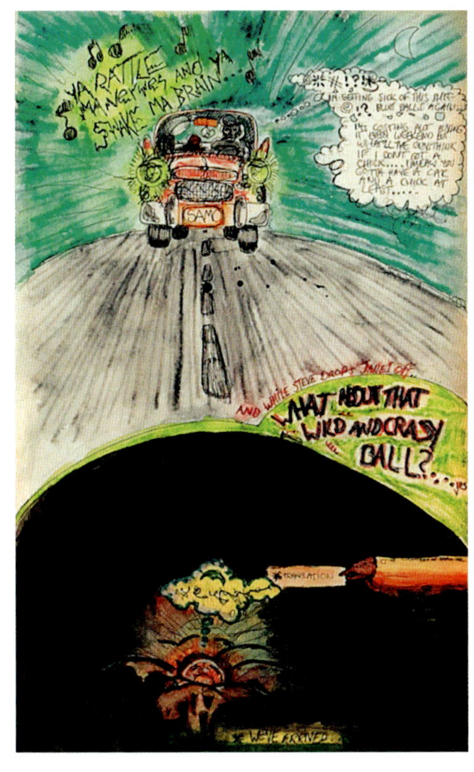
YA RATTLE MA NERVES AND YA SHAKE MA BRAIN....
BLUE BALLS AGAIN
IF I DONT GOT A CHICK.... I MEAN YOU GOTTA HAVE A CAR AND A CHICK AT LEAST.....
SAMO
AND WHILE STEVE DROPS JULIET OFF
WHAT ABOUT THAT WILD AND CRAZY BALL?....
TRANSLATION
WE'VE ARRIVED

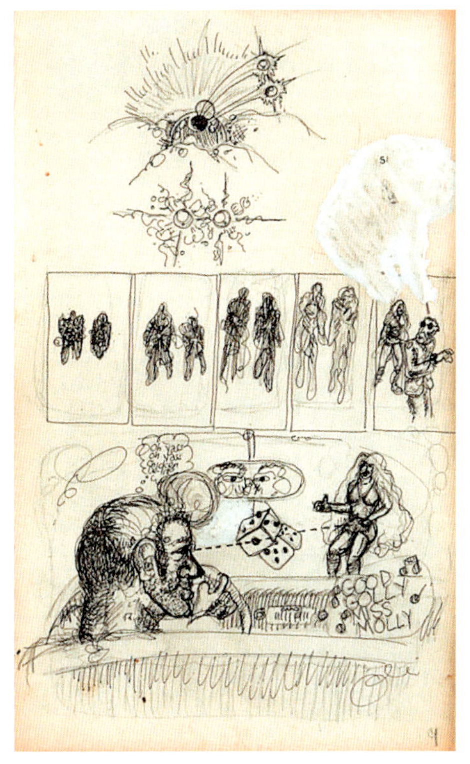
GOOD GOLLY MISS MOLLY

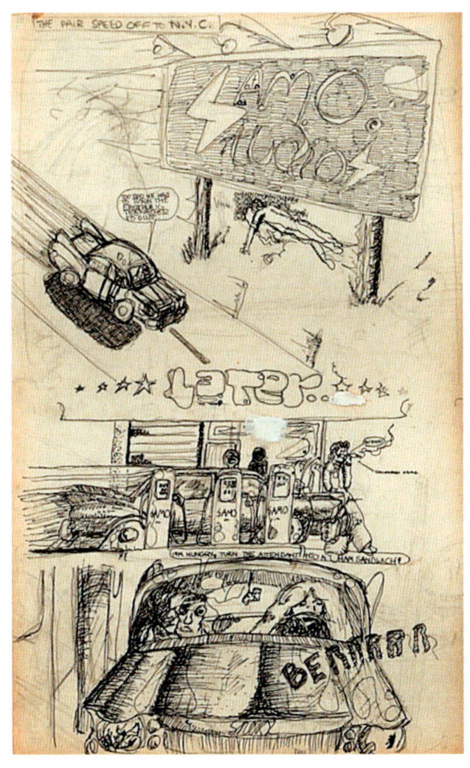
THE PAIR SPEED OFF TO N.Y.C.
later..
SAMO
SAMO
SAMO

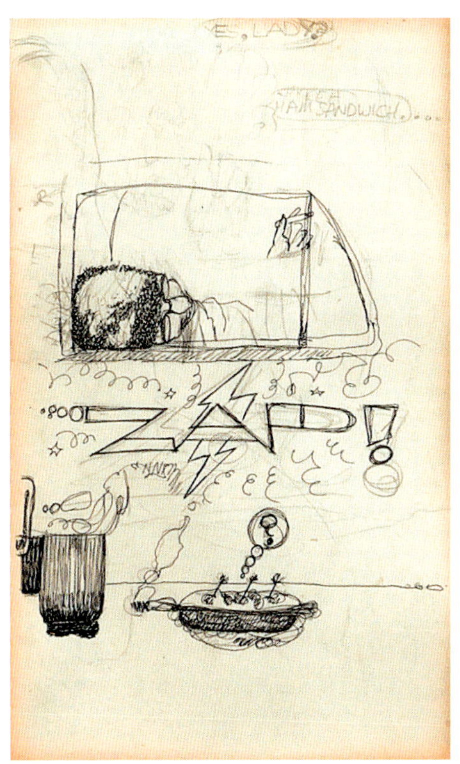
E. LADY
HAM SANDWICH....
ZAP!

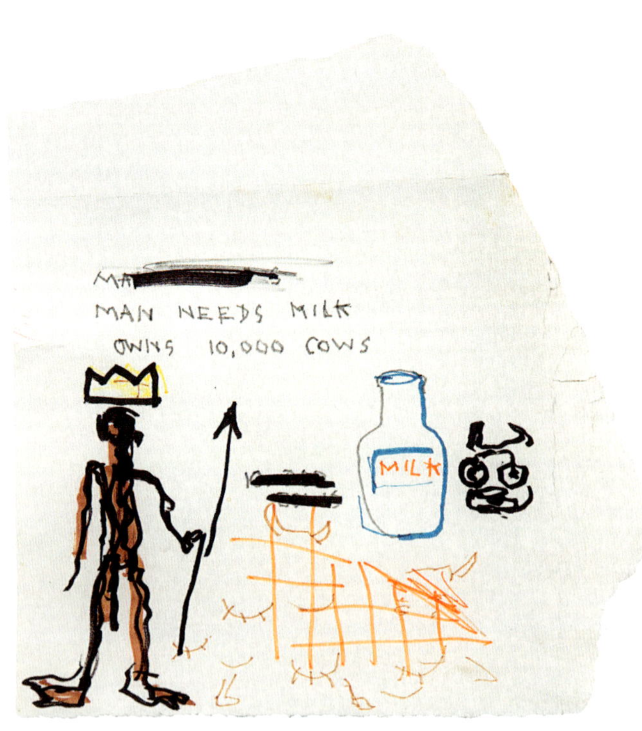

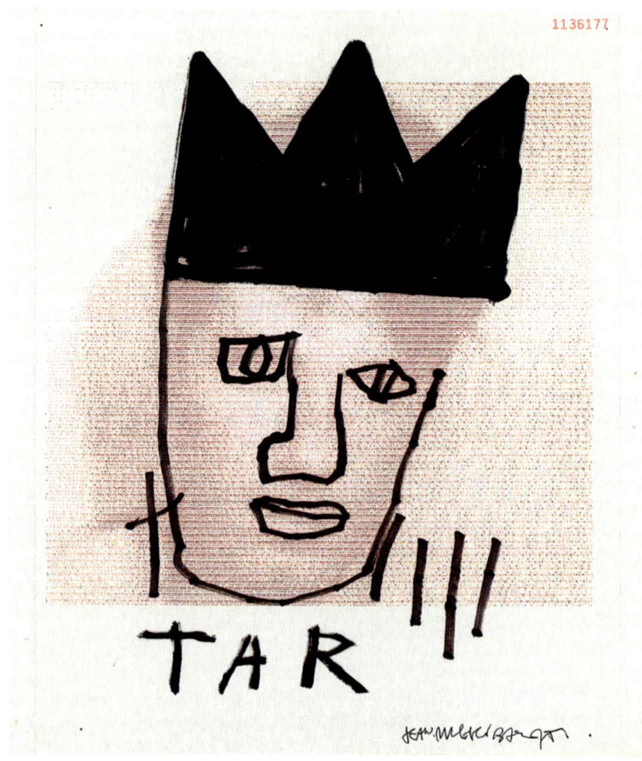

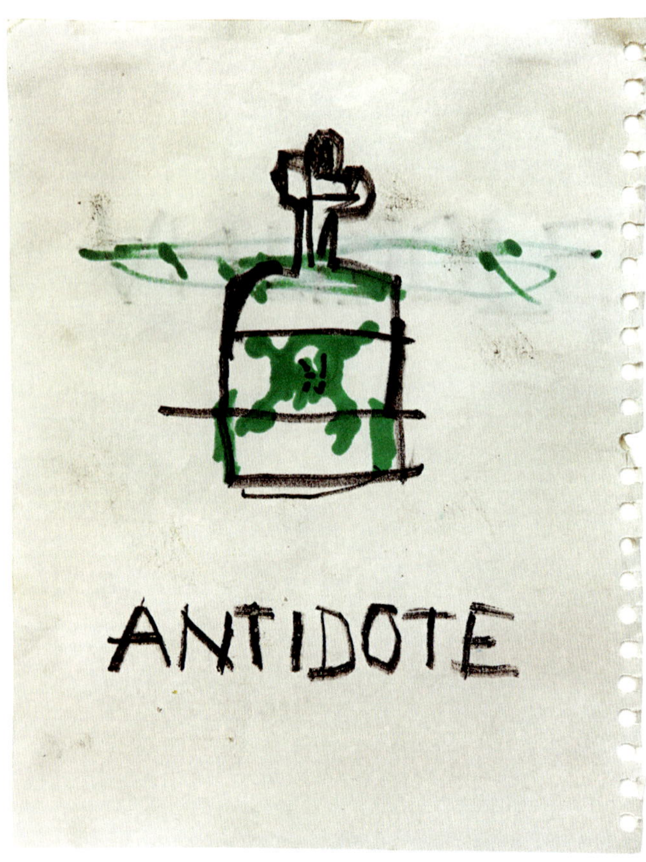

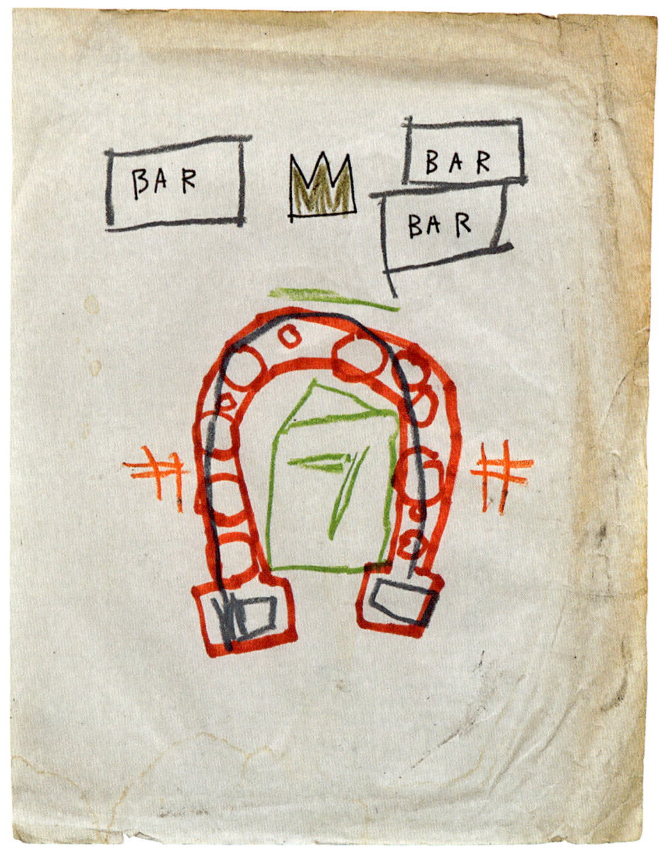

(clockwise from top left) Jean-Michel Basquiat *Untitled (Man Needs Milk)* 1981, mixed media on paper, 30.5 x 20.3 cm; *Untitled (Tar)* 1981, fibre-tipped pen on paper, 29.2 x 21.6 cm; *Untitled (BAR, BAR, BAR)* 1981, mixed media, ink and wax crayon on paper, 27.9 x 20.3 cm; *Antidote* 1981, fibre-tipped pen on paper, 30.5 x 22.9 cm, All works collection of Larry Warsh

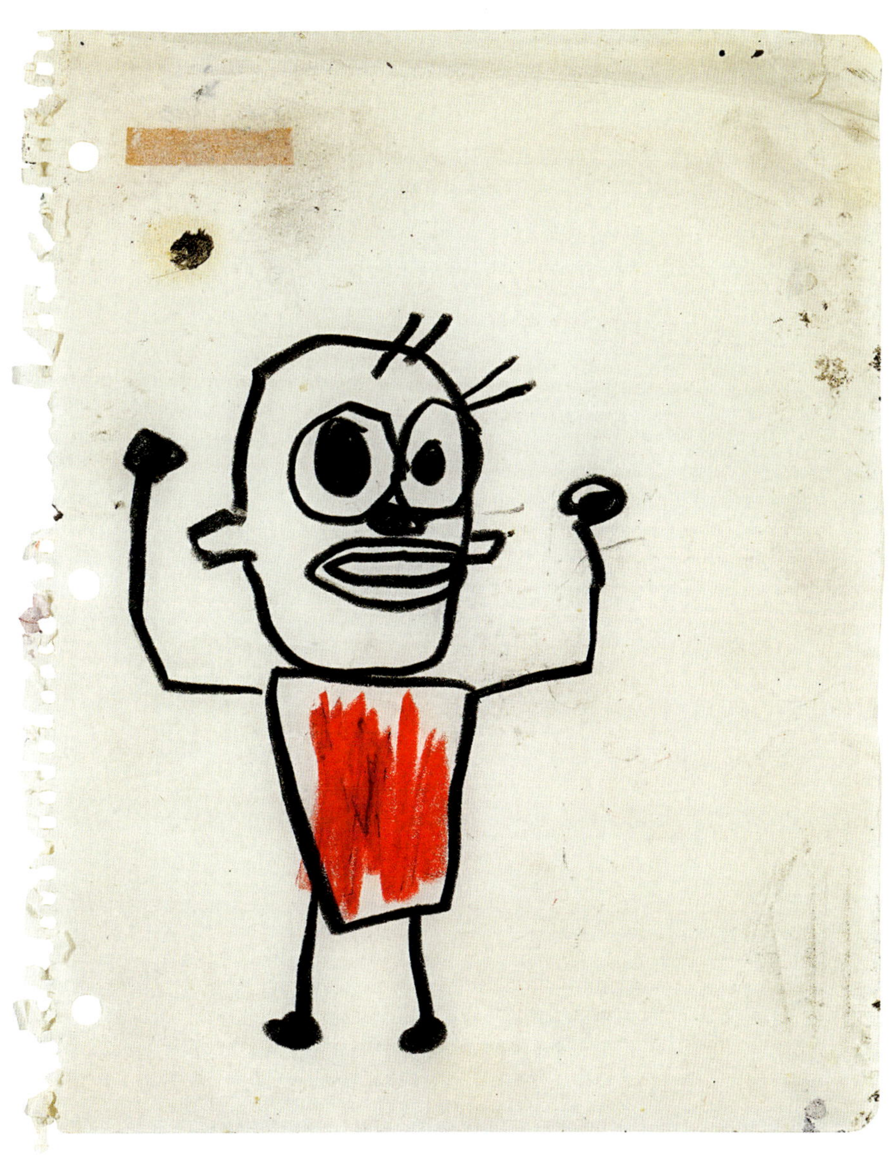

Jean-Michel Basquiat *Untitled* 1982, crayon on notebook paper, 27.9 x 21.5 cm, Collection of Kyoko Tamura

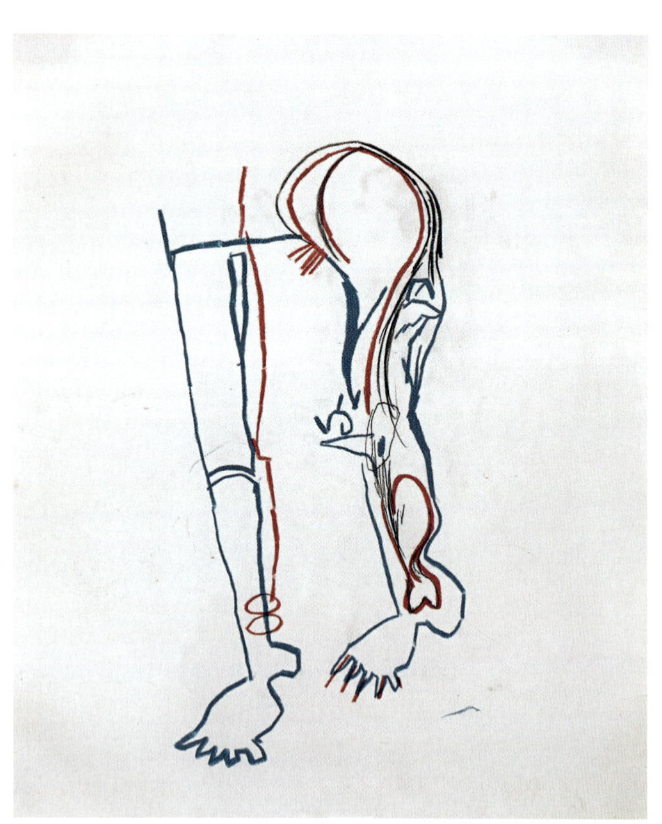

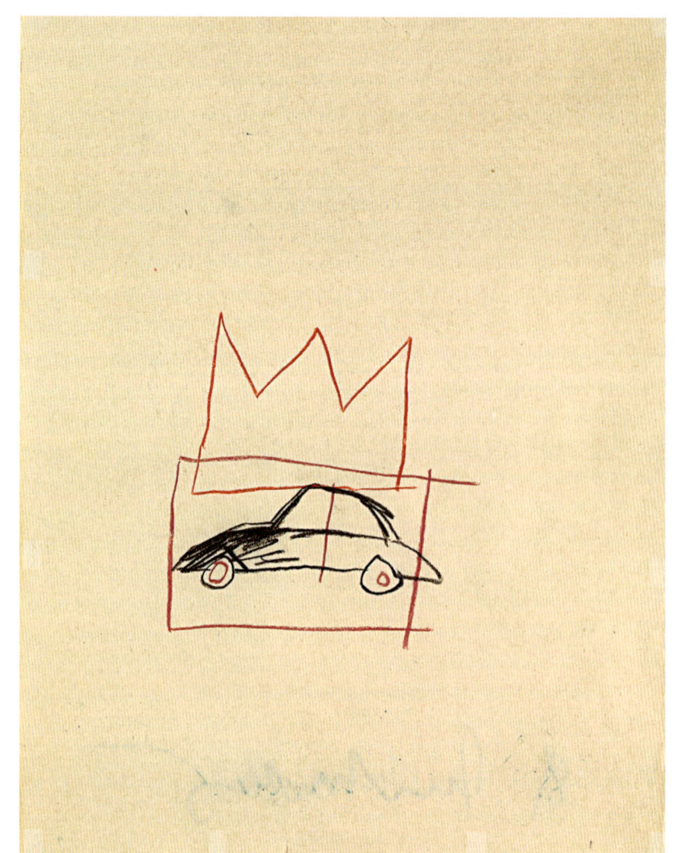

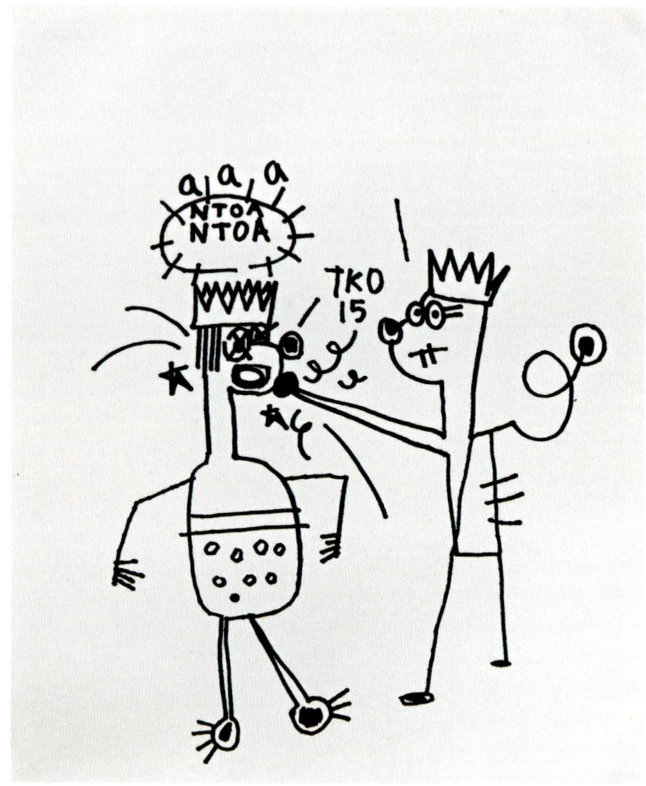

(clockwise from top left) Jean-Michel Basquiat *Untitled (Legs)* 1982, mixed media on paper, 45.7 x 43.2 cm; *Untitled (Crown and Car)* 1981, oilstick on paper, 61.0 x 45.7 cm; *Untitled (TKO)* 1982, sumi ink on paper, 40.6 x 33.0 cm, All works Private collection

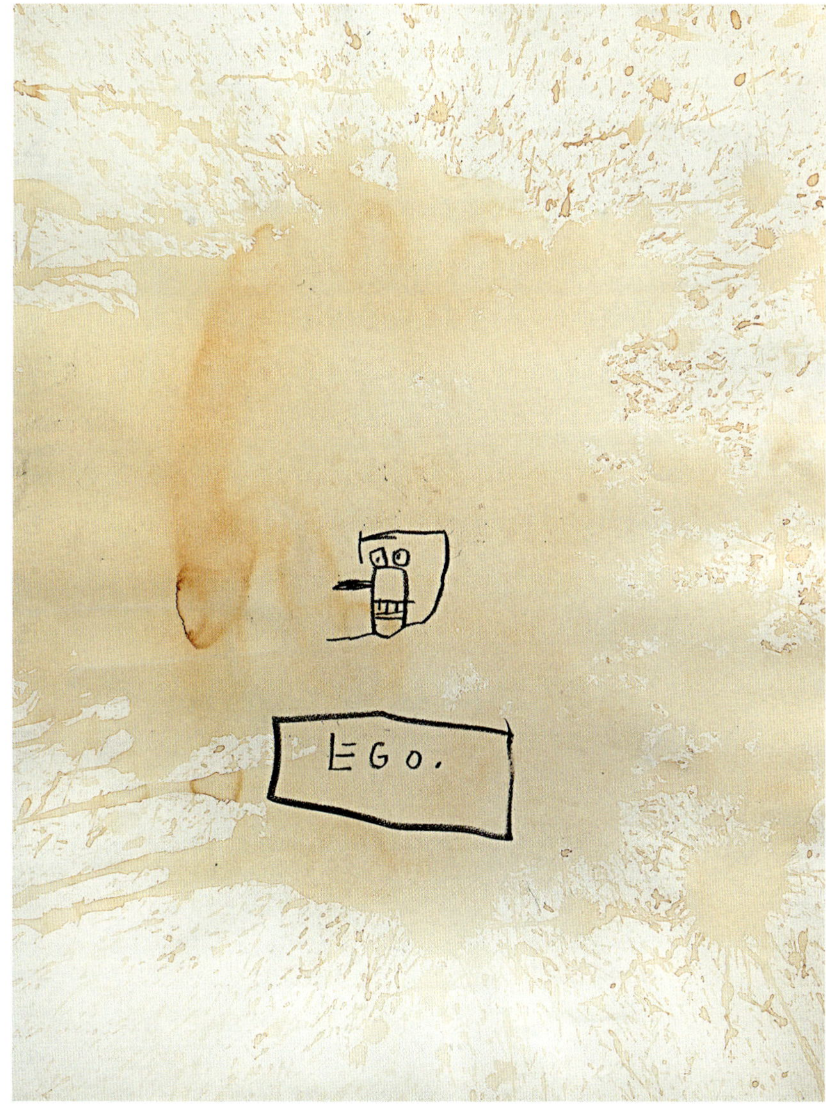

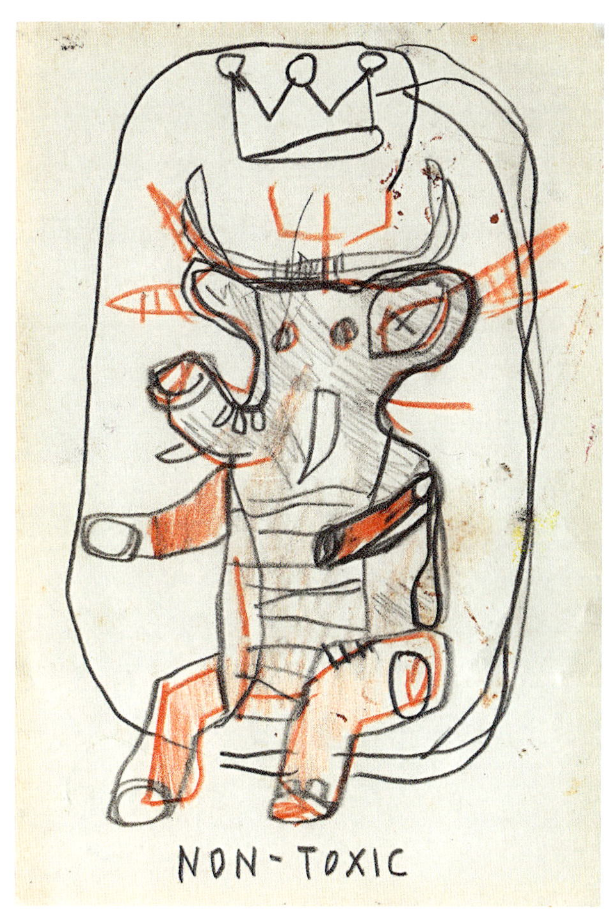

(above left) Jean-Michel Basquiat *Untitled (EGO)* 1983, oilstick and coffee on paper, 76.2 x 55.9 cm, Collection of Larry Warsh
(above right) Jean-Michel Basquiat *Non-Toxic* 1987, pencil and oilstick on paper, 15.0 x 10.0 cm, Private collection

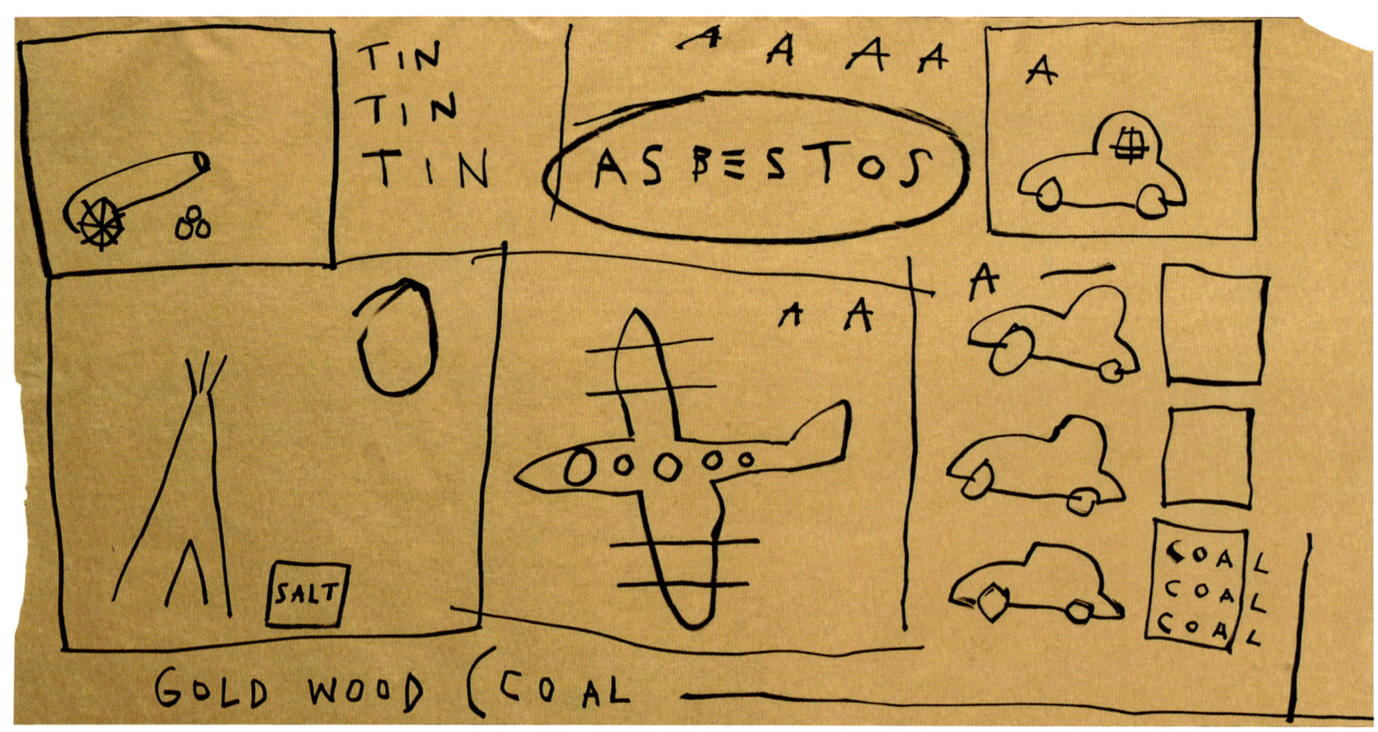

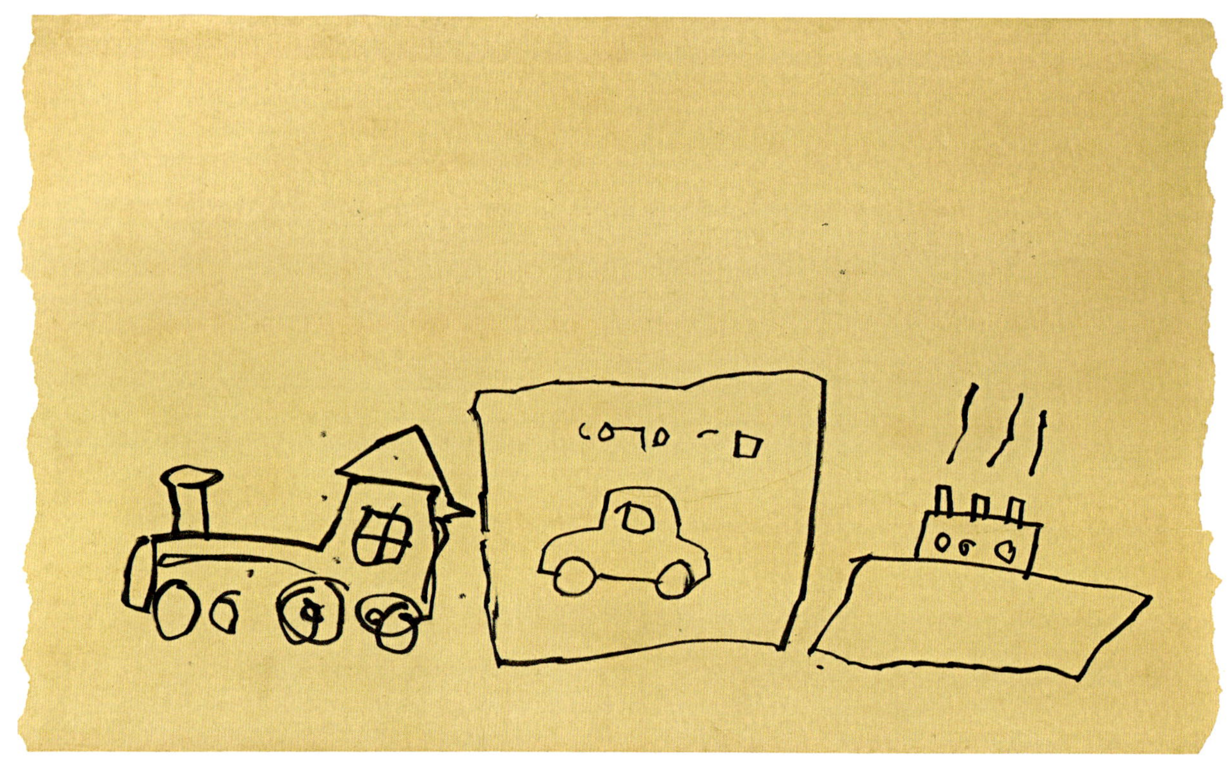

(top) Jean-Michel Basquiat *Untitled* 1981, ink on paper, 74.0 x 153.0 cm, Private collection
(bottom) Jean-Michel Basquiat *Untitled (Train, Car, Boat)* 1981, ink on paper, 71.1 x 116.8 cm, Private collection

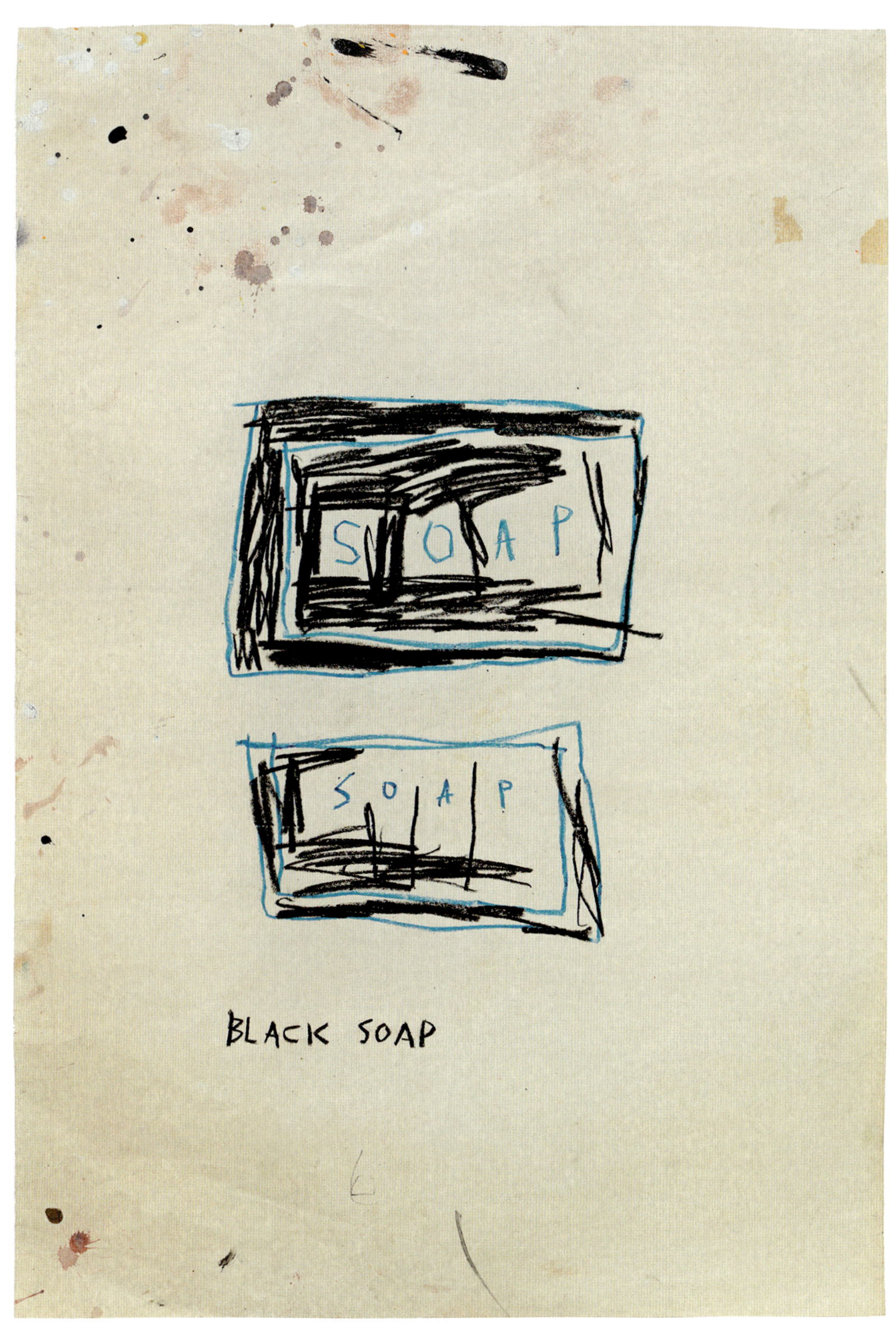

Jean-Michel Basquiat *Black Soap* 1981, mixed media on paper, 90.0 x 60.0 cm, Private collection

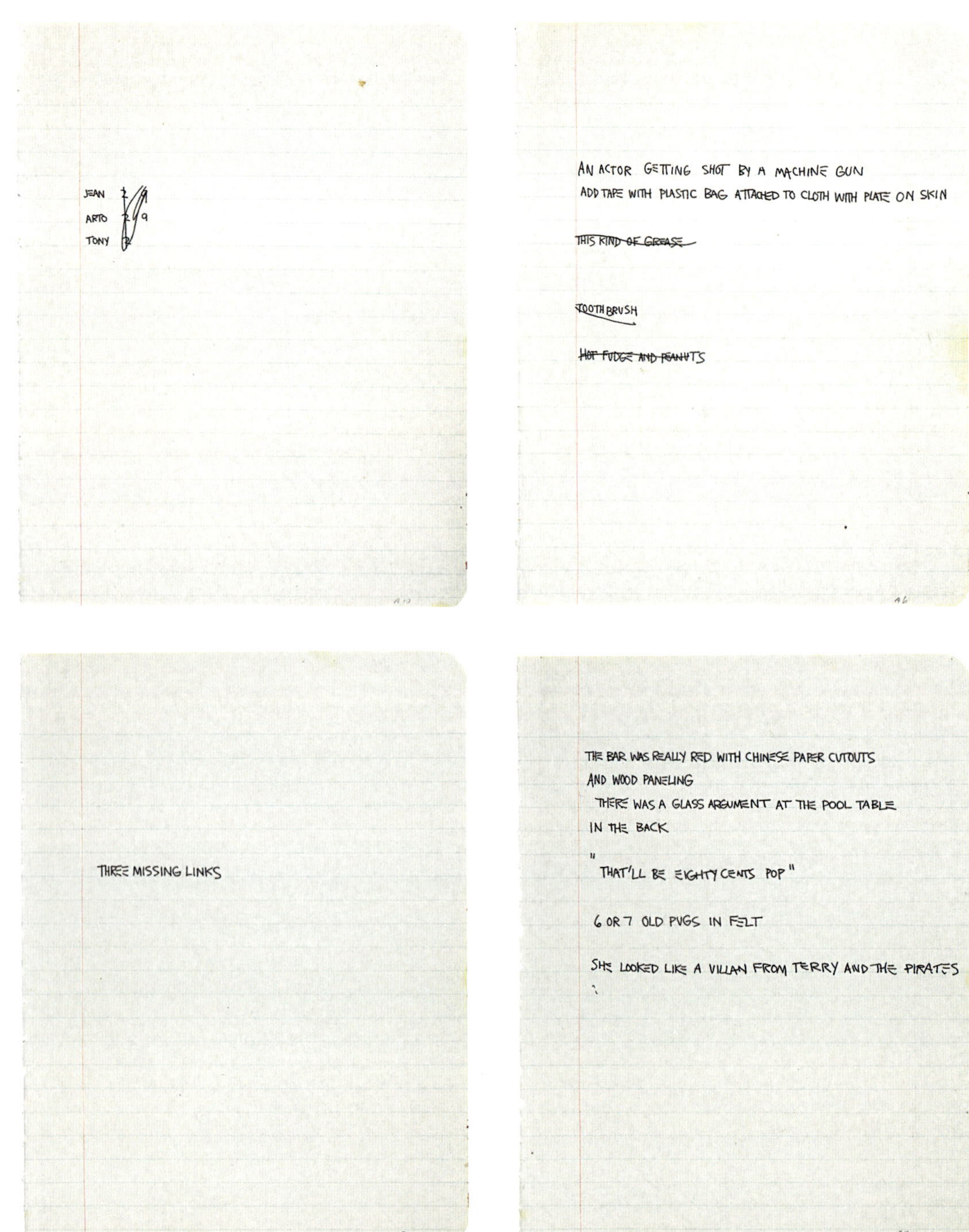

Jean-Michel Basquiat pages from *Notebook 1* 1980–87, fibre-tipped pen, wax crayon and ink on ruled notebook paper, 24.0 x 19.0 cm (each), Collection of Larry Warsh

THIS IS NOT IN PRAISE OF POISON
ING MYSELF WAITING FOR IDEAS
TO HAPPEN· MYSELF· THIS NOT
IN PRAISE OF POISON IS THIS IS NOT

NON
THE NON POISONOUS POISONED
SO SELF RIGHTOU'S POISONED
NO ONE IS CLEAN
FROM RED MEAT TO WHITE
POISON
THIS IS NOT IN PRAISE OF ~~POISON~~
THE BIGGEST BUISNESS
UGLY, FAT LIKE A PIG

THE CUSTOMER IN NEW YORK,
CHICAGO DETROIT

PSALM

Jean-Michel Basquiat page from *Notebook 5* 1980–87, fibre-tipped pen, wax crayon and ink on ruled notebook paper, 24.0 x 19.0 cm, Collection of Larry Warsh

TRUE STORY

SHOT A FOOL'S ~~HEAD OFF~~

"SHOT A FOOL'S HEAD OFF"!

C2

Jean-Michel Basquiat page from *Notebook 5* 1980–87, fibre-tipped pen, wax crayon and ink on ruled notebook paper, 24.0 x 19.0 cm, Collection of Larry Warsh

Jean-Michel Basquiat page from *Notebook 1* 1980–87, fibre-tipped pen, wax crayon and ink on ruled notebook paper, 24.0 x 19.0 cm, Collection of Larry Warsh

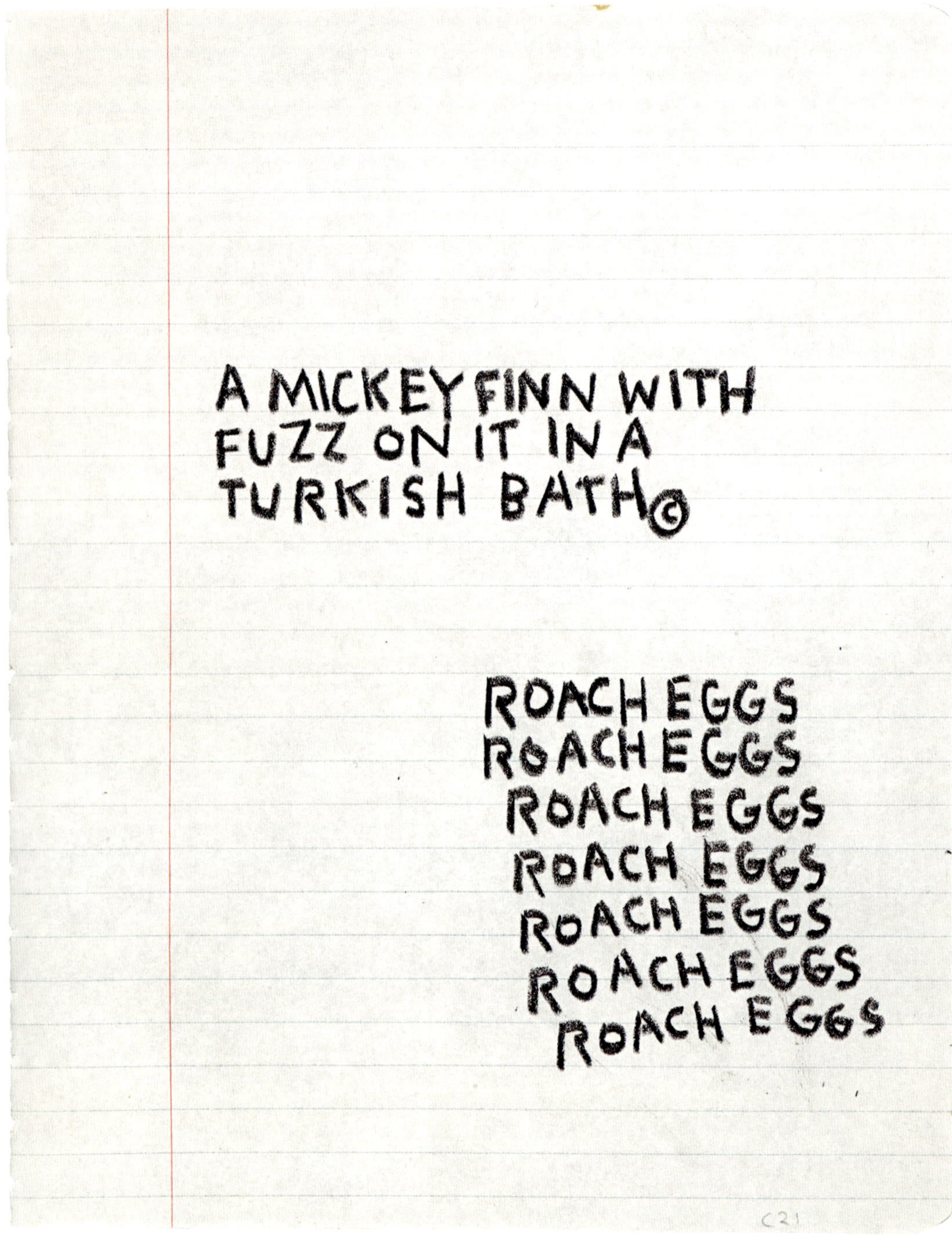

Jean-Michel Basquiat page from *Notebook 5* 1980–87, fibre-tipped pen, wax crayon and ink on ruled notebook paper, 24.0 x 19.0 cm, Collection of Larry Warsh

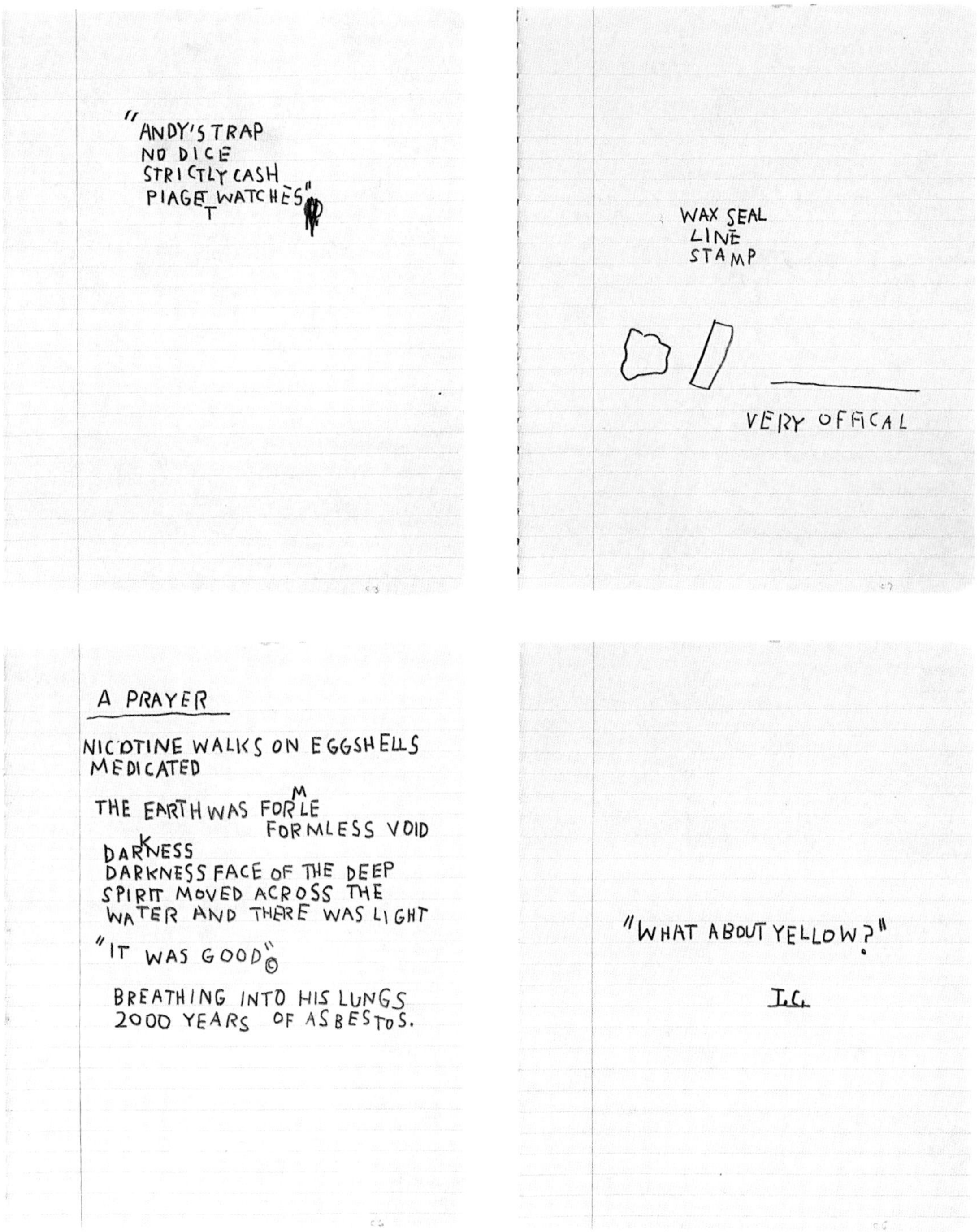

"ANDY'S TRAP
NO DICE
STRICTLY CASH
PIAGET WATCHES"

WAX SEAL
LINE
STAMP

VERY OFFICAL

A PRAYER

NICOTINE WALKS ON EGGSHELLS
MEDICATED

THE EARTH WAS FORMLE
FORMLESS VOID

DARKNESS
DARKNESS FACE OF THE DEEP
SPIRIT MOVED ACROSS THE
WATER AND THERE WAS LIGHT

"IT WAS GOOD" ©

BREATHING INTO HIS LUNGS
2000 YEARS OF ASBESTOS.

"WHAT ABOUT YELLOW?"

I.G.

Jean-Michel Basquiat pages from *Notebook 5* 1980–87, fibre-tipped pen, wax crayon and ink on ruled notebook paper, 24.0 x 19.0 cm (each), Collection of Larry Warsh

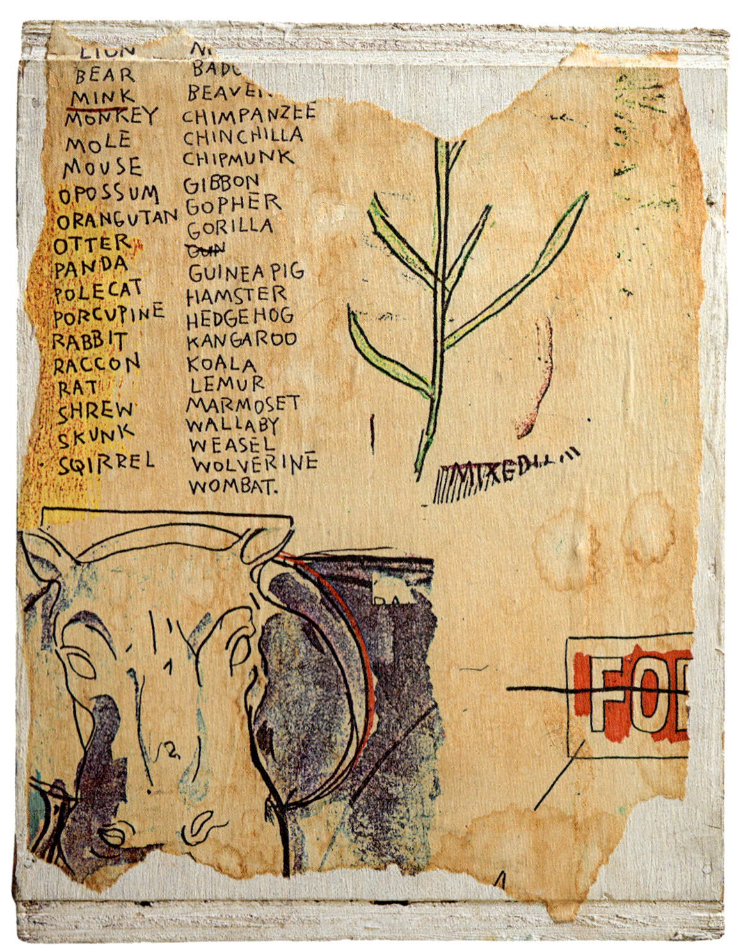

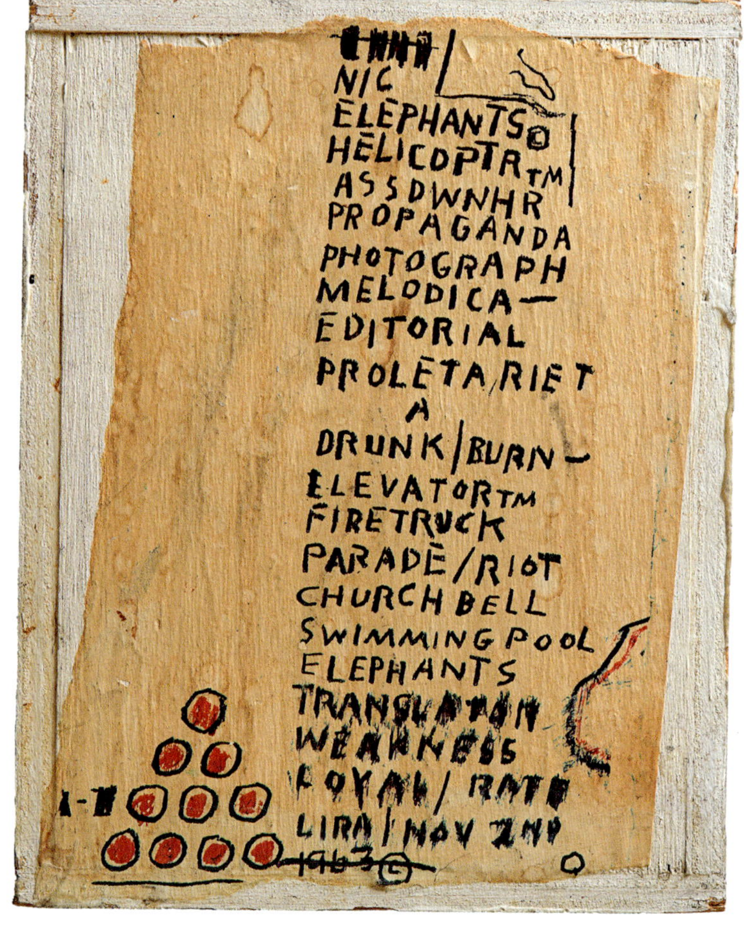

Jean-Michel Basquiat *Untitled* 1985 (detail), xerox collage on wood box, 28.0 x 22.0 cm, Private collection

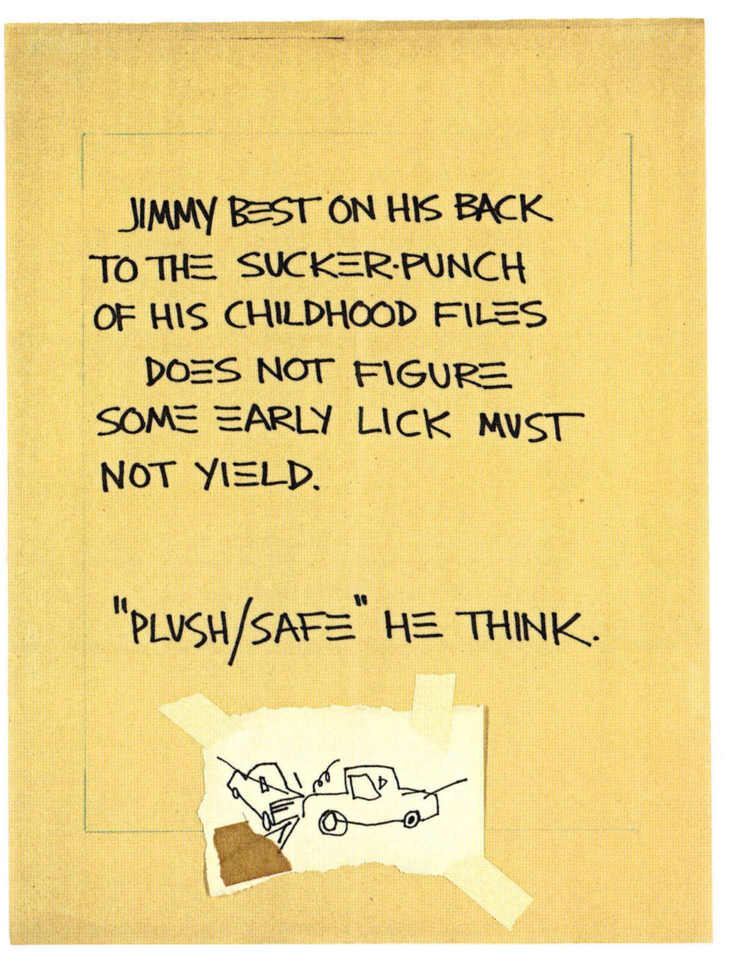

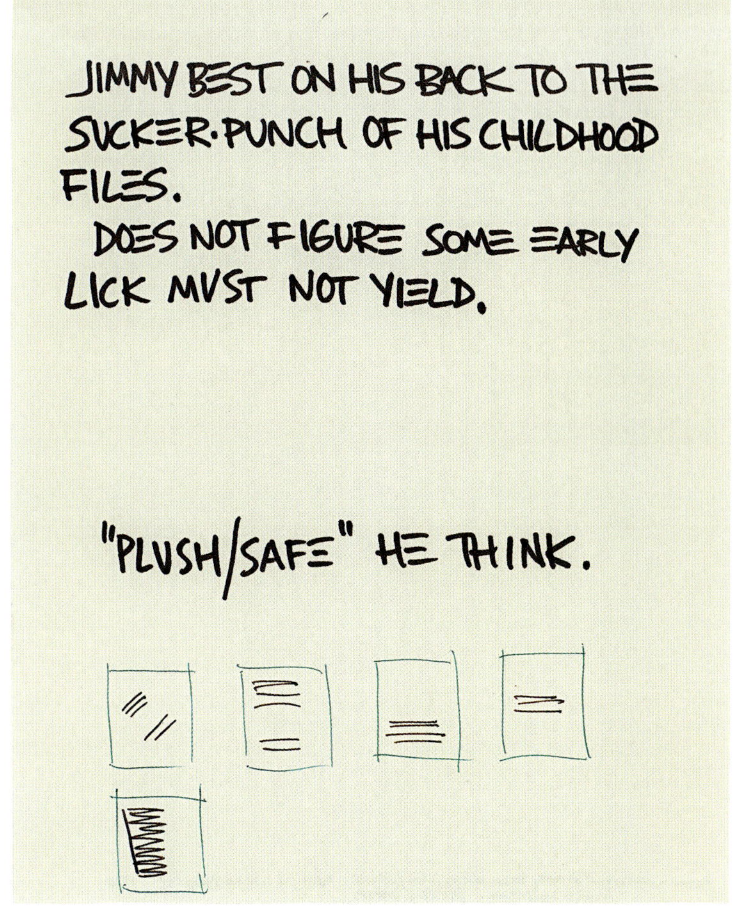

(above left) Jean-Michel Basquiat *Untitled (JIMMY BEST ON HIS BACK)* 1980, mixed media on paper, 61.0 x 47.0 cm, Collection of Larry Warsh
(above right) Jean-Michel Basquiat *Untitled (JIMMY BEST ON HIS BACK)* 1980, ink on paper, 41.9 x 35.6 cm, Collection of Larry Warsh

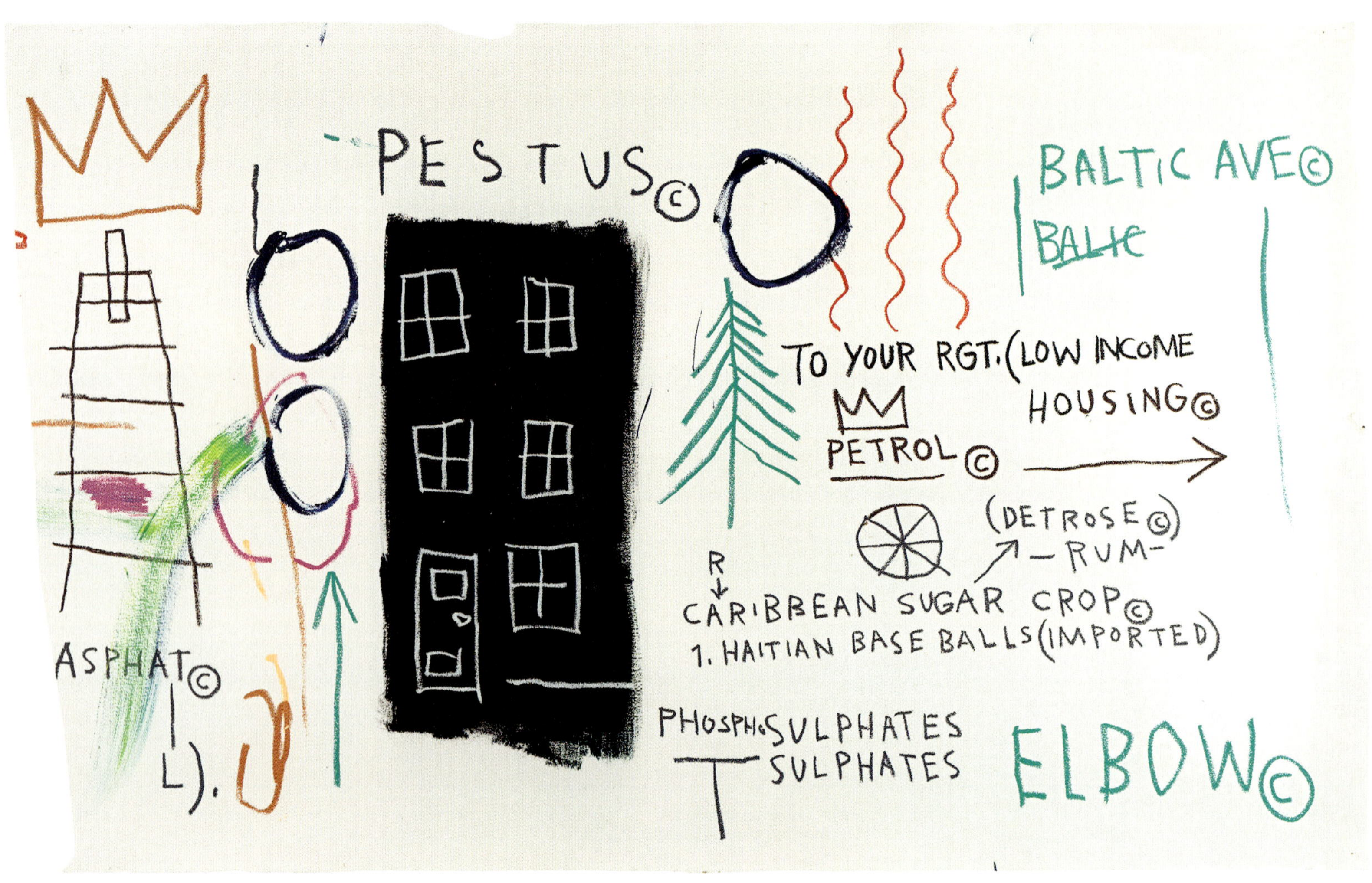

Jean-Michel Basquiat *Untitled (Pestus)* 1982, synthetic polymer paint and oilstick on paper, 115.0 x 183.0 cm, Private collection

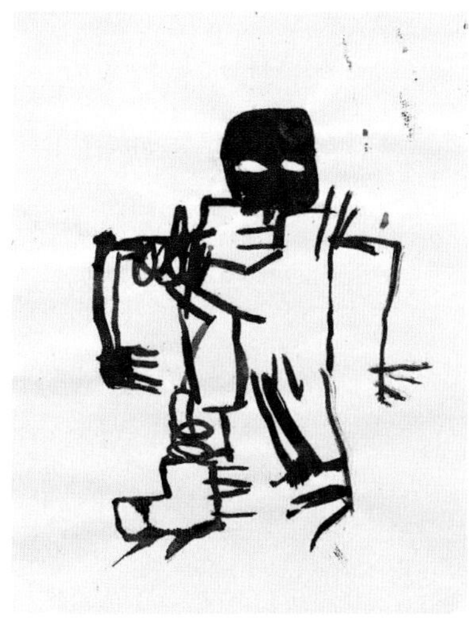
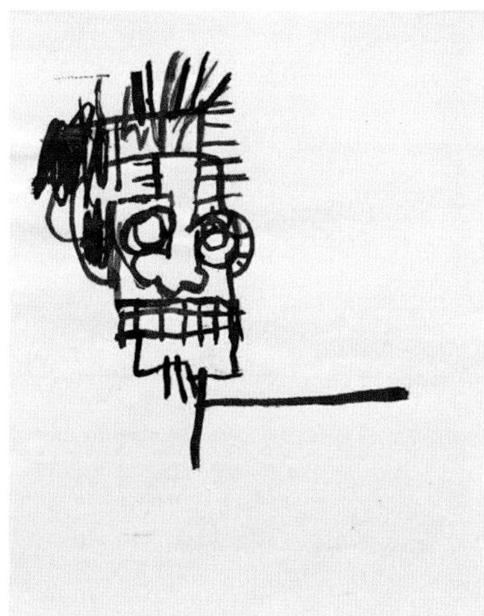
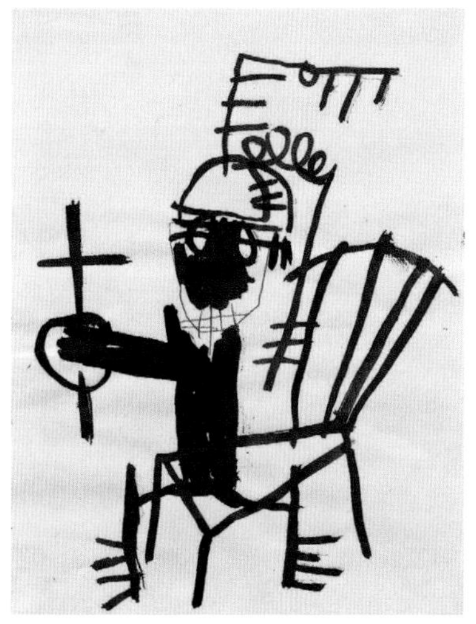
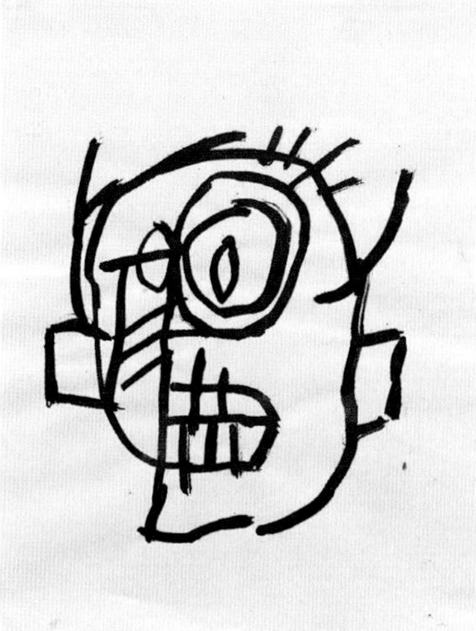
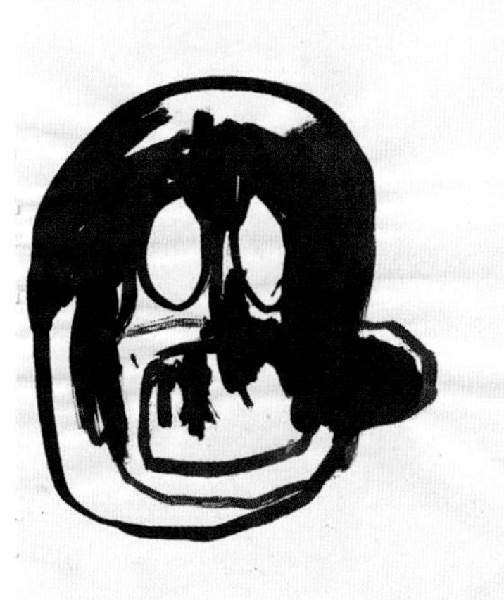
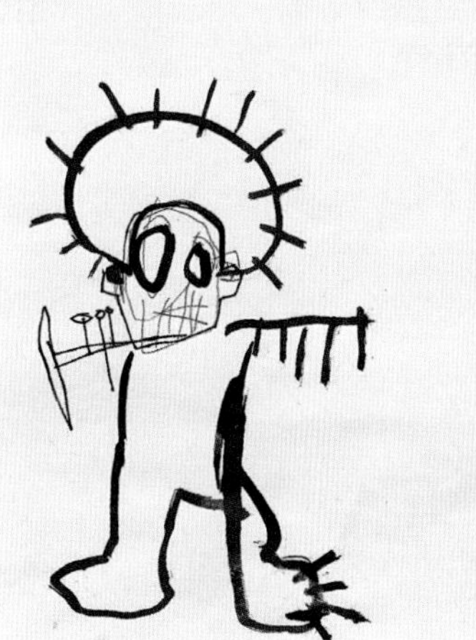
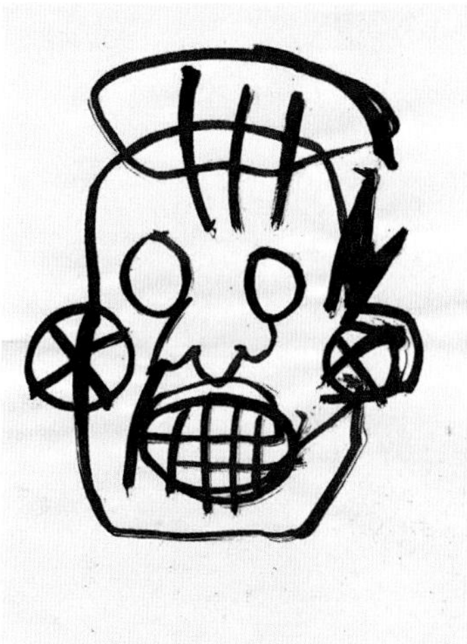

Jean-Michel Basquiat *Untitled* 1981, ink on paper, (a-g) 30.5 x 22.9 cm (each), Private collection

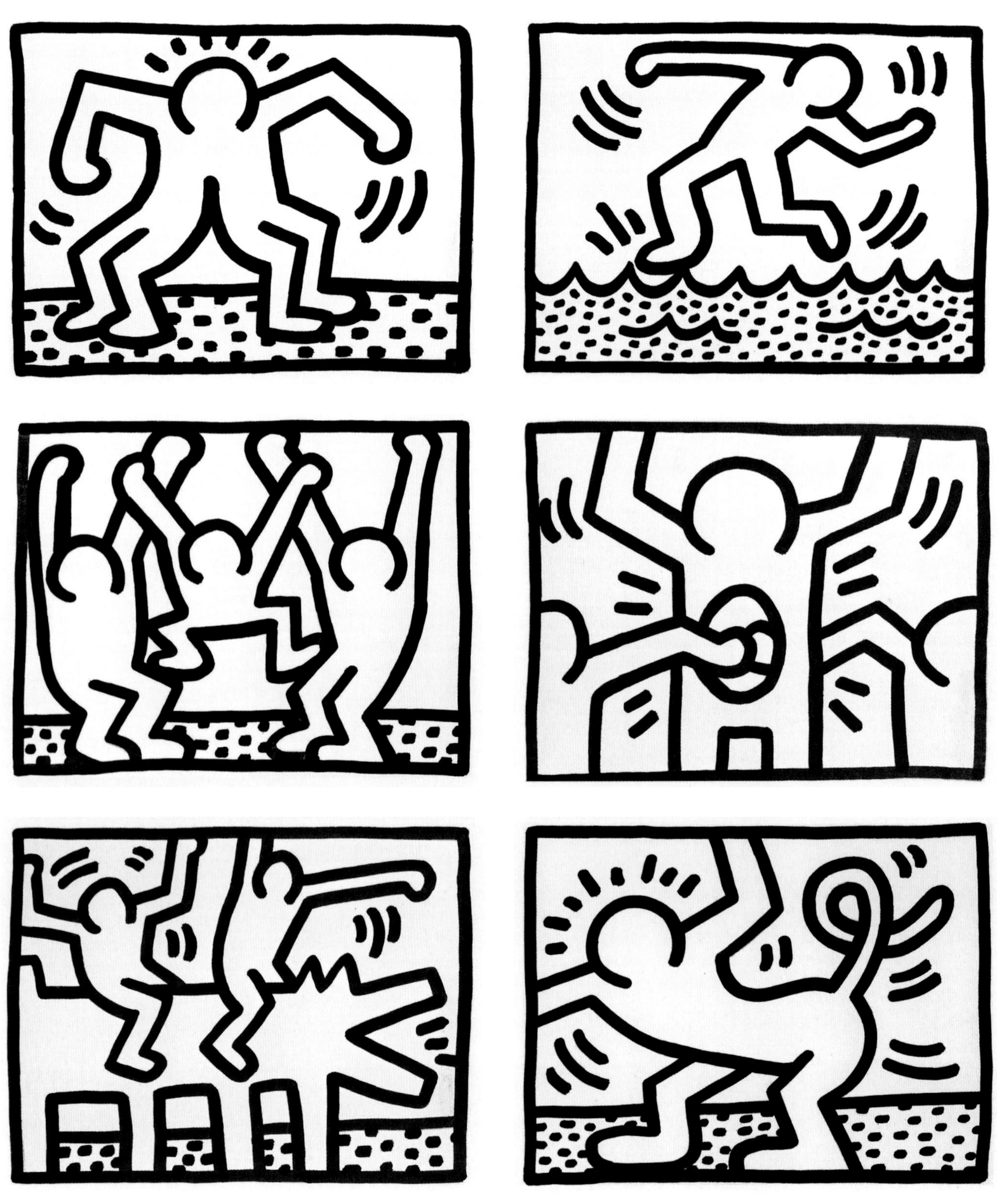

Keith Haring *Untitled* c. 1982, ink on paper, (a–l) 27.9 x 35.5 cm (each), Private collection

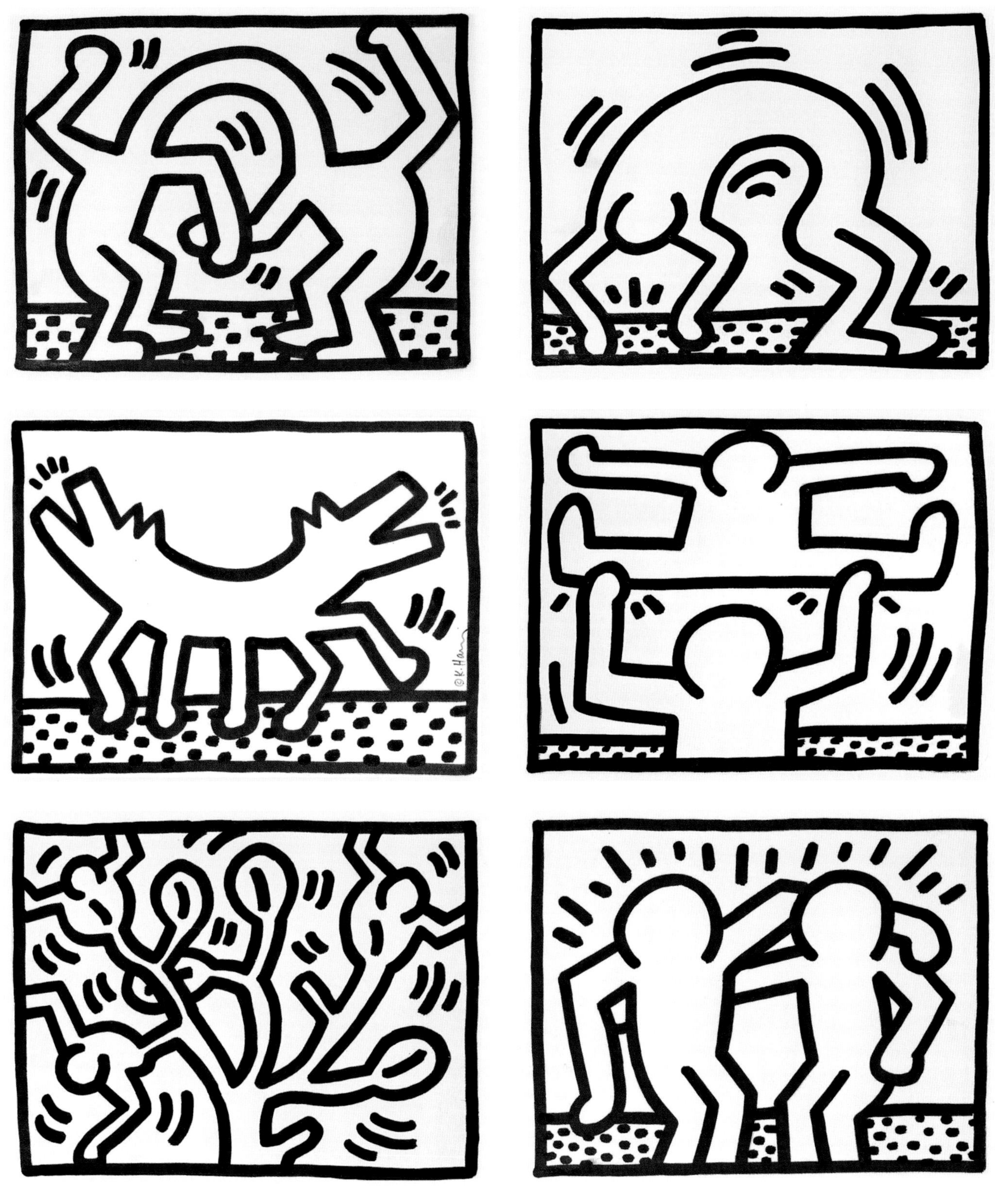

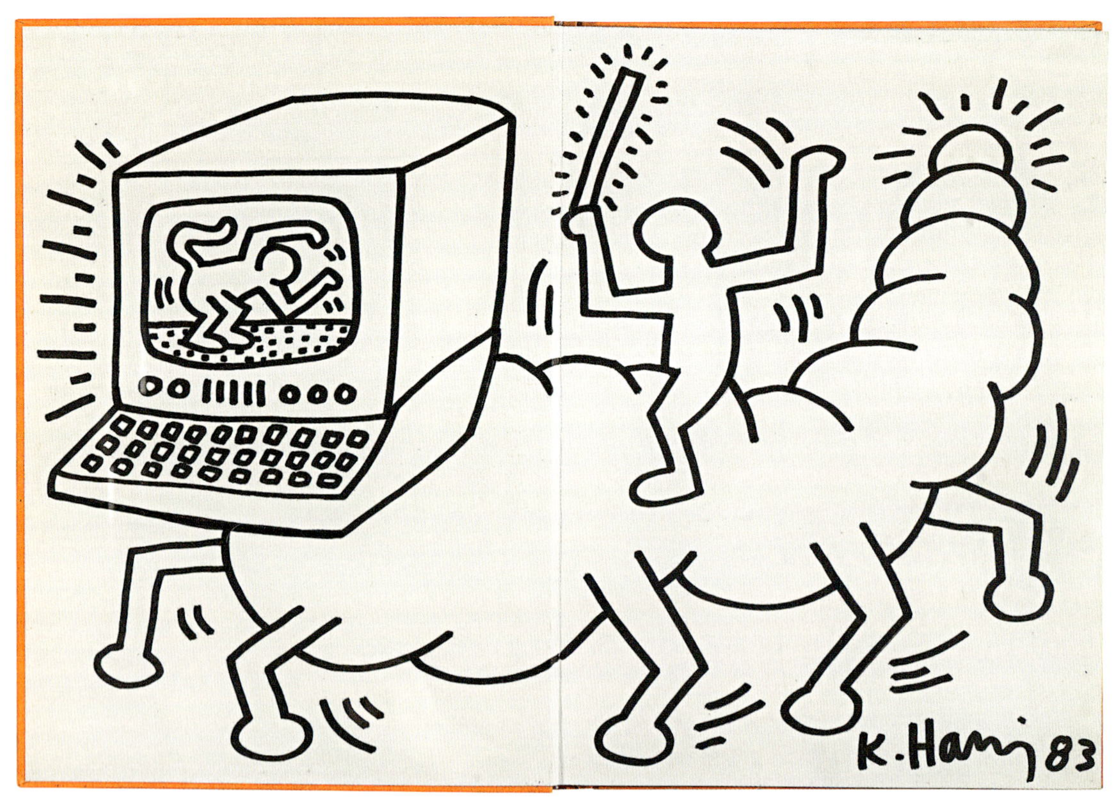

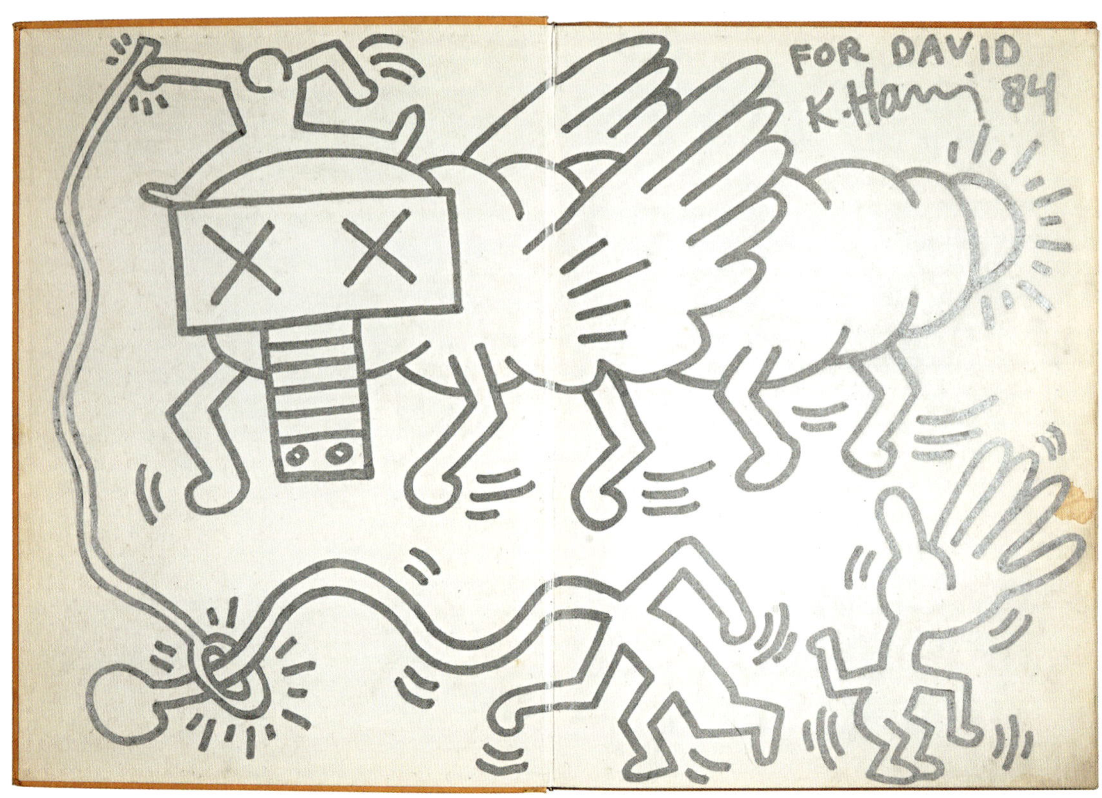

(top) Keith Haring *Untitled* 1983, ink on book cover, 25.4 x 60.9 cm, Private collection
(bottom) Keith Haring *Untitled* 1984, ink on book cover, 60.9 x 76.2 cm, Collection of Larry Warsh

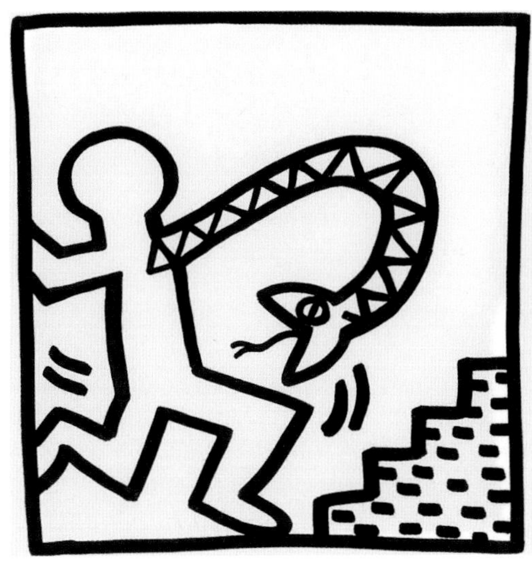

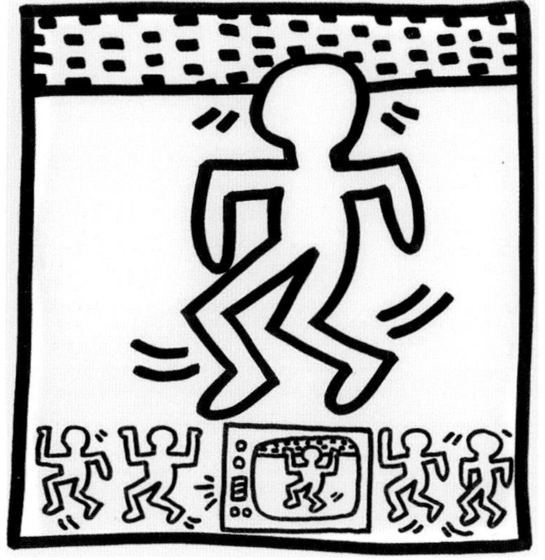

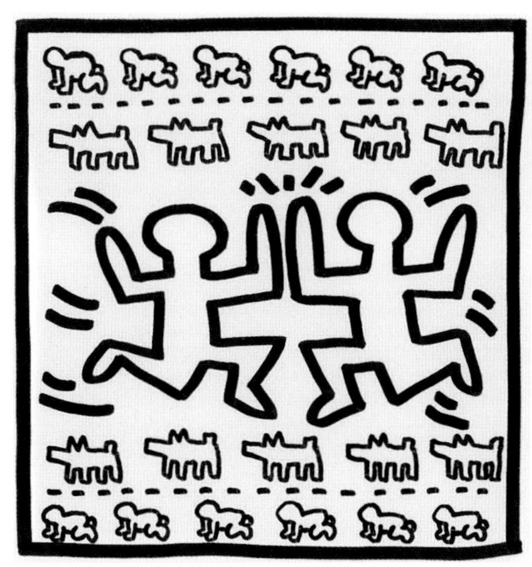

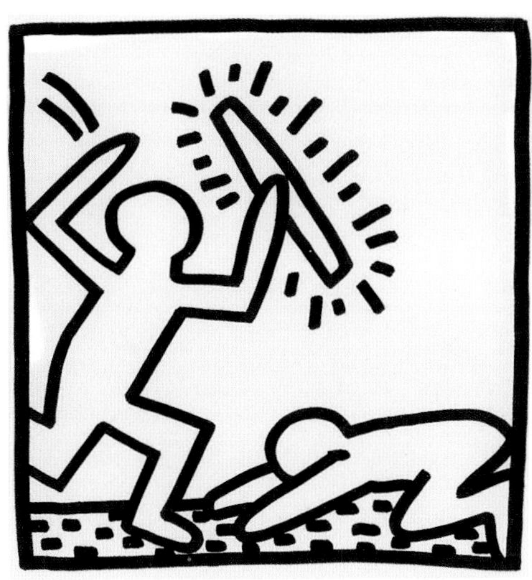

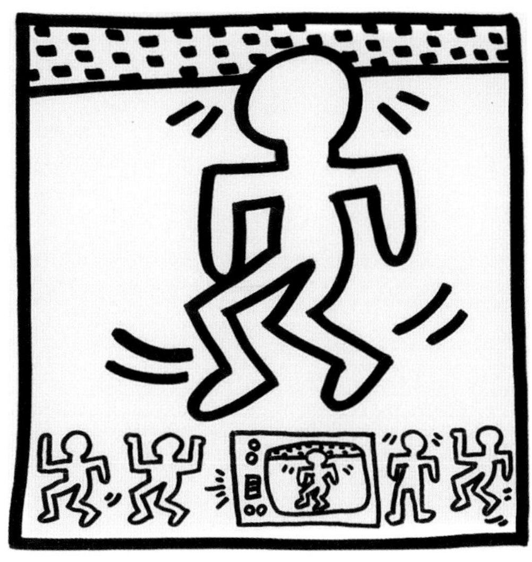

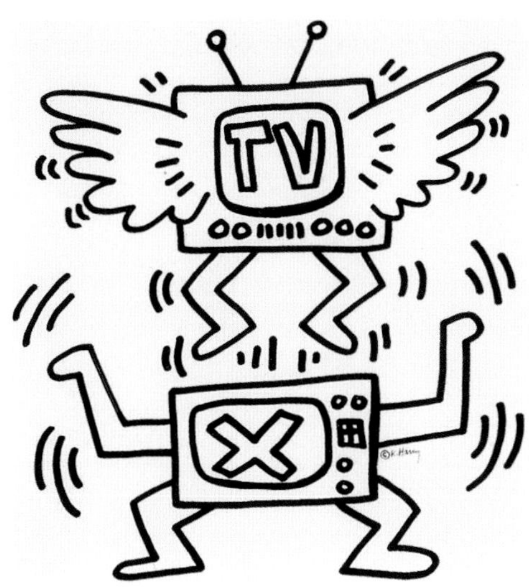

Keith Haring *Untitled* 1982, sumi ink on paper, (a-f) 21.5 x 21.5 cm (each), Private collection

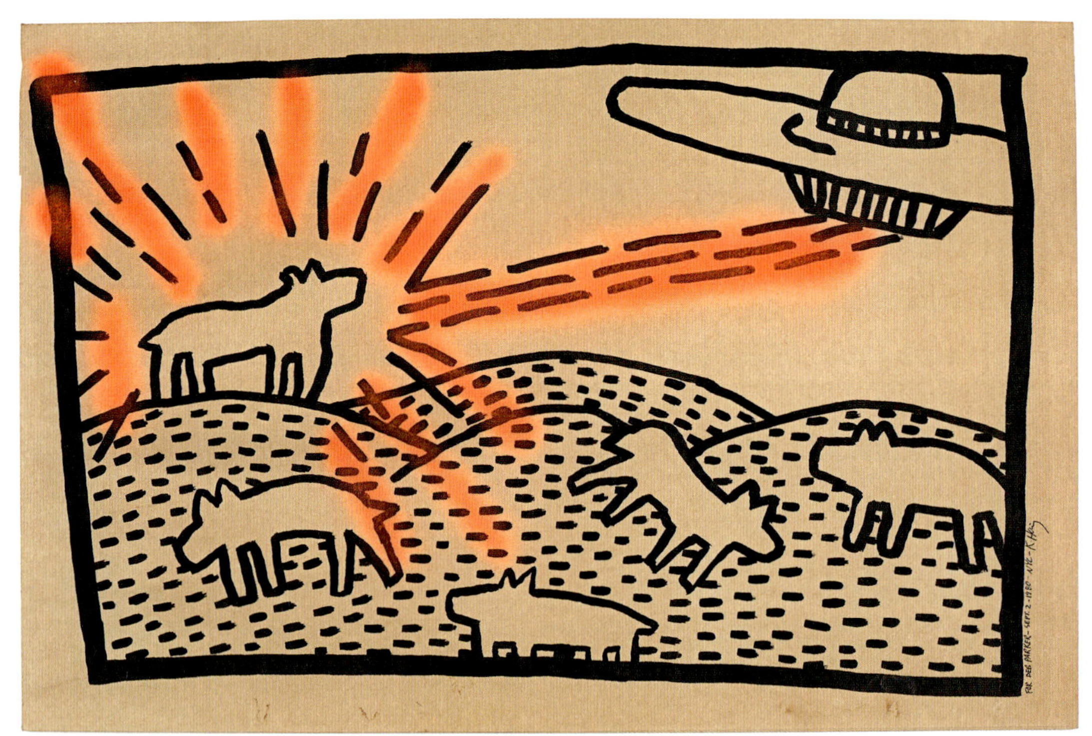

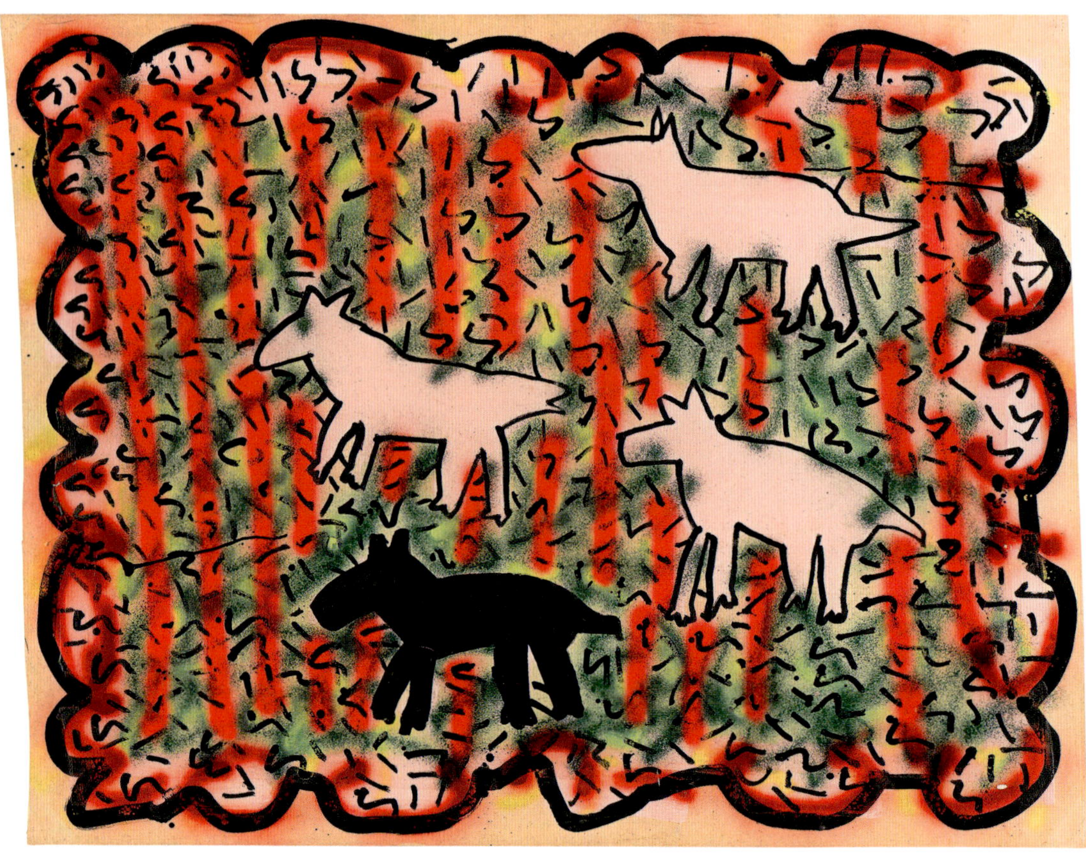

(top) Keith Haring *Untitled* 1980, sumi ink and spray-paint on paper, 66.0 x 102.0 cm, Collection of Larry Warsh
(bottom) Keith Haring *Untitled* c. 1980, spray-paint and ink on paper, 123.2 x 154.9 cm, Collection of Larry Warsh

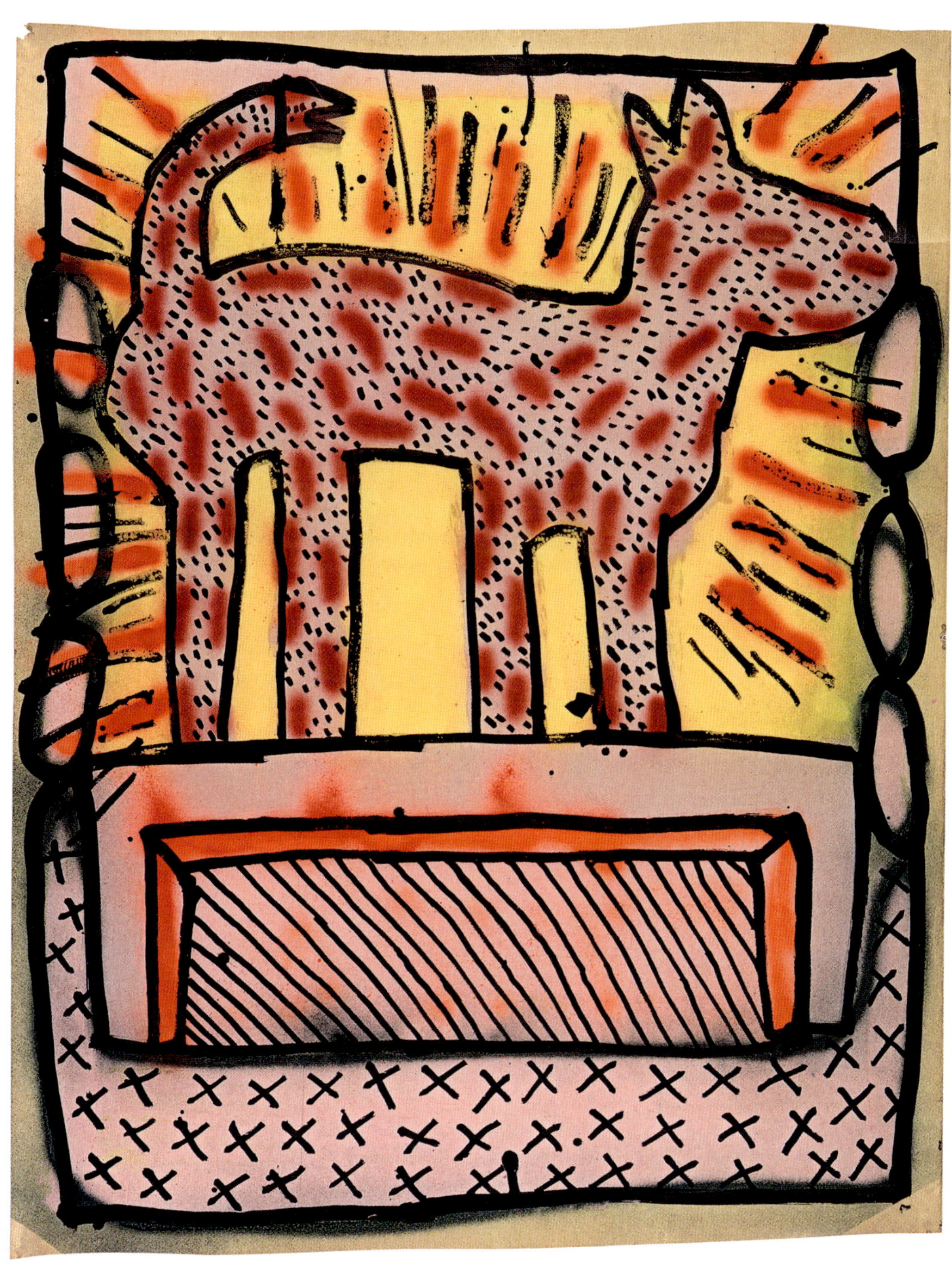

Keith Haring *Untitled* 1980, sumi ink, spray enamel and synthetic polymer paint on poster board, 161.3 x 121.9 cm, The Keith Haring Foundation, New York

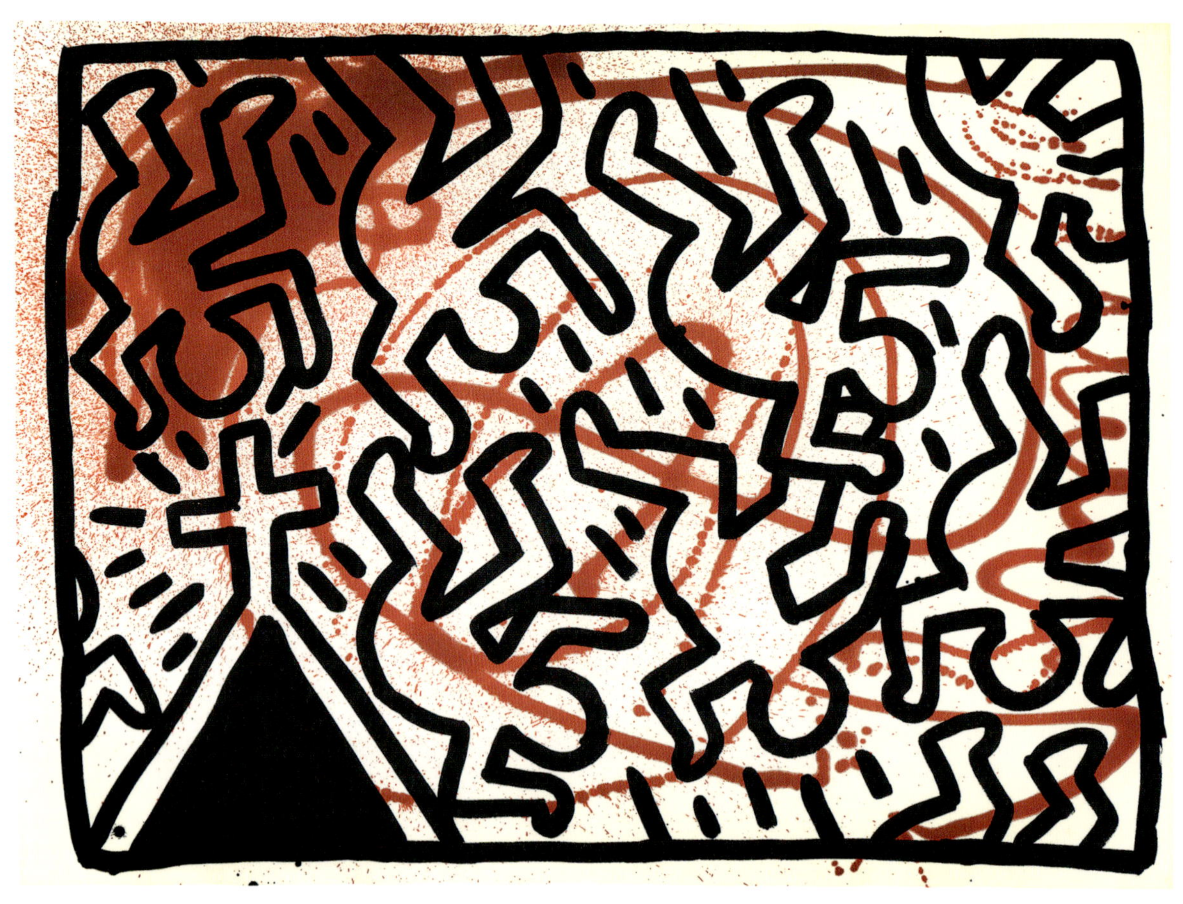

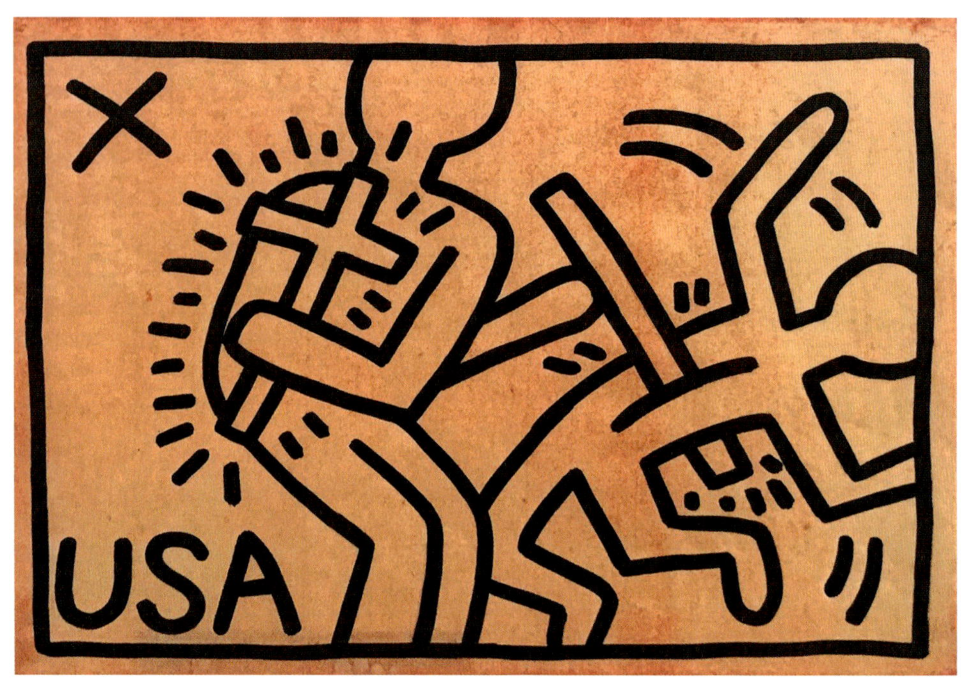

(top) Keith Haring *Untitled* 1981, ink and watercolour on paper, 93.0 x 125.0 cm, Museum MACAN, Jakarta, Indonesia
(bottom) Keith Haring *Untitled* 1983, sumi ink on paper, 38.0 x 51.0 cm, Courtesy Laurent Strouk

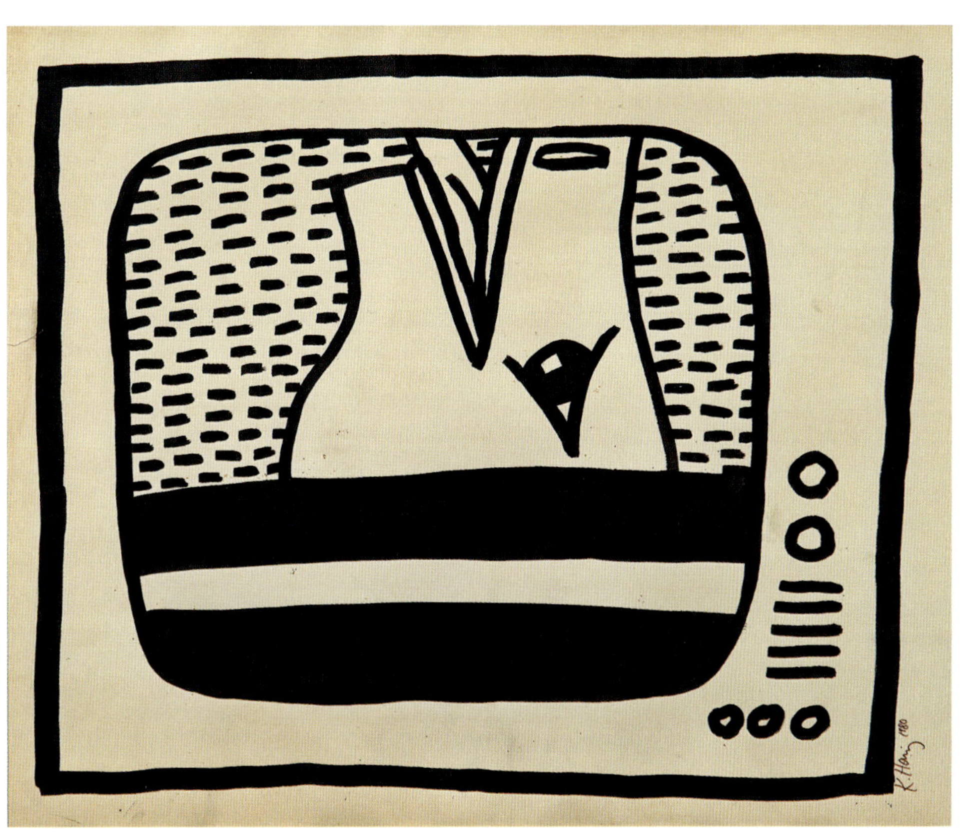

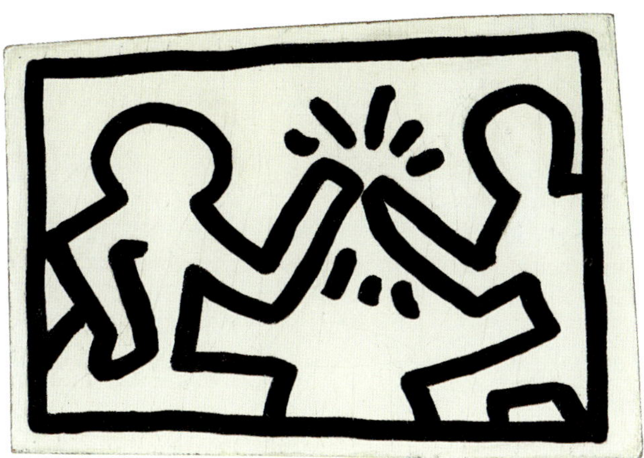

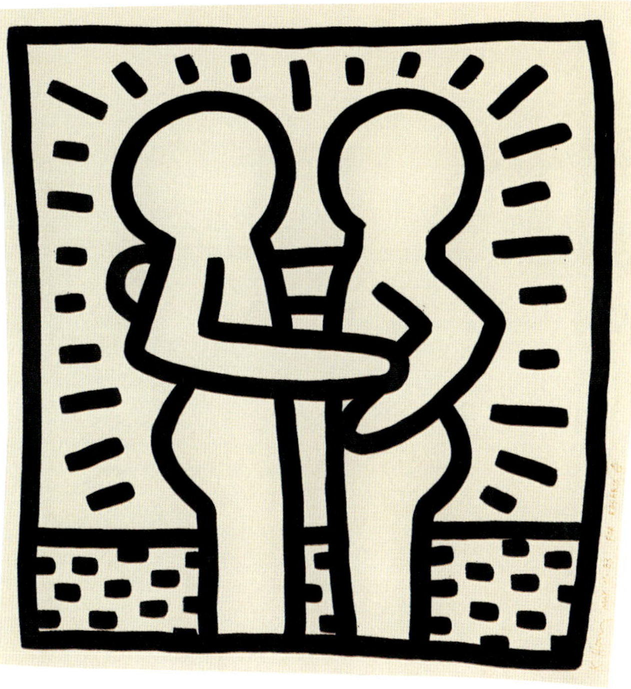

(clockwise from top) Keith Haring *Untitled* c. 1982, ink on paper, 60.9 x 68.5 cm, Collection of Larry Warsh;
Untitled 1983, sumi ink on paper, 52.0 x 50.0 cm, BvB collection, Geneva;
Untitled c. 1984, paint on wood panel, 10.1 x 15.2 cm, Collection of Larry Warsh

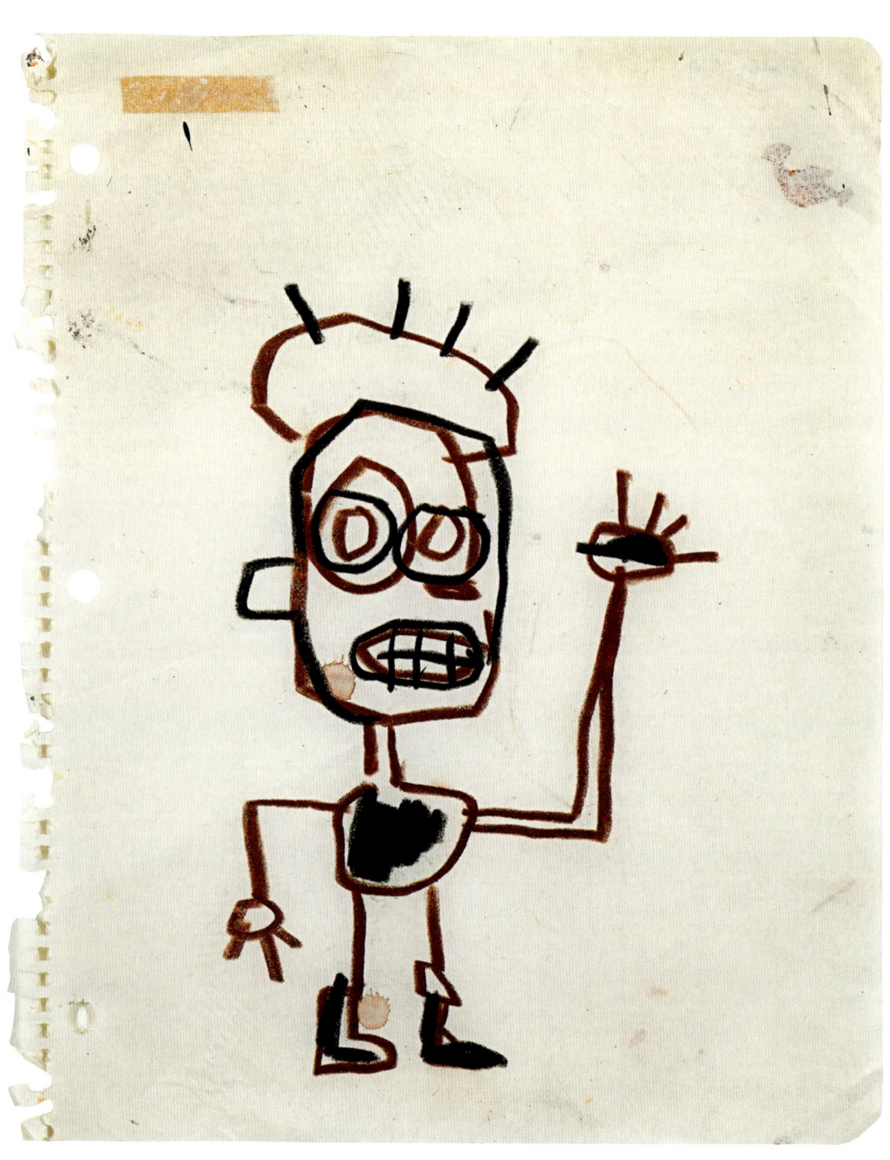

Jean-Michel Basquiat *Untitled* 1982, crayon on notebook paper, 27.9 x 21.5 cm, Collection of Kyoko Tamura

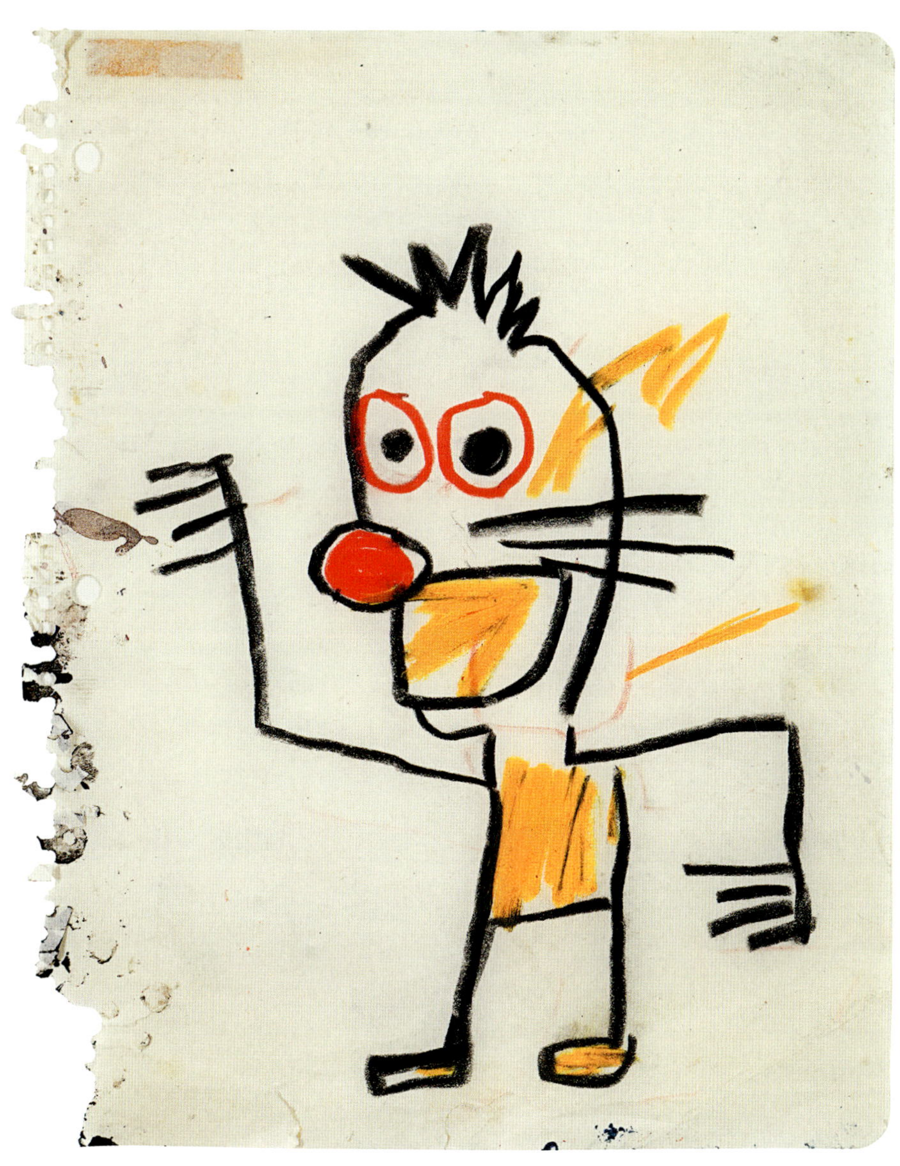

Jean-Michel Basquiat *Untitled* 1982, crayon on notebook paper, 27.9 x 21.5 cm, Collection of Kyoko Tamura

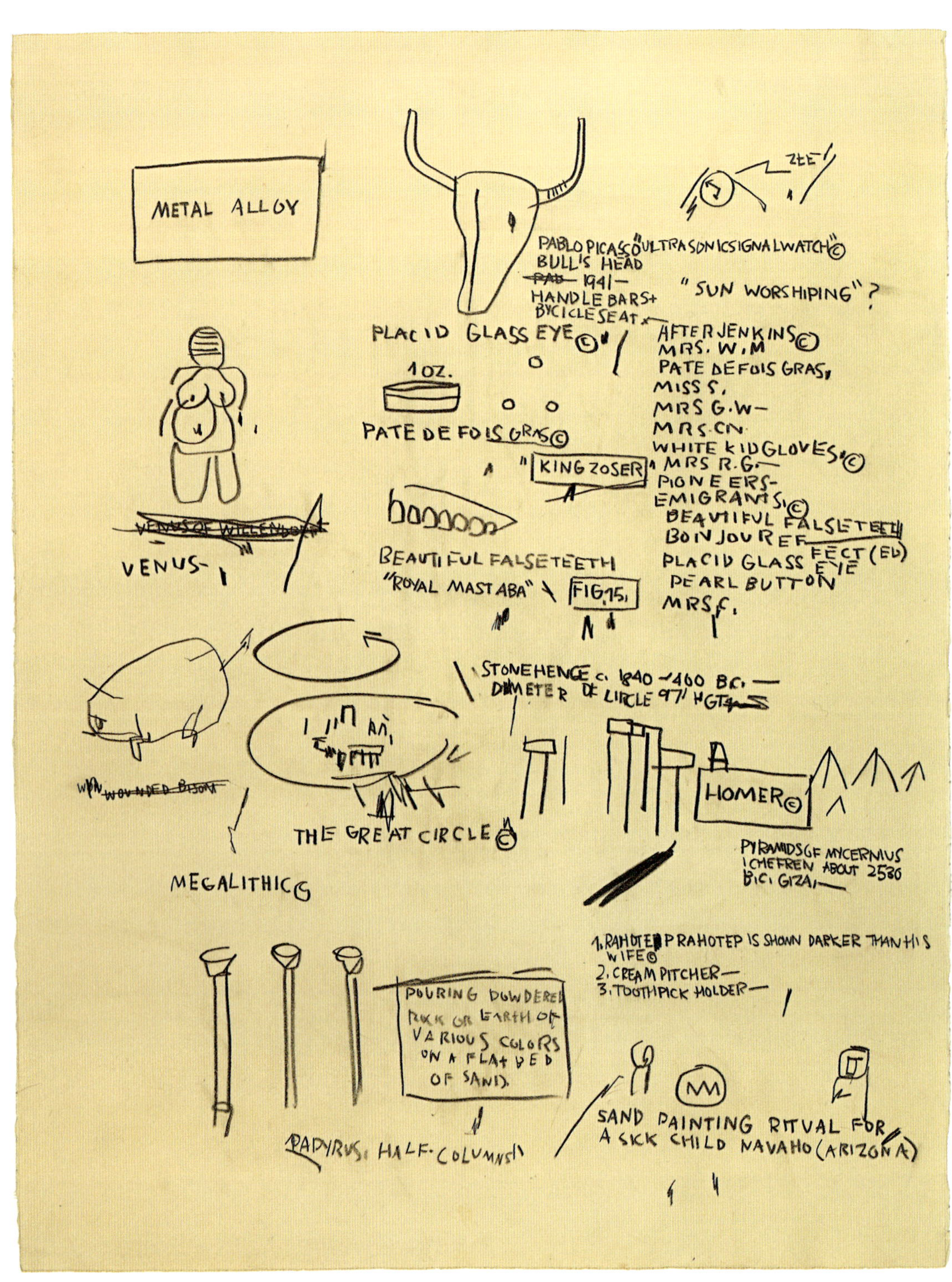

Jean-Michel Basquiat *Untitled (Picasso)* 1984, graphite on paper, 76.2 x 57.1 cm, Collection of Kyoko Tamura

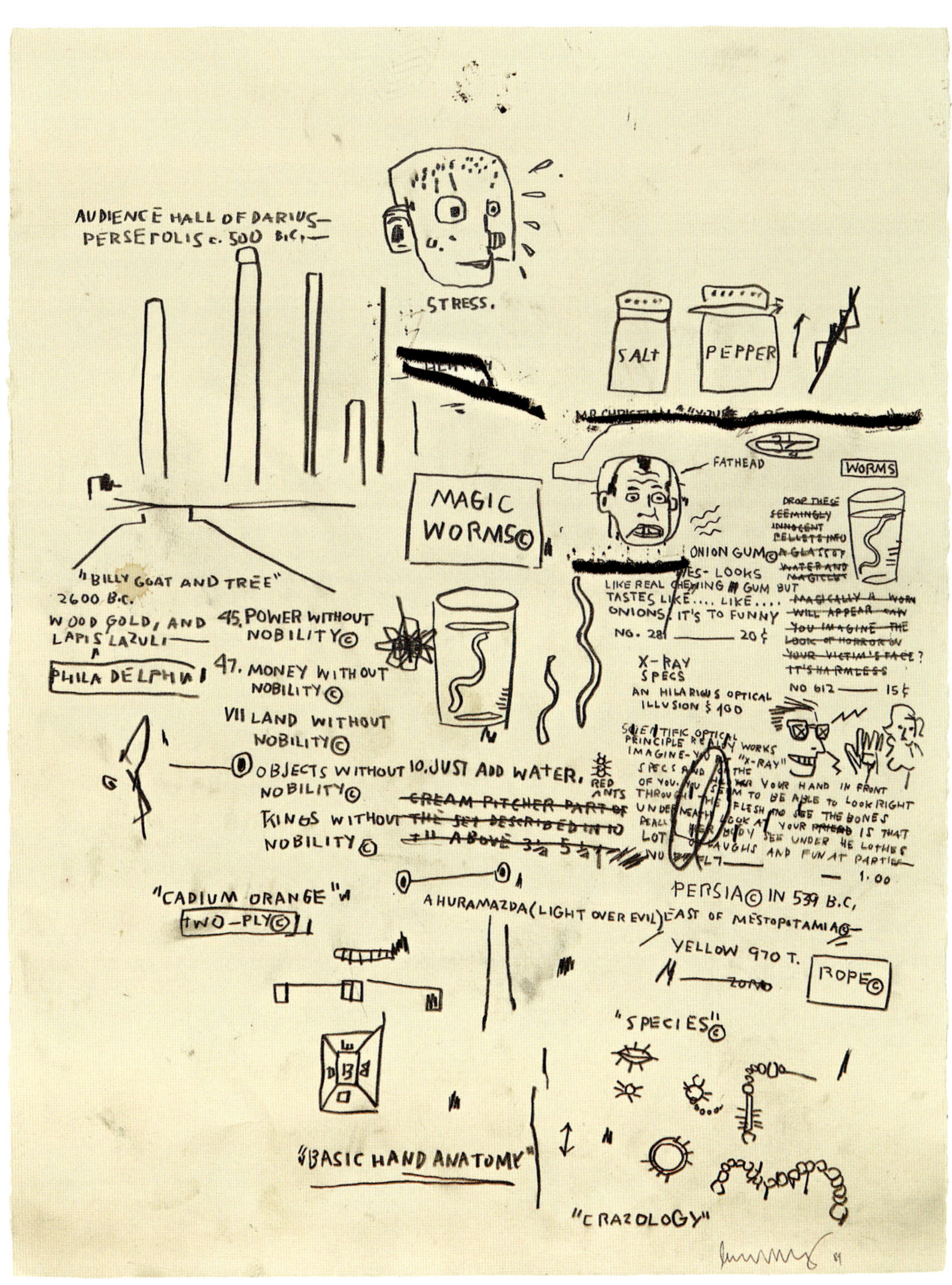

Jean-Michel Basquiat *Untitled (Magic Worms)* 1984, 75.6 x 56.5 cm, graphite and oilstick on paper, Collection of Andy Song

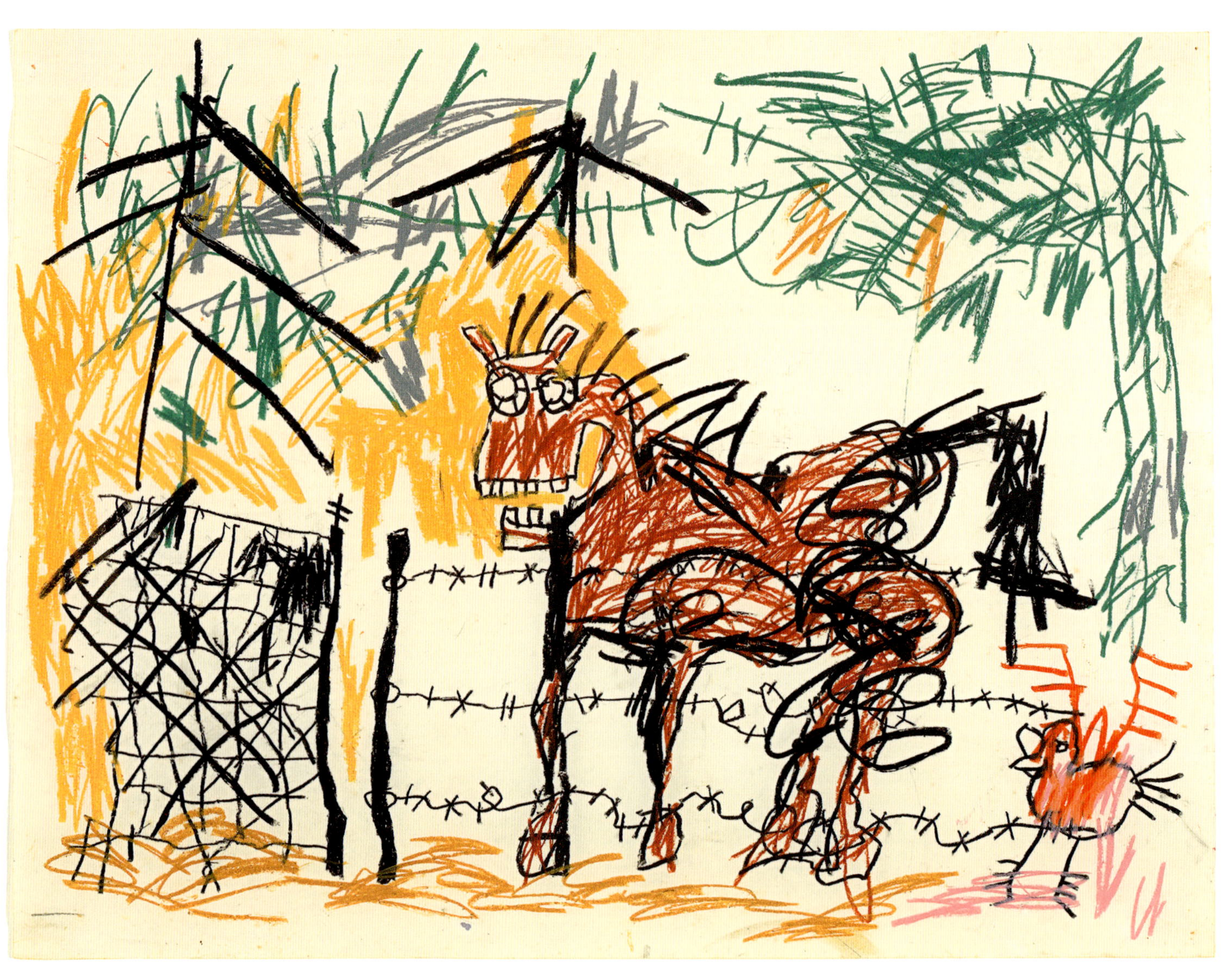

Jean-Michel Basquiat *Untitled* 1981, crayon on paper, 45.0 x 57.2 cm, Collection of Kyoko Tamura

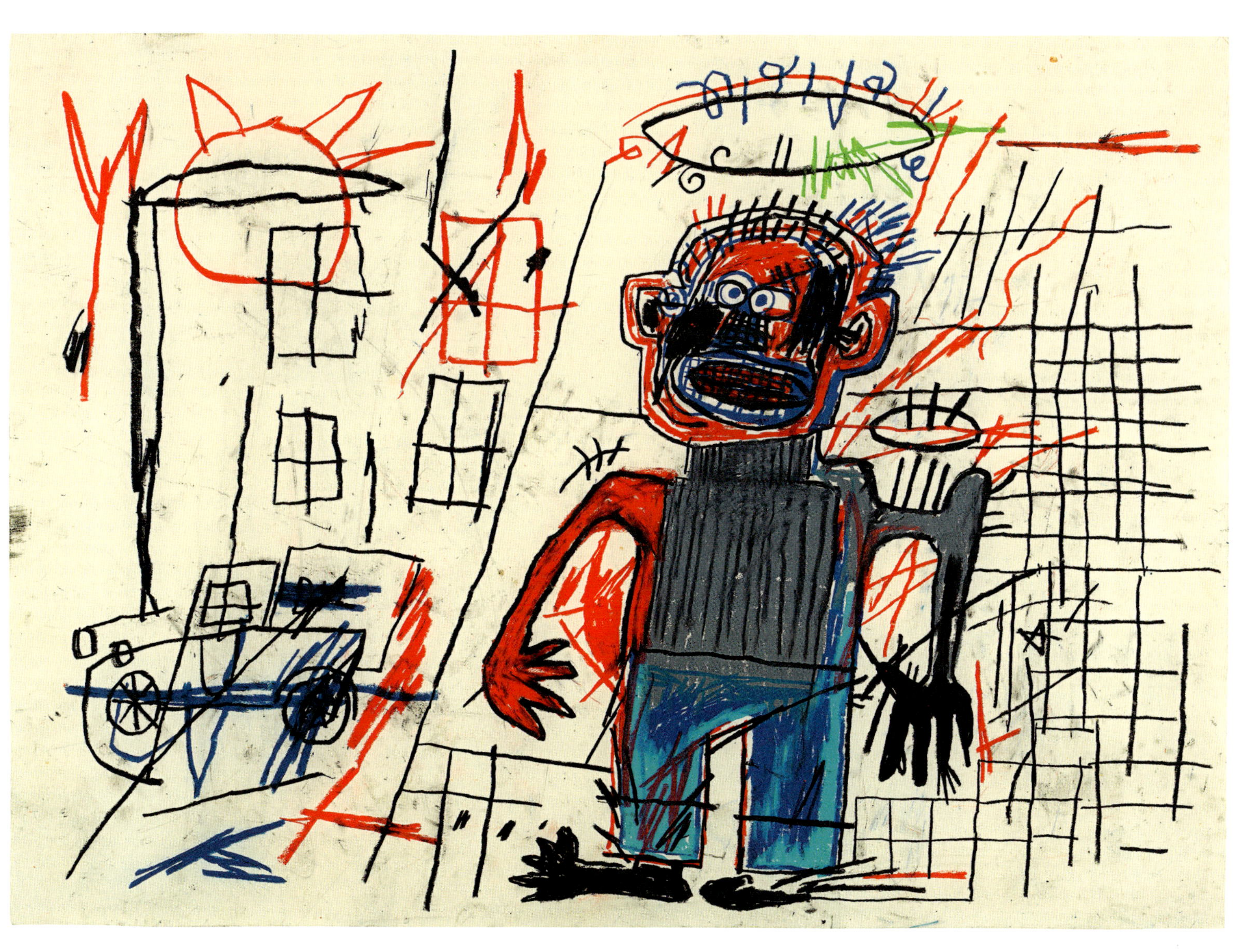

Jean-Michel Basquiat *Warrior* 1982, oilstick on paper, 63.5 x 76.2 cm, Collection of Kyoko Tamura

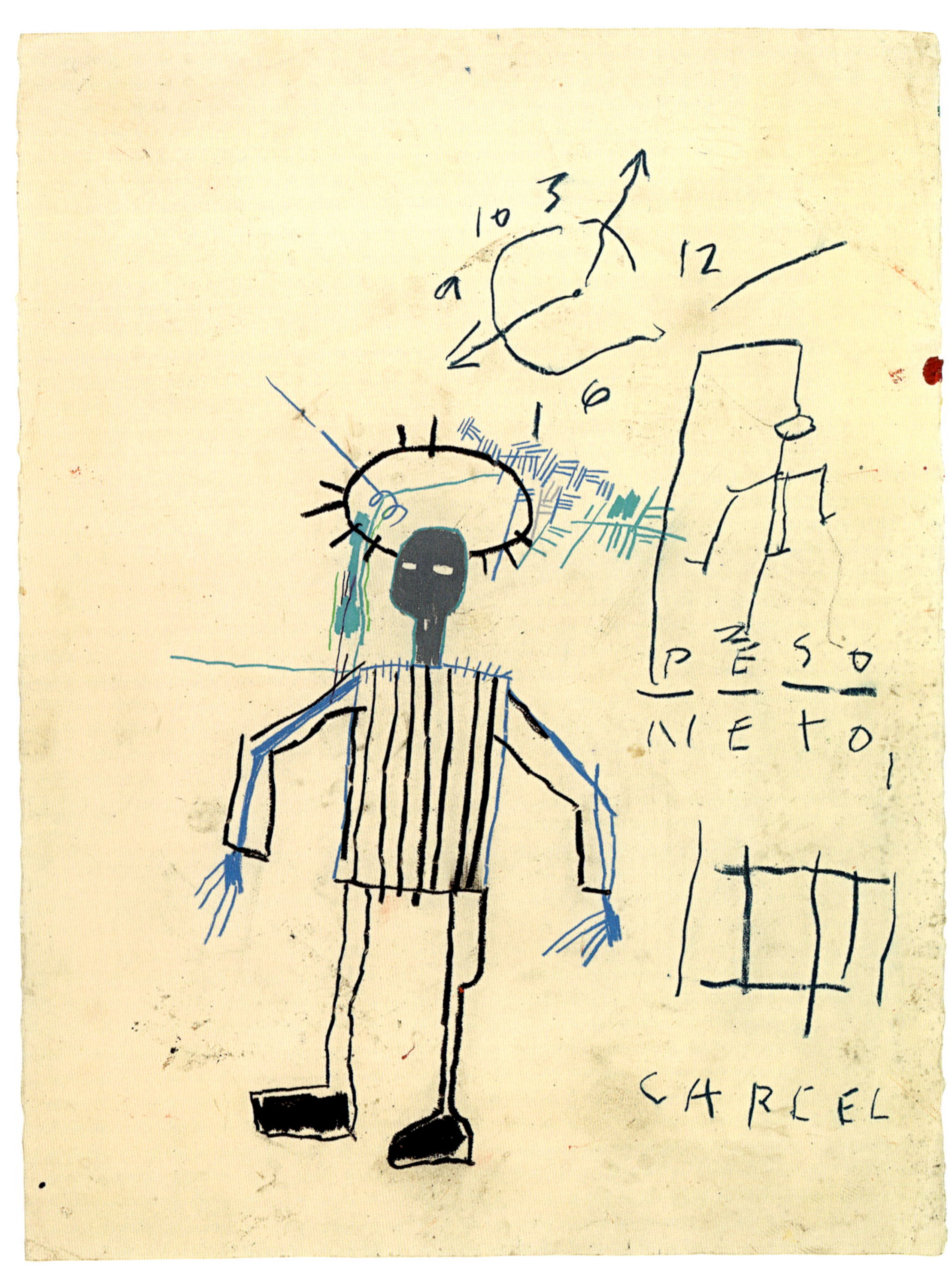

Jean-Michel Basquiat *Untitled (Peso Neto)* 1981, oilstick on paper, 76.2 x 56.5 cm, Collection of Kyoko Tamura

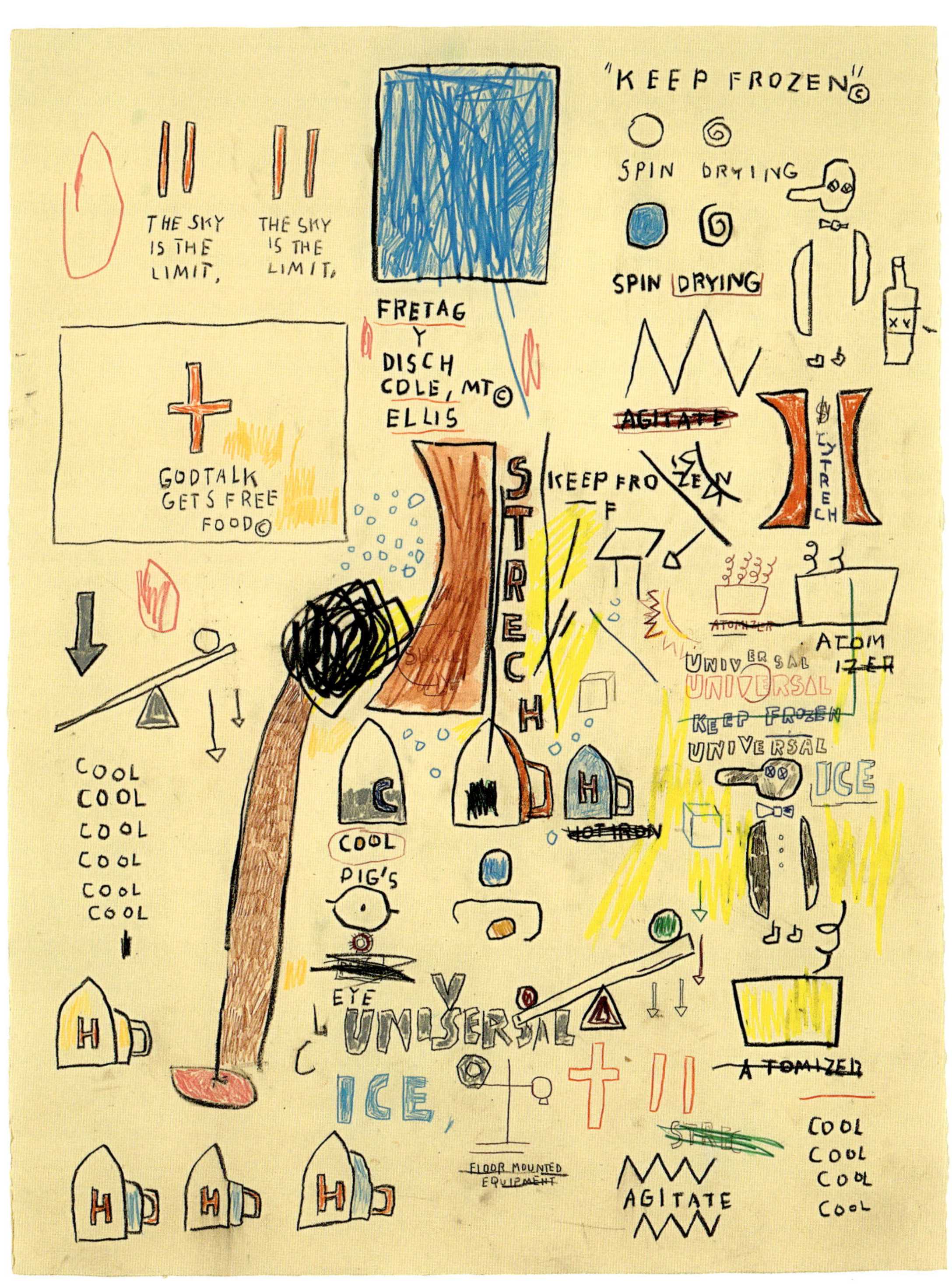

Jean-Michel Basquiat *Untitled* 1987, wax crayon, coloured crayon and pencil on paper, 76.5 x 56.5 cm, Collection of Kyoko Tamura

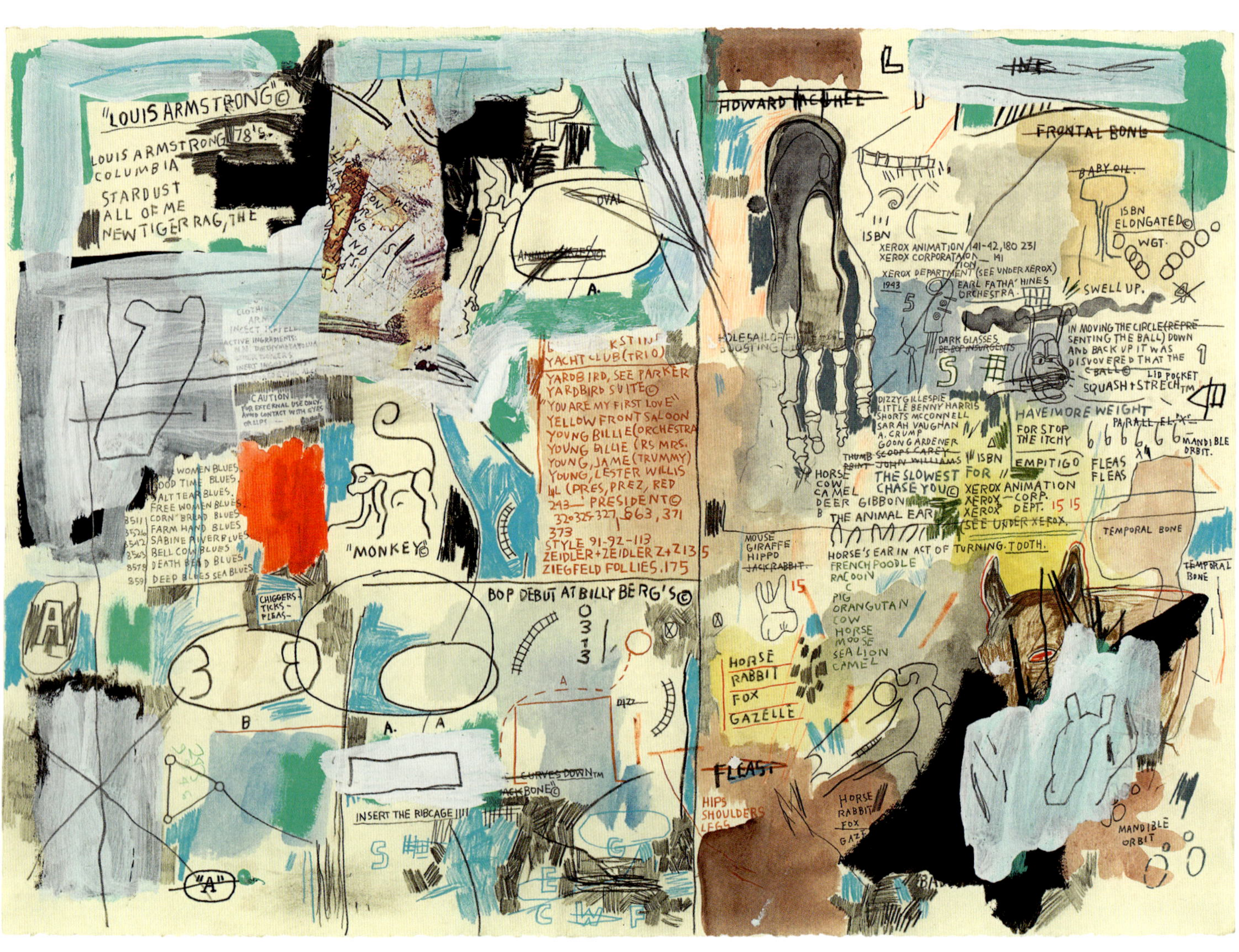

Jean-Michel Basquiat *Untitled (Armstrong)* 1985, mixed media on paper, 56.0 x 76.0 cm, Collection of Kyoko Tamura

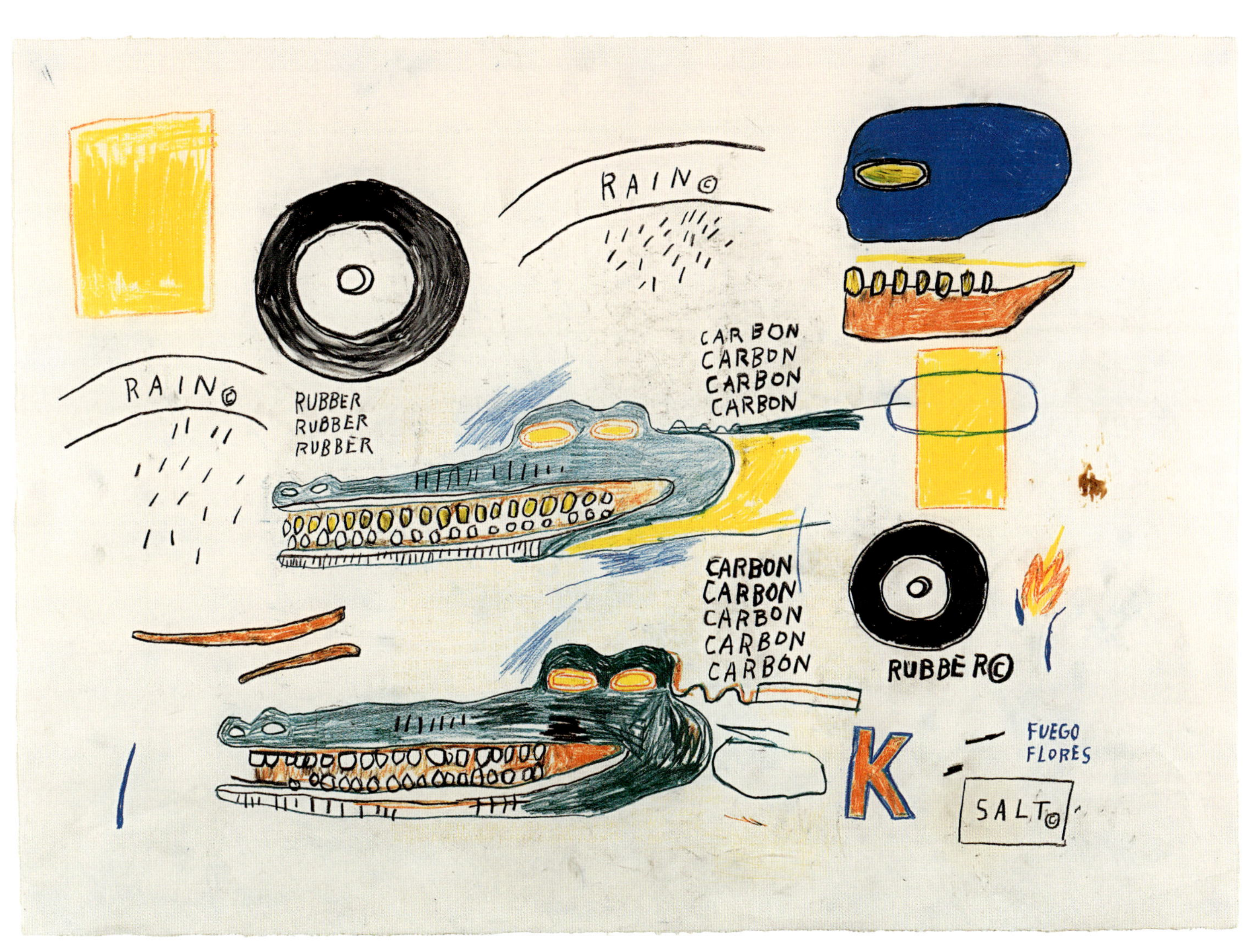

Jean-Michel Basquiat *Izod* 1984, oilstick and ballpoint pen on paper, 55.9 x 76.2 cm, Collection of Kyoko Tamura

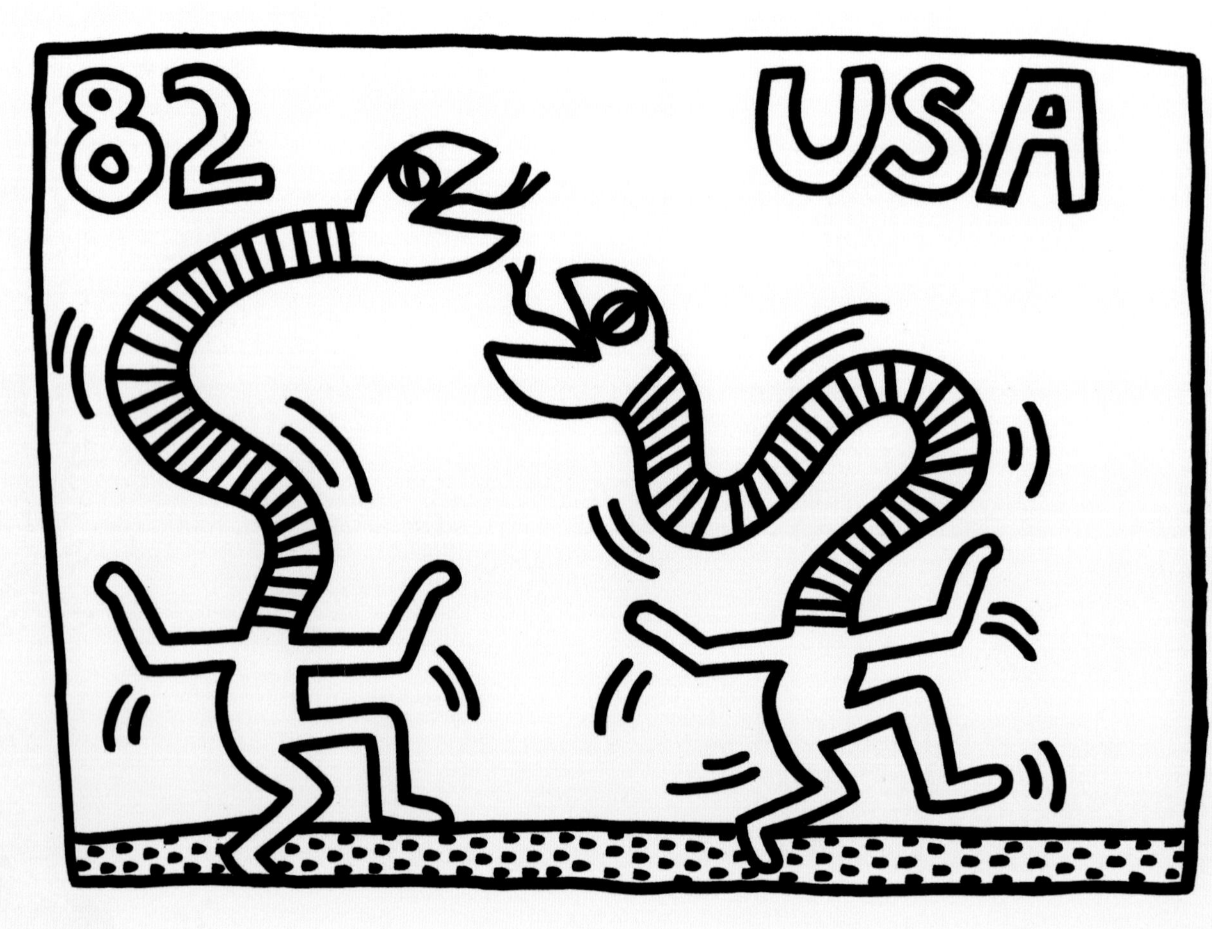

Keith Haring *Untitled* 1982, ink on paper, 97.0 x 127.0 cm, Collection of KAWS

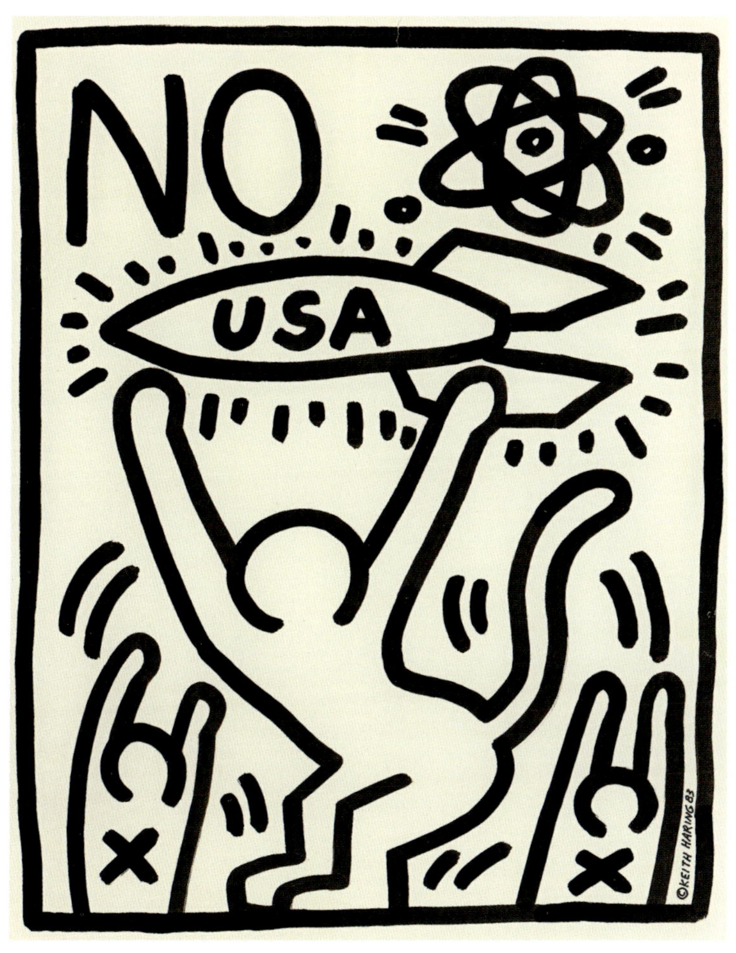

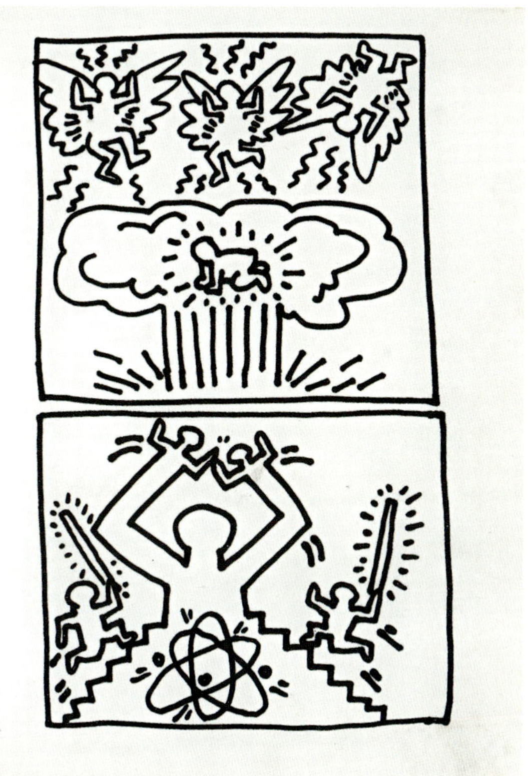

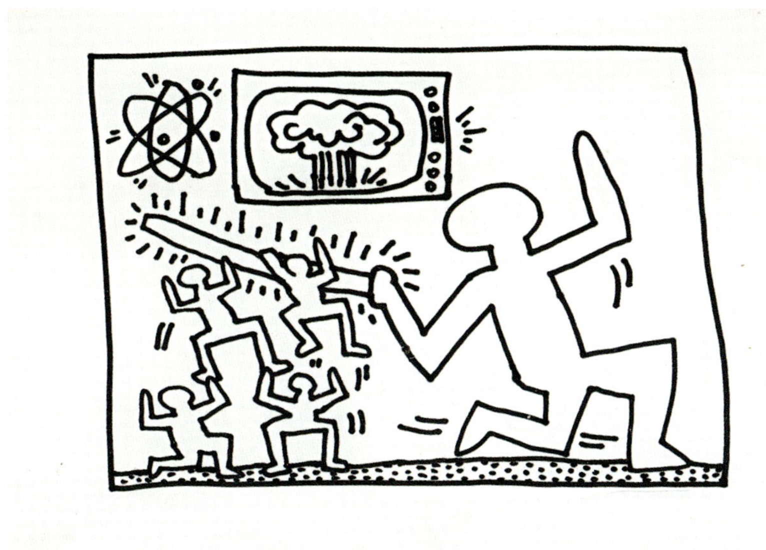

(clockwise from top left) Keith Haring *Untitled* 1983, ink on paper, 63.5 x 48.2 cm, Private collection; *Untitled* 1982, fibre-tipped pen on paper, 30.5 x 22.9 cm, Collection of Larry Warsh; *Untitled* 1982, fibre-tipped pen on paper, 22.9 x 30.5 cm, Collection of Larry Warsh

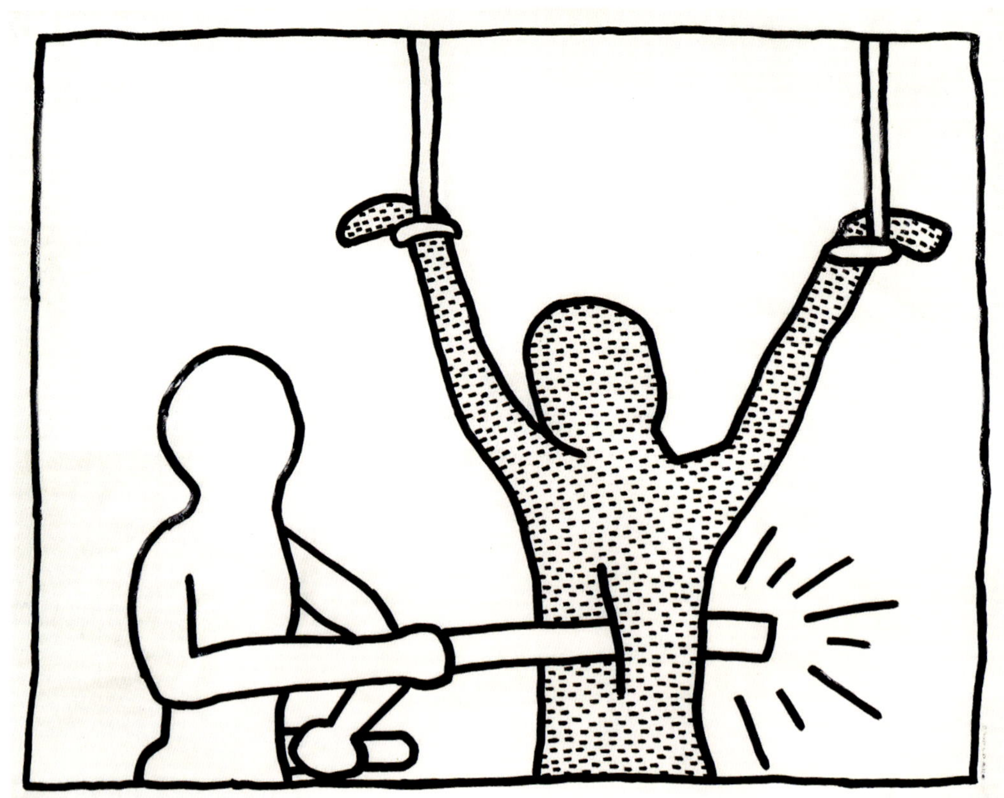

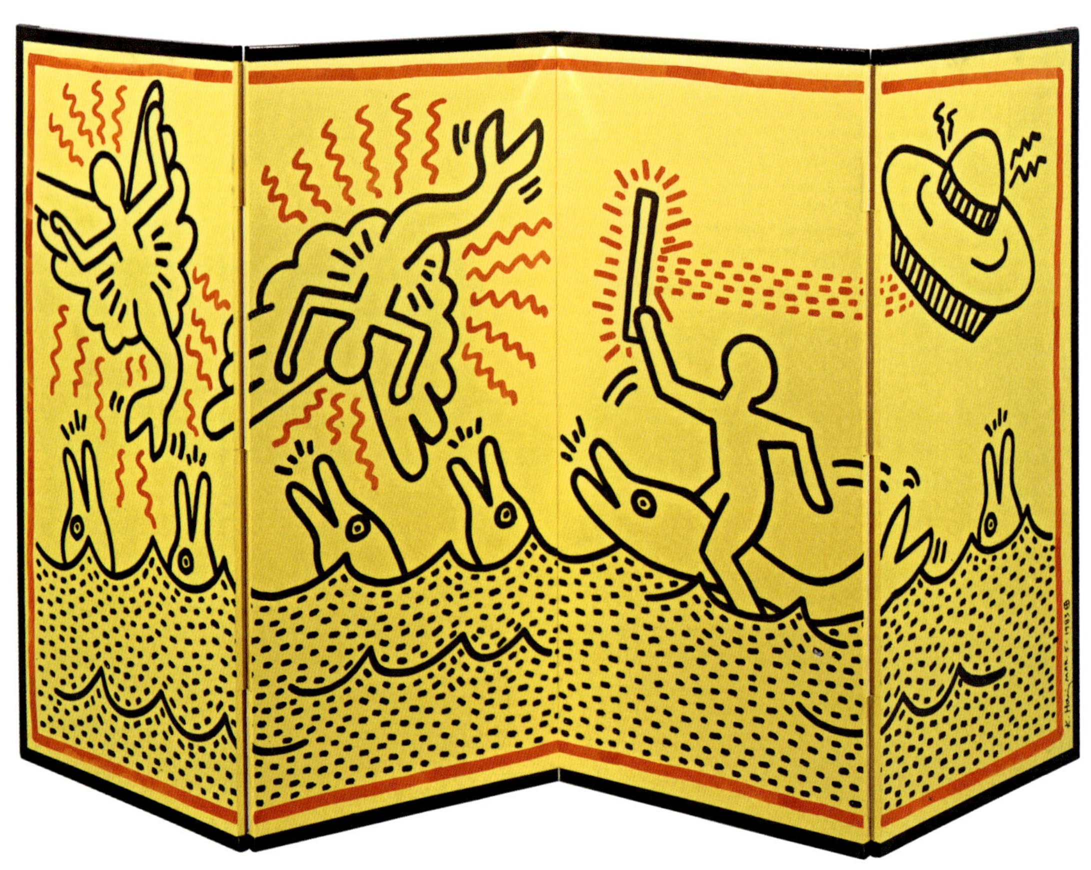

(top) Keith Haring *Untitled* 1981, sumi ink on vellum, 105.4 x 132.1 cm, Collection of Ms Alona Kagan, USA
(bottom) Keith Haring *Untitled* 1983, sumi ink on paper screen, 91.4 x 165.1 cm, Collection of KAWS

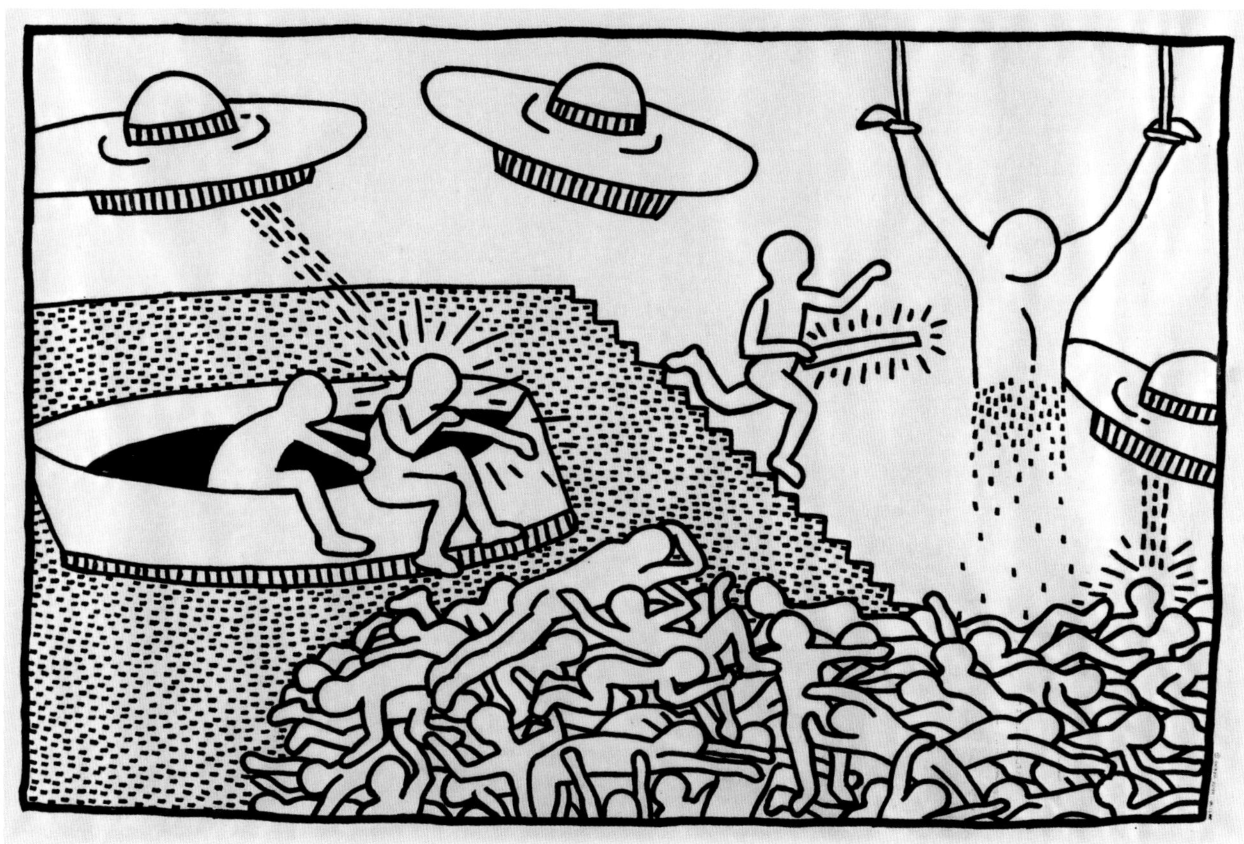

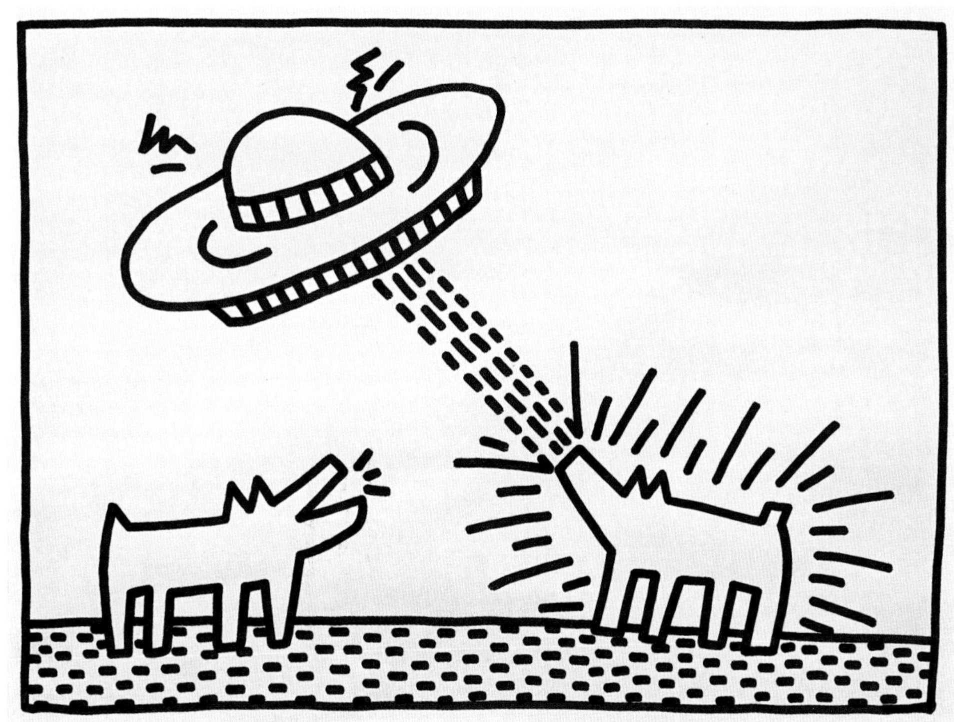

(top) Keith Haring *Untitled* 1981, sumi ink on vellum, 105.4 x 156.2 cm, Collection of Ms Alona Kagan, USA
(bottom) Keith Haring *Untitled* 1981, ink on paper, 55.8 x 76.2 cm, Private collection

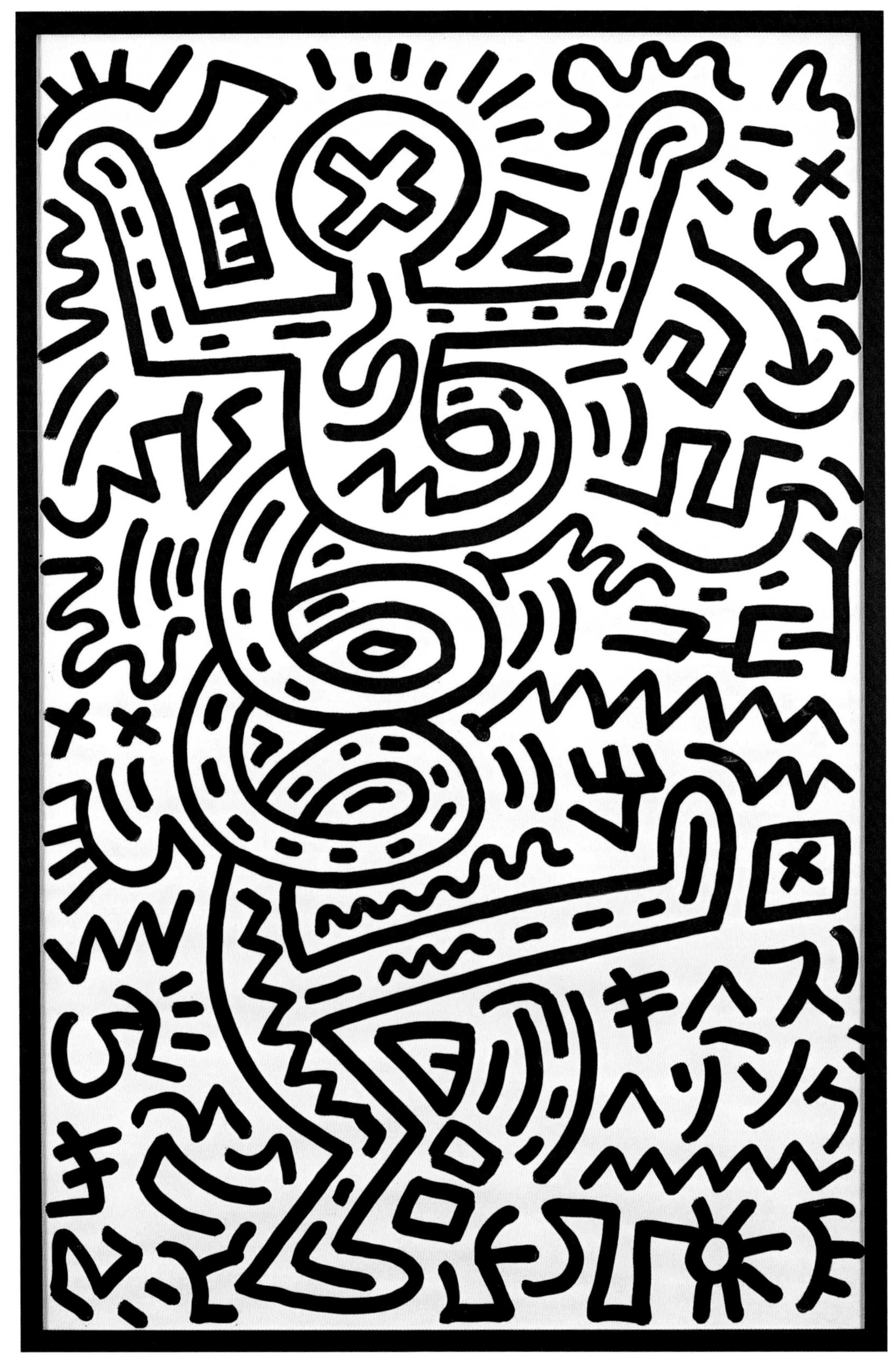

Keith Haring *Untitled* date unknown, sumi ink on paper, 127.0 x 81.3 cm, Collection of Larry Warsh

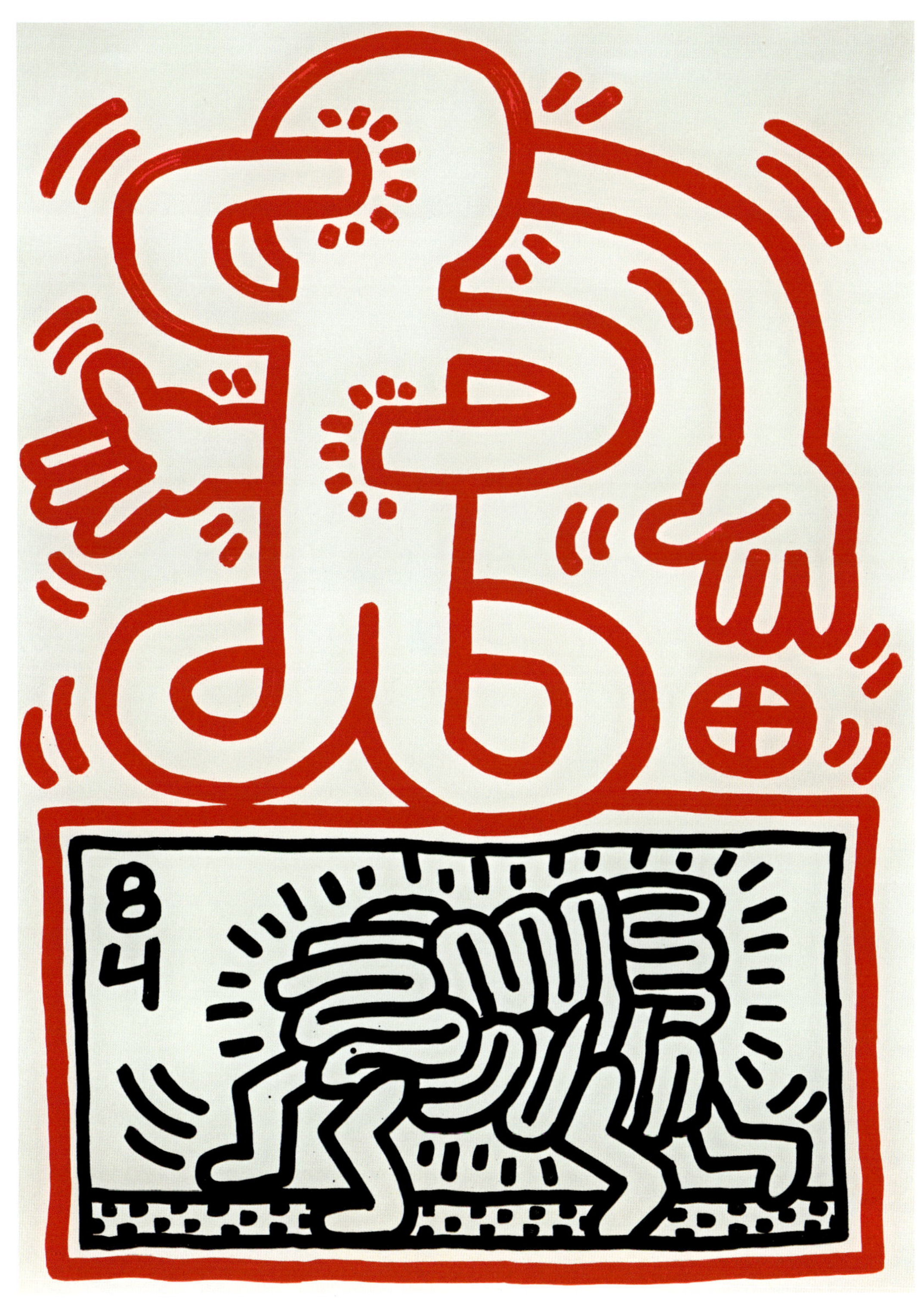

Keith Haring *Untitled* 1984, tempera on paper, 100.0 x 70.0 cm, Private collection, New York

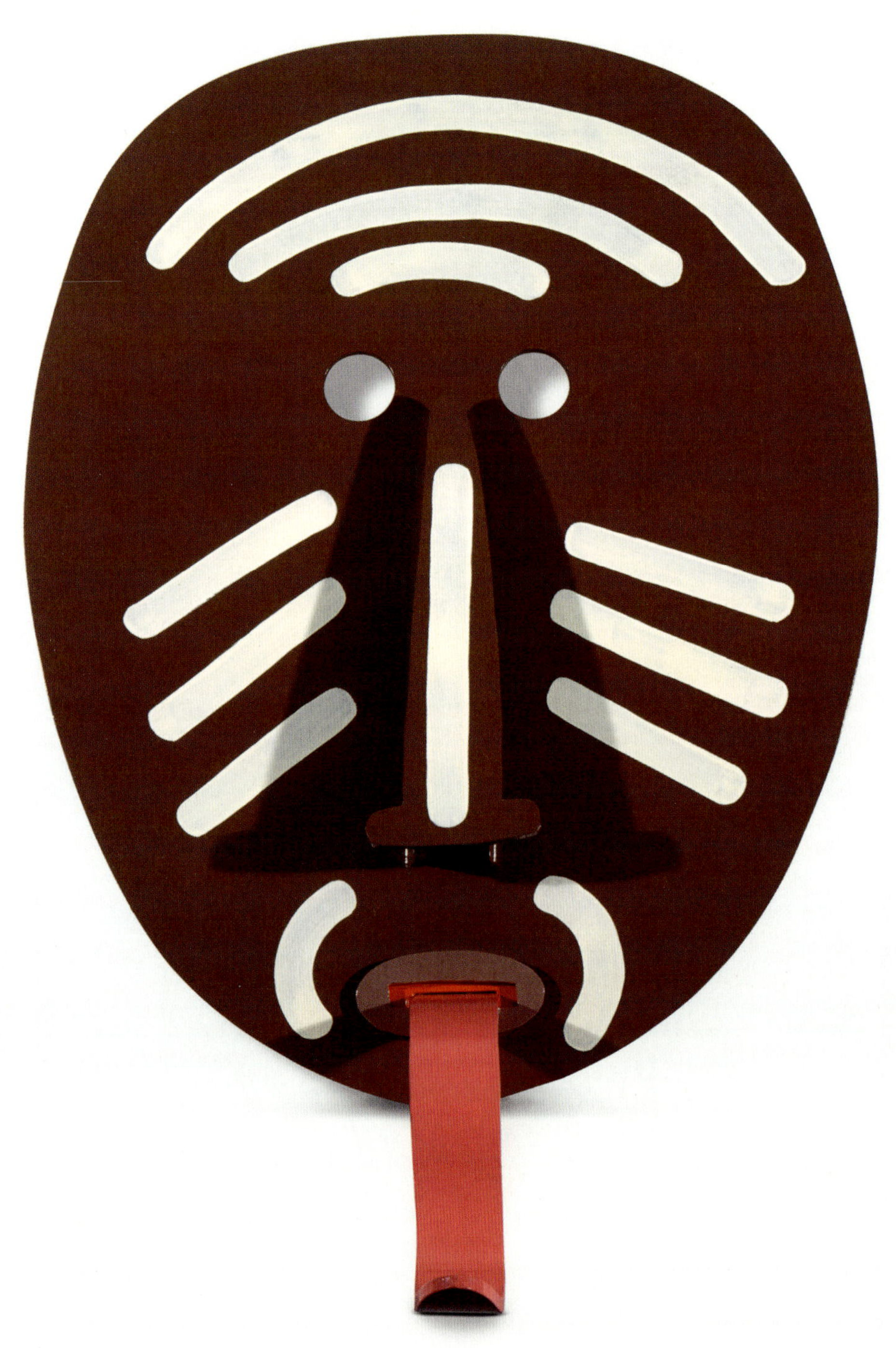

Keith Haring *Untitled* 1987, enamel on metal, 124.5 x 84.0 x 56.0 cm, The Keith Haring Foundation, New York

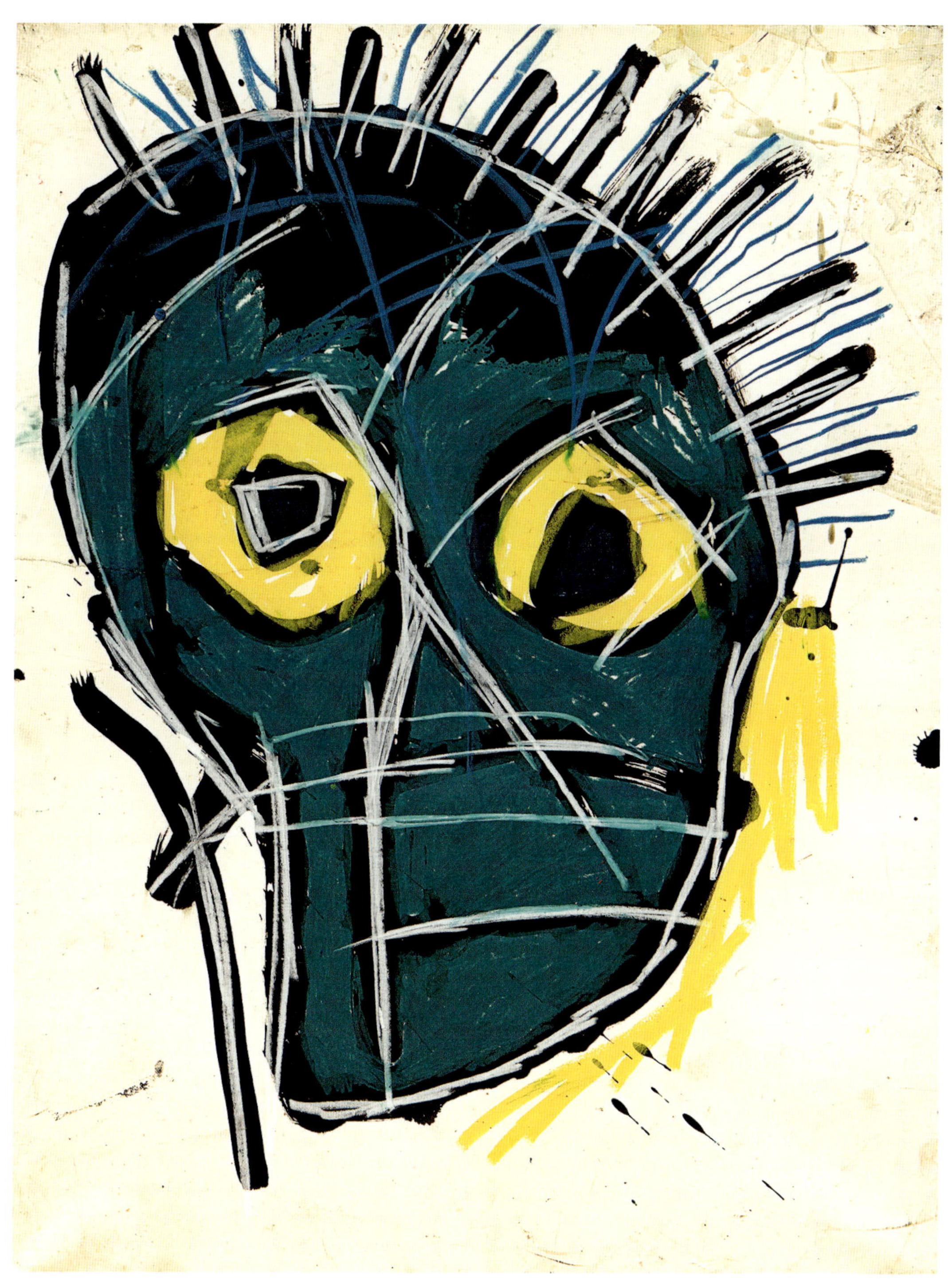

Jean-Michel Basquiat *Untitled* 1983, synthetic polymer paint and oilstick on paper, 76.2 x 55.9 cm, Private collection

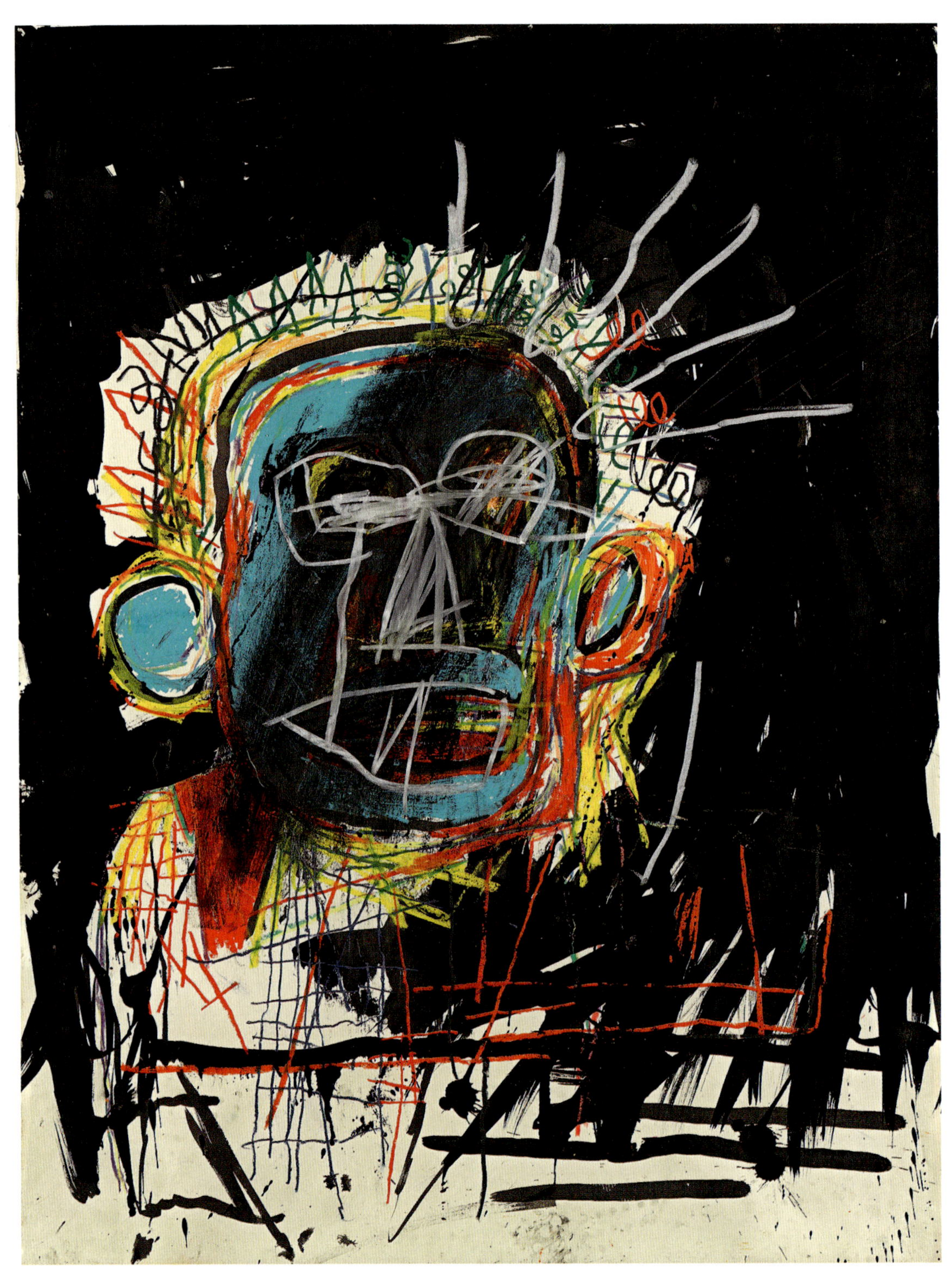

Jean-Michel Basquiat *Untitled (Self-Portrait)* 1982, oilstick and ink on paper, 75.9 x 55.9 cm, Private European collection, courtesy of John Sayegh-Belchatowski

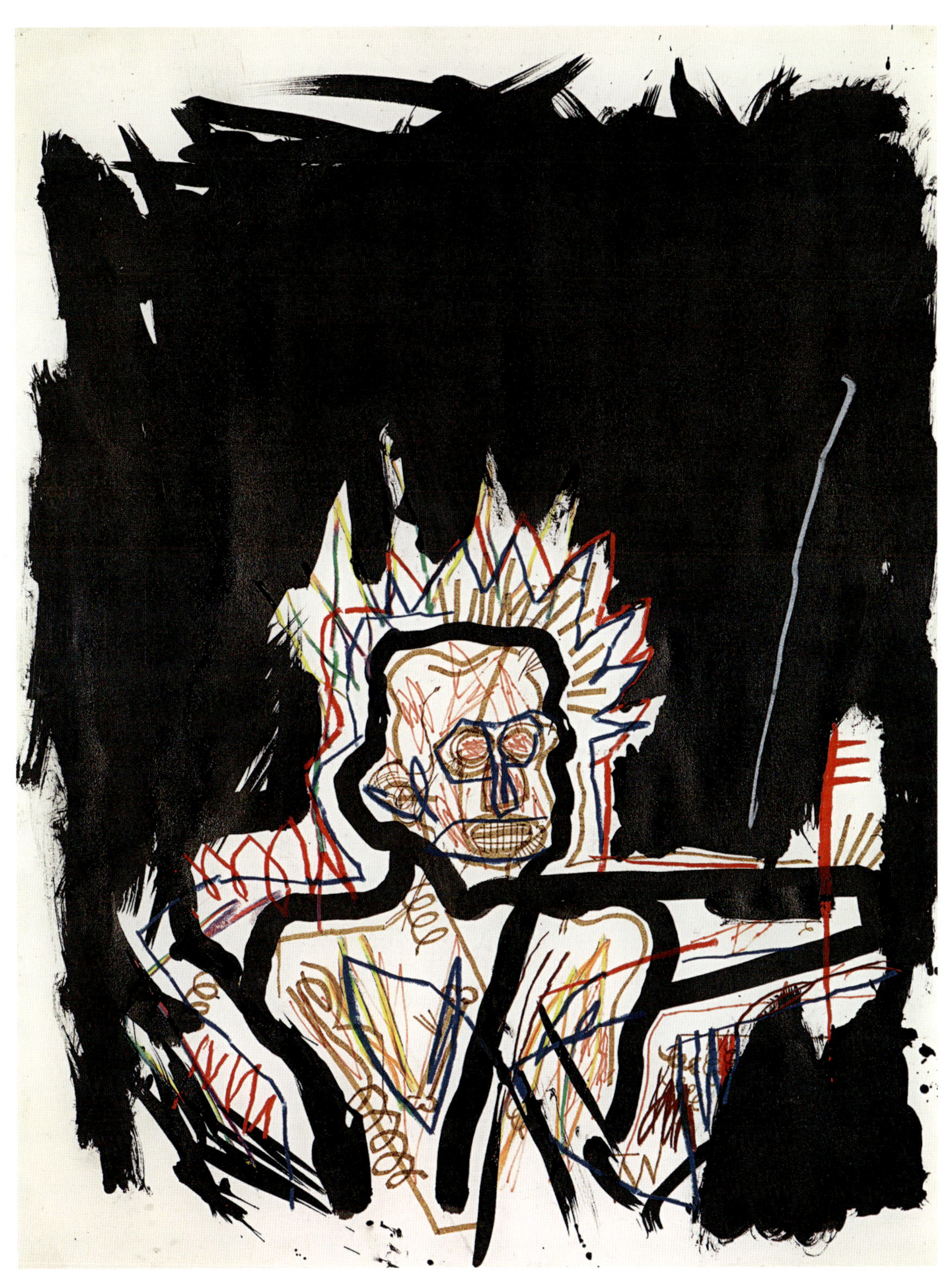

Jean-Michel Basquiat *Untitled (1/2 Black, 1/2 White)* 1982, oilstick and gouache on paper, 75.6 x 55.9 cm, Private collection

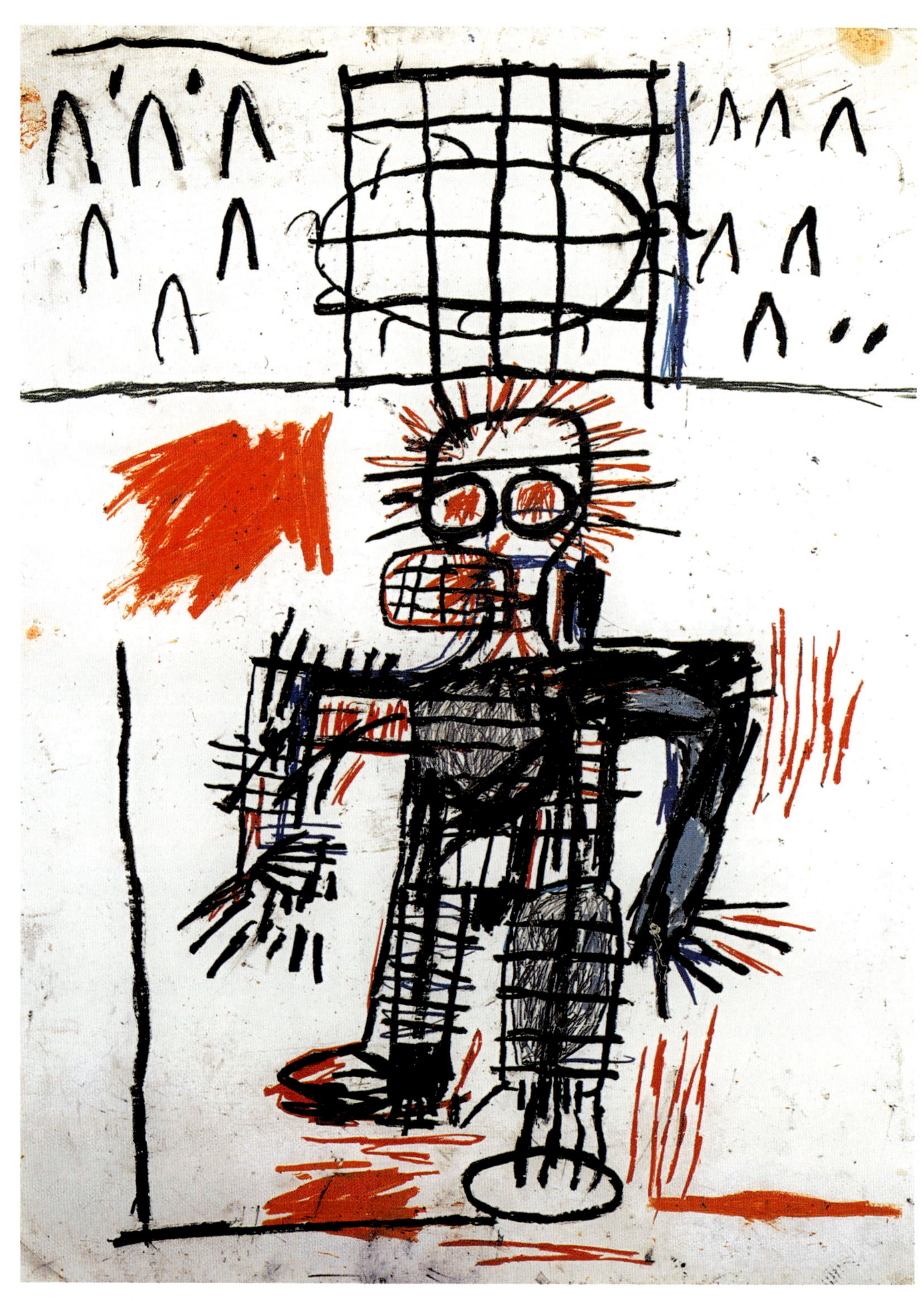

Jean-Michel Basquiat *Untitled* 1982, oil and graphite on paper, 108.5 x 76.8 cm, Private collection

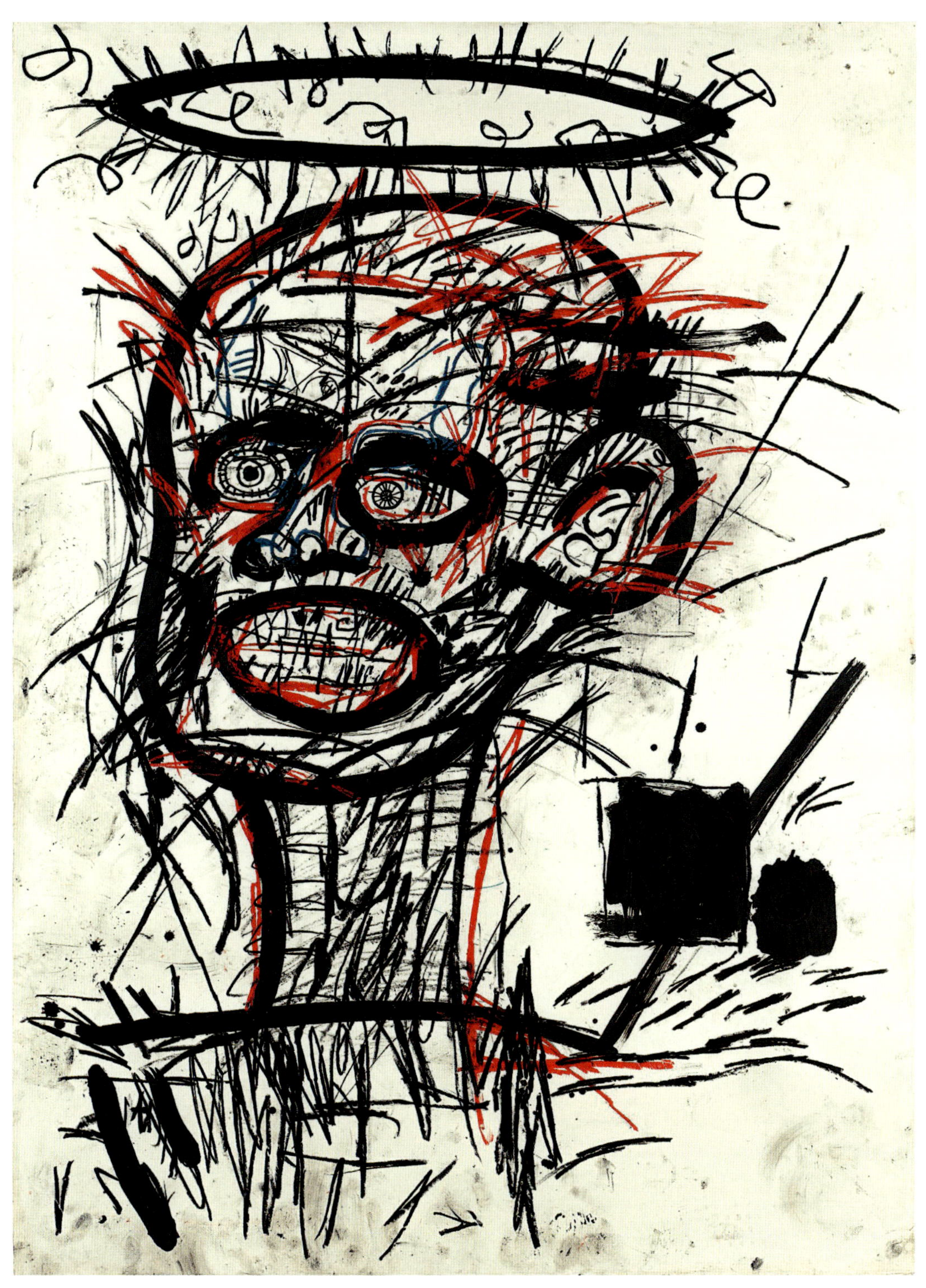

Jean-Michel Basquiat *Untitled* 1982, oilstick and ink on paper, 108.6 x 77.2 cm, Private collection

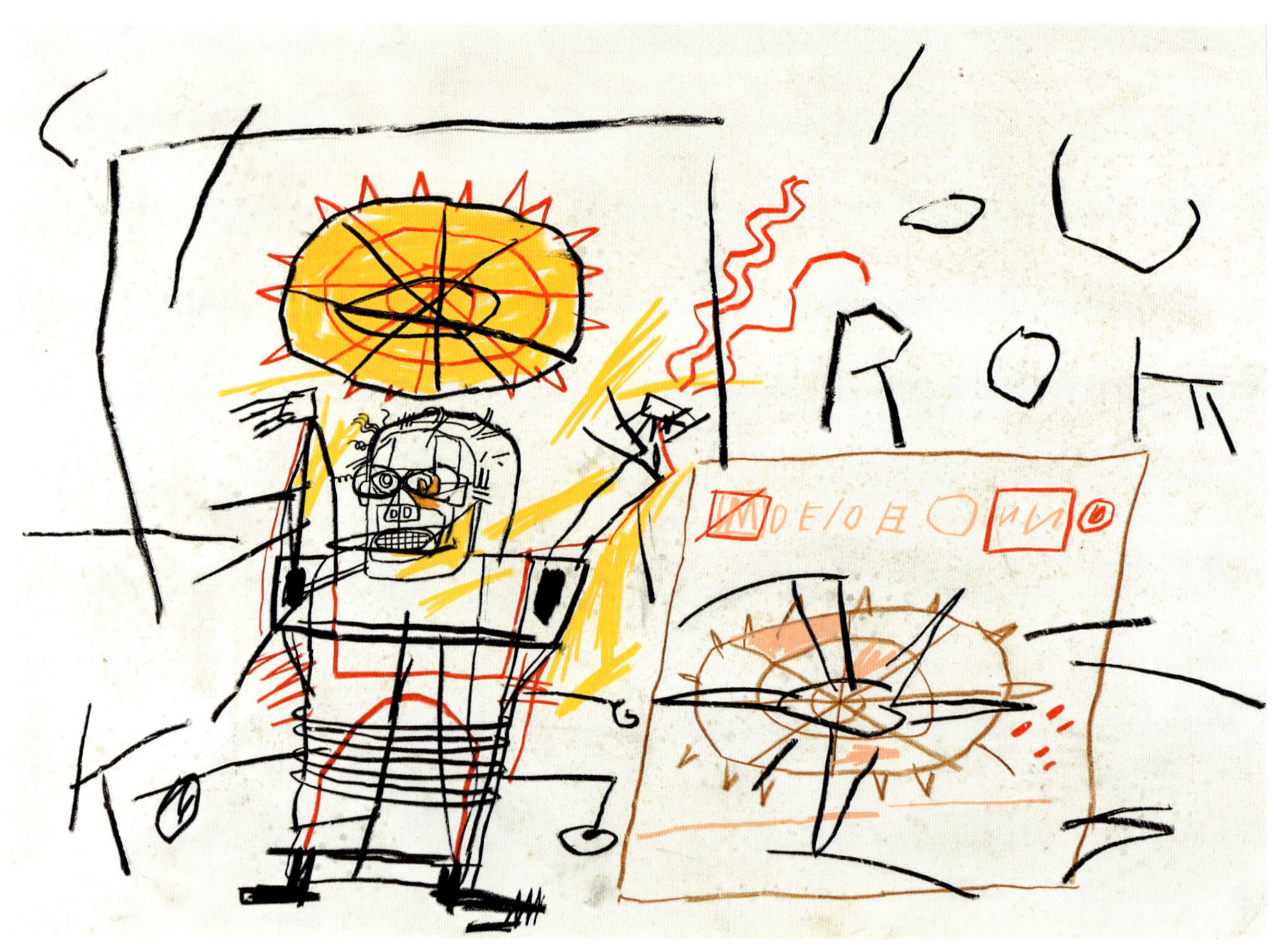

Jean-Michel Basquiat *Untitled* 1982, crayon and oilstick on paper, 54.5 x 75.0 cm, agnès b. collection

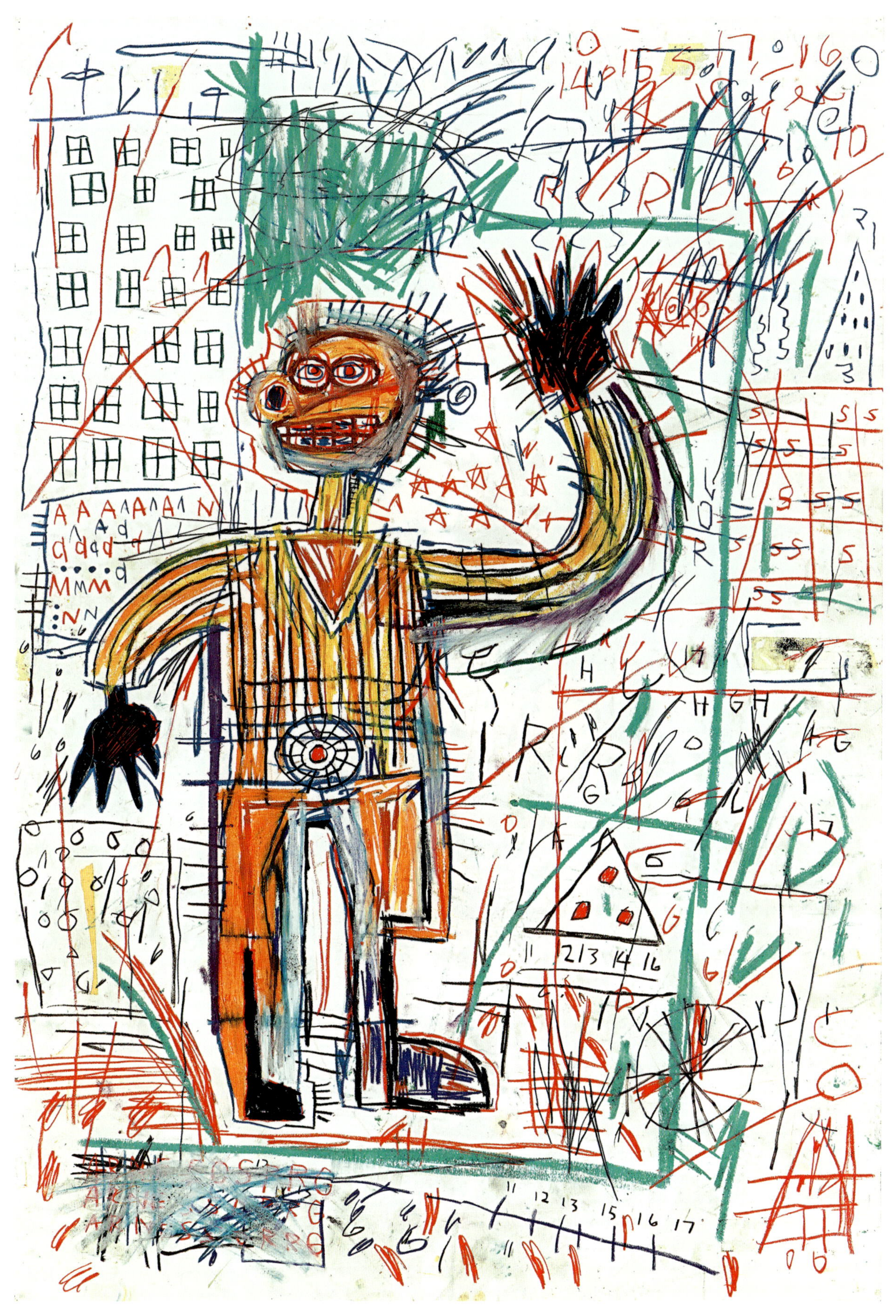

Jean-Michel Basquiat *Untitled* 1982, oilstick on paper, 152.4 x 101.6 cm, Private collection

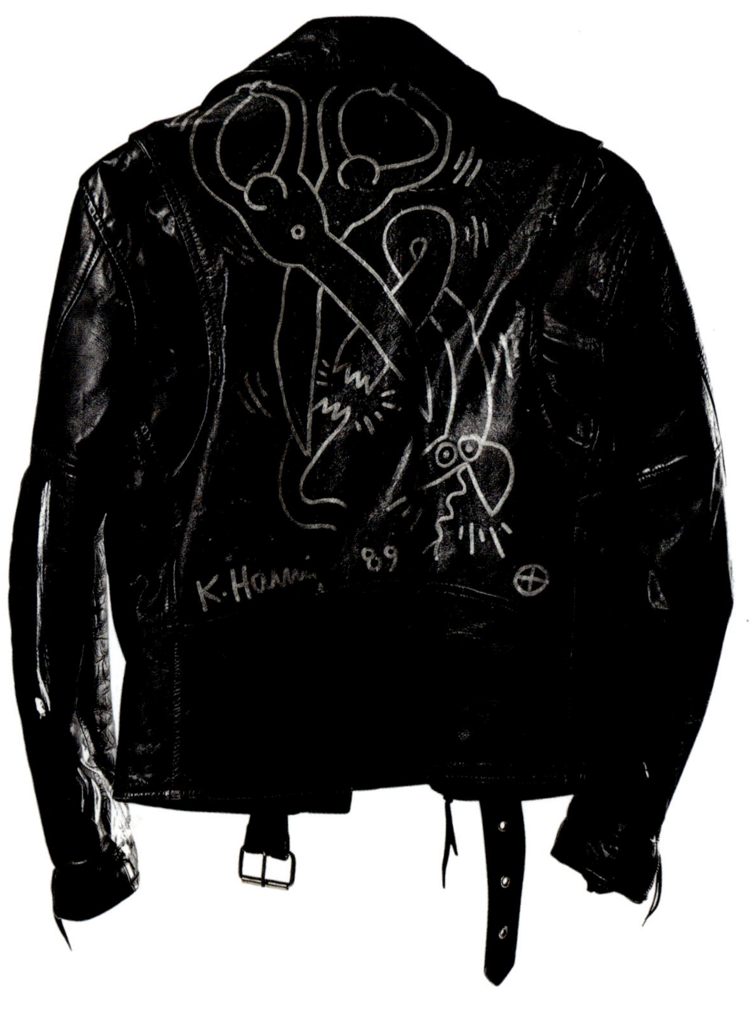

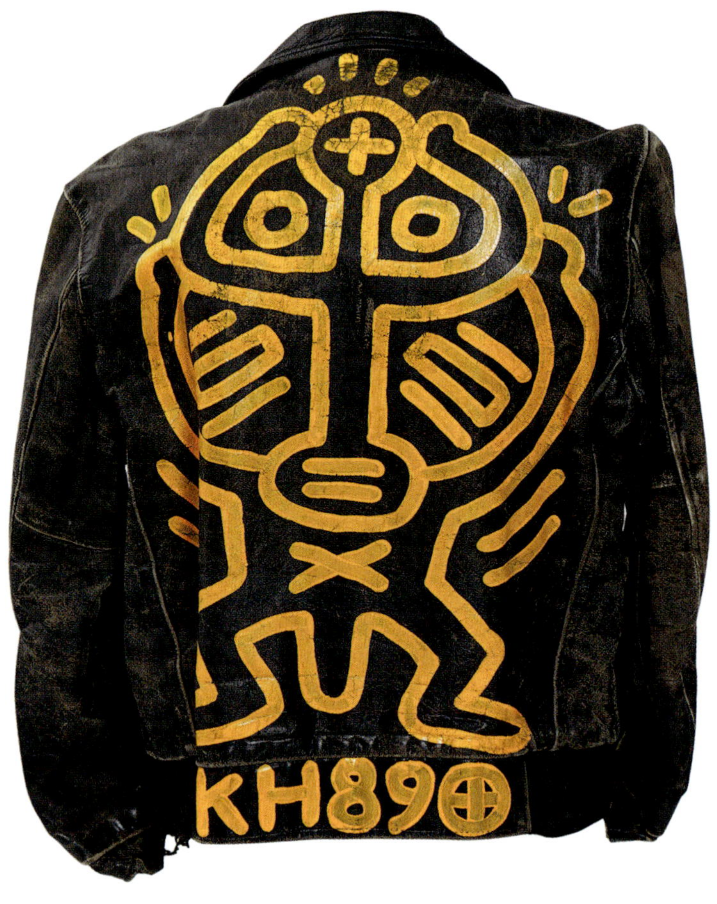

(above left) Keith Haring *Untitled* 1989, paint on leather jacket, 63.5 x 55.8 cm, Private collection
(above right) Keith Haring *Untitled* 1989, paint on leather jacket, 63.5 x 55.9 cm, Collection of Larry Warsh
(opposite) Jean-Michel Basquiat and Keith Haring at Area (detail), New York, 1985

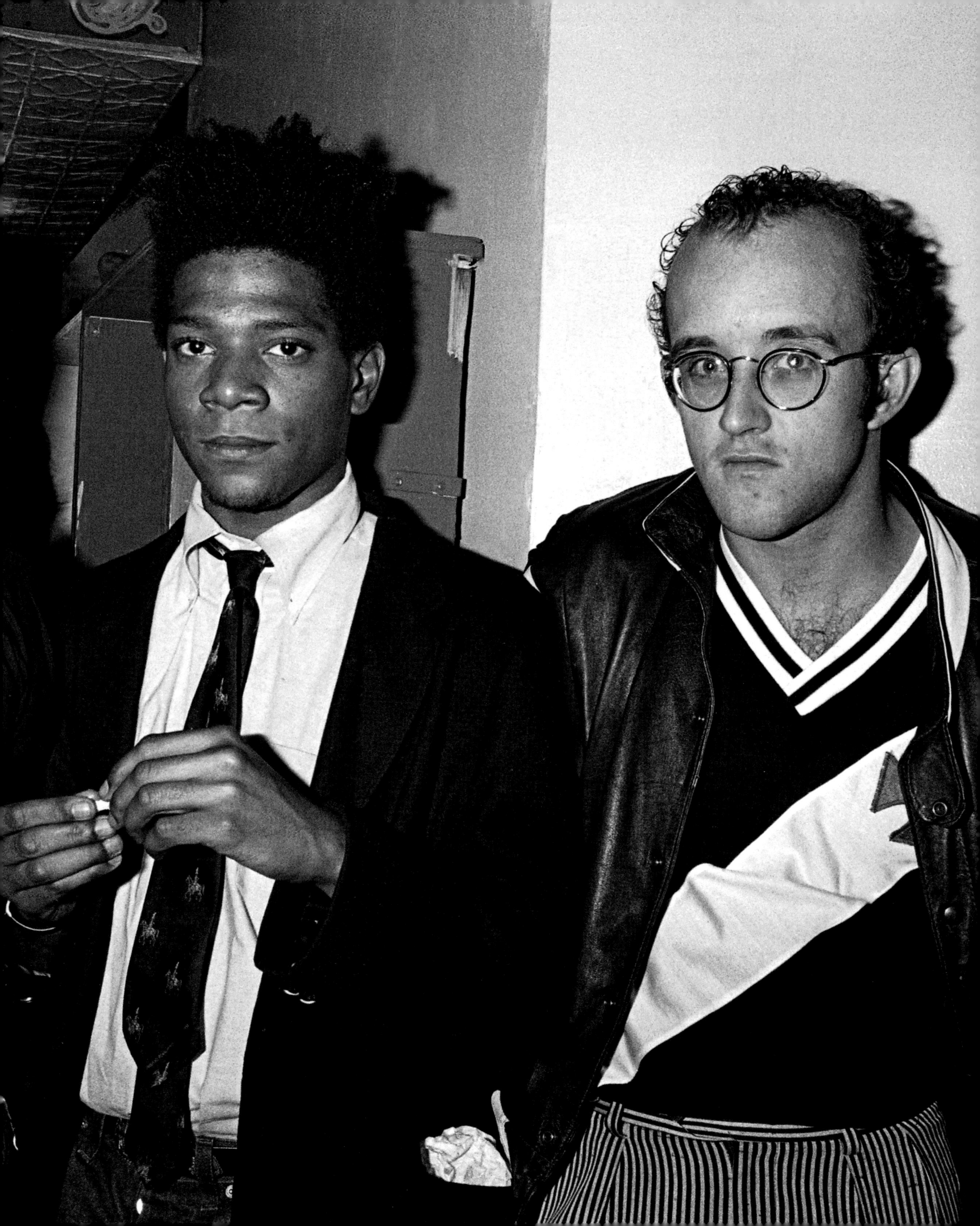

The Art of Friendship

Larry Warsh

During the 1980s – that distant galaxy – I was a younger man coming of age in New York City. I had always enjoyed collecting art, but during those years there was a new focus – the result of a special combination of people, time and place. Looking back, we now understand it as a pivotal moment. It was also during that decade that a clearly recognisable energy was emerging: a core chapter in the history of contemporary art. Those years saw the burgeoning of what we now refer to as the 'downtown scene' (synonymous with the East Village of Manhattan). It was a time of fertile creation, and an era like no other.

The Lower East Side was always abuzz with artistic and social activities and it was also the place where I spent time with many of my friends, people who defined the times – Rene Ricard, Henry Geldzahler, Kenny Scharf, Patti Astor, Kiely Jenkins and Leonard 'Lenny' McGurr (aka Futura 2000), among others. There were always parties, exhibitions and special events and the city was bursting with raw spirit. It was obvious to me that something groundbreaking was taking place, something akin to what we see today in terms of the expansion of popular culture.

There was an implied generosity and a strong sense of continuous interchange and interconnectedness between artists back then, and a feeling of support and care. As Futura 2000 comments: 'Keith [was known] for his wonderful humanity and super generosity, and Jean-Michel for being more than a radiant child, [as] he would later be coined'.[1] Many of the Haring and Basquiat works that I was fortunate to collect are a result of the artists' generosity towards a close circle of friends. Keith, in particular, was always giving artworks to his dearest companions. I think he understood how important it would be for his friends and he even thought about their families and children, too. Whether it was [photographer, stylist, art director] Maripol's or Kenny's or Futura's children, Keith knew his gifts would be cherished by those who loved him.

The serendipitous energy among friends was the catalyst for creativity and a reinforcement of the moment. The friendship

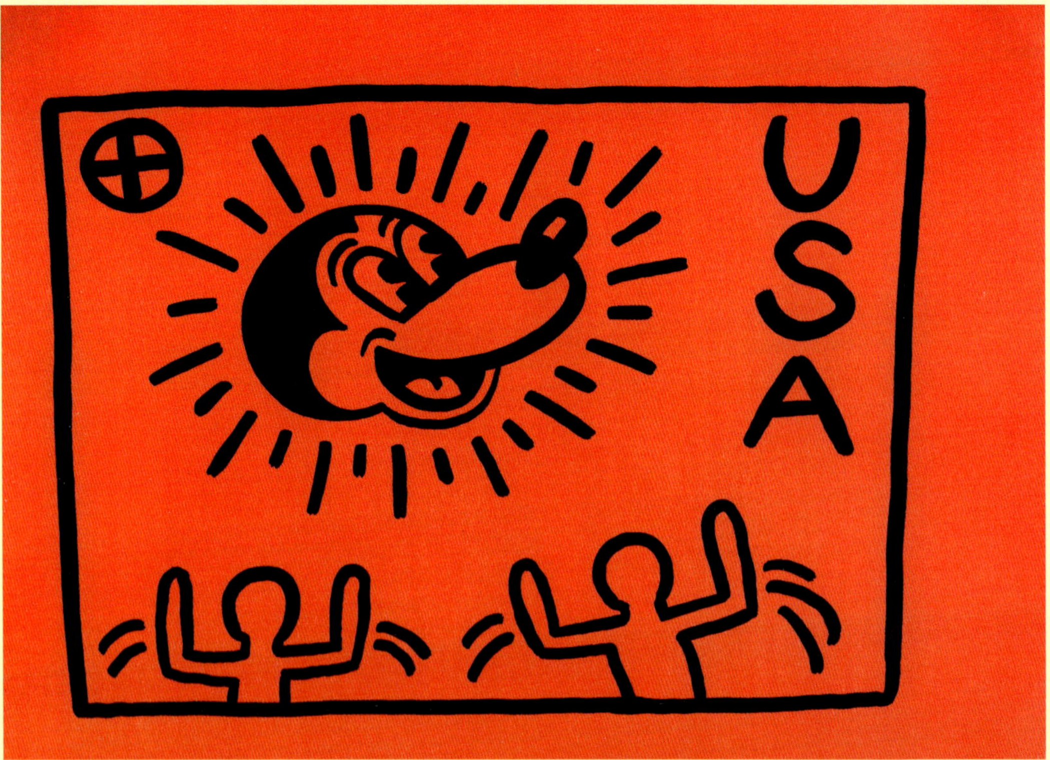

between Keith Haring and Kenny Scharf, for example, was something special and noteworthy. (I used to spend a lot of time with Kenny, in particular, and it was amazing to witness the progression of his art and his rise to fame along with Keith.) There was also a feeling of sincere camaraderie within the city's creative community during those years: artists, celebrities, musicians, dancers, performers, writers, theorists, curators and all the distinguished creative types were connected through the passion and purpose of the day. Although the dark cloud of AIDS hung over the community, it brought everyone closer and engendered a shared sense of responsibility.

Back then, the idea of art as a 'commodity' was not in full force, as it is today. I was lucky to obtain many special pieces that are representative of deep and formative friendships and that as a whole capture a moment and tell a story about that period. As curator and pop cultural critic Carlo McCormick states:

—Given as gifts for any variety of occasions, traded as signs of mutual respect or purchased for token sums as a way of financial support in difficult times, the continuous exchange of work between artists and their peer group has little to do with the kinds of evaluations that are constructed within galleries or auction houses.[2]

During those years, meetings happened naturally – there were no mobile phones, no internet, no hyper-connected social media platforms. But it was equally energising in a different way. One afternoon, while walking in the East Village's famous St Marks Place, I stumbled into the 51X Gallery, and there I met artist Rich Colicchio and we became fast friends. He marched me right over to meet Patti Astor at her Fun Gallery and then the real fun began! Patti was so full of enthusiasm and we immediately got along. Although I fostered many significant friendships during that time, Patti was one of the first people I really connected with and her generosity towards me cannot be overestimated.

Keith Haring *Untitled* 1982, ink on paper, 55.9 x 71.1 cm, Collection of Larry Warsh

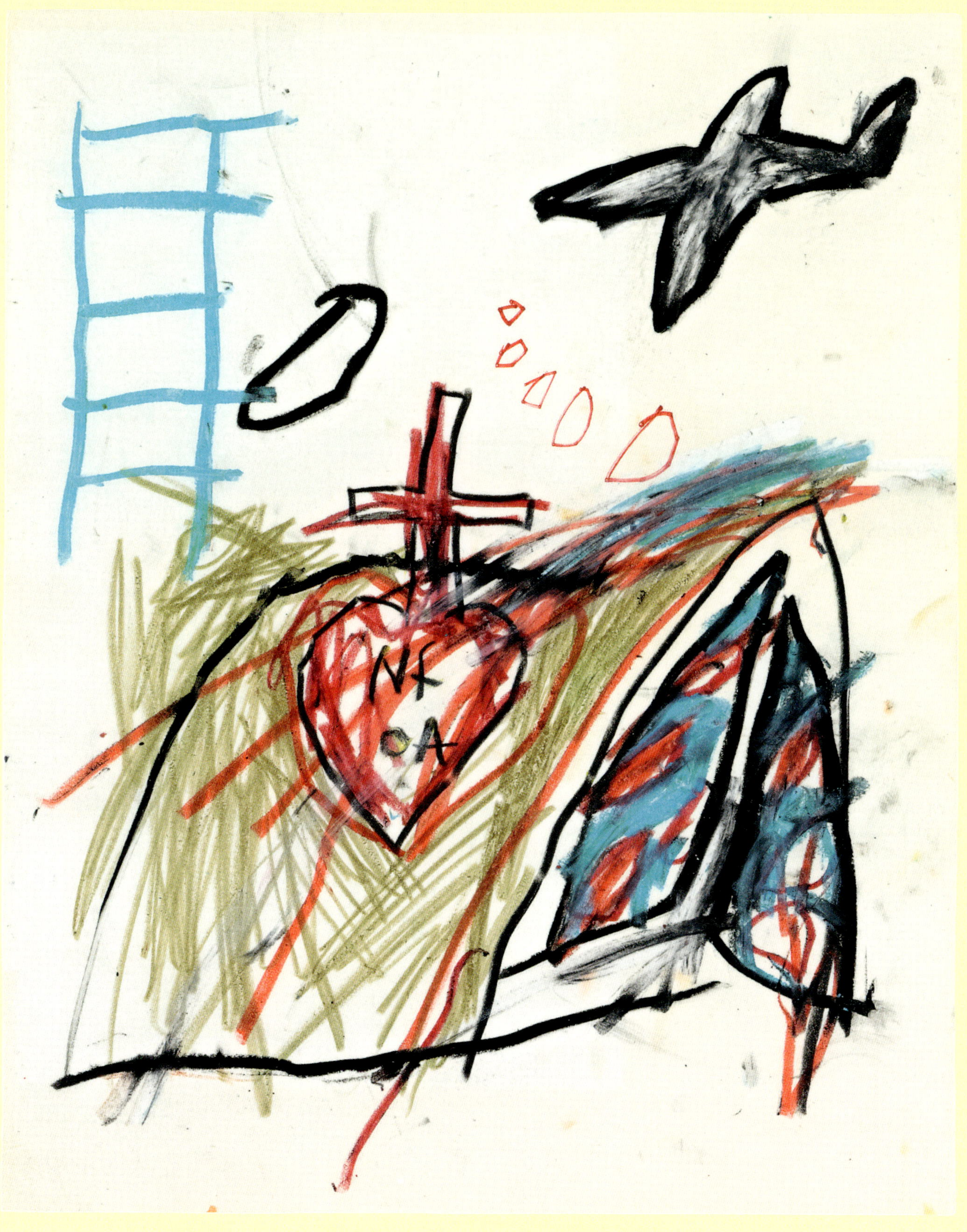

Jean-Michel Basquiat *Untitled (Heart / Henry Geldzahler)* 1981, mixed media on paper, 30.5 x 45.7 cm, Collection of Larry Warsh

Patti's renowned Fun Gallery was an important locus for the revolving crowd of downtown artists and their admiring fans. While all of the works on view in this unprecedented exhibition at the NGV possess a unique narrative, *Untitled (Fun fridge)*, 1982 (p. 225, Collection of Larry Warsh), is one of the most remarkable pieces that came directly from Patti. The fridge was a fixture at her gallery and everyone who hung out there would tag it. Eventually it bore signatures by all the greats: Jean-Michel's famed SAMO© alias, Keith's familiar 'radiant baby' drawing, Kenny's smiling Fred Flintstone head, plus tags by Fab 5 Freddy, Futura 2000 and many others.

The fridge is a living statement of the times and a testimony to the people who imbued the era with its unbridled dynamism. During those days no one could have anticipated what was to come – the meteoric rise and occasional fall of some, and the untimely deaths of others (Keith, Jean-Michel and many more). One of the most poignant works referencing this turbulent period is Francesco Clemente's colourful homage to Keith and Jean-Michel, *Keith and Jean*, c. 1990 (p. 29). With his two close friends in mind, Francesco donated this work for auction at New York's legendary Love Ball of 1989, an AIDS benefit curated by nightlife figure and activist Susanne Bartsch.

As my relationships within the community deepened, so did my understanding of the art being created. My ability to preserve these works is really what helped me analyse the moment with a vision of the future. In this regard, my true mentor and steady ambassador was Rene Ricard. Poet, actor, artist and stalwart figure of New York's downtown cultural scene, Rene was a brilliant person and a passionate thinker. He wrote intensely about art and his ideas were hugely influential on my perspective and journey as a collector. Rene pushed open a lot of conceptual doors for me. He used to visit me at all hours of the night and he was always eager to share his insights. Rene often arrived with an artwork under his arm to show me – a Clemente, a Haring, a Basquiat, sometimes a Scharf and always lots of George Condos. He was like a walking art gallery, and had a fertile imagination and a polished academic mind to boot.

Sometimes he would become so excited about a certain artwork that he would scream about why that particular piece was important and why I should collect it. I recall the time he showed me Basquiat's drawing *Untitled (Man needs milk)*, 1981 (p. 166, top left). He enthusiastically launched into a conversation about race and what this particular work meant with respect to culture and politics. Rene was extremely considerate and conscious of these powerful themes, and the recurring motifs of Basquiat's work are as relevant now as they were then.

Rene was a natural leader within the cultural milieu, and I am forever grateful to him for the education he gave me. He understood the power of Jean-Michel's works and how they were a true foundation for many amazing things to come. Among the most fortuitous occurrences during those years was the time Rene shared Jean-Michel Basquiat's series of rare unknown 'notebooks' (pp. 172–7) with me. From the moment I encountered Basquiat's notebooks, I was blown away by the playfulness, intensity and realness of what I saw on those pages. Basquiat's words were potent and poetic – I knew it was the opportunity of a lifetime to collect those works. I still consider Basquiat's series of notebooks to be among the most consequential works of his entire career – they boldly express his intimate thoughts and singular voice. In Basquiat's hands, words and writing become a dynamic form of art.

Another important mentor of mine was Henry Geldzahler, the American curator of

Keith Haring *Untitled* 1989, fibre-tipped pen on gelatin silver photograph, 35.5 x 27.9 cm, Collection of Larry Warsh
(pictured) Keith Haring *Untitled* 1989, paint on plastic trophy, 116.8 x 15.2 x 15.2 cm, Collection of Larry Warsh

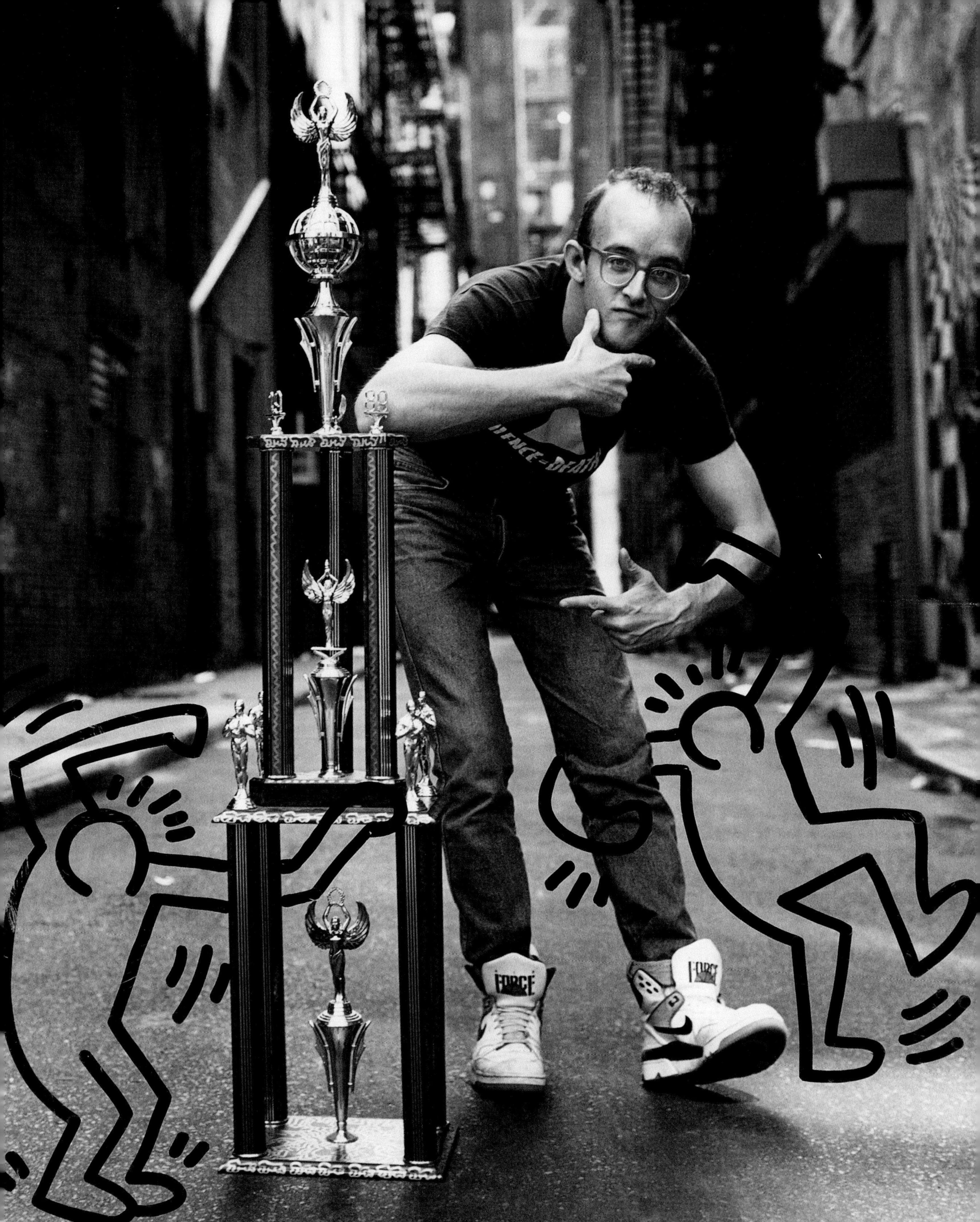
FORCE

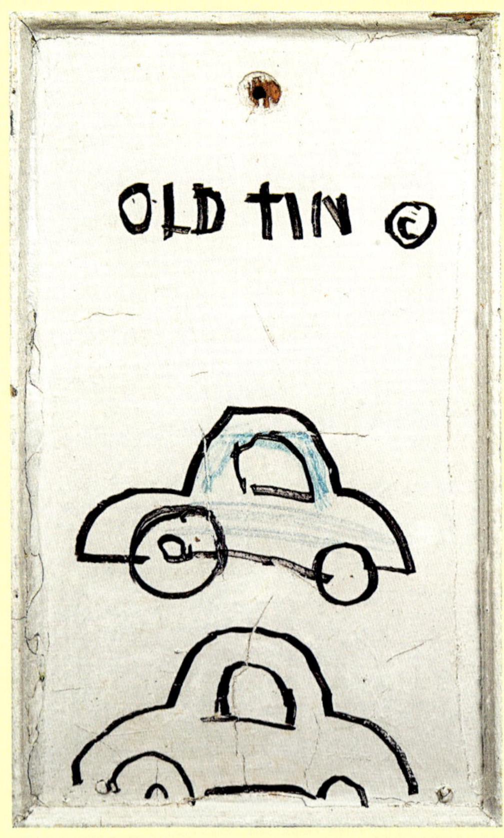

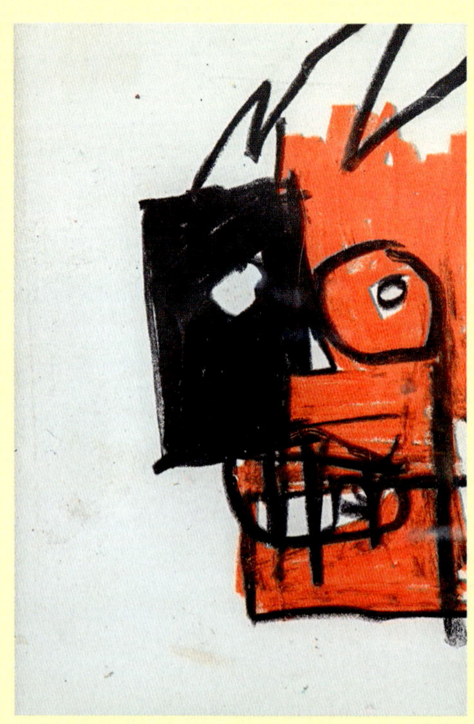

modern and contemporary art, historian and critic. We shared a curious family history and he was like an uncle to me, and I knew him before he befriended Jean-Michel. Henry introduced Jean-Michel to Andy Warhol – the rest is history. (In fact, Henry's connection to the important artist of the 1960s is legendary.) Henry used to show me his collection of special gifts from the earlier generation of New York artists and this was a total inspiration to me. It was a thrill to be associated with some of the moments that were pivotal to the development of global contemporary art.

Bruno Schmidt – the Brazilian-Italian artist, art director and member of the downtown scene – was another significant friend in those years. The friendship between Bruno and Keith is well known – they met while both studying art at the School of Visual Arts (SVA) in New York. Bruno spent a lot of time with Keith and they maintained a strong connection until Keith's untimely passing. During the 1980s, my closest friends became more comfortable sharing their special artworks with me, and Bruno had several early, important pieces by Keith that he knew I would cherish and maintain. It was that type of understanding that led me to add many unusual pieces to my art collection.

The pioneering postmodern graphic designer, teacher and AIDS activist Dan Friedman was also a special friend of mine, and I recall going to his wildly decorated apartment on Fifth Avenue near Washington Square Park, where he first showed me an amazing work by Keith, *Untitled*, 1981 (p. 241). A year later it became one of my most prized possessions.

Early on it occurred to me that these personal artworks by Haring and Basquiat given to their close friends would be the most meaningful things to collect. They are rare examples of Keith's and Jean-Michel's art that are not easily found – they are uncommon, even quirky items that truly characterise the two artists and that contain

(above left) Jean-Michel Basquiat *Old Tin* 1981, paint on wood panel, 66.0 x 38.1 cm, Collection of Larry Warsh
(above right) Jean-Michel Basquiat *Untitled (Red Face)* 1982, mixed media on paper, 17.8 x 12.7 cm, Collection of Larry Warsh

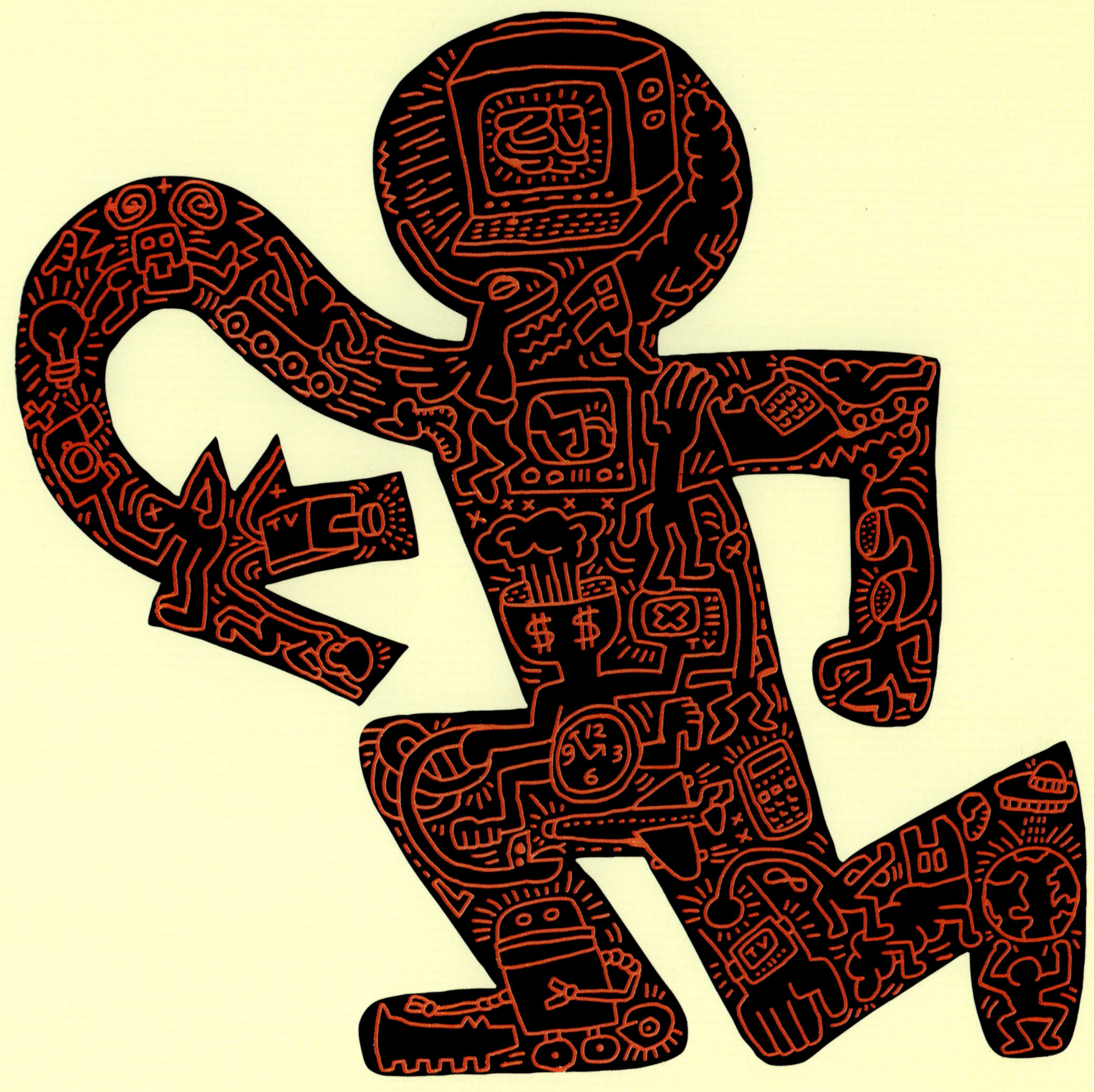

Keith Haring *Untitled* 1983, day-glo paint and enamel on routed wood, 182.9 x 182.9 x 7.6 cm, Collection of Larry Warsh

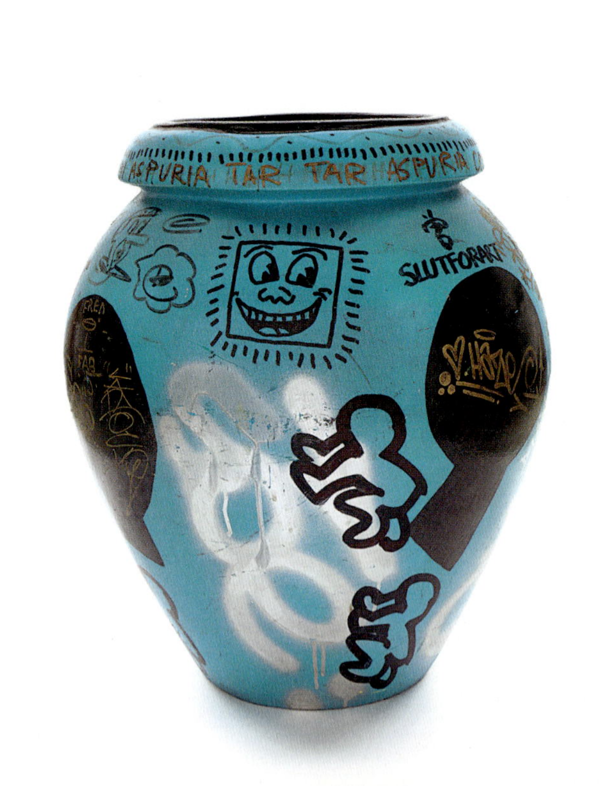

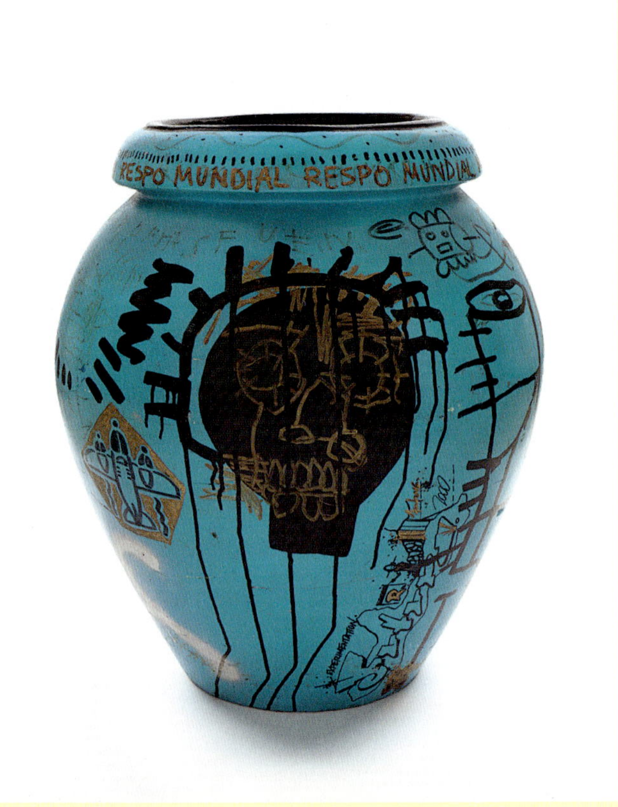

the essence of an extraordinary era. These select pieces also represent a type of art that existed as part of a community and as keepsakes of something far more profound. They are treasured now as relics, but have a greater meaning as mementos of a special unity.

After all these years, I consider these uncommon artworks by Keith Haring and Jean-Michel Basquiat to be symbolic pieces from a 'time capsule' of that momentous period in time. They also simultaneously reflect the genuine art of friendship – they are a living tribute to an abiding generosity that saw these artists give so much of themselves to their friends and to the world.

Peace,
Larry Warsh
New York City
August 2019

Notes

1 Larry Warsh, email correspondence with Leonard 'Lenny' McGurr (aka Futura 2000), 11 April 2019.

2 Carlo McCormick, 'Gifts of friendship and the economy of community', unpublished essay, 21 Jan. 2019.

(above) Keith Haring, Jean-Michel Basquiat, Tseng Kwong Chi, Futura 2000, Kenny Scharf, Fred Brathwaite, Eric Haze, LA II, other artists *Untitled* 1982 (front and back), mixed media, synthetic polymer paint, spray-paint, and fibre-tipped pen on fibreglass, 61.0 x 50.8 cm diameter, Collection of Larry Warsh
(opposite) Keith Haring, Jean-Michel Basquiat and other artists *Untitled (Fun Fridge)* 1982, acrylic, spray-paint and fibre-tipped pen on refrigerator, 182.9 × 71.1 × 71.1 cm, Collection of Larry Warsh

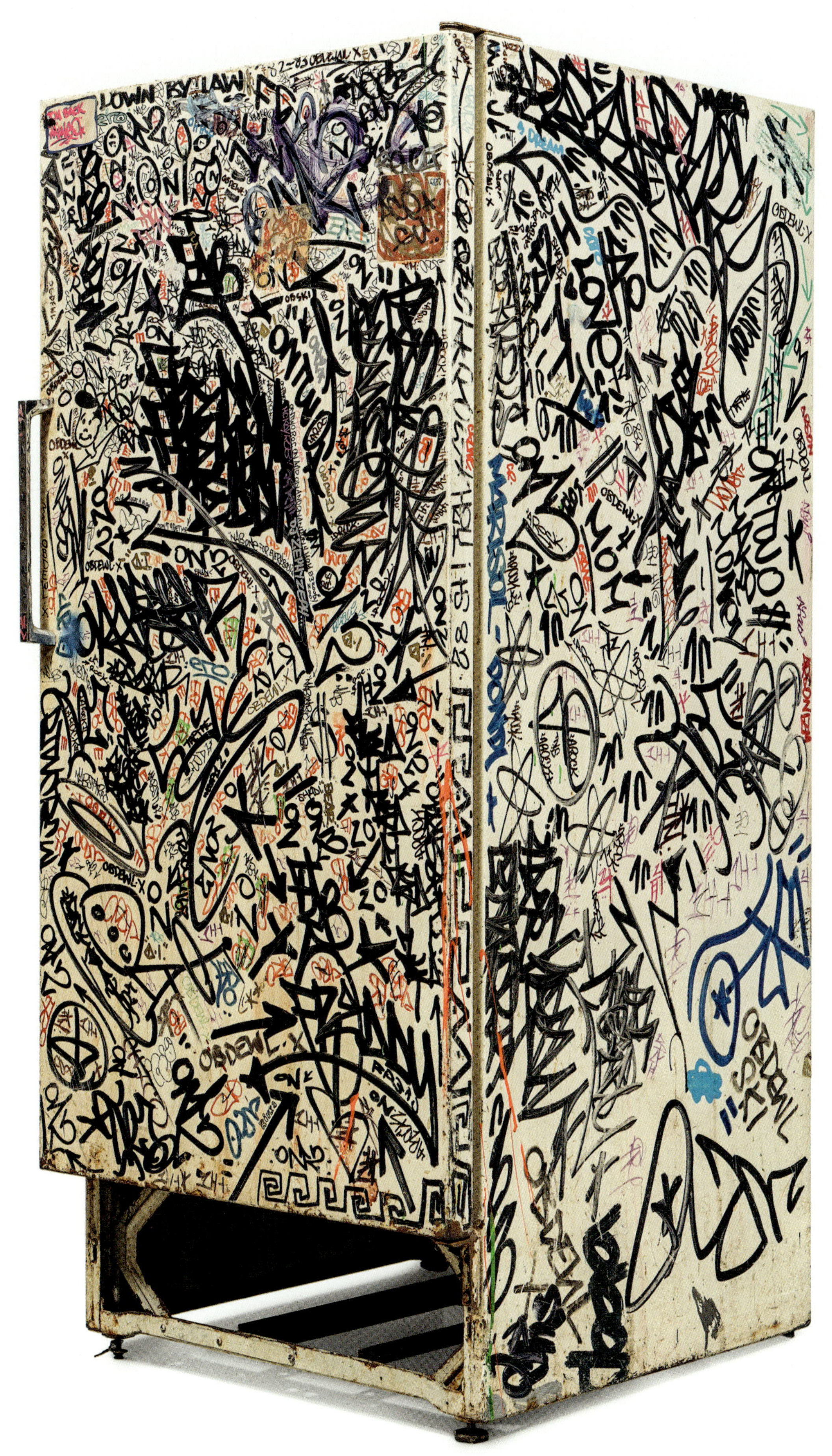
DOWN BY LAW

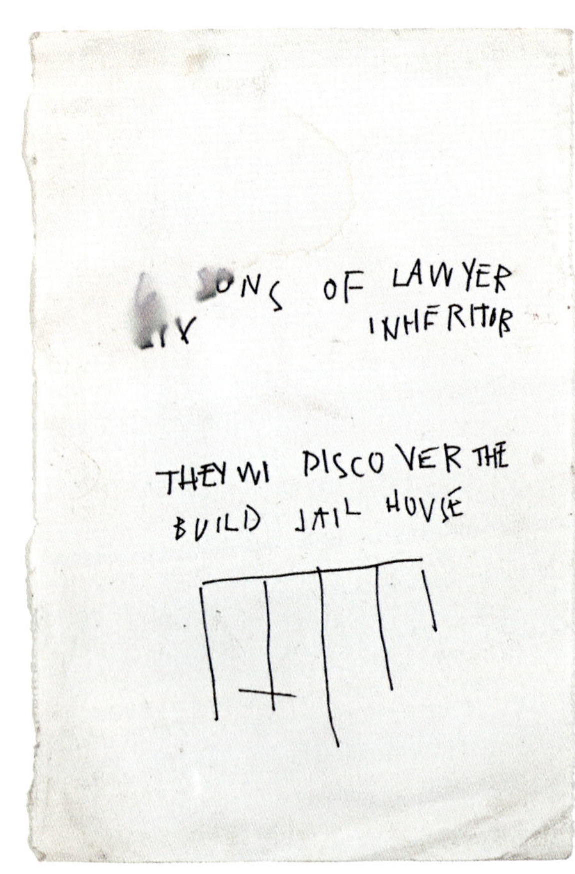

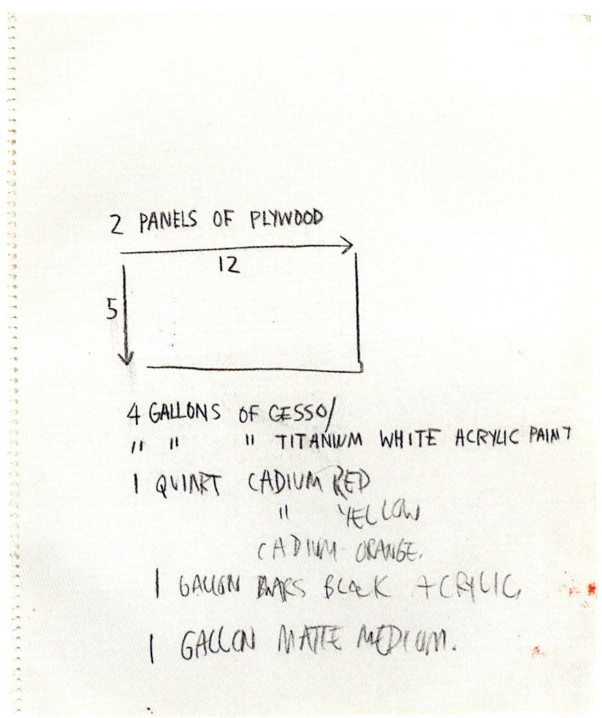

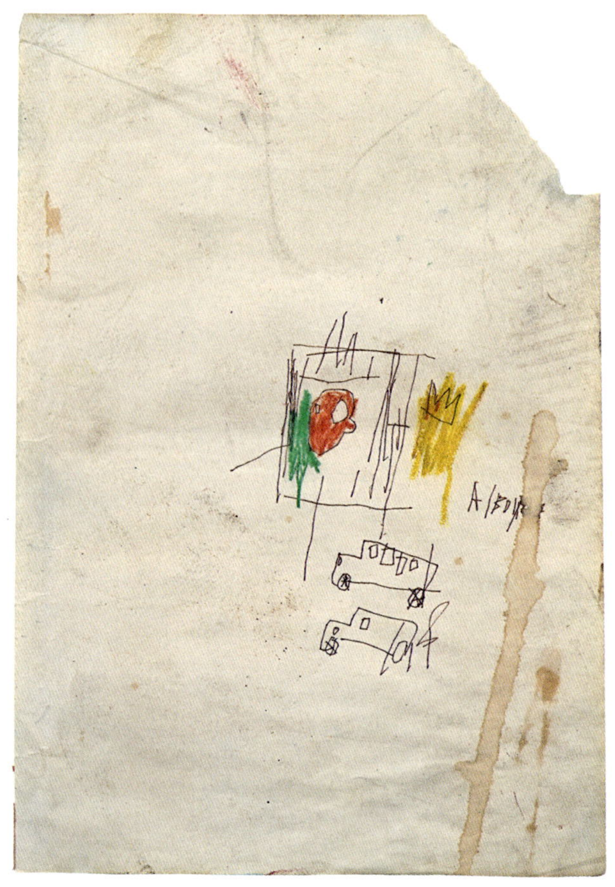

(clockwise from top right) Jean-Michel Basquiat *Untitled (2 Panels of Plywood)* 1982, pencil on paper, 18.3 x 16.5 cm;
Untitled (Two Trucks) 1981, oilstick and mixed media on paper, 35.6 x 25.4 cm;
Untitled (Lawyer) c. 1982–85, ink on paper, 25.4 x 16.5 cm, All works collection of Larry Warsh

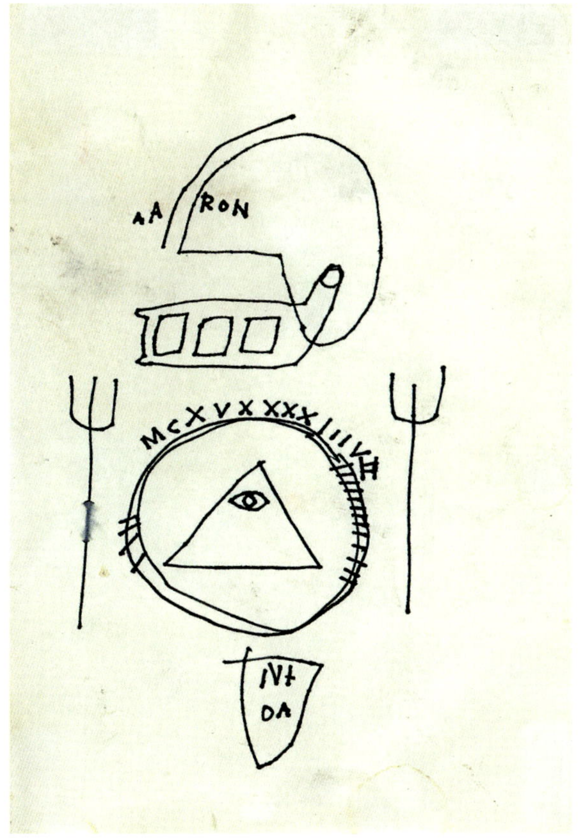

MUTE FINGERS HOLD GLASS SHARDS— SKATING HUNGRY ON CONCRETE
SELLING SKINS TO PAWNSHOP MEDIATORS– WHO IN TURN
EXTRACT FILM CLIPS–EMBARRASING THEM INTO RECLUSE
THAT A DOG LOOKING AT A DOG ON TELEVISION BITE EACH
OTHER.

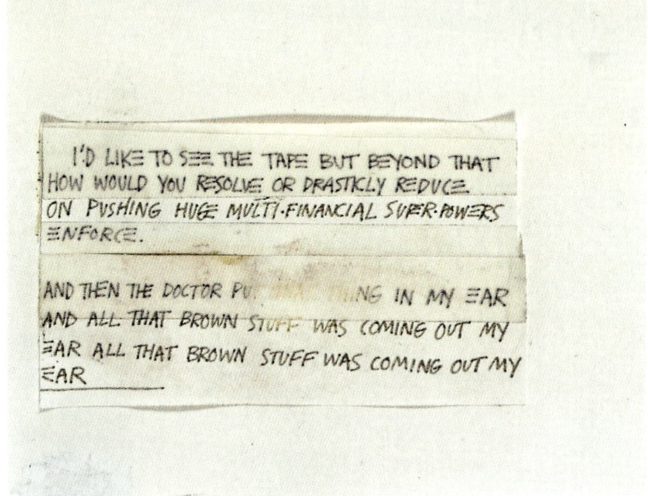

(above left) Jean-Michel Basquiat *Untitled (Ron)* 1982, ink on paper, 22.8 x 15.2 cm, Private collection
(above right) Jean-Michel Basquiat *Untitled (Text)*, 1981, ink on paper, (a) 8.0 x 22.2 cm, (b) 5.1 x 8.9 cm, Collection of Larry Warsh

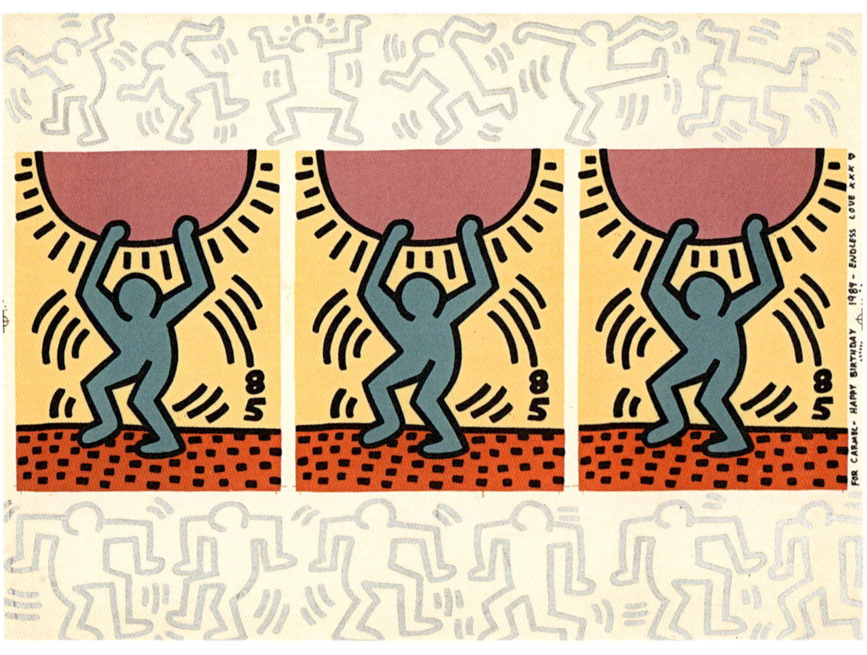

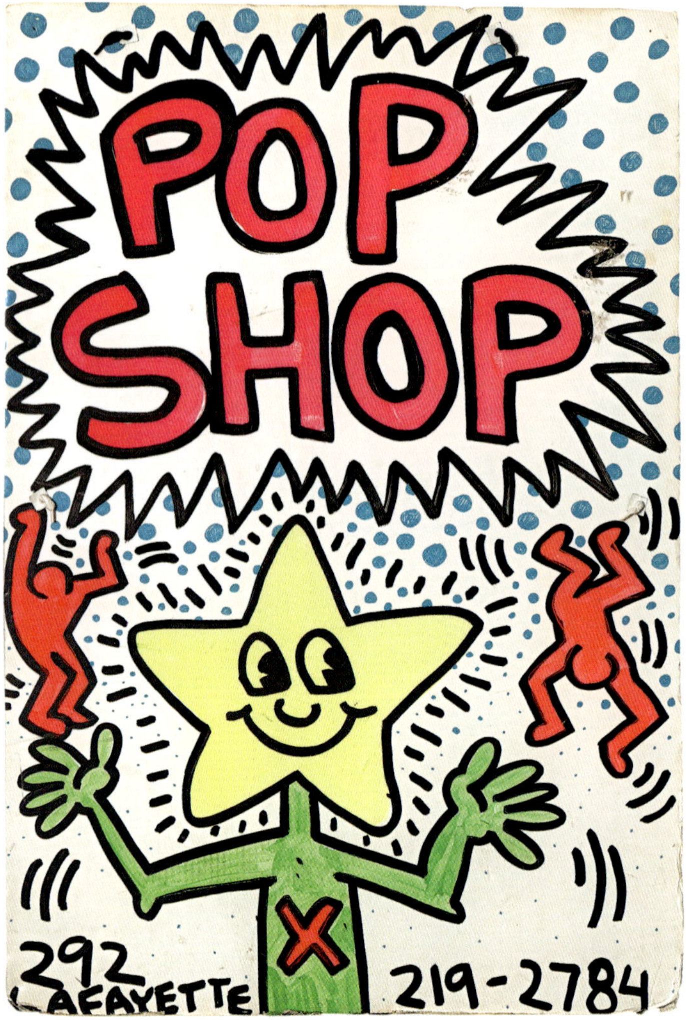

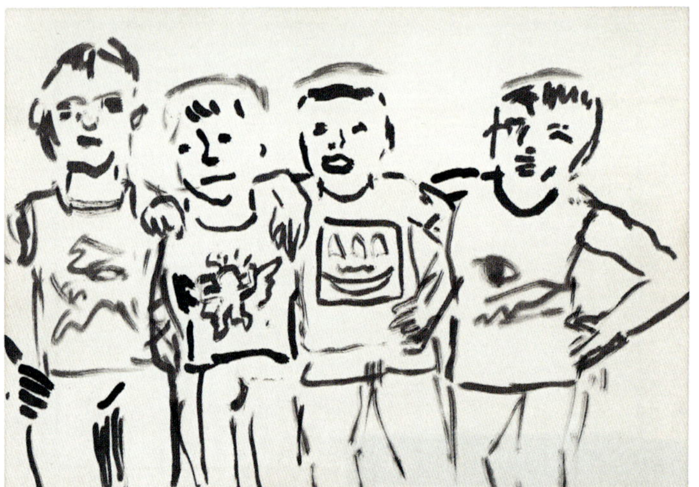

(clockwise from top left) Keith Haring *Untitled* c. 1984, mixed media on paper, 41.9 x 34.2 cm (overall); *Untitled* 1984, fibre-tipped pen on paper, 57.8 x 77.5 cm; *Untitled* 1987 (detail), ink on paper, (a-b) 25.4 x 36.8 cm (each); *Untitled* 1985, ink on paper, 27.9 x 38.1 cm; *Untitled* 1984, mixed media on board, 121.9 x 91.4 cm, All works collection of Larry Warsh

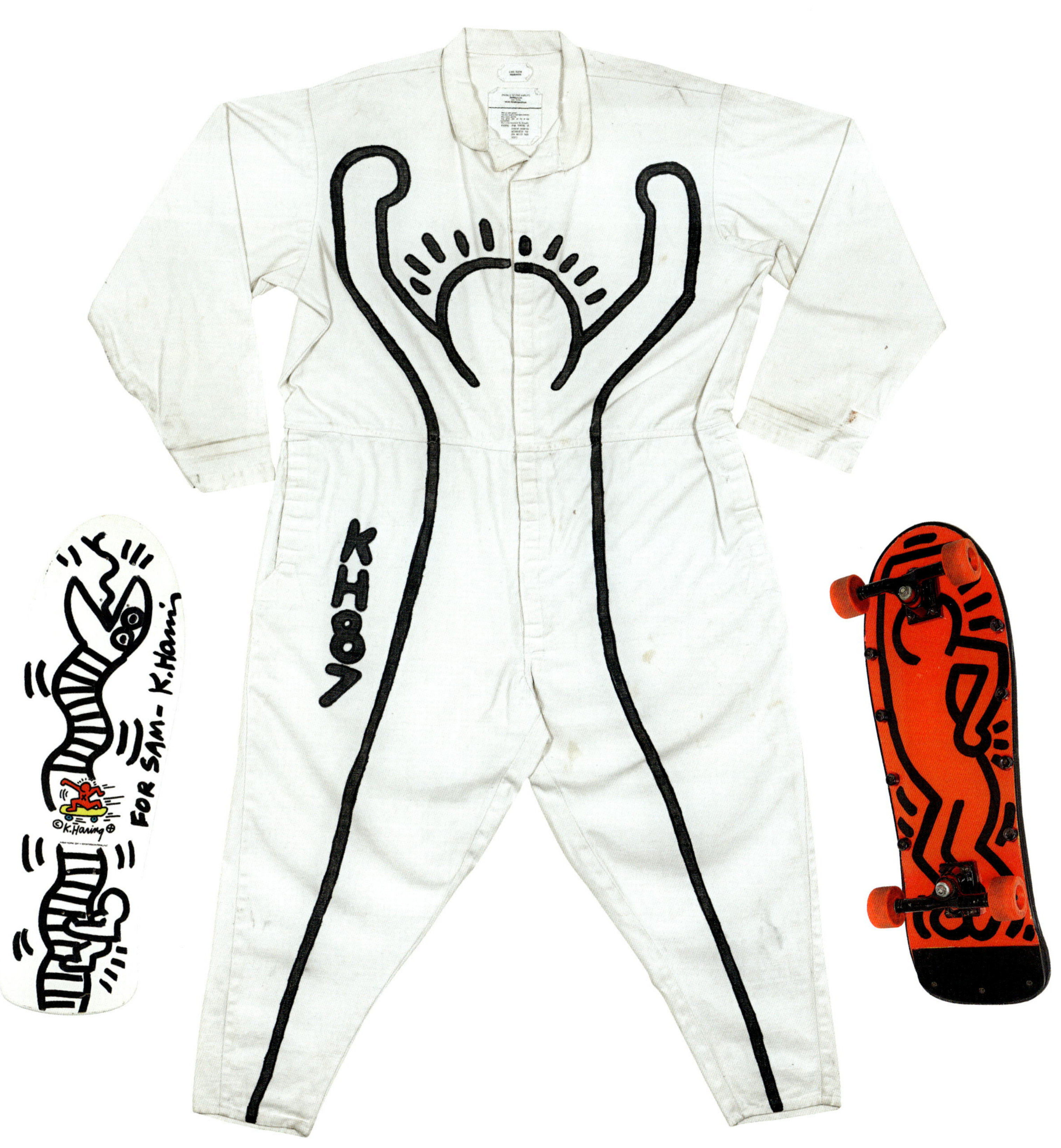

(above left) Keith Haring *Untitled* 1985, fibre-tipped pen on fibreglass skateboard, 76.2 x 25.4 cm, Collection of Larry Warsh
(above centre) Keith Haring *Untitled* 1987, fibre-tipped pen on fabric jumpsuit, 170.2 x 99.0 cm (variable), Collection of Larry Warsh
(above right) Keith Haring *Untitled* 1985, fibre-tipped pen on fibreglass skateboard, 76.2 x 25.4 cm, Collection of Larry Warsh

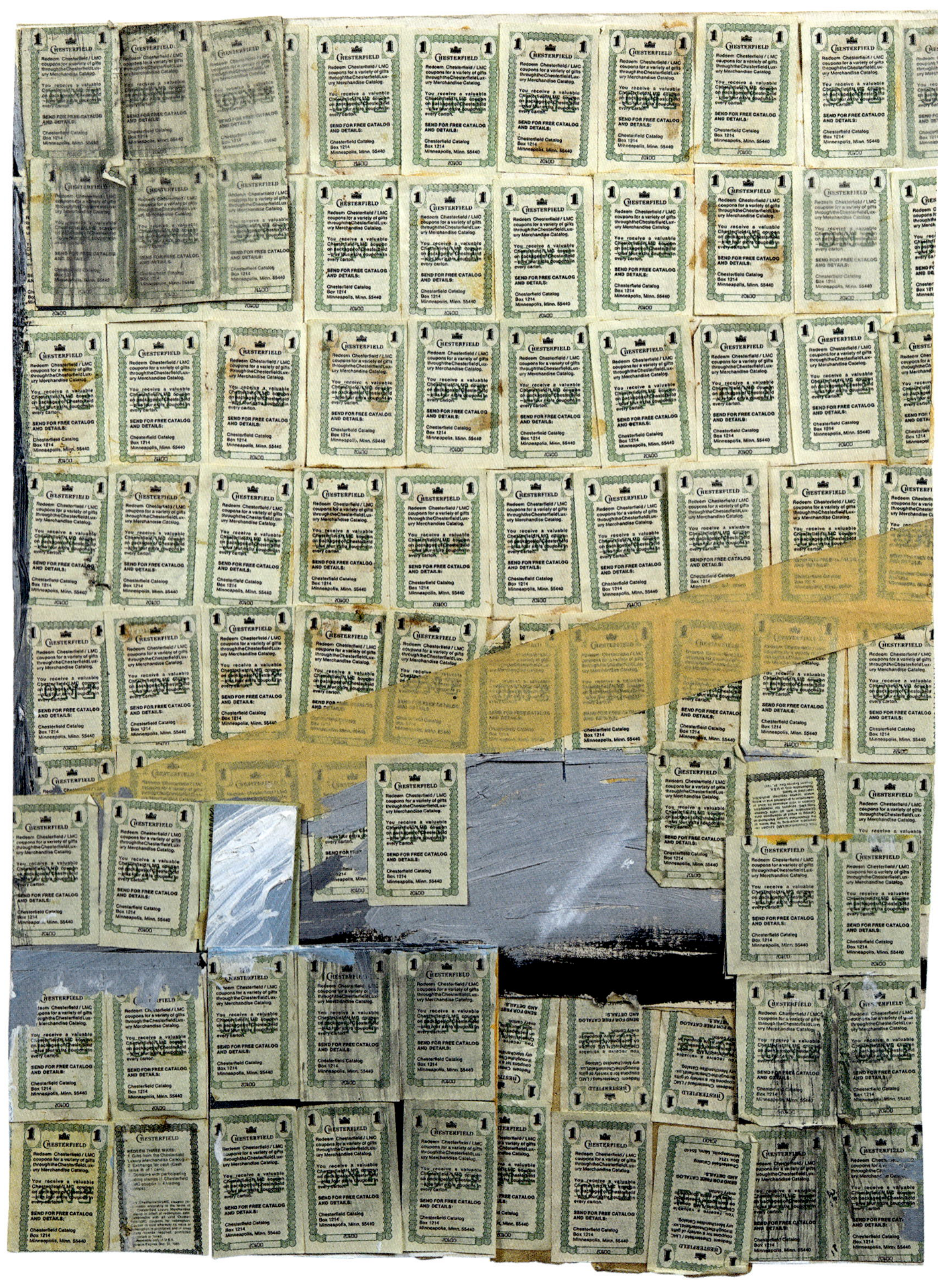

Jean-Michel Basquiat *Untitled (Chesterfield)* 1981, mixed media collage on paper, 61.0 x 45.7 cm, Collection of Larry Warsh

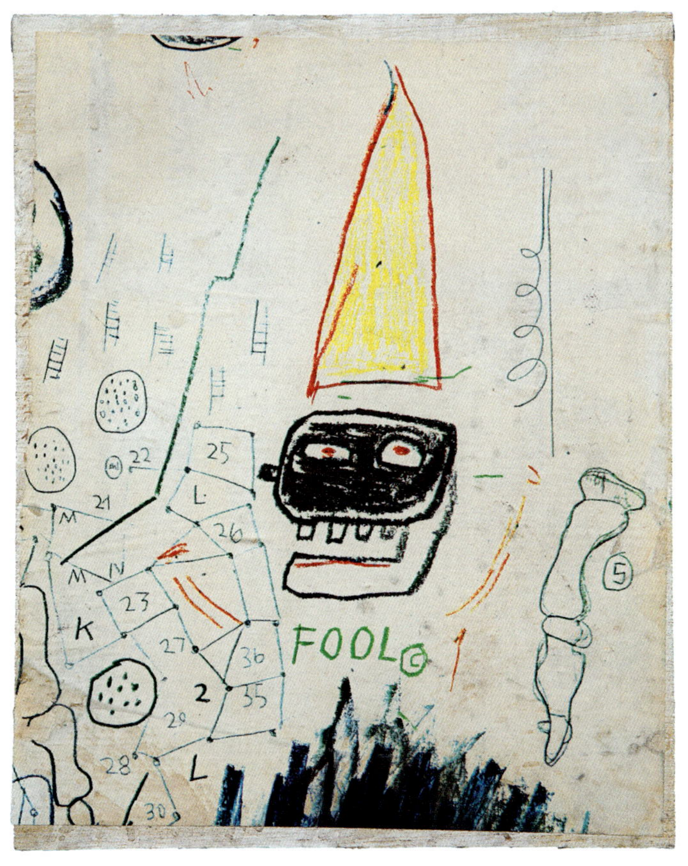

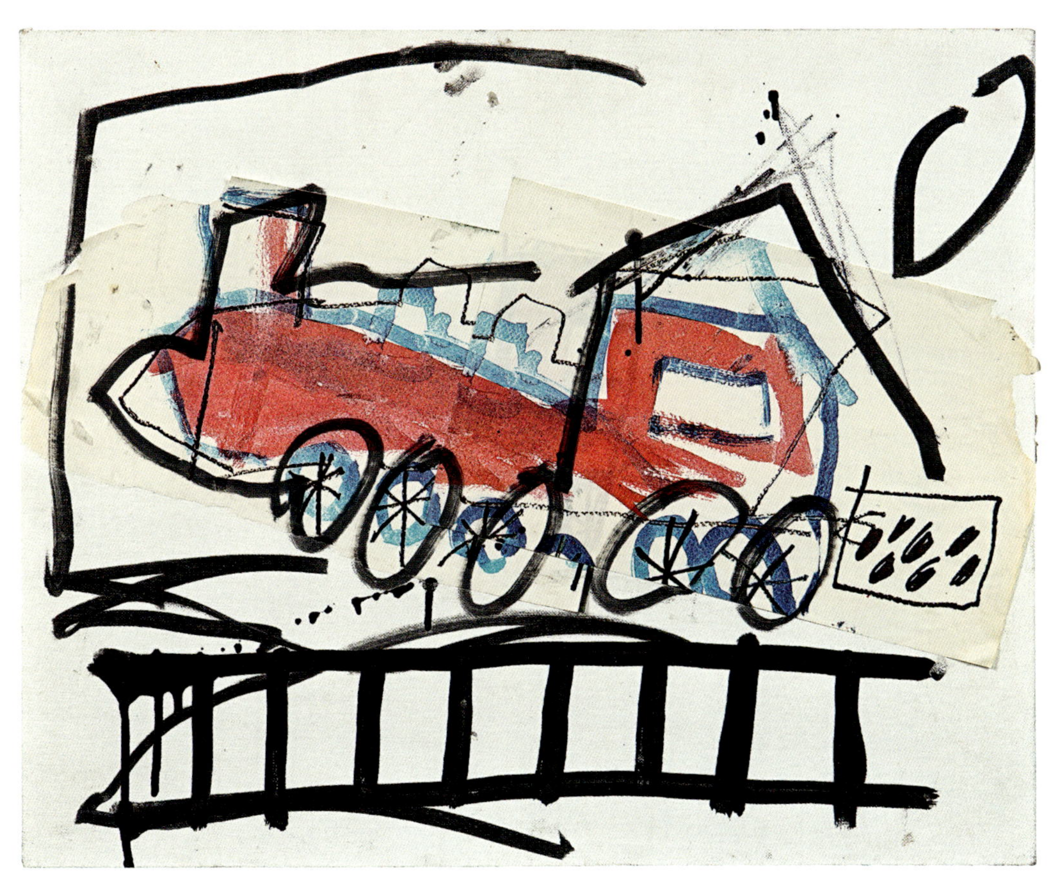

(top) Jean-Michel Basquiat *Untitled (Fool©)* c. 1985, xerox paper on wood panel, 25.4 x 20.3 cm,
Collection of Larry Warsh
(bottom) Jean-Michel Basquiat *Untitled (Train)* 1981, mixed media on canvas, 45.7 x 61.0 cm,
Private collection

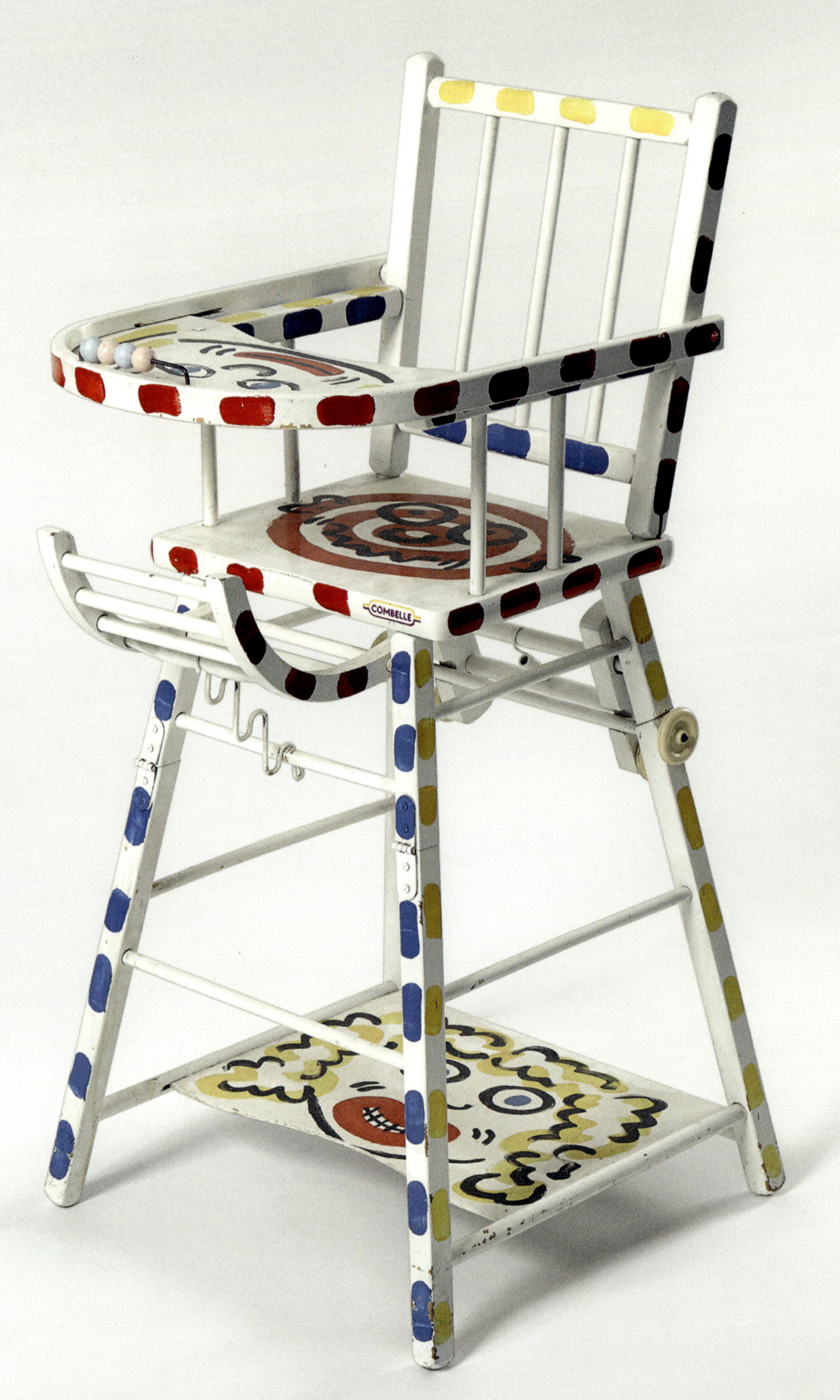
COMBELLE

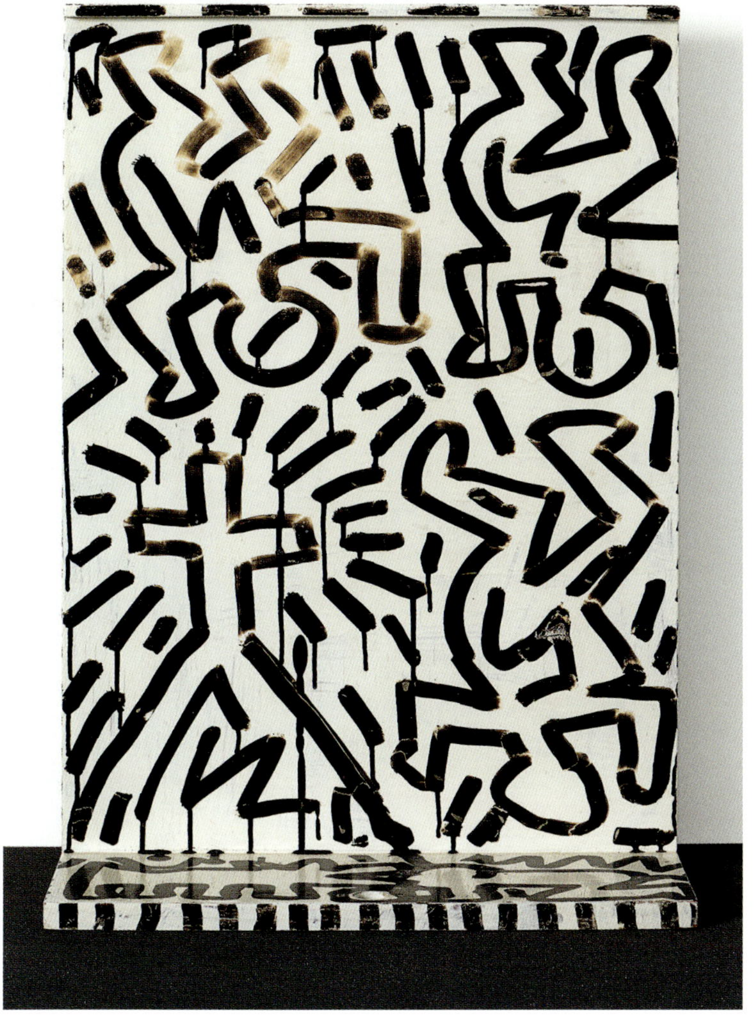

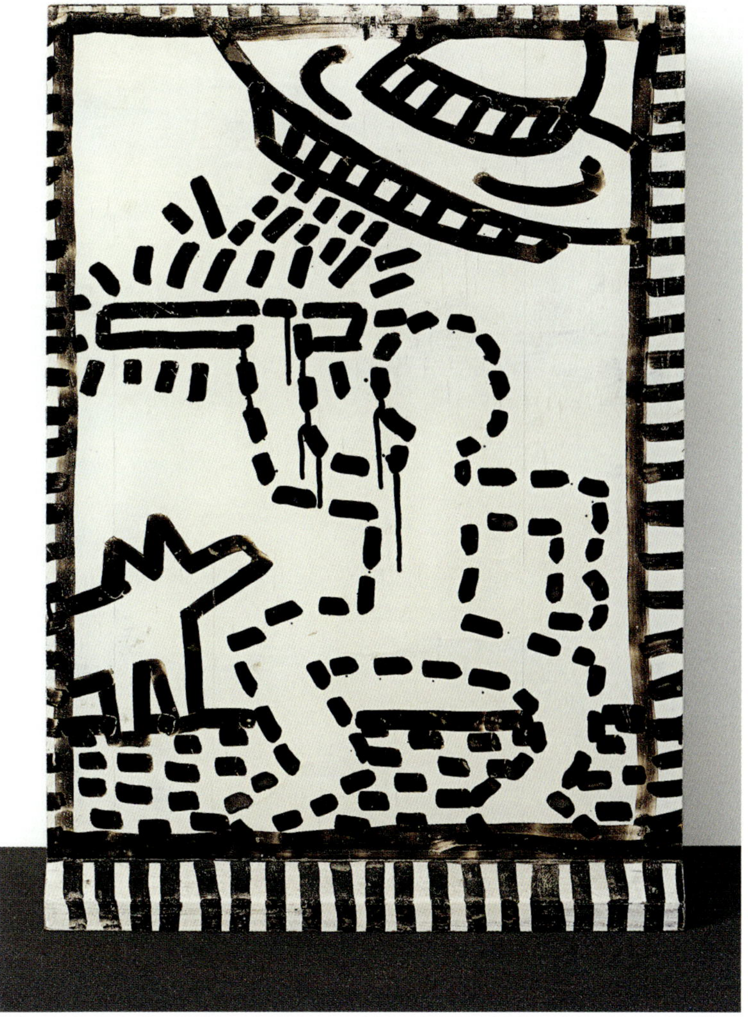

Keith Haring *Untitled* 1981 (back and front), fibre-tipped pen and enamel on wood panel, 58.4 x 40.6 x 17.7 cm, Collection of Larry Warsh
(opposite) Keith Haring *Untitled* c. 1985, synthetic polymer paint on wood high chair, 81.2 x 53.3 x 38.1 cm, Collection of Larry Warsh

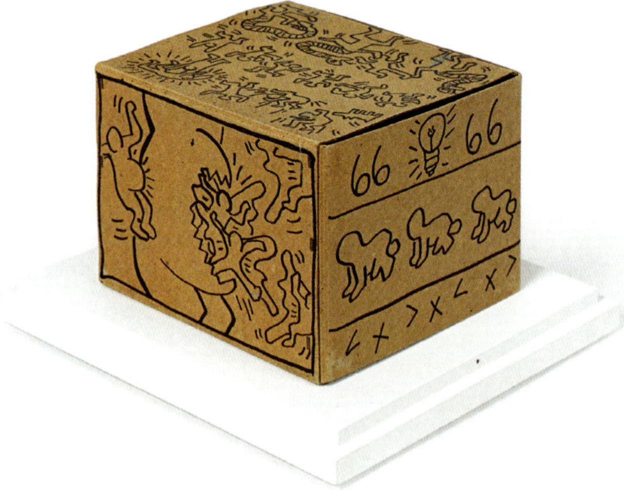

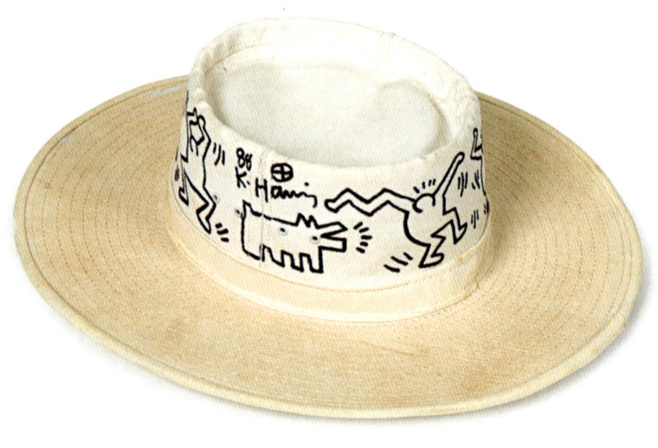

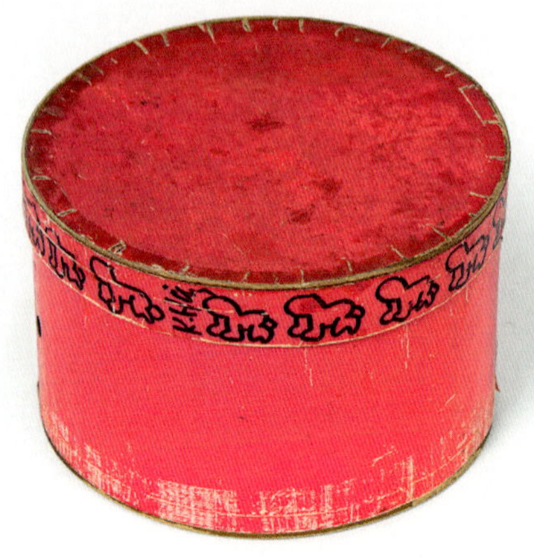

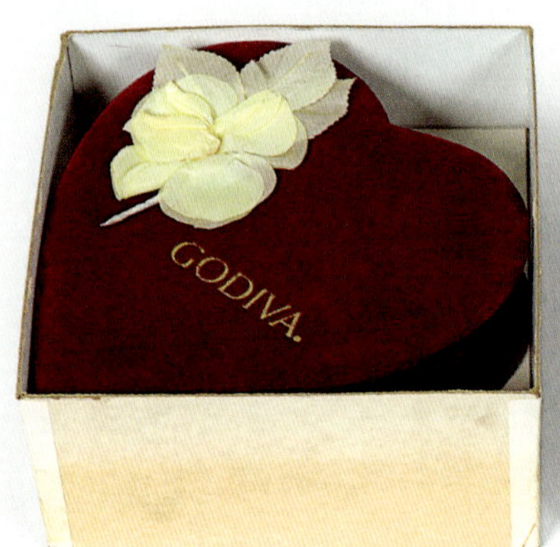

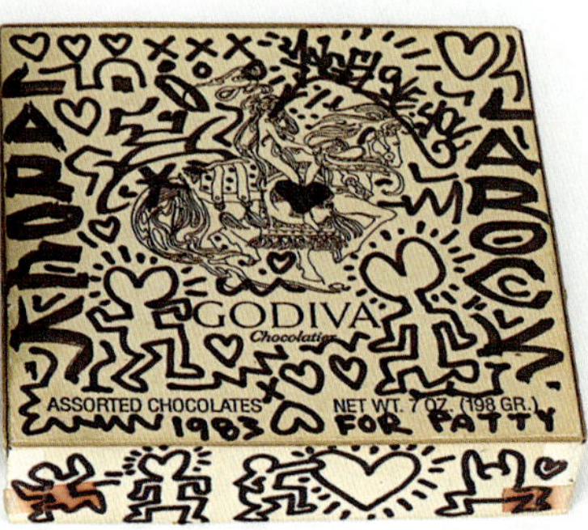

(clockwise from top left) Keith Haring *Untitled* 1984, fibre-tipped pen on cardboard box, 16.5 x 23.5 x 20.3 cm; Keith Haring *Untitled* c. 1985, fibre-tipped pen on canvas hat, 15.2 x 40.6 cm; Keith Haring, LA II *Untitled* 1983, fibre-tipped pen on cardboard box, 25.4 x 25.4 x 10.2 cm; Keith Haring *Untitled* c. 1985, fibre-tipped pen on cardboard box, 15.2 x 21.5 cm, All works collection of Larry Warsh

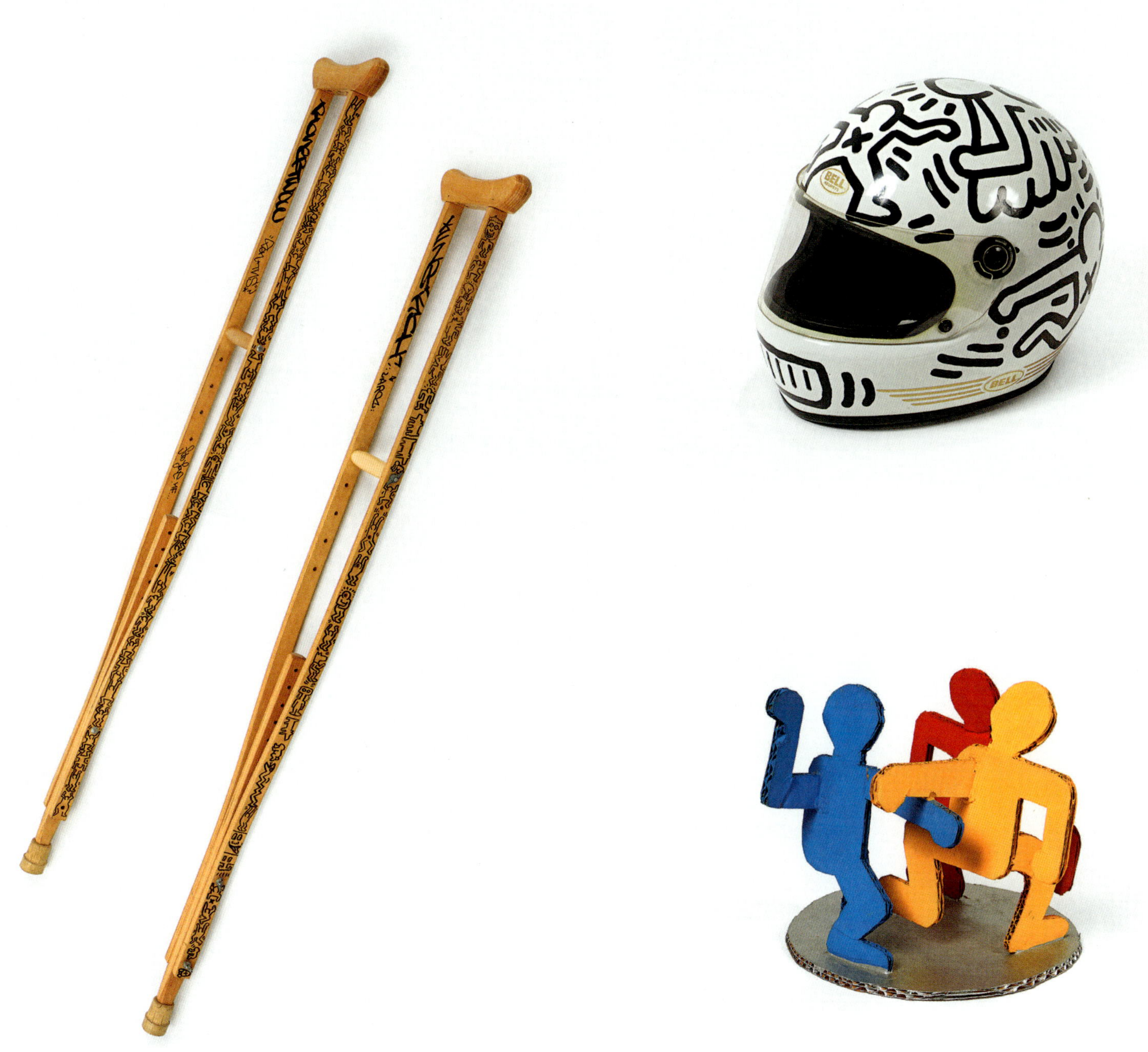

(clockwise from left) Keith Haring *Untitled* c. 1982, fibre-tipped pen on wood crutches, 116.8 x 20.3 cm (variable); *Untitled* c. 1985, fibre-tipped pen on helmet, 36.8 x 25.4 x 22.8 cm; *Untitled* 1984, paint on cardboard, 22.8 x 22.8 cm (variable), All works collection of Larry Warsh

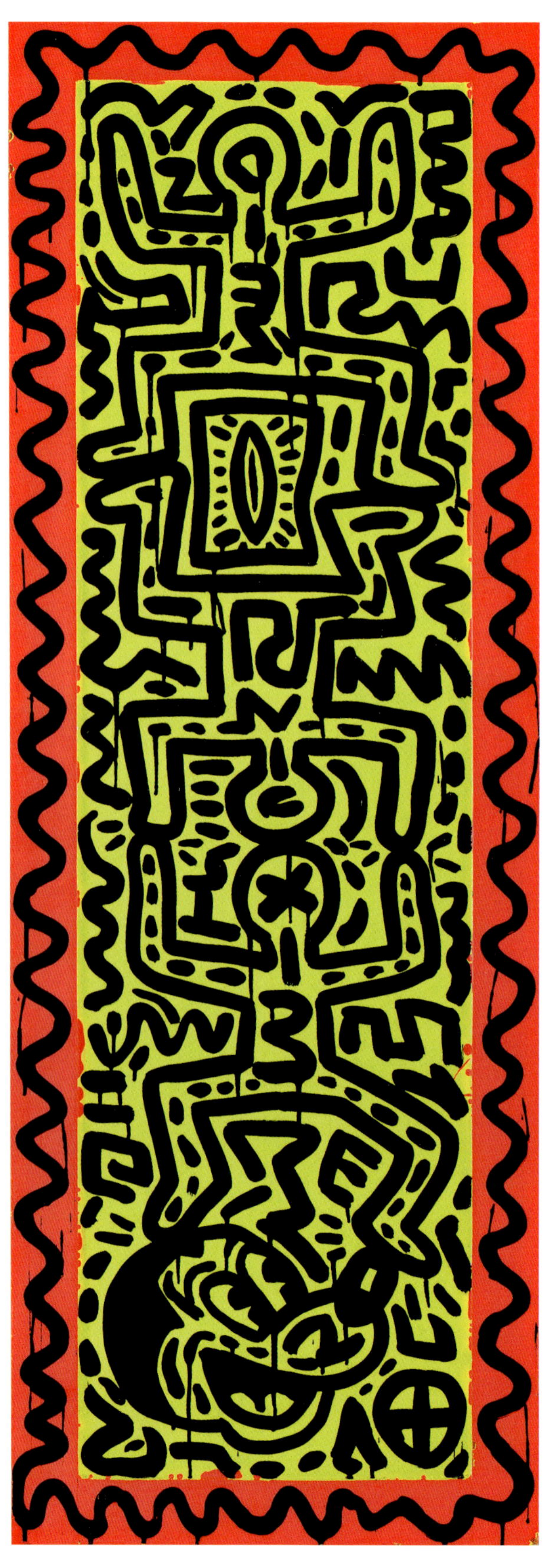

Keith Haring *Untitled* 1982, fibre-tipped pen and enamel on wood panel, 135.0 x 45.0 cm, Courtesy Laurent Strouk
(opposite) Keith Haring *Untitled* 1981, fibre-tipped pen and enamel on child's cot, 101.6 x 139.7 x 76.2 cm, Hal Bromm Gallery

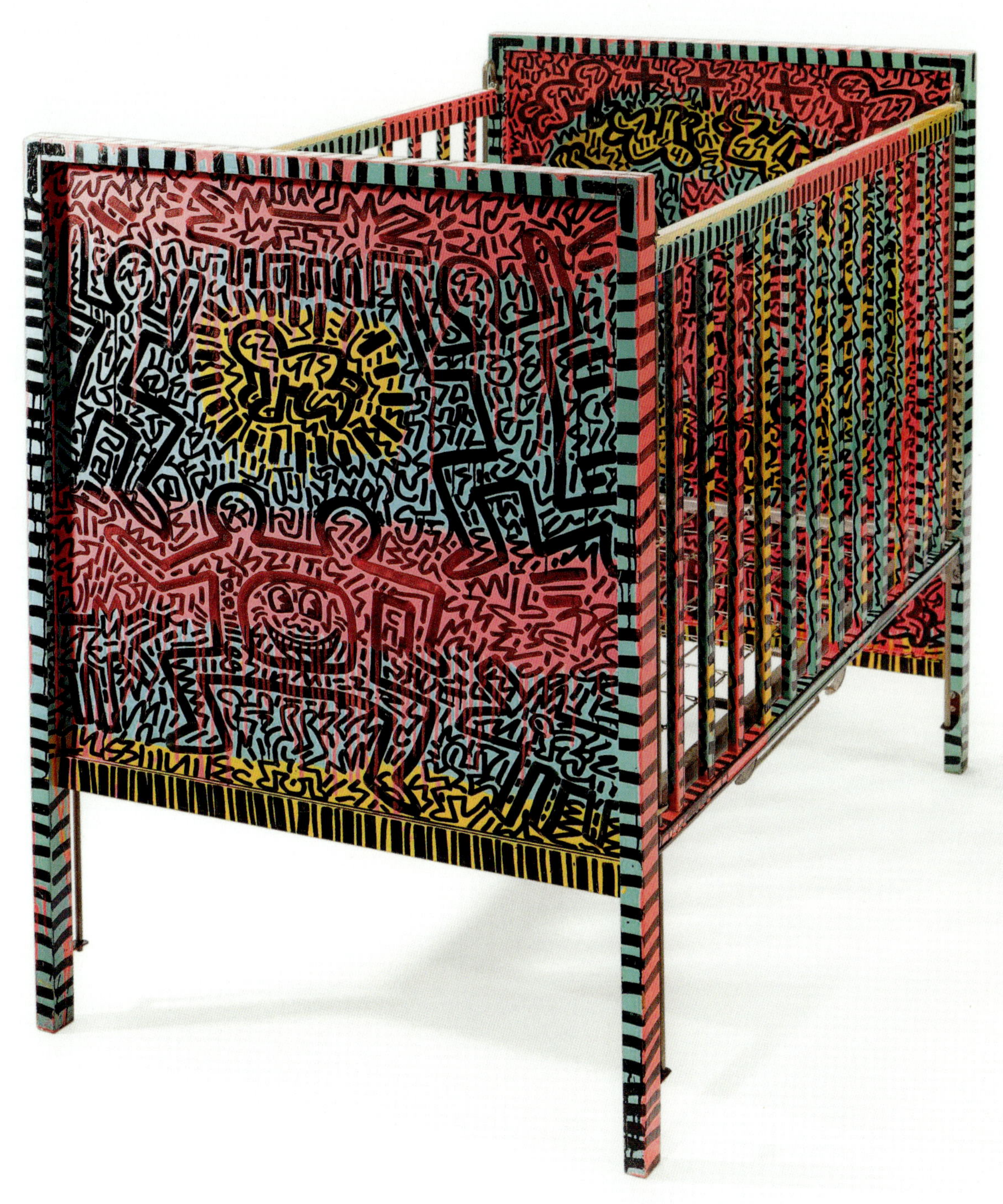

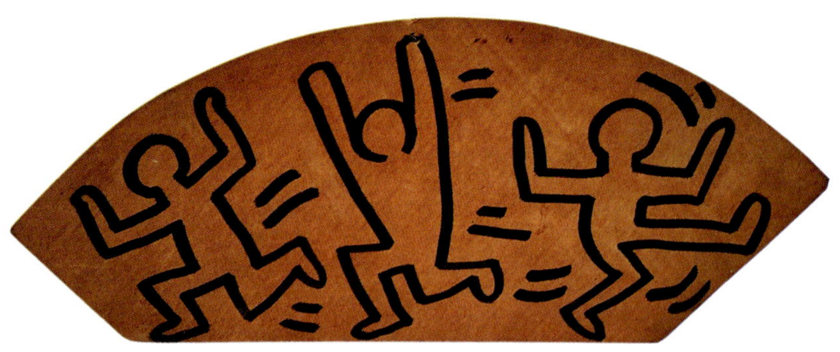

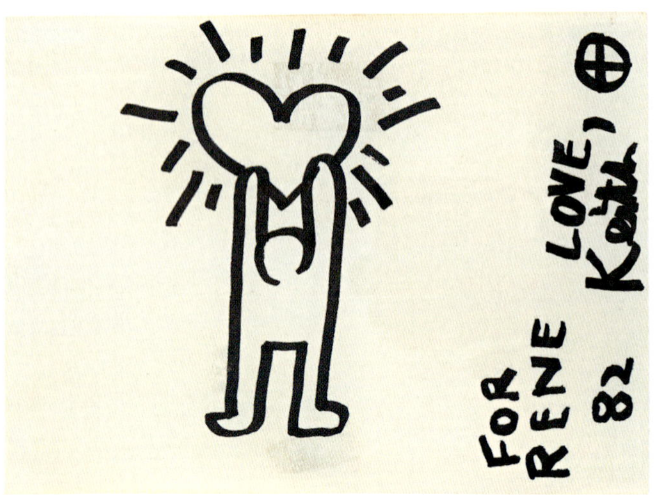

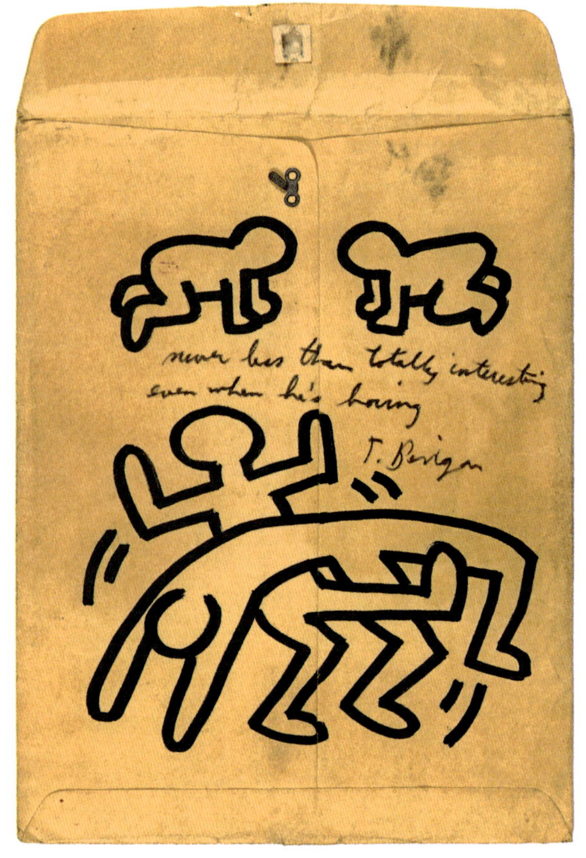

(clockwise from top left) Keith Haring *Untitled* 1983, ink on canvas cloth, 8.6 x 5.5 cm, Private collection; Keith Haring *Untitled* 1982, fibre-tipped pen on wood panel, 15.2 x 38.7 x 1.9 cm, Hal Bromm Gallery; Rene Ricard, Keith Haring, *Untitled* 1982, ink on manila envelope, 35.6 x 24.1 cm, Collection of Larry Warsh; Keith Haring *Untitled* 1982, ink on paper, 22.9 x 30.5 cm, Collection of Larry Warsh

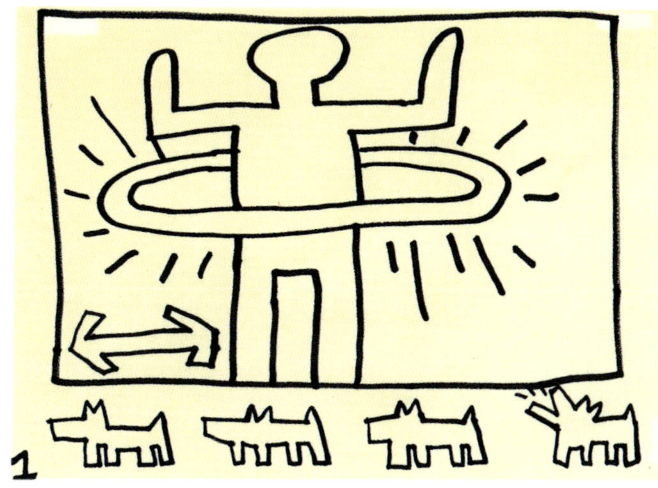

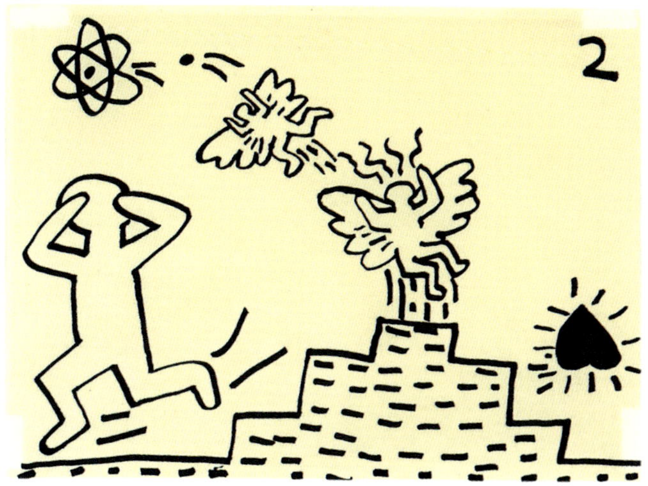

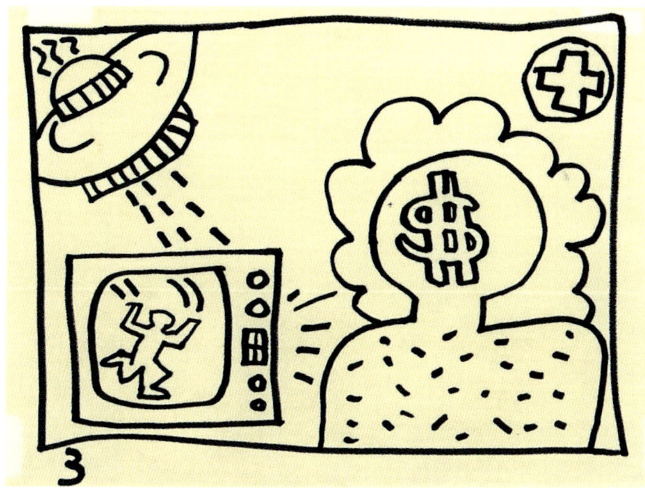

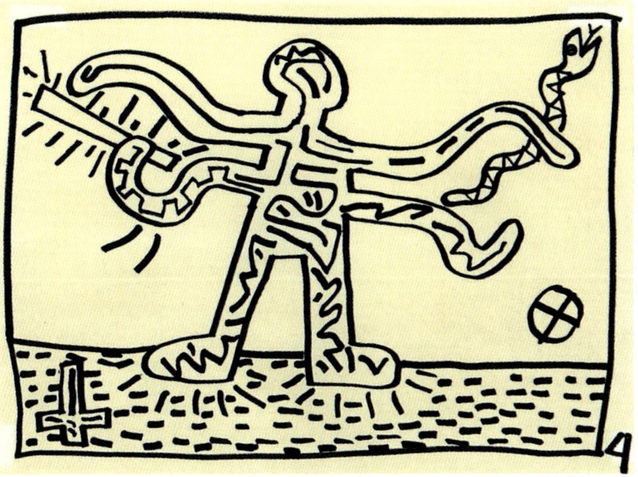

Keith Haring, *Untitled* 1982, ink on paper, (a-d) 22.9 x 30.5cm (each), Collection of Larry Warsh

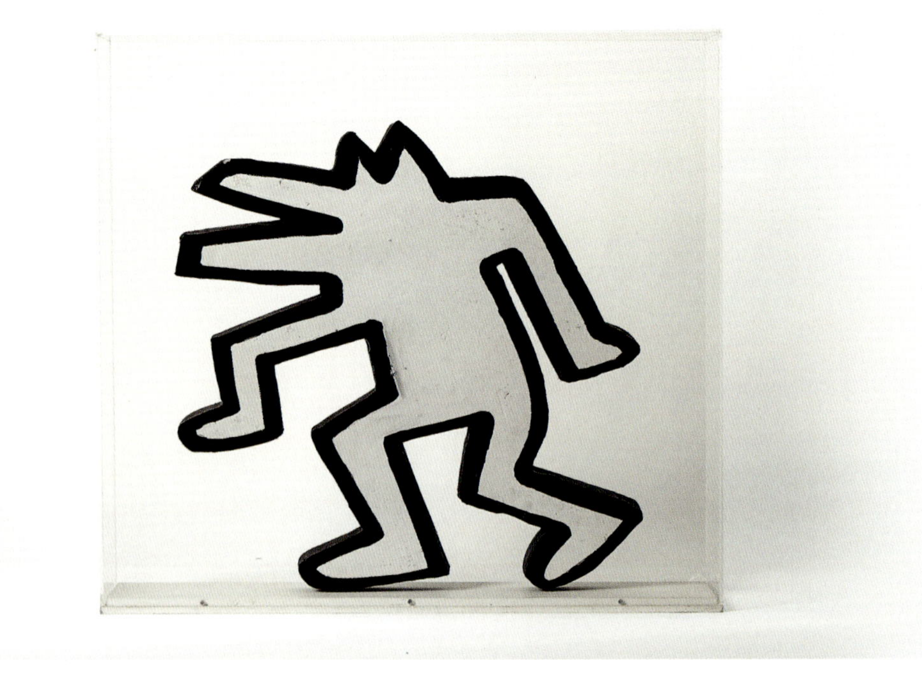

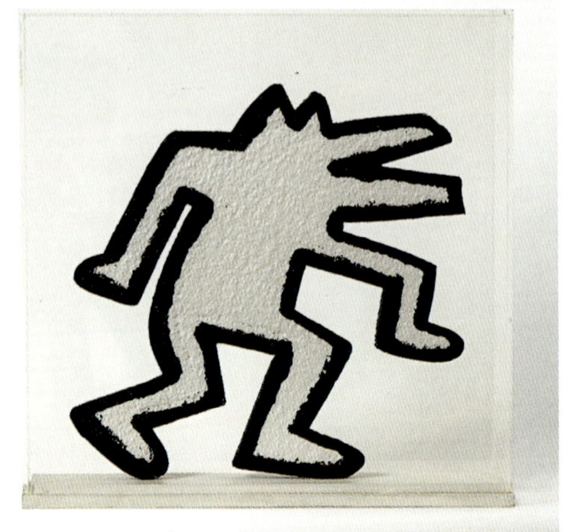

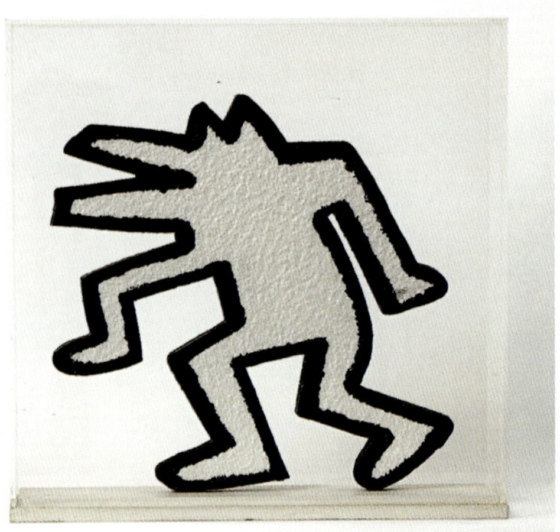

(top) Keith Haring *Untitled* 1985, paint on polystyrene, 72.3 x 77.4 x 16.5 cm, Private collection
(bottom) Keith Haring *Untitled* 1985, paint on polystyrene, (a-b) 33.0 x 33.0 x 2.5 cm (each), Collection of Larry Warsh
(opposite) Keith Haring *Untitled* 1981, fibre-tipped pen, ink and enamel on fibreglass vase, 101.6 x 63.5 x 63.5 cm, Collection of Larry Warsh

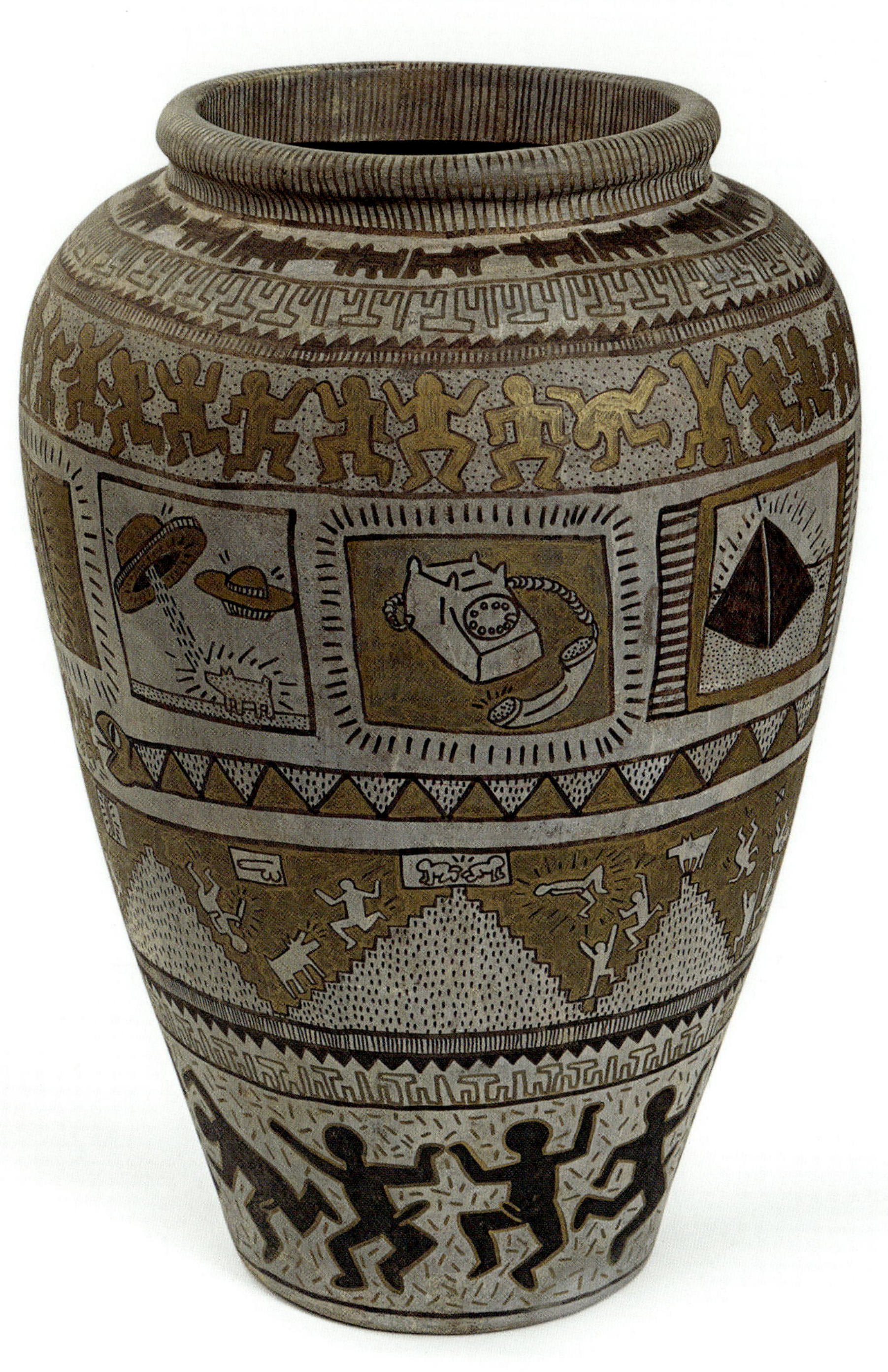

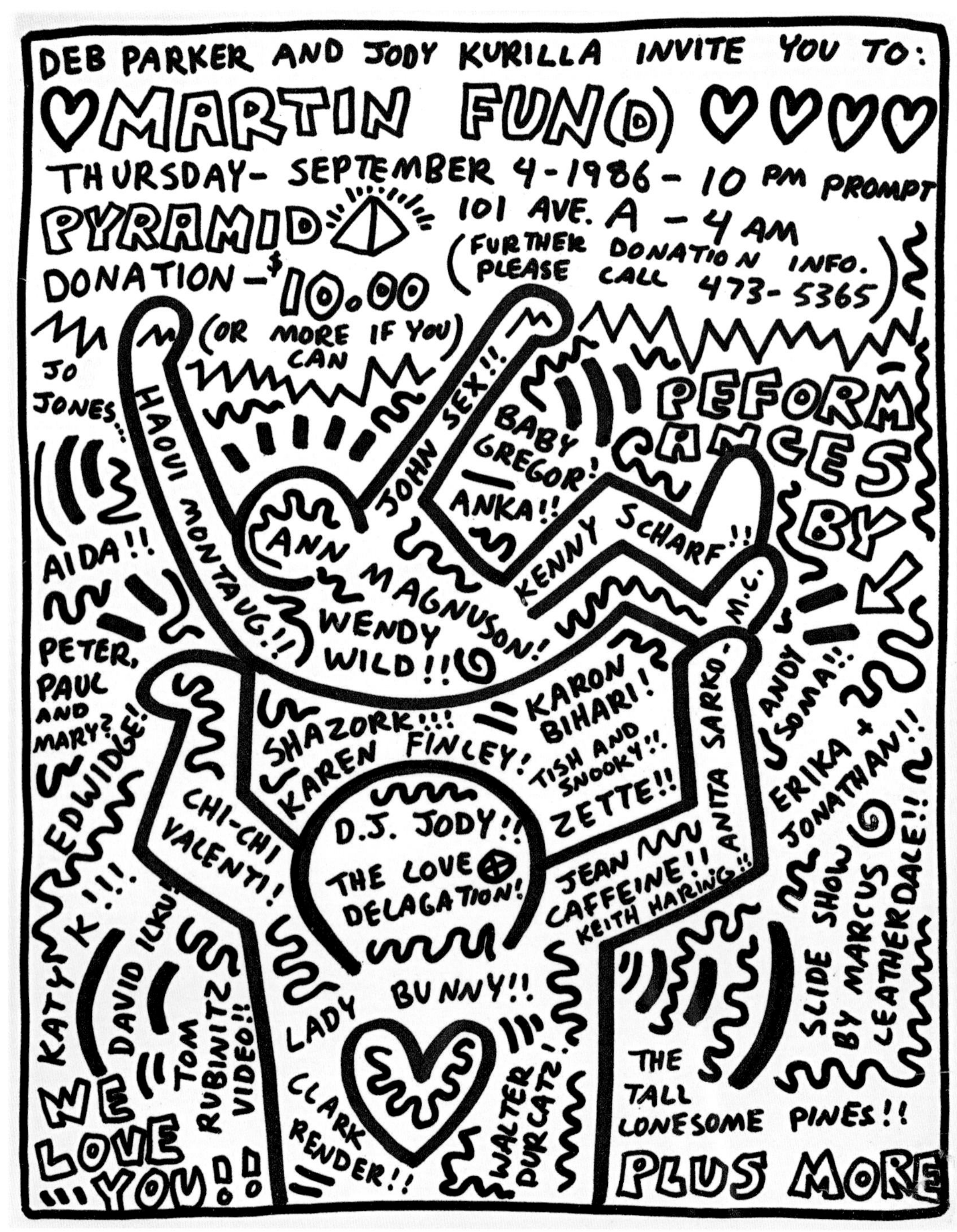

Keith Haring *Untitled* 1986, ink on paper, 43.1 x 35.5 cm, Collection of Larry Warsh

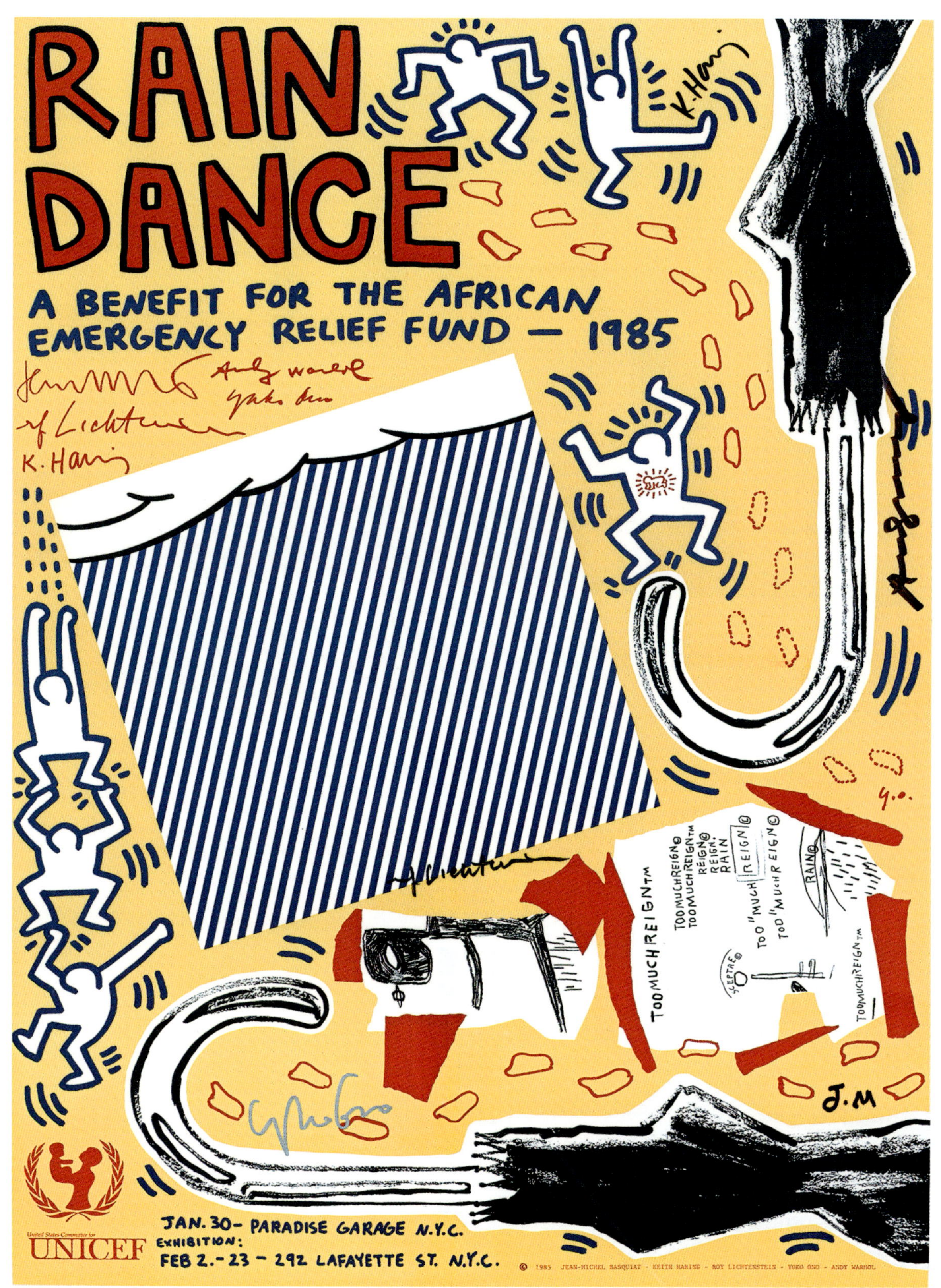

Roy Lichtenstein, Andy Warhol, Yoko Ono, Keith Haring, Jean-Michel Basquiat *Rain Dance* 1985, colour screenprint, ed 100, 88.9 x 66.0 cm, Collection of Larry Warsh

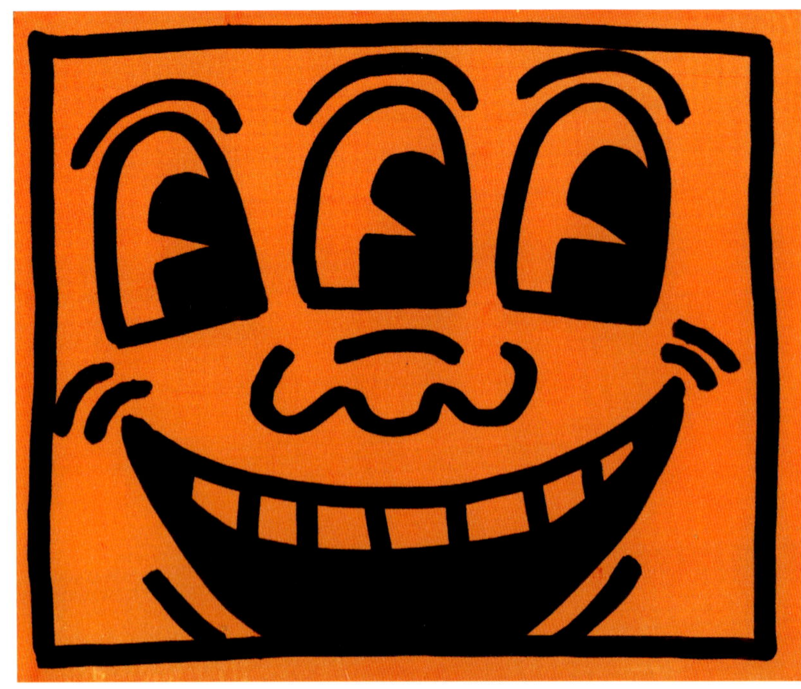

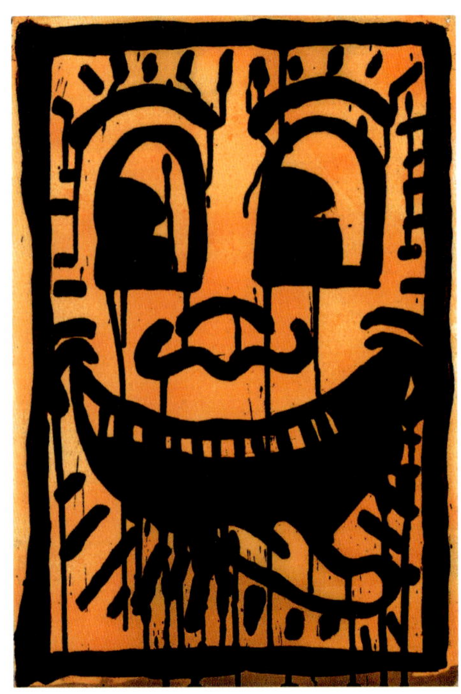

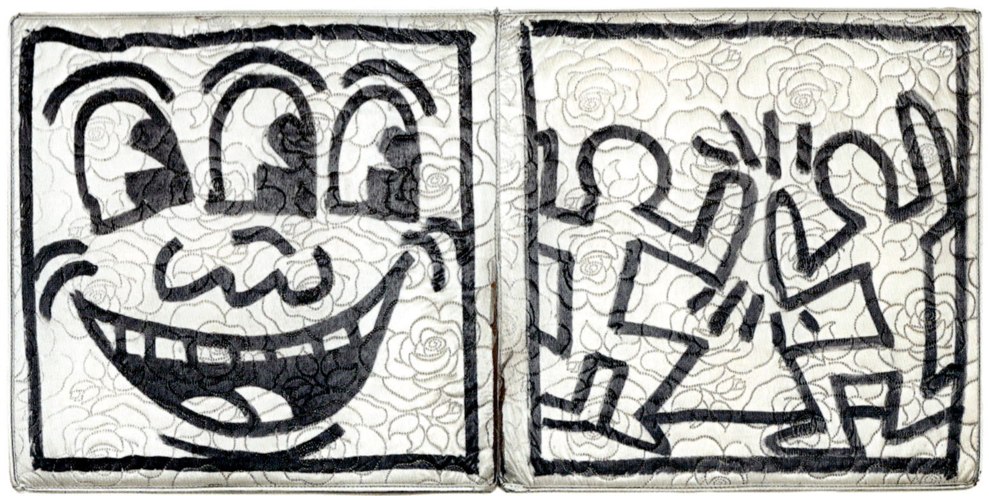

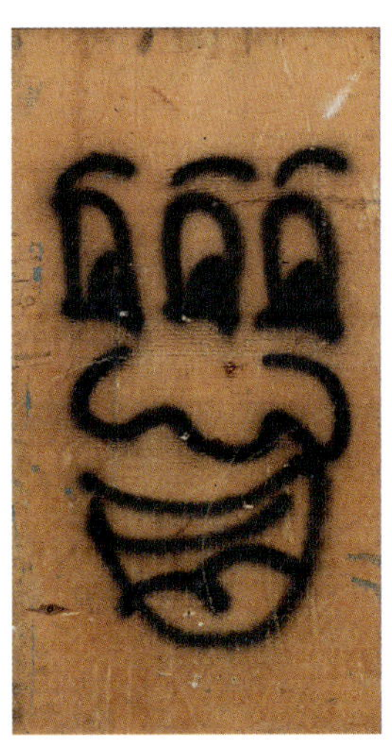

(clockwise from top left) Keith Haring *Untitled* 1982, synthetic polymer paint on wood panel, 35.5 x 35.5 cm, Private collection; *Untitled* c. 1981, ink on paper, 45.7 x 30.4 cm, Collection of Larry Warsh; *Untitled* c. 1982, spray-paint on wood panel, 14.7 x 8.6 x 6.0 cm, Collection of Larry Warsh; *Untitled* c. 1982, mixed media on vinyl, 45.7 x 91.4 cm, Private collection

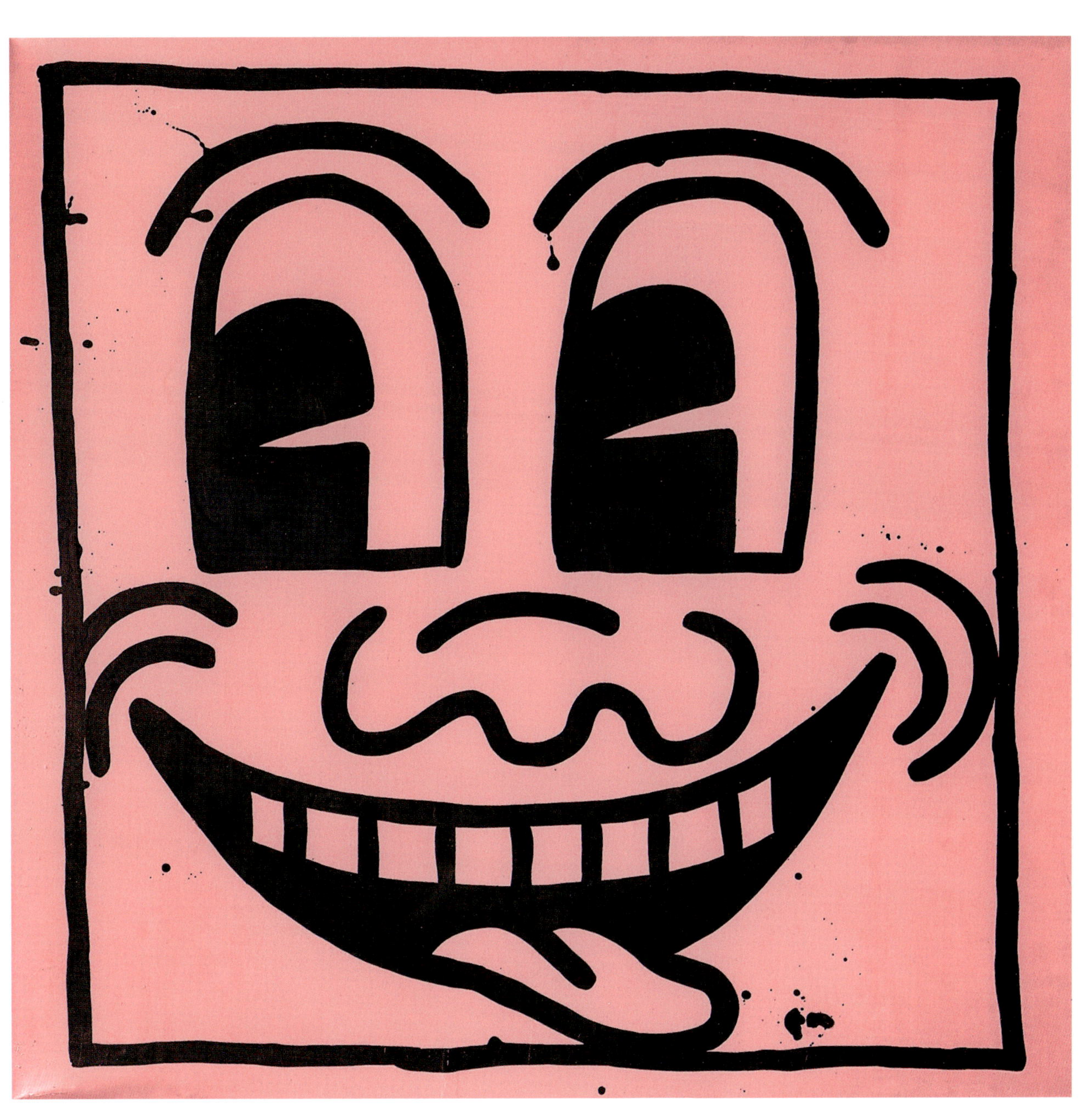

Keith Haring *Untitled* 1981, ink on metal, 121.9 x 121.9 cm, Collection of Larry Warsh

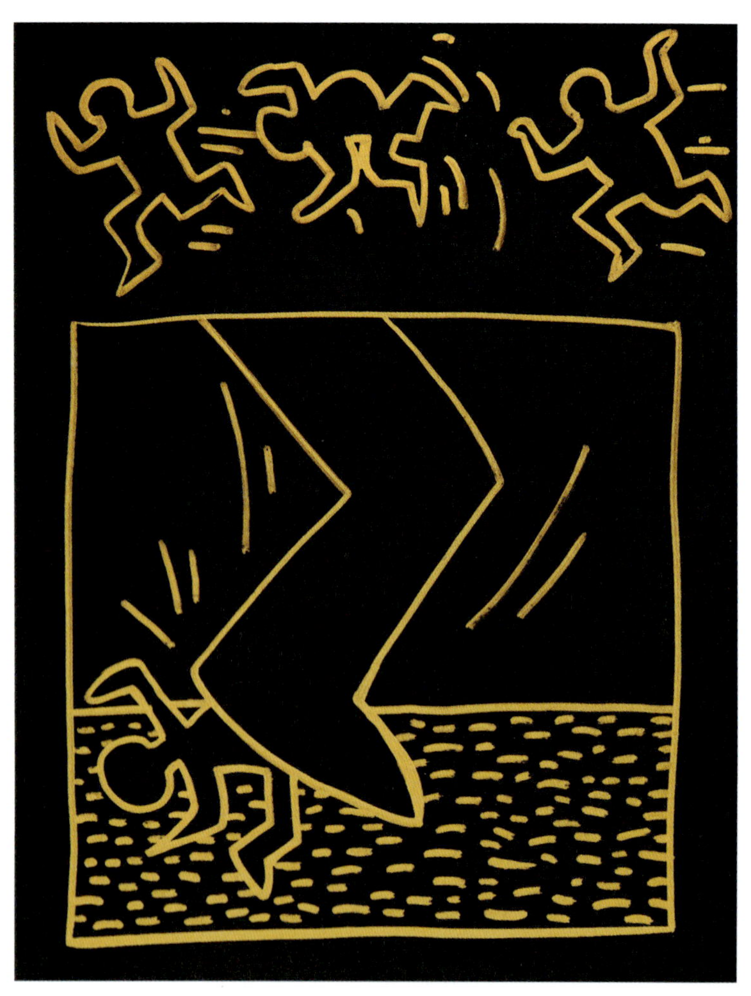

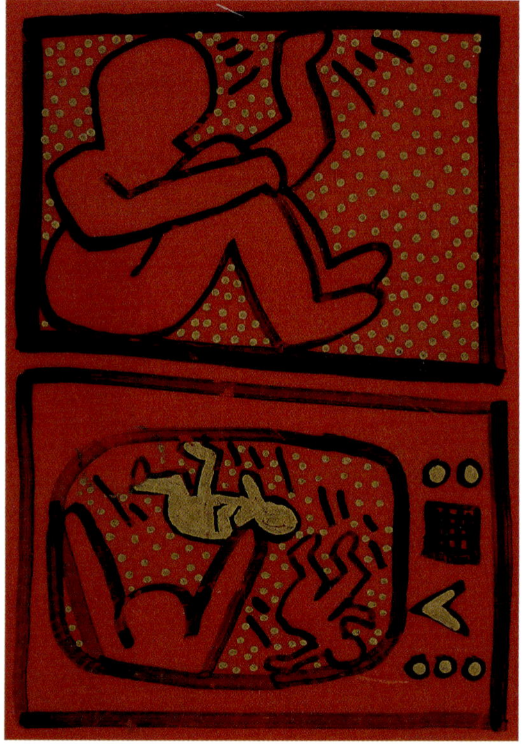

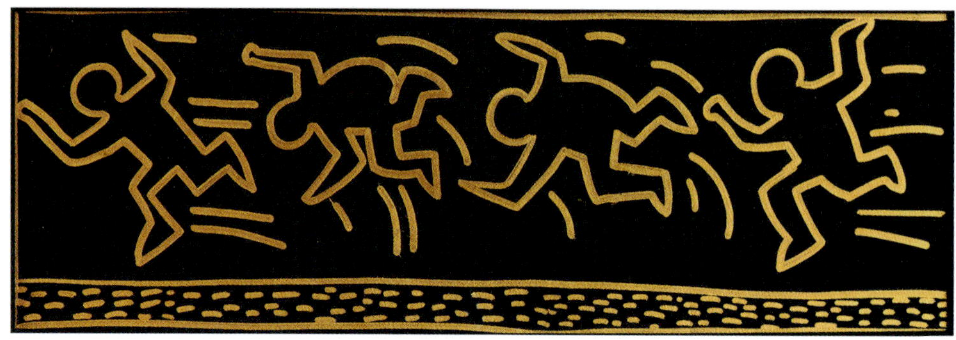

(clockwise from top left) Keith Haring *Untitled* 1982, fibre-tipped pen on composition board, 50.8 x 38.1 cm, Private collection; *Untitled* 1981, fibre-tipped pen on panel, 30.5 x 20.3 cm, Collection of Larry Warsh; *Untitled* 1982, fibre-tipped pen on composition board, 17.7 x 49.5 cm, Private collection

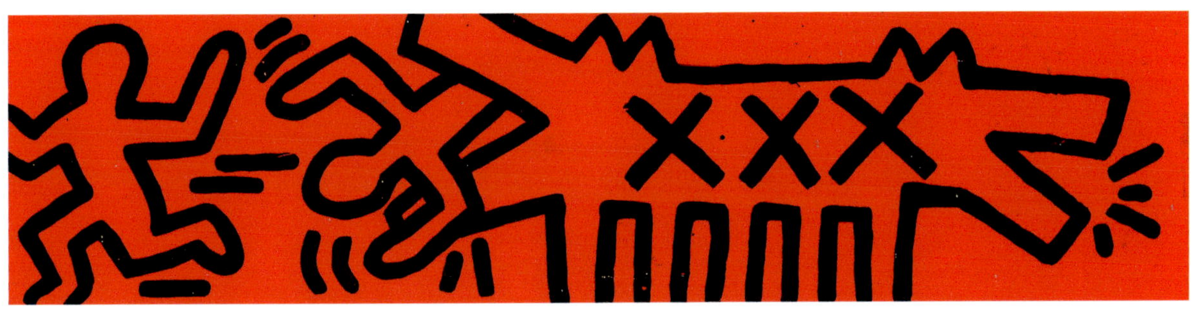

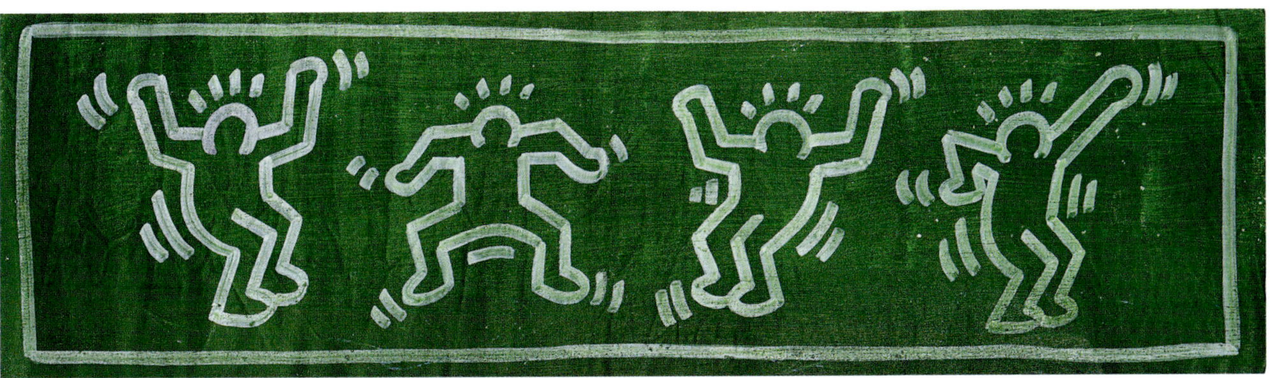

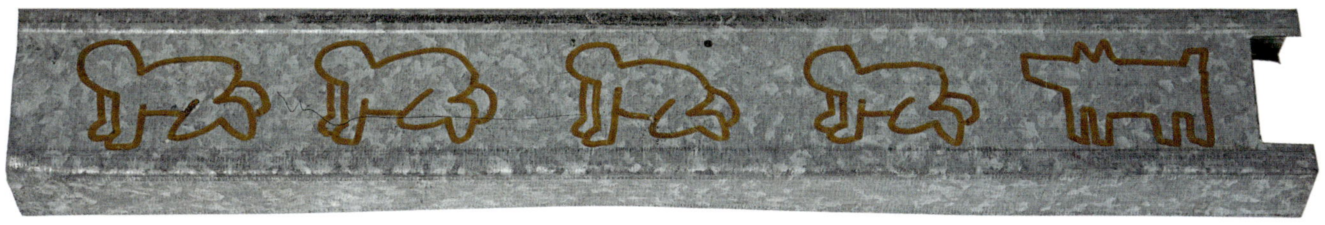

(top to bottom) Keith Haring *Untitled* 1982, synthetic polymer paint on wood panel, 20.0 x 81.8 cm, Courtesy Laurent Strouk; *Untitled* 1983, paint on canvas, 36.8 x 106.6 cm, Private collection; *Untitled* c. 1987, fibre-tipped pen on metal, 6.3 x 43.0 x 3.8 cm, Collection of Larry Warsh

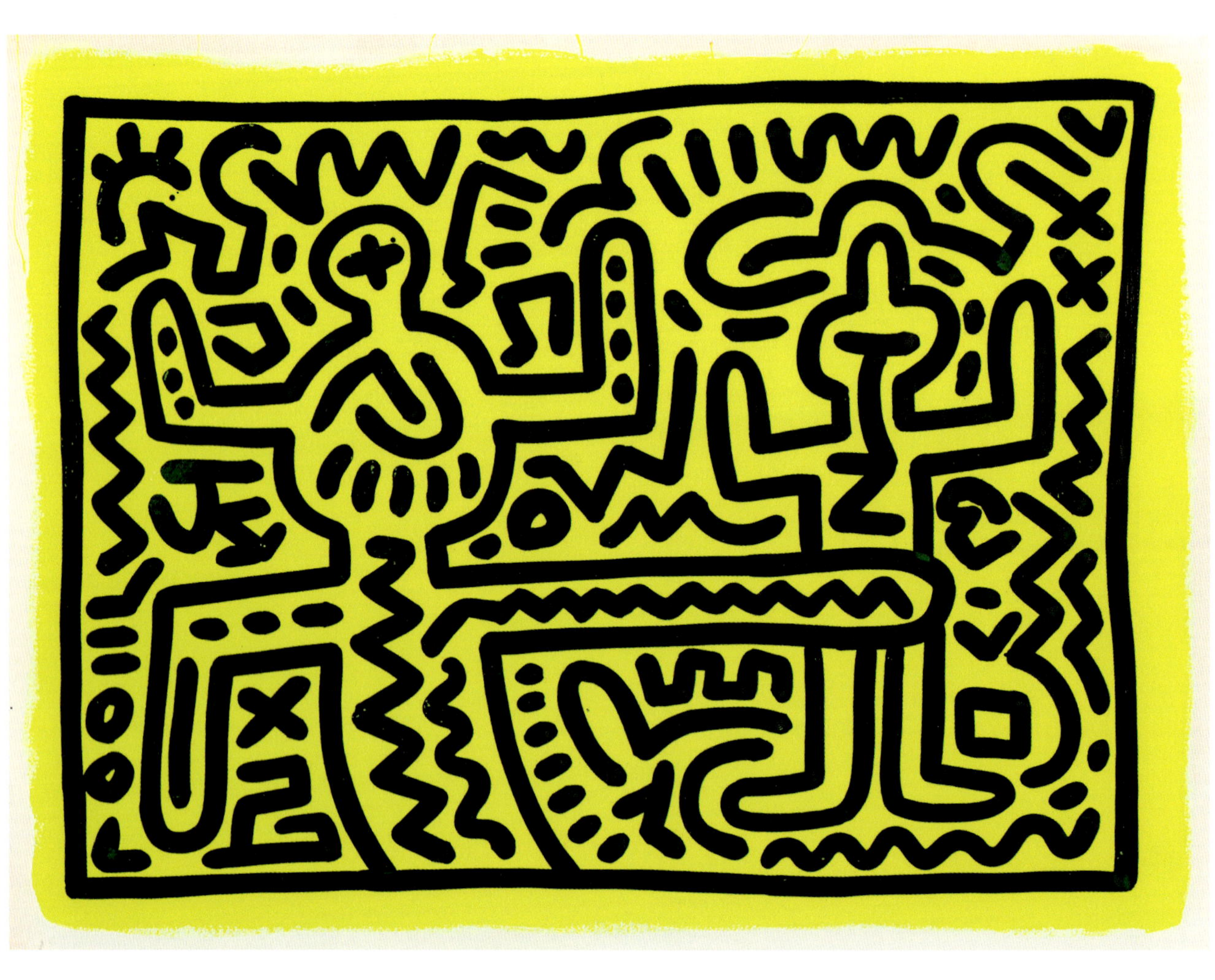

(above) Keith Haring *Untitled* 1982, tempera on paper, 94.9 x 125.1 cm, Private collection, Europe
(opposite) Keith Haring, LA II *Untitled* 1983, ink and day-glo paint on fibreglass, 119.3 x 71.1 x 48.2 cm, Private collection

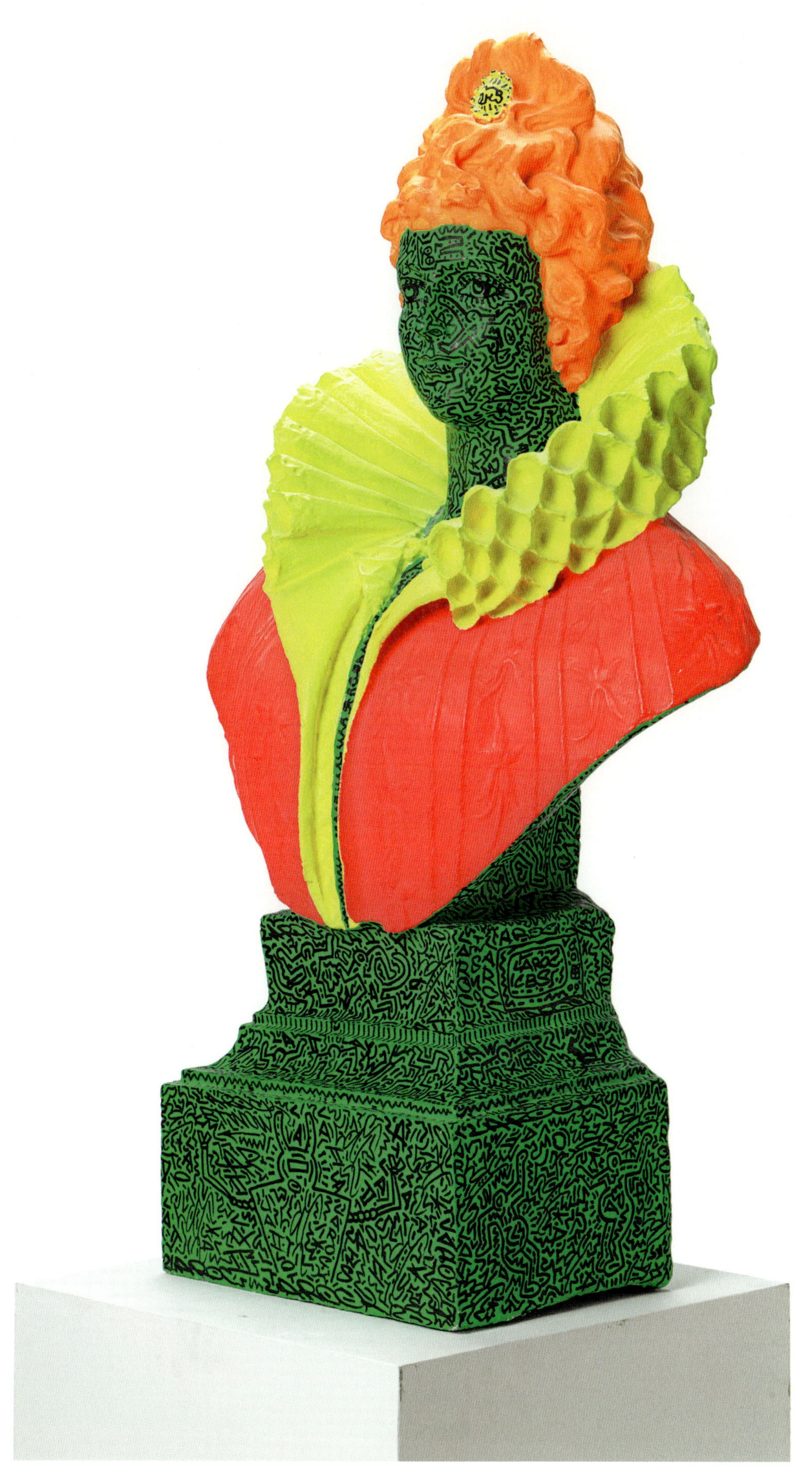

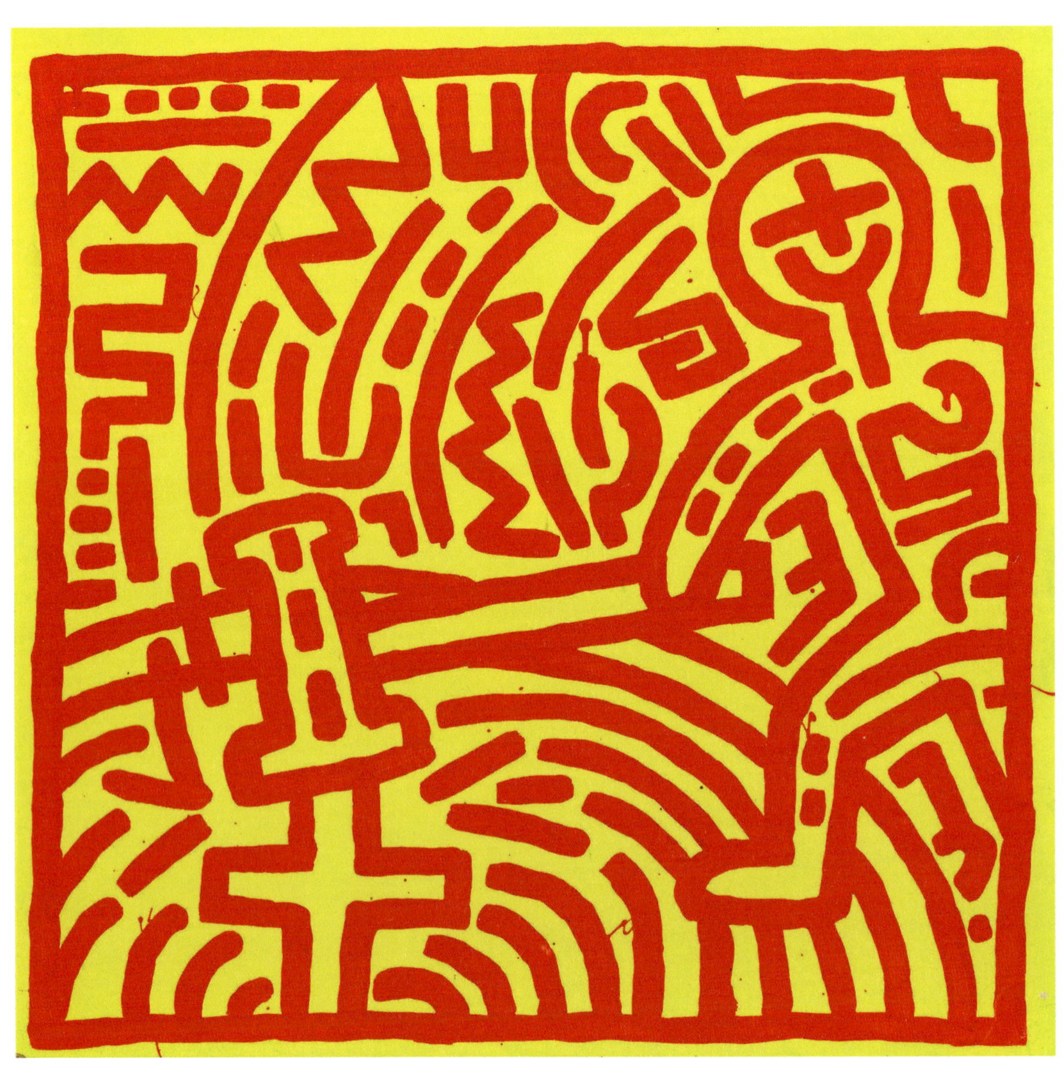

Keith Haring *Untitled (For John Sex)* 1982, synthetic polymer paint and day-glo paint on board, 58.4 x 58.4 cm, Collection of Larry Warsh

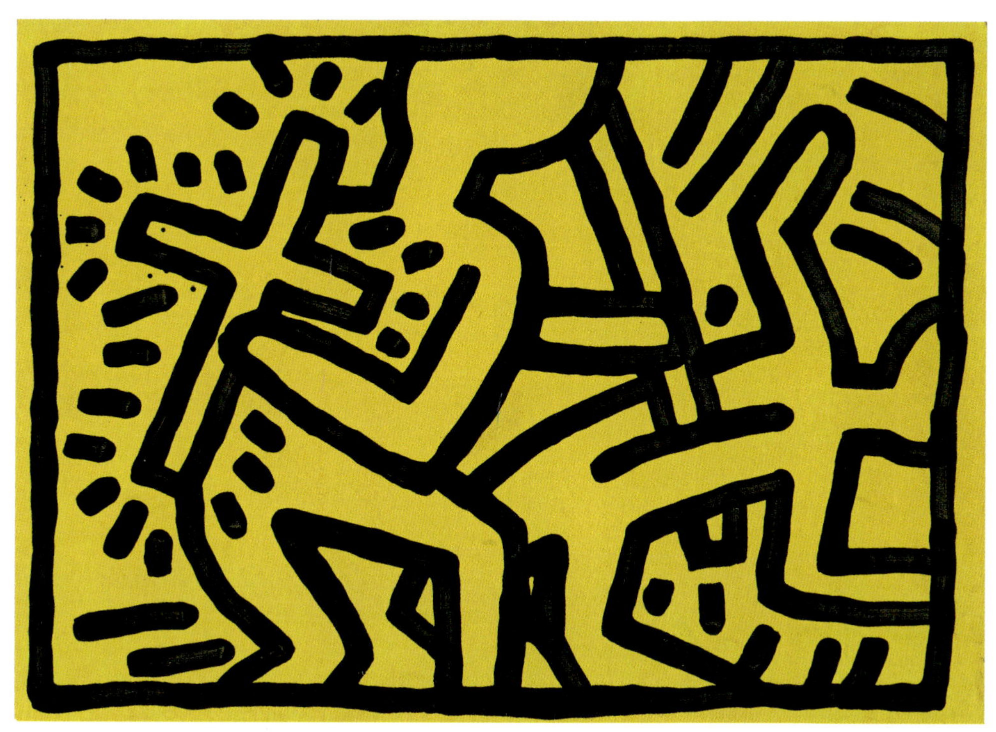

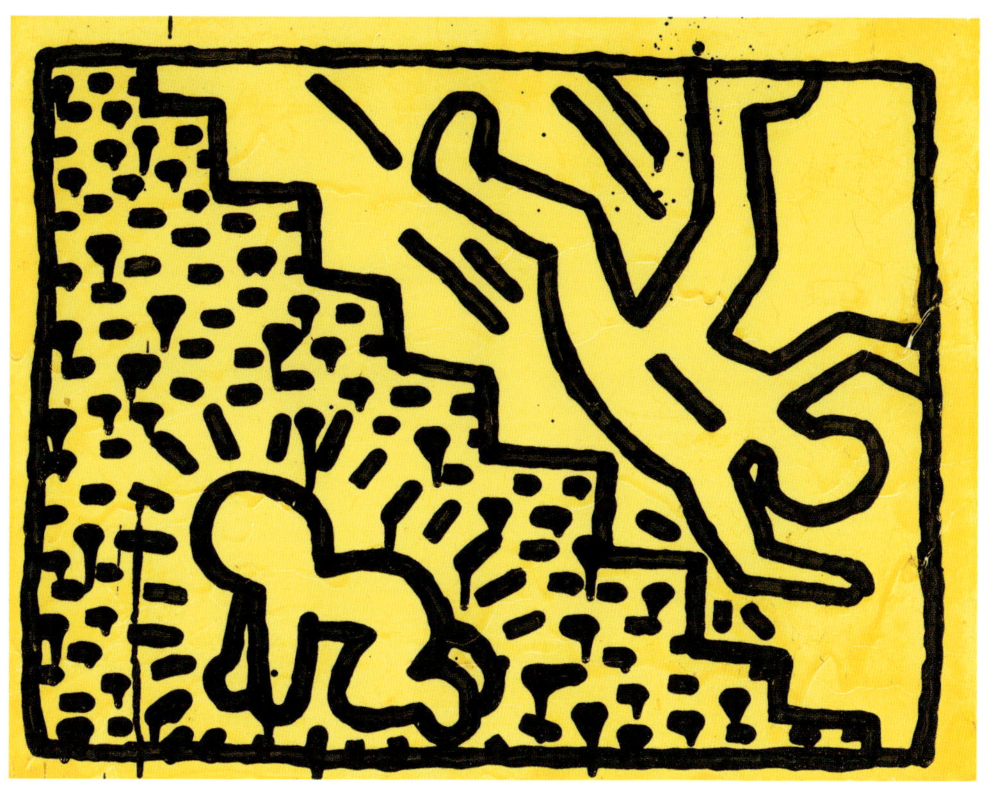

(top) Keith Haring *Untitled* 1982, day-glo on wood panel, 31.0 x 42.5 cm, BvB collection, Geneva
(bottom) Keith Haring *Untitled* 1982, synthetic polymer paint on composition board, 40.6 x 51.1 cm, Collection of Larry Warsh

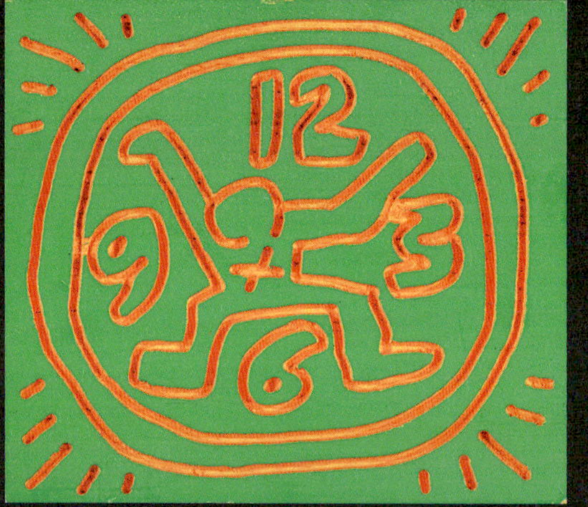

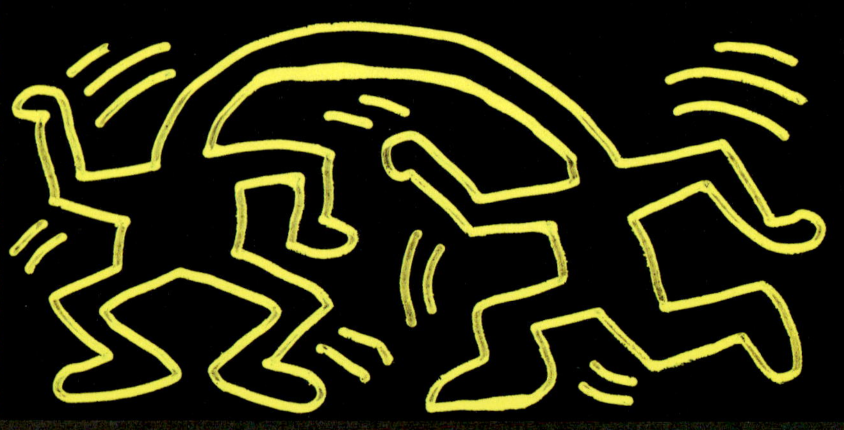

(top to bottom) Keith Haring *Untitled* 1983, day-glo paint on routed wood panel, 30.4 x 31.7 cm;
Untitled 1983, day-glo paint on routed wood panel, 20.3 x 55.8 cm;
Untitled 1983, day-glo paint on routed wood panel, 25.4 x 55.9 cm, All works collection of Larry Warsh

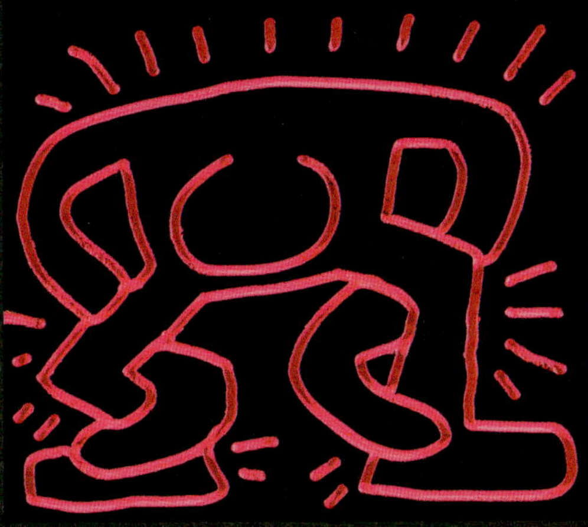

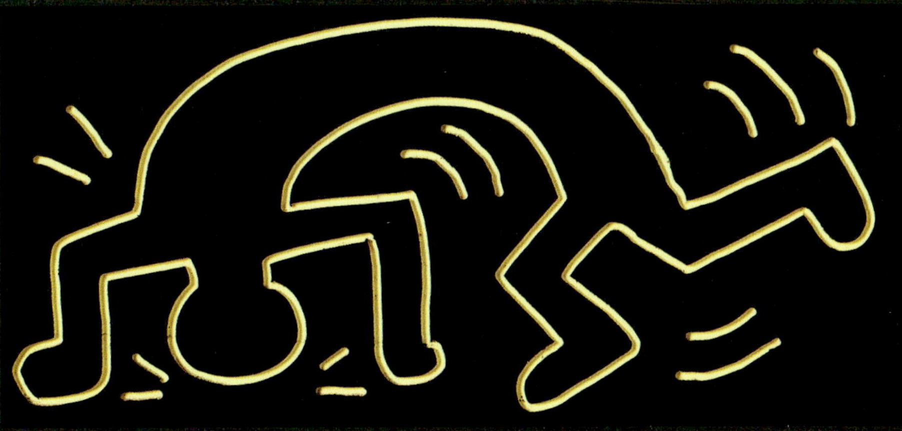

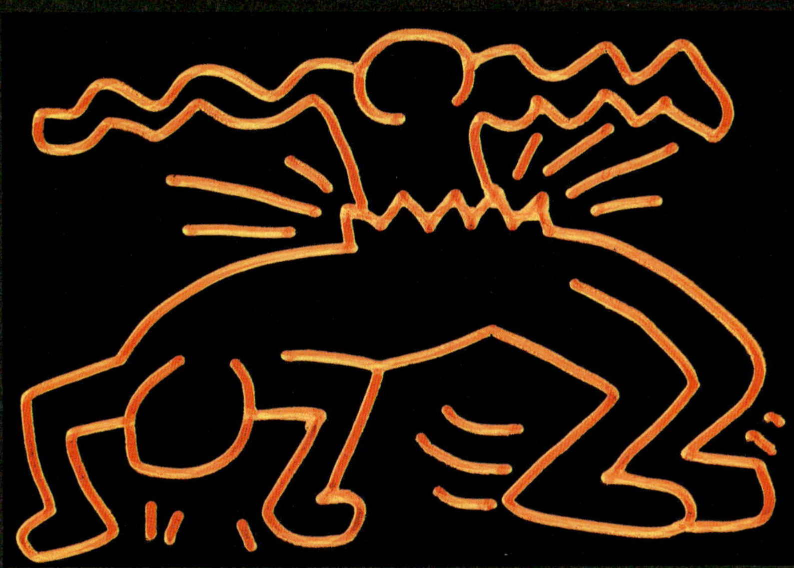

(top to bottom) Keith Haring *Untitled* 1983, day-glo paint on routed wood panel, 30.4 x 31.7 cm;
Untitled 1983, day-glo paint on routed wood panel, 30.4 x 60.9 cm;
Untitled 1983, day-glo paint on routed wood panel, 25.4 x 53.3 cm, All works collection of Larry Warsh

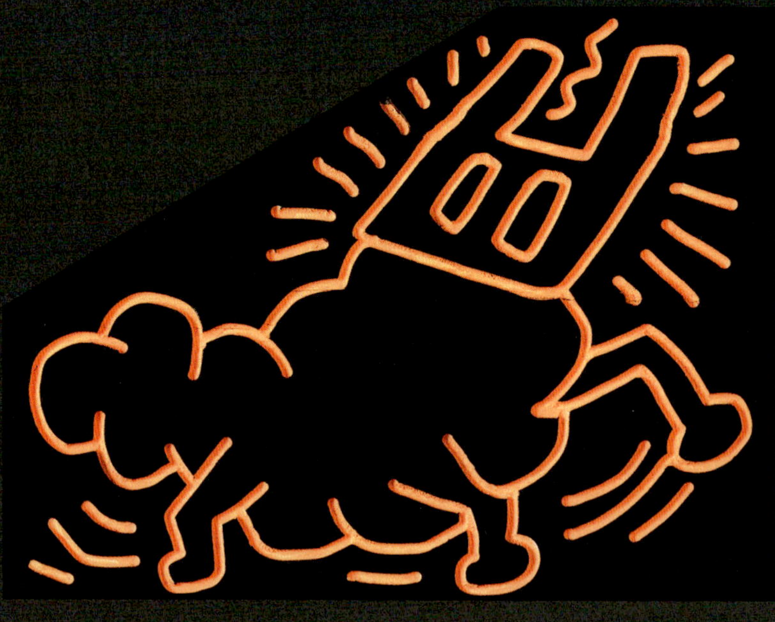

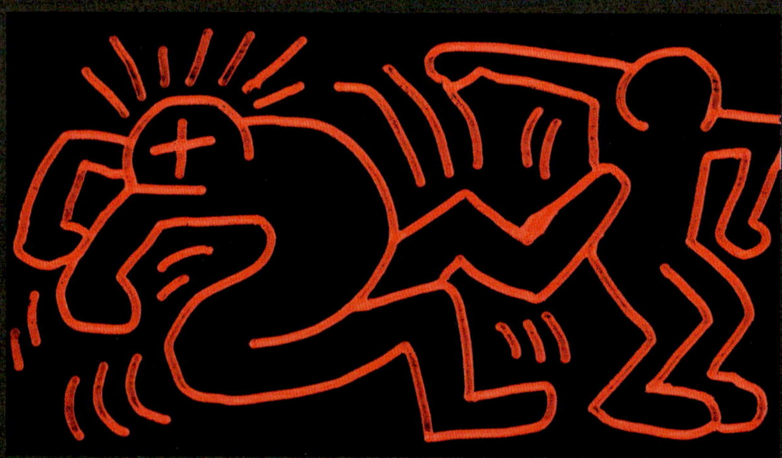

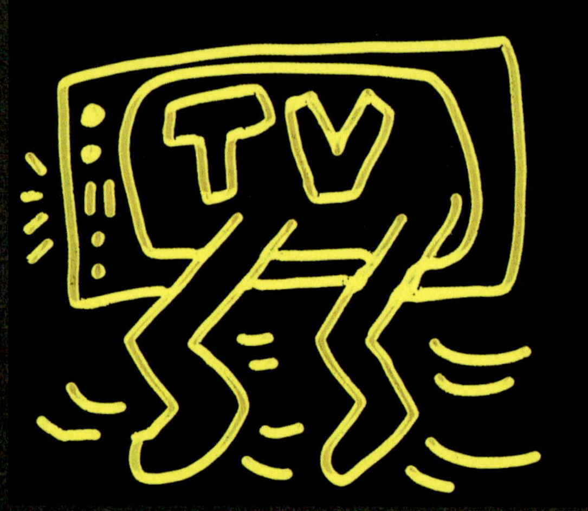

(top to bottom) Keith Haring *Untitled* 1983, day-glo paint on routed wood panel, 31.7 x 50.8 cm;
Untitled 1983, day-glo paint on routed wood panel, 30.4 x 50.8 cm;
Untitled 1983, day-glo paint on routed wood panel, 30.5 x 30.5 cm, All works collection of Larry Warsh

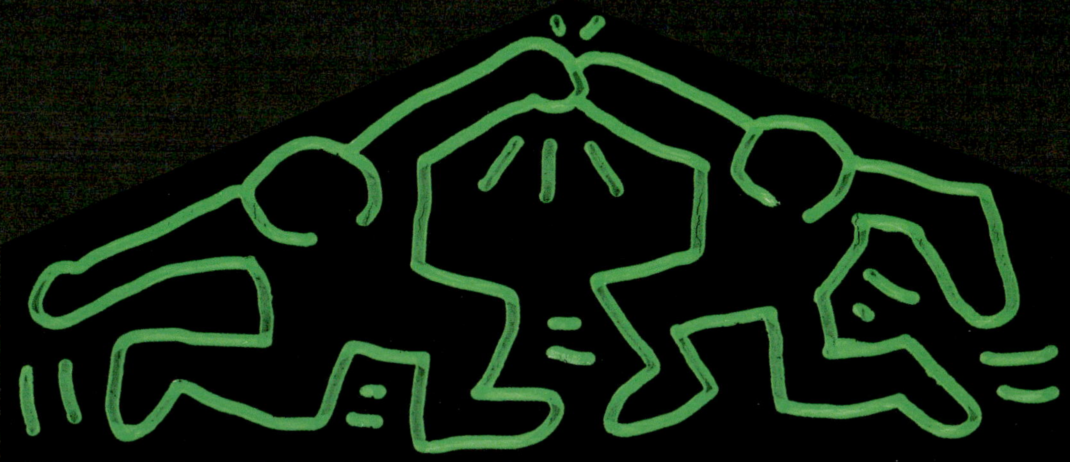

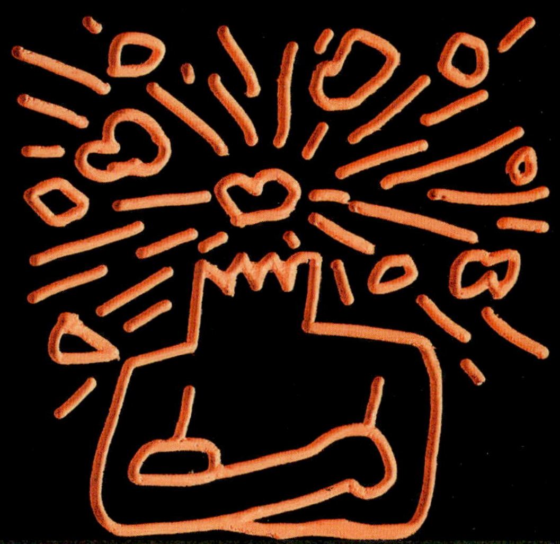

(clockwise from top) Keith Haring *Untitled* 1983, day-glo paint on routed wood panel, 30.4 x 60.9 cm;
Untitled 1983, day-glo paint on routed wood panel, 35.5 x 38.1 cm;
Untitled 1983, day-glo paint on routed wood panel, 40.6 x 30.5 cm, All works collection of Larry Warsh

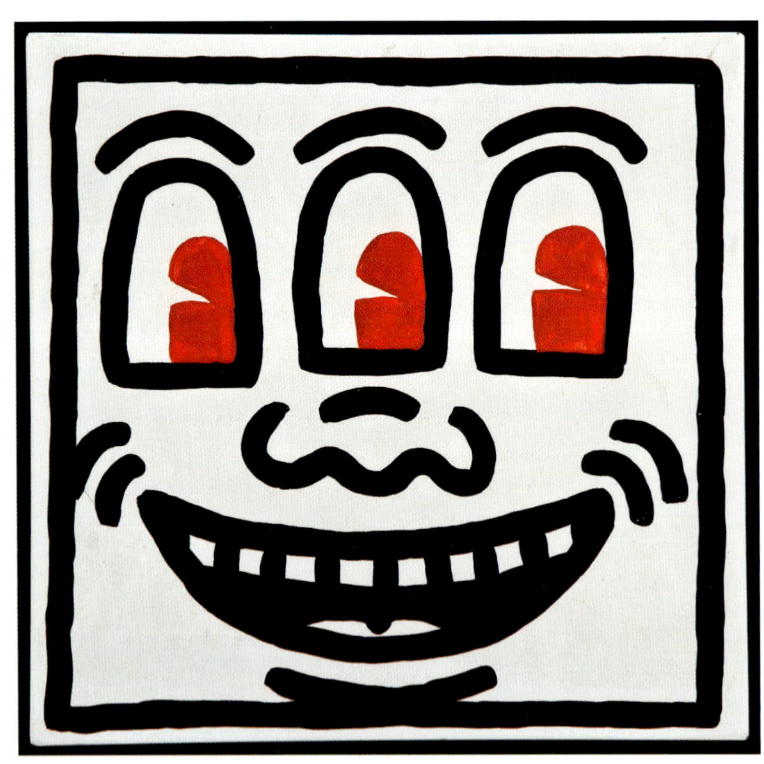

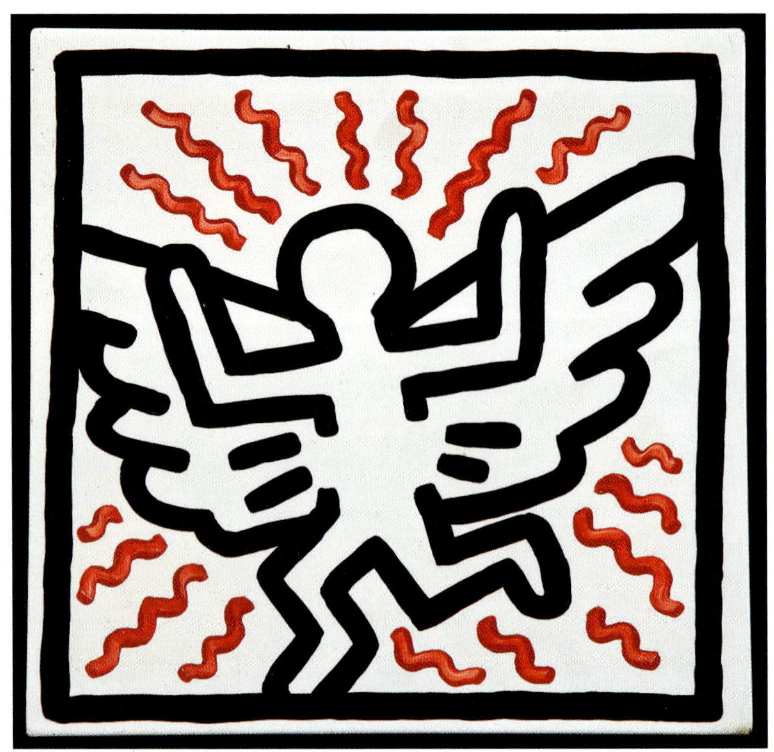

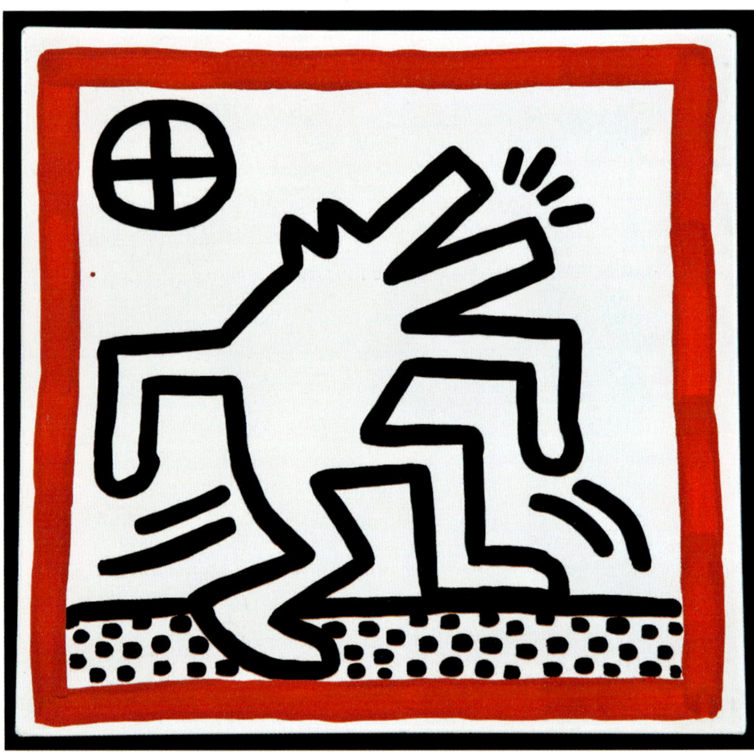

Keith Haring *Untitled* 1982, baked enamel on metal, 30.5 x 30.5 cm (each), Collection of Larry Warsh

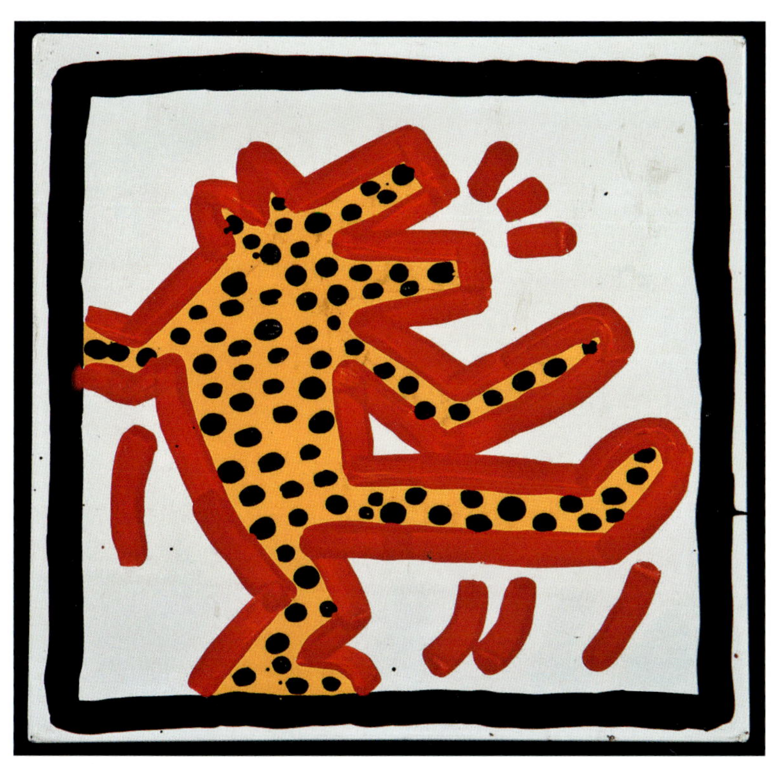

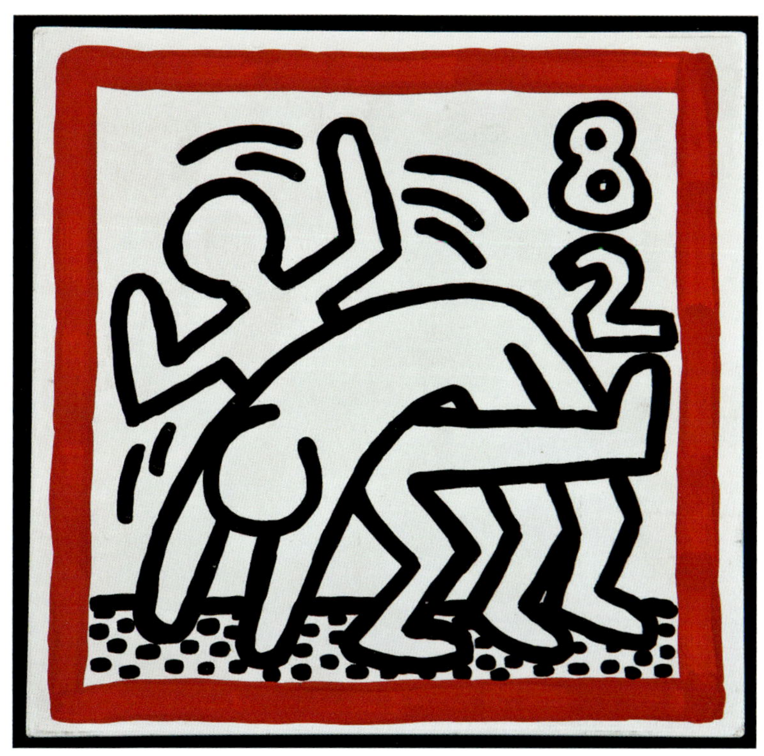
82

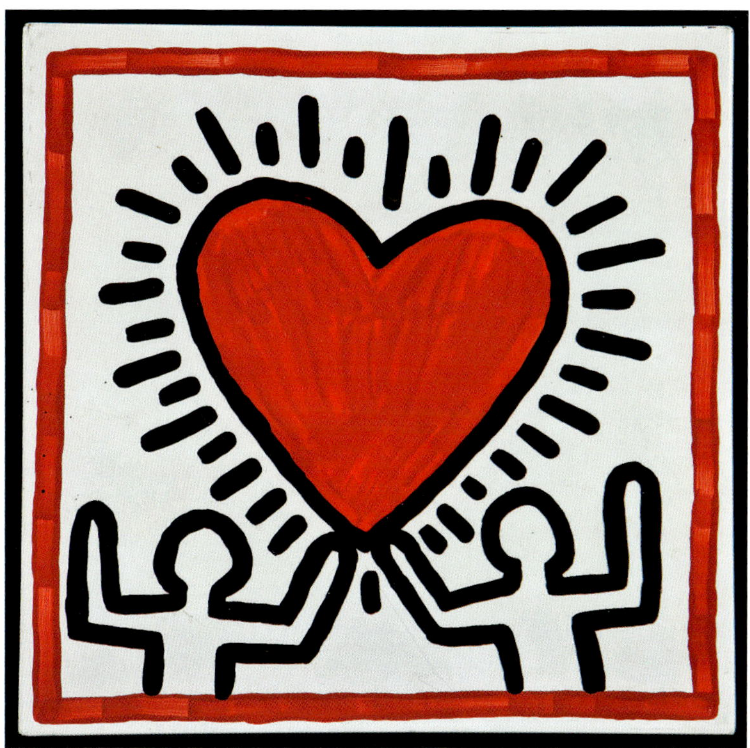

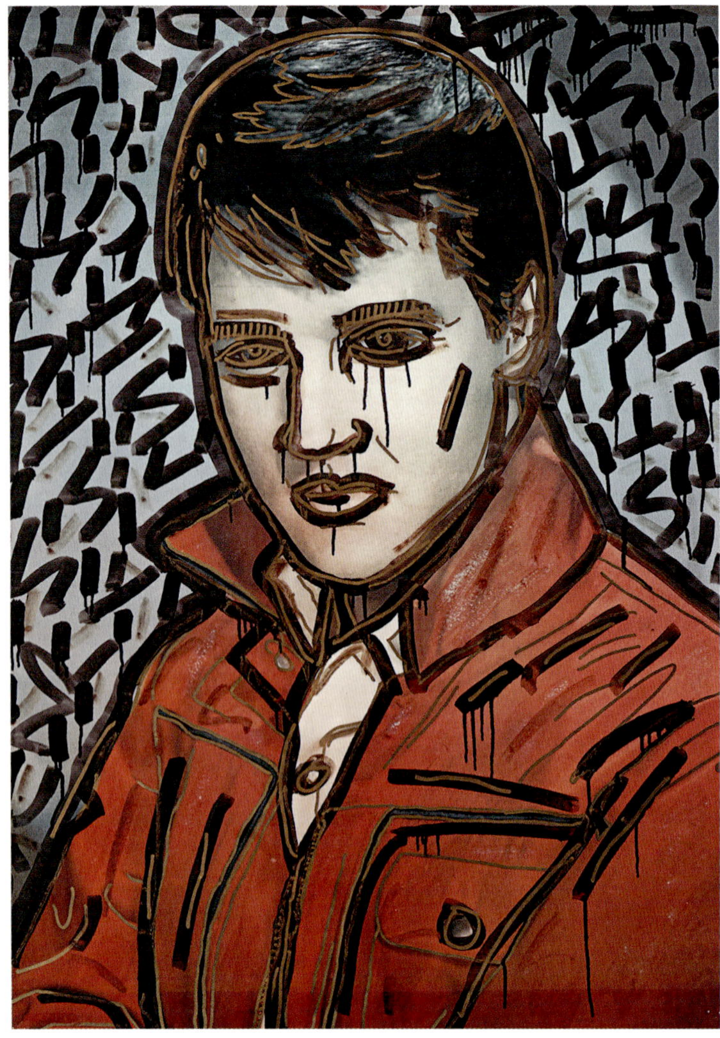

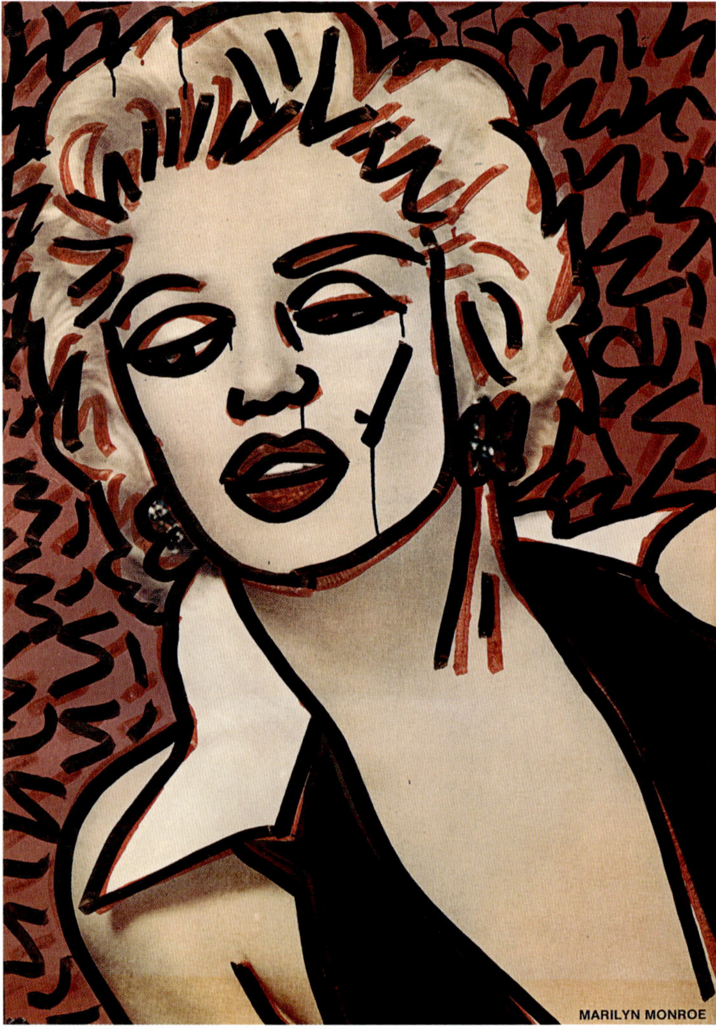

(above left) Keith Haring *Elvis Presley* 1981, ink and tempera on offset lithograph, 96.5 x 66.0 cm, Collection of Larry Warsh
(above right) Keith Haring *Marilyn Monroe* 1981, ink and tempera on offset lithograph, 96.5 x 66.0 cm, Collection of Larry Warsh

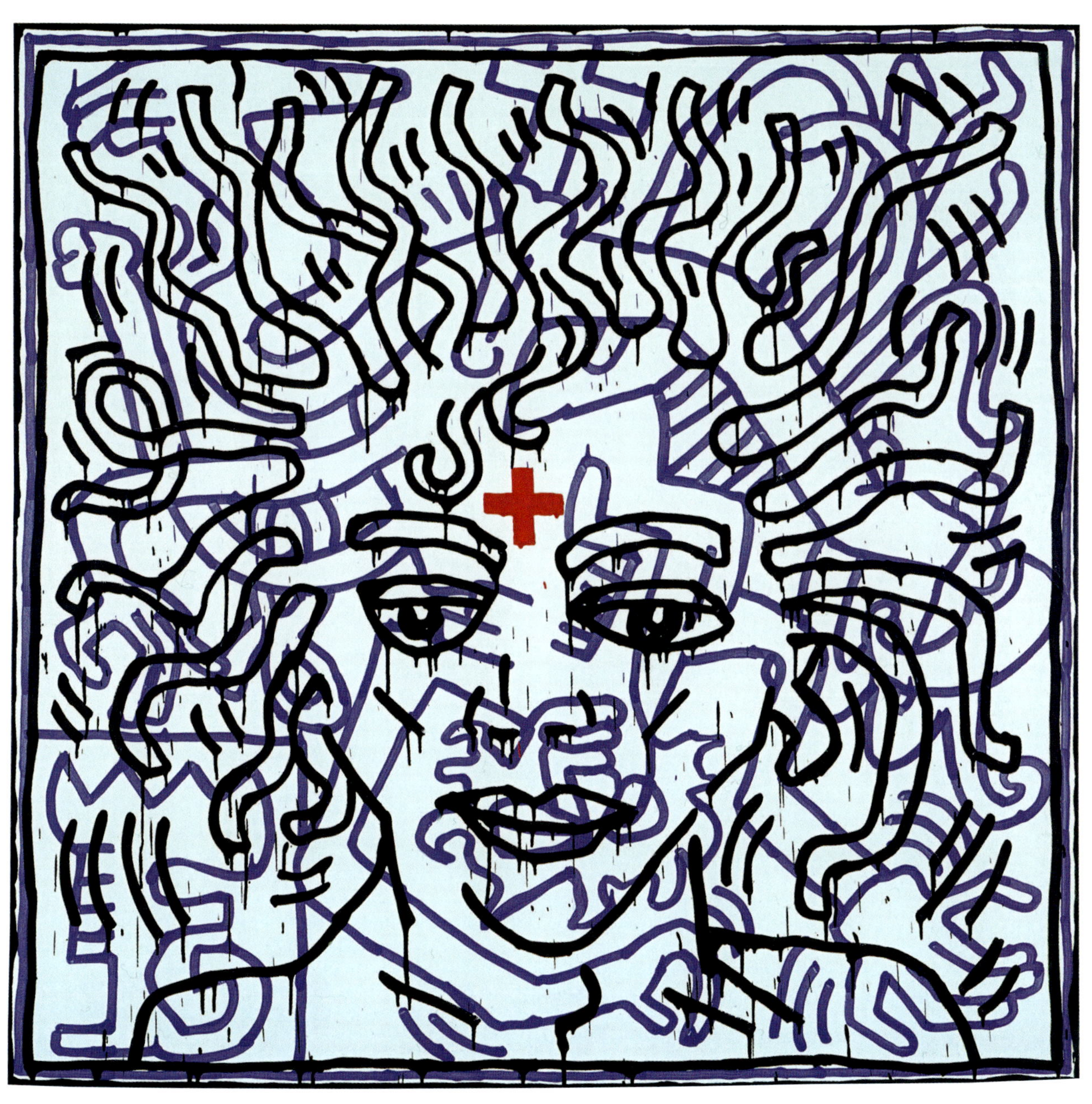

Keith Haring *Untitled* 1984, synthetic polymer paint on muslin, 152.4 x 152.4 cm, Private collection, Europe, courtesy Martos Gallery, New York

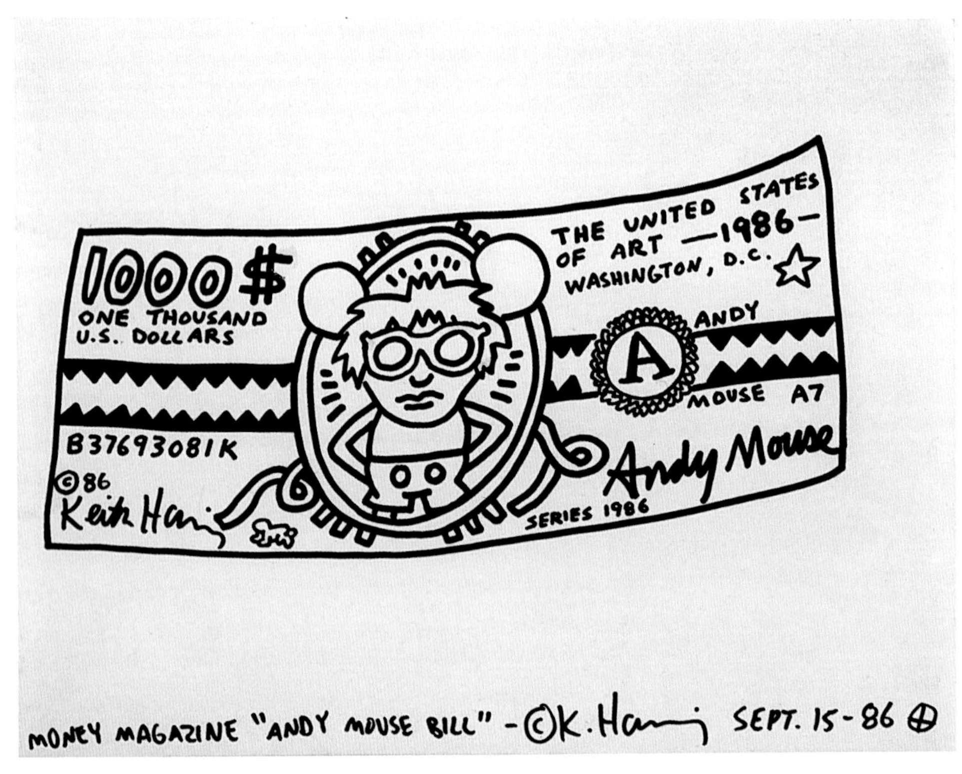

Keith Haring *Money Magazine Andy Mouse Bill* 1986, fibre-tipped pen on paper, 28.0 x 35.6 cm, The Keith Haring Foundation, New York

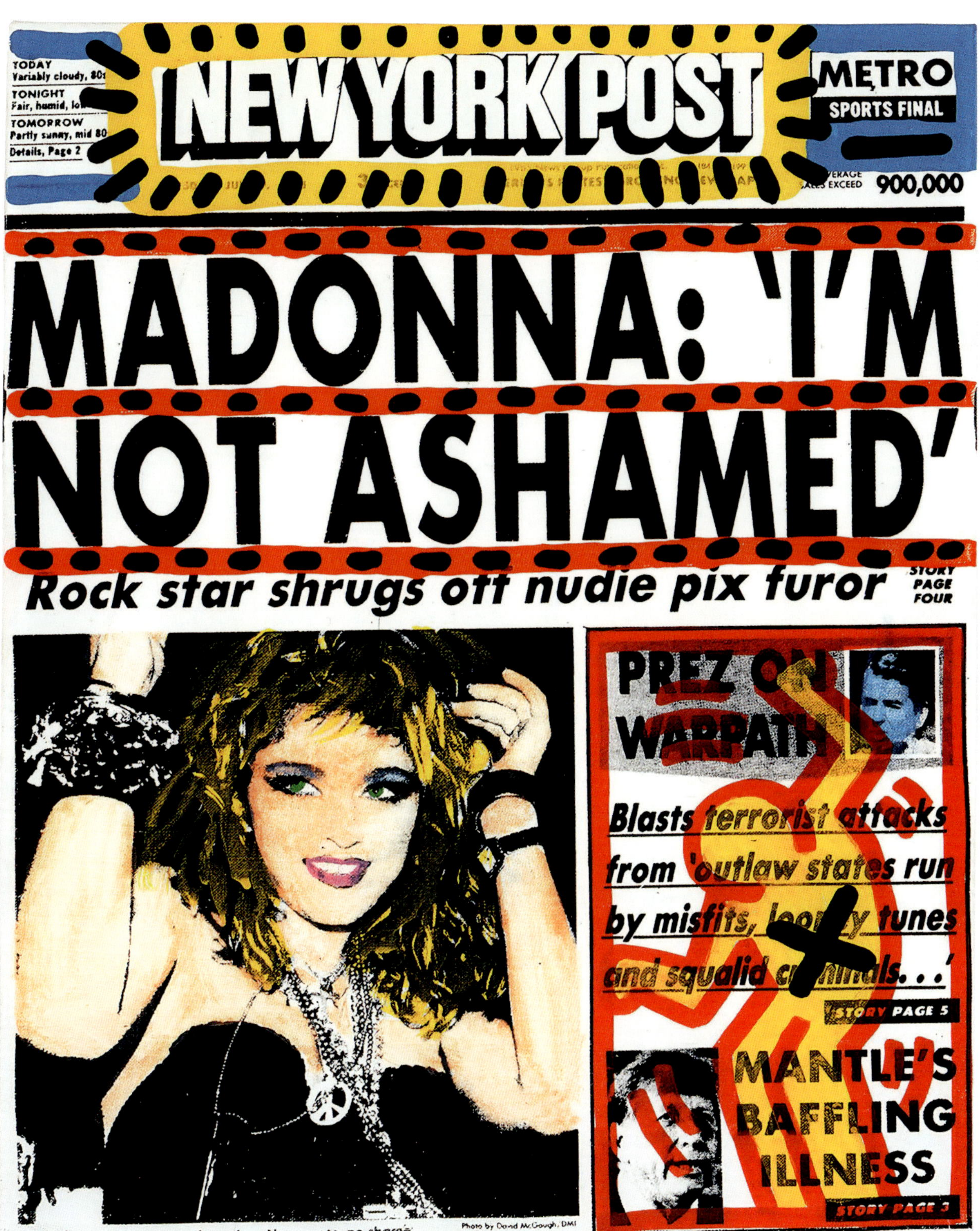

TODAY
Variably cloudy, 80s
TONIGHT
Fair, humid, lo
TOMORROW
Partly sunny, mid 80s
Details, Page 2

NEW YORK POST

METRO
SPORTS FINAL

900,000

MADONNA: 'I'M NOT ASHAMED'

Rock star shrugs off nudie pix furor

STORY PAGE FOUR

PREZ ON WARPATH

Blasts terrorist attacks from 'outlaw states run by misfits, loony tunes and squalid criminals...'

STORY PAGE 5

MANTLE'S BAFFLING ILLNESS

STORY PAGE 3

RAUNCHY STAR Madonna in action: No secrets, no shame.

Photo by David McGough, DMI

(above) Andy Warhol, Keith Haring *Untitled (Madonna, I'm Not Ashamed)* 1985, synthetic polymer paint, day-glo paint and silkscreen ink on canvas, 50.8 x 40.6 cm, The Keith Haring Foundation, New York
(overleaf) Keith Haring, Andy Warhol and Jean-Michel Basquiat, 1984, photographic reproduction from Andy Warhol's 35mm negative

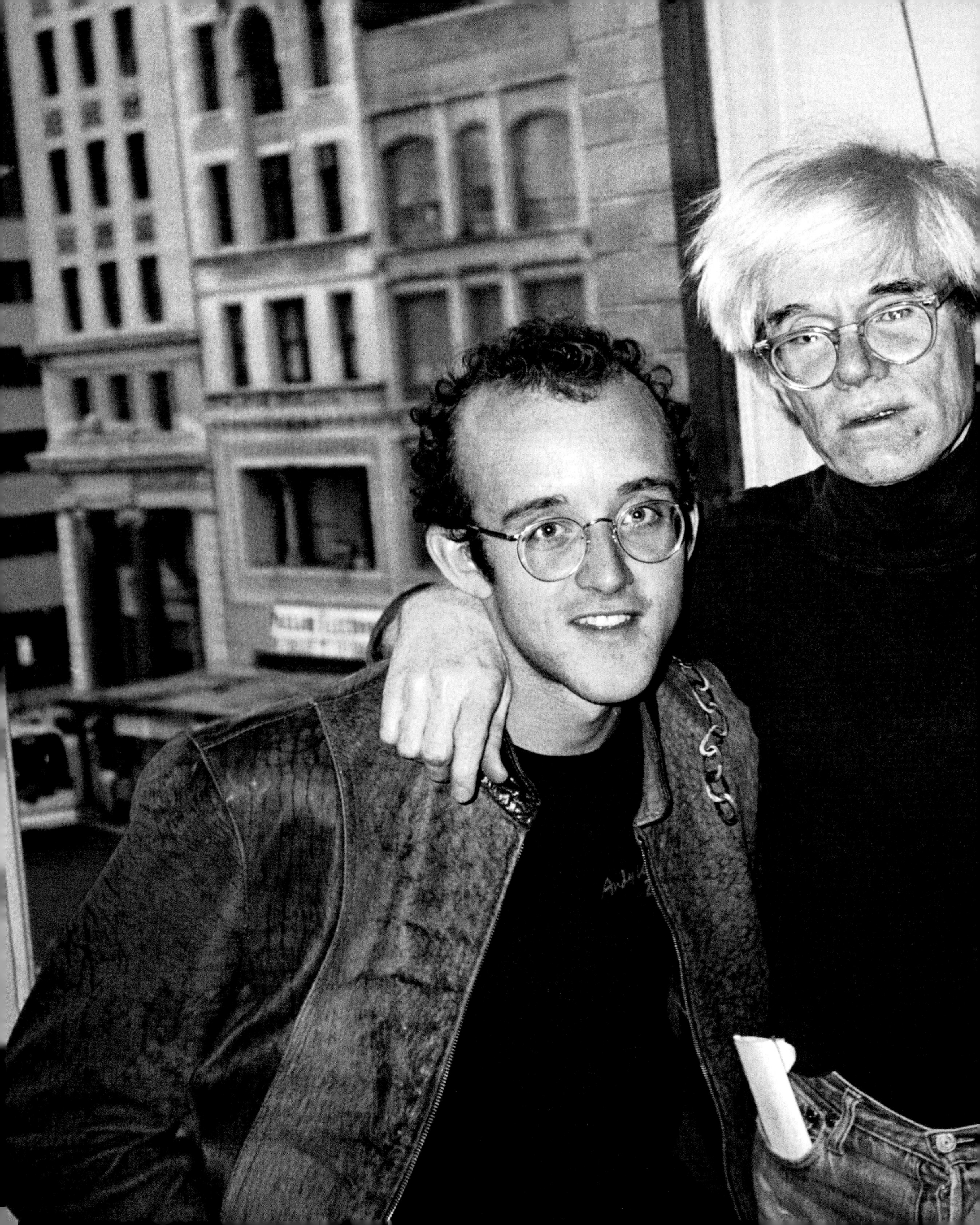

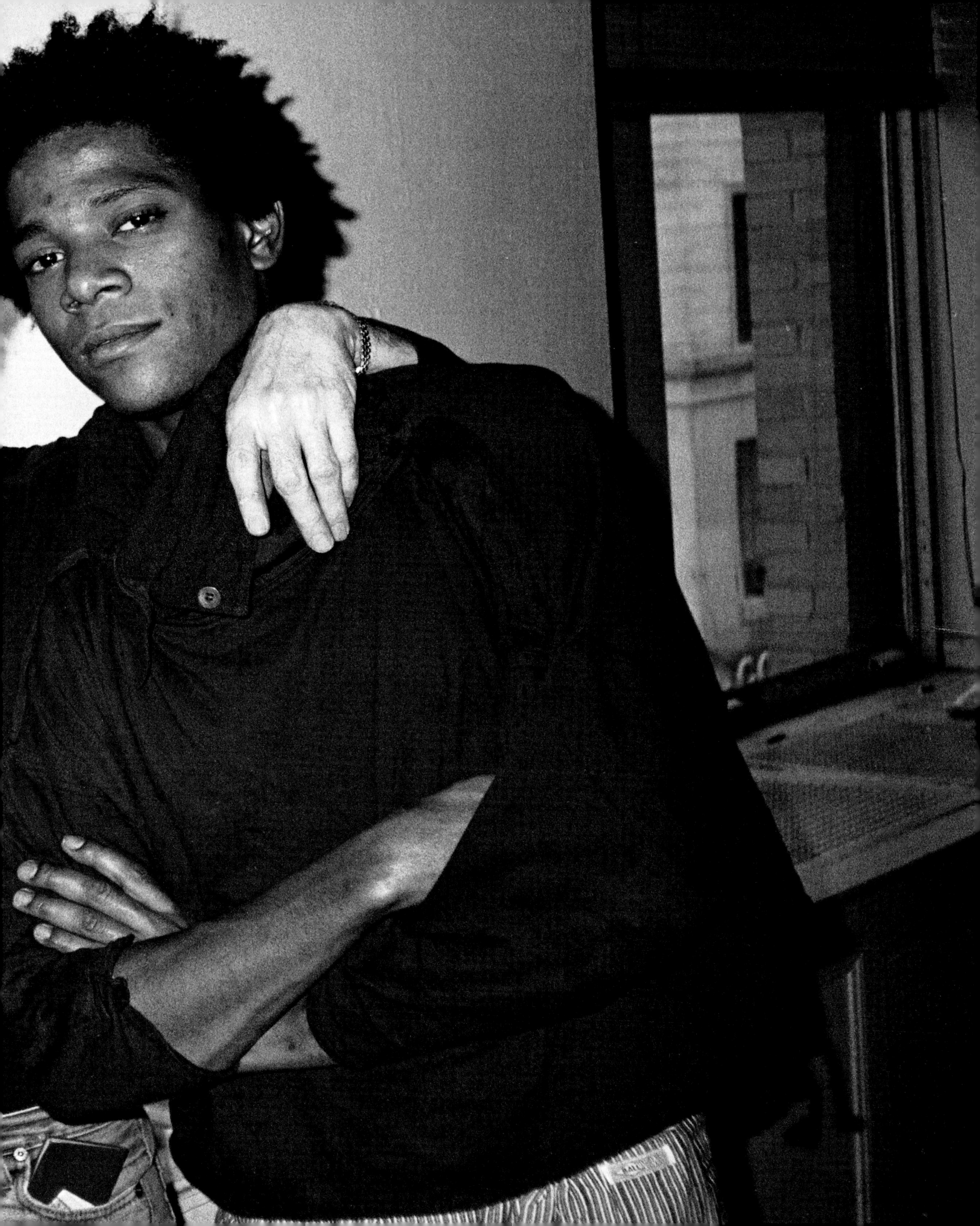

Kool & Blak

Myles Russell-Cook

In 1947, Cuban anthropologist Fernando Ortiz Fernández coined the term 'transculturation' to describe the phenomenon of merging and converging cultures.[1] Transculturation encompasses more than transition from one culture to another; it does not consist merely of acquiring another culture or losing or uprooting a previous culture. Rather, it combines these concepts and includes the idea of the consequent creation of new, hybridised forms of culture. When cultures collide, some things survive, some things are lost and some new things are created. But unlike the collision of cultures that followed Lieutenant James Cook's landing at Botany Bay, Australia, which devastated Aboriginal ways of being, transcultural interactions are not inherently colonial and destructive.

This essay explores the unexpected connections between the work of Keith Haring and Jean-Michel Basquiat in 1980s New York and the art of some contemporary Australian and Aboriginal artists. At first glance, Aboriginal Australia and the art being produced in New York City in the 1980s appear to be entirely unrelated – situated in separate hemispheres and emerging from different cultures and histories. However, New York street art and contemporary Aboriginal art are both firmly part of today's art world, but also maintain strong links to ceremonies, performances and experiences that originate outside the art world and which, historically, have gone unrecognised or been known only to a few.

The first Aboriginal artists to gain recognition by the contemporary art world and market, from 1971 to 1972, were a group of senior Anmatyerre, Pintupi, Warlpiri, and Luritja men working at Papunya in the Western Desert. These artists took designs and motifs that were ephemeral – painted onto bodies, objects and the ground – and rendered them permanent (and saleable) on composition board. The radical act of transferring restricted ceremonial designs onto composition board sparked a shift in perception; what had previously been considered material culture was now recognised as art.[2] In a similar way, Haring and Basquiat found success within the gallery system by rendering permanent the ephemeral designs and motifs of New York street art and nightlife; specifically, the Black and Queer experience of these. What had previously been considered public vandalism or nightlife entertainment was now recognised as art. Both of these traditions, then, are a way of capturing and making permanent an energy and a rhythm that had previously only existed for a short time, on dilapidated walls or ceremonial ground.

Arguably because of these similarities, there have been a number of instances over recent decades where these two traditions have been explicitly connected. Several artists in Australia, for whom their Aboriginality has been a central aspect of their work, have directly engaged with either Haring or Basquiat in their practices, while Haring and Basquiat both engaged with First Nations stories in their work. With this in mind, it is difficult to view the work of Basquiat and Haring and not think about the issue of cultural appropriation. Communications scholar Richard Rogers broadly defines cultural appropriation as 'the use of a culture's symbols, artefacts, genres, rituals, or technologies by members of another culture'.[3] He goes on to identify four distinct types of cultural appropriation: cultural exchange, cultural dominance, cultural exploitation and transculturation. Each of these categories relates to the nature of power relations between the groups involved.

Moreover, Rogers asserts that not all instances of cultural appropriation are inherently colonial and destructive – in the right circumstances, they can be reciprocal and productive. Using Rogers's categories, I contend that the connections between Aboriginal Australian artistic practices and the work of Basquiat and Haring are, on the whole, reciprocal and productive, involving both transculturation and cultural exchange.

Despite a relative lack of reciprocity at the time, the fact that in recent years a number of Indigenous artists have been and continue to be inspired by Haring and Basquiat suggests that in the long run there has been an equitable and reciprocal cultural exchange between these two groups. Furthermore, the particular relationship between Haring and Basquiat and artists such as Gordon Bennett and Reko Rennie is evidence of Aboriginal peoples' cosmopolitan and international curiosity, and their intrepid exploration of ideas from across cultures.

Keith Haring

In 1969, The Metropolitan Museum of Art, New York, acquired from Nelson A. Rockefeller one of the largest collections of so-called 'primitive art'. Haring could not have been unaware of the public attention received by First Nations art in New York in the years after that acquisition. At the same time as the Met was bringing First Nations art to the foreground in an art museum context, Haring was doing a similar thing on the street. It is well known that Haring drew inspiration from a number of First Nations, Black and non-Western artistic practices. His personal library contained numerous reference books on First Nations art, including at least three volumes on Aboriginal art. He was familiar with urban Black and Brown communities through his personal relationships, collaborating with several Black and Brown artists, models and dancers, and had a number of Black and Puerto Rican boyfriends.

Haring's immediately identifiable visual style centres on the human body reduced to a singular, linear shape: flat, graphic and in many instances so stylised that it is rendered essentially raceless. However, Haring's choice to colour some figures solidly, and significantly as black, reinforces that his figures, despite being stylised, are racially charged. Nearly all of Haring's human

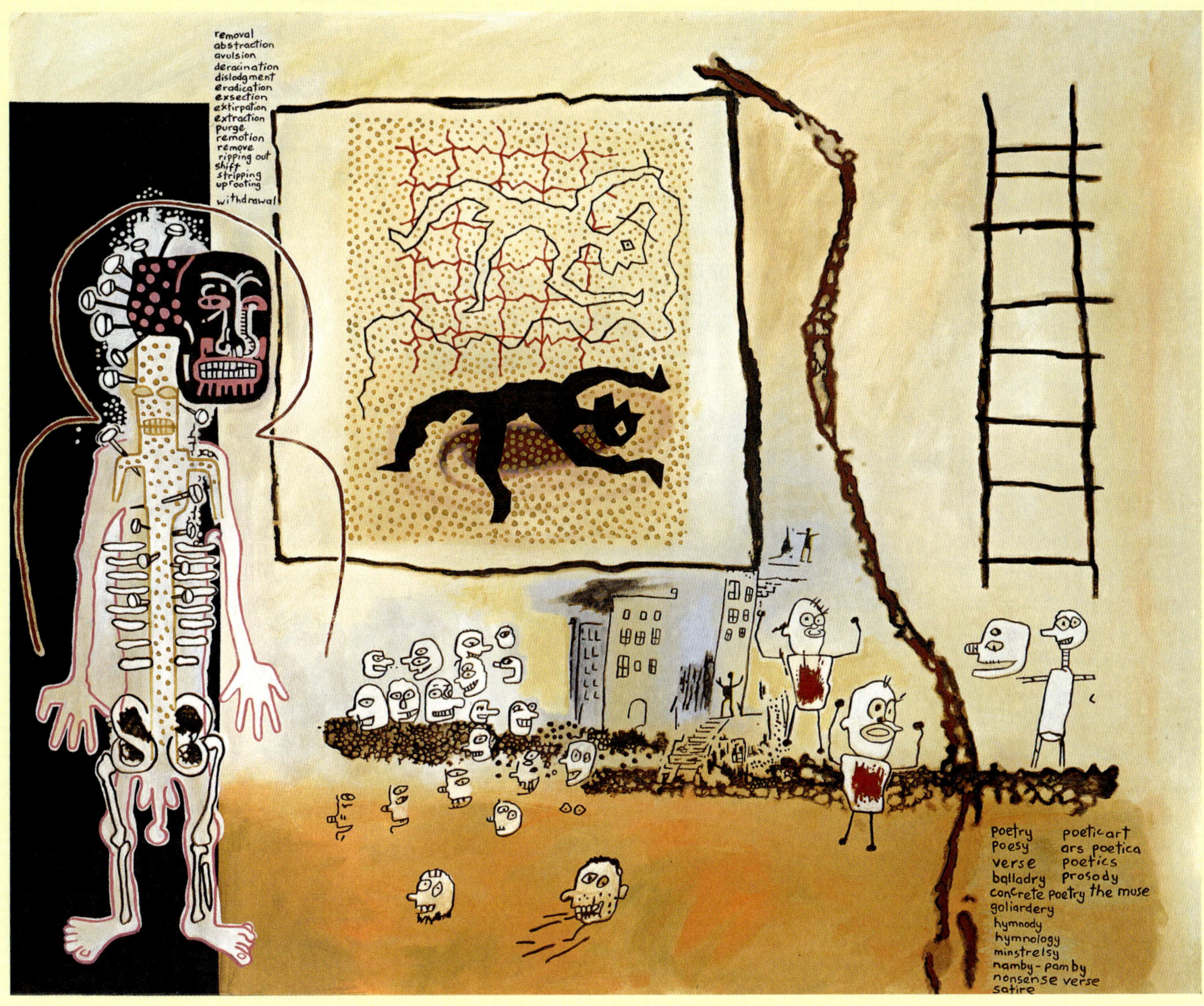

figures are depicted in motion, swept up in the ecstasy of dance, surrounded by small dashes of movement; the artist imbued them with a vibrating intensity and dynamism. Despite the lack of physical signifiers of race in these stylised elemental figures, the particular dance styles Haring depicted usually honoured urban Black or First Nations traditions. These included breakdancing, which ultimately can be traced back to dance practices in the ancient kingdom of Kongo in Central Africa (present-day Angola / Democratic Republic of the Congo), and the Brazilian dance capoeira, based on a martial art developed by African slaves, which can also be traced back to the Kongo. (For a more detailed analysis of the tribal influences on Haring's work, see Robert Farris Thompson's illuminating essay 'Requiem for the Degas of the B-boys, Keith Haring'.)[4]

In February 1984 Haring made his first and only visit to Australia, travelling to Melbourne/Naarm, the lands of the Boon Wurrung and Wurundjeri. While in Melbourne, Haring participated in a number of artistic performances and projects in which he collaborated with the radical expressionists of Roar Studios, together with Howard Arkley, Juan Davila, Robert Jacks and others. Roar Studios was one of Melbourne's earliest

Gordon Bennett *Notes to Basquiat: Poet and Muse* 2000, synthetic polymer paint on canvas, 152.5 × 182.8 cm, National Gallery of Victoria, Purchased through the NGV Foundation with the assistance of Mr Henry Gillespie, Governor, 2001 artist-run studios, and the participating artists were known for painting in a 'raw' and 'primitive' style. As well as executing a mural in Johnston Street, Collingwood, and painting onto the NGV's glass facade (known as the Waterwall[5]), Haring restaged one of his iconic New York performances for one of Australia's largest community events, Melbourne's Moomba Festival. Run by the City of Melbourne, Moomba takes place over four days and includes several community and sports events, as well as discos and parades.

Haring also produced a poster containing the word 'Moomba', which emerged from his interest in the origin of the word. The name 'Moomba' was originally suggested to the festival's white founding committee members by Bill Onus, the Yorta Yorta president of the Aborigines Advancement League. The founding committee members were told that the word means 'Let's get together and have some fun', when in fact it derives from a south-eastern Aboriginal term for 'buttocks'.[6] As Margo Neale has pointed out when discussing the Moomba festival in her biography of Lin Onus, 'encased in the ironies of black humour, a new and surreptitious form of activism is released'.[7] Haring's poster, a cartoon line drawing of three men engaging in anal sex, situated below the word 'Moomba', was his way of engaging with a subversive, playful and ironic display of public activism by Melbourne's Aboriginal people. Haring recognised the need to protest in code, and so was able to participate in a very particular form of Melbourne Aboriginal humour.

Haring's performance at Moomba extends this exploration of the links between his own queer urban New York experience and the Melbourne Aboriginal communities he was engaging with. Footage of the Moomba dance performance is available as part of a 1984 documentary on Haring's time in Australia called *Babies, Snakes and Barking Dogs: Keith Haring in Australia*, a clip of which is available online.[8] The clip features a number of male performers, one of whom is naked but for a jockstrap and entirely painted in Haring's designs. He is surrounded by a group of racially ambiguous dancers wearing Haring-designed hats and T-shirts. At the start the announcer says: 'Up next, rap dancing by Isolation; radio by Kenny Scharf; body jockstrap, hats and T-shirts by Keith Haring'. The raw sexuality of the main dancer is amplified by the ghetto-blaster and rap music.

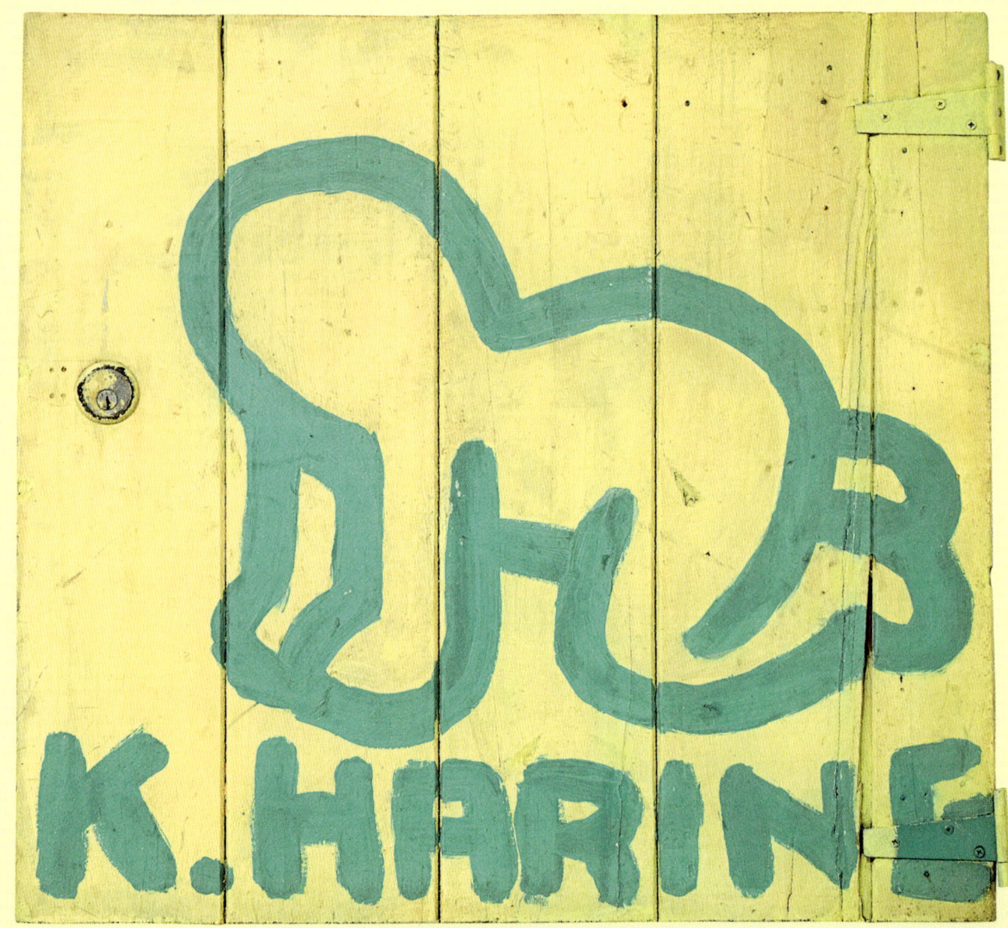

Keith Haring *Untitled* 1984, synthetic polymer paint on wood and metal, 65.2 × 71.7 cm (variable), National Gallery of Victoria, Melbourne

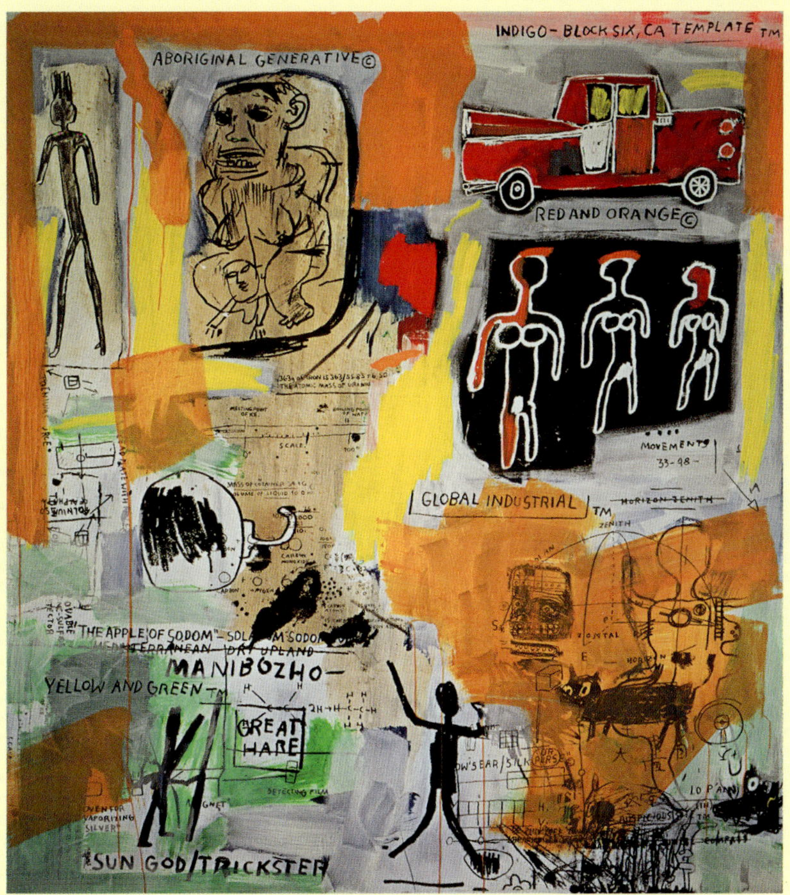

Haring first encountered this combination of queerness, sexuality and party music, energised by Black and Hispanic beats, at the Paradise Garage club in New York, where people of all sexualities and cultural identities would congregate, brought together by art, love, sex and music. By bringing this New York vibe to the Moomba Festival, Haring staged a kind of contemporary corroboree that resonated with both the queer and Koorie communities. In this way, Haring's Moomba performance can be interpreted as a way of emphasising what is shared between First Nations – specifically Koorie – communities and queer communities: the belief that art is deeply entwined with everyday life and the environment in which one lives, and that dance and the painted body are important communal forms of expression, ceremony and resistance.

Jean-Michel Basquiat

Like Haring, Jean-Michel Basquiat was drawn to the intersection of dance, music, performance and visual art. Basquiat's iconography, as well as his political stance, was often informed by his Puerto Rican and Haitian heritage. Evident in his work was a fascination with and critique of racism, colonialism and capitalism, and a commitment to social justice. Again, similar to Haring, Basquiat's personal library reveals some of his sources and reference points. Basquiat's main source of inspiration was *Gray's Anatomy*; his mother had given him a copy while he was in hospital at age seven. However, two other important texts for Basquiat's practice were Burchard Brentjes's *African Rock Art* (1969) and Robert Farris Thompson's *Flash of the Spirit: African and Afro-American Art and Philosophy* (1984). He is also known to have attended the exhibition *'Primitivism' in 20th Century Art: Affinity of the Tribal and the Modern*, both in 1984 at MoMA and when it travelled to the Dallas Museum of Art in 1985. Reflecting his fascination with First Nations material culture, Basquiat's work incorporates references to rock art, fertility idols and masks from multiple non-Western traditions.

Unlike Haring, Basquiat never came to Australia. However, in 1984 he produced a work that fuses references from First Nations cultures across the world. The painting (at left), typical of Basquiat's style, is a dense mashup of images, words, symbols and gestural daubs of colour. In the top left corner, the words 'Aboriginal Generative ©' appear above a drawing of a woman squatting in childbirth. The basis of Basquiat's drawing is an Aztec figurine housed at the Dumbarton Oaks Research Library and Collection in Washington DC. There is nothing to link this image directly with Australia except that in another of Basquiat's works, *Sienna* 1984, the same drawing of

Jean-Michel Basquiat *Untitled* 1984, synthetic polymer paint and silkscreen on canvas, 223.5 x 195.5 cm, Nakanoshima Museum of Art, Osaka

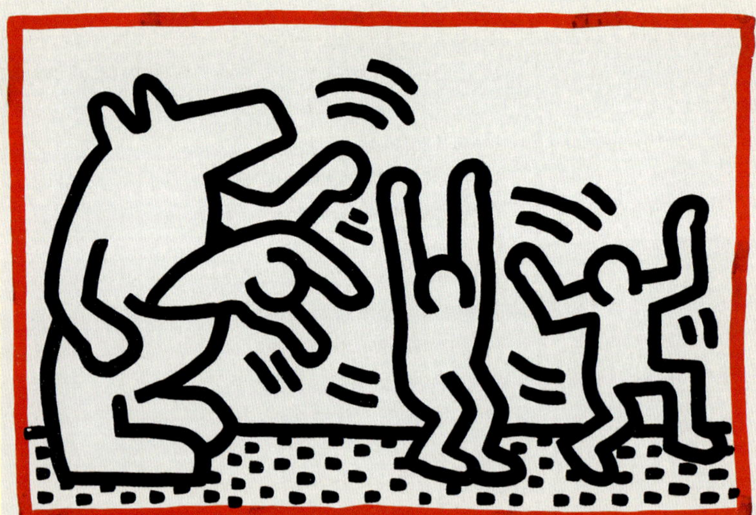

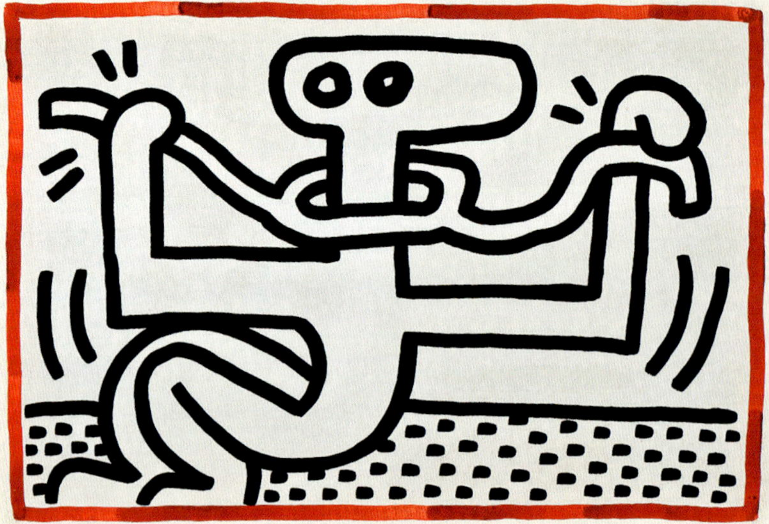

the birthing statue is juxtaposed with the words 'kangaroo woman that makes the rain' (p. 281). Perhaps most interesting, however, is the way in which Basquiat establishes this image of birth and generation as being within a dense web of references to other First Nations cultures. Among his references to advertising, globalisation and capitalism, and schematic bodies reminiscent of rock art and fertility idols, there are a number of words and phrases taken from First Nations ancestral stories. Many indigenous Anishinaabe peoples in what is known today as Canada tell stories about a being called Manibozho, sometimes spelt Nanabozho. Manibozho is referenced three times in Basquiat's painting, with the text 'Manibozho', 'Great Hare' and 'Sun God/Trickster'.[9] The story references the creation of humanity by a shapeshifting sun deity who often takes the form of a hare. Basquiat simplifies and conflates the complex stories associated with this ancestral being who has many names, can take on many forms and exists in multiple planes of reality. Above the references to Manibozho/Nanabozho is the phrase 'The Apple of Sodom'. This refers to a milkweed native to the Dead Sea, which was said to have grown on the site of the destroyed Biblical cities of Sodom and Gomorrah. As well as being a symbol of creation emerging from destruction, the Sodom apple is also a symbol of trickery and deception, since it resembles an apple but, when bitten, contains only dry, fibrous seeds.

These pre-colonial figures and references invite us to think about creation emerging from destruction, through the figure of the trickster. The trickster can be found in First Nations cultures across the world. For the people of the Kulin nation in south-east Australia – the Djadja Wurrung, Taungurong, Wathaurong, Woiwurrung and Boon Wurrung – creation stories centre on two ancestral figures: Bunjil the Eagle and his brother Waa the Crow. The trickster, which might be Waa the Crow, Reynard the Fox, Manibozho the Great Hare, or more recent iterations such as Brer Rabbit, Bugs Bunny or Doctor Who, is invariably a figure representing the use of cunning, creativity and intellect, often marshalling these faculties against forces with superior physical or brute strength. The figure of the trickster has been taken up by African-American writer Henry Louis Gates Jr, in his concept of 'Signifyin''. This theory responds to activist and poet Audre Lorde's powerful statement about the struggle of African Americans living within colonial structures,

(above left) Keith Haring *Untitled* 1984, ink on paper, 51.0 x 73.0 cm, Private collection
(above right) Keith Haring *Untitled* 1984, ink on paper, 51.1 x 73.0 cm, Private collection, New York

that 'the master's tools will never dismantle the master's house'. Henry Louis Gates Jr invokes Western African Yoruba trickster stories about the 'signifying monkey', who fools the lion by using his own words against him, reversing the lion's status as king of the jungle. Gates uses these trickster stories to argue that the master's tools *can* dismantle the master's house when used in a clever, cunning and creative way.

One could argue that this is precisely what Basquiat is himself doing in this painting. Like the shapeshifting trickster god or the Sodom apple, Basquiat is creating something new out of the ruins of history, bringing together fragments of First Nations cultures, symbols of global neo-colonial capitalism, and images of generation and birth to create something new. Basquiat's sampling, remixing and hybridising of different cultures exemplifies what Ortiz refers to as the transcultural: the new things that arise from the resilience and cleverness manifested by First Nations and colonised peoples in order to subvert and resist colonial structures.

Just as Basquiat referenced First Nations stories in his work, his work has gone on to be referenced in the work of Australian artist Gordon Bennett, who in the late 1990s produced his *Notes to Basquiat* series. Bennett's provocative paintings highlight the interconnected and globalised experience of the black body under colonialism and capitalism. Bennett's connection to Basquiat extends beyond this series, with the artist citing several parallels between their lives in a public letter addressed to Basquiat after his death.[10] In this published artist's statement, Bennett openly celebrated the similarities between his own work and Basquiat's, and also referenced their shared love for jazz and rap music. In his letter to

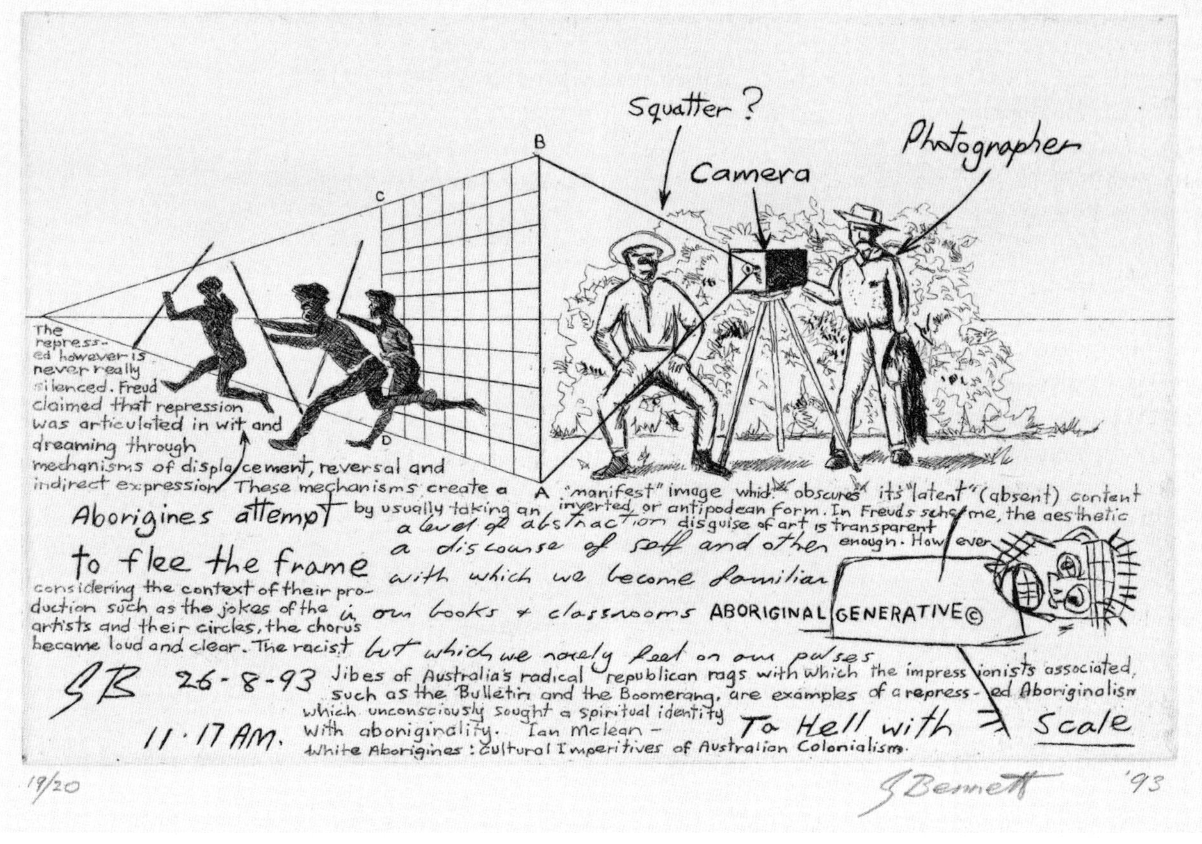

Gordon Bennett *Aboriginal Generative* 1993 (detail), soft ground etching, 19.4 x 29.8 cm (plate), 60.4 x 40.2 cm (sheet), National Gallery of Australia, Canberra, Gordon Darling Australasian Print Fund 1995

Basquiat, Bennett described the transcultural motivations behind his *Notes to Basquiat* series, saying he intended to 'highlight the similarities and cross-connections of our shared experience as human beings living in separate worlds that each seek to exclude, objectify and dehumanise the black body and person'. It is also worth noting that during his life Bennett actively resisted his work being characterised within the context of contemporary Aboriginal art. To his mind, Bennett's work, despite often concentrating on exploring aspects of his Aboriginality, was far more akin to the work of international contemporary artists whose art engaged with, but was not defined by, their race.

Kamilaroi artist Reko Rennie also celebrates the similarities between his work and that of both Haring and Basquiat, employing his own recurring crown motif as a reference to Basquiat, as well as a sign of Aboriginal sovereignty. Rennie has also specifically named Haring as an influence;[11] Rennie's own roots are in street art. These artists smash the stereotype that Aboriginal art derives only from an artist's relationship to Country, and reinforces that Aboriginal artists, whether they are working on Country or in city-based studios, have been, and continue to be, some of the greatest agents of radical change in contemporary art.

These connections between cultures are often discussed solely in terms of exploitation, dominance and power differentials. As demonstrated in this essay, however, people from different cultures can connect in productive and reciprocal ways. Identity politics often focuses on the idea that it is impossible to ever know another person's experience, but through connections like these we are reminded of our shared humanity, and that there are a great many similarities in our experiences that unite us.

Notes

1 Fernando Ortiz Fernández, *Cuban Counterpoint: Tobacco and Sugar*, trans. Harriet de Onís, Duke University Press, Durham, North Carolina, 1995.

2 Judith Ryan, 'From Bark to Neon: Indigenous Art from the NGV Collection', 18 Oct. 2018, *NGV*, Victorian Government, <https://www.ngv.vic.gov.au/essay/black-to-the-future-indigenous-artists-work-forwards/>, accessed 13 Feb. 2019.

3 R. A. Rogers, 'From cultural exchange to transculturation: a review and reconceptualization of cultural appropriation', *Communication Theory*, vol. 16, no. 1, 2006, pp. 474–503.

4 Robert Farris Thompson, 'Requiem for the Degas of the B-boys, Keith Haring', *Artforum*, May 1990, <https://www.artforum.com/print/199005/requiem-for-the-degas-of-the-b-boys-keith-haring-34080>, accessed 1 Feb. 2019.

5 Ted Gott, 'Fragile memories: Keith Haring and the Water Window Mural at the National Gallery of Victoria', 2 June 2014, *NGV*, Victorian Government, <https://www.ngv.vic.gov.au/essay/fragile-memories-keith-haring-and-the-water-window-mural-at-the-national-gallery-of-victoria/>, accessed 24 July 2019.

6 Andrew Montana, *Primitive and Pop: Keith Haring's Australia 1984*, Arcadia, Melbourne, 2017, p. 89.

7 Margo Neale, 'Renegotiating tradition: urban Aboriginal art', in Sylvia Kleinert & Margo Neale (eds), *The Oxford Companion to Aboriginal Art and Culture*, Oxford University Press, South Melbourne, 2000, p. 266.

8 Vimeo, 'Keith Haring: Moomba Festival fashion parade, Melbourne, 1984', *Vimeo.com*, <https://vimeo.com/44861051>, accessed 24 July 2019.

9 A. F. Chamberlain, 'Nanibozhu amongst the Otchipwe, Mississagas, and other Algonkian tribes', *Journal of American Folklore*, vol. 4, no. 14, Jul.–Sep., 1891, pp. 193–213.

10 'Five things to know about Gordon Bennett', *Tate*, <https://www.tate.org.uk/art/five-things-know-gordon-bennett>, accessed 30 July 2019.

11 'Reko Rennie speaking on … the influence of Keith Haring', *Vimeo*, <https://vimeo.com/44858849>, accessed 30 July 2019.

Keith Haring painting the NGV Waterwall, Melbourne, 1984

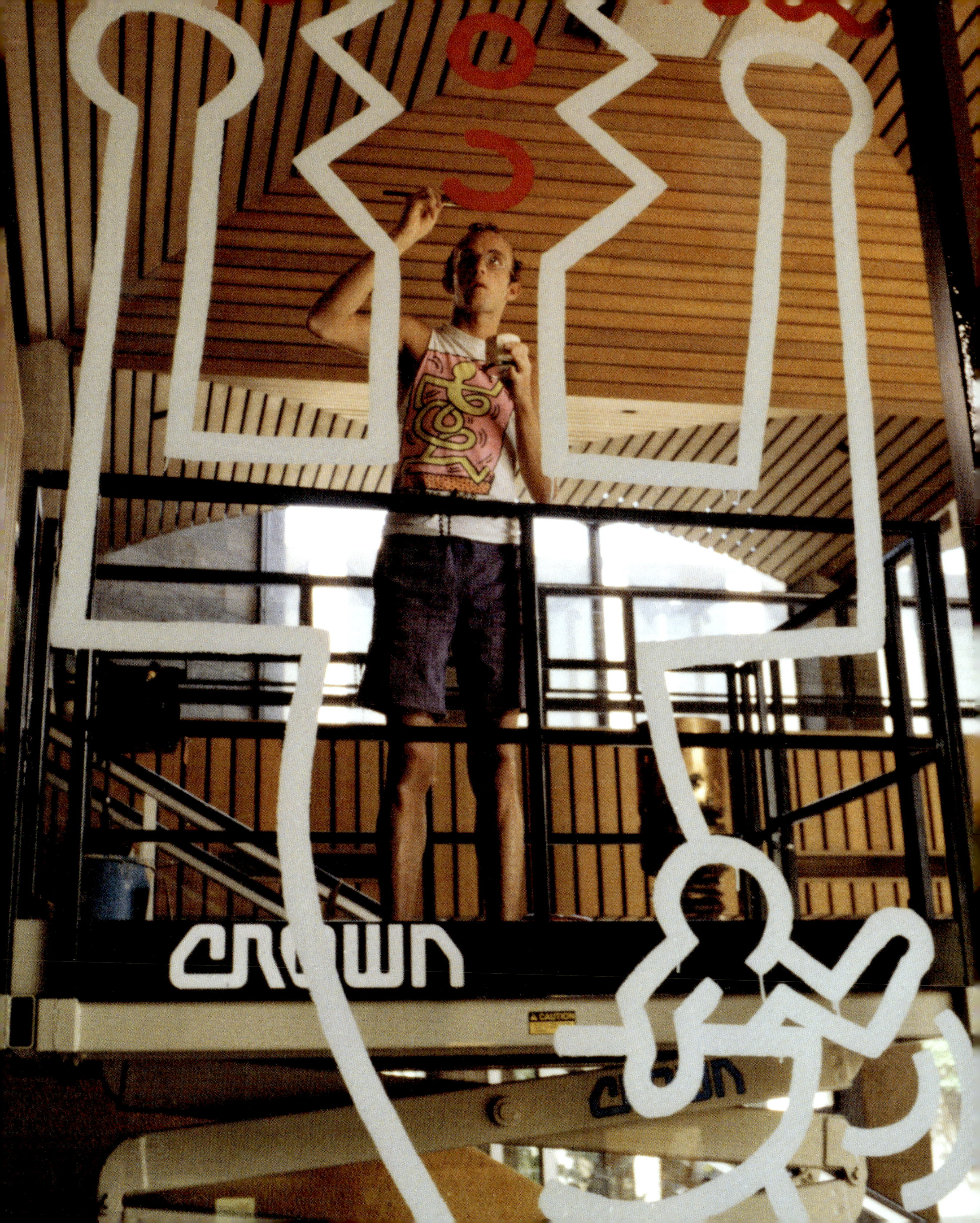
CROWN
CAUTION

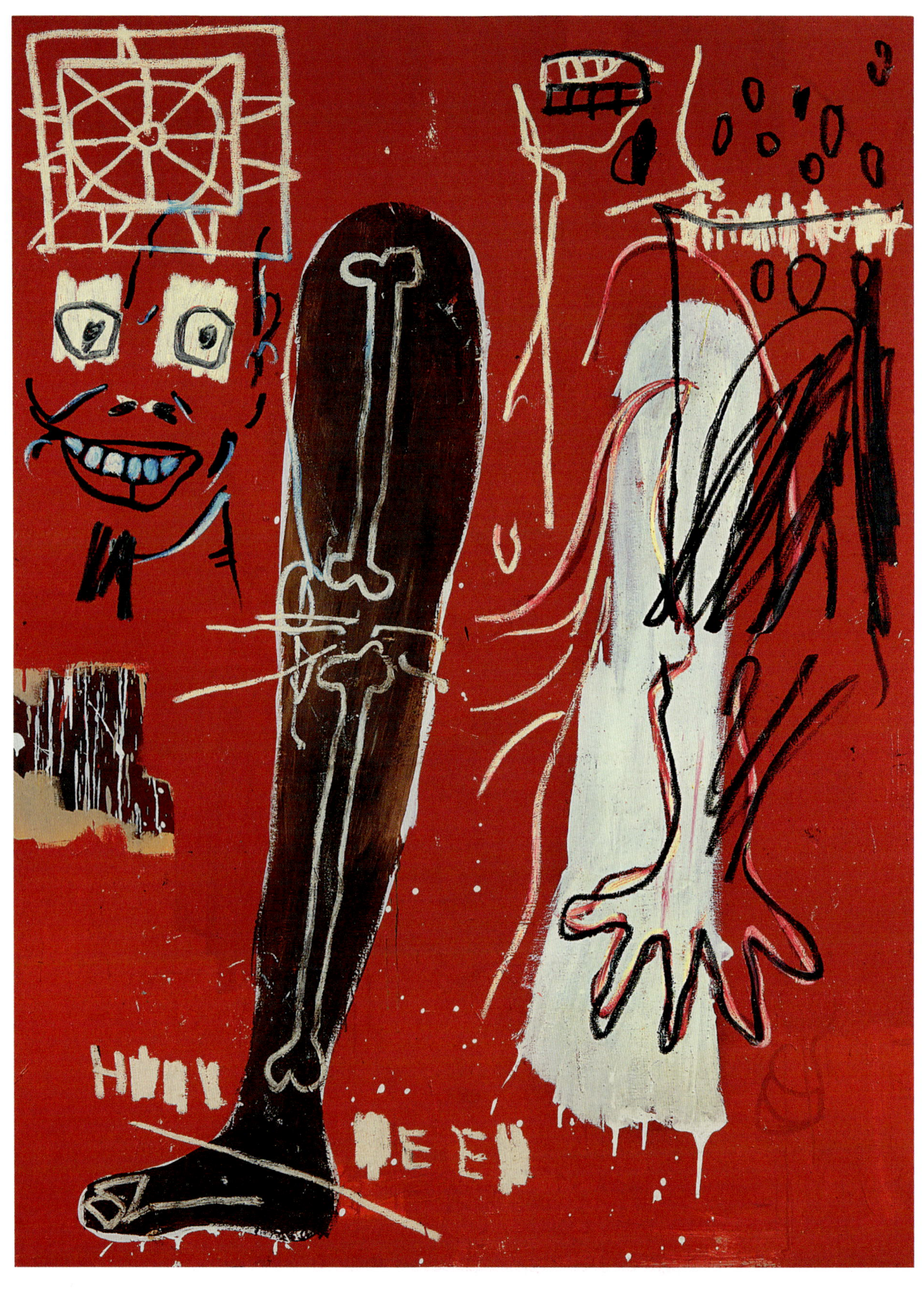

Jean-Michel Basquiat *Untitled (Halloween)* c. 1982, synthetic polymer paint and oilstick on canvas, 211.5 x 151.8 cm, Collection of Andre Sakhai

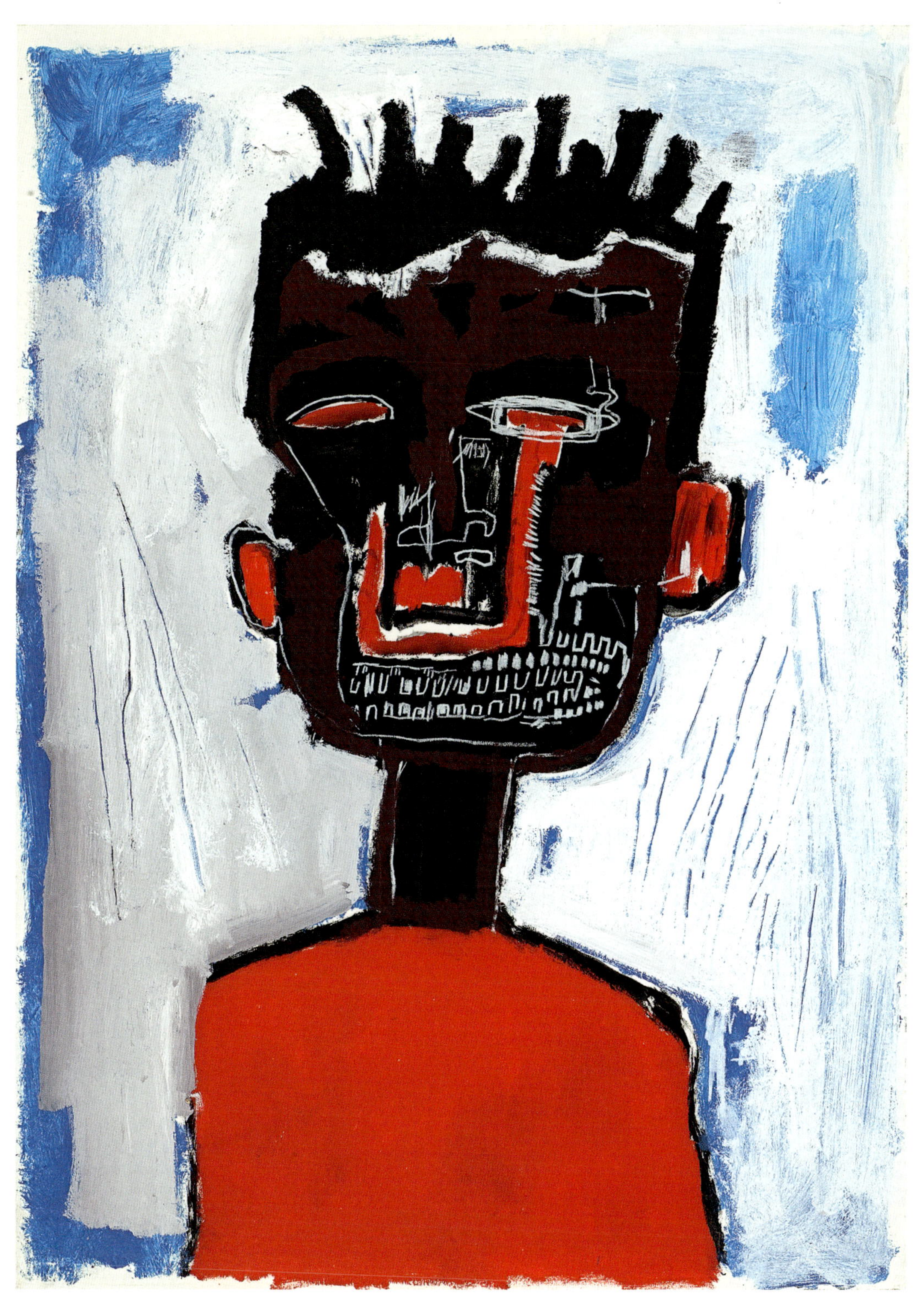

Jean-Michel Basquiat *Self Portrait* 1984, synthetic polymer paint and oilstick on paper on canvas, 98.7 x 71.1 cm, Collection of Yoav Harlap, Israel

Jean-Michel Basquiat *Untitled (Word on Wood)* 1985, oil and pencil on wood, 238.8 x 185.4 cm, Private collection

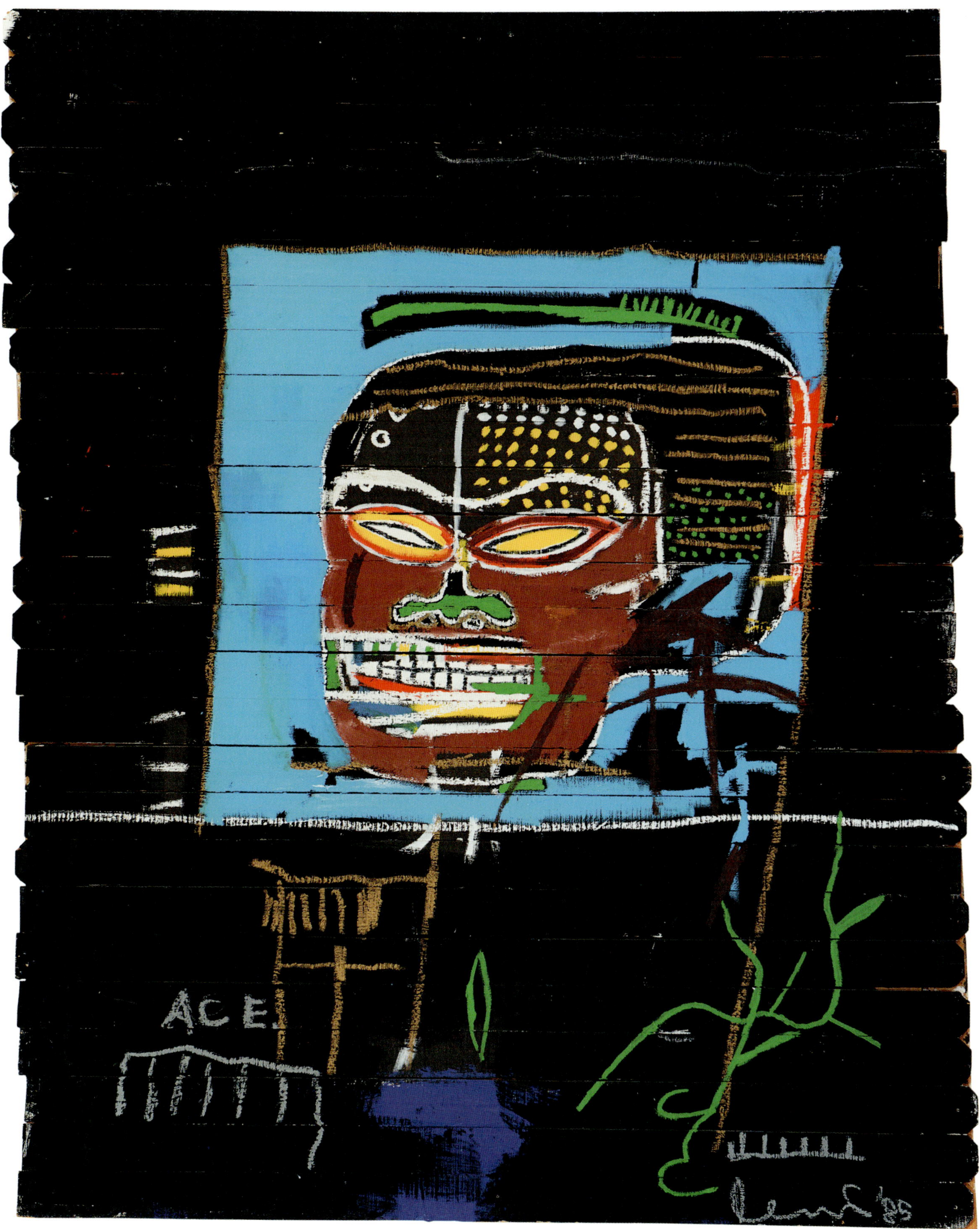
ACE

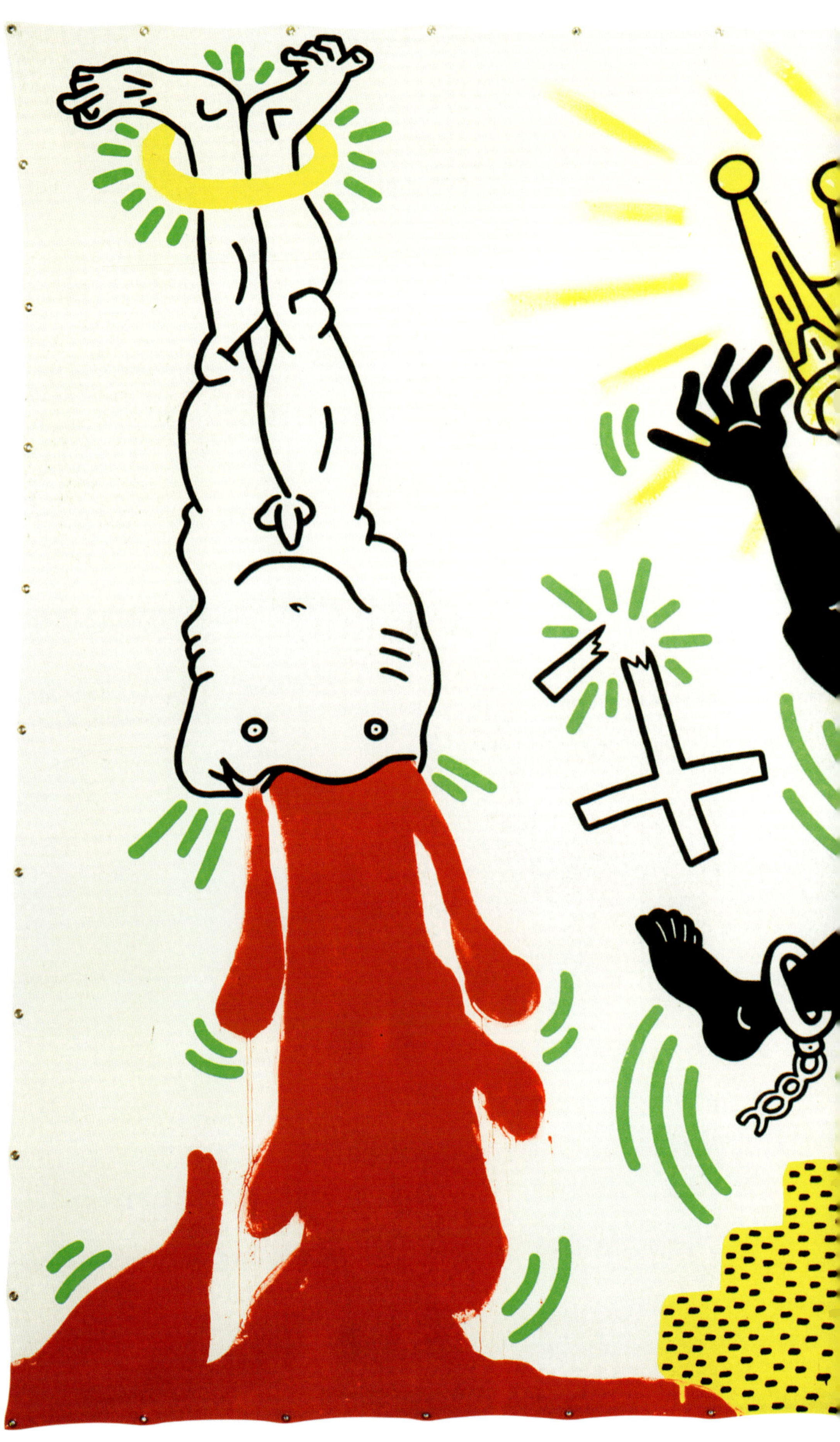

Keith Haring *Prophets of Rage* 1988, synthetic polymer paint on canvas, 304.8 x 457.2 cm, The Keith Haring Foundation, New York

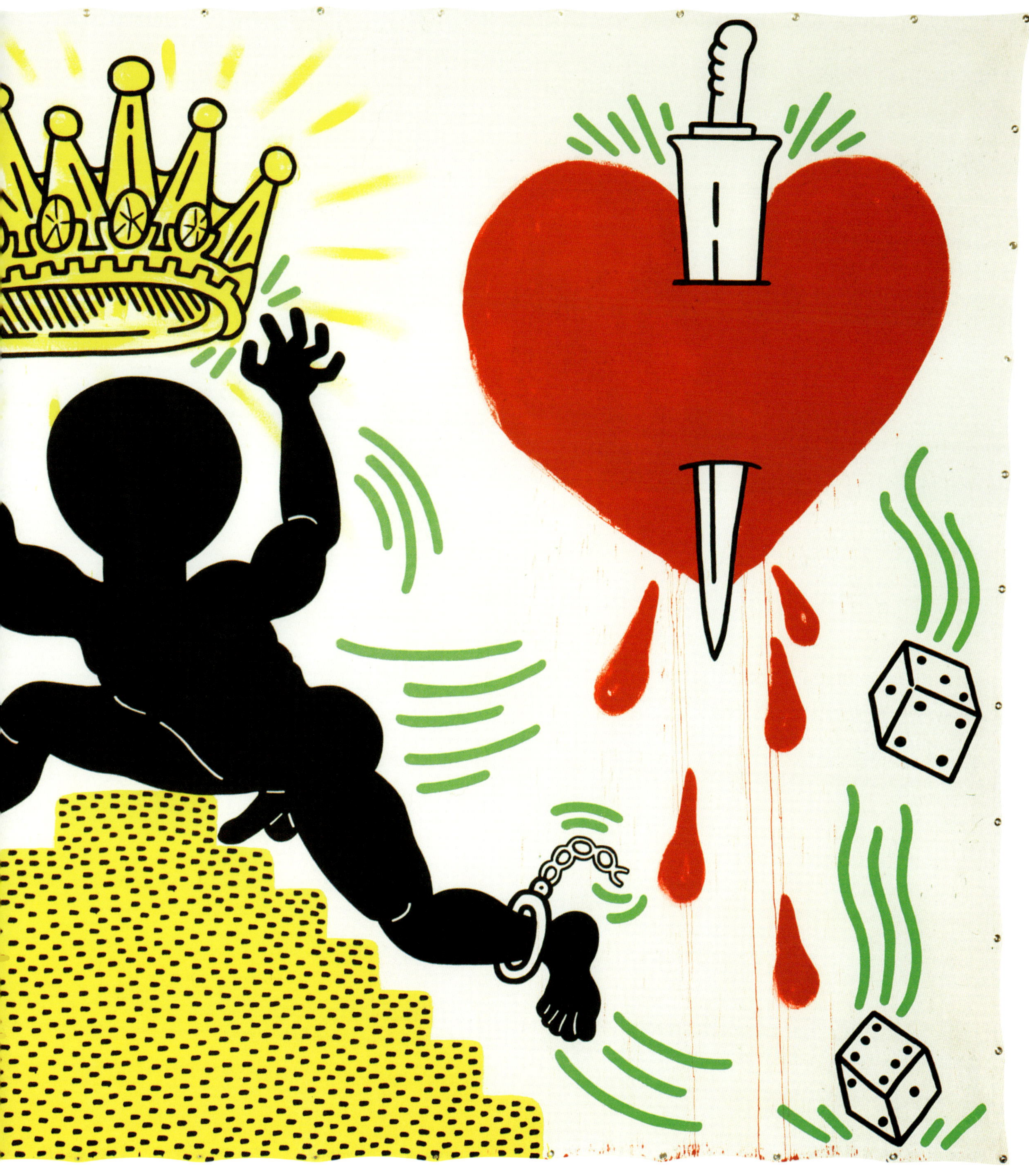

Jean-Michel Basquiat *Sienna* 1984, synthetic polymer paint and oil on canvas, 223.4 x 195.6 cm, Collection ABG

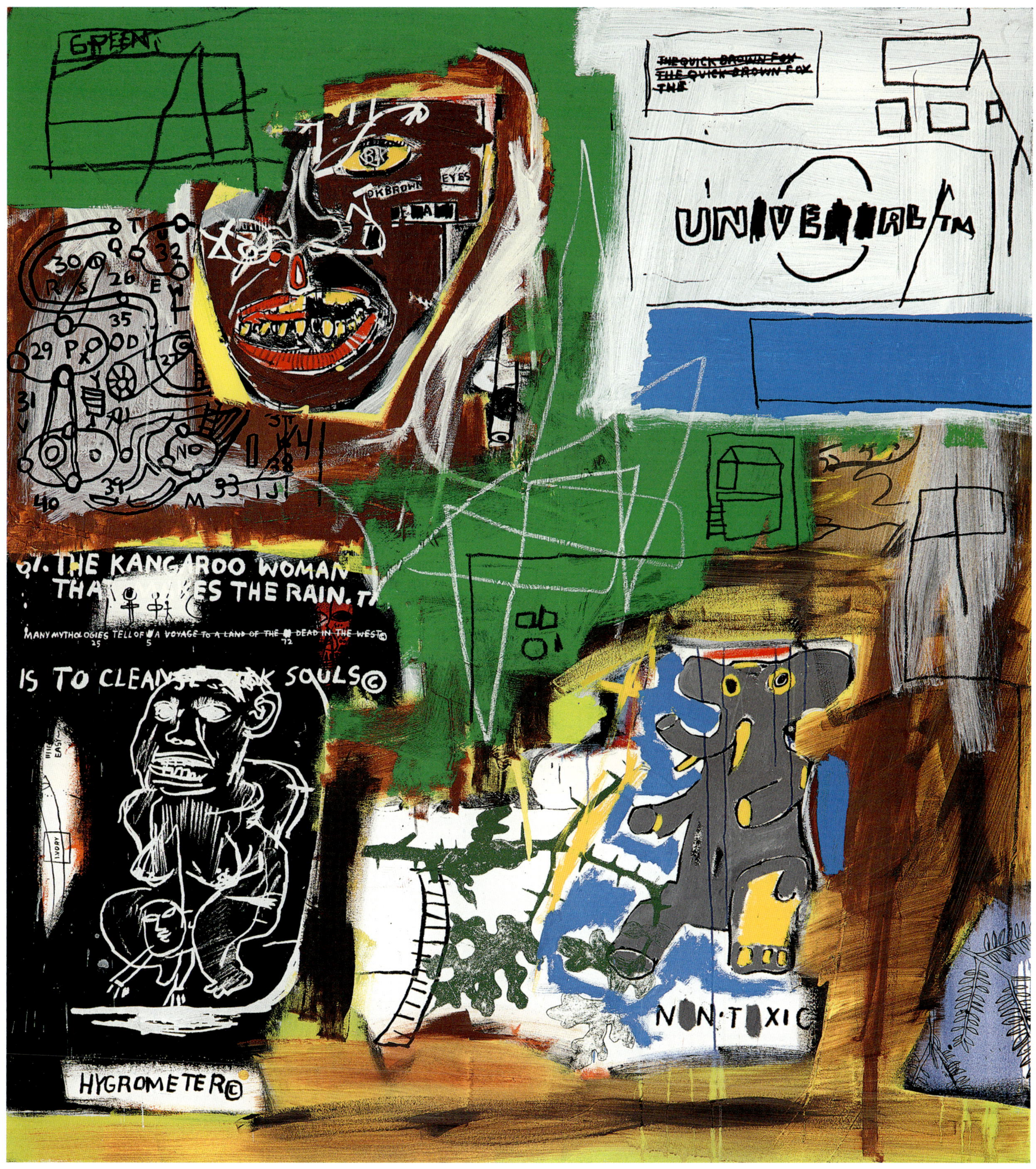
GREEN
THE QUICK BROWN FOX
THE QUICK BROWN FOX
THE
DK BROWN
EYES
97. THE KANGAROO WOMAN
ES THE RAIN.
MANY MYTHOLOGIES TELL OF A VOYAGE TO A LAND OF THE DEAD IN THE WEST©
IS TO CLEAN
SOULS©
HYGROMETER©

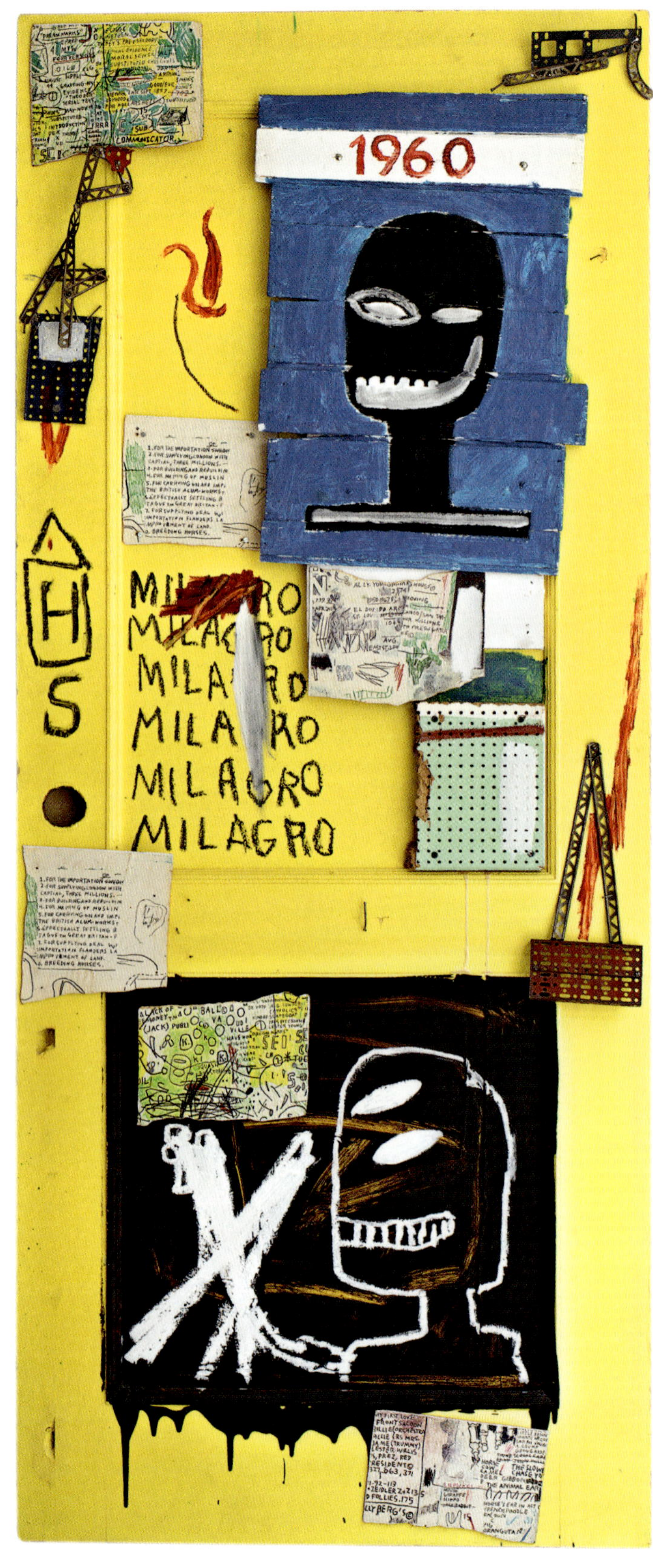

Jean-Michel Basquiat *Yellow Door* 1985–86, oil, colour xerox paper, metal and collaged elements on painted door, 193.4 x 81.3 cm, Private collection

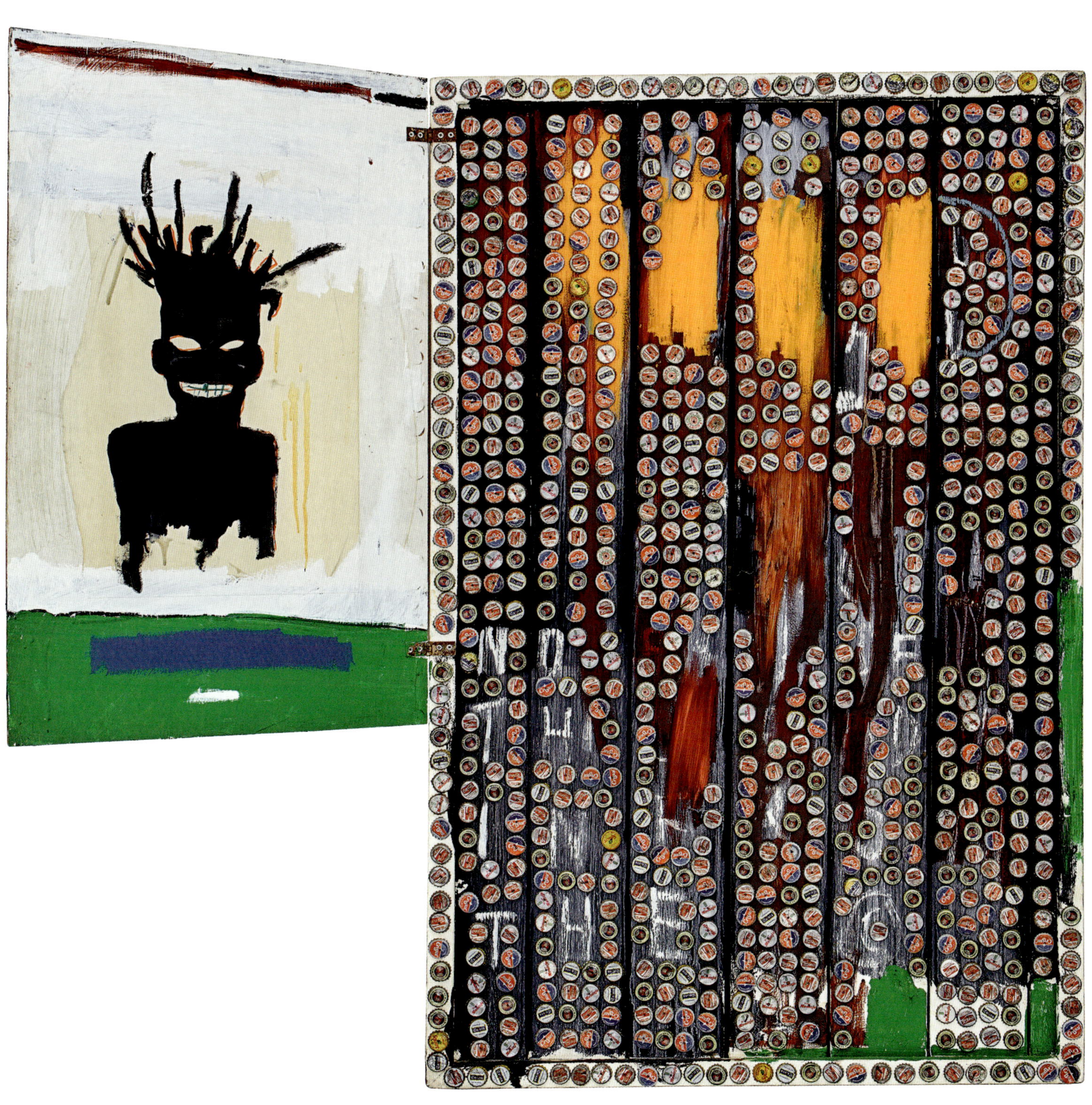

Jean-Michel Basquiat *Self Portrait* 1985, synthetic polymer paint, coloured pencil and bottle caps on wood panel, (a-b) 142.2 x 154.4 cm (overall), Private collection

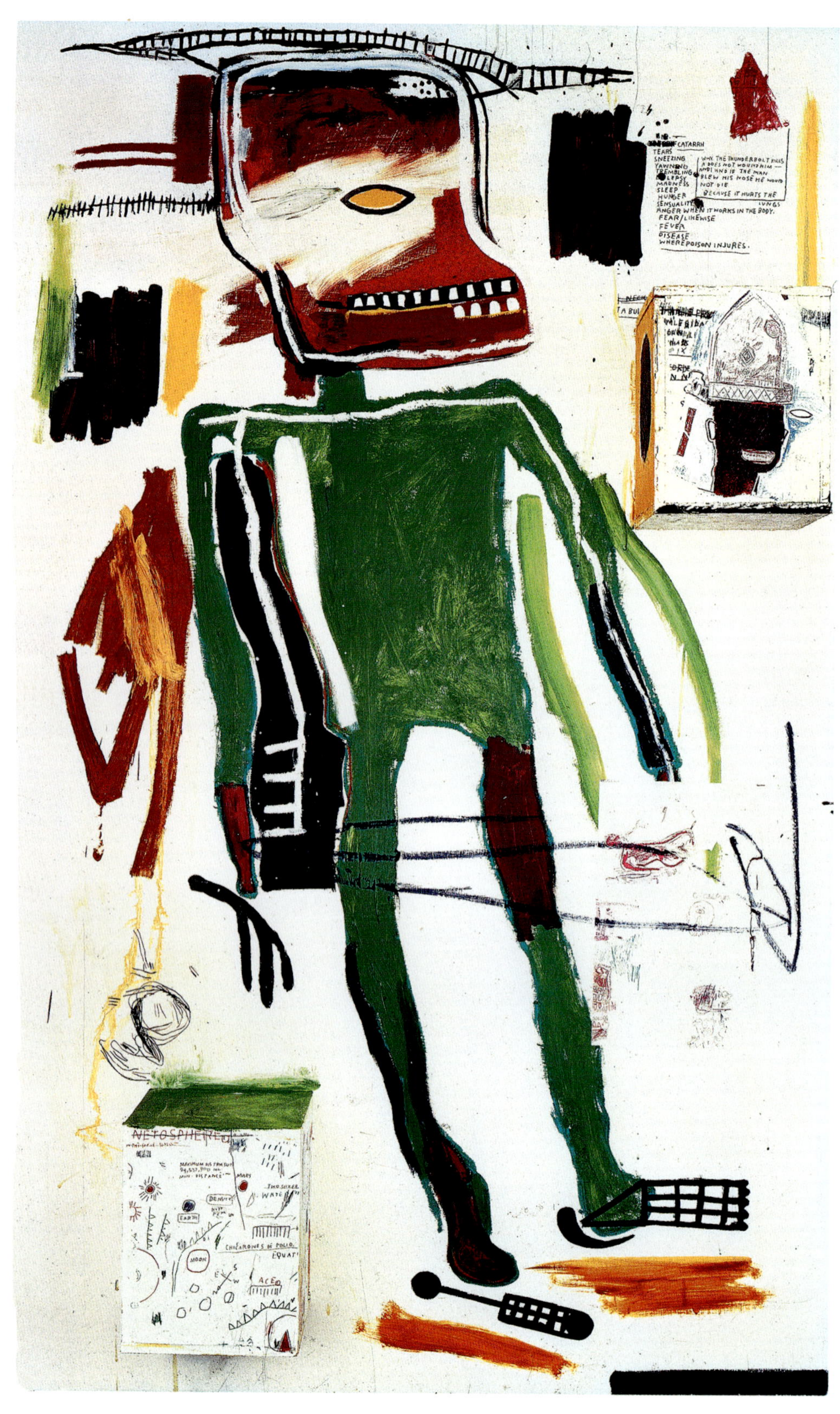

Jean-Michel Basquiat *Because it Hurts the Lungs* 1986, synthetic polymer paint and collage on wood, 183.0 x 107.0 x 21.0 cm, Museum MACAN, Jakarta, Indonesia

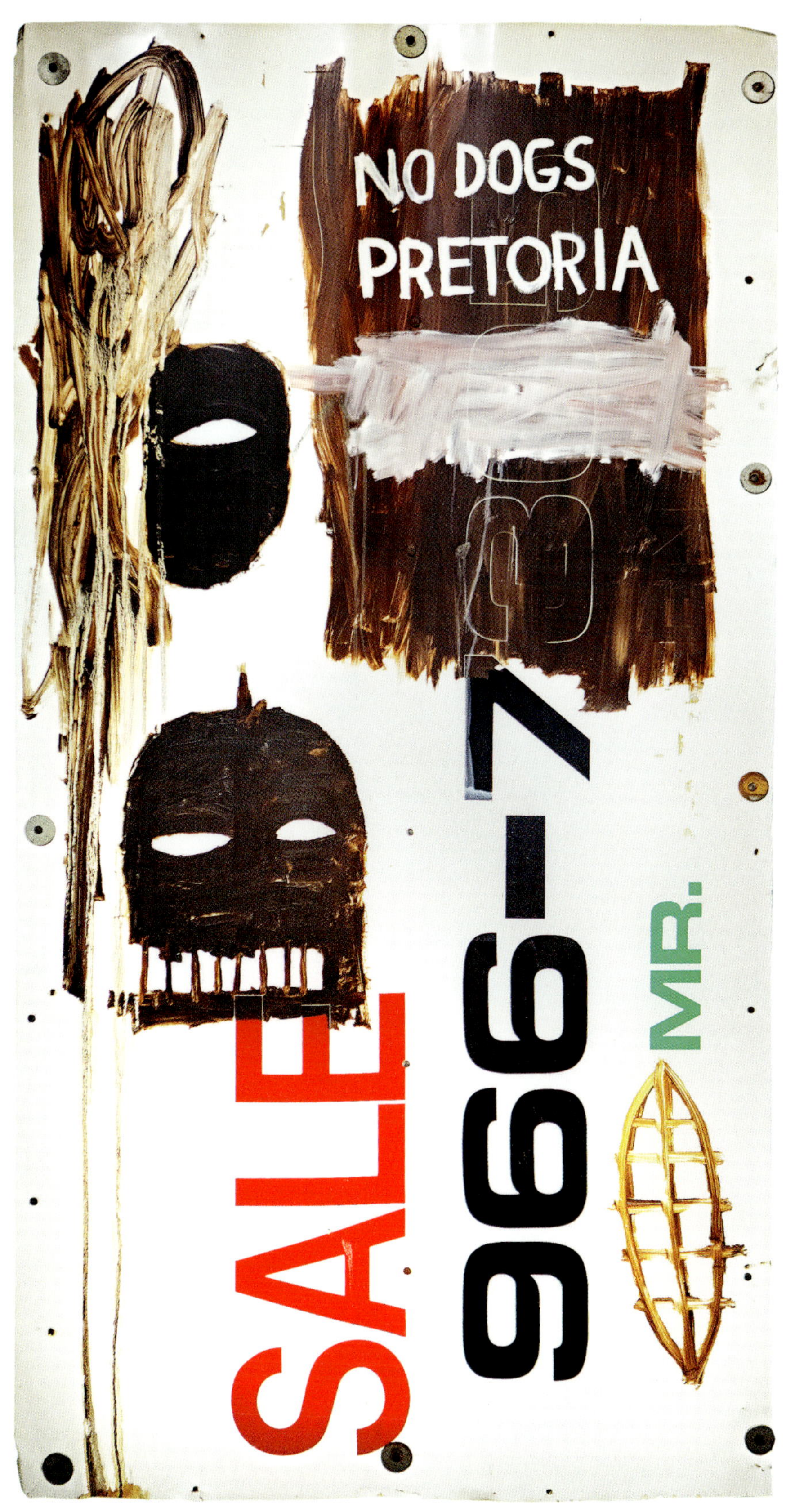

Jean-Michel Basquiat *South African Nazism* 1985, synthetic polymer paint on enamelled metal, 182.9 x 91.4 cm, Private collection

Jean-Michel Basquiat *Untitled* 1984, synthetic polymer paint and oilstick on canvas, 167.5 x 152.5 cm, Collection of Andre Sakhai

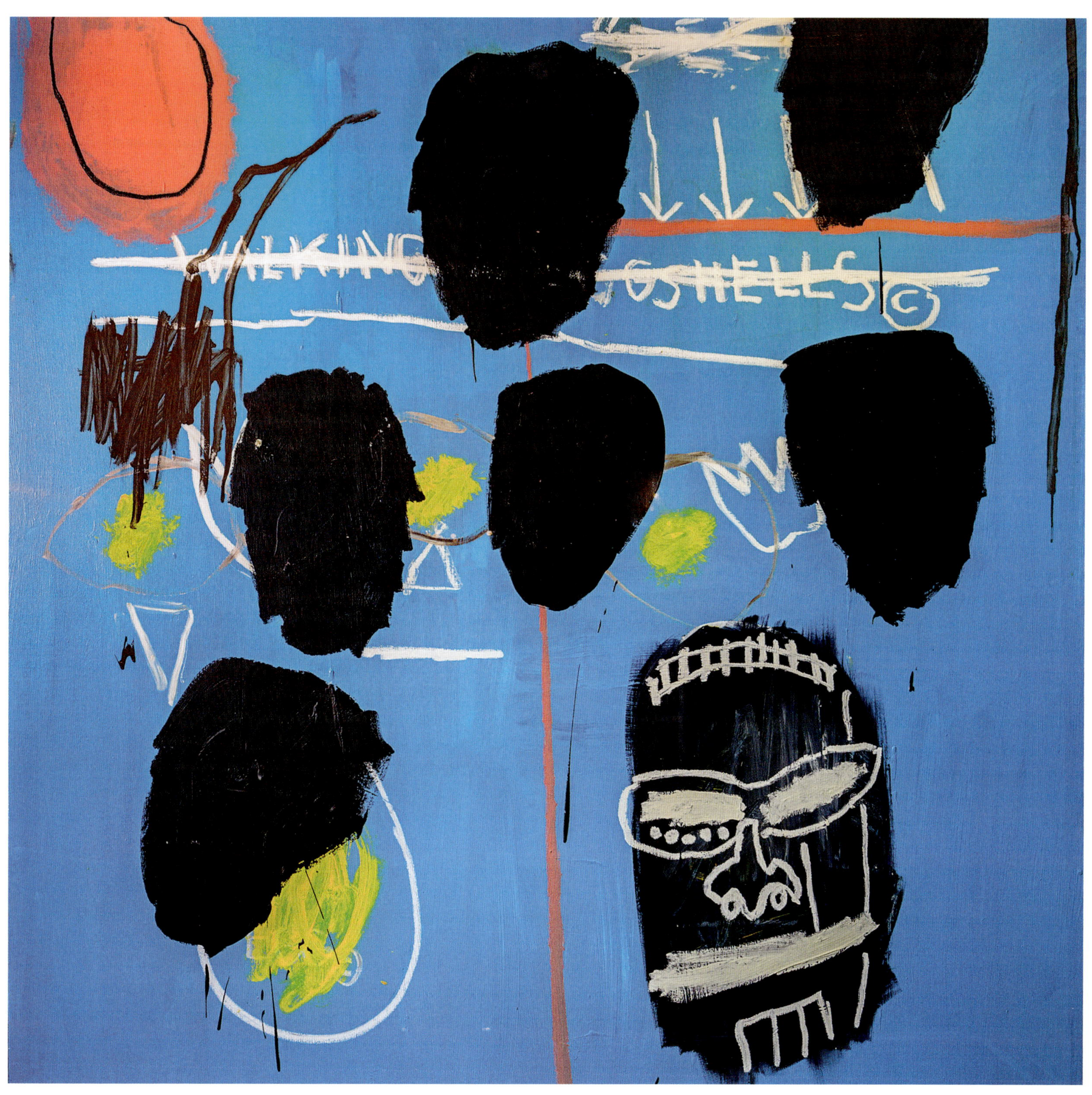
WALKING
SHELLS ©

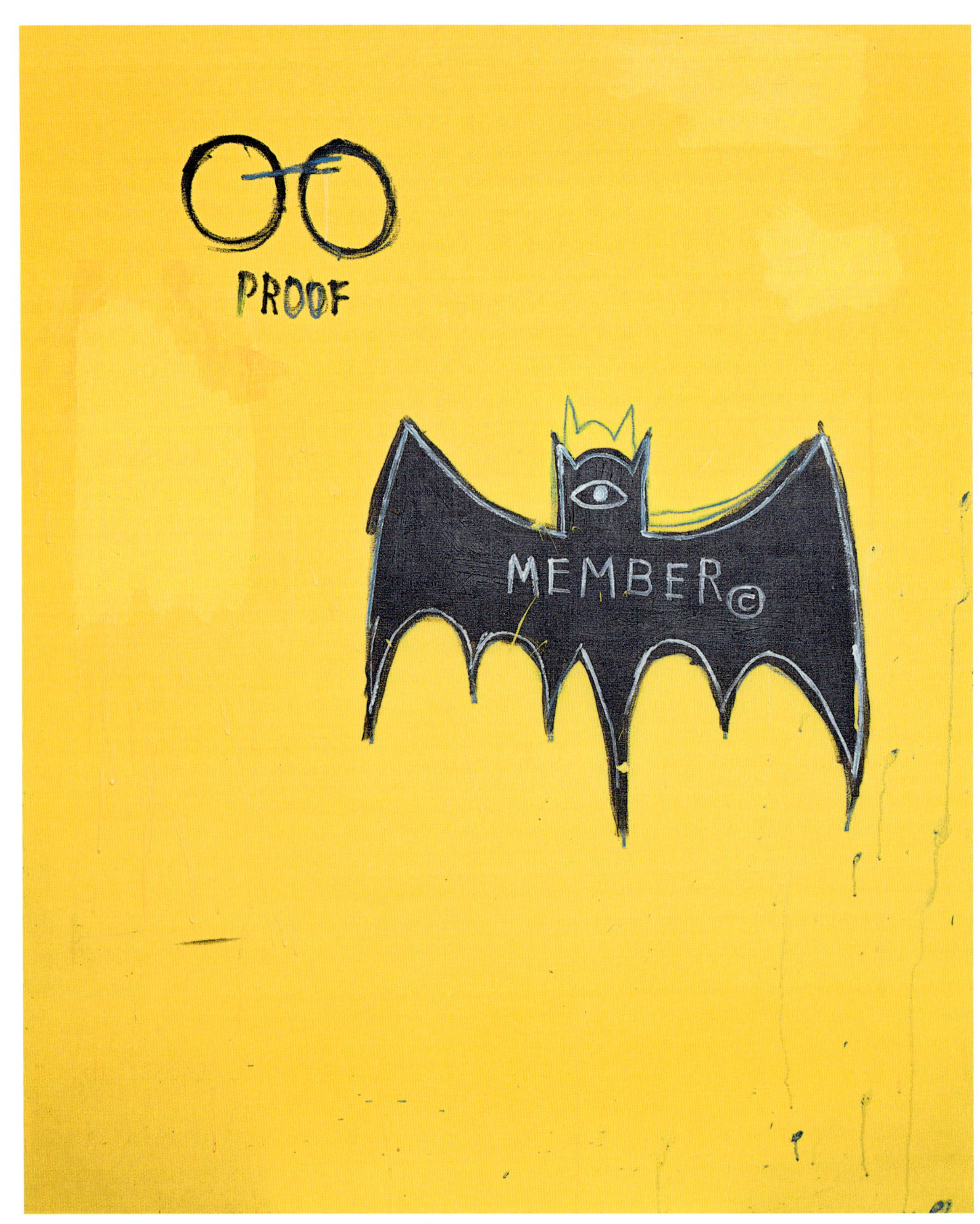

Jean-Michel Basquiat *Item* 1987, synthetic polymer paint and oilstick on canvas, 125.5 x 100.0 cm, Private collection

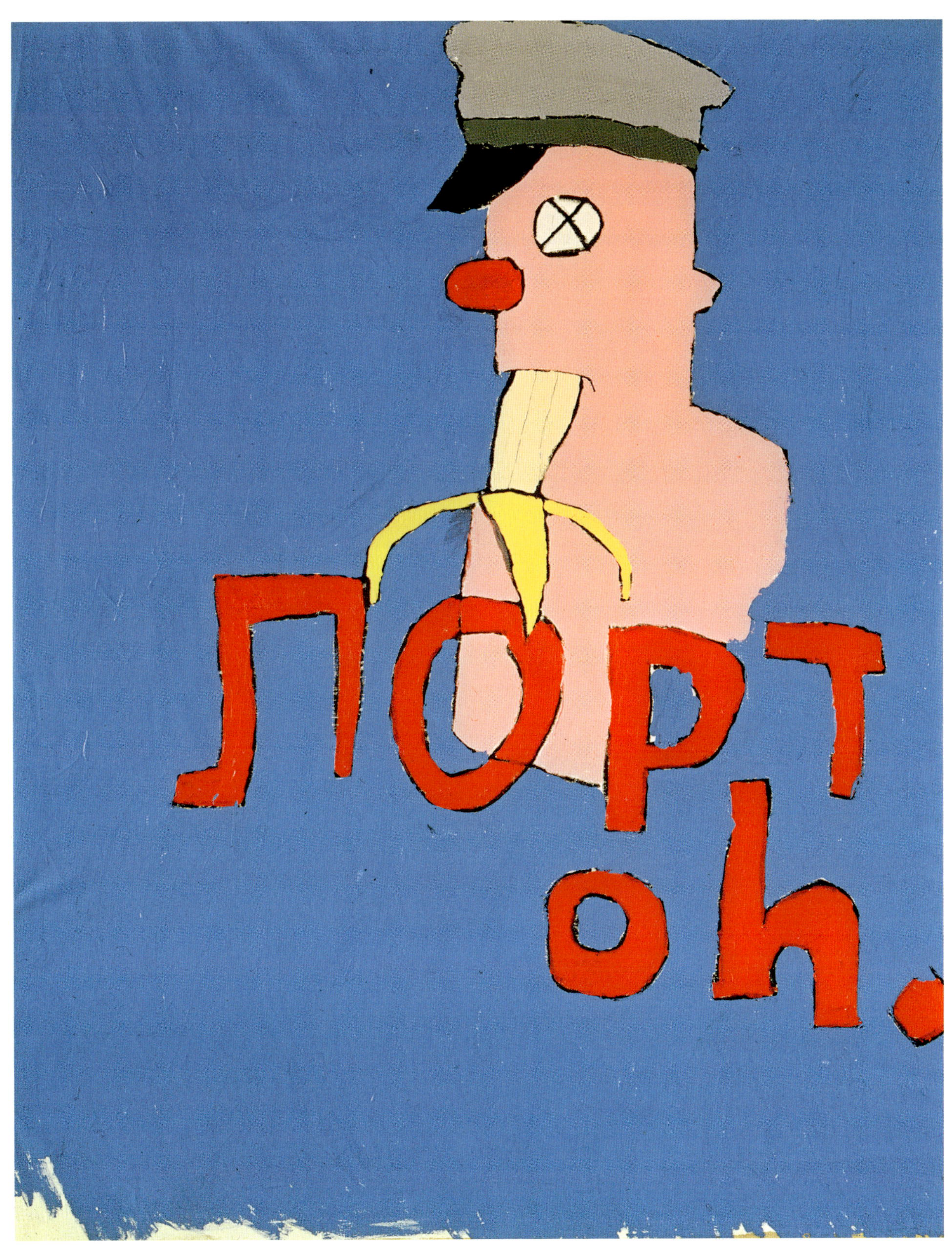

Jean-Michel Basquiat *Glassnose* 1987, synthetic polymer paint and oilstick on canvas, 175.0 x 132.0 cm, Tony Shafrazi Gallery, New York
(overleaf) Jean-Michel Basquiat *Exu* 1988, synthetic polymer paint and oilstick on canvas, 199.5 x 254.0 cm, Private collection

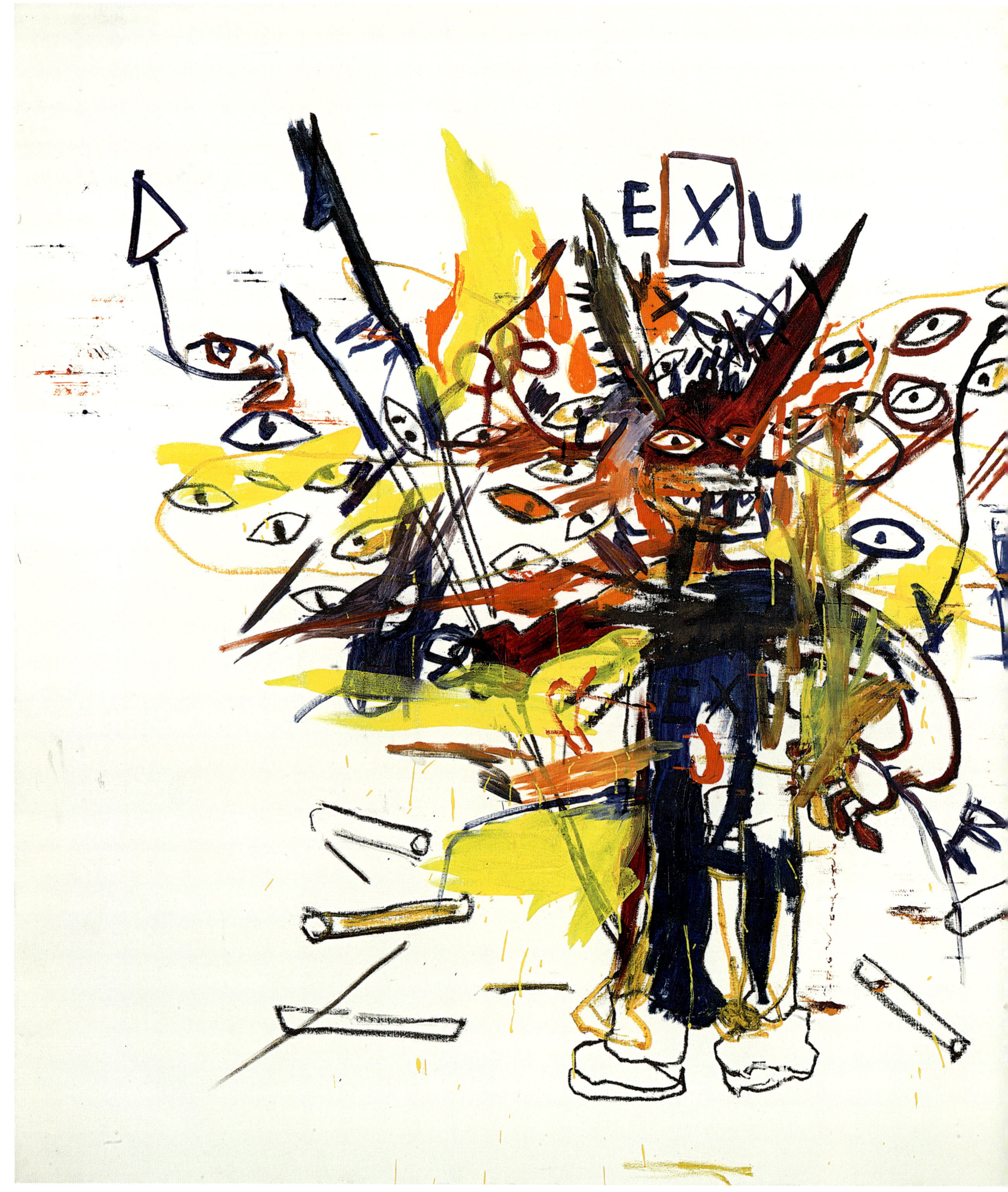
EXU

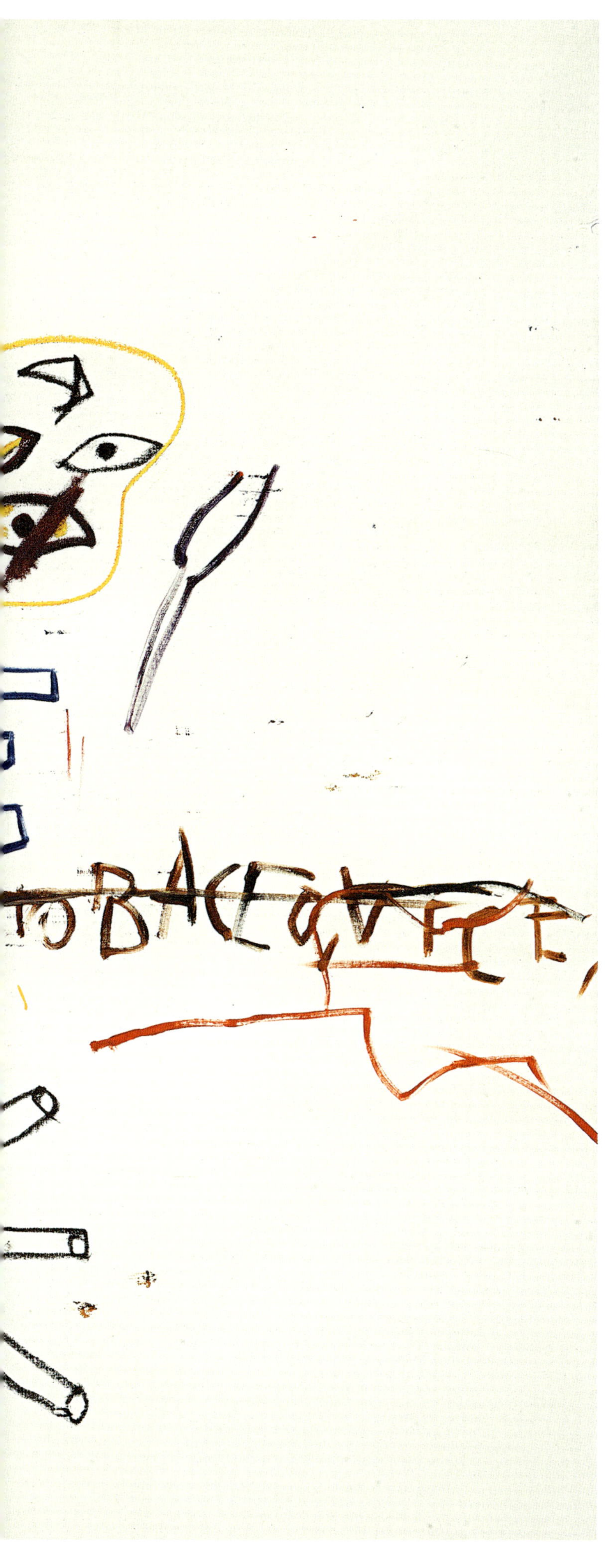

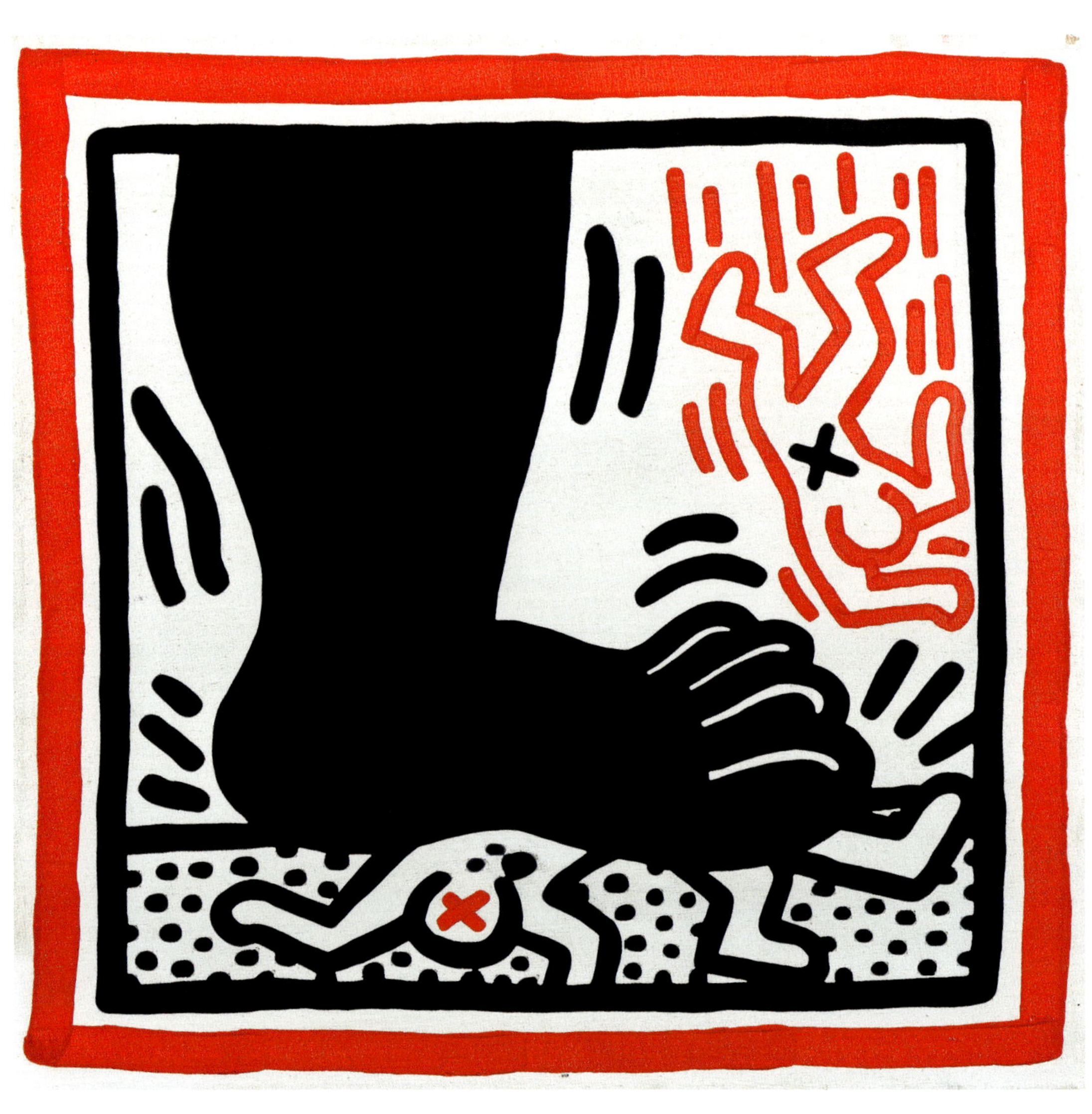

Keith Haring *Untitled* 1985, synthetic polymer paint on canvas, 55.8 x 55.8 cm, Collection of Larry Warsh

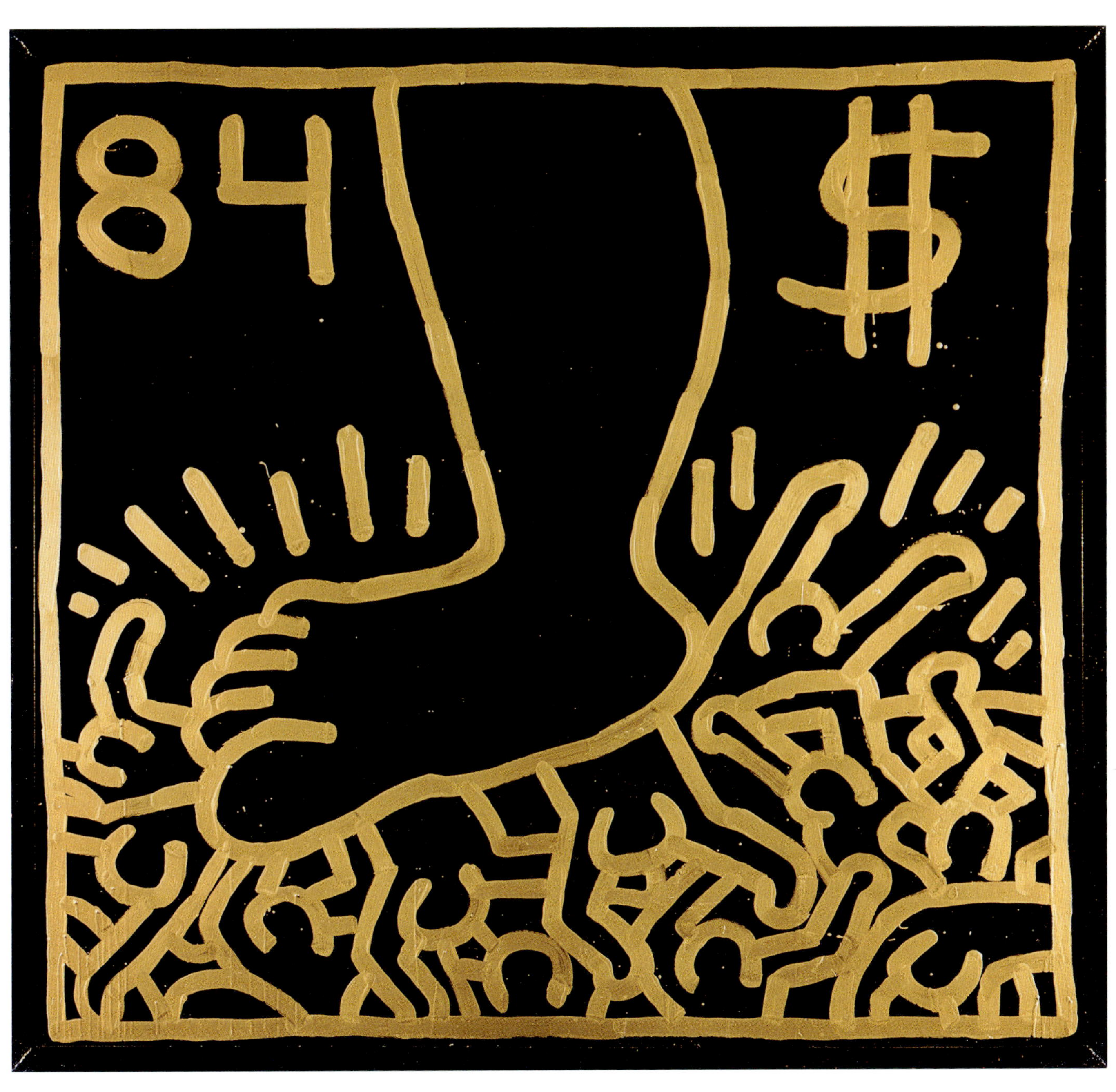

Keith Haring *Untitled* 1984, enamel and paint on metal, 147.3 x 153.7 cm, Private collection

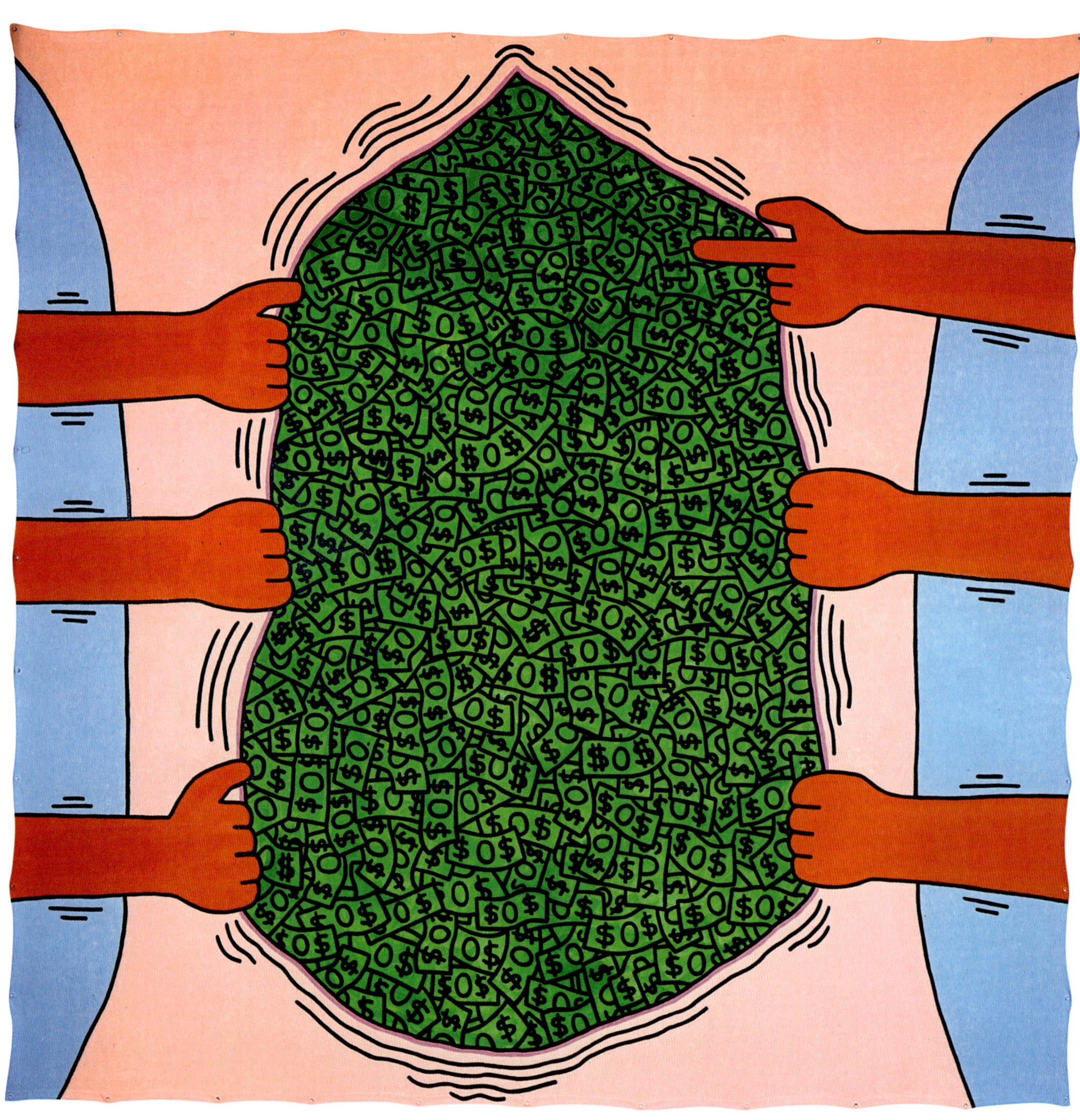

Keith Haring *Untitled* 1985, oil and synthetic polymer paint on canvas tarpaulin, 302.0 x 295.0 cm, Museum MACAN, Jakarta, Indonesia

Keith Haring *Untitled* 1982, synthetic polymer paint on vinyl tarpaulin, 308.6 x 301.6 cm, Private collection

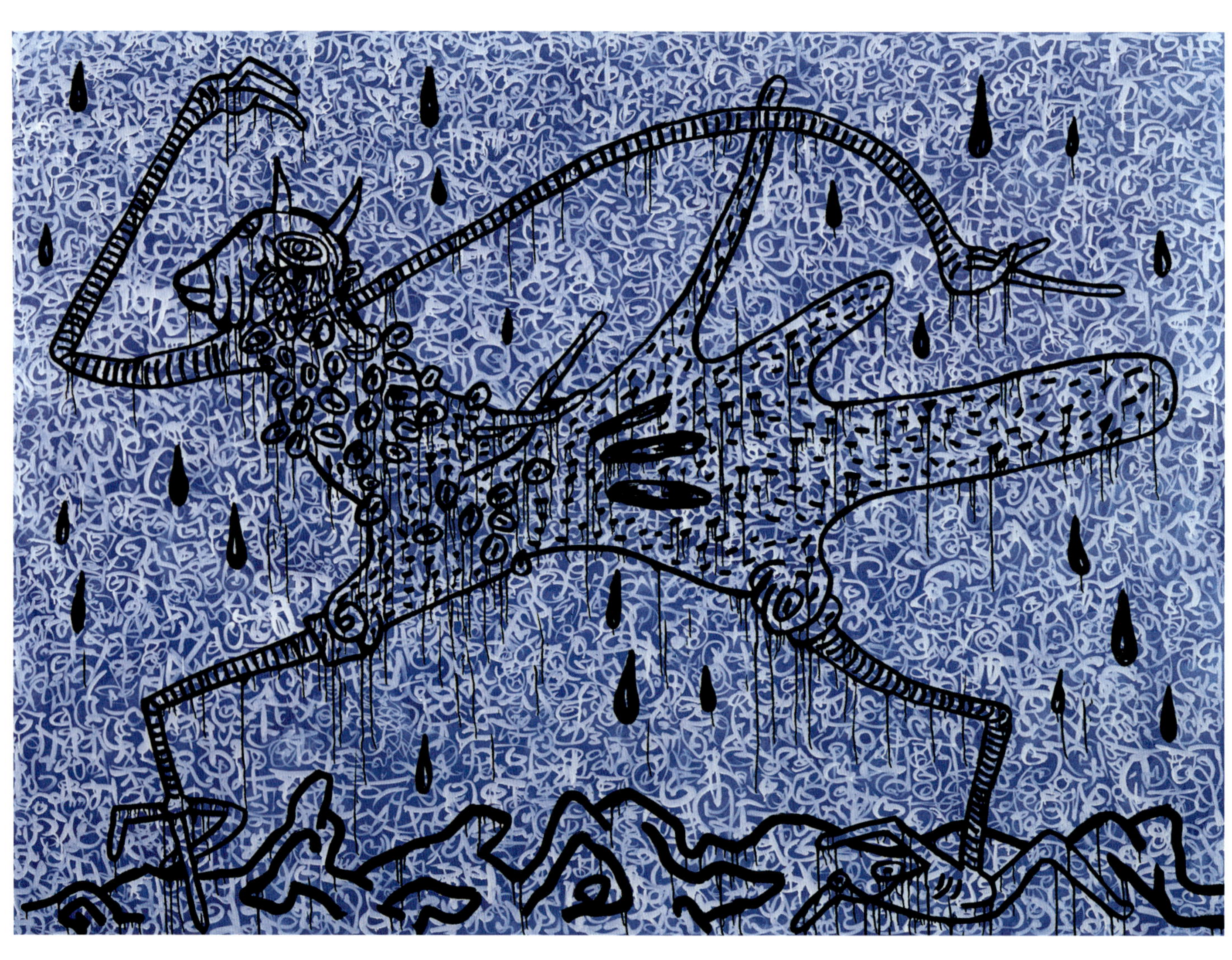

Keith Haring *Walking in the Rain* 1989, synthetic polymer and enamel paint on canvas, 183.4 x 244.6 cm, The Keith Haring Foundation, New York

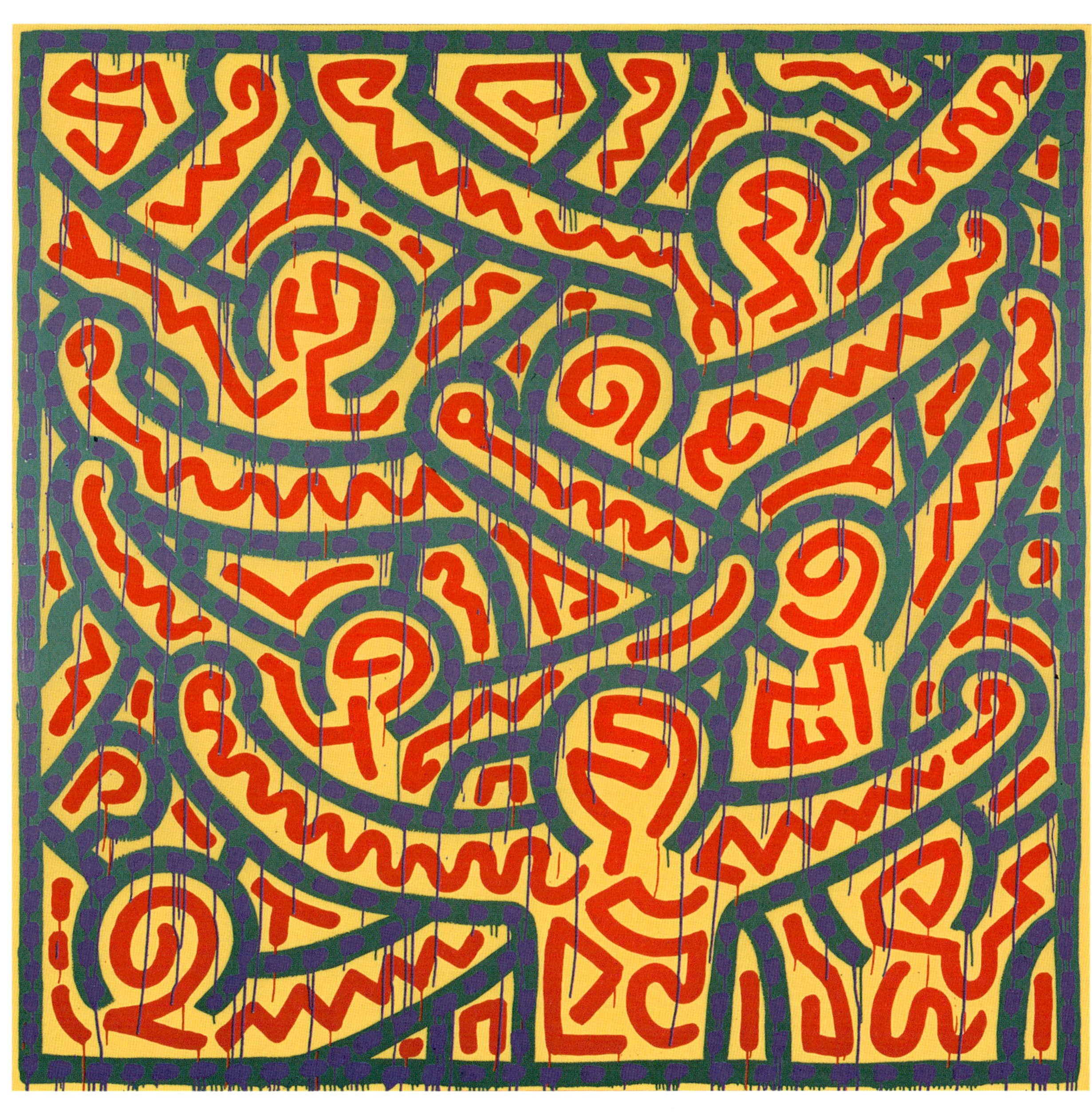

Keith Haring *Untitled* 1989, synthetic polymer paint and enamel on canvas, 182.9 x 182.9 x 8.9 cm,
The Keith Haring Foundation, New York
(overleaf) Keith Haring *A Pile of Crowns for Jean-Michel Basquiat* 1988, synthetic polymer paint on canvas,
304.8 x 304.8 x 304.8 cm, The Keith Haring Foundation, New York

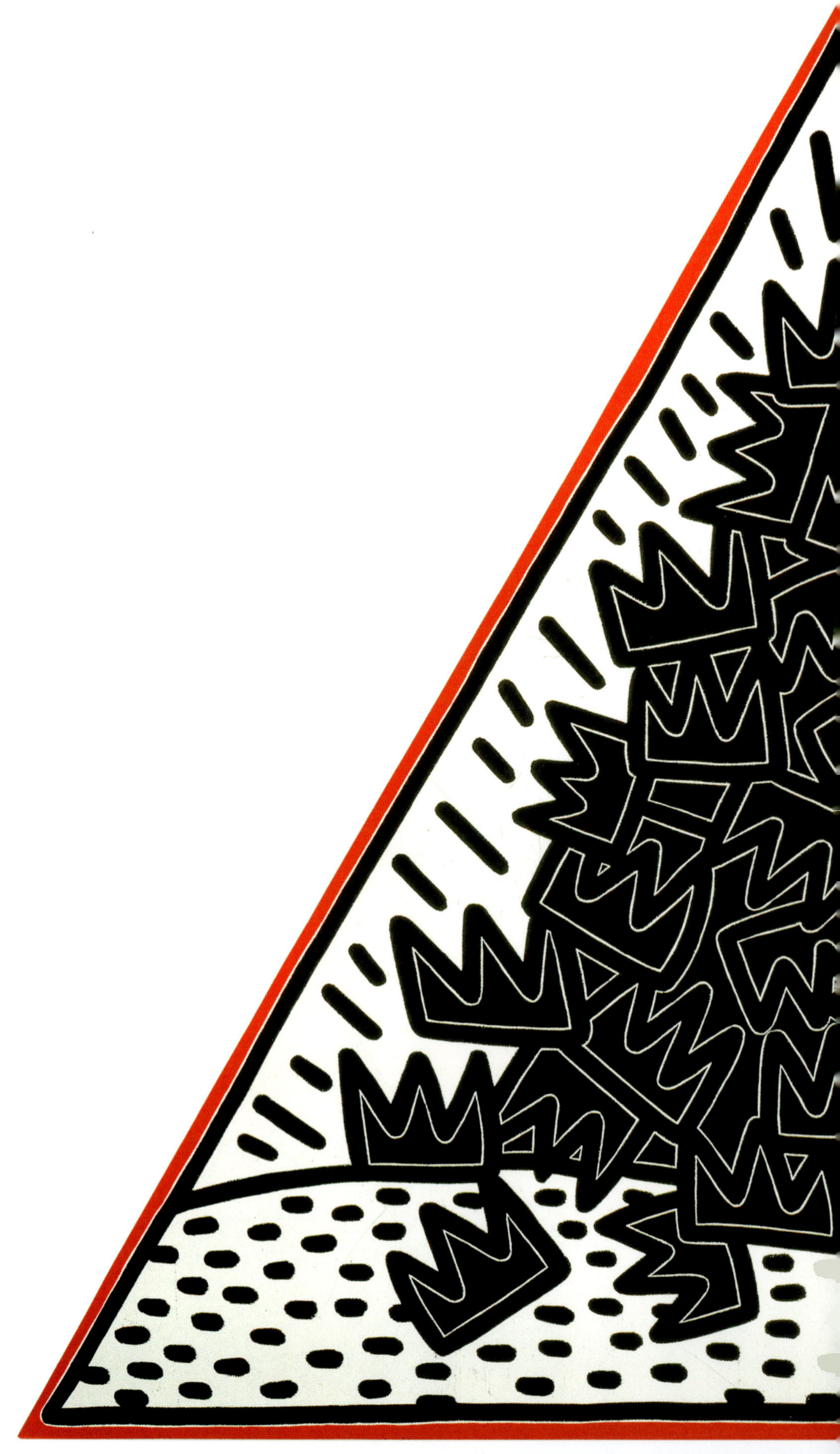

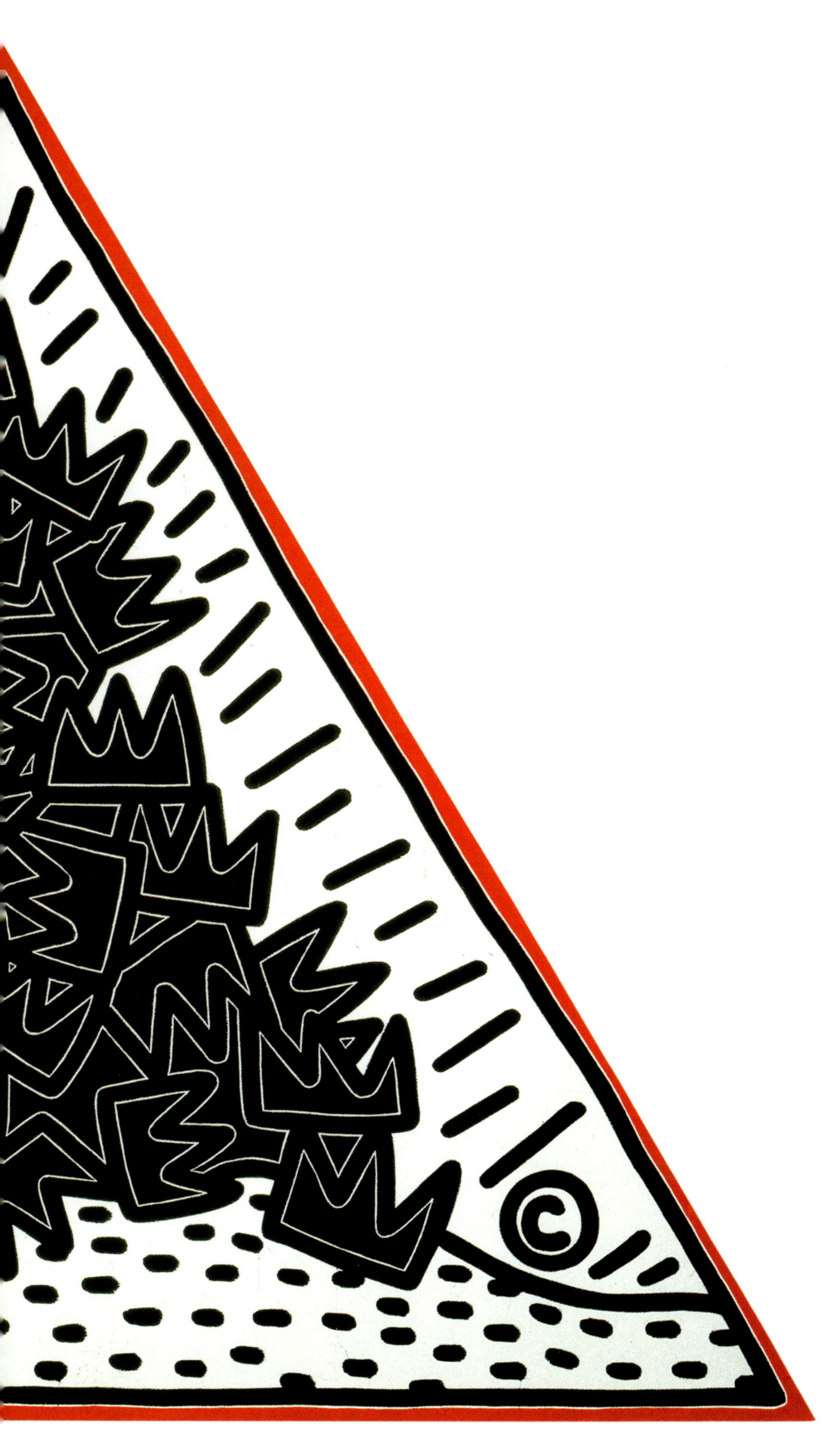

Radiant Desire: Contemplating a Legacy of Cross-racial Contact

Ricardo Montez

In his book *Disidentifications: Queers of Color and the Performance of Politics*, the late art and performance scholar José Esteban Muñoz begins his chapter on Jean-Michel Basquiat and Andy Warhol in 'awe of the ways in which queer children navigate a homophobic public sphere that would rather they did not exist'.[1] 'The survival of children who are both queerly and racially identified is nothing short of staggering', he writes, introducing a framework within which to consider the work of Warhol and Basquiat.[2] Warhol's queer mode of Pop reproduction – his defamiliarising of the iconography of fame constructed by mass media – aligns for Muñoz with Basquiat's treatment of black celebrity, which sees distorted forms and famous names 'enact the disturbing encounter between fame and racist ideology that saturates North American media culture'.[3]

Much of what Muñoz writes, particularly his consideration of the commodity fetish and Basquiat's pointed play with the copyright symbol, reverberates thematically with Rene Ricard's 1981 *Artforum* essay 'The radiant child'. In this essay, the poet-cum-art critic makes a dizzying, contradictory and somewhat convoluted attempt to capture the ethos of art production and consumption in 1980s New York. Ricard sceptically addresses the popularity of graffiti art and contemplates how the graffiti writer's tag speaks to a larger economy in which buyers fetishise the individual artist, whose art they eagerly consume. At the end of the essay, Ricard includes himself in a list of artists, identifying with Basquiat as a fellow survivor. He writes:

> — We are that radiant child and have spent our lives defending that little baby, constructing an adult around it to protect it from the unlisted signals of forces we have no control over. We are that little baby, the radiant child, and our name, what we are to become, is outside us, and we must become 'Judy Rifka' or 'Jean-Michel' the way I became 'Rene Ricard'.[4]

Given Ricard's attention to Keith Haring's signature tag, the radiant baby, at the beginning of the essay, 'Keith Haring' is clearly part of this list of protective names and his baby the inspiration for the essay's title. Where Muñoz identifies Basquiat's use of text and figure as a part of a performance of blackness that calls attention to systems of exploitation and commodification, Ricard similarly positions Basquiat within a mode of performance that underscores the artist's play with a signature that perhaps protects some kind of authentic black self.

What does it mean for Ricard to invoke Haring alongside Basquiat in his meditation on the relationship between artists' signatures, their writing in the world and their existence as art-world commodities? While Ricard puts forward a complicated snapshot of the historical moment in which he writes, he also underscores the ways that race defines the entire system of fame and consumption. Taking a cue from Muñoz's juxtaposition of Warhol and Basquiat, my essay explores signification across the racial lines invoked in Ricard's *Artforum* piece. 'To Whites every Black holds a potential knife behind the back, and to every Black the White is concealing a whip', argues Ricard. 'Our responsibility is to overcome the sins and fears of our ancestors and drop the whip, drop the knife',[5] he writes in his defence of John Ahearn (according to Ricard, this white sculptor was labelled a racist exploiter for his three-dimensional renderings of black and Latinx people from his neighbourhood in the South Bronx). This call by Ricard to move beyond our fixed perceptions of race corresponds in many ways with the utopian project of Keith Haring's art. For as much as Haring became identified with a black and Latinx culture that informed his overall aesthetic, he was complicit in a strain of appropriation that borrowed from the racialised setting of 'the street' to create human forms supposedly free from racial demarcation. The purity of the radiant baby and the dancing figures that appeared in many of his subway chalk drawings, for example, might be understood as energetic, universal forms with an almost primal capacity to speak to the masses, regardless of racial or socioeconomic background.

Haring was a Benetton-era poster boy for neoliberal fantasies of global unity. This is not to suggest that Haring was naive about systems of racial oppression or lacked any sensitivity to the challenges those less privileged than him faced. The art he created on the streets of New York City and the scenes of art production he enabled inspired people from diverse backgrounds. His work often also addressed violence enacted by authorities, something most clearly evidenced in *Michael Stewart – USA for Africa*, 1985, in which the artist explicitly ties the death of a young black graffiti artist following his arrest by police in New York City to apartheid in South Africa. In a journal entry dated 20 March 1987, Haring expresses his outrage at the fact that the officers accused of Stewart's death were acquitted of all charges, and he thinks more broadly about whiteness when he writes:

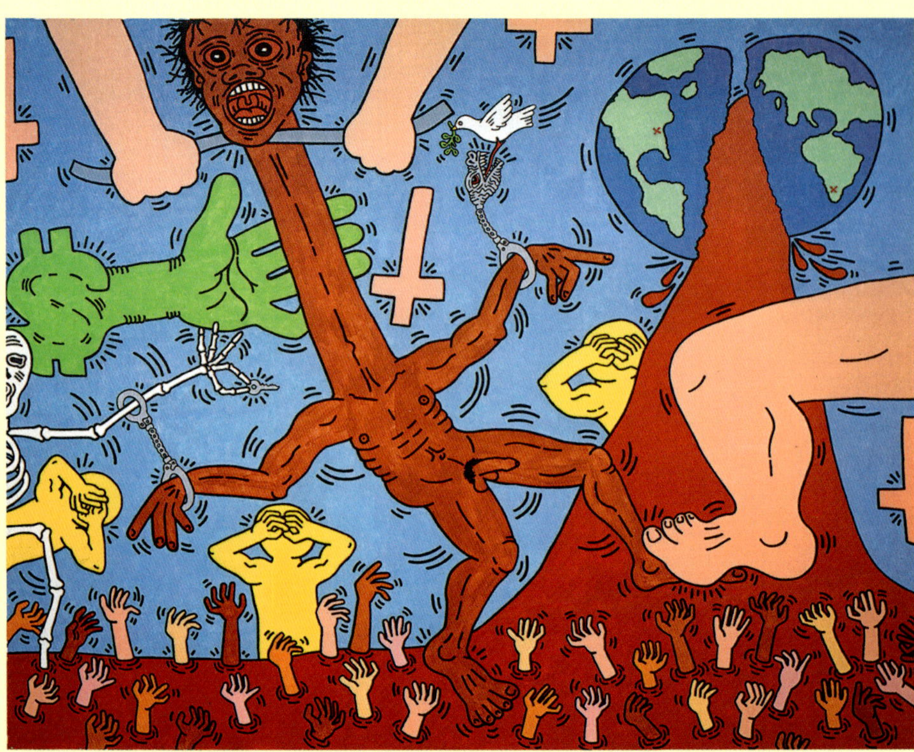

Keith Haring *Michael Stewart – USA for Africa* 1985, synthetic polymer paint and oil on canvas, 304.8 x 304.8 cm, Private collection

— All stories of white men's 'expansion' and 'colonization' and 'domination' are filled with horrific details of the abuse of power and the misuse of people.

I'm sure inside I'm not white. There is no way to stop them, however. I'm sure it is our destiny to fail. The end is inevitable. So who cares if these pigs kill me with their evil disease, they've killed before and will continue to kill until they suck themselves into their own evil grave and rot and stink and explode themselves into oblivion.

I'm glad I'm different. I'm proud to be gay. I'm proud to have friends and lovers of every color. I'm ashamed of my forefathers. I am not like them.[6]

Here, Haring disavows whiteness by claiming some interior sense of self that belies his skin tone, an external mark of privilege, while also aligning himself with the oppressed through his position as a gay man susceptible to the ravages of HIV. The death of Michael Stewart brings to the fore a political consciousness that longs for a better reality. Haring critiques whiteness and in doing so resists complicity with any negative associations of whiteness through the embrace of difference. Haring's move towards depicting racially marked bodies is characterised somewhat differently in his authorised biography. Speaking to John Gruen, Haring discusses his relationship with Juan Dubose, his first significant lover, and states, '[M]y spirit and soul is much closer to the spirit and soul of people of color. And yes, I have an erotic attraction for people of color, because there is no better way to be wholly a part of the experience than to be sexually involved'.[7] Haring's conception of race is necessarily shaped by his sexual desire for bodies of colour, and that desire fuels his political world view. Black and Latinx bodies become sources of inspiration for his artistic practice while at the same time enabling him to imagine that he can inhabit whiteness differently from those who dominate and oppress.

Where Haring believes he can access something beyond whiteness in his work and life, Basquiat's work resists this very paradigm of white liberal access and pointedly destabilises the imagistic and discursive signs that convey blackness. The two artists' different approaches to the problem of race in contemporary society are perhaps most apparent in the way each dealt with the death of Michael Stewart. Haring's tribute to Stewart shows the slain graffiti artist nude, his strangled body stretched across the canvas. The horrifying display recalls historical lynching imagery in the United States, and its foregrounding of Stewart's genitals signals the mythological threat of the black man's sexuality. Even in its criticism of systemic violence, the canvas

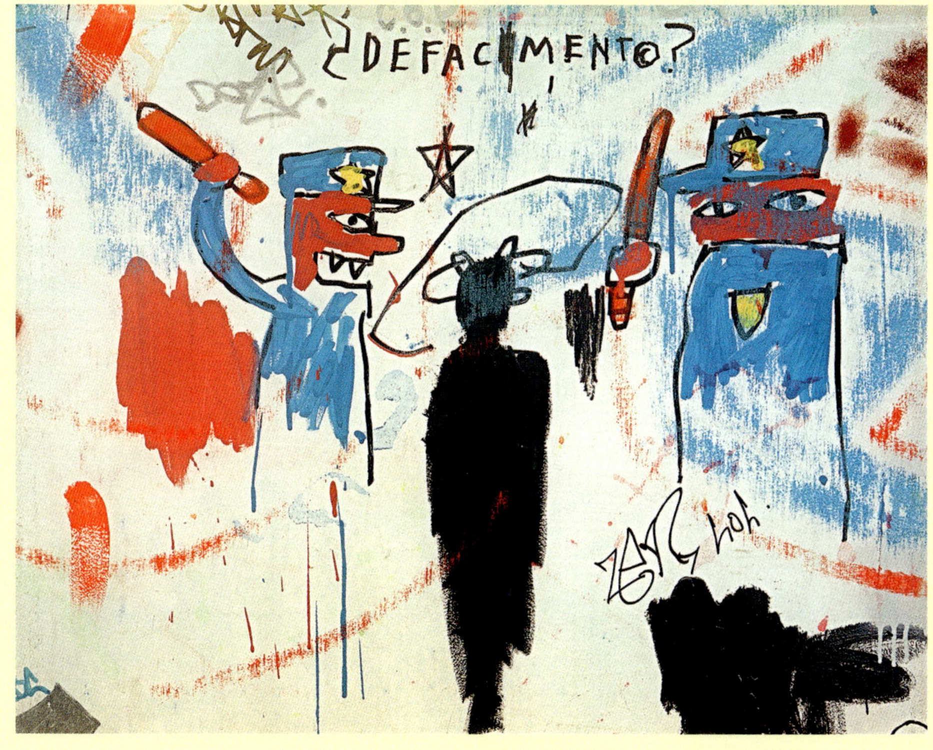

Jean-Michel Basquiat *Defacement (The Death of Michael Stewart)* 1983, acrylic and marker on plasterboard, 63.5 x 77.5 cm (framed), Collection of Nina Clemente, New York

could be seen to be objectifying black flesh in a violent manner and reinforcing an erotic component often central to the apprehension of black suffering and the lessons that might be gleaned from that suffering.

In stark contrast, Basquiat's *Defacement (The Death of Michael Stewart)*, 1983, painted on the wall of Haring's studio shortly after Stewart's death, forgoes any figurative rendering of Stewart's body. Instead a black shadow form lies at the centre of the image and is flanked on either side by crude, cartoonishly sinister representations of police officers wielding clubs. The word 'defacement' scrawled in black letters hovers above these three figures, followed by a copyright symbol that also resembles a hastily written 'o'. The central 'e' appears to have been scratched out, written over with a series of vertical black marks as an 'i' hovers just below the 'm'; these alterations to the word, bracketed by interrogation marks, gesture towards some attempt to signal a Spanish-language form of 'defacement'. Gestural lines surround the central shadow form, suggesting, perhaps, the graffiti for which Stewart was purportedly arrested. The most prominent, decipherable physical features in this painting are the eyes of the police officers and an arm raised, ready to deliver a blow to the spectral form. The shadow is a black space of reflection, projection and mourning. This seems devastatingly appropriate given the fact that the officers were acquitted due to a lack of consistent testimony from witnesses to the crime. Basquiat, like Haring, identified with the graffiti artist who was struck down for his writing on the wall. The question of defacement in the painting and the copyright symbol indicate an unknown potentiality in the street artist's act of expression. How can one know whether one's writing will be celebrated as art or invite authoritarian violence? Haring's nude, strangled representation of Michael Stewart speaks to the ways Stewart circulated in public memory as a famously beaten and murdered black man. Basquiat's refusal to reproduce the scene of violence in shocking detail, his decision to obscure Stewart in shadow, might indicate something about the stakes of representation and a resistance to the erotic draw of black subjection.

To confront the work of Basquiat and Haring one must contend with the racial politics that fed each artist's work and informed their movement between the streets of New York City and the gallery spaces that profited from them. The effect of cross-racial contact is central to the political urgency of the art. When Ricard in 'The radiant child' urges readers to overcome our legacies of racial violence and look beyond the scripts we deploy to make sense of exploitation, he is asking us to imagine the potential for art to explore cross-racial contact as a possible source of political change. 'If going into the ghetto and commemorating its inhabitants is racist', he asks, 'then what do you call people who segregate themselves and plot genocide?'[18] Given his scepticism regarding the art world's embrace of graffiti art, the stark terms in which he contrasts commemoration and genocidal violence feel remarkably naive. For even as Haring might have imagined a different interior self, a non-white other that stood in contrast to the external, protective, adult 'Keith Haring', his form of deeply empathetic cross-racial identification could never wholly negate the systems of oppression he fought.

In 2014, photographer Paige Powell mounted a show at the Suzanne Geiss Company in Soho. Representing a fraction of her extensive photography archive, *Jean-Michel Basquiat: Reclining Nude* allowed visitors to view naked pictures of Basquiat taken by Powell in 1983 when the two were dating. In one photo, Basquiat partially reclines on a futon in front of a television set on a crate and

(opposite) Jean-Michel Basquiat

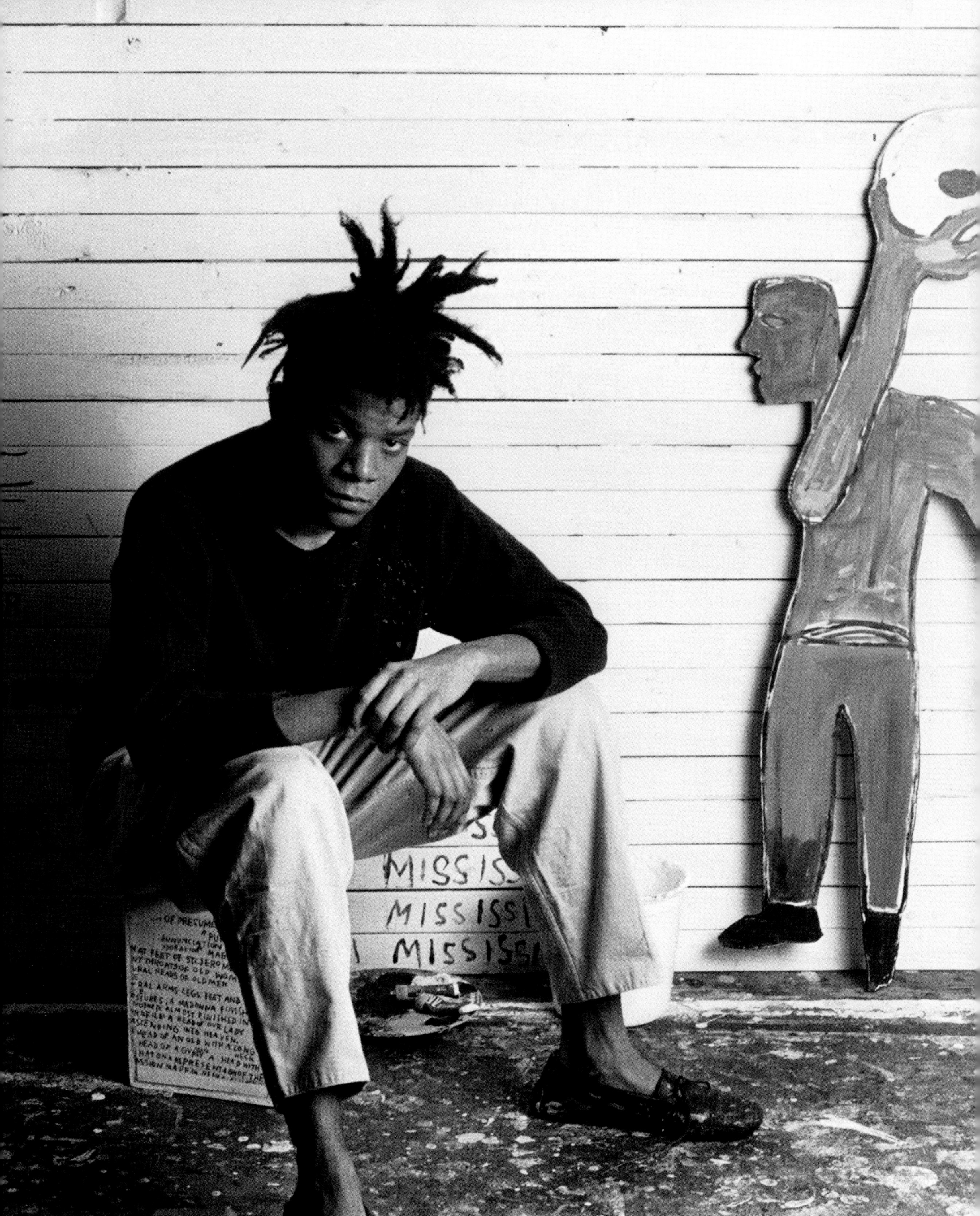

MISSISS
MISSISSI
MISSISSI
OF PRESUME
ANNUNCIATION
AT FEET OF ST. JERO
THROATS OF OLD WOM
HEADS OF OLD MEN
ARMS LEGS FEET AND
A MADONNA FINISH
ALMOST FINISHED IN
A HEAD OF OUR LADY
ASCENDING INTO HEAVEN.
HEAD OF AN OLD WITH A LONG
HEAD OF A GYPSY A HEAD WITH

lights a cigarette. Artworks rest against the wall behind him and some sketches litter the floor in front of the futon. The overall feel of the photographs is relaxed, casual and intimate – a look into the artist's life during what feels like down time with a lover. While none of the shots feel aggressively pornographic, they do place the black artist's naked body in relation to the art he is producing. Basquiat is foregrounded against the line drawings and artwork – tradeable commodities.
The images in some ways make explicit the ways those traded fetish objects were also imbued with value through their relationship to fetishised black flesh. We could look away from Powell's photographs in disgust – how could she so freely display Basquiat's naked black body after his death and take control of his image in such a way? Or, we could sit with the complicated reality they conjure and contemplate the destabilising forces of cross-racial desire that gave us 'Jean-Michel Basquiat' and 'Keith Haring'.

Notes

1 José Esteban Muñoz, *Disidentifications: Queers of Color and the Performance of Politics*, University of Minnesota Press, Minneapolis, 1999, p. 37.
2 During the Twelfth Annual DC Queer Studies Symposium, 'Reflections on *Disidentifications* at 20', held by the Department of Women's Studies at the University of Maryland on 29 March 2019, academic Jennifer Doyle beautifully situated the importance of Muñoz's intervention to Warhol studies by reading the urgent text that begins his consideration of Basquiat's relationship to Warhol.
3 Muñoz, p. 49.
4 Rene Ricard, 'The radiant child', *Artforum*, vol. 20, no. 4, Dec. 1981, p. 43.
5 ibid.
6 Keith Haring, *Keith Haring Journals*, Viking, New York, 1996, p. 124.
7 John Gruen, *Keith Haring: The Authorized Biography*, Fireside, New York, 1991, p. 88.
8 Ricard, p. 43.

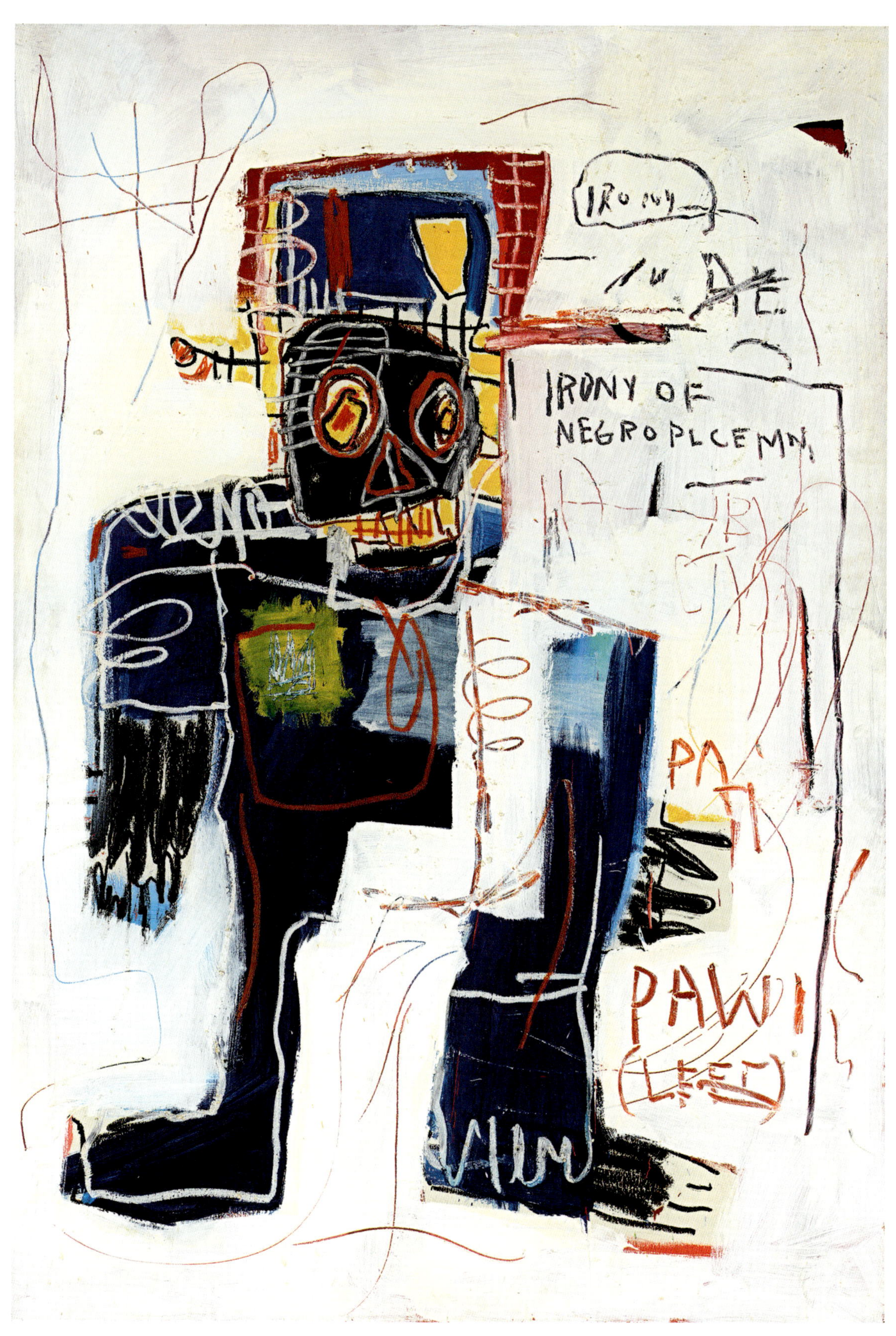

Jean-Michel Basquiat *Irony of a Negro Policeman* 1981, synthetic polymer paint and oilstick on wood, 183.0 x 122.0 cm, AMA Art Collection

The Radiant Child

Rene Ricard, 'The radiant child', *Artforum*, vol. 20, no. 4, Dec. 1981

THE RADIANT CHILD

Jean-Michel Basquiat, *Famous Negro Athlete #47*, 1981, mixed media on paper, approx. 11 × 17″.

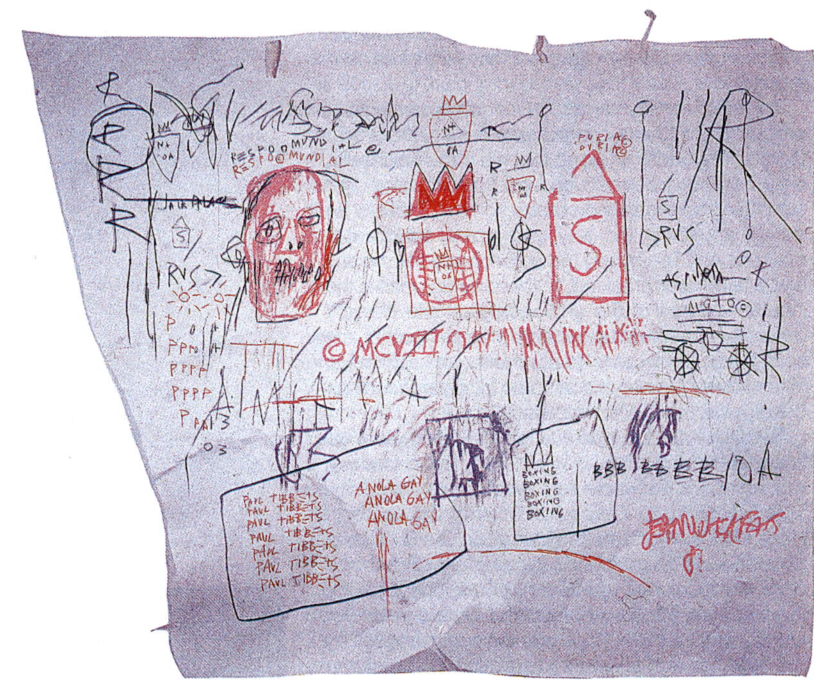

Jean-Michel Basquiat, *Gringo Pilot*, 1981, mixed media on seamless paper, 81 × 103″ at widest point.

Rene Ricard

I remember the first Tags (where is *Taki*?), Breaking (where you spin on your head), Rapping (where I first heard it). I know the names, but are the names important? Where is *Taki*? Perhaps because I have seen graffiti, then seen something else, thrown myself on the dance floor, then gone on to dance another way, I say that the reason for abandoning so much during the '70s was that each fad became an institution. What we can finally see from the '70s buried among the revivals and now surfacing (Tagging, Breaking, Rapping) was at least one academy without program. Distinct to the '70s, graffiti, in particular, was the institutionalization of the idiosyncratic that has led to the need for individuation within this anonymous vernacular. This is why the individuals (*Crazy Legs*) must distinguish themselves.

Artists have a responsibility to their work to raise it above the vernacular. Perhaps it is the critic's job to sort out from the melee of popular style the individuals who define the style, who perhaps inaugurated it (where is *Taki*) and to bring them to public attention. The communal exhibitions of the last year and a half or

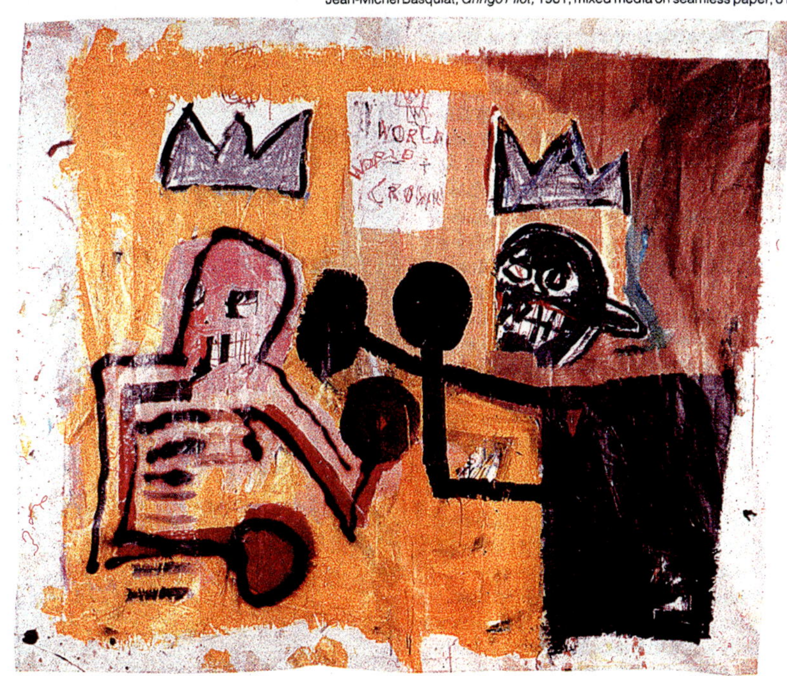

Jean-Michel Basquiat, *World Crown*, 1981, mixed media on canvas, approx. 60 × 72″.

so, from the Times Square Show, the Mudd Club shows, the Monumental Show, to the New York/New Wave Show at P.S. 1, have made us accustomed to looking at art in a group, so much so that an exhibit of an individual's work seems almost antisocial. Colab, Fashion Moda, etc., have created a definite populist ambience, and like all such organizations, from the dawn of modern, have dug a base to launch new work. These are vast communal enterprises as amazing that they got off the ground as the space shuttle and even more, fly-by-night, that they landed on solid ground.

The most accessible and immediately contagious productions in these shows were those of the graffiti stylists. The graffiti style, so much a part of this town, New York, is in our blood now. It's amazing that something so old can be made so new. There is an instant appeal in the way spray paint looks, ditto markers. Any Tag by any teenager on any train on any line is fairly heartbreaking. In these autographs is the inherent pathos of the archaeological site, the cry down the vast endless track of time that "I am somebody," on a wall in Pompeii, on a rock at Piraeus, in the subway graveyard at some future archaeological dig, we ask, "Who was *Taki*?"

Graffiti refutes the idea of anonymous art where we know everything about a work except who made it: who made it is the whole Tag. *Blade*, *Lady Pink*, *Pray*, *Sex*, *Taki*, *Cliff 159*, *Futura 2000*, *Dondi*, *Zephyr*, *Izzy*, *Haze*, *Daze*, *Fred*, *Kool*, *Stan 153*, *Samo*, *Crash*. (*Crash* is still bombing.) But trains get buffed (the *damnatio memoriae* of the Transit Authority), and with the need for identity comes the artist's need for identification with the work, and to support oneself by the work is the absolute distinction between the amateur and the pro. Therefore, the obvious was to raise oneself by the supreme effort of will from the block, from the subway, to the Mudd, to the relative safety and hygiene of the gallery. Because an artist is somebody. Say what you will about group shows and collaborative enterprise: *Das Kapital* was written by one man. This is no graffito, this is no train, this is a Jean-Michel Basquiat. This is a Keith Haring.

Both these artists are a success in the street where the most critical evaluation of a graffito takes place. Jean-Michel is proud of his large *Samo* Tag in a schoolyard, surrounded by other Tags on top of Tags, yet not marked over. This demonstrates respect for the artist as not just a graffitist but as an individual, the worth of whose Tag is recognized. There's prestige in not being bombed over. There are also fake *Samos* and Harings as well as a counter-Haring graffitist who goes around erasing him. The ubiquity of Jean-Michel's *Samo* and Haring's baby Tags has the same effect as advertising; so famous now is that baby button that Haring was mugged by four 13-year-olds for the buttons he was carrying (as well as for his Sony Walkman.) The Radiant Child on the button is Haring's Tag. It is a slick Madison Avenue colophon. It looks as if it's always been there. The greatest thing is to come up with something so good it seems as if it's always been there, like a proverb. Opposite the factory-fresh Keith Haring is Jean-Michel's abandoned cityscape. His prototype, the spontaneous collage of peeling

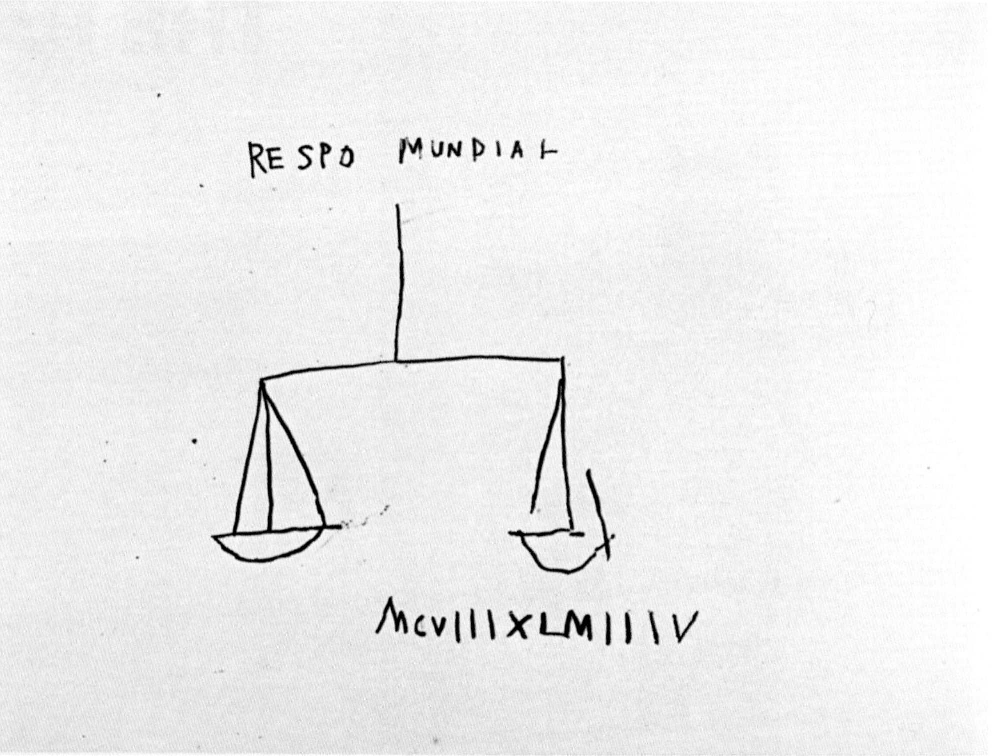

Jean-Michel Basquiat, *Respo Mundial*, 1981, charcoal and marker on rag paper, 50×67".

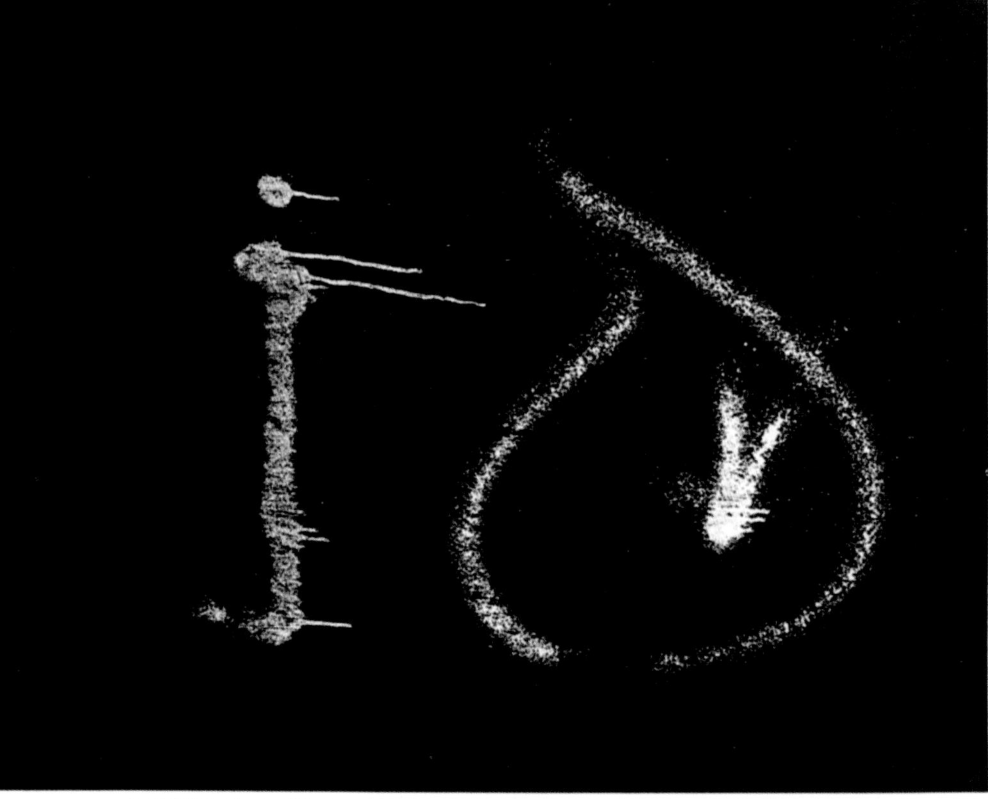

Aaron Siskind, *Chicago*, 1952, silver print, 15¼×19⅜". The Museum of Modern Art, New York, gift of Edwin A. Bergman. *Who was "10"?*

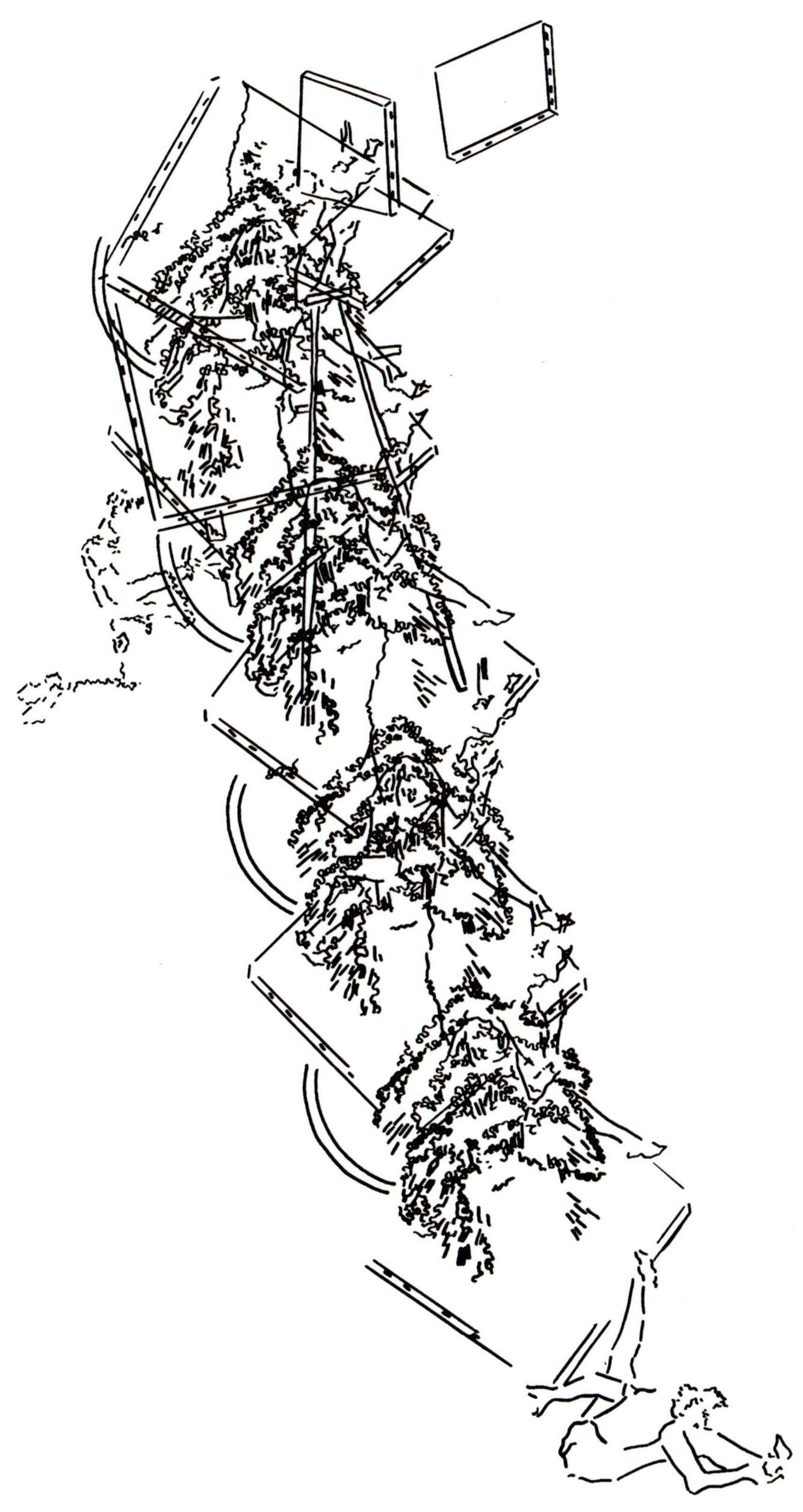

Judy Rifka, *Outro*, 1981, magic marker on acetate, 72 × 24″.

posters, has been there for everyone's ripping off. His earlier paintings were the logical extension of what you could do with a city wall. (For the moment he's stopped the collage.) His is a literal case of bringing something in off the street but with the element of chance removed. I'm always amazed at how people come up with things. Like Jean-Michel. How did he come up with the words he puts all over everything, his way of making a point without overstating the case, using one or two words he reveals a political acuity, gets the viewer going in the direction he wants, the illusion of the bombed-over wall. One or two words containing a full body. One or two words on a Jean-Michel contain the entire history of graffiti. What he incorporates into his pictures, whether found or made, is specific and selective. He has a perfect idea of what he's getting across, using everything that collates to his vision.

Where is *Taki*. When writing or just thinking about say a movement or a style, we automatically attach progenitors of common appearance, attributes of an individual or stylistic precursor to the object of contemplation. I bought an assortment of Wild Style and Plain Style (*Daze Rocks*, etc.) Tags done in marker on a piece of newsprint at the Mudd Club graffiti show because it looked like a late 18th century Chinese literati-type thing, no, maybe more Japanese, yes Japanese. Even the names of the different scripts are like Japanese calligraphic distinctions. (The underlying discipline is getting a character down so good you can repeat it exactly.) This of course leads one into the Zen calligraphic renovations of, say, Mark Tobey, Bradley Walker Tomlin, and just about everybody in the late '40s, early '50s. And you have no choice but to look at things this way because . . . "Does His Voice Sound Some Echo in your Heart." (Source available.) This is the double-headed monster of erudition, half seeing too much and half of it blind.

I asked Jean-Michel where he got the crown. "Everybody does crowns." Yet the crown sits securely on the head of Jean-Michel's repertory so that it is of no importance where he got it bought it stole it; it's his. He won that crown. In one painting there is even a © copyright sign with a date in impossible Roman numerals directly under the crown. We can now say he copyrighted the crown. He is also addicted to the copyright sign itself. Double copyright. So the invention isn't important; it's the patent, the transition from the public sector into the private, the monopolizing personal usurpation of a public utility, of prior art; no matter who owned it before, you own it now. After all, Judy Rifka did not invent the artist's dilemma. I think it's hers for the time being, however.

But influence, when we reach the peak and look down at what we've come from, see mists and clouds under mist, not the base of the mountain. As much as one would like to escape the idea of generation and decade in favor of something better, this provides an easy common way to track development. Where is *Taki*? Graffiti has been around in the way we recognize it now for about ten years and whether one considers this a long or a short amount of time (the

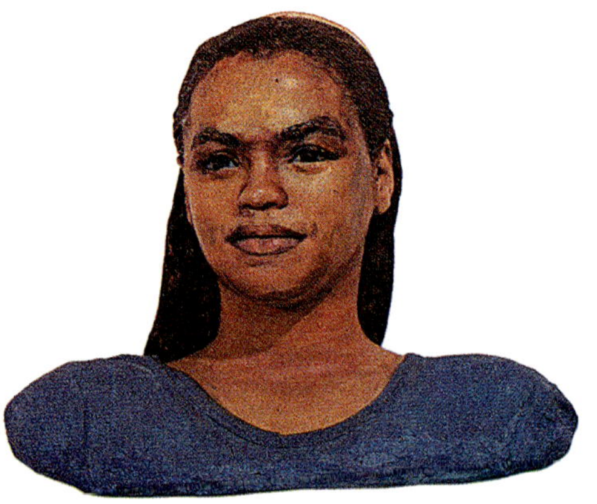

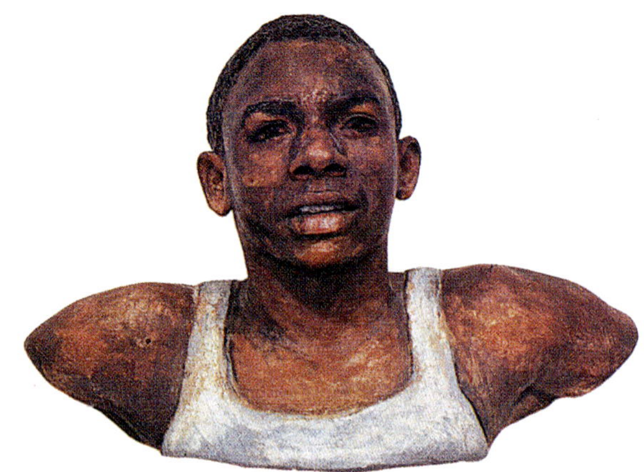

John Ahearn, life-size painted plaster casts, 1981.

Mimmie.

Anthony.

entire High Renaissance from the painting of the Mona Lisa to the Sistine ceiling covered exactly ten years) it is already in its second generation. The transition, however, was neither sudden nor unexpected because in the past ten years we see the full exchange of graffiti from trainstyle to museum candidate. What's unusual is that the gallery bid was not made by the innovators but by the second generation. Graffiti has had a dyslexic development in that the second generation is capitalizing on territory pioneered by its lost innovators. More interesting and more possible to scan than the movement leading up to the picture is, rather, the picture's life after it leaves the artist. The picture must be protected. *(I'm not interested in the prestige of discovery. Part of the artist's job is to get the work where I will see it. I have to be aware of it before I can hype it. I consider myself the metaphor of the public. I'm a public eye. And I only hype the sureshot. The possibility of life without galleries? But how much time, when you really get going, can you spend crating, carrying on correspondences, hiring secretaries, negotiating your appearances in European museums, in fine all the little labors that galleries are supposed to do and that keep you away from your work? There is a place for responsible representation. This is an enormously important season in New York and to make a false step could have severe repercussions for years. In a city comprised of individuals it is important at some point to form the right connections; for your own protection you have to trust someone. Someone else has to have a personal commitment to your work so that it isn't shopped like merchandise. It's cute to be 20 and be pursued when hundreds of young artists are dropping their slides off at these same galleries, but the crass fast-turnover speculators' market can have a deleterious effect on an artist's future career if you don't have protection.* We are no longer collecting art we are buying individuals. This is no piece by *Samo*. This is a piece of *Samo*. *When the work tops a certain mark and the collectors begin their wholesale unloading of your old work in direct competition with your new work you're in trouble with no protection. Every time one of your old paintings is bought one of your new ones isn't. Plus, old more famous pictures always cost more and you don't get a cut off the resale. Of course a record price always helps an artist, but what if the artist has radically changed styles? In any event, it's clear that a good dealer is very careful about where the things land. If there's no personal commitment the chances are that the dealer-as-just-buyer will unload the stuff anywhere for the money, why not, without thought to possible repercussions it could have in the long run. Whereas if the dealer has a stake in your development they will, for example, save the best picture for a possible museum sale rather than just anywhere the cash is flowing. Besides, when anything goes wrong you can blame it on your gallery.)*

"What's with art anyway, that/ We give it such precedence?" (Source available.) Most basic is the common respect, the popular respect for living off one's vision. My experience has shown me that the artist is a person much respected by the poor because they have circumvented the need to exert the body, even of time, to live off what appears to be the simplest bodily act. This is an honest way to rise out of the slum, using one's sheer self as the medium, the money earned rather a proof pure and simple of the value of that individual, The Artist. This is a basic class distinction in the perception of art where a picture your son did in jail hangs on your wall as a proof that beauty is possible even in the most wretched; that someone who can make a beautiful thing can't be all bad; and that beauty has an ability to lift people as a Vermeer copy done in a tenement is surely the same as the greatest mural by some MFA. An object of art is an honest way of making a living, and this is much a different idea from the fancier notion that art is a scam and a ripoff. The bourgeoisie have, after all, made it a scam. But you could never explain to someone who uses God's gift to enslave that you have used God's gift to be free.

What is it that makes something look like art? I can't answer that. I asked someone once why he liked Jean-Michel's work and why it was being singled out for acclaim and he said, "because it looks like art." But then again art doesn't always look like art at first. The way the space shuttle that lifts off doesn't much resemble the space shuttle as it lands.

My favorite Francesco Clemente, for instance, looks just like something in a junk store. It's even painted on one of those premade stretched canvases that are the stock in trade of amateurs. The direct and artless oil paint here, however it looks like a 13-year-old painted it, is very much about being 13. I remember still green ponds like that where I'd go . . . and the anomalous sexuality of the frog, that, no matter what sex it is, a frog's crotch, belly, and thighs, when viewed together, look like a woman. It was brought to my attention that the very thing that freezes this picture compositionally, the flashbulblike shadow of the arm, is what keeps it from being the work of a child; children don't depict cast shadows. Clemente has frozen an instant here, and the sex object of the painting, the frog's crotch, is already underwater. This preservation of a lost moment from childhood, perfectly seen and remembered in a flash, sets this picture apart as art, yet it looks like something in a junk store.

Everybody wants to get on the Van Gogh Boat. There is no trip so horrible that someone won't take it. Nobody wants to miss the Van Gogh Boat. The idea of the unrecognized genius slaving away in a garret is a deliciously foolish one. We must credit the life of Vincent van Gogh for really sending that myth into orbit. How many pictures did he sell. One. He couldn't give them away. Almost no one could bear his work, even among the most modern of his colleagues. In the movie *Lust For Life* there is a scene of Kirk Douglas (as van Gogh) in front of *La Grande Jatte* being treated rudely by Georges Seurat. When I went to the Art Institute of Chicago to see the *Grande Jatte*, it was having a hard time competing with the white walls of the gallery. This habit of putting old pictures up against the white walls is deadly, the walls reflecting more light than the picture, but van Gogh's *Bedroom*

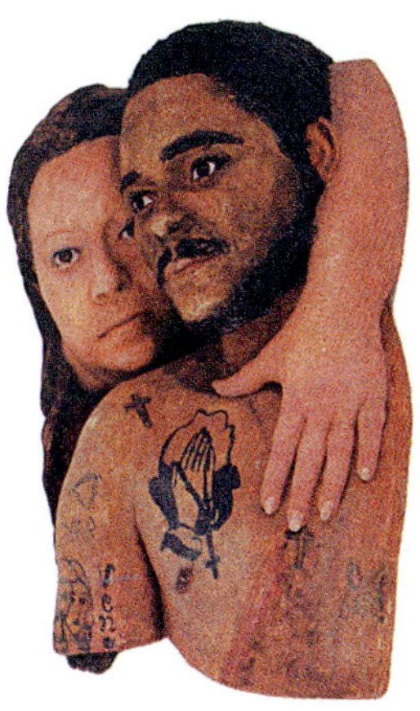

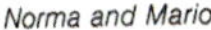
Norma and Mario.

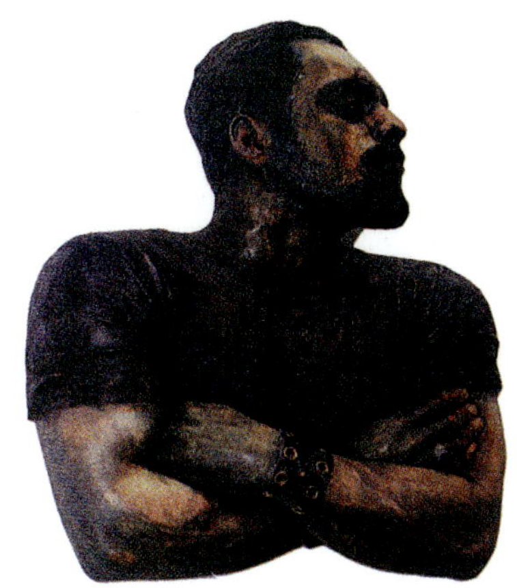
Luis, with bite in forehead.

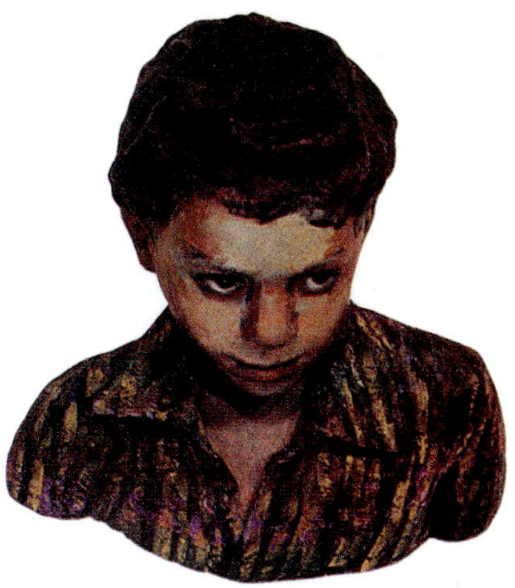
Ephram.

at Arles was on the opposite wall and it was screaming at my back and I turned around and I listened. He has to be the most modern artist, still. Van Goghs don't crack. But everybody hated them. We're so ashamed of his life that the rest of art history will be retribution for van Gogh's neglect. No one wants to be part of a generation that ignores another van Gogh. And yet looking at art history we see that these other guys were pros. They started when they were kids. They sold their work. They worked on commission. There is no great artist in all art history who was as ignored as van Gogh, yet people are still afraid of missing the Van Gogh Boat.

One of the obvious and more interesting developments that insure a nongallery look is the ready-made support, standardized stretchers, artist's panels: the vocabulary of the amateur. The throwaway is the handle absolute of junk, and in using the throwaway one is relieved of the responsibility of constructing one's own outside proportions. Pieces of foam rubber, doors, subway cars, toilet walls make one's considerations, size of image, stroke, etc., purely inner ones. It is impracticable to enter a gallery carting the F train. In the Mudd Club "Beyond Words" show, the most impressive work was either in documentation (photos of bombed trains) or actual junk sprayed over, not the specially-constructed-for-exhibition pieces that looked, frankly, headshop, and it seemed clear to me that whoever was going to get out of the subway was going to have to figure out a way of sophisticating their work into scale, to avoid the cloying naiveté and preciousness that inspire more condescension and "isn't that charming" than, say, awe in the viewer. I don't mean that they have to go big. The sense of scale is innate and relying on found size isn't good enough. When you cut up a roll of canvas you've made your biggest decision. Making something out of nothing is the prime artistic act and I don't mean, "Come to my studio I've got ten refrigerator doors finished."

So what defines the art look? When people say Jean-Michel looks like art, the occult significance of

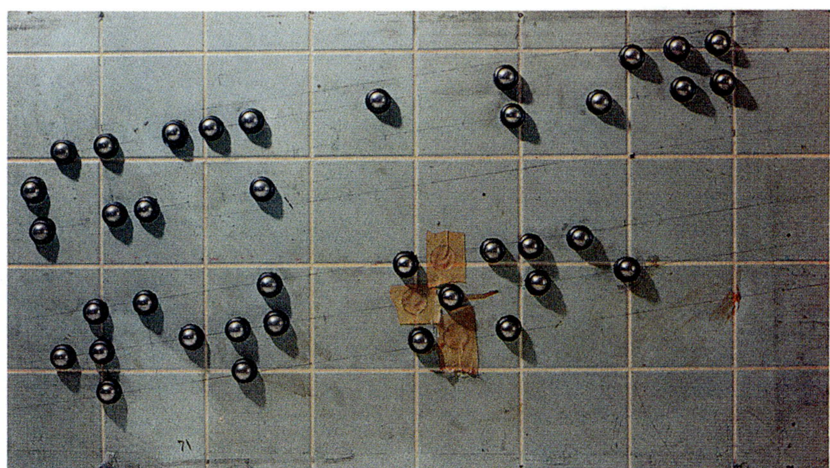
Alain Jacquet, *Bathroom Graffiti*, 1971, ball bearings on Masonite, 18 × 32"

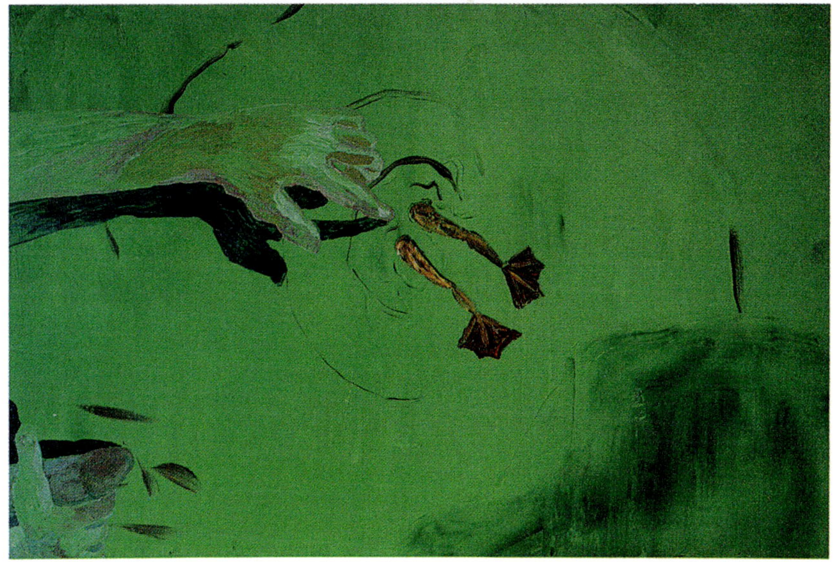
Francesco Clemente, *Titire*, 1980, oil on canvas, 24 × 36". Collection of the author.

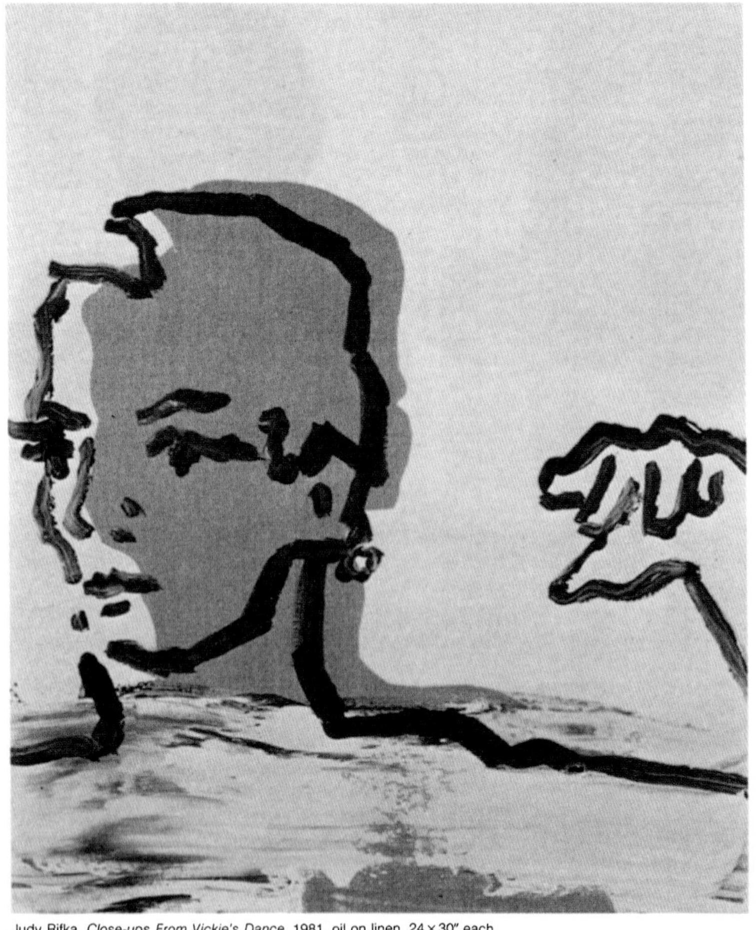

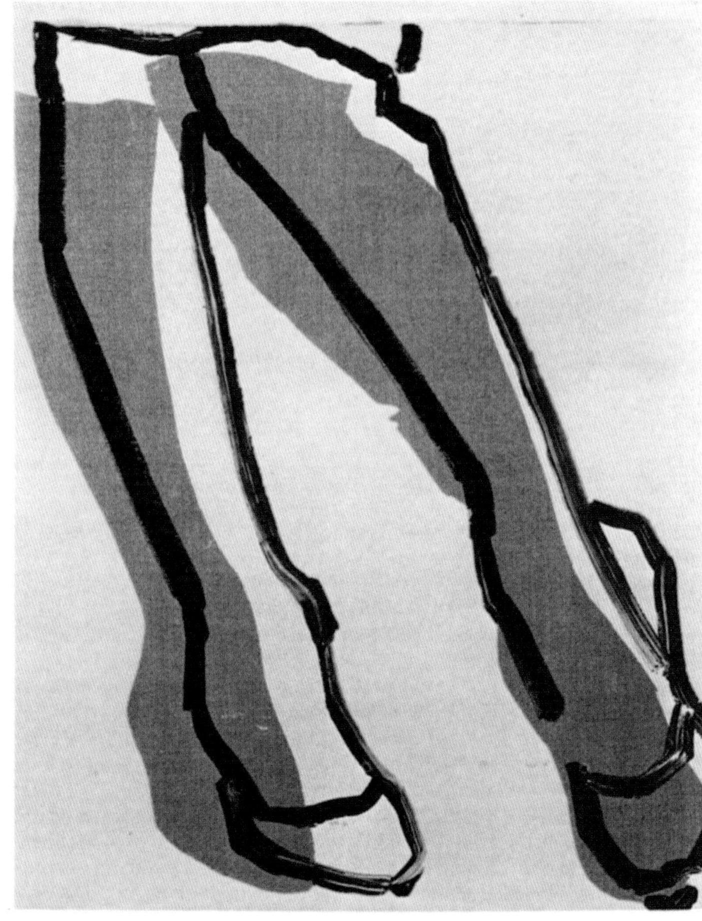

Judy Rifka, *Close-ups From Vickie's Dance*, 1981, oil on linen, 24×30" each.

the comment is that it looks like our expectation of art; there is observable history in his work. His touch has spontaneous erudition that comforts one as the expected does. In the first gallery piece I saw by Jean-Michel (as distinct from his Tag *Samo*) the observable relationship of his drawing to past art alienated me as immediately as it gratified. The superbombers in the same show, with their egregious lack of art history, had the repellent appeal that commands self-analysis in the viewer (me). I didn't want to miss the boat. When you first see a new picture you are very careful because you may be staring at van Gogh's ear. Then I stopped caring about what the pictures should (and might later) look like; regardless of what Jean-Michels look like now, they are transmitting signals that I can receive, that are useful, and finally the graffiti bomb style looks like what it's about and what it's about is packaging.

Bomb style packages itself. At its purest, it's a Tag, a perfect auto-logo, not the artists' names but their trademarks. Designer jeans? You are buying the label proper: the essential iconic self-representation. In any event, the bombers in the show clearly defined a vernacular and made me wonder how long this would take to get off the ground in a big way. Here was, as much as it was predicated on commercial art of the past, the commercial art of the future. Here was the look of the times, this is what packaging should look like: kids would buy it. These guys should get themselves design jobs, before they get ripped off. Several have already worked their way into the applied arts, where they belong: on record covers, doing the art direction for movies, slides behind Rappers, backdrops for Breakers. Sitting by yourself on a wall is different.

An artist's attitude toward the work is telling. It's all hype, sure, but there can be quality in hype and I've caught some sleazy acts. A guy came to my house to deliver a small picture. With a friend. No picture. Broke. "Give me the money I'll come back later with the picture." "OK." While he was there he told me that he was entertaining the idea of giving Andy Warhol a picture. Well, Andy is everyone's culture parent, it's true, but I'm just a poor poet and Andy's turnover must be thousands and thousands a week in prints alone, and it hurt my feelings that I had to pay 50 clams and Andy would get it free. I could see, though, that this boy's climb was on. This was my advice: don't give him the picture. Kids do that. Trade. That's what real artists do with each other. Since Andy's a press junkie, and I see you're getting the taste, call up page six of the *Post* and get a photographer to the Factory on the "Graffiti goes legit/street kid trades Tag for Soup Can" angle. You both get your picture in the paper, Andy comes off looking like friend of youth, you get a press clipping, and it's gravy for all parties. Easily $50 worth of advice. So he left with the money, and, like copping drugs in the street, beat me for the picture. A month or so later, after some friends put on a little muscle, I finally got the doodad, and promptly gave it away. Foolish way to hype yourself. When you're climbing a ladder, don't kick out the rungs.

As much as undervaluation can kill, so can a false sense of the value of your work. Jean-Michel was advised to stop giving it away. But if your friends can't have it, why live? Overprotection is deadly; the stuff has to get out there to be seen. Making money is something between artists and their stomachs. To turn one's work into fetish that is almost indistinct from oneself, to overpersonalize and covet one's own work, is professional suicide. Fear of rip-off is paralysis. One is always ripped off. Keeping work a secret is the psychology of the applied artist, not the fine artist who must live in a dialogue.

Is innovation important? When one compares Jack

Smith's *Flaming Creatures* with Fellini's *Satyricon* we see that Fellini manages with pasty millions a bad reproduction of what Jack Smith achieved with a sequin. The trick is to make it appear that the innovator ripped it off from you. A good example of this principle is the case of Judy Rifka's work at the debut of the '70s. Her single shapes on plywood are among the most important paintings of the decade. Every painter who saw them at the time recognized their influence. She could then be called a painter's painter if feeding ideas to others is what painters' painters do. I suspect that it would be a heartbreaking thing to watch others get credit for your invention. Her researches into Constructivist theory were groundbreaking, but a pioneer is never at a loss for uncharted territory. At the first group show at the Mudd Club I was arrested by a gray painting with a little red blob in it and some drawing on it of Patti Astor from her starring role as Vickie in the movie *Underground USA*. The application of the ground and the way that little red spot was laid on was obviously the work of an extremely sophisticated handler of paint. Although I'd never seen a Judy Rifka of this type the outline of the red left me in no doubt as to its author. There was no visible label and on inquiry I saw I was right. Hers is the poetry of New York. The joy in her new work, the reveling in these characters she creates superimposed on her earlier work, demonstrates that her concerns have dovetailed my own temporary ones: that a picture is only as interesting as its storyline. The Patti Astor iconography is supreme. One must become the iconic representation of oneself in this town. One is at the mercy of the recognition factor and one's public appearance is absolute. (The iconic representation of the artist, in manifestations from sublime to tedious, sublime in Manzoni and Warhol through the tedium of Byars and Beuys, authorship as object, is the precedent for the legitimacy of the Tag. This is the individual as archetype, where we order a "Bud," where every bleach blonde is called "Blondie," the Tag name for the individual Deborah Harry. If Andy Warhol can't be used as an object lesson in how to become iconic then his life has been a waste. We become our name. I have spent my life becoming my name so that it would somehow protect the radiant child it has been created to arm.) Judy's perception of this is accurate. Her multiple-panel pictures are like movies. She has spent the last few years evolving a recognizable cast of characters to people her work. She is the eponymous lead. This is about her life in art, the frustrations and momentary ecstasies of painting a picture; the sub-mafia of artist's assistants; the domestication of pet boys refined into their specific types that become at once the original and the archetype.

Where is *Taki*? We can't escape the etymology or genealogy of art. It's not coincidental that the time that saw the gestation of graffiti was the period of gallery-referential art that flourished (wrong word) in the early '70s. During the era of the white wall, what would have the greater effect on us now was being produced by guerrilla artists bombing trains during their mechanical slumber in Queens. Those teenage prophets are lost in the mists of their own maturity, reminiscent of the way the origin of the blues is lost, the simple expression of the individual followed much later by full-scale commercial exploitation. Contrary to the rules of modern art that hallow the innovator, here is the second generation capitalizing on the innovations of the first. The commercial exploitation of innovation is, conversely, the primary logic of commercial art.

Even as I write, the Transit Authority has unleashed police dogs around the Corona yard, so perhaps there is still hope. Bombing will continue even with the dogs. When it stops you'll know it's played out. If it's still alive the autopsy will kill it. What would happen if subway graffiti were recognized as the native art it is? Would they find *Taki* and declare him a National Living Treasure as the Japanese do their keepers of the flame of native craft? Or if the TA legitimizes it, i.e. encourages it with NEA funding? What happens when the revolution is televised? It bombs out. Train painting has already been severely formalized almost to decadence. It has become historically self-conscious, the progression from expression to Pop; there is a Campbell's Soup can train; sophistication to boredom.

Looking through the Mailer book on graffiti from 1974, was it photographer's optical bias, editorial selectivity, or was the classic period of graffiti as "abstract expressionist," '50s, as the book makes it look when compared to the Pop psychedelic '60s of the train I was on today? It looks so much more severe in the book, metallic style, less balloon style: tougher, *muy switchblade, mas barrio*. But who remembers what it looked like? I remember that it was very sexy, the feeling; I don't remember the look. Eidetic overlays can't be trusted. What did it look like?

Jean-Michels don't look like the others. His don't have that superbomb panache that is the first turn-on of the pop graffitist. Nor does his marker have that tai-chi touch. He doesn't use spray but he's got the dope, and right now what we need is information; I want to know what is going on in people's minds and these pictures are useful. This article is about work that is information, not work that is about information. No

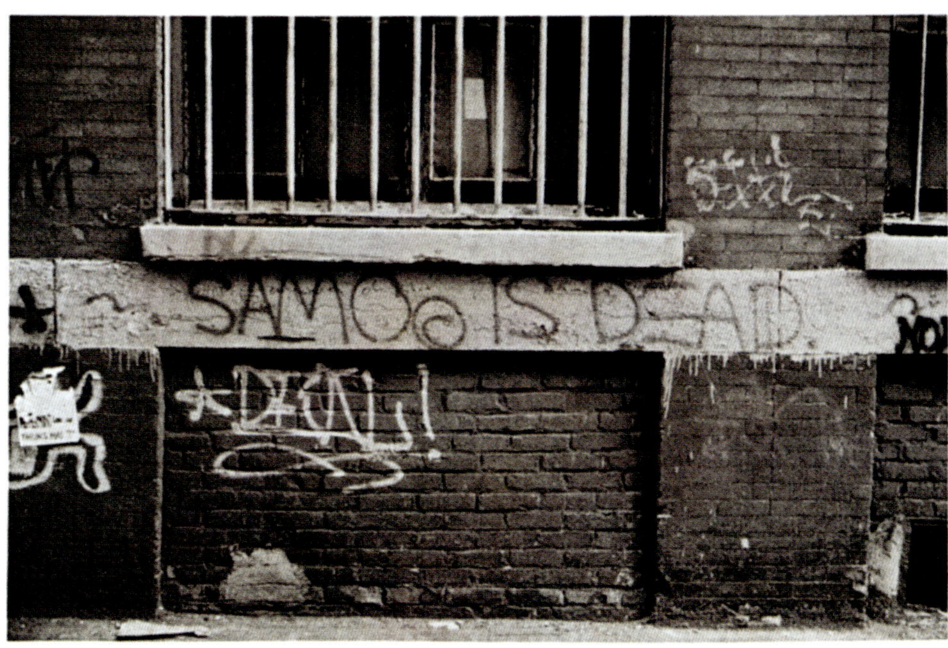

SAMO © is Dead, 1979 an important graffito where the artist refutes his Samo © tag in order to become Jean-Michel Basquiat. See article on Deborah Harry's hair color change. Photo: Charles Hagen.

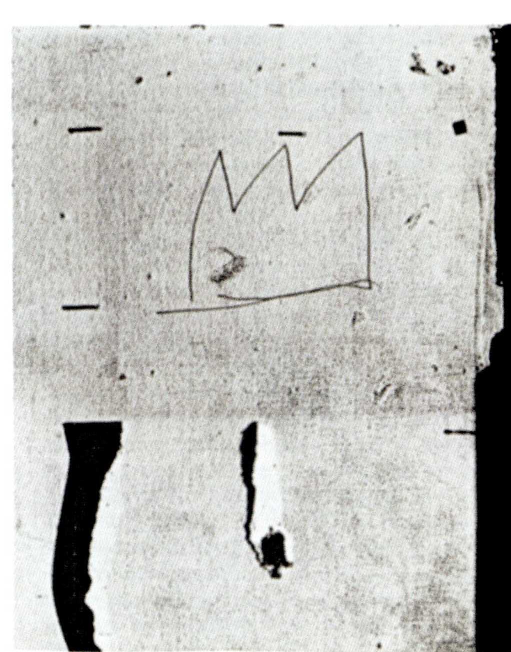

Fake "Samo" crown on wall. Photo: Mary Bachmann.

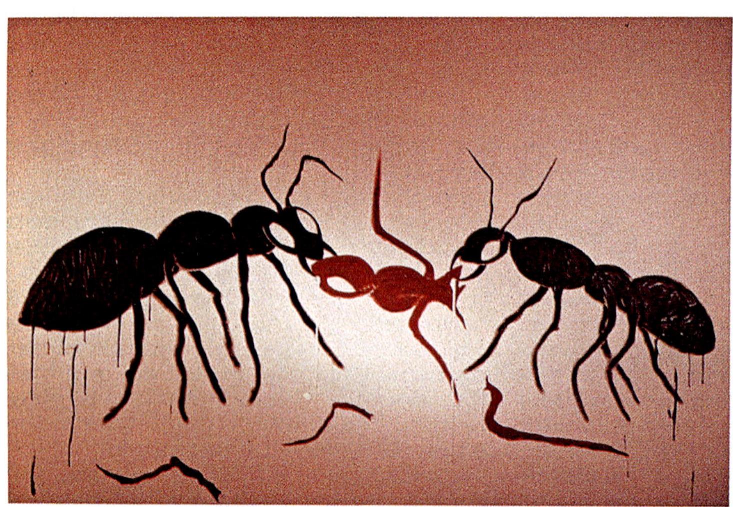

Ronnie Cutrone, *R & B Ants*, 1981, acrylic on raw canvas, 60 × 80". *An incident from human life entomorphosed.*

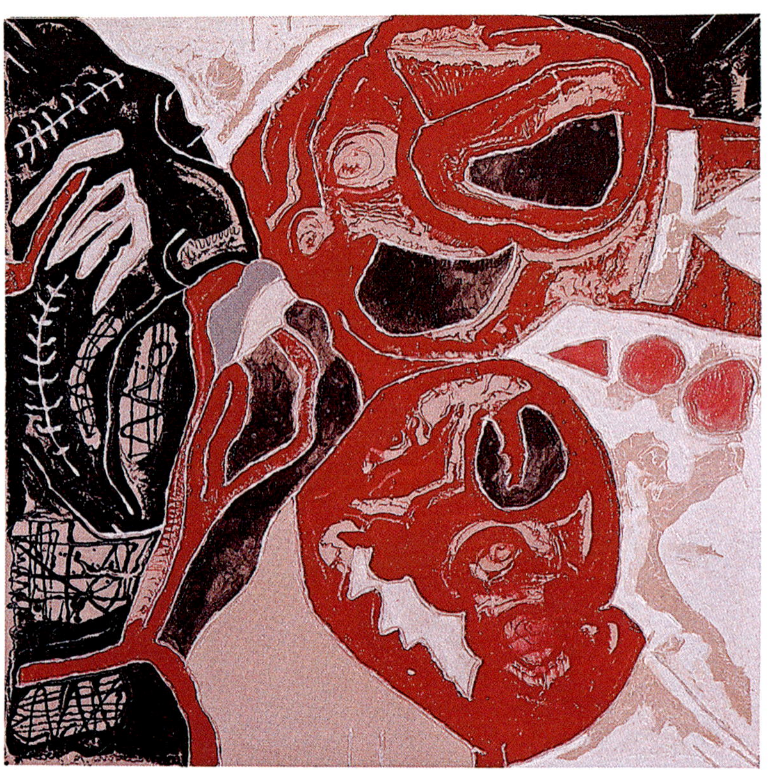

Joe Zucker, *Round 14*, 1981, acrylic, Rhoplex, cotton, on canvas, 72½ × 72½".

matter what the envelope looks like to get it there, the dope's inside. Let the Parisians copy the athletic togs *le look américain jeune Puma sneakaires le graffiti mignon*, style is spin-off; what the pictures are internally about is what matters. If you're going to stand up there with the big kids you've got to be heavy, got to sit on a wall next to Anselm Kiefer next to Jonathan Borofsky next to Julian Schnabel and these guys are tough they can make you look real sissy. There's only one place for a mindless cutie and it ain't the wall, Jack.

Judy Rifka and Jean-Michel Basquiat have both evolved a vocabulary, and so in his way has Keith Haring. In his gray eminence enterpreneurial capacity as director of the Mudd Club shows he was of particular importance in the general dissemination of work by other young artists, and not secondarily his own. His work is faux graphic and looks ready-made, like international road signs. This immediacy is his trump card. It is the already-existing quality of his characters that deceives one into accepting them as already there without the intervention of an individual will. But he did make them up. In their impersonal code they are transmitting a personal narrative. The code is here to be cracked. These poor little characters wigging out from the radioactive communications they are bombarded with are superslick icons of turmoil and confusion. They are without will, without protection from impulses of mysterious source. We can laugh at their involuntary couplings and tiny horrified runnings around because we see them as we cannot see, as the fish cannot see the water, ourselves.

Of course what artists see us as can tell us more about themselves than about us. The second-generation Pop artists who've been popping up behind their more innovative contemporaries show more interest in the(ir) poor victims of cocktail dresses, in the trials and tribulations of dressing up and going out, enchained by our fashion slavery, in Society, than in society. Chief of the Clubbists is Robert Longo who in his own way is concerned with our contemporary solipsism. As an undercover agent of the Fashion Police I am reluctantly placing him under arrest partly for being two years behind the times but really for forgetting that fashion imitates art, and that art that imitates fashion is two removes from the source. Art Deco comes after Cubism. On the subject of Troy Brauntuch, and the use of pictures, his work seems to have been anticipated by an Edwardian novelist: " 'That habit of putting glass over an oil painting,' she murmured, 'makes always such a good reflection particularly when the picture's *dark*. Many's the time I've run into the National Gallery on my way to the Savoy and tidied myself before the Virgin of the Rocks . . .' " (source available).

We need to see ourselves now but not this literally. For some reason we need recognizable evidence of our existence. Something has happened and we need, if not advice, at least a demonstration of the situation and many of our fears are in the words contained in Jean-Michel's pictures—Tar, Oil, Old Tin, Gold—we don't need a lexicon to know what these mean. These morphemes are self-evident.

Phaedrus: Whom do you mean and what is his origin?
Socrates: I mean an intelligent word graven on the soul of the learner, which can defend itself, and who knows when to speak and when to be silent.
Phaedrus: You mean the living word of knowledge which has a soul, and of which the written word is no more than an image?
Socrates: Yes, of course that is what I mean.

—source available.

I'm always amazed by how people come up with things. Like Jean-Michel. How did he come up with those words he puts all over everything? Their aggressively handmade look fits his peculiarly political sensibility. He seems to have become the gutter and his world view very much that of the downtrodden and dispossessed. Here the possession of almost anything of even marginal value becomes a token of corrupt materialism. This is the bum coveting a pair of Guston's shoes. When Jean-Michel writes in almost subliterate scrawl "Safe plush he think" it is not on a Park Avenue facade that would be totally outside the beggar's venue but on a rusted-out door in a godforsaken neighborhood. Plush to whom safe from what?

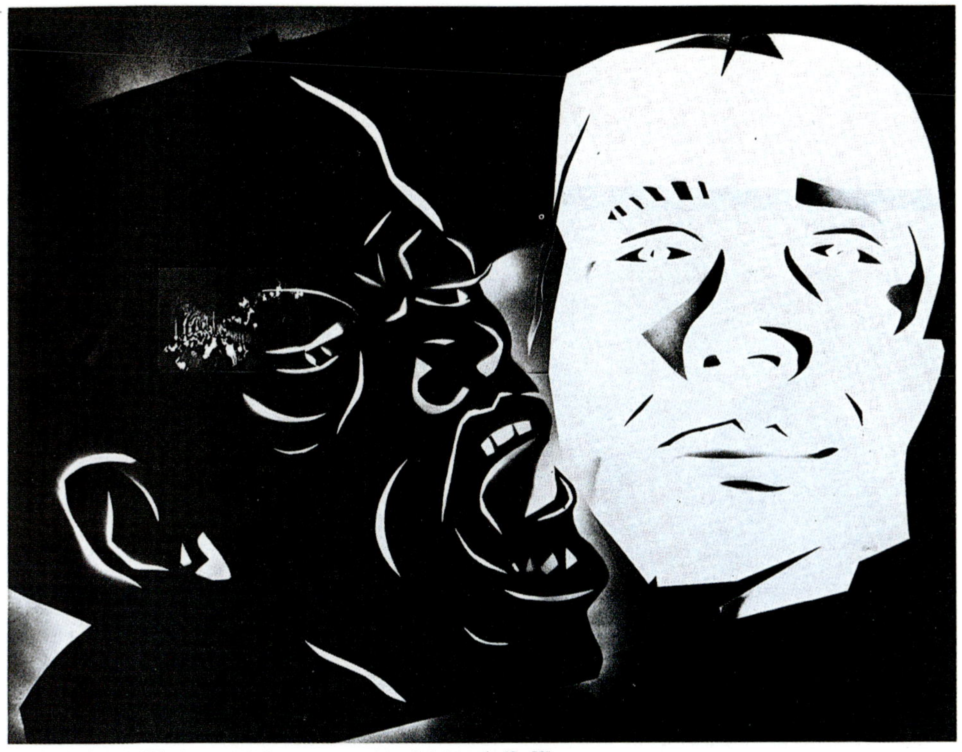

Izhar Patkin, *Collage*, 1981, chrome-coated paper, spray paint and photograph, 40 × 52".

His is also the elegance of the clochard who lights up a megot with his pinkie raised. If Cy Twombly and Jean Dubuffet had a baby and gave it up for adoption, it would be Jean-Michel. The elegance of Twombly is there but from the same source (graffiti) and so is the brut of the young Dubuffet. Except the politics of Dubuffet needed a lecture to show, needed a separate text, whereas in Jean-Michel they are integrated by the picture's necessity. I'd rather have a Jean-Michel than a Cy Twombly. I do not live in the classical city. My neighborhood is unsafe. Also, I want my home to look like a pile of junk to burglars.

Politics can come up by inference in a work, without pointing, without overt dialectic, by the simplest depiction (as in the case of John Ahearn) of an individual. When one looks at Ahearn's pieces, the sensibility is so specific and acute that we feel we would get the same feeling even if it looked entirely different. And his people are about feelings. I don't know how anyone who could afford them would put them in their homes. "Why would the boss want to be reminded at home of the people who keep asking him for a raise?" (source available). They are objects of devotion, of love and its ennobling ability, and are among the rarest and most moving in the history of art. They will command and dominate wherever they are hung and make all art that is anterior to it or that bears a resemblance seem like it was just leading up to Ahearn. They wipe out Segal. They make Duane Hanson seem like a snob and an insensitive jerk. When we look at Hanson's lumpen proles and their dazed stupefaction we feel superior. Ahearns, like most physically dominant art, don't reproduce well. The actual confrontation with the work is overwhelming. They are made to be seen from quite specific angles. Ahearn's work is hung high, and these people up against the white wall of a gallery are looking down at the viewer with dignity, sobriety, querulousness, perfectly precise and specific expressions, fleeting and miraculously caught. The man seems to be looking into the future with intense responsibility as the woman, with her arms around his neck, trusts his ability to confront the world. I am that woman. Ahearn works in the South Bronx the way Caravaggio probably would. He gives his models the first cast. They're poor and they're owed the grace of their image. This is no exploitation and yet I have heard him referred to (by an artist) as a racist, exploiter of his sitters. If going into the ghetto and commemorating its inhabitants is racist, then what do you call people who segregate themselves and plot genocide?

To Whites every Black holds a potential knife behind the back, and to every Black the White is concealing a whip. We were born into this dialogue and to deny it is fatuous. Our responsibility is to overcome the sins and fears of our ancestors and drop the whip, drop the knife. In Izhar Patkin's parable of racial cannibalism we see that when a man with a .45 meets a man with a shotgun I guess the man with the pistol is a dead man.

Where is *Taki*?

I think now about Anya Phillips who so briefly illuminated this fleeting world. I think about clothes worn by people so recently and yet how long ago it all seems that Anya would show up in those cocktail dresses and of all things, a Chinese girl in a blonde wig. And now all the girls in their cocktail dresses who never heard of Anya and how quickly each generation catches the look of its creators and forgets the moral underneath. I think about how one must become the iconic representation of oneself if one is to outlast the vague definite indifference of the world. I think about how every bleach blonde is called Blondie in the street and Deborah Harry's refutation of her iconic responsibility to reify her name as a brunette. We are that radiant child and have spent our lives defending that little baby, constructing an adult around it to protect it from the unlisted signals of forces we have no control over. We are that little baby, the radiant child, and our name, what we are to become, is outside us and we must become "Judy Rifka" or "Jean-Michel" the way I became "Rene Ricard." ■

Rene Ricard's new book of poems is scheduled to appear in the spring.

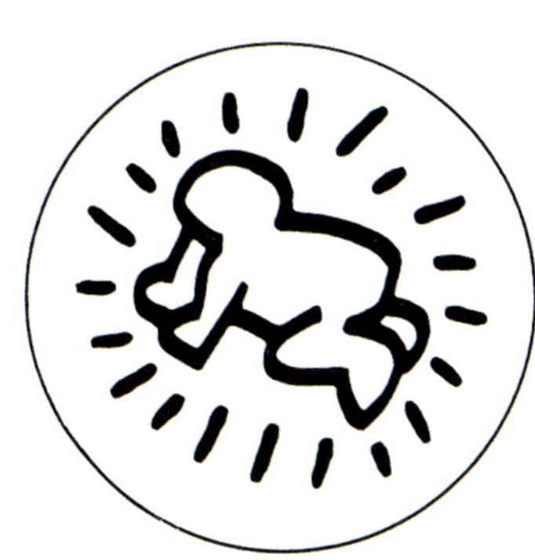

Keith Haring, 1981, button.

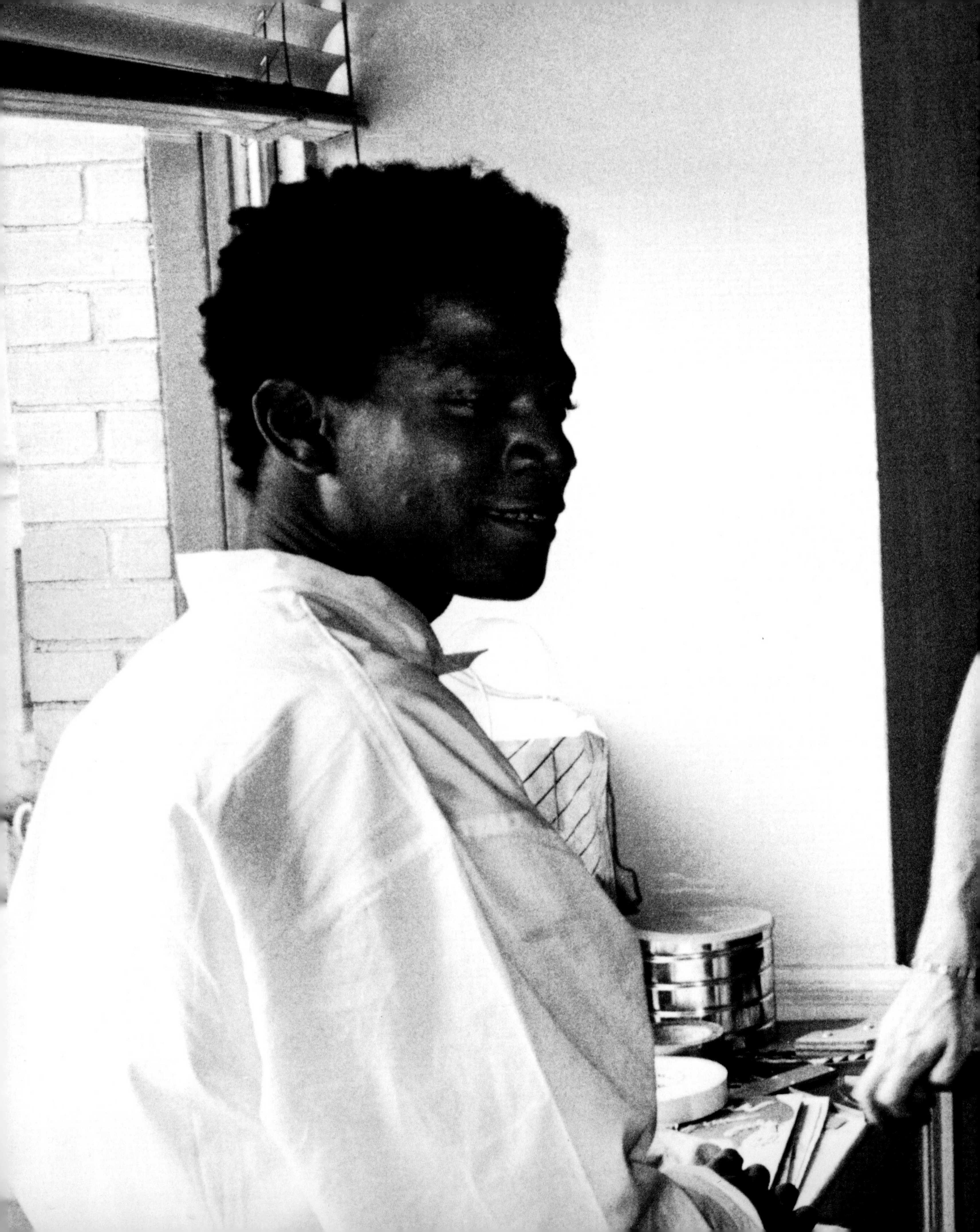

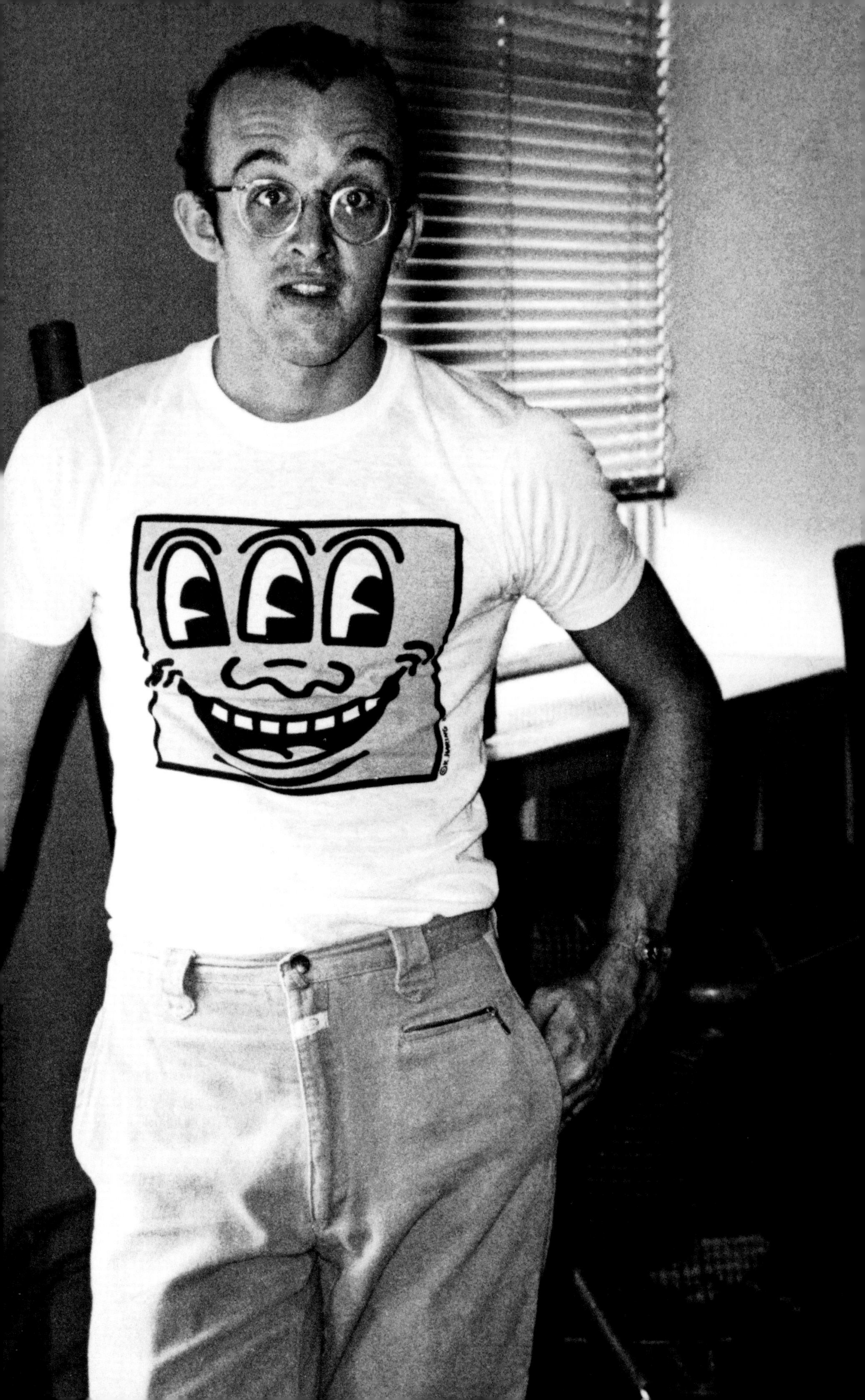

(previous) Andy Warhol *Jean-Michel Basquiat and Keith Haring* 1984, gelatin silver print, 20.3 x 25.4 cm, The Andy Warhol Foundation for the Visual Arts, New York
(opposite) Keith Haring

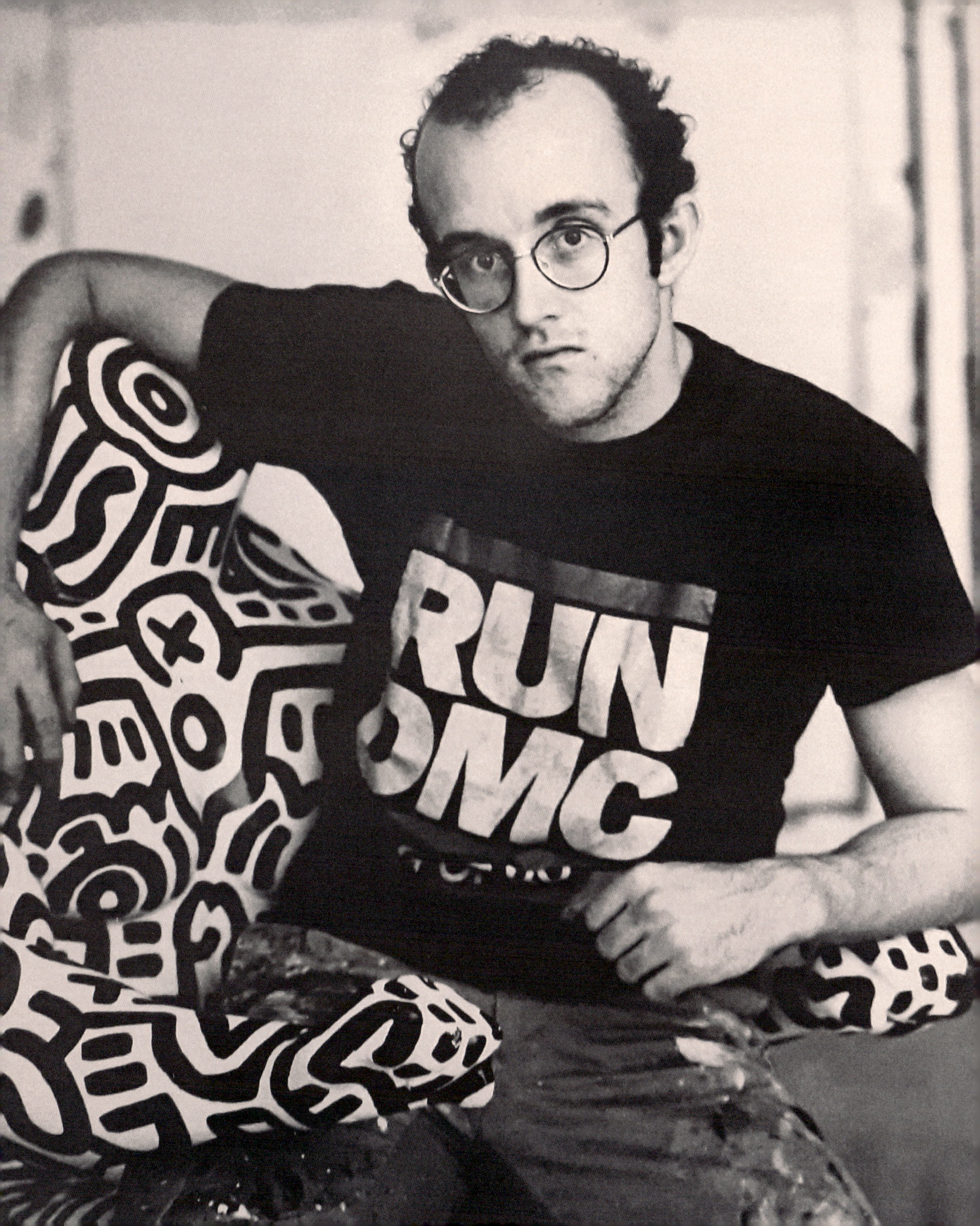
RUN
DMC

Joint Timeline

Compiled by Dieter Buchhart, Anna Karina Hofbauer & Anke Wiedmann

1979 Haring and Basquiat are introduced through Kenny Scharf, a mutual friend.

Around May, Haring performs a eulogy for SAMO© at Club 57, after reading 'SAMO© is dead'.

Haring and Basquiat participate in the *Club 57 Invitational* exhibition at Club 57, organised by Haring.

In June, both artists exhibit works at the *Times Square Show* at 41st Street and 7th Avenue, organised by Colab (Collaborative Projects, Inc.) and Fashion Moda.

1981 From February to April, Haring and Basquiat show works at the *New York/New Wave* exhibition curated by Diego Cortez at P.S. 1 Contemporary Art Center in Queens. Shortly after the opening of *New York/New Wave*, Haring curates the group exhibition *Lower Manhattan Drawing Show* at the Mudd Club, which includes works by Basquiat and Haring.

In April, both artists present works at the *Beyond Words: Graffiti-Based-Rooted-Inspired Works* exhibition held at the Mudd Club, curated by Fab 5 Freddy and Futura 2000, at Haring's invitation.

From October to November, works by Haring and Basquiat are included in the group show *Public Address* at Annina Nosei Gallery, Manhattan.

1982 Basquiat's first solo show at Annina Nosei Gallery opens in March, with Haring helping Basquiat to stretch the canvases on opening night.

In June and July, both artists exhibit in the group show *The Pressure to Paint*, curated by Diego Cortez for Marlborough Gallery, in the group show *Drawings* at Blum Helman Gallery, and in the group show *Fast* at Alexander Milliken Gallery, all in New York.

From June to September, works by Haring and Basquiat are included in the *documenta 7* exhibition in Kassel, Germany.

Through October and November, Haring and Basquiat participate in the exhibition *The Raw Edge: From Penn to Punk*, held at the Cheltenham Center for the Arts, Cheltenham, Pennsylvania, curated by John Laub and Judith Lieb.

Running from October to December, the exhibition *Still Modern After All These Years*, held at the Chrysler Museum, Norfolk, Virginia, includes works by both artists.

Both artists exhibit at *The Crucifix Show* held at Barbara Gladstone Gallery, New York, from December 1982 to January 1983.

1983 In January, the group exhibition *Champions* at Tony Shafrazi Gallery, New York, includes works by Haring and Basquiat.

In March, both artists exhibit in the *Whitney Biennial* at the Whitney Museum of American Art, New York.

Works by Haring and Basquiat are included in *Back to the USA*, held at Kunstmuseum Luzern, Switzerland, between May and July.

In October, Haring travels to Milan to exhibit in a group show in the Salvatore Ala Gallery, organised by Tony Shafrazi. Basquiat is visiting the city at the same time, having travelled there with Andy Warhol. Haring and Basquiat travel to Madrid together.

In December, Haring and Basquiat participate in the *Post-Graffiti Artists* show held at Sidney Janis Gallery, Manhattan, New York.

1984 Haring and Basquiat participate in ART/new york's *Graffiti/Post Graffiti* video, taped at Sidney Janis, Fashion Moda, the Fun Gallery and Tony Shafrazi Gallery.

Works by both artists are included in the *Private Eye* exhibition at the Neuberger Museum of Art, Harrison, New York, which runs from April to June.

In May, Basquiat attends Haring's Party of Life birthday celebration at the Paradise Garage club in New York and both artists participate in the Aldrich Museum of Contemporary Art, Connecticut, exhibition *American Neo-Expressionists*, which runs until September.

The show *Via New York* at the Musée d'art contemporain de Montréal, which runs from May to June, includes works by both artists.

In July–August, works by Haring and Basquiat are presented in the exhibition *Arte di Frontiera: New York Graffiti* at the Galleria d'Arte Moderna in Bologna, Italy.

Haring and Basquiat meet backstage at The Jacksons' Victory Tour in August and both attend Sean Lennon's ninth birthday party, together with Andy Warhol, in October.

In October–December, the works of both artists are included in the exhibition *The East Village Scene*, held at the Institute of Contemporary Art, Philadelphia, Pennsylvania.

Between October 1984 and January 1985, Haring and Basquiat participate in *Content: A Contemporary Focus, 1975–1984* at the Hirshhorn Museum and Sculpture Garden, Smithsonian Institute, Washington DC.

From December 1984 to February 1985, the Museé d'Art Moderne de la Ville de Paris stages *5/5: Figuration Libre France/USA*, which includes works by Haring and Basquiat.

1985 Haring and Basquiat appear separately on MTV: Basquiat participates in the pioneering series *Art Breaks* and Haring paints the studio set during an appearance by Nick Rhodes and Simon Le Bon of pop group Duran Duran.

In January, Haring organises the exhibition *Rain Dance* to benefit the UNICEF Africa Emergency Relief Fund. The exhibition is shown in February at 292 Lafayette Street, which will turn into the Pop Shop one year later. He invites Basquiat to design the poster, along with Roy Lichtenstein, Yoko Ono and Andy Warhol.

Running from March to May, the *XIII Biennale de Paris* includes works by both artists.

In May, Haring and Basquiat, along with Francesco Clemente and Kenny Scharf, are invited to paint murals at the Palladium club in New York where Basquiat attends Keith Haring's birthday party.

In June, the artists meet at the afterparty for Madonna's Virgin Tour concert at Radio City Music Hall, New York.

In September, Haring attends the afterparty of the *Warhol/Basquiat* exhibition at the Tony Shafrazi Gallery.

Works by both artists are included in the exhibition *Vom Zeichnen: Aspekte der Zeichnung 1960–1985*, staged at the Frankfurter Kunstverein and running between November 1985 and January 1986. The exhibition then travels to the Kasseler Kunstverein and the Museum Moderner Kunst in Vienna (now known as Museum Moderner Kunst Stiftung Ludwig).

1986 From January to March, the group show *An American Renaissance: Painting and Sculpture Since 1940* at the Fort Lauderdale Museum of Art, Florida, presents works by Haring and Basquiat.

Between May and July, both artists participate in *Sacred Images in Secular Art* at the Whitney Museum of American Art in New York. Haring's *Untitled* is featured on the cover of the exhibition brochure.

In June, Haring and Basquiat attend a dinner with musicians Grace Jones and Fela Kuti in New York.

In October, Haring and Basquiat contribute customised denim jackets to the AIDS Benefit Auction initiated by Barney's New York as a fundraiser for the St Vincent's AIDS clinic. The jackets are modelled by Iman – wearing Haring's design – as well as Madonna, Debbie Harry, Andie MacDowell and Susan Sarandon, among others.

Between October 1986 and February 1987, the Art Museum Association of America organises the travelling exhibition *Focus on the Image: Selections from the Rivendell Collection*, which includes works by both artists. The show travels to seven regional or university museums across the USA.

1987 Between April and July, Haring and Basquiat's works are included in the exhibition *Avant-Garde in the Eighties* at the Los Angeles County Museum of Art.

From June to August, Haring and Basquiat participate in Austrian artist André Heller's artist theme park project *Luna Luna* in Hamburg, Germany.

1988 In March, Haring and Basquiat contribute painted backdrops and costumes to the Body and Soul dance festival at the Deutsches Theater in Munich, Germany.

In June or July, Haring meets Basquiat by chance on Broadway and takes a photo of him for an article he is writing about street fashion for *Spin* magazine. The photo is published in the September 1988 issue. It is the last time the two see each other.

On 12 August, Basquiat dies. Haring attends Basquiat's funeral and paints *A Pile of Crowns for Jean-Michel Basquiat* the same month.

In November, Haring's eulogy, 'Remembering Basquiat: Keith Haring on a fellow artist – and a friend', is published in *Vogue* magazine.

1990 On 16 February, Haring dies.

In December, Tony Shafrazi Gallery hosts the memorial exhibition *Keith Haring and Jean-Michel Basquiat: Paintings*.

Map: Downtown, New York City

Dieter Buchhart, Anna Karina Hofbauer & Anke Wiedmann

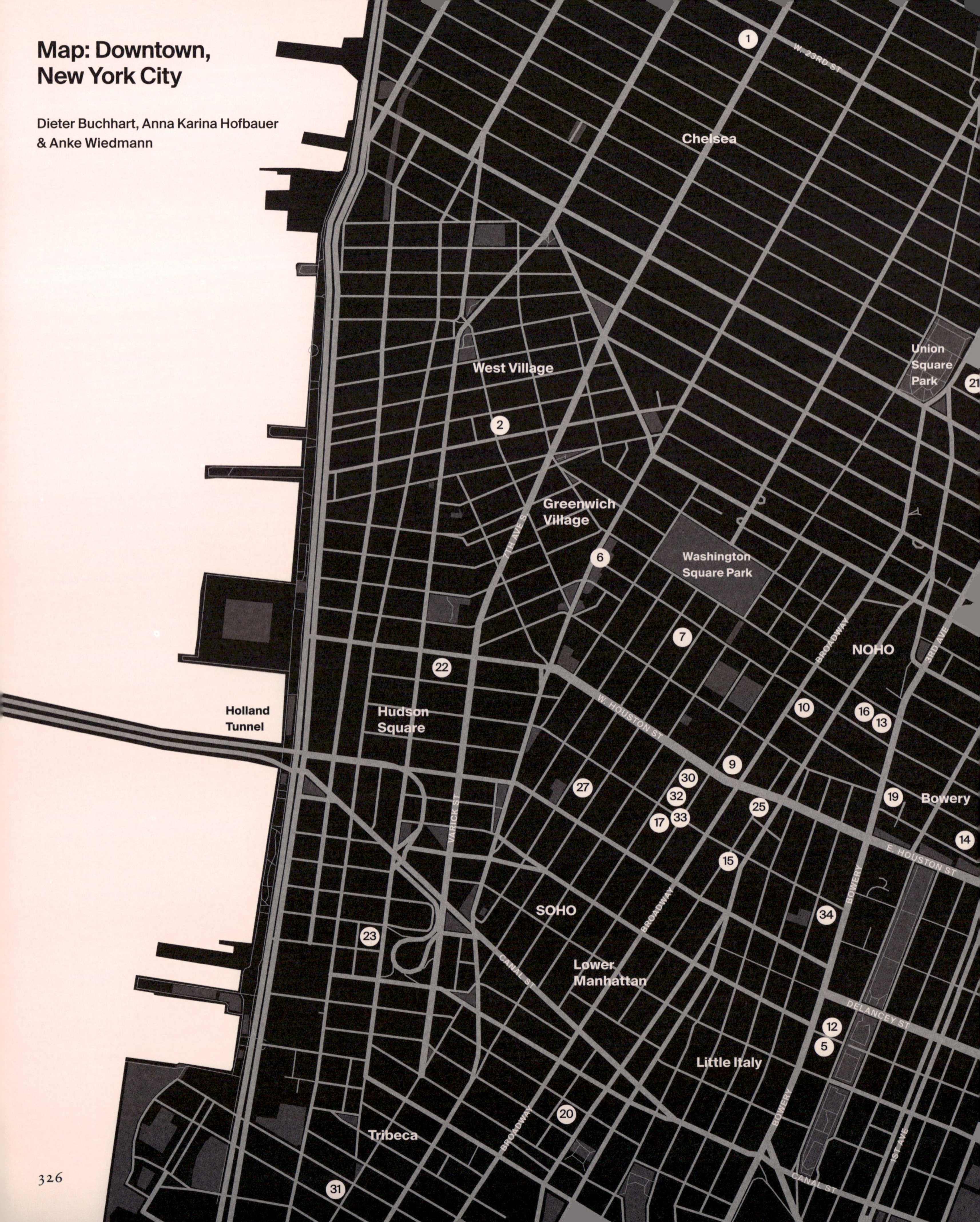

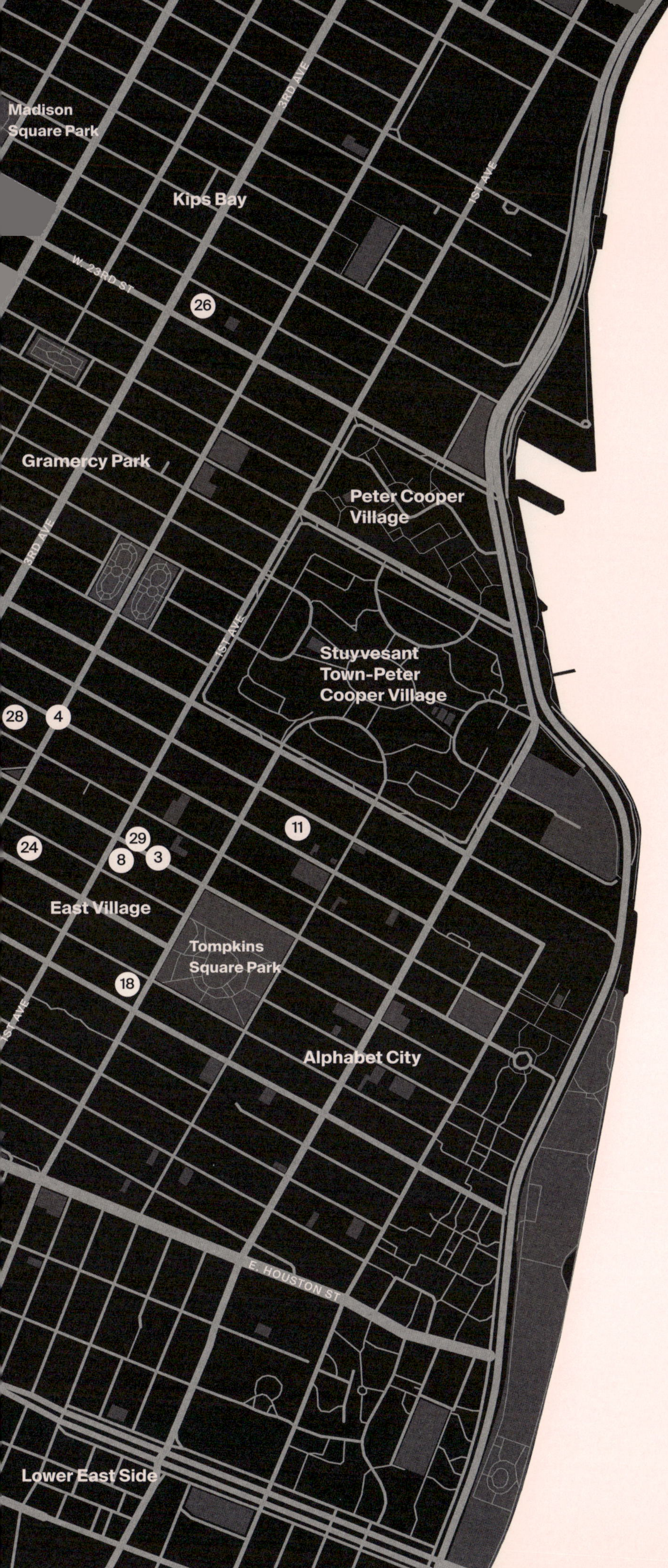

Keith Haring

1 1978 McBurney YMCA: 23rd St between 7th and 8th Ave
2 1978 Haring's apartment: 10th St and Bleecker St
3 1979 Haring's apartment, shared with Drew Straub: 10th St between 1st Ave and Avenue A
4 Summer 1980 Haring's apartment: 2nd Ave and 12th St
5 1981 – mid 1985 Haring's apartment, shared with Juan Dubose and Samantha McEwen: 325 Broome St
6 Mid 1985 – mid 1989 Haring's apartment, shared with Juan Rivera: 6th Ave and 3rd St
7 1989 – until his death Haring's apartment: 542 LaGuardia Place
8 October–November 1980 Artist residency at PS122, 150 1st Ave
5 1981 Haring's studio: 325 Broome St
9 Mid 1984 Haring's studio: 611 Broadway
10 Mid 1985 Haring's studio: 676 Broadway

Jean-Michel Basquiat

11 1979 Alexis Adler and Basquiat's apartment: 527 E. 12th St
12 1980 Stays with Arleen Schloss: 330 Broome St
13 End of 1980 Basquiat's apartment and studio: 54 Great Jones St
14 1981 – January 1982 Basquiat's apartment, shared with Suzanne Mallouk: 68 E. 1st St
15 January 1982 Basquiat's apartment and studio, shared with Suzanne Mallouk: 101 Crosby St
16 Mid 1983 Basquiat's apartment and studio: 57 Great Jones St
13 End of 1980 Basquiat's apartment and studio: 54 Great Jones St
17 c. October 1981 – January 1982 Basquiat's studio at Annina Nosei Gallery: 100 Prince St
15 January 1982 Basquiat's apartment and studio, shared with Suzanne Mallouk: 101 Crosby St
16 Mid 1983 Basquiat's apartment and studio: 57 Great Jones St

Clubs and off spaces

12 Wednesdays at A's (apartment of Arleen Schloss): 330 Broome St
18 Pyramid Club: 101 Avenue A
19 CBGB: 315 Bowery
20 Mudd Club: 77 White St
21 The Palladium: East 14th St between 3rd Ave and Irving Place
22 Paradise Garage: 84 King St
23 Area: 157 Hudson St
24 Club 57: 57 St Marks Place
25 Pop Shop: 292 Lafayette St

Schools, galleries and museums

26 School of Visual Arts: 209 E. 23rd St
27 Mary Boone Gallery: 420 W. Broadway
17 Annina Nosei Gallery: 100 Prince St
28 Fun Gallery (1981 – mid 1982): 225 E. 11th St
29 Fun Gallery (mid 1982 – 1985): 254 E. 10th St
30 Tony Shafrazi Gallery (as of 1981): 163 Mercer St
31 Hal Bromm Gallery: 90 W. Broadway
9 Vrej Baghoomian, Inc.: 611 Broadway
32 Leo Castelli Gallery: 142 Greene St
33 Alexander Milliken Gallery: 96–98 Prince St

Miscellaneous

34 William S. Burroughs's apartment (1974–81): 222 Bowery

Artist Chronologies

Keith Haring

This chronology is derived from various sources, notably the reworked 2018 chronology by Giorgio Verzotti in collaboration with Dieter Buchhart and Julia Gruen. Edited by Anna Karina Hofbauer and Anke Wiedmann

1958 Keith Haring is born on 4 May 1958 in Reading, Pennsylvania, and grows up in neighbouring Kutztown. He is the eldest of four children.

1976 Haring follows his parents' advice and enrols at the Ivy School of Professional Art in Pittsburgh, but drops out after one year to pursue independent art studies.

1978 Haring attends the School of Visual Arts (SVA) in New York, where his teachers include Simone Forti, Keith Sonnier, Joseph Kosuth and Bill Beckley. He develops performances, makes videos and creates large-scale drawings.

1979–81 After attending the SVA, Haring devotes himself to various forms of street art. He pastes photocopies of collages and draws on billboards and other surfaces in public space. He promotes events and organises exhibitions at venues such as Club 57, PS122 and the Mudd Club. These activities and works demonstrate his early sociopolitical awareness.

In June 1980, Haring participates in the *Times Square Show* exhibition.

He creates his first drawings in the New York subway in December 1980, using white chalk to draw on the black paper that covers expired ad hoardings.

In 1981, he begins working with unconventional picture supports: found objects, leather, metal and vinyl tarpaulins.

In August, he receives his first public commission: together with artists including Lady Pink, Futura 2000 and Crash, he paints a mural at PS122.

1982 The New York City Public Art Fund commissions Haring and eleven other artists to create works for a Spectacolor billboard in Times Square.

In April, he contributes drawings to Muna Tseng's *Epochal Songs*, performed at the Riverside Dance Festival. He is also invited to participate in the *documenta 7* exhibition in Kassel, Germany.

On 12 June, at the anti-nuclear rally in Central Park, Haring distributes 20,000 posters he printed in support of the event.

In July, he paints a wall at the corner of Houston Street and the Bowery, which includes dancing figures that recur frequently in his work and specifically reference breakdancing moves.

In October, Haring has his first important solo exhibition at Tony Shafrazi Gallery. His works cover every surface of the gallery. He creates a black light installation and, working with graffiti artist LA II (Angel Ortiz), designs various objects.

1983 Haring participates in the *Whitney Biennial* and his public commissions increase. In February, after the opening of his show at the Fun Gallery, he is invited by Marquette University in Milwaukee, Wisconsin, to paint on a long, white construction fence, behind which the new Haggerty Museum of Art is being built.

Shortly afterwards, he has a solo exhibition at the Watari Gallery in Tokyo and, together with LA II, creates a large mural on a facade opposite the gallery.

In May, he has an exhibition at the Galleria Lucio Amelio in Naples.

He designs the poster for the seventeenth Montreux Jazz Festival, which takes place in July, and executes large drawings during the various concerts. In 1986, he would collaborate with Andy Warhol on the festival poster design.

In October, designer Elio Fiorucci invites Haring and LA II to Milan to decorate the Fiorucci boutique behind the Piazza del Duomo.

Shortly afterwards, Haring travels to London for a solo show at the Robert Fraser Gallery.

Haring collaborates with Vivienne Westwood and Malcolm McLaren on their autumn-winter 1983–84 fashion collection.

1984 Haring participates in the Venice Biennale.

The artist visits Australia between 8 February and 8 March 1984. The National Gallery of Victoria commissions Haring to execute a mural on the Gallery's Waterwall. Haring also creates a permanent mural at the Collingwood Technical College. While in Melbourne, he is asked to contribute to a fashion parade organised by the Fashion Design Council of Australia, for the Moomba Festival. At the invitation of the Art Gallery of New South Wales in Sydney, Haring paints a giant black-on-white mural near the gallery entrance that includes the depiction of a kangaroo. While in Sydney, Haring attends the annual Gay and Lesbian Mardi Gras parade and is photographed by William Yang in front of a float covered in Haring-inspired imagery, alongside David McDiarmid and other Australian creatives.

In May, he organises the First Annual Party of Life at the Paradise Garage club in New York to celebrate his birthday. His friend Madonna wears a leather suit he designed and performs songs from her album *Like a Virgin*.

Haring creates a logo for the New York City Department of Sanitation's anti-litter campaign. At the kick-off in the summer, Haring is publicly thanked by New York mayor Ed Koch, who, ironically, had been a leading advocate of the city's campaign against graffiti.

In October, Haring creates a mural next to the FDR Drive, New York, depicting a large black figure who kicks a much smaller white one that is leading him on a leash. The image will be used for the 1985 anti-apartheid campaign Free South Africa.

The next month, Haring designs the stage set and costumes for the production of Bill T. Jones and Arnie Zane's *Secret Pastures* at the Brooklyn Academy of Music.

While visiting Paris in December for the group exhibition *5/5: Figuration Libre France/USA* at the Musée d'Art Moderne de la Ville de Paris, he draws on advertising spaces in two metro stations.

Afterwards, he travels to Marseille to design the sets for *Le Mariage du Ciel et de l'Enfer*, by Roland Petit, for the Ballet National de Marseille, based on the poem of the same name by William Blake.

1985 In February, Haring curates the exhibition *Rain Dance* for the United States African Relief Fund for UNICEF and organises a benefit party at the Paradise Garage.

The same month, he creates the set design for the Brooklyn Academy of Music production of the ballet *Sweet Saturday Night*.

In May, Haring creates a permanent installation inside the club Palladium – a large backdrop on canvas in fluorescent colours reminiscent of a large puzzle.

Haring's love of music motivates him to do more live paintings during concerts, for example at Live Aid on 13 July in Philadelphia, a concert benefiting famine relief in Africa; performers include Tina Turner and Mick Jagger, among others. In November, while Duran Duran's Nick Rhodes and Simon Le Bon are guest VJs on MTV, Haring paints the set.

In August, he creates a mural at P.S. 97 with a giant ghetto-blaster, surrounded by flying monsters and dancing figures typical of his work.

Together with Grace Jones, Haring develops the concert *Her Grace at Paradise*, performed in October at the Paradise Garage. For the show, Haring paints the pop star's body, who is dressed only in chains, headgear and chest coverings made of metal by David Spada. Later, she wears a skirt made of black and white tubing and a headdress, both constructed with Haring's figures, which were created in 1984, when Warhol asked Haring to body-paint Jones for a photo shoot by Robert Mapplethorpe.

Later that month, Haring opens concurrent shows at the Tony Shafrazi and Leo Castelli galleries. His first solo show in a museum opens in December at the CAPC Musée d'Art Contemporain de Bordeaux and travels on to the Stedelijk Museum in Amsterdam.

1986 Haring and Grace Jones collaborate again, this time on the music video for the song 'I'm Not Perfect (But I'm Perfect for You)'. Haring creates an enormous white skirt with an abstract pattern, while David Spada contributes a bodice and an elaborate headpiece.

In April, Haring opens the Pop Shop on Lafayette Street in Manhattan, where he sells a range of articles and clothes emblazoned with his own imagery, as well as selected works by other artists.

In May, he is invited to Austria to the multidisciplinary art festival Wiener Festwochen, where he collaborates with Jenny Holzer on a poster featuring the words 'protect me from what I want'.

The following month, he creates a 'Crack Is Wack' mural on Harlem River Drive at East 128th Street. Since the mural was created illegally, Haring is fined and must paint over it. In October, he will return to repaint the mural with permission.

In July, he collaborates with the youth organisation CityKids to mark the centenary of the Statue of Liberty. Together with some 1000 young people, he creates an image of the statue on a giant banner.

In August, Haring realises a mural on two levels in the lobby of Brooklyn's Woodhull Hospital.

In October, the Mauermuseum – Museum Haus am Checkpoint Charlie in Berlin invites him to execute a mural on the Berlin Wall. The artist paints over 100 metres of the wall with a human chain in red and black on a yellow background, Germany's national colours. Later in the month, he again collaborates with CityKids, accompanying American schoolchildren to Milan, where his banner CityKids Speak on Liberty is exhibited in the Rotonda della Besana.

1987 In April, Haring designs the set for *Interrupted River*, a dance piece by Jennifer Muller with music by Yoko Ono. The same month, he creates a mural for the paediatric Hôpital Necker-Enfants Malades in Paris.

In May, Haring designs two walls and a carousel for André Heller's contemporary art amusement park *Luna Luna* in Hamburg, which also includes the work of such artists as Jean-Michel Basquiat, Joseph Beuys, Salvador Dalí, David Hockney, Roy Lichtenstein, Sonia Delaunay and Jean Tinguely. Haring's first official commission for a sculpture is installed outside Schneider Children's Hospital in New York.

In June, Haring creates a mural in the cafeteria of the Museum van Hedendaagse Kunst in Antwerp and in September a mural in the Boys' Club of New York on Pitt Street, Lower East Side.

In September, he designs a mural for the Cranbrook Academy of Art in Bloomfield Hills, Michigan, which demonstrates a new style. The entire surface is treated with irregular blotches of colour and new subjects are introduced: jesters, misshapen human bodies, foetuses, masks, men hanged by their feet, skulls, buddhas and naked popes.

Haring lends a design to A&M Records's *A Very Special Christmas* album; proceeds are donated to the Special Olympics.

1988 Haring learns that he is HIV-positive.

Early in 1988, he opens a Pop Shop in Tokyo. The shop interior is completely painted, like its New York counterpart. The shop closes within a year due to the massive increase in cheaper, counterfeit Haring merchandise.

In March, Haring designs the costumes and stage set for the ballet *Tribal Dance*, performed at the Body and Soul dance festival at the Deutsches Theater in Munich. The Public Library Association of New York, with the support of Fox Broadcasting's Channel 5, commissions Haring to design a poster for its literacy campaign. Haring's design for the slogan is 'Fill your head with fun! Start reading!'

For Easter, Haring installs the Creative Keith Haring Fun Center in the garden of the White House. He paints a mural in front of the visitors, which is then donated to the Children's National Medical Center in Washington DC. The Grady Hospital in Atlanta, Georgia, also receives a mural by Haring.

In May, in Phoenix, Arizona, he designs a mural between Washington Street and Adams Street in collaboration with schoolchildren, who colour in his large figure outlines.

In July, Haring revisits P.S. 97 in New York, painting a mural with the phrases 'Don't belieeeve the hype', 'Safe sex or no sex!', 'Respect yourself' and 'Knowledge'.

In October, Haring designs the poster for National Coming Out Day.

1989 In February, Haring paints a mural in the Barrio Chino in Barcelona, with the phrase 'Todos juntos podemos parar el SIDA' ('Together we can stop AIDS'). For the AIDS activist group ACT UP, Haring creates a poster with the familiar phrase 'See no evil, hear no evil, speak no evil'. Above and below the figures, the words 'IGNORANCE = FEAR' and 'SILENCE = DEATH. FIGHT AIDS. ACT UP' are written.

In May, the Museum of Contemporary Art Chicago and the Chicago public schools invite Haring to paint a 150-metre fence together with students. The local television station broadcasts a short documentary on the project, *Off the Wall with Keith and the Kids*, narrated by Dennis Hopper. His week in Chicago is declared Keith Haring Week by mayor Richard M. Daley and Haring creates additional murals at Wells High School and at the Rush-Presbyterian-St Luke's Medical Center. His mural commemorating the twentieth anniversary of the Stonewall riots at The Center (now known as the Lesbian, Gay, Bisexual & Transgender Community Center) in Greenwich Village is likewise completed in May.

In June, the artist is invited to Pisa to create a mural for the church of St Anthony. He covers the entire surface with large complex figures, which the numerous spectators are then allowed to paint. The same month, he and Russian artist Erik Bulatov are invited by the City of Paris to create two large canvases, which are to be mounted to the sides of a zeppelin that will fly above the city as part of the celebrations marking the bicentenary of the French Revolution. For technical reasons, the zeppelin only flies from London, where it was built, to Calais.

In July, the New York City Department of Health commissions the artist to design a poster promoting the city's AIDS hotline.

In August, Princess Caroline of Monaco invites Haring to create a mural in the maternity unit at the Princess Grace Hospital Centre in Monte Carlo. Subsequently, she awards Haring with the honorary title of Chevalier de l'Ordre du Mérite Culturel de la Principauté de Monaco. He is the first American to receive this honour and, at the age of thirty-one, also its youngest recipient.

In November, Haring establishes a foundation to ensure the continuation of his philanthropic work after his death. He appoints as its director his friend and manager of many years, Julia Gruen. The Keith Haring Foundation supports organisations devoted to charitable and educational projects, in particular those that create opportunities for disadvantaged children and/or engage in AIDS and HIV-related education, prevention and care. Haring also charges the foundation with continuing, promoting and protecting his artistic legacy.

In December, Haring creates a mural at the ArtCenter College of Design, Pasadena, on the occasion of the World Health Organization's World AIDS Day.

1990 On 16 February, at the age of thirty-one, Haring dies of AIDS-related complications.

On 16 March, his final work is unveiled – an envelope design commissioned by the World Federation of United Nations Associations, drawing attention to the organisation's efforts to fight AIDS.

On what would have been his thirty-second birthday, a memorial service for Haring is held in the Cathedral of St John the Divine in Manhattan, with more than 1000 people in attendance.

In September, *Future Primeval*, a solo Haring exhibition, premieres at the Queens Museum, New York City, before travelling to two other museums in the United States.

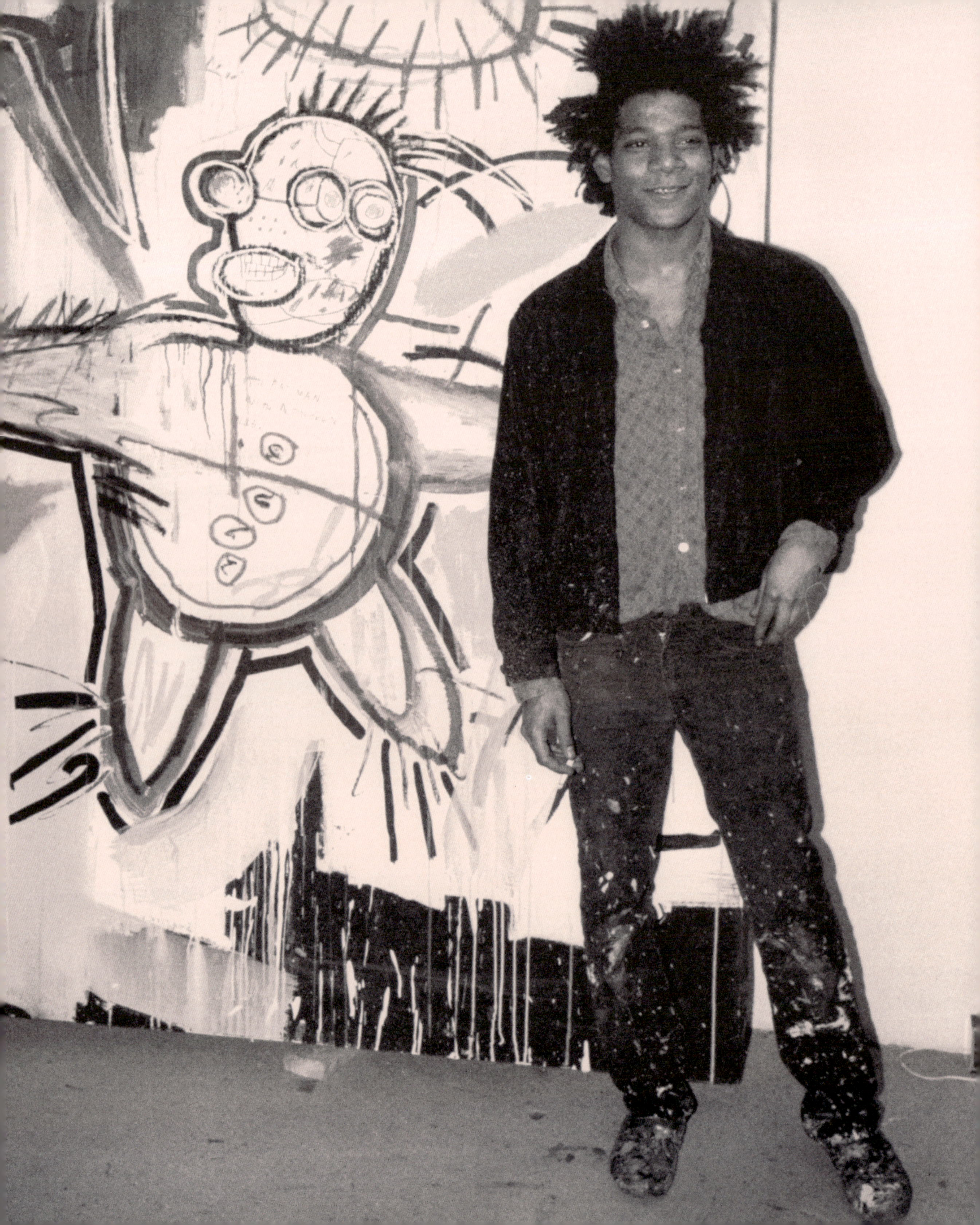

Jean-Michel Basquiat

This chronology is derived from various sources, notably the 1992 chronology by Franklin Sirmans. Compiled by Anna Karina Hofbauer.

1960 Jean-Michel Basquiat is born on 22 December 1960 in Brooklyn, New York. His father, Gérard Basquiat, is Haitian and his mother, Matilde Andrades, was born to Puerto Rican parents. The Basquiats live in Park Slope, Brooklyn.

1964 Basquiat's sister Lisane is born.

1965 Basquiat and his mother often visit the Brooklyn Museum, The Museum of Modern Art and The Metropolitan Museum of Art. His mother continually encourages his interest in art and underlines its importance. Basquiat attends kindergarten at a Head Start school. (Head Start is an early childhood education, health and nutrition program for low-income communities.)

1967 Basquiat's sister Jeanine is born. Basquiat attends Saint Ann's, a private Catholic school in Brooklyn.

1968 Basquiat makes cartoon-like drawings inspired by cars, comic books, Alfred Hitchcock films and the Alfred E. Neuman character from *Mad* magazine.

In May, he is hit by a car while playing ball in the street; Basquiat breaks an arm, suffers various internal injuries and has his spleen removed. He stays at King's County Hospital, Brooklyn, for a month. During his recovery, his mother gives him a copy of *Gray's Anatomy*, which leaves lasting impressions and influences his later work in anatomical drawings and prints.

Gérard and Matilde Basquiat separate; Basquiat and his sisters live with their father.

1974 Following a promotion, Gérard Basquiat and his children move to San Juan, Puerto Rico. Basquiat attends an Episcopalian school.

1976–77 The Basquiat family returns to their townhouse in Boerum Hill, Brooklyn, and Basquiat continues his studies at Edward R. Murrow High School. A few weeks later, he relocates to City-As-School High School, where the focus is on experiential learning through practical knowledge. At City-As-School, he meets Al Diaz, a graffiti artist. Basquiat develops the fictional character called SAMO© and he collaborates with Diaz under this pseudonym.

1978 In June, only one year away from graduation, Basquiat leaves high school and his father's home forever. He stays with friends, frequently at the Canal Street loft of British artist Stan Peskett. He is introduced to Fred Brathwaite (Fab 5 Freddy) and actor Danny Rosen.

1979 Basquiat and Diaz end their collaboration as SAMO©, and 'SAMO© is dead' appears spray-painted on walls in Soho. Basquiat begins to sell handpainted postcards, in collaboration with Jennifer Stein and sometimes John Sex.

In May, Basquiat, along with Shannon Dawson, Vincent Gallo and Michael Holman, forms the band Channel 9, later renamed Gray. Basquiat plays clarinet and synthesisers.

In the autumn, while strolling around the School of Visual Arts, Basquiat meets Keith Haring and Kenny Scharf. Basquiat and Haring become close friends.

1980 In June, Basquiat shows his work publicly for the first time in the *Times Square Show*, a group exhibition held in a vacant building in Times Square.

Jean-Michel Basquiat in his studio at the Annina Nosei Gallery, May 1982

Writer Glenn O'Brien selects Basquiat to play the lead role in the film *New York Beat* (eventually released in 2000 as *Downtown 81*). The film is loosely based on Basquiat and the downtown art scene surrounding him.

1981 From February to April, Basquiat is part of the *New York/New Wave* exhibition organised by Diego Cortez at P.S. 1 Contemporary Art Center in Long Island City.

In April, Basquiat as SAMO© is shown in the group exhibition *Beyond Words: Graffiti Based-Rooted-Inspired Works*, organised by Fab 5 Freddy and Futura 2000 at the Mudd Club, New York.

In May, Basquiat travels to Europe for the first time for his first solo show. It is staged at Galleria Mazzoli, Modena, Italy. Here, too, the works are shown under the name SAMO©.

In September, Annina Nosei invites Basquiat to participate in the November group show *Public Address* at her gallery in New York. Several weeks before the opening, she offers him the basement of her gallery as a studio. Following the exhibition, where the entire rear gallery is reserved for Basquiat's work, Nosei becomes Basquiat's dealer.

In December, the first extensive article on Basquiat, 'The radiant child' by Rene Ricard, is published in *Artforum*.

1982 In January, Basquiat moves with Suzanne Mallouk to 151 Crosby Street in Soho.

In March, he has his first solo show in the US, at the Annina Nosei Gallery, New York. He participates in the group exhibition *Transavanguardia: Italia/America* at the Galleria Civica del Comune, Modena.

In April, his second solo show is held at the Larry Gagosian Gallery in Los Angeles.

In May, Basquiat leaves the Annina Nosei Gallery. In late spring, Bruno Bischofberger becomes his main gallerist, without the two having met in person, and they agree that he will be his worldwide exclusive art dealer, an agreement that will last until Basquiat's death.

In June, *documenta 7* takes place in Kassel, Germany; Basquiat is the youngest of the 176 artists exhibiting.

In September, Basquiat has the first of six solo exhibitions during his lifetime at Galerie Bruno Bischofberger, Zurich.

On 5 October, Bischofberger formally introduces Basquiat to Andy Warhol.

In November, Basquiat has a solo show at the Fun Gallery, New York, featuring around thirty works. Basquiat makes his first visit to Japan this year.

1983 In January, Basquiat is part of the group show *Champions* at the Tony Shafrazi Gallery, New York.

In February, the Annina Nosei Gallery organises a solo show with paintings from their stock, completed before May 1982.

In March, Basquiat has a solo show at Larry Gagosian Gallery in Los Angeles. Also in March, he participates in the *Whitney Biennial* at the Whitney Museum of American Art, New York, where he is the youngest artist included.

In June 1983, Basquiat travels to Japan, models for fashion designer Issey Miyake and is photographed by Yutaka Sakano. He goes on to model for Comme des Garçons in 1987.

In October, he has a one-man show at Galerie Bruno Bischofberger, Zurich. That same month, Basquiat is included in the exhibition *Expressive Painting after Picasso* at the Galerie Beyeler, Basel. His work is presented alongside that of artists such as Pablo Picasso, Joan Miró, Jean Dubuffet, Willem de Kooning and Francis Bacon. Basquiat's work features on the cover of the exhibition catalogue. Also in October, he is in the group show *Mary Boone and Her Artists* at the Seibu Museum of Art, Tokyo.

In November, Basquiat has his first exhibition in Japan at the Akira Ikeda Gallery, Tokyo, organised by Bruno Bischofberger.

In December, Bischofberger initiates a group of fifteen collaborative works between Andy Warhol, Francesco Clemente and Basquiat, and they begin work on them that month.

1984 In January, Basquiat leaves to set up a studio in Hana, Maui, Hawaii, to which he frequently returns.

In March, Basquiat participates in the group show *Painting Now* at Akira Ikeda Gallery in Nagoya and also takes part in its summer show in August at their Tokyo gallery.

In May, he has his first of two solo exhibitions at the Mary Boone/Michael Werner Gallery in New York in partnership with Galerie Bruno Bischofberger.

In August, he has his first solo museum exhibition at the Fruitmarket Gallery in Edinburgh. The exhibition travels to the Institute of Contemporary Arts, London, and the Museum Boijmans Van Beuningen in Rotterdam. Basquiat travels together with Bischofberger and his wife, Yoyo, to Scotland.

In September, the exhibition *Collaborations: Jean-Michel Basquiat, Francesco Clemente, Andy Warhol* is shown at Galerie Bruno Bischofberger, Zurich, featuring all fifteen collaborations by the three artists. Basquiat continues collaborating with Andy Warhol until mid 1985, together producing over 150 paintings. In October, Basquiat participates in the group show *Painting Now: The Restoration of Painterly Figuration* at Kitakyushu Municipal Museum of Art, Japan.

In December, he participates in the exhibition *5/5: Figuration Libre France/USA*, at the Musée d'Art Moderne de la Ville de Paris.

1985 In January, Basquiat's work is presented in a solo exhibition at Galerie Bruno Bischofberger, Zurich, and in *Collaborations: Jean-Michel Basquiat, Francesco Clemente, Andy Warhol* at the Akira Ikeda Gallery, Tokyo.

In February, he shows *Drawings* at the Akira Ikeda Gallery in Nagoya. On 10 February, Basquiat appears on the cover of *The New York Times Magazine* as part of Cathleen McGuigan's article 'New art, new money'.

In March, he has his second and last show at Mary Boone/Michael Werner Gallery in New York. Robert Farris Thompson writes an essay for the exhibition catalogue.
The Annina Nosei Gallery, New York, shows *Jean-Michel Basquiat: Paintings from 1982*.

In May, Basquiat is commissioned, through the recommendation of Henry Geldzahler, together with Francesco Clemente, Keith Haring and Kenny Scharf, to do art installations for Palladium, a new club on East 14th Street opened by Studio 54 founders Ian Schrager and Steve Rubell. For the opening of the Michael Todd Room at the club, Basquiat paints two huge, mural-size paintings.

Galerie Bruno Bischofberger publishes the catalogue *Jean-Michel Basquiat: Drawings* featuring thirty-two works made in winter 1982–83, which are later called the *Daros Suite*.

In September, the exhibition *Andy Warhol and Jean-Michel Basquiat: Paintings* at the Tony Shafrazi Gallery shows sixteen collaborative works. At Shafrazi's suggestion, the two artists pose together in boxing trunks and gloves for a poster advertising the show.

In November, Basquiat travels to Tokyo to prepare for a December solo show, *Paintings*, at Akira Ikeda Gallery, Tokyo. During this trip, he visits the legendary Cay restaurant in Aoyama, Tokyo, leaving behind a drawing on the wall, like Roy Lichtenstein and Keith Haring before him.

1986 In January, Basquiat returns to Los Angeles for what is to be his last show at the Larry Gagosian Gallery.

In March, he participates in the group exhibition *Naivety in Art* at Setagaya Art Museum in Tokyo, which travels to the Tochigi Prefectural Museum of Fine Arts in Tochigi.

In April, the artist has a solo exhibition at Galerie Bruno Bischofberger, Zurich, with a selection of twenty-five drawings from 1984 to 1986.

In August, *Jean-Michel Basquiat: Bilder 1984–86* is shown at Galerie Thaddaeus Ropac, Salzburg, and in September, a group of collaborations by Basquiat and Warhol are shown at the Akira Ikeda Gallery, Tokyo, both organised by Bruno Bischofberger.

In autumn, Basquiat undertakes his only trip to Africa, accompanied by Jennifer Goode and her brother Eric. They are joined by Yoyo and Bruno Bischofberger. Bruno, at Basquiat's request, has organised an exhibition in Abidjan, Ivory Coast, titled *Jean-Michel Basquiat*, at the Centre Culturel Français. Afterwards, Basquiat, Bruno, Yoyo, Jennifer and Eric fly to Korhogo in the north of the country to meet people from the Senufo tribe.

In November, *Jean-Michel Basquiat: Drawings* opens at the Akira Ikeda Gallery, Tokyo, and a second museum show opens at the Kestner-Gesellschaft in Hanover. The show includes more than sixty paintings and drawings. At age twenty-five, Basquiat is the youngest artist ever to be given an exhibition there.

In December, he is part of the group show *Drawings* at Akira Ikeda Gallery in Nagoya. Bischofberger shows ten collaborative works by Basquiat and Warhol.

1987 In January, the exhibition *Jean-Michel Basquiat: Oeuvres récentes* is shown at Galerie Daniel Templon, Paris. In February, *Jean-Michel Basquiat: New Works*, organised by Bischofberger, is shown at Akira Ikeda Gallery, Tokyo.

On 22 February, Andy Warhol dies, at the age of fifty-eight, from complications during gall bladder surgery at New York Hospital. Basquiat paints *Gravestone*, 1987, in homage to his friend.

In May, *Jean-Michel Basquiat: Drawings* shows at the Tony Shafrazi Gallery, New York.

In June, a selection of drawings is shown at Galerie Thaddaeus Ropac, Salzburg.

In September, the group exhibition *Relief & Sculpture* is shown at the Akira Ikeda Gallery, Nagoya, and in October, a solo show, *Jean-Michel Basquiat*, opens at the PS Gallery, Tokyo.

1988 In January, Basquiat has solo shows at the Galerie Yvon Lambert, Paris, and Galerie Hans Mayer, Düsseldorf, and, in April, at the Vrej Baghoomian Gallery, New York.

In May, Basquiat travels to Maui, Hawaii, to attempt to treat his drug addiction.

The last exhibition in his lifetime, *Jean-Michel Basquiat: Paintings, Drawings*, is held at the Galerie Thaddaeus Ropac, Salzburg, in June and July.

In June, he returns to New York.

On Friday 12 August 1988, Basquiat dies at his Great Jones Street loft at age twenty-seven. Basquiat's private funeral is held on 17 August at the Frank E. Campbell Funeral Chapel on Madison Avenue and 81st Street, attended only by immediate family and close friends. He is buried at Green-Wood Cemetery, Brooklyn. On 5 November, a memorial gathering is held at St Peter's Church on Lexington Avenue and 54th Street, attended by around 300 of Basquiat's friends and admirers.

List of Works

Note to the reader
This list refers to works exhibited in the National Gallery of Victoria exhibition *Keith Haring | Jean-Michel Basquiat: Crossing Lines* (1 December 2019 – 13 April 2020). This list of works is arranged chronologically by artist. Works produced in the same year are listed alphabetically by title. All measurements are in centimetres to the first decimal point, height (x) width for two-dimensional objects, height (x) width (x) depth or height (x) diameter for three-dimensional objects. Numbers in brackets at the conclusion of the caption indicate page on which the work is illustrated.

Keith Haring
American 1958–1990

Untitled c. 1980
spray-paint and ink on paper
123.2 x 154.9 cm
Collection of Larry Warsh
(p. 186)

Lick Fat Boys 1980
black and white video, sound, 3 min
The Keith Haring Foundation, New York

Mob Flees at Pope Rally 1980
newspaper collage
21.6 x 27.9 cm
The Keith Haring Foundation, New York
(p. 47)

Ready to Kill 1980
newspaper collage
21.6 x 27.9 cm
The Keith Haring Foundation, New York
(p. 46)

Reagan Son $50G Sex 1980
newspaper collage
21.6 x 27.9 cm
The Keith Haring Foundation, New York
(p. 46)

Ronald Reagan Accused of TV Star Sex Death 1980
newspaper collage
21.6 x 27.9 cm
The Keith Haring Foundation, New York
(p. 47)

Untitled 1980
sumi ink, spray enamel and synthetic polymer paint on poster board
161.3 x 121.9 cm
The Keith Haring Foundation, New York
(p. 187)

Untitled 1980
sumi ink and spray-paint on paper
66.0 x 102.0 cm
Collection of Larry Warsh
(p. 186)

Elvis Presley 1981
ink and tempera on offset lithograph
96.5 x 66.0 cm
Collection of Larry Warsh
(p. 258)

Marilyn Monroe 1981
ink and tempera on offset lithograph
96.5 x 66.0 cm
Collection of Larry Warsh
(p. 258)

Untitled 1981
ink and watercolour on paper
93.0 x 125.0 cm
Museum MACAN, Jakarta, Indonesia
(p. 188)

Untitled 1981
fibre-tipped pen and enamel on child's cot
101.6 x 139.7 x 76.2 cm
Hal Bromm Gallery
(p. 237)

Untitled 1981
vinyl ink on tarpaulin
182.8 x 182.8 cm
Private collection, Europe, courtesy Martos Gallery, New York
(p. 83)

Untitled 1981
synthetic polymer paint on canvas
127.0 x 127.0 cm
Private collection, New York
(p. 77)

Untitled 1981
fibre-tipped pen, ink and enamel on fibreglass vase
101.6 x 63.5 x 63.5 cm
Collection of Larry Warsh
(p. 241)

Untitled 1981
sumi ink on vellum
105.4 x 156.2 cm
Collection of Ms Alona Kagan, USA
(p. 203)

Untitled 1981
sumi ink on vellum
105.4 x 132.1 cm
Collection of Ms Alona Kagan, USA
(p. 202)

Untitled 1981
paint on wood panels
215.9 x 152.4 cm
Collection of Larry Warsh
(p. 55)

Untitled 1981
fibre-tipped pen on panel
30.5 x 20.3 cm
Collection of Larry Warsh
(p. 246)

Untitled 1981
ink on metal
121.9 x 121.9 cm
Collection of Larry Warsh
(p. 245)

Untitled 1981
enamel and ink on wood panel
52.1 x 53.3 cm
Private collection
(p. 132)

Untitled 1981
fibre-tipped pen and enamel on wood panel
58.4 x 40.6 x 17.7 cm
Collection of Larry Warsh
(p. 233)

Untitled 1981
ink on paper
55.8 x 76.2 cm
Private collection
(p. 203)

Untitled 1982
vinyl paint and vinyl ink on vinyl tarpaulin
213.4 x 213.4 cm
Private collection
(p. 79)

Untitled 1982
oil on wood panel
43.1 x 48.3 cm
Private collection
(p. 132)

Untitled 1982
synthetic polymer paint on composition board
40.6 x 51.1 cm
Collection of Larry Warsh
(p. 251)

Untitled 1982
day-glo on wood panel
31.0 x 42.5 cm
BvB collection, Geneva
(p. 251)

Untitled 1982
synthetic polymer paint on vinyl tarpaulin
213.5 x 220.0 cm
J W Power Collection, The University of Sydney, managed by Museum of Contemporary Art, purchased with funds from the J W Power Bequest, 1982
(p. 78)

Untitled 1982
baked enamel on metal
109.2 x 109.2 cm
Museum MACAN, Jakarta, Indonesia
(p. 80)

Untitled 1982
baked enamel on metal
109.2 x 109.2 cm
Private collection
(p. 81)

Untitled 1982
baked enamel on metal
109.2 x 109.2 cm
Collection of Larry Warsh
(p. 80)

Untitled 1982
baked enamel on metal
109.2 x 109.2 cm
Collection of Larry Warsh
(p. 81)

Untitled 1982
fibre-tipped pen and enamel on wood panel
135.0 x 45.0 cm
Courtesy Laurent Strouk
(p. 236)

Untitled 1982
ink on paper
22.9 x 30.5 cm
Collection of Larry Warsh
(p. 238)

Untitled 1982
ink on paper
(a–d) 22.9 x 30.5 cm (each)
Collection of Larry Warsh
(p. 239)

Untitled 1982
tempera on paper
94.9 x 125.1 cm
Private collection, Europe
(p. 248)

Untitled 1982
fibre-tipped pen on wood panel
15.2 x 38.7 x 1.9 cm
Hal Bromm Gallery
(p. 238)

Untitled 1982
fibre-tipped pen on paper
27.9 x 21.6 cm
Hal Bromm Gallery
(p. 53)

Untitled 1982
synthetic polymer paint on vinyl tarpaulin
308.6 x 301.6 cm
Private collection
(p. 295)

Untitled 1982
baked enamel on metal
(a–j) 30.5 x 30.5 cm (each)
Collection of Larry Warsh
(pp. 82, 256, 257)

Untitled 1982
baked enamel on metal
30.5 x 30.5 cm
Courtesy Laurent Strouk
(p. 82)

Untitled 1982
fibre-tipped pen on composition board
50.8 x 38.1 cm
Private collection
(p. 246)

Untitled c. 1982
ink on board
101.6 x 127.0 cm
Collection of Larry Warsh
(p. 120)

Untitled 1982
fibre-tipped pen on paper
30.5 x 22.9 cm
Collection of Larry Warsh
(p. 201)

Untitled 1982
synthetic polymer paint on wood panel
35.5 x 35.5 cm
Private collection
(p. 244)

Untitled 1982
chalk on paper
220.0 x 114.0 cm
Collection of Larry Warsh
(p. 61)

Untitled c. 1982
ink on paper
60.9 x 68.5 cm
Collection of Larry Warsh
(p. 189)

Untitled 1982
ink on paper
55.9 x 71.1 cm
Collection of Larry Warsh
(p. 218)

Untitled 1982
ink on paper
97.0 x 127.0 cm
Collection of KAWS
(p. 200)

Untitled 1983
day-glo paint on routed wood panel
30.4 x 31.7 cm
Collection of Larry Warsh
(p. 252)

Untitled 1983
day-glo paint on routed wood panel
25.4 x 55.9 cm
Collection of Larry Warsh
(p. 252)

Untitled 1983
day-glo paint on routed wood panel
25.4 x 53.3 cm
Collection of Larry Warsh
(p. 253)

Untitled 1983
day-glo paint on routed wood panel
30.4 x 31.7 cm
Collection of Larry Warsh
(p. 253)

Untitled 1983
day-glo paint on routed wood panel
30.4 x 60.9 cm
Collection of Larry Warsh
(p. 255)

Untitled 1983
day-glo paint on routed wood panel
30.5 x 30.5 cm
Collection of Larry Warsh
(p. 254)

Untitled 1983
day-glo paint on routed wood panel
30.4 x 50.8 cm
Collection of Larry Warsh
(p. 254)

Untitled 1983
day-glo paint on routed wood panel
40.6 x 30.5 cm
Collection of Larry Warsh
(p. 255)

Untitled 1983
day-glo paint on routed wood panel
31.7 x 50.8 cm
Collection of Larry Warsh
(p. 254)

Untitled 1983
day-glo paint on routed wood panel
35.5 x 38.1 cm
Collection of Larry Warsh
(p. 255)

Untitled 1983
day-glo paint on routed wood panel
30.4 x 60.9 cm
Collection of Larry Warsh
(p. 253)

Untitled 1983
day-glo paint on routed wood panel
20.3 x 55.8 cm
Collection of Larry Warsh
(p. 252)

Untitled 1983
synthetic polymer paint on leather
134.6 x 294.6 cm
Private collection
(p. 128–9)

Untitled 1983
sumi ink on paper screen
91.4 x 165.1 cm
Collection of KAWS
(p. 202)

Untitled 1983
sumi ink on paper
38.0 x 51.0 cm
Courtesy Laurent Strouk
(p. 188)

Untitled 1983
sumi ink on paper
52.0 x 50.0 cm
BvB collection, Geneva
(p. 189)

Untitled 1983
vinyl paint on vinyl tarpaulin
307.0 x 302.0 cm
Collection of KAWS
(p. 127)

Untitled 1983
day-glo paint and enamel on routed wood
182.9 x 182.9 x 7.6 cm
Collection of Larry Warsh
(p. 223)

Untitled 1983
paint on canvas
36.8 x 106.6 cm
Private collection
(p. 247)

Untitled 1983
enamel on routed wood panel
28.0 x 29.0 cm
Collection of Misha and Anna Moeremans d'Emaus
(p. 20)

Untitled 1984
enamel on sheet metal
145.4 x 152.1 cm
Private collection
(p. 76)

Untitled 1984
ink on terracotta vase
54.6 x 44.5 x 44.5 cm
Collection of Larry Warsh
(p. 137)

Untitled 1984
synthetic polymer paint on canvas
38.0 x 38.0 cm
Courtesy Laurent Strouk
(p. 133)

Untitled 1984
synthetic polymer paint on canvas
33.5 x 33.5 cm
Private collection
(p. 133)

Untitled 1984
synthetic polymer paint on muslin
152.4 x 152.4 cm
Private collection, Europe, courtesy Martos Gallery, New York
(p. 259)

Untitled 1984
tempera on paper
100.0 x 70.0 cm
Private collection, New York
(p. 205)

Untitled 1984
enamel and paint on metal
147.3 x 153.7 cm
Private collection
(p. 293)

Untitled c. 1984
paint on wood panel
10.1 x 15.2 cm
Collection of Larry Warsh
(p. 189)

Untitled 1984
synthetic polymer paint on wood and metal
65.2 × 71.7 cm (variable)
National Gallery of Victoria, Melbourne
Presented by the Department of Economic Development, Jobs, Transport and Resources, Victoria, 2017 (2016.138)
(p. 268)

Untitled 1984
metallic and enamel paint on composition board
166.0 × 86.5 cm
National Gallery of Victoria, Melbourne
Gift of Jason Yeap OAM and Min Lee Wong through the Australian Government's Cultural Gifts Program, 2015 (2015.286)
(p. 114)

Untitled 1984
metallic and enamel paint on composition board
166.0 × 86.5 cm
National Gallery of Victoria, Melbourne
Gift of Jason Yeap OAM and Min Lee Wong through the Australian Government's Cultural Gifts Program, 2015 (2015.285)
(p. 114)

Untitled 1984
chalk on paper
220.0 x 114.0 cm
Collection of Larry Warsh
(p. 62)

Andy Mouse 1985
fibre-tipped pen on plexiglass
81.2 x 105.4 cm
Courtesy Laurent Strouk
(p. 16)

Untitled 1985
synthetic polymer paint on canvas
55.8 x 55.8 cm
Collection of Larry Warsh
(p. 292)

Untitled 1985
synthetic polymer paint on canvas
150.0 x 150.0 cm
Collection of Ms Alona Kagan, USA
(p. 126)

Untitled 1985
synthetic polymer paint on canvas
228.6 x 599.4 cm
Private Collection, Europe, courtesy Martos Gallery, New York
(pp. 146–7)

Untitled 1985
paint on polystyrene
(a-b) 33.0 x 33.0 x 2.5 cm (each)
Collection of Larry Warsh
(p. 240)

Untitled 1985
oil and synthetic polymer paint on canvas tarpaulin
302.0 x 295.0 cm
Museum MACAN, Jakarta, Indonesia
(p. 294)

Untitled 1985
fibre-tipped pen on fibreglass
76.2 x 25.4 cm
Collection of Larry Warsh
(p. 229)

Untitled 1985
chalk on paper
220.0 x 114.0 cm
Collection of Larry Warsh
(p. 63)

Untitled 1985
fibre-tipped pen on fibreglass
76.2 x 25.4 cm
Collection of Larry Warsh
(p. 229)

Untitled c. 1985
fibre-tipped pen on helmet
36.8 x 25.4 x 22.8 cm
Collection of Larry Warsh
(p. 235)

Untitled 1986
mixed media and paint on television and shopping cart
101.6 x 71.1 x 35.6 cm
Collection of Larry Warsh
(p. 13)

Untitled 1986
ink on paper
43.1 x 35.5 cm
Collection of Larry Warsh
(p. 242)

Money Magazine Andy Mouse Bill 1986
fibre-tipped pen on paper
28.0 x 35.6 cm
The Keith Haring Foundation, New York
(p. 260)

Untitled 1987
enamel on metal
124.5 x 84.0 x 56.0 cm
The Keith Haring Foundation, New York
(p. 206)

Untitled 1987
ink on paper and box of chalk
54.6 x 38.1 cm (overall)
Collection of Larry Warsh
(p. 88)

Untitled 1987
ink on paper
12.7 x 15.2 cm
Collection of Larry Warsh
(p. 37)

Malcolm X 1988
synthetic polymer paint, enamel and collage on canvas
152.4 x 152.4 cm
Private collection, New York
(pp. 4–5, 27)

A Pile of Crowns for Jean-Michel Basquiat 1988
synthetic polymer paint on canvas
304.8 x 304.8 x 304.8 cm
The Keith Haring Foundation, New York
(pp. 298–9)

Prophets of Rage 1988
synthetic polymer paint on canvas
304.8 x 457.2 cm
The Keith Haring Foundation, New York
(pp. 278–9)

Untitled 1988
synthetic polymer paint on canvas
126.0 x 97.0 cm
Courtesy Laurent Strouk
(p. 133)

Untitled 1988
ink on paper
26.0 x 17.8 cm
Collection of Kermit and Lisa Oswald
(p. 33)

Untitled 1989
synthetic polymer paint and enamel on canvas
182.9 x 182.9 x 8.9 cm
The Keith Haring Foundation, New York
(p. 297)

Untitled 1989
paint on cotton jacket
(a-b) 63.5 x 55.9 cm (variable) (each)
Collection of Larry Warsh
(p. 112)

Untitled 1989
ink on paper
11.4 x 15.2 cm
Collection of Larry Warsh
(p. 37)

Untitled 1990
synthetic polymer paint and fibre-tipped pen on terracotta vase
60.3 x 27.9 x 27.9 cm
Collection of KAWS
(p. 137)

Untitled 1990
ink on paper
40.6 x 30.5 cm
Private collection
(p. 37)

Walking in the Rain 1989
synthetic polymer and enamel paint on canvas
183.4 x 244.6 cm
The Keith Haring Foundation, New York
(p. 296)

Ephemera from The Keith Haring Foundation, New York
medium variable
dimensions variable
The Keith Haring Foundation, New York
(partially illustrated, p. 9)

Jean-Michel Basquiat
American 1960–1988

Samo 1978
ink on paper
30.5 x 22.9 cm
Collection of Emmanuelle and Jérôme de Noirmont
(p. 163)

Stoned on Samo 1978
ink on paper
30.5 x 22.9 cm
Collection of Emmanuelle and Jérôme de Noirmont
(p. 163)

The Comic Book 1978
watercolour, ink and pencil on paper
(a–h) 35.6 x 21.6 cm (each)
Private collection
(pp. 164–5)

Untitled 1979
ink stamp, coloured pencil and xerox collage on paper
42.0 x 33.0 cm
Private collection

Untitled 1979–80
ink on paper
(a-b) 28.6 x 22.9 cm (each)
Private collection

Untitled 1979–80
ink on paper
(a-b) 28.6 x 22.9 cm (each)
Private collection

We Have Decided the Bullet Must Have Been Going Very Fast 1979–80
synthetic polymer paint, blood, ink and collage on paper
42.5 x 35.5 cm
Private collection
(p. 41)

Notebook 1 1980–87
cover: mixed media on board
pages: fibre-tipped pen, wax crayon and ink on ruled notebook paper
(a-ll) 24.0 x 19.0 cm (each)
Collection of Larry Warsh
(partially illustrated, pp. 172, 175)

Notebook 5 1980–87
cover: mixed media on board
pages: fibre-tipped pen, wax crayon and ink on ruled notebook paper
(a-x) 24.0 x 19.0 cm (each)
Collection of Larry Warsh
(partially illustrated, pp. 173, 174, 176, 177)

Untitled 1980
enamel, spray-paint and oilstick on enamelled metal
243.8 × 122.1 cm
Whitney Museum of American Art, New York
Gift of an anonymous donor (97.95)
(p. 101)

Untitled 1980
graphite, collage, adhesive tape and plastic on paper
29.9 x 38.1 cm
Private collection

Untitled (Duchamp) 1980
collage on paper
26.7 x 21.0 cm
Collection of Larry Warsh
(p. 40)

Untitled (JIMMY BEST ON HIS BACK) 1980
mixed media on paper
61.0 x 47.0 cm
Collection of Larry Warsh
(p. 179)

Untitled (JIMMY BEST ON HIS BACK) 1980
ink on paper
41.9 x 35.6 cm
Collection of Larry Warsh
(p. 179)

Untitled (Map) 1980
mixed media collage
26.7 x 34.0 cm
Collection of Larry Warsh
(p. 36)

Untitled (Keith Haring) 1980–81
oilstick and fibre-tipped pen on paper
45.7 x 30.5 cm
Private collection, courtesy Tony Shafrazi Gallery, New York
(p. 39)

Antidote 1981
fibre-tipped pen on paper
30.5 x 22.9 cm
Collection of Larry Warsh
(p. 166)

Black Soap 1981
mixed media on paper
90.0 x 60.0 cm
Private collection
(p. 171)

Irony of a Negro Policeman 1981
synthetic polymer paint and oilstick on wood
183.0 x 122.0 cm
AMA Art Collection
(p. 307)

Just as a Shot Cracked Out 1981
pencil and oilstick on paper
76.0 x 56.0 cm
Collection of Diego de Noirmont
(p. 162)

Masque 1981
synthetic polymer paint and oilstick on canvas
142.0 x 125.0 cm
Collection of Ben and Debra Ashkenazy, New York
(p. 70)

Number 4 1981
synthetic polymer paint, oilstick and paper collage on canvas
167.0 x 137.0 cm
Collection of Andre Sakhai
(p. 71)

Old Tin 1981
paint on wood panel
66.0 x 38.1 cm
Collection of Larry Warsh
(p. 222)

Pork 1981
synthetic polymer paint, oil and oilstick on wood and glass door
210.8 x 85.4 cm
Private collection
(p. 64)

Untitled (Chesterfield) 1981
mixed media collage on paper
61.0 x 45.7 cm
Collection of Larry Warsh
(p. 230)

Untitled 1981
ink on paper
74.0 x 153.0 cm
Private collection
(p. 170)

Untitled 1981
crayon on paper
45.0 x 57.2 cm
Collection of Kyoko Tamura
(p. 194)

Untitled (BAR, BAR, BAR) 1981
mixed media, ink and wax crayon on paper
27.9 x 20.3 cm
Collection of Larry Warsh
(p. 166)

Untitled (Crown and Car) 1981
oilstick on paper
61.0 x 45.7 cm
Private collection
(p. 168)

Untitled (Heart / Henry Geldzahler) 1981
mixed media on paper
30.5 x 45.7 cm
Collection of Larry Warsh
(p. 219)

Untitled 1981
ink on paper
(a-g) 30.5 x 22.9 cm (each)
Private collection
(p. 181)

Untitled (Man Needs Milk) 1981
mixed media on paper
30.5 x 20.3 cm
Collection of Larry Warsh
(p. 166)

Untitled (Peso Neto) 1981
oilstick on paper
76.2 x 56.5 cm
Collection of Kyoko Tamura
(p. 196)

Untitled (Tar) 1981
fibre-tipped pen on paper
29.2 x 21.6 cm
Collection of Larry Warsh
(p. 166)

Untitled (Text) 1981
ink on paper
(a) 8.0 x 22.2 cm
(b) 5.1 x 8.9 cm
Collection of Larry Warsh
(p. 227)

Untitled (Train) 1981
mixed media on canvas
45.7 x 61.0 cm
Private collection
(p. 231)

Untitled (Train, Car, Boat) 1981
ink on paper
71.1 x 116.8 cm
Private collection
(p. 170)

Untitled (Two Trucks) 1981
oilstick and mixed media on paper
35.6 x 25.4 cm
Collection of Larry Warsh
(p. 226)

A Panel of Experts 1982
synthetic polymer paint and oil pastel on paper on canvas and wood
152.5 x 152.0 cm
Montreal Museum of Fine Arts
Gift of Ira Young (1990.28)
(p. 86)

Cantasso 1982
synthetic polymer paint on canvas and wood
156.0 x 156.0 cm
Collection of Georges Saier
(p. 84)

Donut Revenge 1982
synthetic polymer paint, oilstick and paper collage on canvas
243.2 x 182.9 cm
Private collection
(p. 144)

Jack Johnson 1982
synthetic polymer paint and oilstick on canvas
120.5 x 96.5 cm
Private collection
(p. 87)

Portrait of A-One A.K.A. King 1982
synthetic polymer paint on canvas and wood
182.8 x 184.0 cm
Private collection
(p. 65)

Totem 1982
synthetic polymer paint, oilstick and paper collage on canvas on wood panel
203.0 x 63.5 x 10.0 cm
Collection of Yoav Harlap, Israel
(p. 85)

Versus Medici 1982
synthetic polymer paint and oil wax crayon on canvas
213.0 x 136.0 cm
Private collection
(p. 141)

Untitled 1982
synthetic polymer paint and oilstick on wood panel
183.0 x 122.5 cm
Private collection
(p. 145)

Untitled 1982
crayon on notebook paper
27.9 x 21.5 cm
Collection of Kyoko Tamura
(p. 190)

Untitled 1982
crayon on notebook paper
27.9 x 21.5 cm
Collection of Kyoko Tamura
(p. 191)

Untitled 1982
crayon on notebook paper
27.9 x 21.5 cm
Collection of Kyoko Tamura
(p. 167)

Untitled 1982
crayon and oilstick on paper
54.5 x 75.0 cm
agnès b. collection
(p. 212)

Untitled 1982
oilstick on paper
152.4 x 101.6 cm
Private collection
(p. 213)

Untitled 1982
oil and graphite on paper
108.5 x 76.8 cm
Private collection
(p. 210)

Untitled 1982
oilstick and ink on paper
108.6 x 77.2 cm
Private collection
(p. 211)

Untitled (1/2 Black, 1/2 White) 1982
oilstick and gouache on paper
75.6 x 55.9 cm
Private collection
(p. 209)

Untitled (2 Panels of Plywood) 1982
pencil on paper
18.3 x 16.5 cm
Collection of Larry Warsh
(p. 226)

Untitled #27 (Lee Harvey Oswald) c. 1982
oilstick on paper
55.9 x 76.2 cm
Private collection
(p. 105)

Untitled (Lawyer) c. 1982–85
ink on paper
25.4 x 16.5 cm
Collection of Larry Warsh
(p. 226)

Untitled (Legs) 1982
mixed media on paper
45.7 x 43.2 cm
Private collection
(p. 168)

Untitled (Pestus) 1982
synthetic polymer paint and oilstick on paper
115.0 x 183.0 cm
Private collection
(p. 180)

Untitled (Pollo Frito) 1982
synthetic polymer paint, oil and enamel on canvas
(a–b) 152.4 x 306.1 cm (overall)
Private European collection, courtesy of John Sayegh-Belchatowski
(pp. 72–3)

Untitled (Red Face) 1982
mixed media on paper
17.8 x 12.7 cm
Collection of Larry Warsh
(p. 222)

Untitled (Ron) 1982
ink on paper
22.8 x 15.2 cm
Private collection
(p. 227)

Untitled (Self-Portrait) 1982
oilstick and ink on paper
75.9 x 55.9 cm
Private European collection, courtesy of John Sayegh-Belchatowski
(p. 208)

Untitled (TKO) 1982
sumi ink on paper
40.6 x 33.0 cm
Private collection
(p. 168)

Warrior 1982
oilstick on paper
63.5 x 76.2 cm
Collection of Kyoko Tamura
(p. 195)

Untitled (Pecho/Oreja) 1982–83
synthetic polymer paint, oilstick and paper collage on canvas
183.0 x 183.0 cm
Onyx Art Collection
(pp. 138–9)

Ramm:ell:zee vs. K.Rob, Beat Bop 1983
vinyl record and album cover
30.0 x 30.0 cm (album cover)
Collection of Jennifer von Holstein
(p. 121)

Boone 1983
paper collage, fibre-tipped pen and oil wax crayon on composition board
104.0 x 30.5 cm
Private collection
(p. 26)

Hollywood Africans in Front of the Chinese Theater with Footprints of Movie Stars 1983
synthetic polymer paint and oilstick on canvas on wood panel
90.0 x 207.0 cm
The Estate of Jean-Michel Basquiat, New York
(p. 106)

Ishtar 1983
synthetic polymer paint, wax crayon and photocopy collage on canvas and wood
182.9 x 352.0 cm (overall)
Collection Ludwig, Ludwig Forum für Internationale Kunst, Aachen
(pp. 142–3)

Seascape 1983
synthetic polymer paint and oil pastel on paper on canvas and wood
92.4 x 91.2 cm
Montreal Museum of Fine Arts
Gift of Ira Young (1990.29)
(p. 134)

Untitled 1983
synthetic polymer paint and oilstick on paper on canvas and wood
91.5 x 91.5 cm
The George Economou Collection
(p. 135)

Untitled 1983
synthetic polymer paint and oilstick on paper
76.2 x 55.9 cm
Private collection
(p. 207)

Untitled 1983
oilstick and ink on paper
75.6 x 55.9 cm
Private collection
(p. 130)

Untitled (Cold Blooded Killer) 1983
wax crayon on paper
59.7 x 45.7 cm
Private collection
(p. 104)

Untitled (EGO) 1983
oilstick and coffee on paper
76.2 x 55.9 cm
Collection of Larry Warsh
(p. 169)

Untitled (World Famous) 1983
crayon on paper
57.1 x 76.2 cm
The Estate of Jean-Michel Basquiat, New York
(p. 38)

Farina 1984
synthetic polymer paint and oilstick on canvas
218.4 x 172.7 cm
Collection of Sabina and Robert Franklin
(p. 131)

Izod 1984
oilstick and ballpoint pen on paper
55.9 x 76.2 cm
Collection of Kyoko Tamura
(p. 199)

Plastic Sax 1984
synthetic polymer paint, colour oilstick, xerox paper and collage on canvas
152.4 x 123.2 cm
agnès b. collection
(p. 107)

Self Portrait 1984
synthetic polymer paint and oilstick on paper on canvas
98.7 x 71.1 cm
Collection of Yoav Harlap, Israel
(p. 275)

Sienna 1984
synthetic polymer paint and oil on canvas
223.4 x 195.6 cm
Collection ABG
(p. 281)

Untitled 1984
synthetic polymer paint, oilstick and xerox collage on wood
125.5 x 94.0 cm
Private collection
(p. 140)

Untitled 1984
synthetic polymer paint and oilstick on canvas
167.5 x 152.5 cm
Collection of Andre Sakhai
(p. 287)

Untitled (Magic Worms) 1984
75.6 x 56.5 cm
graphite and oilstick on paper
Collection of Andy Song
(p. 193)

Untitled (Picasso) 1984
graphite on paper
76.2 x 57.1 cm
Collection of Kyoko Tamura
(p. 192)

Self Portrait 1985
synthetic polymer paint, coloured pencil and bottle caps on wood panel
(a-b) 142.2 x 154.4 cm (overall)
Private collection
(p. 283)

South African Nazism 1985
synthetic polymer paint on enamelled metal
182.9 x 91.4 cm
Private collection
(p. 285)

Untitled (Armstrong) 1985
mixed media on paper
56.0 x 76.0 cm
Collection of Kyoko Tamura
(p. 198)

Untitled (E) 1985
ink, oilstick and watercolour on paper
15.6 x 23.5 cm
The Estate of Jean-Michel Basquiat, New York
(p. 36)

Untitled (Fool©) c. 1985
xerox paper on wood panel
25.4 x 20.3 cm
Collection of Larry Warsh
(p. 231)

Untitled (I Swear to God) c. 1985
ink on postcard
14.0 x 11.4 cm
Collection of Larry Warsh
(p. 43)

Untitled 1985
xerox collage on wood box
28.0 x 22.0 cm
Private collection
(p. 178)

Untitled (Word on Wood) 1985
oil and pencil on wood
238.8 x 185.4 cm
Private collection
(p. 277)

Yellow Door 1985–86
oil, colour xerox paper, metal and collaged elements on painted door
193.4 x 81.3 cm
Private collection
(p. 282)

Because it Hurts the Lungs 1986
synthetic polymer paint and collage on wood
183.0 x 107.0 x 21.0 cm
Museum MACAN, Jakarta, Indonesia
(p. 284)

Untitled (Left Entrance Hall) 1986
pencil, oilstick and gouache on paper
106.0 x 75.0 cm
Private collection
(p. 115)

Untitled (Monkey) 1986
oil on denim jacket
81.3 x 62.2 cm
Private collection
(p. 112)

Glassnose 1987
synthetic polymer paint and oilstick on canvas
175.0 x 132.0 cm
Tony Shafrazi Gallery, New York
(p. 289)

Item 1987
synthetic polymer paint and oilstick on canvas
125.5 x 100.0 cm
Private collection
(p. 288)

Non-Toxic 1987
pencil and oilstick on paper
15.0 x 10.0 cm
Private collection
(p. 169)

Untitled 1987
wax crayon, coloured crayon and pencil on paper
76.5 x 56.5 cm
Collection of Kyoko Tamura
(p. 197)

Exu 1988
synthetic polymer paint and oilstick on canvas
199.5 x 254.0 cm
Private collection
(pp. 290–1)

Keith Haring
American 1958–1990
Jean-Michel Basquiat
American 1960–1988
Untitled 1980
fibre-tipped pen on paper
96.5 x 127.0 cm
Private collection
(p. 14)

Untitled 1981
fibre-tipped pen and spray-paint on paper
106.7 x 121.0 cm
The Keith Haring Foundation, New York
(p. 68)

Untitled 1981
fibre-tipped pen and spray-paint on paper
106.7 x 142.3 cm
The Keith Haring Foundation, New York
(p. 69)

Untitled 1982
ink on rubber printing blanket
62.9 x 88.9 cm
The Keith Haring Foundation, New York
(p. 15)

Keith Haring
American 1958–1990
Jean-Michel Basquiat
American 1960–1988
Other artists
Untitled (Symphony No. 1) c. 1980–83
mixed media, spray-paint and paper on plywood
122.6 x 219.7 cm
Collection of Larry Warsh
(p. 60)

Jennifer Stein
American born 1957
Jean-Michel Basquiat
American 1960–1988
42 postcards 1979
mixed media on cardboard
dimensions variable
Collection of Jennifer von Holstein
(partially illustrated, pp. 42–5)

Tseng Kwong Chi
Born Hong Kong, lived America, 1950-1990
Futura 2000
American born 1955
Keith Haring
American 1958–1990
Kenny Scharf
American born 1958
Fred Brathwaite
American born 1959
Jean-Michel Basquiat
America 1960–1988
Eric Haze
American born 1961
LA II
American born 1967
Other artists
Untitled 1982
mixed media, synthetic polymer paint, spray-paint and fibre-tipped pen on fibreglass vase
61.0 x 50.8 cm diameter
Collection of Larry Warsh
(p. 224)

Kenny Scharf
American born 1958
Fred Brathwaite
American born 1959
Jean-Michel Basquiat
American 1960–1988
LA II
American born 1967
Other artists
Art is the Word 1981
spray-paint and fibre-tipped pen on composition board
186.7 x 121.9 cm
Noirmontartproduction collection
(p. 67)

Keith Haring
American 1958–1990
LA II
American born 1967
Sarcophagus 1983
synthetic polymer paint and fibre-tipped pen on fibreglass
249.0 x 86.0 x 56.0 cm
Private collection
(p. 136)

Untitled 1983
ink and day-glo paint on fibreglass
119.3 x 71.1 x 48.2 cm
Private collection
(p. 249)

World's End, London (manufacturer)
British 1979–1984
Vivienne Westwood (designer)
British born 1941
Malcolm McLaren (designer)
British 1946–2010
Keith Haring (designer)
American 1958–1990
Outfit; jacket, T-shirt, skirt and scarf
1983–84, autumn–winter *Witches* collection
cotton, Velcro
(a) 55.0 cm (centre back) (jacket)
(b) 53.0 cm (centre back) (T-shirt)
(c) 53.0 cm (centre back) (skirt)
(d) 164.0 x 15.0 cm (scarf)
National Gallery of Victoria, Melbourne
Purchased through The Art Foundation of Victoria with the assistance of Just Jeans Pty Ltd, Member, 1999
(1999.366.a-d)
(p. 113)

Keith Haring
American 1958–1990
Other artists
Untitled c. 1982
mixed media on composition board
243.8 x 121.9 cm
Collection of Larry Warsh
(p. 66)

Andy Warhol
American 1928–1987
Keith Haring
American 1958–1990
Untitled (Madonna, I'm Not Ashamed) 1985
synthetic polymer paint, day-glo paint and silkscreen ink on canvas
50.8 x 40.6 cm
The Keith Haring Foundation, New York
(p. 261)

Keith Haring
American 1958–1990
David Spada
American 1961–1996
Grace Jones's Hat 1984
ink on metal
89.0 x 61.0 cm
The Keith Haring Foundation, New York
(p. 111)

Ornaments for Grace Jones's costume 1984
ink on metal
(a-n) 25.4 x 15.3 cm (variable) (each)
Collection of Larry Warsh
(p. 110)

Roy Lichtenstein
American 1923–1997
Andy Warhol
American 1928–1987
Yoko Ono
Japanese born 1933, works in United States 1953–
Keith Haring
American 1958–1990
Jean-Michel Basquiat
American 1960–1988
Rain Dance 1985
colour screenprint, ed 100
88.9 x 66.0 cm
Collection of Larry Warsh
(p. 243)

Rene Ricard
American 1946–2014
Keith Haring
American 1958–1990
Untitled 1982
ink on manila envelope
35.6 x 24.1 cm
Collection of Larry Warsh
(p. 238)

Acknowledgements & Contributors

Executive Management Team
Tony Ellwood AM, Director
Andrew Clark, Deputy Director
Donna McColm, Acting Assistant Director, Curatorial and Collection Management
Don Heron, Assistant Director, Exhibitions Management and Design

Curatorial Team
Tony Ellwood AM, Director
Andrew Clark, Deputy Director
Don Heron, Assistant Director, Exhibitions Management and Design
Dr Miranda Wallace, Senior Curator, International Exhibition Projects
Meg Slater, Curatorial Project Officer, International Exhibition Projects
Pip Wallis, Curator, Contemporary Art
Dr Dieter Buchhart, Exhibition Curator
Dr Anna Karina Hofbauer, Co-Curator
Anke Wiedmann, Curatorial Assistant

Special Curatorial Advisors
Estate of Jean-Michel Basquiat
The Keith Haring Foundation, New York

Special Advisor
Larry Warsh

Project Team and Staff
Misha Agzarian, Associate Director, Fundraising, and staff
Marion Joseph, Associate Director, Media and Public Affairs, and staff
Alison Lee, Associate Director, Governance, Policy, Planning and IT, and staff
Jane Zantuck, Associate Director, Marketing, and staff
Anna Last, Senior Account Manager, Corporate Partnerships, and Adriana Gomberg, Senior Development Manager, Corporate Partnerships, and staff
Michael Burke, Manager, Exhibitions and Collections Operations, and staff
Lucy Hastewell, Head of Facilities and Operations, and staff
Tony Henshaw, Manager, Facilities, and staff
Paul Lambrick, Chief Financial Officer, and staff
Matthew Lim, Manager, Multimedia, and staff
Trish Little, Senior Cataloguer
Nicole Monteiro, Exhibitions Manager, and staff
Paula Nason, Head of Registration, and staff
Toby Newell, Manager, Commercial Operations, and staff
Megan Patty, Head of Publications, Photographic Services and Library, and staff
Ingrid Rhule, Manager, Exhibition Design, and staff
Jackie Robinson, Manager, Graphic Design, and staff
Garry Sommerfeld, Manager, Photographic Services, and staff
Michele Stockley, Head of Learning, and staff
Michael Varcoe-Cocks, Head of Conservation, and staff

Contributors

Dr Dieter Buchhart is a curator and art theorist, and Exhibition Curator on *Keith Haring | Jean-Michel Basquiat: Crossing Lines*. He holds PhD degrees in art history and restoration (science). He is the curator of numerous international exhibitions, including solo exhibitions of the work of Keith Haring and Jean-Michel Basquiat. From 2007 to 2009 he was the director of the Kunsthalle Krems, near Vienna. Since 1999, he has worked as an art critic, publishing monographs and interviews for *Kunstforum International* and other art publications. His research foci range from art around 1900 and Expressionism, to art from the 1980s and contemporary art. He is based in Vienna.

Dr Anna Karina Hofbauer is a freelance curator and art critic, and Co-Curator on *Keith Haring | Jean-Michel Basquiat: Crossing Lines*. She holds a PhD in art history. Her research areas range from modernism to contemporary art, with a focus on participatory art and relational aesthetics. She has co-curated exhibitions on modern and contemporary art featuring artists such as Edvard Munch, Jean-Michel Basquiat, Keith Haring, Yoko Ono, Felix Gonzales-Torres, Damien Hirst, Mark Dion, Olaf Nicolai, Ernesto Neto and Rirkrit Tiravanija. She lives and works in Vienna.

Ricardo Montez is Associate Professor of Performance Studies in the Schools for Public Engagement at The New School, New York. His research examines the performance of race, ethnicity and sexuality in visual culture and media. *Keith Haring's Line: Race and the Performance of Desire*, his forthcoming book, will be published by Duke University Press.

Rene Ricard (1946–2014) was an American poet and painter. His work has appeared in influential literary, art and popular publications. He is acknowledged to have launched the careers of Jean-Michel Basquiat and Keith Haring. His breakthrough 1981 essay for *Artforum* magazine, 'The radiant child', is reproduced in this volume.

Myles Russell-Cook is Curator of Indigenous Art at the National Gallery of Victoria. He is jointly responsible for the NGV's collections of Aboriginal and Torres Strait Islander art and the art of Oceania, pre-Hispanic America and Africa. Much of his influence and inspiration comes from his maternal Aboriginal heritage in Western Victoria with connections into Tasmania and the Bass Strait Islands.

Larry Warsh has been active in the art world for more than thirty years as a publisher and artist-collaborator. An early collector of Keith Haring and Jean-Michel Basquiat, Warsh was a member of the Basquiat Authentication Committee from its establishment in 1984 until its dissolution in 2012. Warsh was a lead organiser for the exhibition *Basquiat: The Unknown Notebooks*, which debuted at the Brooklyn Museum, New York, in 2015, and later travelled to several American museums. He has loaned artworks by Haring and Basquiat from his collection to numerous exhibitions worldwide, and he served as a curatorial consultant on *Keith Haring | Jean-Michel Basquiat: Crossing Lines* for the NGV. The founder of Museums Magazines, Warsh has been involved in many publishing projects, including original monographs on the work of Keith Haring, Jean-Michel Basquiat and Ai Weiwei. He is the editor of *Basquiat-isms* (2019) and *Jean-Michel Basquiat: The Notebooks* (2015).

Anke Wiedmann is the Curatorial Assistant on *Keith Haring | Jean-Michel Basquiat: Crossing Lines*. She holds a degree in art history and cultural studies, and as a freelance research and curatorial assistant specialises in modern and contemporary art. She has worked on major exhibitions of artists, including Haring and Basquiat, for institutions such as the Barbican Centre, London; the Albertina Museum, Vienna; and the Mori Arts Center Gallery, Tokyo. As managing editor, she has worked on numerous publications, including the forthcoming catalogue raisonné of Mel Ramos's prints.

Linda Yablonksy is a critic and journalist based in New York. She has been covering the art world for more than twenty-five years as a contributor to *The New York Times*, *The Art Newspaper*, Artforum.com, *W Magazine*, *Art News* and many other publications. She is also the author of *The Story of Junk: A Novel* (1997), numerous essays for exhibition catalogues and a forthcoming biography of the artist Jeff Koons.

Interviewees

Patti Astor is co-founder of the Fun Gallery (1981–85), New York, whose roster of artists included Keith Haring and Jean-Michel Basquiat. She is also a dancer, having been accepted into the Cincinnati Ballet at the age of fourteen and later touring Europe with her self-developed dance act. As an actor, she studied under Nicholas Ray, director of *Rebel Without A Cause*, starred in the films *Wild Style* (1983) and *Underground USA* (1981), and went on to appear in a dozen low-budget films, earning herself the title of 'Queen of The Downtown Screen'. Astor has self-published a memoir about her life, *Fun Gallery ... The True Story* (2012).

George Condo is an American visual artist working in painting, sculpture, drawing and printmaking. Along with Jean-Michel Basquiat and Keith Haring, Condo was instrumental in the international revival of figurative painting from the 1980s onwards. Solo exhibitions of Condo's work have been staged at the New Museum, New York; Hayward Gallery, London; Schirn Kunsthalle, Frankfurt; The Phillips Collection, Washington DC; Musée Maillol, Paris; the Louisiana Museum of Modern Art, Denmark; and the Staatliche Museen zu Berlin-Museum Berggruen, among others. His works are in the permanent collections of many international art museums, including The Metropolitan Museum of Art, The Museum of Modern Art and The Solomon R. Guggenheim Museum, all in New York, and Tate Modern, London.

Diego Cortez is a curator and agent. In 1973, he earned an MFA in new media (video, film and performance) at the School of the Art Institute of Chicago, where he studied under artists including Stan Brakhage, Nam June Paik and Kenneth Anger. Cortez curated the landmark no wave exhibition *New York/New Wave* for New York art space P.S. 1 in 1981. He was also co-founder of the Mudd Club, together with Steve Mass and Anya Phillips. He has lectured at Yale University and collaborated on the publication *Autonomia: Post-Political Politics* (1980) with Sylvère Lotringer and Christian Marazzi.

Jenny Holzer has been a practising artist for more than forty years, presenting her work in public places and international exhibitions including 7 World Trade Center, the Venice Biennale, the Guggenheim Museums in New York and Bilbao, the Whitney Museum of American Art and the Louvre Abu Dhabi. Writing is her primary medium and the public dimension is integral to the delivery of her work, starting in the 1970s with the New York City posters, and continuing through her recent light projections on landscape and architecture. Holzer received the Leone d'Oro at the Venice Biennale in 1990, the Crystal Award at the World Economic Forum in 1996 and the Barnard Medal of Distinction in 2011. She holds honorary degrees from Williams College, the Rhode Island School of Design, The New School and Smith College. She lives and works in New York.

Photo: akg-images pp. 141, 303; Licensed by Art + Commerce, Art © Estate of Jean-Michel Basquiat. Licensed by Artestar, New York pp. 58–9; © Artforum, December 1981, 'The Radiant Child', by Rene Ricard pp. 309–17; Courtesy of the Art Gallery of Ontario p. 171; Photo: Art Issue Editions pp. 12, 36 (bottom), 37 (right), 40, 60–3, 80 (bottom), 81 (bottom), 82 (left, top and bottom), 88, 108, 112 (top), 136 (left, top and bottom), 137 (right), 166, 168 (top right, bottom), 169 (right), 170 (top), 172–9, 181–4 (top), 186 (bottom), 189 (top), 201 (top left), 203 (bottom), 218–25, 226 (right), 230–1, 238 (top left), 242, 247 (middle), 250–1, 252 (middle), 253 (top and bottom), 254 (middle and bottom), 255 (top and bottom), 256 (middle, bottom), 257 (top, bottom left), 258, 259, 292; Courtesy of Estate of Jean-Michel Basquiat and Artestar, New York pp. 2–3, 26, 34, 36 (top), 38, 41, 106, 145, 210, 281, 284, 290–1, 307; © The Estate of Gordon Bennett / Image: National Gallery of Victoria pp. 267, 271; Photo: David Bordes p. 28; Photo: Carl Brunn pp. 142–3, 148–9; Photo © Ben Buchanan pp. cover, vi–vii, 215; Photo © Geoffrey Burke / National Gallery of Victoria p. 273; Photo: Marion Busch pp. 75, 335; Courtesy BvB collection, Geneva pp. 35, 189 (bottom right), 251 (top); Image © 2004 Christie's Images Limited p. 115; Image © 2007 Christie's Images Limited p. 170 (top); Image © 2008 Christie's Images Limited p. 133 (bottom left); Image © 2013 Christie's Images Limited p. 133 (top left); Image © 2016 Christie's Images Limited pp. 104, 105, 211; © George Condo 2019 © Keith Haring Foundation. Courtesy of George Condo, Skarstedt New York/London and Sprüth Magers Berlin/London/Los Angeles p. 95; © George Condo 2019. Courtesy of the Artist, Skarstedt New York/ London and Sprüth Magers Berlin/London/Los Angeles p. 93; Photo: Carl Ferrari p. 209; Courtesy Hal Bromm Gallery pp. 53, 237, 238 (top right); Photos © Michael Halsband pp. xvii, 221; Image courtesy of the Keith Haring Foundation, New York pp. 4–9, 15, 27, 46–7, 52, 68–9, 77, 79–80 (top), 81 (top), 83, 111, 126–7, 133 (right), 136 (right), 137 (left), 187, 202–3 (top), 206, 260, 278–9, 293–9; Photo © George Hirose p. xi; Photo © Timothy Hursley pp. 22, 96–7, 103; Photo: Image Art Studio, Hong Kong pp. 167, 190–2; Photo: Jean François Rogeboz p. 169 (right), p. 288; Photo: Flavio Karrer, 2019 p. 180; Photo © Vijya Kern / Courtesy of Artstübli Gallery, Basel pp. 56–7; Photo: Mathias Kessler pp. 29, 37 (left, top and bottom), 43 (right), 54–5, 66, 109–10, 120, 168 (top left), 184 (bottom), 185–6 (top), 189 (bottom left), 201 (top right, bottom), 204, 214, 226 (left), 227, 228–9, 232–5, 238 (bottom), 239–41, 243–6, 247 (bottom), 253 (bottom), 254 (top), 255 (bottom right), 256 (top), 257 (bottom right), 260; Photo © Eric Kroll p. 122; Photo © Annie Leibovitz / Trunk Archive p. 19; Photo: Mark French Photography p. 192, 194–6, 198–9; Photo © Maripol p. 153; Courtesy of Martos Gallery, New York pp. 11, 83, 146–7, 205, 259; Courtesy Menzies Art Brands p. 270 (left); Courtesy Montreal Museum of Fine Arts pp. 86, 134; Photo: Tseng Kwong Chi © Muna Tseng Dance Projects, Inc., Art © Keith Haring Foundation, Art © Estate of Jean-Michel Basquiat. Licensed by Artestar, New York p. 74; Photo: Tseng Kwong Chi © Muna Tseng Dance Projects, Inc., Art © Keith Haring Foundation pp. 17, 23, 24–5, 89; Courtesy of the Museum of Contemporary Art, Sydney p. 78; Courtesy Museum MACAN, Jakarta, Indonesia p. 188 (top); Courtesy Nakanoshima Museum of Art, Osaka p. 269; National Gallery of Victoria pp. 113, 268; Photo: Mikael Olsson p. 20; Courtesy of the owner pp. 14, 16, 21, 33, 64, 65, 67, 71, 76, 82 (right), 84, 92, 107, 126–9, 132, 135, 140, 162–3, 188 (bottom), 197, 200, 212, 236, 247 (top), 277, 282, 285, 287; Image copyright 2016 Phillips Auctioneers LLC. All Rights Reserved pp. 130, 193, 274; Photo: Justin Piperger p. 121; Photo © Sabina Sarnitz pp. 116, 17, 305, 321; Photo © Didi Sattmann / Getty Images p. 51; Photo: Peter Schälchli, Zürich p. 139; Photo: Courtesy of Sotheby's, Inc. © 2019 pp. 70, 72–3, 112 (bottom), 141, 164–5, 208; Photo: Courtesy The Yoav Harlap Collection, all rights reserved pp. 85, 275; Andy Warhol © The Andy Warhol Foundation for the Visual Arts, Inc. pp. 156–7, 262–3, 318–19; Photo: Tom Powel Imaging p. 213; Courtesy Tony Shafrazi Gallery, New York pp. 39, 289; Courtesy Jennifer von Holstein pp. 42–3 (left), 44–5, 121; Photo: Joshua White p. 131; Digital image Whitney Museum of American Art / Licensed by Scala p. 101; Photo: W&K – Wienerroither & Kohlbacher, Wien, w-k.art p. 207; Narelle Wilson / National Gallery of Victoria p. 114; Photo: Max Yawney p. 283.

First published by the Council of Trustees
of the National Gallery of Victoria
180 St Kilda Road
Melbourne, Victoria 3004, Australia
ngv.melbourne

Keith Haring | Jean-Michel Basquiat: Crossing Lines is edited by Dieter Buchhart with texts by various contributors.
First published in association with the exhibition held at NGV International, 180 St Kilda Road, Melbourne.

Distributed throughout the world excluding Australia and New Zealand by
Princeton University Press
41 William Street, Princeton, New Jersey 08540
6 Oxford Street, Woodstock, Oxfordshire OX20 1TR
press.princeton.edu
In association with No More Rulers
nomorerulers.com
@nomorerulers

NO MORE RULERS

All Rights Reserved
ISBN 9781925432725
Library of Congress Control Number: 2021942544
British Library Cataloging-in-Publication Data is available
This book has been composed in Suisse Int'l

Head of Publications, Photographic Services and Library:
Megan Patty
Manager, Graphic Design Projects: Thomas Deverall
assisted by Tristan Main
Map illustration: Cally Bennett
Editor: Rowena Robertson with Dr Anita Pisch
Proofreader: Natalie Book
Publishing Coordinator: Julia Rodwell with Meg Slater
Pre-press: National Gallery of Victoria
Production and Lithography: Colour & Books
Printing: Wilco Art Books
Printed in the Netherlands

10 9 8 7 6 5 4 3 2